THE COLLECTED WORKS OF MAX HAINES

VOLUME 4

MAX HAINES
1993–1995

Penguin Books

PENGUIN BOOKS

Published by the Penguin Group

Penguin Books Canada Ltd, 10 Alcorn Avenue, Toronto, Ontario,
Canada M4V 3B2
Penguin Books Ltd, 27 Wrights Lane, London W8 5TZ, England
Penguin Putnam Inc., 375 Hudson Street, New York, New York 10014, U.S.A.
Penguin Books Australia Ltd, Ringwood, Victoria, Australia
Penguin Books (NZ) Ltd, cnr Rosedale and Airborne Roads, Albany,
Auckland 1310, New Zealand

Penguin Looks Ltd, Registered Offices: Hammondsworth, Middlesex, England

First published, 2000

1   3   5   7   9   10   8   6   4   2

Manufactured in Canada

CANADIAN CATALOGUING IN PUBLICATION DATA

Haines, Max
The collected works of Max Haines

Contents: v. 4.

ISBN 0-14-029515-1 (V. 4)

1. Murder. I. Title.

HV6515.H355 1985   364.1'523   c86-008656-9 rev

Visit Penguin Canada's website at www.penguin.ca

For Shawn, Jay, Alexandra, and Fayth

CONTENTS

PART 1

ENGLISH DOCTORS

FROM DOCTORS WHO KILL

DR. JAMES BELANEY

A few eyebrows were raised when Dr. James Cockburn Belany up and married beautiful Rachel Skelly of Sunderland, England. You see, Dr. Jimmy was 43; Rachel was an unsoiled virgin of 20. The pair wed on February 1, 1843.

Rachel's widowed mother owned several properties, as well as a portfolio chock full of stocks and bonds. Mum was so flush that Dr. Jimmy gave up his practice to devote full time to the administration of her fortune. In fact, the newlyweds moved into Mother's home presumably to live happily ever after.

The doctor and Rachel were married only five months when Mother suddenly took ill. Her son-in-law took care of her medical needs. Dr. Jimmy didn't do that good a job. Mrs. Skelly died a short time after being stricken. Dr. Jimmy stated that the dear soul was carried away by "bilious fever," whatever that is.

Ah, but even the Grim Reaper has his brighter side. All of Mrs. Skelly's worldly goods were left to Rachel. Not one to let grass grow under his feet, Jimmy saw to it that Rachel drew up a will with him as beneficiary.

With the coming of spring, Jimmy planned a trip to Germany to take part in his favorite sport, falconry. He had a bit of a problem. Rachel was somewhat pregnant, but this inconvenience was overcome when it was decided that she would spend some time in London while Jimmy continued on to Germany.

Excitedly, plans were drawn up. On June 3, Jimmy and Rachel rented rooms at a Mrs. Heppingstall's home in London. A Captain Clark and his daughter, who were friends of the doctor, lived close by. It was Jimmy's plan to spend a few days in London with Rachel while she became acquainted with the Captain's daughter, who would act as her companion during his absence.

On the day of her arrival, a Tuesday, Rachel was in fine spirits. She attended the theatre that evening with her husband, Captain Clark and his daughter. Next day, Rachel didn't feel well. She stayed in bed, but the following day, Thursday, was up and about and felt so well she went shopping at 10 in the morning and didn't return home until 5 o'clock.

Later that evening, Dr. Jimmy called on an old friend, a surgeon named

Donaghue. Dr. Jimmy explained that he had been taking tiny quantities of prussic acid for medicinal purposes for years and required a small quantity. Next morning, Dr. Donaghue sent a one ounce bottle of the deadly poison to Jimmy's rooms.

Early on Saturday morning the landlady, Mrs. Heppingstall, heard the happy couple moving about in their rooms. Shortly after 7 a.m., Dr. Jimmy requested a tumbler of hot water and a spoon. Mrs. Heppingstall brought them to his rooms. At about 7:30, Dr. Jimmy walked out of his bedroom into an adjoining sitting room and proceeded to write some letters.

Thirty minutes later, Dr. Jimmy screamed for help. Mrs. Heppingstall came on the fly. She found Rachel lying unconscious in bed, frothing at the mouth. Dr. Jimmy was excited, but did not seem to react to the seriousness of the moment. Mrs. Heppingstall hurriedly instructed her maid, Sarah Williams, to fetch Captain Clark. Meanwhile, Rachel went into convulsions. When Mrs. Heppingstall implored Dr. Jimmy to do something, he replied, "It is no fit. It is a disease of the heart from which her mother died some months ago."

Finally Clark arrived, took one look and dashed out, returning moments later with his own physician, Dr. Garrett. They were too late. Rachel died with her head on Mrs. Heppingstall's shoulder. Dr. Garrett informed the bereaved husband that an inquest and autopsy would be necessary.

The results of the autopsy indicated that Rachel had died from prussic acid, which was found in her stomach. An inquest revealed enough incriminating information to charge Dr. Belany with his wife's murder.

Dr. Jimmy's trial, which began on August 21, 1844, became a celebrated one, chiefly because the jury was asked to weigh a preponderance of circumstantial evidence against one basic possibility.

An array of witnesses was called to the stand and swore that Dr. Jimmy and Rachel had been an ideal couple who had apparently been very much in love. Preliminaries dispensed with, everyone got down to the business at hand.

Sarah Williams, Mrs. Heppingstall's maid, told the court that she had found the prussic acid bottle and a used tumbler on a small table near Rachel's bed. The neck of the bottle was broken. After Rachel's death Sarah had also found broken glass on the steps of the front door, but not in the room where Rachel died. Later the prussic acid bottle was nowhere to be found. Dr. Jimmy stated that he had thrown it away in a vacant field, but it was never recovered.

Dr. Garrett testified that Jimmy had called on him several times after his wife's death inquiring about the cause of death. On one occasion he told Garrett that he had been taking three drops of prussic acid daily for years and had purchased some from Dr. Donaghue before Rachel died.

He went on to explain that on the day of the tragedy he was attempting to take his daily dose when he broke the neck of the prussic acid bottle while taking out the stopper. Some of the acid spilled on the bedroom floor. Trying to be careful with the remainder, he poured it into a tumbler and left the room to write letters. Dr. Jimmy told Garrett, "I heard a scream. I immediately went in a found my wife in convulsions. She said, 'Oh, dear me! I have taken some of the strong drink out of the tumbler. Give me some cold water.'"

It must be pointed out that this statement was given to Garrett before the autopsy revealed that prussic acid had been the cause of death. It is well known that prussic acid gives off a strong smell of bitter almonds. Dr. Garrett stated that he did not smell bitter almonds when he entered Rachel's bedroom. If some had been spilled on the floor, the odor would have been obvious.

There you have it. It was definitely proven that Dr. Jimmy purchased prussic acid, that Rachel drank the prussic acid, and that Jimmy stood to inherit his wife's fortune upon her death.

A guilty verdict appeared certain until the solicitor general instructed the jury: "The question you have to decide is whether the prussic acid had been taken by the wife by mistake or whether the accused had been guilty of the capital offence of administering it to her or purposely placing it in her way in order that she might take it herself."

The jury took only one hour to find the defendant not guilty. However, matters didn't end with the verdict. Dr. Jimmy, who most probably was guilty of murder, was so hated by the public that he was forced to leave London for Sunderland the day of his release. He arrived home in time to witness his effigy being set on fire in front of his house. Three days later, his home was burned to the ground by an angry mob. Dr. James Belany was fortunate to escape with his life. It is reported that he made his way to Newcastle and was never heard of again.

DR. WILLIAM PALMER 1855

POISONERS as a group have always plied their dubious profession under an extreme disadvantage. They simply have to obtain their poison somewhere. Invariably a chemist or pharmacist ends up on the witness stand pointing a finger at the accused exclaiming, "He said it was to get rid of rats," or some other innocuous expression designed to lend legitimacy to the purchase.

That is, unless the accused happens to be a *doctor*.

Dr. William Palmer was born on October 21, 1824 in Rugeley, England and took his medical degree in London. During his student days he gained quite a reputation as a gambler with a particular affinity for the ponies. He returned to Rugeley and married a colonel's daughter, Annie Brooks. Everything went along well with the doctor and his wife as he established a large and profitable practice. Dr. Palmer neither smoked nor drank, and who are we to criticize if he bet a bob or two on the horses now and then. The Palmers lived in a big house, and he appeared to have everything any man could want.

Then one day an annoying lady from Rugeley presented him with an illegitimate child. Being a man of medicine he thought it would be a good idea to give the newborn child a physical examination. The child died of convulsions shortly after the visit to the doctor's office.

Dr. Palmer and Annie proceeded to have five children during the course of their marriage, and all but one died of convulsions. The eldest, Willie, through the luck of the draw, outlived dear old Dad.

After the initial pleasures of married life had worn off, Dr. Palmer started to bet heavily on the horses. Then, as now, it was very difficult to beat the nags and he got deeper and deeper into debt. Finally his mother-in-law, Mrs. Thornton, was approached for a loan. She sent him 20 pounds, and in effect told him to get lost. William, never one to pass up a mark, invited Mrs. Thornton to come stay with him and Annie. She was dead within two weeks, and the Palmers inherited nine houses. The doctor was furious when he found out they were in need of repair.

Then Dr. Palmer invited an acquaintance of his, Mr. Bladon, to visit. He owed Bladon several hundred pounds, which he promised to pay back during his stay. Poor Bladon was hardly settled in the house before he passed away suddenly during the night, writhing with convulsions. Dr. Palmer was obviously distressed at losing his friend. He brought in a colleague, Dr. Bamford, during that last horrible night, and it was Dr. Bamford who signed the death certificate with the cause of death being English cholera. In all fairness, we should point out that 80-year-old Dr. Bamford was a tottering, half-blind gentleman who looked up to Dr. Palmer and was flattered at being consulted. Kindly Dr. Palmer took care of his friend's funeral arrangements. He was even decent enough to tell Bladon's widow that while her husband owed him huge sums of money, under the circumstances, he would forget the debt.

Another gentleman named Bly was hounding Palmer for £800 when he was invited down to Rugeley for a visit. Exit Bly.

Around now, Mrs. Palmer was beginning to wonder. First her children, and now it seemed that everyone who walked into their front door was being carried out. She didn't have all that long to worry. Mrs. Palmer attended a concert in Liverpool on the night of September 18, 1854 and took a slight chill. Dr. Palmer prescribed bed rest. Their servant, Eliza Thorn, was preparing Mrs. Palmer's meals, but the considerate doctor insisted on carrying them upstairs and feeding his wife. The patient vomited continuously and grew weaker. Dr. Bamford was called in and was told by Dr. Palmer that his wife had English cholera. She was dead in two weeks. Dr. Bamford duly signed the death certificate, and Palmer collected £13,000 in insurance money.

By now William had his own string of horses, and the added expense of trainers, stables and jockeys. His horses can best be described as slow. The doctor was spending money faster than he could kill people.

William, who never drank himself, had a brother who was an alcoholic. He convinced his brother that he would give him a loan which the brother would never have to pay back. William would take out insurance on his life, and when he died Dr. Palmer would get his money back. The brother, Walter, who was in a daze most of the time, went for it. Dr. Palmer sobered him up long enough to pass the physical exam required by the insurance company. You guessed it. Walter passed away, and Dr. Palmer again collected £13,000 insurance.

Still the flow of money coming in wasn't enough, and soon Dr. Palmer was borrowing from loan sharks and paying 60 per cent interest. The money lender, Mr. Pratt, demanded money on certain dates, and unlike previous lenders, he would not be put off.

One day at the race track, Dr. Palmer met John Parsons Cook. Now Cook was a friend cut from the same cloth as Palmer. He had his own stable and was a hard-drinking playboy. One day at the races Cook had a long shot come in by a nose. The men had a champagne supper and some further drinks to celebrate. During the celebration Palmer gave Cook some brandy, and he immediately took ill. When it came time to return to Rugeley, Palmer suggested that Cook return with him. There were comfortable lodgings at the Talbot Arms, right across the street from his own house. Cook thought the doctor most obliging, and the two men left together.

Once installed at the Talbot Arms, Cook's illness became worse. The more Dr. Palmer prescribed for him, the worse he became. Finally he died. After he passed away, Palmer produced cheques in his favor signed by Cook. The doctor was making his usual hasty funeral arrangements for his friend, when a spoil-sport arrived on the scene. Cook's stepfather, a Mr. Stevens, advised Palmer that he would make all the arrangements. In fact, he thought the whole thing smelled to high heaven. Stevens was going to have a post mortem performed on Cook's body and an inquiry into his death.

On Friday, December 14, the results of the post mortem were presented at the inquiry. No strychnine was found in the body, but the cause of death was given as tetanus which was the result of the administration of strychnine. A verdict of wilful murder was returned against Dr. Palmer.

The whole of England talked of little else but the Dr. William Palmer case. There were many who couldn't believe that the gambler and mass murderer described by the newspapers was the same gentle doctor they knew. The bodies of his wife Annie and his brother Walter were exhumed. Annie's body was found to contain antimony. While no poison was evident in Walter's body, it was believed that he met his death by the administration of prussic acid. Traces of this acid would have evaporated since death.

Dr. Palmer's house and the Talbot Arms became so notorious that an enterprising photographer set up his equipment in front of the two establishments. For a small sum you could have your picture taken with the murder buildings in the background. Dr. Palmer was speedily found guilty of murder. In 1855, there were still public executions in England. Before a howling crowd, shouting "Poisoner, poisoner!" Dr. Palmer was hanged. He was 31 years old.

DR. THOMAS SMETHURST 1859

AFTER a lengthy period of time, it is a rare crime that continues to hold the essential elements of mystery, intrigue and, above all, the burning question of the accused's innocence or guilt.

It is 134 years since Dr. Thomas Smethurst's star shone ever so brightly on the stage of murderous infamy. The good doctor was not a big man, nor was he particularly attractive. His one outstanding feature was his luxuriant crop of red hair. While still a student, Thomas met and married Mary Durham, who was a mature 51 and twenty years his senior. From the outset, there is no evidence that the doctor and his wife had anything but a conventional marriage.

Dr. Smethurst obtained his medical degree from the University of Erlangen and practised for years in both London and Ramsgate before selling his practice in 1853. For the next six years, he travelled extensively on the continent and in general, we are safe in assuming, led the good life.

In 1859, Thomas and Mary were living in quarters in a Bayswater rooming house. It was here that Thomas met Isabella Bankes, a fellow roomer. Let's consider Isabella's balance sheet for a moment. She was single, rather attractive in a delicate sort of way, was pleasant company, had a substantial income and was a relatively young 42. All of these assets compared favorably with Mrs. Smethurst, who had seen 74 summers come and go.

Ask any accountant; every balance sheet has some liabilities. Isabella had one flaw. She was subject to stomach trouble and often had to leave the dining room table to vomit. There is some evidence that this condition ran in the woman's family.

Isabella was charmed by the glib medic and there is little doubt that she fell in love. The basis of Thomas' attraction to Isabella was not as clear cut or well defined. We do know that the couple carried on to such an extent that the land-lady of the rooming house, Mrs. Smith, asked Isabella to leave the premises.

Mrs. Smith must have mulled over in her mind the moral dilemma of a mar-ried man and a single woman hugging and kissing each other in front of other guests in her house against the loss of income if she tossed Miss Bankes out on her ear. The morals of the era won out. Isabella left. A short time later, Dr. Smethurst joined her. What Mrs. Smethurst thought of all this is unknown. It is a possibility that she was not aware of the other woman in her husband's life. Isn't it an axiom of the triangle business that the wife is always the last to know?

Dr. Thomas Smethurst and Isabella Bankes were married at Battersea Church and set up housekeeping in Richmond. It is inconceivable that Isabella wasn't aware that the man she was marrying was already married. Sly dogs in murderous plots have been known to pull off such deceptions, but on balance, Isabella simply had to know.

It wasn't long after the wedding that Isabella started to feel ill, which wasn't at all surprising. She had never been what you would call a healthy woman. Dr. Smethurst ministered to his new wife, but when she displayed a decided lack of improvement, he called in another doctor on the recommendation of his landlady, Mrs. Robinson.

Dr. Julius conferred with Smethurst and Isabella. He learned that she was suffering from excessive vomiting and diarrhea. He prescribed bismuth and common grey powder. When Isabella not only showed no improvement, but grew steadily worse, Dr. Julius suspected that somehow his patient was suffering from irritant poisoning. Dr. Julius called in his associate, Dr. Bird, to see Isabella. After Dr. Julius advised Dr. Bird of his suspicions, Dr. Bird agreed that the patient may have been poisoned.

It was seventeen days after Dr. Julius was first brought into the case that Dr. Smethurst called on a Richmond lawyer. On April 30, he showed up at the office of lawyer Senior with Isabella's will. It was handwritten by Smethurst. He suggested that Senior witness the signing the next day and do whatever lawyers do to make the will binding and legal. The following day, Senior called at the Smethursts', where he executed a proper will signed by Isabella Bankes, leaving her entire estate to Thomas Smethurst. She signed the will Isabella Bankes, not Isabella Smethurst, which leads one to believe that she knew very well she had taken part in a bigamous marriage.

While all this was going on, Isabella's health continued to deteriorate. The team of Julius and Bird called in yet another physician, Dr. Todd. He suggested that there was a real possibility that the patient was being poisoned and ordered that a stool be examined. This specimen was tested by Dr. Alfred Taylor, professor of chemistry at Guy's Hospital and a well known authority on such matters.

On May 2, 1859, based on this renowned doctor's findings, Dr. Smethurst was arrested and charged with administering poison. Dr. Smethurst told the court that his wife might die because of his absence. The presiding magistrate listened to his plea and released the prisoner on his own recognizance, but not before officials accompanied him to his home and confiscated all the bottles, vials and containers they could find. These were turned over to Dr. Taylor for examination. Next day, Isabella Bankes died. Dr. Taylor advised authorities that he had found arsenic in one of the bottles turned over to him for analysis. Dr. Smethurst was arrested and charged with murder.

In the years since Dr. Smethurst stood trial in London's Old Bailey, it is doubtful if any of the succeeding trials held there were more interesting or controversial than the Smethurst trial.

The prosecution contended that Isabella Bankes' death had been the culmination of an elaborate plot. As proof of this they produced a letter written by the accused man to his legal wife, telling her that it was his wish to be reunited with her and that it wouldn't be long before his wish would be fulfilled.

The fact that Dr. Smethurst stood to gain financially by Isabella's death weighed heavily against him. Isabella owned a property valued at £1800 which was left outright to Smethurst. However, the interest on £5000 she had been collecting ceased upon her death and reverted to other members of her family. Most sensational of all was the autopsy result. At the time of her death, Isabella was five to seven weeks pregnant.

An array of doctors took the witness stand for the prosecution, attesting to the state of Miss Bankes' internal organs. All agreed that the condition of these organs was compatible with irritant poisoning and nothing else.

It was left to Dr. Alfred Taylor, far and away the leading authority at the trial, to cause the greatest sensation and, some would say, embarrassment to the medical profession. Dr. Taylor stated that he had found no arsenic in any of Miss Bankes' internal organs. Under cross examination, he admitted that his previous statement given to a magistrate that he had found arsenic in one of the bottles seized on the day Smethurst was arrested was erroneous. Dr. Taylor said that a

mistake had been made. He told the court that when he gave his original statement, he believed it to be true. Since then, he had discovered that while performing the tests for arsenic in that particular bottle he had used a copper gauze
containing impurities which, in effect, had produced arsenic.

This was an explosive admission. Possession of poison is one of the salient
elements in gaining convictions in poison cases. It was Dr. Taylor's original
statement which had led to Dr. Smethurst being tried for murder. Now this vital
piece of evidence had been revoked.

To be fair, as soon as he became aware of his grave error, Dr. Taylor had
informed both the prosecution and the defence. In subsequent testimony, Dr.
Taylor told the court that he had discovered minute quantities of antimony in one
of the deceased woman's organs. One suspects that those in court wondered if
the doctor hadn't made another mistake. Despite Dr. Taylor's error, other doctors
swore that the condition of Isabella's organs could have been caused only by irritant poisoning.

The defence claimed that the Crown had not proven that Dr. Smethurst was
in possession of either arsenic or antimony, nor had it proven that he had administered the deadly poison. They went on to point out that cutting off his rights
to the interest on Isabella's £5000 was not the action of a man who killed for
financial gain. As for the £1800 left to him, this sum would eventually have
been his had Miss Bankes lived. The defence professed that, taking everything
into consideration, Smethurst would have been better off financially had Miss
Bankes not died. Then there was Miss Bankes' history of bilious attacks, general delicate health and pregnancy to consider.

To substantiate their claim, the defence paraded to the witness stand a distinguished group of doctors who swore that, in their opinion, after examining all
the facts, Isabella had not been murdered, but had died of natural causes. Of the
seventeen doctors who were called to the stand during the trial, ten claimed the
victim was poisoned, while seven stated that she had died of natural causes.

The English jury deliberated only forty minutes before finding Dr.
Smethurst guilty of murdering Isabella Bankes. The presiding judge expressed
his agreement with the jury's verdict before passing the death sentence.

Once the verdict was made public, both the legal and medical communities
challenged the justification for the death sentence. While all agreed that the

doctor was a first class cad and might very well have killed his wife, they were adamant in their opinion that, based on the evidence, he should not have been convicted. Several expressed the opinion that even if conviction was warranted, the death sentence should not have been applied. Prestigious medical organizations wrote to officials stating their objections to the conviction. One example, representative of many, appeared in the Dublin Medical Press. Dripping with sarcasm, it reads:

"So much for the position to which the members of the medical profession, in their capacity as witnesses in criminal trials, have been degraded by Drs. Todd, Taylor, Julius, Bird, and Co. They have not left behind them one fixed opinion to guide the public press. The man who, par excellence, was looked upon as the pillar of medical jurisprudence; the man who it was believed could clear up the most obscure case, involving medico-legal considerations, ever brought into a court of justice; the man without whose assistance no criminal suspected of poisoning could be found guilty in England; the man whose opinion was quoted as the highest of all authorities at every trial where analysis is required, is the same who has now admitted the use of impure copper in an arsenic test where a life hung upon his evidence, the same who has brought an amount of disrepute upon his branch of the profession that years will not remove, the ultimate effects of which it is impossible to calculate, which none can regret with a deeper feeling of sorrow than ourselves, though, perhaps, in the end, a lesson may be taught which will not be lost upon the medical jurists, and which may tend to keep the fountain of justice clear and unpolluted. We must look now upon Professor Taylor as having ended his career, and hope he will immediately withdraw into the obscurity of private life, not forgetting to carry with him his favorite arsenical copper. He can never again be listened to in a court of justice, and should henceforth leave the witness-box to the occupation of others."

Scores of such documents were forwarded to the Home Secretary, who in turn sent all the documents, several of them learned treatises on the subject of poisons and the condition of Miss Bankes' internal organs, to Sir Benjamin Collins Brodie, the most prominent medical authority in England. Dr. Brodie studied all the material and came to the conclusion that although the medical evidence threw suspicion on Dr. Smethurst, there was no positive proof of his guilt.

As a result of this report, it was suggested to Queen Victoria that she take the rare step of granting Dr. Smethurst a free pardon. The Queen took the advice and the doctor was freed.

Dr. Smethurst wasn't totally out of the woods. In November 1859, he was charged with bigamy, found guilty and sentenced to one year in prison at hard labor. The man of medicine served his time. Two years after his release, he took legal action to collect on Isabella Bankes' will. The court ruled the document valid. Dr. Thomas Smethurst collected the proceeds of his late wife's will.

DR. GEORGE LAMSON 1882

To perform murder in Victorian England and have the case still considered to be a classic is no mean feat. In those days young people often died due to maladies caused by unsanitary conditions, contaminated water, and tainted food. Those who didn't die of natural causes were often eased into oblivion with the help of some poison or other which was not readily detected. An innovative approach was required to stand out in such a crowd.

Dr. George Lamson was such a trail blazer. At the age of 20 he was studying medicine in Paris. In 1878, by the time he was 28, he was practising medicine in London, England, and had taken a wife.

Pretty Kate John was everything a Victorian wife should have been—pleasant, gracious, devoted, and loyal to her handsome, educated husband. Kate's younger brother, Hubert, died of natural causes a year after the couple's marriage. This tragedy did have a silver lining. Hubert left the Lamsons an amount of money which enabled the good doctor to purchase a medical practice in Bournemouth.

Kate had another brother, Percy. Sixteen-year-old Percy had curvature of the spine, which left him paralyzed from the waist down. Confined to a wheelchair, he was placed in a private school, Blenheim House in Wimbledon, where he seemed to fit in well with the other boys.

All went well for some time. Being a doctor, and husband to a woman who deeply cared for her afflicted brother, it was only natural that Dr. Lamson displayed a certain concern for Percy. On December 3, 1881, he visited Blenheim House.

The principal of the school, William Bedbrook, fetched Percy when the doctor arrived. Dr. Lamson had brought some treats. From a black bag he produced some hard fruit candy and a fruitcake. The doctor cut the cake with a penknife, offering a slice to Percy and the principal, as well as taking a slice himself. All three almost finished the cake at the one sitting.

During the course of idle conversation, Dr. Lamson mentioned that he had recently returned from America and had brought back something new—gelatin capsules. The gelatin dissolved after the capsule was swallowed, effectively doing away with the disagreeable taste of some medicines. Both the principal and Percy tried one. The principal's was empty, but Percy's was filled with sugar from a sugar bowl sitting on a table nearby. He swallowed it without tasting the sugar at all.

The doctor terminated his visit and left the school, informing the principal that he had to catch a train later that night for Florence.

That evening Percy complained of heartburn and went to bed. Later he began to vomit and convulse violently. Two doctors were summoned, but they could do nothing for the boy. At 11:20 that same evening Percy died.

On December 6, a post mortem was held, and it was the opinion of the doctors that Percy had been poisoned. Dr. Lamson was located in Paris. Once informed of the death in the family he immediately returned to London. By that time the story of his visit to the school was known to the authorities. He was arrested and charged with murder.

On March 8, 1882, Lamson's murder trial began in London's Old Bailey. The prosecution quickly established that Percy had been done in by aconite, one of the most lethal poisons known to man. Dr. Lamson had purchased aconite shortly before his visit to the school. He also was deeply in debt and stood to gain financially from Percy's death.

In all murder cases involving poison, the prosecution must establish that the victim was in fact poisoned, and that the accused administered the poison. It was this second point that proved to be a sticky wicket. Bedbrook, the principal, was present at all times during Lamson's visit. The hard candies weren't touched. All three ate the cake. The sugar, which went into the capsule consumed by Percy, came from the school's own sugar bowl.

Despite this little problem, and the doctor's insistence throughout that he was innocent, he was found guilty and sentenced to hang. The sentence was carried out on April 28, 1882. The day before he was hanged Dr. Lamson confessed in writing to the murder of his brother-in-law. He never did state how he had administered the poison, and the solution to the case has baffled criminologists down through the years.

Here is the diabolical method most accepted by those who have closely studied the case. The speculation is that the doctor injected aconite into a raisin, which he then placed back into the cake. He marked the part of the cake containing the fatal raisin, making sure he gave the piece to his victim.

DR. HAWLEY CRIPPEN 1910

THE 35 years between 1875 and 1910 gave rise to a multitude of strange and unusual murders. There were so many people stabbing, strangling and cutting up their fellow men that one hardly knows where to begin. But most of these gentlemen, while they are certainly noteworthy, left their victims where they fell. They didn't experience that blood-chilling confrontation with what has until recently been a fellow human being, and the utterly bothersome task of disposing of the body. So from this era of mass murderers we have plucked a mild, unassuming little man named Dr. Hawley Harvey Crippen.

Hawley was born in Clearwater, Michigan, in 1863, and from the very beginning of his academic career he was considered to be a good student. He was singleminded in his desire to become a doctor, and to this end he studied medicine in Cleveland and New York. After he qualified, he did post-graduate work, becoming an eye and ear specialist. Then he completed his education with further studies in London, England, before returning to the United States, where, between 1885 and 1893, he moved frequently, practising in Detroit, Salt Lake City, New York, St. Louis, Toronto, and Philadelphia.

In 1887, the doctor married one Charlotte Bell, who died, presumably of natural causes, in 1890. After his wife's death, Crippen returned to New York, where he again set up his practice. Dr. Crippen was now a mature 31 years old. He was five feet, seven inches tall, with a decidedly receding hairline, protruding eyes that stared out from behind thick-lensed spectacles, and a small, well-kept moustache. While not altogether a ladies' man, Crippen was neat in appearance and a pleasant, intelligent conversationalist. When he was practising in New York he met a 17-year-old medical secretary called Kunigunde Mackamotzki, who had had the good sense to change her name to Cora Turner. The doctor took one look at Cora's substantial bust, slim waist and well turned ankle and was smitten. The love-struck pair were married almost immediately.

By 1899, the Crippens were living in Philadelphia, and it was here that Cora let the mild Hawley in on a little secret—she wanted to be an opera star. Now,

Crippen was no student of voice, but he had heard his wife sing and knew she had a pleasant soprano warble. On occasion, at parties, he would become rather proud when she rendered a tune or two, but an operatic career—that was something else. The little doctor looked quizzically at his wife. Yes, she said, she seriously wanted to study music. Hawley suggested that they relax in the bedroom and continue the discussion about singing another day. No, said Cora, there would be no sex in the Crippen household until she was promised that he would finance her singing lessons. She received a firm promise that very night.

Soon Crippen found that every cent he made was going for singing lessons for his wife. Cora was extremely serious when it came to her career, even to the point of taking the professional name of Belle Elmore. A few years passed, and Cora's singing lessons had practically bankrupted the distraught Crippen. Besides the financial difficulties her singing had brought him, deep down in his heart he didn't think she was all that good.

By 1900, the couple had been husband and wife for eleven years. Like all of us, they had grown older; the doctor was now a worry-racked 42, and his once receding hairline was in full flight, while Cora, at 28, had begun to put on weight and was becoming slovenly in her appearance. More than that, as the months went by, she started to find fault with Hawley. Little by little she had become an overweight nag; and to make matters worse, she had failed to make a name for herself in the singing world. As she became more frustrated with her career, she more and more frequently denied Crippen that which every husband figures is his right. At the Crippen residence, conjugal bliss had given way to continual bickering.

Then the doctor decided to do something about his dilemma. He was offered, and accepted, the position of manager at Munyon's Patent Remedies in London, England. He figured the move would keep him one step ahead of his creditors, as well as providing him and Cora with a welcome change which might improve the climate of their marriage. Cora had other ideas; she felt that at last she would get an opportunity to appear on the stage of the British Music Hall.

The Crippens arrived in London and took furnished rooms in Bloomsbury. Even before they were comfortably settled, Cora started making the rounds of booking agents, trying to get a high-class singing position. She soon lowered her sights, and was satisfied to accept any singing job she could get. But she had one major drawback. While she made placid Hawley buy her expensive clothing to enhance her appearance when auditioning, she simply couldn't sing. She managed to obtain a few engagements in provincial halls, reaching the pinnacle of her career when she appeared on the same bill as George Formby, Sr., at the Dudley New Empire. A short time after this appearance, she was booed off the stage during another performance. Cora was finding out that the road to fame and fortune was a rocky one.

In 1905, the couple moved from Bloomsbury to 39 Hilldrop Crescent in the Holloway district. It was around this time that 22-year-old Ethel Le Neve became Dr. Crippen's private secretary. The doctor, now in his forties, fell hard for the winsome Ethel, and she for her part was not averse to the positive vibes coming her way from the little doctor. By 1907, Ethel and Hawley were lovers, and not only in the physical sense, for it is a fact that they sincerely loved and cared for each other. Crippen was charmed by the passive, unassuming Ethel, who gave so willingly of herself, in sharp contrast to the domineering, aggressive Cora. And that closed bedroom door in the Crippen residence had to be an additional factor.

Further aggravating an already explosive situation, Cora started to invite her theatrical acquaintances over to Hilldrop Crescent. Cora and her friends hardly missed a day whooping it up, while the mild-mannered doctor would shrug and pay the bills. One day after the gang had left the house, Hawley meekly mentioned to Cora that maybe she should cut down on the expensive food and drink she was serving her friends. Crippen received a blast that could be heard as far away as Stonehenge on a clear day, for even suggesting such a thing. On occasion Cora would do more than party; some evenings she stayed out until the early morning hours, and Crippen knew full well she was having affairs with her broken-down Thespian buddies. On the other hand, Cora was aware that her meek husband was playing around, and if his infidelity managed to keep him out of her hair, so much the better. And so life went on at Hilldrop Crescent, both husband and wife leading separate lives, each tolerating the other's indiscretions.

On January 17, 1910, Dr. Crippen strolled in to Lewis and Burrowes, Chemists, on Oxford Street. He purchased five grains of hyoscin hydrobromide, which, in small doses, is used as a sedative. The clerk had Crippen sign the poisons register—taken in large doses hyoscin hydrobromide is a deadly poison—and remembered the transaction because he could not recall ever having sold such a large amount of the drug before. It can be administered in tea or coffee, and is tasteless. Its effects in massive doses are loss of consciousness, paralysis, and death in a matter of hours.

Two weeks later, on the night of January 31, Cora and Hawley had another couple over for an intimate little dinner party followed by a game of cards. Clara and Paul Martinetti were retired entertainers, who were really friends of Cora's. They had a pleasant enough evening, and left at about one thirty in the morning. The Martinettis were the last people to see Cora alive.

The first sign that all was not normal at the Crippen household came when an organization Cora belonged to—the Music Hall Ladies' Guild—received a letter of resignation advising them that she had to rush to America to take care of a seriously ill relative. The letter was signed by Crippen using his wife's professional name, Belle Elmore, per H.H.C. By word of mouth the news spread that Cora was away in America. Some of her close friends remarked that it was strange that she didn't call someone with an explanation. Still, serious illnesses do strike suddenly and the entertainment set seemed satisfied for the time being.

Then Dr. Crippen commenced to make moves which were not designed to enhance our opinion of his intelligence. He pawned some of Cora's jewelry for £200. On February 12, Ethel Le Neve moved into the house on Hilldrop Crescent, causing tongues to wag. As if that wasn't enough to raise an eyebrow or two, Hawley showed up at a Music Hall Ladies' Ball with Ethel. Only a blind man could have failed to notice that the brooch Ethel was sporting over her left breast was the property of Cora Crippen. Cora's friends didn't like the look of things, and started to ask the doctor embarrassing questions. They simply couldn't get over the idea of Cora leaving without so much as a goodbye. Crippen told the ladies that a relative of his who lived in San Francisco was seriously ill. He had been told that this relative had mentioned him in his will, and as the sum involved was substantial, Cora and he thought that one of them should go to California to protect their interests. He couldn't go due to his workload, so Cora had made the trip. That story pacified the ladies for a few more weeks.

Then the Music Hall Ladies' Guild received a telegram from Dr. Crippen advising them that dear Cora herself was seriously ill in California. An official of the Guild, a Miss Hawthorne, visited Hilldrop Crescent, and found the mild little doctor half crazy with worry. She left the house with tears in her eyes feeling guilty that suspicious thoughts about Crippen should ever have entered her mind.

A few days later Miss Hawthorne received another telegram from Crippen, this time advising her that the worst had happened—Cora had passed away from pneumonia. The ladies of the Guild inquired as to where the funeral would be held; they wanted to send flowers. Dr. Crippen told them that the body was to be cremated and the ashes would be sent back to London. He then inserted a memorial notice in The Era, a theatrical newspaper. Immediately after he placed the notice, he left for a short trip to Dieppe, France. When Cora's friends dropped around to his office, they noticed that Ethel wasn't at her desk. The ladies talked about Ethel's absence for a moment or two, but the consensus of opinion was that it was most natural for Crippen to have given his secretary some time off while he was away.

Ethel, however, had accompanied her lover to France, and was continually at his side, consoling and comforting him. She couldn't help but notice that the doctor carried a large leather hatbox with him when he boarded the boat for the English Channel crossing. When she inquired about the box while in Dieppe, the doctor replied that he had misplaced it during the crossing, and it never entered her mind again.

When the pair returned to London, Crippen found that the suspicions concerning his wife's disappearance had grown. It seems that Mr. Nash, a friend of Cora's, had just returned to London from New York. He had been there while Cora had supposedly passed through the city on her way to California. Nash knew Cora well, and knew how she felt about their mutual friends in New York. He found it incredible that she had never once contacted them. When he told Miss Hawthorne of his suspicions, they decided to contact Scotland Yard.

It was over four months since Cora had last been seen when Chief Inspector Walter Dew and Sergeant Arthur Miller knocked on the door of 39 Hilldrop Crescent. Dr. Crippen amicably invited the officers in for a cup of tea. In a somewhat hesitant manner Inspector Dew broached the reason for their visit. It seems some friends had become suspicious when they noticed Miss Le Neve wearing a piece of jewelry belonging to his wife. Dr. Crippen cleared his throat—there was something he had to explain to the officers—you see, his wife wasn't dead at all; she had run off with a music hall performer named Bruce Miller. She had been "carrying on" with him for some time, and had finally picked up and left without a word to any of her friends. He had been too ashamed and embarrassed to tell anyone the truth, so he had made up the story of his wife's death. In reality, he thought the two lovers had headed for Chicago.

"Now, doctor, about Miss Le Neve and the jewelry?" Crippen didn't bat an eyelash. He explained that his wife had left in such a hurry she had left her jewelry behind. With a knowing wink Crippen admitted that he had taken up with Ethel Le Neve after his wife ran away, and he was now her lover.

The Inspector looked at the sergeant and the sergeant looked at the inspector. The whole story had a ring of truth to it. The two men conducted a cursory examination of the entire premises and found nothing suspicious. They advised Crippen to place an advertisement in a Chicago paper to assist in finding his wife and still the gossip once and for all. Crippen assured them that he would take their advice. The policemen apologized to Dr. Crippen for the disturbance and returned to the station satisfied that no crime had been committed.

On July 11, 1910, three days after the police visit to Crippen's house, Miss Hawthorne called Inspector Dew for a progress report on the Crippen affair. Dew told Miss Hawthorne that Cora had run away with another man, and that the whole matter was not of concern to the police. Miss Hawthorne informed Dew that something was wrong. Crippen and Le Neve had disappeared. Dew was forced to look into the case again. This time he found out that shortly after his meeting with Crippen on the previous Saturday, July 8, the doctor had written notes to his business associates resigning his position, cleaning out his office, and together with Ethel Le Neve had dropped from sight.

The doctor, who had appeared cool as a cucumber from the first day his wife was noticed to be missing, had finally panicked. Dew questioned Crippen's fellow employees and found a young man who had performed an unusual errand for him. The doctor had asked his colleague to purchase an entire outfit of clothing to fit a boy of sixteen. The young man gave a detailed description of the articles he had purchased for Crippen—brown tweed suit, boots, a hat and an overcoat. After some reflection, Dew came to the conclusion that the clothing had been purchased to disguise Ethel Le Neve in her flight with Crippen. On

Tuesday, July 12, Scotland Yard decided to make a thorough search of 39 Hilldrop Crescent. For three days the police peered into and poked at the house while the garden was being dug up. On the third day some loose bricks were discovered under the coal bin in the cellar. The remainder of the floor had mortar between the bricks. The loose bricks were removed, and under a few inches of clay, the police found the remains of Mrs. Crippen—really just "a mass of flesh" wrapped in a pyjama jacket. The body had been dissected and the head was missing.

Inspector Dew checked back on Crippen's actions and found the chemist where he had purchased the hyoscin hydrobromide. Chemical analysis of Cora's remains confirmed that she had met her death as the result of the administration of this drug. On July 16, a warrant was issued for the arrest of Crippen and Le Neve for murder and mutilation. The story was a sensation, and became even more newsworthy because no one seemed to know where to look for the two fugitives. In England, during the time Crippen and Le Neve were at large, little else was discussed. Everyone had a theory about the missing pair, and they were constantly being spotted throughout England and the continent by both the police and the public.

In reality, Dew was on the right track. Crippen had dressed his lover as a boy, and the two of them had left the country, heading for Rotterdam, Holland. The doctor used the alias of John Philo Robinson, and Ethel took on the identity of his son George.

They made their way to Antwerp, Belgium, where on July 20 they booked passage for Quebec City, Canada, on the SS Montrose.

It is quite possible that the fugitives would have made good their escape had it not been for the captain of the Montrose. Almost from the first hour the pair boarded his ship, the captain noticed the unnatural actions of the Robinsons. He watched the way they held hands, which seemed decidedly odd for a father and son. The second day out of Antwerp he noticed how feminine young Robinson's movements were when he caught a tennis ball on deck. By July 22, the captain was sure that he had Crippen and Le Neve on his ship. Captain Kendall radioed his suspicions to the managing director of the Canadian Pacific Shipping Co. in Liverpool, who passed the message along to Scotland Yard. Several messages went back and forth, and Scotland Yard became convinced that they had located the wanted pair. On July 23, Inspector Dew boarded the Laurentic, a much faster ship than the Montrose, at Liverpool. It was calculated that Dew would overtake his quarry just before the Montrose docked in Canada. The case now took on the aspect of a race. Each day the press carried the relative positions of both ships, vividly illustrating the relentless pursuit of the Montrose by the Laurentic. The distance between the two ships diminished steadily as the Montrose approached Canada.

It is well to remember that the passing of radio messages was relatively new to the public. Guglielmo Marconi had established wireless communication across the Atlantic in 1901. This added feature of the chase captured the imagination, not only of England, but of the entire world. At the time of Crippen's flight for freedom, only about one hundred ships were equipped with radios. Within six months over six hundred ships were so equipped and it is believed the Crippen case was instrumental in making radios a legal requirement for ocean going vessels.

While all this was going on, Crippen and Le Neve thought they had succeeded in evading the authorities, and didn't even know that Cora's body had been discovered. Finally, on July 31 the Laurentic caught up with the Montrose off Father Point, Quebec. Dew boarded the ship and arranged with Captain Kendall to meet Crippen in the captain's quarters.

"Good morning, Dr. Crippen, I am Chief Inspector Dew."

"Good morning, Mr. Dew," replied Crippen.

"You will be arrested for the murder and mutilation of your wife, Cora Crippen," stated Dew.

"I am not sorry, the anxiety has been too much."

The dramatic confrontation between detective and murderer was over. Extradition proceedings were dispensed with speedily, and the couple were returned to England to stand trial. Crippen's trial took place in October 1910, and took four days to complete. Public interest in the Crippen trial was greater than in any other heard in London's famous Old Bailey. Huge crowds spilled out onto the street. People stood waiting for hours to catch a glimpse of the accused. The proceedings had all the right ingredients—a love triangle, promiscuous relations, poison, a mutilated body, a missing head, drama on the high seas, a beautiful young girl, and a man of medicine gone wrong.

When it was all over Dr. Crippen was found guilty of the murder of his wife. He was executed on the gallows at Pentonville on November 23, 1910. His last request was that a photograph of Ethel be buried with him, and this request was granted and carried out. Crippen went to his death proclaiming Ethel's innocence.

Two weeks after Crippen's trial, Ethel Le Neve stood trial as an accessory after the fact at the Old Bailey. The evidence against her was flimsy, and it is doubtful if she ever realized that she was doing anything more than running away with her lover. Ethel steadfastly professed that she did not even know of Mrs. Crippen's death. She was acquitted, and left for Canada on the day Dr. Crippen was executed.

After five years she returned to England using an assumed name, Ethel Nelson. She married clerk Stanley Smith, and lived a quiet life in Croydon, South London. Only her husband and one other close friend ever knew her real identity. In 1967, 57 years after the Crippen-Le Neve trials, a gentle, grey-haired grandmother, lying close to death in Dulwich hospital, made a last request, that a locket containing a picture of Dr. Hawley Crippen be placed in her casket. So Ethel Le Neve passed from this earth.

DR. JOHN ADAMS 1950

DR. John Bodkin Adams, 58, had practised medicine for over 35 years in the resort town of Eastbourne, England. He never married, and lived alone in a large Victorian home with only a housekeeper to care for his needs. The doctor had a lucrative practice and was considered to be a pillar of the community. Yet he was to become the central figure in one of the most sensational murder cases ever to unfold in England.

The doctor's life was to become entwined forever with that of a patient, Mrs. Edith Alice Morell. An elderly lady, Mrs. Morell was visiting her son in Cheshire in June 1948, when she suffered a stroke. Taken to the Cheshire General Hospital, she was in great distress, and was given a quarter grain of morphine each day for the nine days she stayed in hospital. On July 5 she was transferred by ambulance to Eastbourne, where she came under the care of Dr. Adams, who remained her doctor until her death on November 13, 1950, at the age of 81. Mrs. Morell's body was cremated, and that, for all intents and purposes, was that.

Six years passed before any further notice was paid to Mrs. Morell and the manner of her death. In 1956 rumors spread in and around Eastbourne that many of Dr. Adams' patients who had died had left him bequests in their wills. These rumors came to the attention of the authorities and it wasn't long before Scotland Yard dispatched senior investigators to look into Dr. Adams and his medical practice. As a result of their inquiries the doctor was arrested and charged with Mrs. Morell's murder.

The murder case that unfolded captured the imagination of the English-speaking world. While many doctors have stood trial for murder in England, rarely had a doctor been accused of murder while ministering to a patient. In fact, the last such case took place over a hundred years earlier, when the infamous Dr. Palmer of Rugeley was convicted of murder. The Adams trial lasted seventeen days, making it the longest murder trial to take place in England up to that time.

Mrs. Morell's stroke had left her partially paralyzed. Eventually she was able to get around with assistance, but required nurses around the clock. Although the alleged crime was six years old at the time of the trial, the nursing records detailing frequency of injections and quantities of drugs administered were available. All medication, whether injected by the nurses or not, was given under the doctor's instructions.

It was established that Dr. Adams was a beneficiary in Mrs. Morell's will. He stood to gain a prewar Rolls Royce, as well as an amount of silver valued at £275. After Mrs. Morell's death Dr. Adams did, in fact, come into possession of these two items.

From the time Mrs. Morell came under Dr. Adams' care, she received a quarter grain of morphine and a quarter grain of heroin daily. No doubt she became somewhat addicted to the good feeling these drugs gave her, for generally speaking, Mrs. Morell was an irritable and demanding patient.

During September 1950, when Mrs. Morell had only seven weeks to live, her medication was drastically altered by Dr. Adams. He instructed that she be given increased quantities of both morphine and heroin. Mrs. Morell received 10 grains of heroin on November 8, 12 grains on November 9, and 18 on November 11. On November 12, the day before she died, Mrs. Morell received three and a half grains of heroin and two grains of morphine.

Was Mrs. Morell's dosage of these drugs increased in order to end her life or was the doctor doing everything possible to alleviate pain for a dying patient? The line is a thin one, which many physicians have to walk. Maybe it was even thinner in 1950 than it is today.

Other pertinent events that occurred during Mrs. Morell's illness came to light. Dr. Adams had known he was in his patient's will. At one point he had gone to Scotland for a vacation and Mrs. Morell, in a fit of anger, changed her will, leaving him nothing. Later Dr. Adams returned to her good graces and was placed back in her will. There is little doubt that Dr. Adams was concerned about his patient's will. He had discussed the matter with Mrs. Morell's lawyer on several occasions, and at one point suggested that the lawyer draw up a new will and get Mrs. Morell's son to agree to it at a later date. Mrs. Morell's lawyer turned down such a shady proposition.

Conversely, there was the matter of the competent nurses who took care of Mrs. Morell during her long illness. Not one of them spoke up or suggested that during her last weeks Mrs. Morell's dosage was too high. Even Dr. Adams' partner, Dr. Harris, who filled in for his colleague while he was in Scotland, continued the regime of morphine and heroin. His explanation was that it is customary, all things being equal, to continue medication as prescribed by the regular doctor.

What could be the doctor's motive for murder? He had a lucrative practice and was well respected. Why would he purposely set out to destroy a partially paralyzed elderly woman who had a limited life expectancy? There were those who believed that Dr. Adams set out to make Mrs. Morell totally dependent on him after he realized that she was addicted to drugs. By abruptly increasing her dosage he intended to influence her in any way he wished concerning her will. It must be remembered that Mrs. Morell was an extremely wealthy woman. When her will was finally probated, her estate amounted to £175,000. A tidy sum today, in 1950 this amounted to a fortune.

Detectives uncovered a form, signed by Dr. Adams, which had secured Mrs. Morell's cremation. One of the questions of the form was, "Have you, as far as you are aware, any pecuniary interest in the death of the deceased?" The doctor answered in the negative, although it is quite clear that he was aware he would receive the Rolls and the silver under the terms of Mrs. Morell's will. Mrs. Morell was cremated the day after her death.

It took six years before the doctor was asked his reason for lying on the cremation form. His only explanation was that he had not lied from any sinister intent, but only to circumvent red tape and get on with the cremation.

On the day of Dr. Adams' arrest he made a statement that was to haunt him throughout his trial. In response to being advised of his rights he told a Scotland Yard detective, "Murder? Can you prove it was murder?" Not exactly the utterance of an innocent man.

During the Adams trial it was revealed that Mrs. Morell was not in pain while under the doctor's care. Expert medical opinion stated that morphine and heroin should be used only if the patient is suffering agonizing pain. Mrs. Morell was irritable and had trouble sleeping. Other drugs should have been used, and furthermore, Dr. Adams, as a competent physician, would know this. In fact, two expert medical witnesses swore that the dosages prescribed by Dr. Adams were certain to cause death.

Dr. Adams' defence attorneys produced experts of their own, who stated that it is impossible to tell exactly how an 81-year-old partially paralyzed woman died. Remember, Mrs. Morell's body had been cremated, so it was impossible to perform an autopsy. The defence doctors claimed that it is quite common for an individual who has suffered one stroke to suffer a second, fatal one. In fact, this was suggested to the jury as an alternative to murder. This theory was ridiculed by the prosecution and contributed the only levity to an otherwise grim affair. Crown attorneys likened this second stroke theory to the instance of a man walking on a railroad track and being struck by a train. Is it reasonable to assume he had a heart attack a moment before the train struck, and therefore death was not due to a train accident but to a heart attack?

The crux of the Adams' trial revolved around the definition of murder. Murder is an act in which the intent is to kill, and that does in fact kill. A doctor attending a dying patient is compelled to take those measures necessary to relieve pain and suffering, and if his efforts incidentally shorten life, that is not murder. If he deliberately and knowingly cuts off life, that is murder. In the Adams case it was totally irrelevant if life was shortened by a day or by a year. If the intent to kill was there, it was murder. If a doctor errs in his judgment, and institutes measures that effectively terminate life, that is not murder. Intent was of the essence in the Adams case.

Despite the suspicious circumstances surrounding Dr. Adams and his particular brand of medicine, he received the benefit of reasonable doubt. The jury took only 44 minutes to find him not guilty.

The trial of Dr. Adams for Mrs. Morell's murder stands alone, and I have tried to relate the salient points of the tedious trial as fairly as possible. However, the reader should know that, at the time, Dr. Adams came under strong suspicion for the deaths of two other patients. In fact, at the preliminary hearing that preceded the Morell trial, it was alleged that Adams murdered two other rich patients, a Mr. and Mrs. Hullett. While Adams was in custody, the bodies of these two suspected victims were exhumed, but as the Crown took no action against Adams in this regard, we can only assume nothing incriminating was found.

After his acquittal of the murder of Mrs. Morell, Dr. Adams was arrested and charged with sixteen counts of forging medical prescriptions and contravention of the Cremation and Dangerous Drugs Acts. He pleaded guilty to fifteen of these charges and was fined £2,400.

As a result of these disclosures, the General Medical Council of England had Dr. Adams' name struck off the Register of Medical Practitioners. John Bodkin Adams never practised medicine in England again.

DR. PETER DRINKWATER 1959

DR. Peter Drinkwater seemed to have the world by the tail when he completed his medical training at St. Bartholomew's Hospital in London, England in 1959. Within a year, he married and, together with his wife Christine, set out to conquer the world. The doctor joined the Royal Army Medical Corps. For five years he served in Germany and later in British Guyana. Then something went wrong.

During the latter years of his term in the army the handsome young doctor deteriorated rapidly. He drank with a vengeance, mixing his drinks with drinamyl and amphetamines. After he attempted suicide by placing a pistol to his head and threatening to pull the trigger, he was returned to England and discharged.

Dr. Drinkwater joined an existing medical practice in Reading, where he continued his wild lifestyle. He had been fined several times for reckless driving when he struck and killed an elderly cyclist. The man was dragged 40 yards before the doctor stopped his vehicle and ascertained that the cyclist was dead. Dr. Drinkwater then drove away, neglecting to report the accident until 30 minutes later. After this latest brush with the law, his driver's licence was suspended for three years.

It was during this time that the doctor began to pay a great deal of attention to one of his patients, blonde, shapely Carole Califano. Carole lived in apparent harmony with her hubby, Gerrard, until Peter Drinkwater came upon the scene. Gerrard owned a chain of hairdressing salons, which provided him and his wife with more than an adequate living. As time passed, the doctor evidently provided Carole with more earthy pleasures. Whatever the reason, Carole became infatuated with Drinkwater and Drinkwater became infatuated with Carole.

In May 1971, Christine Drinkwater divorced her husband on the grounds of cruelty. Seems the good doctor habitually came home loaded to the gills with booze and drugs. He liked to beat up Christine just for fun. She took their two children with her when she left.

Three months later, Carole Califano left her husband and eight-year-old daughter, Bridgetta. She moved in with Dr. Drinkwater. In the months preceding the move, Carole had been taking drugs given to her by her lover. Those who knew her well claimed that she was now under the complete domination of Peter Drinkwater.

For about a year, Carole was something of a zombie in the doctor's hands. Her continued use of drugs often threw her into a state of depression. On July 2, 1972, Dr. Drinkwater frantically called another medic, Dr. King, and implored him to rush over to his home in Hemsby, Norfolk. Drinkwater said it was an emergency, and sure enough it was. Carole was lying face down on her bed. She was dead.

Peter Drinkwater told the first detective at the scene that Carole had been extremely depressed because he had been in contact with his wife. She believed that he was about to break up their relationship, which was not the case. Obviously distressed, she had decided to end it all with an overdose of drugs. The investigator bought that one for the time being. An autopsy indicated that Carole had died as the result of four substances taken in combination.

Once again, Dr. Drinkwater was interviewed. This time he told a different story. He and Carole had argued about her suspicion he was returning to his wife. He grew exasperated and filled a syringe with a fatal dose of drugs. Then he told her to go ahead if she wanted to end it all. Naturally, he stressed that he never dreamed she would actually carry out her suicide threat. Now he was racked with guilt.

There matters would have stood forever had police not decided to search the Drinkwater bungalow. They uncovered Polaroid photographs of Carole alone and with Peter in pornographic poses. An English court was later to describe them as "lewd and bizarre."

For the third time, the doctor was questioned. He gave yet another version of the events leading up to his mistress' death. He admitted that he had injected the fatal drugs, but had done so at Carole's request. Dr. Drinkwater explained that Carole had asked him to render her unconscious so that he might take the pornographic poses. She had often made the same request and he had complied with her wishes.

It was quite a story, but it wasn't believed. Dr. Peter Drinkwater was taken into custody and charged with Carole Califano's murder. In December 1972, he stood trial for murder at St. Albans.

The doctor was the star of the show. From the witness stand, he explained that he and Carole had had normal sex relations right up until a month before Carole's demise. In fact, they had intended to get married when both were free to do so. Drinkwater had even given Carole a wedding ring as proof of his honorable intentions.

Despite this gesture, Carole grew despondent, mainly over her inability to gain custody of her daughter, who had been sent to Italy to live with one of her husband's relatives.

To ease the tension of the relationship, Drinkwater purchased a Polaroid camera, not to take obscene pictures of Carole, but to have some pure, clean fun. A couple of weeks after he purchased the camera, Carole suggested they take some erotic photos.

They decided to get high before embarking on their photographic adventure. He injected Carole with pentathol, while he downed amphetamine tablets to get in the mood. Drinkwater testified that he had become so high he was incapable of working the simple camera mechanism. Carole, who had been rendered unconscious was disappointed next morning when he told her the photographs had not been taken.

That same day, the doctor attended to his medical practice fortified by pills. Surprisingly, his practice did not suffer, nor did his patients ever realize that on most days he was under the influence of alcohol, drugs, or both. With office hours concluded, the doctor downed a couple of gin and tonics at a nearby pub and picked up a bottle of wine to take home.

He and Carole were sharing the wine when, according to Drinkwater, she suggested they continue the erotic picture session of the previous night. He went on to state that Carole said the picture session would serve to cement their relationship. She also suggested that he use pentathol to put her under. He removed Carole's clothing and carried her into the bedroom where he gave her another injection to ensure that she would be asleep when he posed her body.

Next morning, Dr. Drinkwater woke up to find Carole lying face down in bed beside him. He assumed she was asleep. After getting up to make tea, his head cleared. He ran to her side and took her pulse. Carole was dead. In a futile effort to revive her, he injected a respiratory drug directly into her heart.

Dr. Drinkwater then told the court how he sobbed at the bedside of his only true love. He emphasized that at no time did he intend to murder Carole. He only intended to comply with her wishes to take erotic photographs.

The doctor went on to say that he panicked and made up the suicide story. He placed the body exactly as he found it, tidied up the scene, and called Dr. King. He believed Carole must have suffocated during the night. Above all, he wanted to keep the pornographic photos and erotic activities of the night before from investigators.

Prosecution attorneys painted Dr. Drinkwater as a cold-blooded killer, who lied at the least provocation. The defence asserted that at no time did he intend to kill Carole.

In the end, the jury was asked to delve into the doctor's drug-hazed mind. Did he intend to murder Carole? It would still be murder if death ensued from an action on his part which he knew might cause physical harm. On the other hand, if there was no intent to kill or physically harm the victim, but merely to put her to sleep, the correct verdict would be manslaughter.

After close to six hours deliberation the benevolent English jury found Dr. Peter Drinkwater innocent of murder but guilty of manslaughter. He was sentenced to 12 years imprisonment.

PART 2

U.S. MULTIPLE MURDERERS

FROM MULTIPLE MURDERERS

LEE ANDREWS

No one had a bad word to say about Lee Andrews. Why should they? After all, around Grandview, Kansas, he was reputed to be a bright boy with an even brighter future.

Lee graduated from high school with the highest marks ever achieved by a Kansas student. His IQ was in the near genius category. Like many big men, Lee was kind and gentle. At over six feet and 260 pounds, he was an imposing figure in the tiny community.

Lee regularly accompanied his parents and his sister Jenny to the Grandview Baptist Church. He often had long chats with his minister, the Reverend V.D. Dameron. They discussed religion and world events. Rev. Dameron, who was Lee's father's best friend, often thought that everyone should be blessed with a son like Lee Andrews.

After entering the University of Kansas, Lee became an honor student. For relaxation, he played the bassoon in the university band.

Who knows when Lee Andrews first thought that there were pursuits in life other than scholastic ones. In hindsight, the germ of the idea was probably planted in his mind when his parents' home was burglarized. Big Lee figured that with brains and imagination, he could plan and carry out the perfect crime. Why wander further afield than his own family? His parents always had a couple of thousand dollars in their bank account. Then there was the 250-acre spread his father owned. Lee figured it had to be worth $50,000. If they were to die suddenly, he and Jenny would inherit their entire estate. Of course, if Jenny were to die at the same time, Lee would be left as sole heir.

For months, the ideal son fantasized about killing his family, inheriting their worldly goods and leading the good life. Right off, he would purchase a car and clothing; not jeans or t-shirts, but made-to-measure suits. He would quit university and travel the world. There would be no clues. This would be the perfect murder.

Lee considered poisoning his family, but dismissed poison as too risky. No, he would shoot them and fake a robbery. The police would be no match for him. As the only surviving member of the family, he would be the recipient of much sympathy. It was ironic. His parents had given him a .22 repeater rifle last Christmas to go with his German Luger. He would snuff out their lives with their Christmas present. Lee figured the very best time to kill his family would be during the Thanksgiving break, when he would be home from school.

On Friday, November 28, 1958, Lee prepared to commit the triple murder. As he talked to his father that afternoon, he idly glanced out the living room window. He noticed that the bread man had made a delivery to a neighbor and was slowly making his way to the Andrews home to deliver the usual weekend supply. How silly, thought Lee. There would be no one alive to eat the bread. He ran outside and told the bread man that they wouldn't be requiring their usual delivery that weekend.

Thanksgiving dinner went off without a hitch. Lee's dad made a mini speech, saying how happy he was to have his family together for Thanksgiving dinner. Lee kept waiting for an excuse to leave the room. Just as he was about to leave, his mother started to clear the dishes. This was no good at all. For his particular purposes, Lee wanted all the members of his family to be together. At last, his mother and Jenny joined him and his father.

Lee got up, excused himself and went to his bedroom. He loaded his .22 rifle and silently placed the German Luger into his pocket. His plan was now in motion. To simulate a burglary, he pushed out his screen and opened the window. Then he opened the drawers of his dresser.

The young boy with the bright future proceeded to the living room, his purpose clear, his mind unclouded. The killings were well planned. In the living room, Jenny watched as her mother adjusted the controls of the TV. Mr. Andrews was engrossed in the daily paper.

No one paid attention to Lee. He stood in the doorway and calmly slammed four slugs into his mother. She died instantly. Jenny turned.

Lee fired three times. One of the slugs smashed into Jenny's brain, killing her before she crumpled to the living room floor. Mr. Andrews managed to rise and move into the kitchen before bullets entered his back. He staggered. Lee followed, firing as he went until his father sprawled dead on the floor. Standing over his father, Lee fired into his body again and again. An autopsy would later reveal that the dead man had been shot 17 times. The house became deadly quiet.

Calmly following his preconceived plan, Lee drove his father's car to the Kaw River and threw away his two weapons. He smiled as he heard the splash. So much for incriminating weapons.

Lee continued to his room at the University of Kansas in Lawrence. He spoke to his landlady, being careful to mention that he was there to pick up his typewriter and that it had taken him a long time to get there due to the icy condition of the roads. That took care of one witness who would place him in Lawrence at the time of the murders, but you couldn't be too sure in this business. Lee took in a movie called Mardi Gras, and talked for some time to a girl behind the confectionery counter. On the way home, he purchased gasoline, making sure to get a receipt. That should do it for alibi witnesses.

Lee arrived home about 1 a.m. He called police, who arrived at the house 10 minutes later. They found Lee sitting in the sun room, petting the family dog. When the police inquired as to the nature of the emergency call, Lee didn't say anything. He just nodded toward the living room. Inside the house were the bodies of the Andrews family.

Police turned to Lee. The bright boy with the bright future didn't realize that most people, who stumble on the bodies of their sister and parents, are usually upset. Lee was cool as a cucumber. He related his story without shedding a tear. He had had Thanksgiving dinner with his family, had gone to Lawrence to pick up a typewriter, had taken in a movie and had filled the family car with gas on his way home. He volunteered that burglars must have entered the house through his bedroom window.

Investigators followed Lee to his bedroom. They expected to find the room in shambles. Instead, they noticed that while drawers were pulled out, nothing had been scattered about the room. This was the tidiest burglary the police had ever encountered. They were also surprised to learn that nothing had been stolen from the house.

The big lumbering boy didn't seem to care that his entire family had been murdered. It wasn't natural. The police questioned Lee in detail about his activities. He told them that he had been to Lawrence—his landlady would verify that. He had taken in a movie—the girl at the confectionery counter would verify that. He had purchased gas on the way home. Sure, he had a receipt.

It was all too much. The boy had left so many tracks a Boy Scout could have traced his movements. Lee was informed that he was a prime suspect in the triple murder. When he was taken to jail, he asked to speak to his father's best friend, Rev. Dameron. In minutes, the minister was brought up to date on the crime. Like police, he was amazed at Lee's nonchalant demeanor.

Lee had not planned it this way, not at all. Rev. Dameron seemed to be as suspicious as the police. It was obvious that he believed that Lee had committed the murders. When the reverend asked, "You didn't do it, did you?" Lee replied in his usual calm manner, "Yes, I did."

Now that Lee had confessed to the murder, his minister pressed him for his motive until the boy admitted that he had wanted his family's money. Lee was convicted of the murders of his family and was sentenced to death. He never displayed any remorse for what he had done. On November 30, 1962, 22-year-old Lee Andrews was hanged at Lansing Prison.

The entire town of Grandview attended the Andrews funeral. Lee wasn't one of their number. Throughout his incarceration and trial, he remained calm and collected. His lawyers attempted to prove that he was insane at the time he committed the murders and that he had acted impulsively. The state produced the bread man, who testified that Lee had cancelled the usual bread delivery on the afternoon of the murders. Only Lee knew there would be no one alive at the Andrews home after the Thanksgiving Day meal.

DAVID BERKOWITZ

SELDOM has an individual criminal managed to hold an entire city in a grip of terror. Jack the Ripper did it by killing and mutilating five prostitutes in London, England, in the autumn of 1888. In more recent times the Boston Strangler assaulted and murdered 13 women. In so doing, he kept the entire city of Boston in a state of fear.

It takes a series of unusual criminal acts to make the good citizens of New York City sit up and take notice. Almost every bizarre occurrence perpetrated by man has taken place in Gotham. The natives are accustomed to the unusual.

When Bette and Tony Falco gave birth to little David Richard on June 1, 1953, they had already decided to put their newborn son up for adoption. The details had all been arranged.

Pearl Berkowitz was an active woman who, at 38, had been informed by her doctors that she could never conceive. Her husband Nathan, a hardware store owner, had often discussed adopting a child with his wife. It was Pearl and Nathan who drove David Richard home from the hospital. They didn't know the soft, cuddly bundle Pearl held so gently was a potential monster. Eighteen months later David Richard Falco legally became David Richard Berkowitz.

David grew up to be a quiet, introverted little boy. In hindsight, many friends and neighbors who knew him during his formative years later came forward with some anecdote or other illustrating a streak of meanness or cruelty in David as a child. In actuality there was probably nothing to distinguish David from thousands of other children being brought up in like circumstances.

When David was 14 his mother died of cancer, after a long and painful bout with the dreaded disease. Pearl had been a kind and loving mother, and we have every reason to believe that her son was truly affected by her death. In 1971, when Nathan remarried, David displayed open resentment toward his stepmother.

His father's marriage coincided with David's joining the army. David, who had always expressed patriotic sentiments toward his country, was shipped off to Fort Dix, New Jersey. During rugged basic training he showed some skill with a rifle. Pursuing his natural aptitude, he soon qualified as a sharpshooter.

From Fort Dix, David was sent to Fort Polk, Louisiana, for advanced training. On December 13, 1971, he was shipped to Korea, where he served with the 17th Infantry, 1st Battalion. After his tour of duty, David was posted to Fort Knox, Kentucky. On June 24, 1974, he was discharged from the U.S. Army after serving three years.

David returned to his parents' apartment in the Bronx. He was mildly surprised to find out that they were trying to sell their apartment in order to retire to Florida. By the end of the year David had found a one-bedroom apartment for himself at 2161 Barnes Ave. in the Bronx. He registered at the Bronx Community College in February 1975, where he attained a high C average. During the summer he worked for his uncle as a sheet metal worker. To all outward appearances, David Berkowitz was going to make something of himself.

Donna Lauria was an attractive, 18-year-old with shoulder-length brown hair. Donna and her friend Jody Valente were sitting outside Donna's apartment building double parked in Jody's car. It was 1:10 a.m. on a hot July morning in 1976. Donna's parents walked by and entered the apartment building. Without warning, a man appeared beside the automobile occupied by the two girls. He pointed a long barrelled revolver at Donna's head and fired. Donna Lauria was dead without ever knowing what had happened. A .44 calibre slug slammed into Jody's left thigh. Despite bleeding profusely, her wound was not serious. No one knew it at the time, but the killer later to be known and feared as the Son of Sam had claimed his first victim.

A short time later David Berkowitz left his sheet metal job.

Rosemary Keenan and Carl Denaro, a pair of 20 year olds, had promised to meet friends at a tavern in Flushing. It was about two in the morning when they drove into the tavern parking lot. Carl was about to open the car door when a bullet crashed through the car window and lodged in his head. Fortunately the slug missed Carl's brain. His friends from the tavern rushed him to the nearest hospital, where an emergency operation, lasting over two hours, saved his life. The senseless attack on Carl Denaro and his girlfriend was not connected at the time with the Lauria-Valente shooting.

On a cool November night two teenagers, Joanne Lomino and Donna

DeMasi, sat on Joanne's front steps talking about boyfriends and job opportunities. The two girls had taken in a movie and had finished off their night out with hamburgers. Now they were preparing to part. Out of the darkness a man approached the girls. He appeared to be of average height, about 30 years old, and wore a green army-type three-quarter length coat. The man extracted a revolver from his belt and began shooting.

The first slug entered Donna's neck and shattered her collarbone. She fell to the sidewalk. Joanne took a slug directly into her back. Of the five shots fired at the girls, three went astray. Donna DeMasi recovered from the attack, but Joanne Lomino will forever remain paralyzed from the waist down. The mad killer who used a .44-calibre revolver had struck again.

John Diel was a 30-year-old bartender. He and his girlfriend, Christine Freund, had a lot to talk over. They were planning to get engaged in two weeks time. Now, as they sat talking well past midnight on the morning of January 30, they had no way of knowing there would be no engagement party. Christine would be dead in a matter of hours. Two explosions interrupted their conversation, sending a shower of windshield glass cascading into the interior of the car. Diel lifted his girlfriend's limp form out of the car and gently placed her on the ground. At 4:30 a.m. Christine died in hospital from bullet wounds to the head.

The wanton attacks had all been treated as individual cases. Now the cases were cross checked, and police attributed the attacks to the frenzy of one man. Lauria, Valente, Denaro, Lomino, DeMasi, and Freund. A monster with a .44-calibre revolver was loose on the streets of New York. No wonder the police could find no motive for the individual attacks. The madman didn't even know the victims. He killed at random.

David Berkowitz applied for a job at the Bronx General Post Office. He scored an exceptional 85.5% on the post office test. David got the job on a part-time basis at $7 an hour.

Virginia Voskerichian was a 19-year-old student at Columbia University. She lived in fashionable Forest Hills Garden with her parents. One evening in March, as she walked home, the crazed killer shot her dead with his .44-calibre revolver.

Back at the Bronx Post Office David Berkowitz often talked of the .44-calibre killer to fellow employees. It seemed to be one of the few topics pleasant, quiet David liked to talk about.

Valentina Suriani lived at 1950 Hutchinson St., only a few streets from the killer's first victim, Donna Lauria. Valentina attended Lehman College, where she was majoring in acting. Her fiancé, Alexander Esau, parked his car early on the morning of April 19. Both fell under the rage that burned within the .44-calibre killer. This time he left a sealed envelope beside the bodies of his victims. The contents of the letter were not revealed by the police at the time. From it police knew that the killer had no intention of curtailing his murderous rampage.

The killer then wrote to Daily News columnist Jimmy Breslin, signing his letter Son of Sam. The letter was authentic, having been written by the same crazed mind which had composed the letter found beside Valentina Suriani's body.

In April 1977, within days of the Suriani-Esau murders, a man not connected with any victim, Sam Carr, received an anonymous letter at his home at 316 Warbuton Avenue. in Yonkers. It contained gibberish about his Labrador retriever being a menace, saying that the dog should be removed from his home. Carr mentioned the crazy letter to members of his family and then dismissed the incident from his mind. He then received another more threatening letter, but still did nothing about it.

On April 27, someone shot Sam Carr's Labrador retriever. The dog, Harvey, had been severely wounded in the thigh. Carr was to spend over $1,000 to save his dog, but the bullet remained lodged in Harvey's thigh. After this incident, Carr took the letters to the Yonkers police. They attributed the letters and the shooting as the work of a schizophrenic, but did not connect the incident to the mass killings which were now under the jurisdiction of a task force formed exclusively to capture the .44-calibre killer.

David Berkowitz had moved. He now lived at 35 Pine St. in Yonkers. His apartment building backed on to Sam Carr's back yard.

Sal Lupo and Judy Placido frequented the same discotheque in Queens. They had never dated, but knew each other rather well and often danced together. Judy was in a good mood. She had just graduated from St. Catherines Academy that day. Now, it was after 3 a.m. Sunday morning, June 26. One of the main topics of conversation that evening was the crazed murderer who killed without reason.

Sal asked Judy if he could drive her home. Judy, still wearing her special graduation dress, was thrilled to accept the ride. Before Sal could turn the ignition key in his car four slugs poured into the interior of the car. The wound inflicted to Sal's arm was not serious. Judy had taken one bullet behind the right ear. One lodged close to her spinal cord, and the third pierced her right shoulder. All three bullets were removed from Judy's body, and miraculously she recovered. The bullets were .44-calibre and had been fired from the same weapon which had felled the other victims.

David Berkowitz did commendable work at the post office. He often told fellow employees that he sure hoped the police would catch that Son of Sam fellow. A year had passed since the first Son of Sam murder.

Sixteen-year-old Stacy Moskowitz of Brooklyn had been asked out by the best looking boy she had ever dated. Robert Violante, a recent graduate of Brooklyn's New Utrecht High, was by any standards a handsome young man. Before seeing a play, Stacy brought Robert home to meet her family.

After the play and a bite to eat, the young people parked alongside the Shore Parkway at Bay 14th St. Several other cars were parked there. Four successive explosions roared into the open car window. Robert received a bullet in the temple which exited at the bridge of his nose. He recovered, but will only have partial sight for the rest of his life. Stacy Moskowitz died later in hospital.

David Berkowitz left his job at the post office a few days later and never returned.

On the night of Stacy Moskowitz' murder, Mrs. Cacalia Davis took her dog Snowball for a walk. As she walked she fixed her gaze on a young man approaching from the opposite direction. They passed within touching distance of each other. Mrs. Davis noticed that the young man's right arm was stiff. Later she found out it was because Son of Sam carried his .44-calibre revolver up his sleeve.

Next day, when Mrs. Davis became aware of the murder which had taken place close to her home, she was positive that it was Son of Sam whom she passed on the sidewalk. She informed the police of her suspicions. When she told her story she mentioned that during her walk with Snowball she had noticed a cop writing out a traffic ticket for a car parked too near a hydrant.

Police checked on all traffic tickets issued in the early morning hours in that area. There were only three. Two had been issued to respectable citizens in their late sixties. The third was issued to David R. Berkowitz.

Son of Sam, who had terrorized an entire city for over a year was to be taken into custody because he had parked too close to a hydrant. When picked up, Berkowitz' car yielded a sub-machine gun, a rifle with several boxes of ammunition, and a .44 Charter Arms Bulldog small revolver. Later it was proven that the .44 was the weapon which Son of Sam had used for over a year.

Why had David Berkowitz killed six innocent individuals and wounded seven others? He had no choice. You see, the devil who lived in Sam Carr's Labrador retriever Harvey commanded him to kill.

David Berkowitz was adjudged unfit to stand trial by reason of insanity. No doubt he will spend the rest of his life in custody.

KEN BIANCHI & ANGELO BUONO

YOLANDA Washington couldn't support her baby on the money she earned as a waitress. That's why she turned to prostitution. Her beat was Sunset and Vista in Hollywood, California. Yolanda did pretty well at her profession, averaging somewhere between $500 and $1,000 a week. Not bad for a 19-year-old. It beat depending on tips in a restaurant.

On October 17, 1977, at 11 p.m. Yolanda let herself be picked up. Next day her body was found on a Los Angeles hillside. She had been strangled to death before being tossed out of a car. Semen samples indicated that two men had had sexual relations with her before death.

Judy Miller was only 15, but was already a part-time prostitute who sold whatever charms she possessed along Hollywood Blvd. in order to keep herself supplied with pot and pills. On October 31, Judy disappeared from her usual haunts. Her nude body was found near La Crescenta just outside of L.A. She had not been thrown from a car, but had been carried to her final resting place. Footprints indicated that two men, one holding the body by the arms, the other by the head, had carried Judy to where she was found. Judy had been gagged, bound, and strangled. She had also been raped. Police did not connect Judy's death to that of Yolanda Washington's.

Lissa Kastin, 21, unlike the first two victims, was neither a prostitute nor a drug user. She worked as a waitress, and also for her father's construction firm on a part-time basis. Her real ambition was a career in show business and Lissa was making some headway. She and some other girls had formed a dance group and were good enough to obtain bookings in several local clubs. Lissa's body was found on the side of a hill in Glendale. She had been bound, raped, and strangled to death. Physical evidence at the scene of the crime indicated that two men were responsible. Detectives met to discuss the similarities of the three recent murders.

The killing spree continued. Jane Evelyn King, 28, an actress and part-time model, was murdered on November 9. Her body was discovered two weeks later near the Golden State Freeway.

Two friends, Dolores Cepeda, 12, and Sonja Johnson, were last seen near the Eagle Rock Shopping Centre on November 13. Their bodies were found on a hillside near downtown Los Angeles.

No one remembers who coined the phrase The Hillside Strangler, but the name stuck. Women of all ages took precautions against the madmen who raped and strangled without mercy. Throughout Los Angeles women walked in groups, husbands picked up wives after work, while many women carried weapons and warning devices. The Hillside Strangler was the main topic of conversation in L.A., but still the killings continued.

On November 19, Kristina Weckler, 20, an art student, was strangled to death before being deposited in Highland Park. Lauren Wagner, 18, was murdered November 28.

A break in the pattern occurred with the murder of 17-year-old Kimberly Martin. Despite her tender years, Kim was a hardened, experienced prostitute. Because of the Hillside Strangler's well-known penchant for prostitutes, Kim decided to protect herself in the pursuit of her risky profession. She secured employment with a nude modelling agency, which was in reality a front for a call-in prostitution service.

Girls like Kimberly would wait for calls from the agency, and would be sent out to perform their unique services. The advantage to Kim would be the screening done by the agency before giving her the assignment. Supposedly this procedure would eliminate the weirdos.

Kim obtained an assignment from the agency on December 13. Her body was found on a hillside near downtown L.A. While investigating the murder, detectives obtained the address of Kim's last assignment. It turned out to be a vacant apartment in the Tamarino Apartments.

The apartment had been wiped clean of fingerprints, but police believed that Kim's murderers had waited for her in the unoccupied apartment. They felt that the victim had been bound and beaten before being led out of the apartment to be strangled elsewhere.

Police questioned all the tenants in the apartment building, and found out that several tenants had heard noises coming from the vacant apartment on the night of Kim's disappearance. No one had investigated.

Many of the tenants detected that the police officers questioning them were unnecessarily gruff and abrasive in their manner. Several officers felt a degree of animosity towards people who did not want to get involved. If someone had reported the scuffle, the vicious killers might have been caught in the act.

It was refreshing to interrogate clean-cut handsome Ken Bianchi, even though he hadn't heard any noises. He was most co-operative and understanding. Bianchi seemed concerned about the safety of his pregnant live-in girl friend, Kelli Boyd. Ken hardly ever let Kelli walk alone on the streets after the questioning.

Death took a holiday over the Christmas season. It wasn't until February 17, 1978, that 20-year-old Cindy Lee Hudspeth's nude body was found strangled in the trunk of her car in Glendale. No one knew it at the time, but the notorious Hillside Strangler, whose exploits were now being reported throughout the world, had struck in L.A. for the last time.

Kelli Boyd gave birth to her baby. She and Ken Bianchi named the boy Sean. After the baby was born Kelli informed Ken that she was returning to her home town of Bellingham, Washington, to give her baby a proper home with her family. Ken was heartbroken. He loved Sean and couldn't believe Kelli would leave him. Kelli explained that Ken didn't earn enough to support a family, and besides, he seemed more concerned with visiting and playing cards with his cousin Angelo Buono than raising a family.

Kelli left. Ken wrote letters and poems, pleading for another chance. Kelli relented, and Ken joined her in Bellingham to begin a new life. The good citizens of the community, located just south of Vancouver, had no way of knowing it at the time, but the Hillside Strangler was now among them.

On Friday, January 12, 1979, two Western Washington University students, Karen Mandik and Diane Wilder, were reported missing. Both girls were responsible, serious students, whose absence caused immediate concern. Their known movements were carefully traced. On Thursday Karen, who worked part-time at a department store, left the store and picked up Diane, who was her roommate. The girls had a chance to earn some easy money that night. A wealthy family who were travelling in Europe normally had their home fully protected by an alarm system operated by a highly respectable protection agency. Apparently the alarm system had failed, and Karen had received an offer of $100 to house-sit for two hours while the alarm was being repaired. Karen brought

Diane along for company. When Karen failed to return to the department store, police were notified.

Detectives found out that Karen had received her generous house-sitting job from Ken Bianchi, a young man whom she had met some months before when he worked as a security guard at the department store. Ken had moved to a good job with a protection company.

Detectives learned that Bianchi had lied in order to get the use of a company van on the night of the girls' disappearance. He had told a fellow worker that he was taking the van into a garage for repairs, but the garage had no record of repairing the vehicle. Karen's phone number was found on a piece of paper in Ken's home.

At 4:30 p.m. on the day following the missing person's report, the two girls were found murdered in Karen's car, parked in a wooded side street. They had been strangled. Detectives immediately arrested Ken Bianchi while they continued to amass evidence against him. By now the similarities between the Bellingham double murder and the handiwork of the Hillside Strangler was recognized. Clean-cut Ken Bianchi was quite possibly a monster in disguise.

On March 21, 1979, Bianchi gave a highly detailed confession of the murders while in a hypnotic state. He claimed that he was not Ken when he murdered but was controlled by his other half, Steve. Bianchi claimed that while he was Steve he and his cousin Angelo Buono had killed all ten Hillside Strangler victims in Los Angeles. He later confessed in minute detail to the double murder in Bellingham.

Doctors were divided in their opinion. Was Ken Bianchi a bona fide example of a multiple personality, or was he conning the doctors in an attempt to save his skin?

As the investigation into Buono's past was being undertaken, the judicial system as it applied to Bianchi was slowly grinding to a conclusion. For the Bellingham killings he received two consecutive life sentences. He was then shunted off to L.A., where he received several additional life terms. Bianchi's lawyers had made a deal. Their client escaped the death sentence in return for his testimony against Buono. It is doubtful that Bianchi will ever be a free man again.

Ken Bianchi has repudiated all his confessions since his conviction and has become a shaky and less than credible witness for the state against his cousin

Angelo, who has steadfastly maintained his innocence. Since Bianchi has admitted and subsequently denied involvement in all of the murders, he is obviously a liar, which weakened his usefulness as a prosecution witness against Buono.

Despite the lies, the evidence against Buono proved to be overwhelming. He was tried, found guilty, and sentenced to nine life terms in prison with no possibility of parole.

ARTHUR BISHOP

THE area in and around Salt Lake City was caught in a grip of fear. Was it possible that here, in the very centre of the Mormon faith, a mad serial killer was preying on little boys?

On October 14, 1979, four-year-old Alonzo Daniels left his apartment, as he did most days, to play in the backyard. Mrs. Daniels, who had a clear view of her son from her kitchen window, observed Alonzo imitating an airplane taking off from the ground. She smiled and went on with her chores.

A few minutes later, she glanced out the window. Alonzo was nowhere to be seen. Mrs. Daniels ran out to the yard. Alonzo had vanished. She would never see her son alive again.

Neighbors searched the yard and the apartment building basement. Police interviewed the occupants of the entire building. Adjacent buildings were searched. A youngster had apparently been carried away in broad daylight without being seen by anyone and without leaving a trace.

Thirteen months later, 11-year-old Kim Peterson told his parents that a man he had met at a skating rink had offered to purchase his skates. Kim wanted a new pair. This was his chance to add to the monies he had already saved.

On November 9, 1980, Kim informed his parents that he had been offered $35 for his old skates. He ran out of the house, shouting over his shoulder that he had an appointment to meet with the prospective purchaser on a street corner. When Kim failed to return home, his parents notified police.

Detectives interviewed everyone at the skating rink who could have seen Kim speaking to an older man. Several witnesses recalled seeing him. The man he was talking to was chubby, wore blue jeans and an army-type jacket. Most thought he was between 25 and 35 years of age.

Several witnesses agreed to undergo hypnosis in order to better describe the suspect. In this way, police learned that he was six feet tall, 200 pounds, with bushy eyebrows. That's as far as they got. The investigation wound down.

A year later, on October 20, 1981, four-year-old Danny Davis went shopping at a supermarket with his grandfather. The little boy was hardly out of his grandfather's sight, yet he vanished.

Store employees and customers frantically searched for the youngster. Police were summoned. They were successful in locating several customers who remembered seeing a little boy fitting Danny's description playing with a gumball machine. Ominously, they also recalled a male adult helping Danny work the machine.

That evening, as searchers roamed the desert and nearby hills, the temperature dropped to zero. It was imperative they locate the missing youngster, as he might die of exposure if left out all night. He was wearing only a t-shirt, thongs and a pair of light blue trousers.

Next day, police divers searched Big Cottonwood Creek. Every pond and ditch was combed without results. Posters throughout Utah displayed Danny's photo. The hunt for Danny Davis was the largest ever conducted in and around Salt Lake City up to that time.

While the investigation into Danny's disappearance yielded no useful clues, it made officials aware that all three youngsters had disappeared within two weeks of Hallowe'en in three consecutive years. As Hollowe'en of 1982 approached and passed, they breathed a sigh of relief. It was possible that the man who plucked boys out of their backyards, off street corners and out of supermarkets had relocated or died.

Their relief did not last long. On June 22, 1983, Troy Ward, celebrating his sixth birthday, was abducted from the play area of Liberty Park. After an extensive search, the best the police could come up with was a witness who saw a boy matching Troy's description leaving the park with a young smiling man. The youngster and the man got along so well the witness thought the stranger was the little boy's father.

By now, slayings in neighboring states were being checked for similarities with the Salt Lake City crimes. No connection could be found between these crimes and the ones committed in and around Salt Lake City. The Hallowe'en theory was thrown out as a coincidence.

Graeme Cunningham, 13, was excited about going on a camping trip with a teenaged buddy and an older man, Roger Downs, 32, a highly-respected accountant. Two days before they were to leave on the trip to the Lake Tahoe area, Graeme disappeared.

Downs and Graeme's friend went on the camping trip. They appeared to be genuinely surprised when they returned to learn that Graeme had not been located. Police questioned Downs as to his relationship with the missing boy. Initially, Downs could offer no useful information, but gradually police detected discrepancies in his story. Little by little, he broke down. After a night of questioning, Roger Downs confessed to sexually attacking and murdering the five boys.

Next day, Downs led police to the gravesites of Alonzo Daniels, Danny Davis and Kim Peterson. Displaying great willingness to co-operate, Downs next led police some 100 kilometres to Big Cottonwood Creek, where he pointed out the burial sites of Troy Ward and Graeme Cunningham.

Downs would only tell police that he had killed the boys because he was afraid they would tell their parents of his sexual advances.

A thorough check of the mild-mannered accountant's past revealed that his real name was Arthur Bishop. Bishop was born in Hinckley, a small town in Utah. In high school, he was an honor student, an Eagle Scout and a devout Mormon. He graduated with honors in accounting from Stevens Henager College.

Then, something went drastically wrong. In February 1978, Arthur was accused of embezzling more than $8,000 from a car dealership where he was employed. He pleaded guilty and was placed on five years' probation. Arthur promptly skipped and was excommunicated from the Mormon Church.

He roamed the country working at odd jobs and changing his name frequently. Using the name Roger Downs, he settled in Salt Lake City.

Arthur Bishop was charged with five counts of first degree murder. At his trial, the jury deliberated only five hours before finding him guilty of all five murders. Bishop has never displayed any remorse for his horrible crimes. In fact, during his taped confession, he said, "I'm glad they caught me, because I'd do it again."

Bishop was sentenced to death. In compliance with Utah law, he was given the choice of death by firing squad or lethal injection. He chose lethal injection.

As this is written, Arthur Bishop languishes on Death Row awaiting his execution.

TED BUNDY

THE delays had come to an end. Theodore Robert Cowell Bundy had a date with Florida's electric chair.

In January 1989, Florida's governor, Bob Martinez, signed the official death warrant shortly after the U.S. Supreme Court turned down Bundy's final appeal. Sternly, the governor stated, "Bundy is one of the most notorious killers in our nation's history. He has used legal manoeuvring to dodge the electric chair for ten years."

Ted Bundy was brought up in Tacoma, Washington. There was nothing in his youth to indicate that the handsome charmer would become a notorious serial killer, known simply as "Ted" to the law enforcement agencies of four states.

He graduated from Wilson High School with a B average, attended the University of Puget Sound, switching to the University of Washington for his sophomore year. In 1972, Ted graduated and, for a short time, worked for the King County Law and Justice Planning Department. While thus employed, ironically, he wrote a pamphlet on rape.

Ted entered the University of Utah Law School. A few months later, young girls began to disappear without a trace. Lynda Ann Healy, 21, a University of Washington student, vanished from her apartment. On March 19, Donna Munsen, 19, a student at Evergreen State College, disappeared on her way to a music recital. A month later, Susan Racourt, 18, left Central State College at Ellenburg to take in a movie. She was never seen again. On May 6, Roberta Parks, 22, walked out of the Student Union building of Oregon State University and vanished.

Ted, who by now had quit law school, obtained employment with the Emergency Service in Olympia. Girls continued to disappear. On June 1, Brenda Ball, 22, vanished after leaving a bar with the express intention of going home. Georgann Hawkins, 18, left her sorority house at the University of Washington. She, too, was never heard of again. Slim, handsome Ted Bundy continued to counsel troubled individuals all that summer down at Emergency Service.

In August, Ted left his job to continue his law studies in Salt Lake City.

Soon, girls in that area began to vanish. An old girlfriend of Ted's back in Seattle read about the rash killings in Utah. She was troubled. Witnesses claimed that a young man who called himself Ted was known to have attempted to pick up girls. He would approach them, wearing a plaster cast on one arm, and ask for assistance placing a small boat on top of his tan Volkswagen. The Ted she had known in Seattle drove a tan Volkswagen.

With many misgivings, she called police. After she told them of her suspicions, they decided to check out Ted Bundy at the University of Utah Law School. Their cursory check of Ted's records and application at the school indicated that the former girlfriend had either made a mistake or was one of those vindictive women who was seeking revenge. After all, this guy had a recommendation letter on file from no less a personage than Washington's Governor Don Evans.

On November 8, 1974, something happened to Ted that had never happened before. One of his victims escaped. Carol Da Ronch, 18, was approached by a young man who claimed to be a police officer. He told the girl that someone had been apprehended burglarizing her car and asked her to accompany him to the police station to identify the stolen goods. Carol got in the Volkswagen. She then asked the police officer to identify himself. Instead, the man pulled out a pair of handcuffs and a pistol. He threatened, "Be still or I'll blow your brains out!"

Carol didn't hesitate. She jumped from the car, stumbled and fell. Her assailant had also left the car and now stood over the fallen girl. Carol got up, scratching at her attacker's face as he attempted to control her. The terrified girl ran to the centre of the street and managed to hail a passing motorist. Her potential abductor raced to his Volkswagen and sped away.

Now that they had a surviving witness, police were anxious to show photos of suspects to the badly frightened girl. Carol failed to pick anyone who resembled her attacker. Inexplicably, she was not shown Ted Bundy's photograph.

Ted moved on to Colorado. Soon after, Julie Cunningham, 22, Denise Oliverson, 23, and Melanie Cooley, 21, vanished. At the Wildwood Inn near Aspen, a Michigan nurse, Caryn Campbell, 23, disappeared from the corridors of the inn. Her terribly mutilated nude body was found some ten miles away months later. A brochure from the Wildwood Inn would later be found in Ted's

Volkswagen. Also, credit card purchases would indicate he had been in the area when all four women disappeared.

Police attempted to find Ted, now wanted for questioning, but it would be nine months before he would be taken into custody by a highway patrol officer whom Ted attempted to evade. Inside his car, Ted had little goodies, such as a crowbar, handcuffs, a nylon stocking and an ice pick.

Ted Bundy was arrested. Current photos were taken of him and, together with other photos, were shown to Carol Da Ronch. She pulled out Ted's photo without hesitation. "This is the man!" she shouted.

Ted Bundy, now a likely suspect in the murders of girls in Washington, Colorado and Utah, as well as in the kidnapping of Carol Da Ronch, was released on $15,000 bail.

Law enforcement agencies of three states were sure they were all looking for the same man, yet they didn't have any direct proof. This changed when the material vacuumed from the floor of Ted's van revealed pubic hair which matched that of Melissa Smith, the murdered daughter of Midvale, Utah's police chief. They also found hair which matched that of Carol Da Ronch and Caryn Campbell. Together with the Wildwood Inn pamphlet and credit card purchases from Colorado, police felt they had enough evidence to proceed with the prosecution of the Colorado killings.

Meanwhile, Ted was tried and found guilty of kidnapping Carol Da Ronch. He was also sentenced to 60 days in jail for evading a police officer. While in custody, he was charged with the murder of Caryn Campbell. At the time, Bundy stated, "I have never killed, never kidnapped, never designed to injure another human being. I am prepared to use every ounce of my strength to vindicate myself."

Charming Ted was now a prime suspect in a grand total of 32 cases involving missing and murdered women. Over the years several decomposed bodies were found and identified. Others have never been found.

Ted informed the court that he wished to represent himself in future court appearances. As a result, he was given access to the Glenwood Springs Library. One day, left alone to pore over law books, he jumped out a window to the pavement 20 feet below. Ted managed to steal a Cadillac, but was soon picked up and hustled back to jail.

Ted wasn't through escaping from jail. His second attempt was far more successful than the first. He managed to lose a great deal of weight in a short time. Now slimmer than usual, he squeezed up into the false ceiling in his cell and crawled to freedom.

In the following weeks, Ted travelled by car, bus and plane, making his way to Chicago. On New Year's Day, 1978, he took in the Rose Bowl game on TV in a bar in Ann Arbor, Michigan. His old school, the University of Washington, won the game.

A week later, the most wanted man in America made his way to Tallahassee, Florida, and took a room a few blocks from Florida State University under the name Chris Hagen.

It was killing time in Florida.

In the wee hours of January 15, Nita Jane Neary returned to her university dormitory after a date. A man, clutching a two-by-four piece of wood brushed past her on his way out. Nita rushed upstairs in time to see 21-year-old Karen Chandler, soaked with blood, stagger out of her room. Nita looked into her friend's room. She saw Cathy Kleiner lying on her bed with blood gushing from her head.

Soon, 40 coeds were milling about, ministering to their wounded friends. There was more. Margaret Bowman, 21, lay motionless in death. A maniac had crushed her skull and twisted a pair of panty hose around her neck. Lisa Levy, 20, had been sexually attacked and beaten to death. Her killer had bitten deeply into her breasts and buttocks.

Ted Bundy became unnerved at the police activity taking place so close to his rooming house. He left that very night, checking into a Holiday Inn in Lake City, about 100 miles down the road from Tallahassee. Next day, 12-year-old Kimberley Leach disappeared from her school. No one connected her disappearance with the slaughter which had taken place in Tallahassee.

Five days later, an alert Pensacola police officer picked up Ted in a stolen Volkswagen. He claimed to be Kenneth Misner, a Florida State student. He had 22 credit cards to prove it. Next day, the real Kenneth Misner called police to report his wallet and credit cards stolen.

When Ted's photo appeared in the paper, he was recognized in the rooming house back in Tallahassee as Chris Hagen. A fellow roomer had seen the man he knew as Chris enter the rooming house at 4 a.m. on the morning of the killings. Fingerprints identified the bogus Kenneth Misner and Chris Hagen as escaped convict Ted Bundy.

Florida authorities didn't want to release Ted to another state. They endeavored to build an airtight case against their man. They managed to do just that.

Dental technicians were given teeth mark impressions taken from Lisa Levy's body. They matched in every detail impressions taken from Ted's teeth. The Florida jury which heard the Bundy case took only six and a half hours to find him guilty. They recommended death in the electric chair.

In February 1980, Ted stood trial once more for murder, this time for the murder of 12-year-old Kimberley Leach. Once again, he was found guilty and sentenced to die.

For ten years, Ted danced around Florida's infernal machine. He had several dates with death, on occasion coming within days of being executed. The story of his life and his killing spree was dramatized in a made-for-television movie starring Mark Harmon.

At 7 a.m. on Tuesday, January 24, 1989, Ted Bundy was executed in Florida's electric chair.

DALE BURR

BACK in 1983, Dale Burr's farm was considered one of the finest in Johnson County, Iowa. Every farmer around Lone Tree would be quick to tell you that Dale deserved everything he had acquired over the years. True enough, his father had given him a prosperous 160-acre spread as a wedding present when he married Emily Wacker, but Dale had worked hard and had expanded the farm to well over 500 acres.

Dale had helped his son John to acquire a 200-acre farm close to his own. The Burrs had two other children, Sheila and Julia. Sheila had married and moved to Arkansas, while Julia had become a teacher and had left the farm as well.

Dale Burr's farm was a rich productive unit, raising corn, beans and pork. His spread was valued at around $2 million, but that was academic. Dale was a purchaser of land, not a seller. He had been born into farm life. It had been good to generations of Burrs before him and it was good to him and his family.

What went wrong?

In one season, between 1983 and 1984, prices paid to farmers for their crops dropped drastically, in many cases almost a dollar a bushel. Such a drop can be disastrous to a farmer producing tens of thousands of bushels.

To expand their farms, large landholders had borrowed from local banks to finance their latest acquisitions. There was nothing wrong with this time proven method of expanding one's farm, but by the mid-1980s, two factors turned bank debt into a nightmare. Prices of crops fell and the value of land dropped appreciably.

Loans for seed money, which had been routine for years, became a humiliating experience for farmers. They were constantly being told that the amount of their loans was fast approaching the value of their collateral, which was usually their farms and the buildings on them.

Dale's son required a bank loan. He had used up all his credit, but his father had no difficulty borrowing the funds. Dale gave the nearby Hills Bank and

Trust Co. a mortgage on a portion of his property. When his own cash flow wasn't enough to meet current expenses, he mortgaged more of his property at the Hills Bank.

Bank president John Hughes was a married man with two teenaged daughters. Mostly he was well liked in Hills and Lone Tree, but there was one thing. John Hughes was a stickler for collateral. He wanted his loans covered. There was no way his bank would go under because of the economic disaster that was sweeping the rural communities of the United States. He wasn't above foreclosing and selling off farmers' assets to repay bank loans. It was common knowledge that one sentimental banker who had loaned farmers money on their good word had committed suicide rather than foreclose on personal friends. That would never happen to John Hughes.

After Dale had exhausted his credit at government agencies and the bank, Hughes wrote him a scorching letter, warning him to curtail some of his farming methods and become more efficient. There would be no more bailouts for him or his son. The two men met on several occasions to discuss the problem, but nothing was finalized.

Dale didn't view his obligation as an honest debt which must be paid. He understood only one thing; he and his family before him had worked the soil for generations and now a banker was threatening to take it all away. There was more than money involved. There was humiliation and disgrace. At age 62, Dale Burr had difficulty raising enough money to purchase groceries. He borrowed $500 from his daughter Julia. Then he acted.

On Monday, December 9, 1985, Dale dug his old model 31 Remington out of his basement and shot his wife of over 30 years directly through the heart. He sat down at the kitchen table and a wrote a note to his son: "John, I'm sorry, I just couldn't stand all the problems." It was signed 'Dad.'

Dale jumped into his 4X4 and headed for town. He drove directly to the Hills Bank, where he attempted to cash a $500 cheque. When assistant vice president Roger Reilly told him his account was overdrawn by $55, Dale gave Reilly $60 in cash and was given a receipt. He then chatted with a few other customers and left the bank.

Calmly, Dale drove down the street and purchased a box of shotgun shells. Once again he drove into the bank's parking lot. He loaded his Remington and shoved the weapon down the leg of his coveralls. Dale, who had once had a bank balance in the hundreds of thousands of dollars now had loans against his farm that he couldn't possibly repay. This same bank, which had once solicited his business, wouldn't honor his $500 cheque.

Dale limped towards President John Hughes office. He stood in the doorway, pulled his Remington from his coveralls, quickly aimed, fired, and blew off the left side of John Hughes' head. He moved a few feet to Roger Reilly's office, pointed the gun at Roger and said, "I'm going to get you too!" Roger could only reply, "Dale, please, you can't do this!"

Bank officer Dale Kretchmar, who had been talking to Roger when John Hughes had been shot, flung out his arms, striking the barrel of the Remington. Reilly dove under a desk. Dale stared at Kretchmar, who firmly thought he was about to be shot. Instead, the desperate man backed out of the office and walked out of the bank. He tossed his Remington onto the front seat of his 4X4 and drove away. Dale had one more score to settle.

Years earlier, in 1983, farmer Rich Goody and John Burr had had a dispute over a section of the Goody farm. Rich had sued John and had been awarded some $6,000, which Dale had to pay. In Dale's eyes, the entire incident had been a demeaning experience. Now he sped in his pickup to the Goody farm. The two men met outdoors. Dale shot Rich fully in the face from a distance of 15 feet. The blast spun the man around. Another shot plowed into Rich's back, killing him instantly. Dale jumped into his vehicle and drove away.

Just then Deputy Sheriff David Henderson received word on his police radio that Dale Burr had shot John Hughes and was heading towards his general area. Henderson spotted the wanted man before the message was completed. He turned on his siren, but Dale continued on for another half mile before pulling over to the side of the road. Henderson parked a cautious 30 yards away.

Dale placed the butt of his Remington on the floor and positioned the barrel against his chest. He pulled the trigger, but the weapon slipped. The blast shattered some ribs and hit his left arm, but was not fatal. Desperately, he managed to eject the shell and reload the Remington. This time he was successful.

Other policemen joined Henderson. Dale Burr was long past the concerns of this world. In the space of one hour he had killed his wife, the president of a bank, a fellow farmer and himself.

RICHARD CHASE

RICHARD Chase was born in 1950, the second of two children, to a middle-class couple in Sacramento, California. As a teenager, he was a fair student and managed to graduate from Mira Loma High School. He tried college, but his grades deteriorated and he dropped out. Somewhat of a string bean, Richard didn't bother bathing and let his hair grow to his shoulders. He smoked marijuana daily.

At age 20, Richard moved out of his parents' home into an apartment with two roommates. His behavior was so erratic that his roommates asked him to leave. On one occasion he was reported to police for shooting a gun. In an unrelated incident, he was taken into custody after running down a street completely nude.

By the time he was in his mid-twenties, Richard would fight with anyone who disagreed with him. He visited various hospitals, complaining about a variety of symptoms. At this stage in his checkered career, the idea of steady employment was out of the question. Employers would take one look at the scraggly young man and say thanks, but no thanks. From time to time Richard admitted himself into psychiatric institutions, where he was diagnosed as schizophrenic, but not a danger to himself or others. On these occasions, he or his parents facilitated his discharge.

Over the years Richard displayed an abnormal interest in blood. He believed that drinking it would cure his various ailments. Sometimes he killed birds and drank their blood. He captured small dogs and carried them to his apartment, where they were put to death for their blood.

Four days after Christmas 1977, Richard decided to kill a human being. It would be an experiment just to see if he could accomplish the task. The blood drinking would come later.

Ambrose Griffin was a 51-year-old engineer, who lived on Robinson St. in a suburb of Sacramento. He didn't deserve to die, yet he was killed as he innocently walked from his home to his car. Someone drove by his house, took aim with a .22 calibre handgun and fired. Ambrose, a family man without an enemy in the world, fell dead on the driveway of his house.

Neighbors along Robinson St. were questioned. No one had noticed the killer or his vehicle. Richard Chase had killed for the first time.

On January 23, 1978, several individuals saw a skinny dirty man walking down Tioga Way. He stopped at 2360, the home of Teresa and David Wallin, and tried the front door. It was unlocked. Teresa had just arrived home loaded down with a bag of groceries. She spun around, dropped the groceries and faced the man pointing the semi-automatic .22 at her. There was no talk. Richard Chase aimed and fired. Teresa fell to the floor. Richard leaned over and fired a second shot into her skull. He dragged her into the bedroom, where he extensively mutilated her body.

David Wallin walked into his home and found his wife dead. Unlike the murder of Ambrose Griffin, this time the killer left a clue—a distinctive bloody shoe print on the floor. There were also several small bloody circles on the floor near the body, but the significance of these circles was not apparent at the time.

Four days after the Wallin murder, Richard Chase struck again. Thirty-eight year-old divorcee Evelyn Miroth was excited for her six-year-old son Jason. A good friend and neighbor on Merrywood Dr., Neone Grangaard, was planning to take Jason, along with her own children, into the nearby Sierra Nevada mountains to play in the snow. Evelyn was a bit disappointed at not being able to get away herself. She had promised to baby-sit 22-month-old David Ferreira that morning. David's mother, Karen, had dropped the baby off at Evelyn's home.

Evelyn's boyfriend, Danny Meredith, would be visiting her later that day. She would walk Jason over to Neone's house just across the street in a few minutes. The two neighbors could see each other's front doors from their own homes.

When a half an hour passed with no sign of Evelyn or Jason, Neone decided to go over to find out what was holding them up. No one answered the door. How inconsiderate of Evelyn to go out without cancelling her son's trip to snow country, Neone thought. She mentioned the slight to another neighbor, Nancy Turner. Nancy tried Evelyn's back door. It was open. She walked into the house and let out a scream that could be heard throughout the subdivision.

Danny Meredith was lying in the hall. He had been shot to death, as had little Jason Miroth. Evelyn's body was horribly mutilated. There were the telltale bloody circles on the carpet near the body. A police physician thought the circles had been made with human blood, possibly the overflow of a small pail or container.

Distinctive bloody shoe prints matched the prints found in the Wallin home. There was no doubt in investigators' minds that a madman was killing and mutilating individuals in a confined area of Sacramento. There was no connection between victims. The killer was choosing them at random.

Another ominous element entered the case when police learned that little David Ferreira was nowhere to be found. Obviously, the killer had taken the baby with him after he had killed the other three people in the house.

Over 50 detectives were actively engaged in following leads. It was routine police work which finally uncovered a clue to the killer's identity. Detectives questioned everyone who worked or lived in the area. One woman, Nancy Holden, told police that she had been approached in a shopping mall by a tall, dirty man whom she identified as an old high school classmate. She had barely recognized the man, who had acted so strangely, even though she had been out on one date with him as a teenager. His name was Rick Chase.

At the time, it wasn't much of a lead. There were hundreds of tall dirty men in California. When Chase's name was checked out through motor vehicles, it was learned that he lived at 2934 Watt Ave., only a few blocks from the scenes of the murders.

Chase was picked up and his apartment was searched. At the time of his arrest, he was carrying the .22 calibre semi-automatic which had taken so many lives. He was also in possession of Danny Meredith's wallet containing Meredith's credit cards. A pair of Chase's athletic shoes had made the bloody prints found in both the Wallin and Miroth homes.

The interior of Chase's apartment was spattered with blood. Dog bones were strewn about the filthy premises. As for Chase, he admitted to capturing dogs and drinking their blood, but despite the evidence against him, he denied killing anyone. He claimed he had no idea of the fate of little David Ferreira.

On March 24, 1978, less than a mile from Chase's apartment, a janitor at the Arcade Wesleyan Church peered into a cardboard box lying in a pile of garbage on the church grounds. David Ferreira's fate was no longer a mystery.

On January 2, 1979, Richard Chase stood trial on six counts of murder. He admitted from the witness stand that he had killed so that he could drink his victims' blood. He pleaded not guilty by reason of insanity in order to escape the death penalty, but was found guilty and sentenced to death in California's gas chamber.

Chase was lodged on Death Row in San Quentin Prison. The prison physician prescribed three daily 50 mg tablets of doxepin hydrochloride to combat depression. Richard Chase saved up his daily dose for three weeks. He consumed his entire supply at one time and successfully committed suicide.

JEFFREY DAHMER

DURING the day he worked at the Ambrosia Chocolate Co. in Milwaukee. At night he killed people and cut up their bodies.

Jeffrey Dahmer had always been a bit different. As a kid in Akron, Ohio, he loved to dissect insects and small animals. When his middle-class parents divorced in 1978, Jeffrey was attending Ohio State University. He dropped out after only one semester. That same year, 18-year-old Jeffrey committed his first murder.

Stephen Hicks had hitchhiked to a rock music concert 30 miles from his home in Coventry, Ohio. Then he simply disappeared off the face of the earth. His parents offered a reward to anyone who could lead them to their son, but no one came forward with information. Stephen, one day a typical teenager, next day had ceased to exist.

It would be 13 years before his parents would learn that Jeffrey Dahmer had given their son a lift after the concert. The boys drove to Jeffrey's house for a few beers, but when Stephen attempted to leave, Jeffrey struck him over the head with a barbell and proceeded to strangle his unwary companion. Jeffrey had nothing against Stephen. He just didn't want him to leave.

Jeffrey dragged the body outdoors into a crawl space between the ground and the floor of the house. He cut the body into pieces and poured acid over the parts. It took a few weeks before he was able to remove excess flesh from the bones, which were then crushed with a sledgehammer. Once the bones were in tiny pieces, they were scattered over his backyard.

Out of sight, out of mind. Jeffrey joined the U.S. Army and served overseas in Germany for three years before being discharged for excessive drinking. In 1982, he moved in with his grandmother in West Allis, a suburb of Milwaukee.

For the next few years, Jeffrey drank heavily and was in and out of trouble with the law. He was given suspended sentences for his sex-related crimes. Once he lowered his trousers in a crowd. On another occasion, he was accused of masturbating in public.

Almost 10 years had passed since the murder of Stephen Hicks. That strange urge which he had managed to suppress for so long again had to be satisfied. It was 14-year-old James Doxtator's misfortune to cross Jeffrey Dahmer's path. Doxtator was accustomed to selling his body to wierdos for a price. Jeffrey picked him up with the promise that he would pay well if the boy would pose for nude pictures. Doxtator was drugged, strangled and dismembered. Acid was applied to his body, which was eventually pulverized with a sledgehammer.

Jeffrey Dahmer frequented gay bars where men were susceptible to being picked up. Richard Guerrero was one such man. He disappeared after falling into the deadly grasp of the man with the unnatural compulsion to kill and mutilate.

It became increasingly difficult and inconvenient to bring men to his grandmother's home. Jeffrey moved into the Oxford apartments at 808 N. 24th St. in Milwaukee. Later he would move into apartment 213, an address which would one day be flashed around the world.

Not everyone lured to Jeffrey's apartment was murdered. A few boys sensed that drugs had been placed in their beer or coffee and raced out of the apartment. One boy, a Laotian named Sinthasomphone, pressed charges. As a result, Jeffrey found himself convicted of sexual assault. He received a five-year jail sentence, but was allowed out on day parole so that he could continue working at his job at the chocolate factory. Ten months later, he was given full parole.

The killings continued. Anthony Sears, Ray Smith, Edward Smith, Ernest Miller and David Thomas all were reported missing in the 18-month period between March 1989 and September 1990. Jeffrey would later claim that he had had sex with these men before strangling them.

By now, Jeffrey Dahmer had developed an extraordinary trait, one which places him in a unique category among serial killers who keep trophies of their kills. While trophy collecting is common amongst serial killers, most keep items such as a glove or wallet. Jeffrey kept heads and entire limbs. Anthony Sears' skull was painted and stored in a refrigerator. Other heads, limbs and organs were kept as mementos of sex and murder.

Months passed. Neighbors complained of the odor emanating from the Dahmer apartment. Jeffrey satisfied them with plausible excuses and promises that he would remedy the situation. No one took any concrete action. The killing spree went on unabated. Curtis Straughter, 18; Errol Lindsey, 19; and Tony

Hughes, 31, all ended up as victims of the human monster who retained portions of their bodies as trophies.

Konerak Sinthasomphone, 14, coincidentally the younger brother of the boy responsible for Dahmer's earlier imprisonment for sexual assault, was a student at Pulaski High School. He was picked up by Jeffrey Dahmer and enticed into unit 213 at the Oxford apartments. Konerak was given a beer laced with a knock-out drop. He fell unconscious and was subjected to a sexual attack. Noticing that he was out of beer, Jeffrey left to pick up a six-pack. While he was gone, Konerak regained consciousness and staggered, bleeding and naked, out of the apartment and down into the street, where he was spotted by Dahmer.

Others also witnessed the scene and called the police. Three patrolmen, John Balcerzak, Joe Gabrish, and Richard Porubcan were soon at the scene of the incident. All three officers were experienced members of the Milwaukee Police Force. Throughout their careers they have received several citations for heroism and acting beyond the call of duty.

Jeffrey had to talk fast. He assured the officers his gay lover was a drunken adult and that there was really nothing amiss. The officers accompanied Jeffrey to his apartment, unaware that the body of Tony Hughes lay decaying in the bedroom at the time of their visit.

Jeffrey showed the officers Polaroid pictures of Konerak posing in a skimpy bathing suit. The officers assumed they had been called to a domestic dispute between two consenting males. They were tragically wrong. After they left, Jeffrey strangled Konerak Sinthasomphone to death.

All three officers would later be suspended with pay for their actions that night. The three policemen maintained that there appeared to be a loving relationship between the two participants and that there were none of the usual warning signs that anything was drastically wrong.

The brief brush with the law didn't discourage Jeffrey. On June 30, 1991, Matt Turner was murdered in the apartment. Jeremiah Weinberger, Oliver Lacy, and Joseph Bradehoft met the same fate. All four heads were later found in the refrigerator.

On July 22, 1991, police officers Robert Rauth and Rolf Mueller were in their patrol car when they were flagged down by Tracy Edwards. Edwards wanted the cops to get him out of the handcuffs he was wearing. He told the officers a wild story of a man who had threatened to cut out his heart and eat it. The officers had the frightened man lead them to Jeffrey Dahmer's apartment.

The first thing to hit the officers was the vile odor of the apartment. They questioned Jeffrey and radioed headquarters to do a routine check on their suspect. Word came back that Dahmer had a felony conviction against him. The officers looked around the filthy apartment. One of them opened the refrigerator door and within hours the world was privy to the secret life of Jeffrey Dahmer.

Once in custody, Dahmer admitted to having committed 17 murders in all and to having practised cannibalism.

In February 1992, he was found guilty of 15 murders and was sentenced to 15 consecutive life sentences. On November 28, 1994, Jeffrey Dahmer was beaten to death in prison by a fellow inmate.

LAURIE DANN

WINNETKA, Illinois, was a good place to live, a good place to bring up a family. The pleasant Chicago suburb of 14,000 was a safe haven, relatively free of the violence which has reached epidemic proportions in major U.S. cities. That is, until May 20, 1988, when Laurie Dann went berserk.

It wasn't supposed to happen that way. Born Laurie Wasserman, the daughter of an affluent accountant, she was a graduate of exclusive New Trier East High School. She went on to the University of Arizona before returning to Chicago.

In 1980, Laurie dated Russell Dann, whom she married two years later. For awhile she seemed content to be the suburban housewife ensconced in her quarter of a million dollar home, but the marriage gradually deteriorated. In 1984, the Danns divorced and Laurie returned to her parents' home.

The signs were there if only someone had paid attention. Laurie commenced to behave in an irrational manner.

Her ex-husband, Russell Dann, was stabbed while he slept in bed. The wound was serious and Russell was hospitalized. Later, he revealed that Laurie had admitted stabbing him. Russell realized that his ex-wife was unstable and didn't press the matter. Besides, there was no definite proof that Laurie had committed the crime.

A short time later, Laurie, for no apparent reason, began phoning an Arizona University grad whom she had dated while attending university. The old acquaintance, who was now a medical doctor, was amazed at the string of calls. When Laurie threatened his wife and children, he contacted his lawyers, who wrote to her parents, advising them of the unnatural series of phone calls. Questioned by local authorities, Laurie swore she was pregnant by the doctor, whom she had not seen for over five years.

At any time during this period of irrational behavior, someone could have suggested professional help for the mature woman who was obviously deranged. But things don't always work out that way. In hindsight, Laurie should have received treatment. As events unfolded over the years, she was thought of as a harmless oddball.

In 1987, Laurie advertised herself as a competent baby-sitter. Those who hired her recommended her to friends. Occasionally, there were incidents, such as the time one couple found that their sofa had been slashed after Laurie had been baby-sitting for them. Laurie swore she had no knowledge of the damage, which was reported to the police. They felt that Laurie may have had a hand in the vandalism, but had no proof.

Now caught up in a veritable frenzy of strange behavior, Laurie moved out of her parents' home and took an apartment on the Northwestern University campus. Almost immediately, there were complaints of raw meat being left to spoil in various locations in the apartment building. University officials asked Laurie to move.

Meanwhile Laurie had gained a measure of notoriety as a baby-sitter. There were complaints of theft of food and damage of property. She became known to the police as a very troubled individual. Her father paid for any damage attributed to her. She wrote threatening missives to her ex-husband's parents. The Danns implored the Wassermans to have Laurie institutionalized. Again, with the benefit of hindsight, we can see the avenue which should have been taken. Looking at events as they occurred, who can blame a parent for not wanting to institutionalize a daughter? One must remember that despite her strange behavior, Laurie could turn on the charm when the occasion arose.

Laurie moved to Madison, Wisconsin, and became a part-time student at the University of Wisconsin, where she lived in a dormitory. She was considered a loony by the other students. Laurie rode the elevators up and down for hours. Sometimes she showed up in the dining room in her pyjamas and slippers.

In March 1988, Laurie was apprehended while shoplifting. After spending the night in jail, she was sentenced to perform community service. Within weeks of being sentenced, she set fire to the rooms of two fellow students.

By April, Laurie, who was now well-known to the local police, may have been considered something more than a troubled oddball to the authorities. Known by the FBI to have purchased three pistols years earlier, they thought it advisable to pay her a visit. They were too late.

On May 14, Laurie slashed a fellow student's clothing. Because the semester was over the next day, most students had left their living quarters. Laurie was found in a storage bin in the basement of the school. Police were summoned. Next day, the FBI dropped by to question Laurie. She was gone.

On May 19, Laurie Dann showed up at the home of Padraig and Marian Rushe. The Rushes had previously used Laurie as a baby-sitter and never suspected her of any wrongdoing. When Laurie offered to take two of the five Rushe children to a fair the following day, the Rushes consented.

On May 20, the evil machinations at work in Laurie's brain predicated that she rise at 7 a.m. It would be an eventful day.

Laurie delivered packages of fruit juice to eight suburban homes. All contained arsenic. At two other homes, she left plates of Rice Krispies on the doorstep. Both contained arsenic. At 9 a.m., Laurie picked up Patrick Rushe, 8 and his little brother, Carl, 4. She gave the two boys cartons of milk, but the milk didn't taste good and the youngsters only took a sip before placing them on the seat of the car. Fortunately, there were no casualties as a result of Laurie's poison attempts.

Laurie drove to Ravinia School and set fire to a plastic bag filled with gasoline, which she placed near the school. Returning the two Rushe children to their home, Laurie bid a cheerful goodbye to Mrs. Rushe, who was busy in the laundry room. As soon as Laurie left, the laundry room stairs burst into flames. Marian Rushe miraculously tore out an entire window frame and, together with her two children, managed to escape the fire.

Laurie Dann, armed with a .22-calibre Beretta, a .357 Magnum and a .32-calibre Smith and Wesson revolver, drove to Hubbard Woods School. She walked into the boys' washroom and shot the first little boy to enter the room. Robert Trossman, 6, took the full force of the .357 Magnum in the chest and stomach. Laurie tossed the gun to the floor beside the form of her first victim. Unbelievably, Robert survived.

Laurie entered a classroom and gave an order to teacher Amy Moses. Ms. Moses refused to respond. Laurie pulled out two pistols. Amy Moses couldn't quite comprehend the situation. She found herself in a hand-to-hand struggle with a mysterious woman who had two guns. Laurie broke loose and opened fire on a group of children. Lindsay Fisher, eight; Peter Munro, eight; Kathryn

Miller, seven; and Mark Teborek, eight, were wounded. Little Nicholas Corwin, eight, took the time to push a friend out of Laurie's line of fire. The friend escaped unscathed, but Nicholas was shot through the heart and died instantly.

Laurie dashed out of the school, jumped into her Toyota and roared down a dead-end street. She hit a tree. Deserting her car, she ran into the home of Ruth and Raymond Andrews. The Andrews were talking to their son Philip, 20, a student at the University of Illinois. Wielding two pistols, Laurie hurriedly explained that she had just been raped. The Andrews were unable to comprehend the entire situation, but all three realized that something terribly wrong had just taken place. They cajoled Laurie into calling her parents. She told her parents the police were closing in on her, as indeed they were.

By gestures, Philip Andrews conveyed the message to his parents to leave the room while Laurie was still on the phone. Once his parents were safe, Philip made a desperate grab for the .22 calibre Beretta. Laurie shot him in the chest. Philip staggered outside before collapsing. Although seriously wounded, he survived.

Meanwhile, a SWAT team surrounded the Andrews' home. It wasn't until seven that evening that they stormed the house. In an upstairs bedroom, they found the body of Laurie Dann. Earlier in the day, she had placed the .32 calibre Smith and Wesson in her mouth, pulled the trigger and ended her troubled life.

No one knows why the pent-up evil that filled Laurie's mind exploded in a classroom on a quiet day in May in a quiet suburb of Chicago. There is no reasonable explanation, except for the terrible mental illness that drove her to murder and suicide.

ALBERT DE SALVO

THE Hillside Strangler kept the city of Los Angeles in a reign of terror. Wayne Williams, who murdered young children in Atlanta, Georgia, terrorized that city. But nothing before or since has ever held a city in the grip of fear quite like the Boston Strangler did back in 1962.

From June 1962, to January 1964, the citizens of Boston and its suburbs talked of little else but the weird, sexually motivated murders of women ranging in age from 19 to 85.

The sale of locks escalated rapidly. Some apartments resembled armed camps, yet a cunning, deranged man talked his way into hundred of apartments to molest, rape and, in 13 instances, kill innocent women.

On the evening of June 14, 1962, Juris Slesers, 25, a research engineer at M.I.T., climbed the stairs to his mother's third floor apartment at 77 Gainsborough St. The 55-year-old Anna Slesers had been looking forward to her son's visit. She had prepared his favorite dishes for dinner.

Anna didn't answer Juris' knock. Inside the apartment, she lay on the floor, dead. Juris broke down the door to the apartment and found his mother's body. It was not a pleasant sight. Anna lay on her back. Her robe appeared to be open on purpose, displaying her nudity. She had been strangled with her bathrobe cord, which had been knotted around her neck and tied in a bow.

The house had been ransacked, indicating to police that the killer may have been robbing the apartment when Anna, who was preparing to take a bath, heard something, opened the bathroom door and was attacked. There was water in the bathtub. Anna had not been raped, but had been sexually molested. The door to her apartment had not been forced. Would Anna greet a stranger in her bathrobe?

No one knew it at the time, but the Boston Strangler, as he was soon to become known, had murdered for the first time.

Two weeks later, on June 30, the temperature in Boston hit 90 degrees F. Nina Nichols, 68, was on the phone speaking to her sister when the buzzer to her apartment sounded. She told her sister, "Excuse me, Marguerite, there's my buzzer. I'll call you right back." Nina Nichols never called back. She answered the door and became the Boston Strangler's second victim. The building janitor eventually opened the door with a passkey and found her body.

Nina Nichols had been strangled with her own nylon stocking, which had been grotesquely knotted into a bow around her neck. Her underclothing had been pulled up to her waist, exposing her nude body. Although her apartment had been ransacked, no money, jewelry or other valuables appeared to be missing.

That same night of June 30, Helen Blake, 65, was strangled to death. When neighbors couldn't contact her, they called police. Helen was found on her bed, face down, nude except for her pyjama top. She had been strangled with her nylon stockings and brassiere, which had been tied around her neck in the familiar bow. She had been sexually assaulted.

Now the rash of murders were attributed to one man, dubbed the Boston Strangler. Each murder was stranger than the last. The victims were unknown to each other. Although their apartments had been ransacked, nothing appeared to be missing. Why were the victims exposed and made to look ridiculous in death? Who was this man who seemed to be able to talk any woman into opening the door of her apartment? Who was the Boston Strangler? No one knew. The murders continued.

Ida Irga, 75, was strangled on August 19. Next day, Jane Sullivan, 67, met her death at the hands of the Strangler. That winter, on December 5, Sophia Clark, 20, was murdered. Over three weeks later, Patricia Bissette, 23, was killed in the Strangler's unique way.

It should be noted that another murder, at first not thought to be the work of the Boston Strangler, but later attributed to him, took place during the summer of 1962. Eighty-five-year-old Mary Mullen died of a heart attack in the Strangler's arms before he had a chance to strangle her.

The series of weird murders were the main topic of conversation in the greater Boston area. Delivery men had a difficult time performing their duties. Parcels were left outside doors. Men walked their dates to their front doors and waited until their companions had securely locked themselves in.

The killings continued. March 9, 1963, Mary Brown, 69; May 6, 1963, Beverley Samans, 23; September 8, 1963, Evelyn Corbin, 58; November 23, 1963, Joann Graff, 23; January 4, 1964, Mary Sullivan, 19. In all, 13 innocent victims fell to the madness that was the Boston Strangler. Who was he?

Albert De Salvo was born in Chelsea, a suburb of Boston. His father, who was a wife-beater, taught little Albert the art of shoplifting when the lad was five years old. Albert was in and out of trouble during his early years. At 16, he joined the army, where he served for over eight years. During a five-year stint in Germany, he married. At the conclusion of his army service, he returned with his bride, Irmgard, to live near Boston. They had two children, a boy and a girl.

In 1961, Albert achieved some degree of infamy posing as the Measuring Man. He would knock on an apartment door, first making sure that the lady of the house was home alone. Flashing his boyish grin, he would explain that he was recruiting models for a project where they could earn $40 an hour. To add credibility to his patter, he would produce a measuring tape, explaining that nudity was not involved. The modelling was for evening gowns.

If the lady of the house refused, Albert would bow and move along. If she consented, he measured her from every conceivable angle. He would then shake hands, with a promise that a woman from his agency would be in contact.

No crime was actually committed. No woman from the agency showed up. However, on one occasion, Albert was spotted dashing through an alleyway by an alert police officer. Once in custody, he admitted to being the Measuring Man. He explained that he meant no harm. It just gave him a thrill to talk to and measure women. Albert was sentenced to 18 months for attempted breaking and entering. He was paroled from the Middlesex County House of Correction in April 1962, after serving 11 months.

Another weirdo was out on the streets. Albert now became the Green Man, as well as the Boston Strangler. Dressed up in a green uniform, he gained entrance to the apartments of even the most careful women. Once inside, he molested and raped his victims, after apologizing for the intrusion. Many women didn't report the Green Man's crimes, so we will never know how many women the Green Man raped. Police estimate over 300. Albert was later to say between 600 and 1000. We do know that he often raped four women on the same day.

One victim gave such a detailed description of her attacker's face that an artist's sketch was matched to a photograph of the old Measuring Man. The similarities were startling. Albert De Dalvo was picked up and questioned. Under urging by his wife, he confessed to being the Green Man. He had committed scores of crimes, which were never attributed to him, sometimes ranging into Connecticut, New Hampshire and Rhode Island. At no time did Albert De Salvo admit that simultaneously to being the Green Man, he was operating and killing as the Boston Strangler.

While awaiting trial, Albert began to act in an irrational manner, often talking to his wife and police officers in his cell in the middle of the night. After a sanity hearing, he was incarcerated in the Bridgewater State Hospital until deemed fit to stand trial.

In Bridgewater, Albert became friends with two-time killer, George Nassar, an unusual inmate who had an IQ of 150. Albert bragged incessantly to Nassar about his successes with women while posing as the Measuring Man and the Green Man. Initially, Nassar paid little attention, but when Albert claimed to be the Boston Strangler, he listened more closely. He soon came to believe that Albert was telling the truth. Nassar contacted his lawyer, F. Lee Bailey, considered one of the finest defence lawyers in the country.

Bailey took on Albert's case. He listened to his story, which was full of details only the authentic Boston Strangler could know. There was no doubt about it. Albert De Salvo was the Boston Strangler.

Albert was deemed competent to stand trial. He was found guilty of assault and sex crimes committed as the Green Man. As a result, he was sentenced to life imprisonment, but never stood trial for the 13 murders he committed as the Boston Strangler.

In 1967, Albert again made headlines when he escaped from Bridgewater. Newspapers, radio and television blared out the warning that the Boston Strangler was at large. Albert listened to the hunt on his transistor radio before walking into a clothing store and giving himself up to a clerk.

On November 26, 1973, Albert De Salvo was stabbed to death by a fellow inmate in prison.

MARK ESSEX

MARK Essex was raised in a fine home by fine parents in the fine Midwest town of Emporia, Kansas. From the time he joined the U.S. Navy in 1969, until January 1973, something turned Mark Essex into a raging killer.

While in the navy, Mark completed a three-month dental assistant's course. The 21-year-old black man with the solid background let it be known that he intended to become a dentist.

But the navy held many surprises for Mark. He was unaccustomed to racial prejudice and was ill-equipped to cope with the petty indignities passed out by the white servicemen. Mark soon discovered that blacks were given the distasteful duties. The whites treated the black servicemen as inferiors.

In 1970, Mark couldn't stand the discrimination and abusive behavior any longer. He left the navy without leave and returned to Emporia. The young man who returned to his parents was a bitter individual. The world outside his sheltered Midwest existence was not what he imagined. With a minister's help, his parents managed to talk Mark into returning to the navy after he had brooded at home for a month.

Court-martialled, he was confined to the naval base for one month and sentenced to forfeit $90 pay each month for the next two months. Mark's court-martial trial dwelt on two salient issues, namely Mark's above-average ability at his dental work and the amount of racial abuse he had encountered in the service. However, the punishment devastated Mark and reinforced his now deep-rooted belief that all whites were the black man's natural enemy.

Discharged from the navy, Mark once more returned to his home town, where he stayed with his parents until 1972. He then took several trips to New York, before moving on to New Orleans. While in New York, Mark picked up a .44-magnum carbine and a .38-calibre Colt revolver. In New Orleans, he took a vending machine repair course.

Mark was somewhat a lone brooder until November 16, 1972. That was the day a university demonstration in Baton Rouge culminated in two black students being shot by police. The Baton Rouge incident firmly committed Mark to a course of action from which there was no return. He wrote his parents, affirming his commitment to the cause of the black man in America. Mark even decorated the walls of his apartment with racial slogans.

On New Year's Eve of 1972, Mark secreted himself across the street from the New Orleans police department's Central Lockup and opened fire with his Ruger .44-magnum semi-automatic carbine. One shot struck police cadet Al Harrell, 19, in the chest, killing him. Ironically, Harrell was one of the few black cadets attached to the New Orleans police force. The same bullet exited Harrell's body and hit Lt. Horace Perez in the ankle. In a matter of minutes, scores of police were looking for the mysterious sniper, but the madman had disappeared.

A few blocks away from the Central Lockup building, two policemen were checking out an alarm that had sounded in the offices of a factory building. Unknown to the police, Mark Essex lurked in one of the offices. A shot rang out, and Officer Edwin Hosli slumped to the floor. Two months later he would die of his wounds.

Thirty-five police officers surrounded the factory. Shots ricocheted off the walls, but once again, the sniper made good his escape. This time police found bloodstains, indicating that their quarry had been wounded.

Police followed the sniper. It wasn't that difficult. He left a trail of bullets, as if inviting police to follow. The trail led to the First New St. Mark Baptist Church. However, not wanting to have another shootout that night, the police retreated from the area. Once more, the sniper had eluded capture.

A week passed. On January 7, Mark walked into a grocery store managed by Joe Perniciaro and shot him in the chest. Mark ran from the store and commandeered a car idling at a stop sign. He then drove to Howard Johnson's Hotel in downtown New Orleans.

Mark proceeded up an outside staircase to the 18th floor of the hotel before he could gain entrance. Lugging his rifle with him, he briskly walked by three black hotel employees. He reassured them with the comment, "Don't worry, I'm not going to hurt you black people. I want the whites."

Dr. Robert Steagall had the bad luck to cross Mark's path. Mark shot him the chest and arm. Betty Steagall knelt to comfort her husband. As she did so, Mark shot her in the head. He then entered the Steagalls' room and set fire to the curtains.

Mark made his way down to the 11th floor, where he met bellman Donald Roberts and office manager Frank Schneider. The two men took one look and ran for their lives. Bullets slammed into the walls. One struck Frank Schneider in the head, killing him instantly.

The sniper shot at anyone he met. General manager Walter Collins, accompanied by janitor Lucino Llovett, went looking for the sniper. They found him on the 10th floor. Collins was shot in the back.

Meanwhile, as the slaughter progressed, someone called police, who arrived along with the fire department. A ladder was raised outside the building. Lt. Tim Ursin was climbing the ladder when Mark spotted him. Ursin was shot in his left arm. The wound was severe enough to necessitate the later amputation of the arm.

One can imagine the chaos the shooting caused in a large hotel. Guests screamed and ran for their lives. Occasionally, police would shoot at a moving object on an upper floor. The number of police mounted until well over 600 surrounded the building. Mark kept moving, setting fires in rooms as he spread havoc throughout the hotel. Firemen, attempting to battle the flames, feared for their lives; not only from the sniper but from the indiscriminate police gunfire.

Several men were wounded by the sniper. Patrolman Charles Arnold opened a window of a building directly across the street from the hotel. As he did so, a bullet smashed into his face. Robert Beamish, a hotel guest, was shot in the stomach. Officer Kenneth Solis was shot in the shoulder. When Sgt. Emanuel Palmisano came to Solis' aid, he was shot in the back. Patrolman Paul Persigo wasn't so lucky. He was shot dead by the sniper.

The strange scenario unfolding in New Orleans took on an unreal aura. Armed civilians joined the large crowd that stared up at the smouldering top floors of Howard Johnson's. Many shouted encouragement to the sniper.

Finally, the police advanced upward in the hotel, but not without paying a price. Deputy Superintendent Louis Sirgo was shot dead on the 16th floor. The sniper retreated to the roof. The first policeman to gain the roof was Officer Larry Arthur. He was shot in the abdomen, while the gunman shouted, "Free Africa! Come on up, pigs!"

Tear gas was fired to the rooftop without effect. To taunt police, Mark shouted, "I'm still here, pigs!"

A helicopter was brought in to stamp out the sniper. Unbelievably, Mark's fire drove off the first few passes. An armored helicopter carrying two Marine sharpshooters and three police officers was then used. The sharpshooters poured bullets into the roof. Several volleys almost killed police officers who were hiding in stairwells and behind abutments. Nine policemen were wounded by their colleagues' fire.

Darkness descended on New Orleans. The armored helicopter, with its sharpshooters, made pass after pass at the lone sniper. A bullet wounded Mark, who then came out from cover and attacked the helicopter, firing from the hip. Bullets poured into Mark's body—from the helicopter, from the roof, from the stairwells.

In all, over 200 bullet holes were found in the unrecognizable mass that was once Mark Essex. In his wake, he left nine dead and 10 wounded. Mark Essex's body was returned to Emporia, Kansas, where he was buried in an unmarked grave.

LARRY EYLER

BY the summer of 1983, police were certain that a serial killer was operating in the greater Chicago area and across the border in Indiana. The bodies of young men between the ages of 16 and 28 were turning up in epidemic proportions.

On May 9, 1983, Dan McNeive, a 21-year-old hustler, was found stabbed to death in a field in Henderson County, Indiana. The many stab wounds on his body were typical of the injuries found on the dozen victims discovered during the previous year. Dan frequented gay bars and had often been seen in the company of gay men. Most of the victims were homosexuals and were well known in the gay communities of Chicago and Indianapolis.

A task force was formed to take over the investigations already underway. This force spread out, checking gay bars in several localities within 150 miles of Lake Michigan. In this way, the name Larry Eyler first came to the attention of police. An anonymous phone call suggested him as a suspect because he had been in some trouble five years earlier.

At that time, Larry worked in a liquor store and frequented gay bars. In 1978, he had picked up a hitchhiker in Terre Haute, had driven him to a field outside town and had threatened the man with a knife. Larry's captive was handcuffed and stabbed repeatedly. Despite the handcuffs and his serious wounds, the injured man was able to roll off the back of Larry's pickup truck and escape. He spent several days in the intensive care unit of a local hospital and was fortunate to survive the attack.

After posting bond of $10,000, Larry was released from custody. When his trial date approached, his lawyer offered the victim $2,500 to cover his medical expenses and wages lost because of his hospitalization. The young man accepted the cash and agreed not to press charges. Larry, who had been planning to plead guilty to aggravated assault, changed his plea to innocent. The case was dismissed. Larry paid $43 in court costs.

The task force investigation brought many suspects into their net, but Larry Eyler's name always rose to the surface. Although he lived in Terre Haute, he roamed the Indiana/Illinois border where most of the bodies were recovered. The victims had usually been stabbed. Many had indentations around their wrists, leading investigators to believe they had been handcuffed before being murdered. The bodies were found in woods and fields near highways. Larry continually travelled these roads and it was well known in the gay community that he was deeply involved in bondage. Despite the fact that police were keeping an eye on Larry, bodies continued to show up, all bearing the tell-tale multiple stabbings.

On September 30, 1983, task force detectives staked out a gay bar on North Clark St. in Chicago. Inside, Larry Eyler was having a midday beer. He came out and drove away in his 1982 Ford pickup. Detectives followed. Larry cruised at a snail's pace, obviously looking for a male companion. When fog settled on the seamy north side, the detectives lost their quarry. They did, however, report to task force headquarters that their prime suspect was in Chicago and apparently was on the prowl.

Meanwhile, Larry had picked up a drifter. As soon as the man was in the vehicle Larry propositioned him. He wanted to tie the man up and would pay him $100 for his trouble. Larry promised that the fun and games wouldn't hurt. Finally, the drifter agreed to the proposition. Larry parked the truck and the two men walked the short distance into a field. The drifter didn't like the proximity to the road and suggested they find a more secluded spot. Larry agreed.

The two men were walking back to the truck when State Trooper Kenneth Buehrie just happened to pull up. He thought the circumstances were suspicious and decided to question the two men, as well as to radio for a vehicle registration check. He was informed that Larry Eyler was a prime suspect in a serial murder investigation.

Larry was taken into custody and detained in a cell while police searched his truck. The soles of Larry's shoes corresponded with footprints made at the scene of one of the murders. A bloodstained hunting knife, some rope and a key for unlocking handcuffs were found in the truck. Despite the grave suspicion that they had the right man in custody, police doubted that they could hold him based on the evidence. Larry admitted to his bondage fetish and informed his interrogators that he had cut his finger on his hunting knife weeks earlier. The drifter told police that he had gone willingly with Larry. After being held for 12 hours, Larry Eyler was released.

Next day, Larry's home in Terre Haute was searched. Telephone records revealed that he had called a male lover in Chicago before each one of the serial killer's victims was murdered. While in Chicago, Larry lived with this lover.

When the body of Ralph Calise was found, authorities felt that there was enough cumulative evidence to arrest Larry Eyler and charge him with Calise's murder. Larry hired respected lawyer David Shipper to defend him on the murder charge. There was far more at stake than a single murder. Police were certain they were dealing with a monster who had killed 19 times with seeming immunity from prosecution.

At a pretrial hearing held in January 1984, defence lawyer Shipper tore the initial police investigation to shreds. Larry had been held in custody for over 12 hours without being charged with any crime. Police had searched his truck without obtaining a warrant. Although Larry had cooperated fully with police, he had been handcuffed. No one had advised him of his rights.

The presiding judge decided that the search and treatment Larry received was illegal, making most of the subsequent evidence against him inadmissable. The court didn't get to hear about the bag of rope in Larry's truck, nor did they hear about the bloody knife. The judge reduced bail from $1 million to $10,000. Larry's family deposited the required 10% and Larry walked out of court practically a free man. True, the decision to reduce bail would be appealed, but that could be 18 months down the road. Larry's friends and relatives rejoiced. The families of many victims wept openly in court.

A friend fixed Larry up with an apartment at 1628 West Sherwin Ave. in Chicago. To one and all he announced that he was beginning a new life. However, he continued his love trysts with his regular lover and often picked up transients.

On August 21, 1984, the janitor of Larry's apartment building thought several plastic bags of garbage were unusually heavy. On his way to tossing them into a dumpster, he decided to open one. Inside he discovered the dismembered body of 15-year-old male prostitute Daniel Bridges. The garbage belonged to none other than Larry Eyler.

Police were called. They immediately recognized the name. Had a suspected serial killer become so brazen that he had killed in his own apartment and had attempted to dispose of the body behind his own building?

A search of Larry's apartment revealed that it had been freshly painted. Despite the new paint job, bloodstains were found, which proved to be the same blood type as the victim's. In addition, Larry had been seen lugging the garbage bags outdoors.

In October 1986, the entire despicable life led by Larry Eyler was paraded before a jury. The evidence led to no other conclusion but guilt. Larry was sentenced to death for the murder of Daniel Bridges. Many believe that he was responsible for a total of 21 victims.

Larry offered to plead guilty to all 21 murders in exchange for a life sentence. His offer was rejected. In March 1994, Larry Eyler died of AIDS in a Pontiac, Illinois prison.

JOHN WAYNE GACY

JOHN Wayne Gacy would grow up to be the manager of a chain of southern fried chicken stores, a successful shoe-store manager, a respected member of the Junior Chamber of Commerce, a performing clown, a precinct captain in the Democratic Party, and the owner of his own prosperous contracting business. He also was to become one of the most prolific mass murderers in the history of the United States.

John's formative years hold no clue to his future bizarre behavior. Gregarious, fun-loving John Gacy was an average student who took a job as a shoe salesman after graduating from Northwestern Business College in Chicago.

In 1964, when he was 22, he was so highly regarded by the shoe firm that he was transferred to Springfield, Illinois, where he was made manager of the company's retail outlet. A few months later he was dating and eventually married co-worker Marlynn Myers.

John, who always had a weight problem, tipped the scales at approximately 220 pounds and stood only five-feet, eight-inches tall. His sparkling personality more than made up for his chunky appearance. He joined the Junior Chamber of Commerce, where he was one of the hardest working and most popular members of the local chapter.

When his father-in-law offered him a job in Waterloo, Iowa, working for his chain of southern fried chicken franchise stores, John jumped at the opportunity. Soon he was effectively running the chain, often working sixteen hours a day. John joined the Jaycees and quickly became a valuable member of the organization. He was named chaplain as well as chairman of the group's prayer breakfast. Marlynn gave birth to two healthy children, a son John and a daughter Elaine.

In the spring of 1968 the veil of respectability which shielded John Gacy's world began to crumble. A local boy claimed that while he was working for John in one of the food outlets, he had accompanied the older man to his home. Mrs. Gacy and the children were not in.

After providing his visitor with a few drinks, John suggested oral sex. When the boy refused, John threatened him with a knife and fastened him to a bed with chains. Gacy proceeded to choke the young lad until he was almost unconscious, abruptly releasing him and allowing him to leave the house.

A second boy told much the same story. His experience culminated with being forced to perform unnatural sex acts. John was arrested, and after much plea bargaining, was charged with committing sodomy. Understandably, at this time his wife left him.

John was sentenced to ten years imprisonment at the Iowa State Reformatory for men at Anamosa. Anamosa boasted one of the first Jaycee chapters formed in an American prison. John threw himself into chapter work with the same vigor he had employed at Waterloo. As a result he became president of the organization. Eighteen months after entering prison, John was paroled.

Still under thirty, John returned to Chicago. For a while he lived with his mother, having gained employment as a cook in a nearby restaurant. Four months after his release, with his mother's help, John purchased his own home at 8213 West Summerdale Avenue in suburban Norwood Park.

On February 12, 1971, a short time after moving into his own home, John was charged with disorderly conduct by Chicago police. A teenaged admitted homosexual claimed that John picked him up, drove him to his home, and attempted to force him to perform unnatural sex acts. When his accuser failed to show up in court, the charges against John were dropped.

No one has ever been able to explain why the Iowa Board of Parole was not made aware that Gacy had been charged with a sex crime in another state. Still on parole on the sodomy charge, Gacy's activities certainly would have been curtailed had a routine check been carried out. Unfortunately, the board was never informed. One month later Gacy was officially discharged from parole.

On the surface it appeared that Gacy was rebuilding his life. He met Carole Hoff, the divorced mother of two little girls, who would soon become the second Mrs. Gacy. He made friends with his neighbors. Everyone liked big John Gacy.

What no one knew, and could not possibly conceive, was the horrible fact that the most prolific mass murderer in U.S. history was already killing boys and burying them under the crawlspace of his home. It is believed that the first murder took place on the night of January 3, 1972. The killings were to last for the next seven years.

After John and Carole became husband and wife, she and her two children were to remain in the death house for the next four years. Carole was completely unaware that John could only gain sexual gratification by killing. She was well aware that her husband was forever doing carpentry jobs around the house, making additions to this, enlarging that. Many men do the same thing. She never gave it a second thought.

Around this time a strange musty odor became noticeable in the Gacy household. John claimed it was a broken sewer tile. The old tile was replaced, but the odor didn't abate until John closed off the vents leading from the crawlspace.

Meanwhile, John was a considerate husband to Carole and a good father to her two children. Around the neighborhood he gained something of a reputation as a party giver. A couple of times a year he would throw a big barbecue. It wasn't uncommon for these feasts to be attended by more than a hundred friends and neighbors. John loved to dress up as a clown and entertain the neighborhood children.

Gacy left his job as a cook and opened his own business, P.D.M. Contractors, Inc. It was successful from the beginning. John hired experienced older men for skilled tasks, but drew his manual labor from young boys who were willing to work for low wages. His construction company expanded rapidly, and soon John was bidding on and obtaining contracts worth up to $100,000. He purchased a Cadillac and became active in the Democratic Party.

All the while renovations were taking place at the Gacy home. John built a storage shed at the end of the garage. It was customary to see young boys coming and going. Everyone knew John hired them for his construction company.

Carole became disenchanted with her marriage. Her husband spent all his time either working at his business or working for the Democrats. He seemed to prefer the company of young boys to hers. She filed for divorce and left her husband on March 2, 1976.

For seven years boys and young men had been picked up by Gacy off the streets or were befriended when they applied for employment with his construction company. He gratified his strange sexual desires before killing them and burying them on his own property.

Robert Piest was a conscientious high-school student who worked in a drug-store on a part-time basis. At 8:00 p.m., when his mother called at Nissons Pharmacy in Des Plaines to pick up her son on the evening of December 11, 1978, Robert asked her to wait in the store for a few moments. He had to talk to a man named John Gacy about a contracting job which paid quite a bit better than his present job at the drugstore. Gacy was waiting in his pickup truck in the parking lot. Robert left the store, telling his mother that he would be back in a few moments. He never returned.

Mrs. Piest searched the parking lot. She questioned Robert's friends. No one could help her. Finally she called the police. Next day detectives were exten-sively questioning John Gacy about the missing boy. Gacy denied having any knowledge about the disappearance. When detectives were informed of Gacy's criminal record, they obtained a warrant to search his home.

Rows of bodies, some little more than skeletons, were found buried in the crawlspace of the house. Others were found buried under the recreation room, while still others were buried in the garage. In all, twenty-nine bodies were removed from Gacy's property. Four other victims had been thrown in nearby rivers.

Gacy's murder trial concluded on March 13, 1980, when he was convicted of murdering thirty-three young men and boys, more than any other person in U.S. history.

In May 1994, John Wayne Gacy was executed by lethal injection in Statesville Penitentiary near Joliet, Illinois.

GERALD GALLEGO

THEY told little nine-year-old Gerald Gallego that his father had died in a car accident. They lied.

Gerald was a bad little boy. By the time he was 13 he displayed an abnormal tendency toward sadism and sex. A few months after his thirteenth birthday, he was incarcerated by the California Youth Authority for having sex with a six-year-old girl.

Gerald went on to spend most of his formative years behind bars. He married seven different women between prison sentences, often without benefit of divorce. We need only concern ourselves with his seventh wife, Charlene, who strangely relished her husband's wild lifestyle. Unlike Gerald, Charlene came from a secure, loving family, who were well respected in the Sacramento, California area. For reasons only she understands, she fell in love and married Gerald Gallego.

Charlene was 24, Gerald 32, when the pair graduated from child molesting, rape, and robbery to wanton serial killing.

On September 11, 1978, Rhonda Scheffler, 17 and Kippi Vaught, 16 set out in the Schefflers' family car for a shopping mall in Sacramento. The girls never returned home. Two days later their bodies were found about 15 miles outside the city. They had been beaten with a tire iron and shot in the head with a .25 calibre pistol. Both had been sexually abused.

Nine months later, on April 24, 1980, Stacy Redican and Karen Chipman-Twiggs vanished from another Sacramento shopping mall. Their decomposed bodies were found in July by picnickers 75 miles north of Reno. They had been beaten about the head with sufficient force to crush their skulls.

Linda Aquilar, 21, was five months pregnant when she disappeared while hitchhiking from Port Orford, Oregon. Her body was recovered from a shallow grave a few miles south of Gold Beach. She had been bound hand and foot with nylon rope. An autopsy revealed that death had been caused by vicious blows to the head with an iron object. She had been buried while still alive.

In hindsight, we are connecting the murders, but at the time separate investigations were being conducted in all three cases. They were not considered to be related. The crimes took place in different locales and the victims were from vastly different backgrounds. One victim was pregnant and was apparently picked up by her killer while hitchhiking. The others were abducted from shopping malls.

Waitress Virginia Mochel walked out of the Sacramento bar where she worked into the parking lot toward her car. While walking those few yards, she disappeared. Virginia's body was found three months later just outside Sacramento. Her arms were securely tied behind her back.

Customers at the bar were questioned. Many remembered that Virginia had spoken to a man and woman several times while they drank. The man, who said he was a bartender, was outgoing and loud, while his companion was docile and spoke very little. That's about all the police had to go on. The killings didn't stop.

Mary Beth Sowers and her fiancé, Craig Miller, attended California State University in Sacramento. They were a popular young couple who had every reason to look forward to a happy and prosperous future. Craig had been named Man of the Year at the university for 1979.

Mary Beth and Craig attended the Sigma Phi Epsilon Founders Day dinner at the Carousel, a well-known Sacramento restaurant. Mary Beth was resplendent in a formal gown. Craig was decked out in a tuxedo.

Arm in arm, they left the restaurant at midnight. Out of the darkness, a woman lurched toward them. Too late, they saw she was pointing a handgun in their direction. The woman ordered them into a parked 1977 Olds. An adult male occupied the front passenger seat.

The woman with the gun jumped into the driver's seat and sped away, but not before a friend of the students witnessed the abduction. He had gone over to investigate and had received a slap from the woman before she jumped into the vehicle. The alert friend jotted down the licence number and phoned police. The number was fed into the police computer. A few minutes later they had the name of the registered owner—Charlene Gallego.

The car containing the two abducted students pulled onto a secluded road in El Dorado County. Craig was ordered from the vehicle and told to lie face down on the road. The man, now equipped with a handgun, fired three shots into the back of the hapless student's head.

Mary Beth Sowers cowered in horror while her fiancé was murdered in cold blood. She was then driven to a Sacramento apartment where she was raped.

The man's companion waited outside the bedroom door. Mary Beth was taken from the apartment and driven a few miles outside the city, where she too was shot three times in the head.

The day after these murders, Charlene Gallego was questioned by police. She told them very little other than that she was drunk the night before and couldn't remember anything that had happened. The police had no idea they were involved in a murder investigation. They only knew they had a report that two students had left a fraternity dinner under suspicious circumstances. As far as they were concerned, it could be nothing more than university student hijinks.

Later that same day, when Craig's body was found, police raced back to Charlene's apartment. She and the Olds were long gone. A few inquiries revealed that Charlene's husband was one Gerald Gallego, a man with a long police record, including many sex crimes.

Charlene contacted friends, attempting to have them wire money to her. Police were notified and were waiting for the Gallegos in a Western Union office in Omaha, Nebraska. Returned to California, both initially pleaded not guilty to charges of murder and abduction. A few weeks after they were taken into custody, the body of Mary Beth Sowers was found in a little-used field.

Charlene, who was seven months pregnant at the time of her arrest, gave birth to a boy while in jail. The baby Gerald Jr., was given to relatives to raise.

Months passed. Charlene was removed from the dominating personality of her husband. Slowly she revealed the details of the killing spree. At the same time, she plea-bargained for her life. She would receive a prison sentence of 16 years and eight months for the murders of Craig Miller and Mary Beth Sowers and another concurrent sentence of 16 years and eight months in the deaths of Stacy Redican and Karen Chipman-Twiggs in Nevada. She would be immune from prosecution on all other charges. In return she would tell all she knew about her husband's involvement in the killings.

Charlene told plenty. Sometimes she had been used as a lure to entice girls into their car. Other times she used a gun. The motive for the crimes had been

Gerald's perverted sexual desire. In all cases he had his way with the victims while Charlene watched or waited until he was satisfied. The victims were then killed.

In the summer of 1982, Gerald Gallego stood trial for the murder of Craig Miller and Mary Beth Sowers. The trial lasted three and a half months. Gallego was found guilty and sentenced to die in California's gas chamber.

Because of California's reluctance to execute its killers, it was decided that Gerald should stand trial in Nevada for the murders committed there. It was felt that there was a better chance that Nevada would carry out his execution. Once again, he was tried, found guilty and sentenced to death. He is presently awaiting execution on Death Row in Nevada State Prison in Carson City. Charlene is serving her time next door in Nevada Women's Correctional Centre. There is no contact allowed between husband and wife.

Why was nine-year-old Gerald Gallego told that his father had died in a car accident so many years ago? Ironically Gerald Sr. was a 28-year-old convict when his son was nine. After gaining his release from San Quentin, he killed a man who was booking him into jail. After making his way to Mississippi, he was recaptured. Gerald Sr. tossed lye in a guard's face and stomped the blinded officer to death.

In 1955, the senior Gallego was the first man executed in Mississippi's new gas chamber. Should his son eventually be executed, it will be the first time a father and a son have been tried, found guilty and executed for multiple murder.

BELLE GUNNESS

BELLE Paulsen's father was a magician who travelled the length and breadth of Norway with his magic act. Belle was born in 1859 and grew up to be a slim, well-behaved child who became adept at tightrope walking, delighting her father's audiences with daring stunts on the taut wire. When her father retired from the transient life of a magician and bought a farm, Belle found the change from being a performer to the solitude of rural life unbearably boring. Now an impetuous teenager, she decided to emigrate to the United States.

After she arrived in the U.S., Belle, a shapely 24-year-old, met Mads Sorensen, a Swede, who courted her and won her hand in marriage. The couple settled in Chicago, Illinois, and the marriage commenced to bear fruit in the form of two offspring, Lucy and Myrtle. Two years after the marriage, Mads had a heart attack and died. There was a small group of friends and relatives in the close-knit Scandinavian community who never for a moment thought that it was a heart attack that had put an end to Mads. They whispered that he had been poisoned, and they fingered the widow as the administrator of the deadly potion. But even though Belle collected $8,500 in insurance money and sold Sorensen's home for $5,000, nothing came of the distasteful rumors.

The now well-heeled Belle and her two children moved to Austin, Illinois, where they purchased a new home. One cold night the house mysteriously caught fire, and while the insurance company suspected that the fire wasn't accidental, there was no proof of any monkey business and they paid off.

Belle moved back to Chicago in the grip of an obsession. She had somehow acquired a ravenous appetite, and ate to such an extent that she started to gain weight rapidly. She became fatter and fatter, until the scales tipped 200 lbs. This five-foot, seven-inch dumpling was no longer recognizable as the slender Norwegian girl who had married Mads Sorensen. Her face had been plain to begin with, but now it became bloated and ugly. In Chicago, she purchased a candy store, which soon burned to the ground. Again with some misgivings, the insurance company paid off. We can imagine Belle, relaxing with a box of chocolates, figuring that the greatest prerequisite for success in the world of commerce was to have a quick hand with a match.

With the proceeds of her fires she purchased a 48-acre farm about a mile from La Porte, Indiana, and quite by chance had an unexpected addition to her family. Antone Olson had recently lost his wife, and felt ill-equipped to take care of his daughter Jennie. Belle, who had known the Olsons for years in Chicago, was only too happy to take Jenny in, and as she put it, "treat her like one of my own."

Belle soon ballooned to a substantial 230 lbs. She worked her farm and gained a sort of local fame by butchering her own farm animals, particularly hogs, and selling the meat in the nearby town of La Porte. In April 1902, she met Peter Gunness, who, like Belle, was Norwegian. We don't know where Peter came from, but he settled in on the farm and appears to have been well liked by his neighbors and people who came in contact with him in La Porte.

The neighbors had only a short time to make any judgment about Peter, for only seven months after he married Belle, disaster struck. It came in the form of a sausage grinder, and it struck poor Peter square on the head, killing him instantly. The grinder sat on a high shelf and, as luck, or whatever, would have it, Peter picked a spot directly under the grinder to rest his weary bones. Coincidentally enough, the grinder chose this opportune moment to totter and fall, striking Peter a fatal blow to the head.

During his short but noteworthy appearance upon the stage with Belle, the unlucky Norwegian managed to accomplish three things. He changed Belle's name from Belle Brynhilde Paulsetter Sorensen to Belle Gunness, for which he earns our gratitude. He was also thoughtful enough to insure his life for $4,000, which Belle reluctantly allowed to be pressed into her chubby hands. And he wasn't fully acclimatized to his new surroundings in the grave when Belle discovered that she was heavy laden with child, as they used to say. "Son of a bitch," Belle hissed between her teeth when she discovered the dirty trick he had pulled on her from the grave. The object of her dilemma popped into the world in 1903, and was named Phillip for no particular reason.

After the birth of her son, Belle settled down to farming, and occasionally hired a transient hand to help her. Most stayed for a short time and moved on. There was something strange and sinister about working for the quiet, puffing butterball, who could not only pitch hay with the best of men, but who also seemed to take a delight in butchering her own hogs. Rough and tough as these men were, Belle's actions didn't appear natural to them.

Belle worked hard, but a chubby nymphomaniac needs a man around the house. Like so many men and women in similar circumstances, Belle gravitated to advertising in matrimonial journals. This direct approach had produced many good husbands and wives, so we cannot completely condemn the practice of selecting a partner by mail order. But it would be as well to warn the lovesick advertiser that a certain risk is involved in communicating with a total stranger. Belle reduced the risk factor, but unfortunately her male partners weren't quite as cautious. She refined the ads and eliminated a lot of riffraff with her no-nonsense approach.

For example: "Comely widow who owns a large farm in one of the finest districts in La Porte County, Indiana, desires to make acquaintance of a gentleman equally well provided, with view of joining fortunes. No replies by letter considered unless sender is willing to follow answer with personal visit. No triflers please."

The number of men attracted to ads of this nature is uncertain. For one thing, we will never know how many men showed up at the widow's doorstep, took one look at Belle's 230 lbs., and said thanks, but no thanks. Conversely, we have no way of knowing how many prospective suitors didn't measure up to Belle's standards. She obviously preferred men of Scandinavian extraction who had accumulated some cold, hard cash.

In answer to one of her ads, a Norwegian named John Moo arrived from Minnesota in 1906. John must be placed in the missing, presumed dead category, for he was seen and met by neighbors as the bridegroom apparent, and just as suddenly as he appeared on the scene, he vanished. During the inquiries that followed, not a trace of him could be found, and Belle claimed she had no idea where he went when he left the farm.

Another native of Norway, George Anderson, travelled from a small village in Missouri to meet Belle. By now she had developed a line that could charm the birds out of the trees. Mr. Anderson had taken the precaution of not bringing his nest-egg with him, but admitted later to being completely captivated by his hostess. She wined and dined him in the grand manner. Visions of the good life on the farm danced before his eyes, giving a rosy tinge to her obvious shortcomings.

One night at the farmhouse, Anderson was startled out of a deep sleep. There, towering over him by candlelight, was the huge form of Mrs. Gunness with a strange, wild look in her eyes. As he awoke she ran from the room, and Anderson, scared half out of his wits, made the wisest move of his life. He got out of bed, put on his pants, ran all the way to the station in La Porte, and went back to Missouri on the next train.

Not quite as fortunate was Bud Budsberg, another native of Norway, who arrived at Belle's door in 1907. Mr. Budsberg had travelled from Iola, Wisconsin, with $2,000 in his poke. Despite extensive inquiries conducted by relatives back in Wisconsin, Bud was never heard from again. He simply crossed Belle's threshold and disappeared.

Nothing seemed very permanent on the Gunness farm. But there was one exception; Belle had finally found a hired hand who didn't move on like the rest. He was a French Canadian named Ray Lamphere, who was not only willing to tolerate Belle as an employer, but actually fell in love with her. Ray, who had the personality of a born follower, was of average height and had a handlebar moustache and bulging eyes that made him look as if he was always afraid of something, as well he might have been. It is pretty certain that Belle kept Ray around the farm for a variety of reasons, not the least of which was instant sex. Her other gentlemen friends had developed the annoying habit of disappearing, but steady, if not heady, Ray was always available. Jealous though he was of the other men who were continually coming to the farm, Ray was secure in the knowledge that he would outlast them all.

At about this time neighbors noticed that a large eight-foot-high fence had been put up around the farmhouse. The shutters on the windows were closed for weeks on end, and it was well-known that the basement was equipped as a slaughterhouse for Belle's hogs. She had a large table down there, as well as a pulley system for raising the carcasses of slaughtered animals. Along one wall hung a top-quality set of butchers' knives and cleavers.

The parade of suitors continued. Andrew K. Helgelein arrived from Aberdeen, South Dakota, with $3,000 in a bulging wallet. This gentleman differed from those who had come before in that he got under Ray Lamphere's skin. For some reason, Ray, who had become accustomed to seeing his beloved being courted by other men, couldn't take it when Helgelein and Belle were together.

Ray and Belle argued bitterly about this, and Ray packed up his belongings and left the farm in a tantrum.

He went to La Porte and started gossiping about his former lover and employer. Nothing serious, mind you, but enough so that when word of his loose tongue got back to Belle she had him arrested and tried to have him judged insane and committed to an institution. A sanity hearing actually took place, and Lamphere was declared sane. He made up with Belle, and returned to the farm. He commenced to pick another fight; this time Belle had him arrested for trespassing. Lamphere was found guilty of this offence and paid a fine.

Still in La Porte, the French Canadian continued to badmouth Belle, even mentioning to a farmer, Bill Slater, "Helgelein won't bother me no more. She fixed him for keeps."

By coincidence Helgelein had disappeared the day before this conversation took place. Then something happened that was even more vexing than Ray Lamphere shooting off his mouth in town. For the first time in all her years on the farm, Belle was the recipient of a serious threat, in the form of inquiring letters from Mr. Asle Helgelein of Mansfield, South Dakota, who was the brother of the missing Andrew. Belle met his pointed questions with the claim that Andrew had gone back to Norway, to which Asle replied, "Rubbish."

With the heat definitely on, Belle hitched up the team, drove into La Porte and paid a visit to her lawyer, M.E. Leliter. On April 27, 1908, Belle asked the lawyer to draw up her will, leaving her estate to her three children, with the proviso that should she outlive her children, the money would go to a Norwegian orphanage in Chicago. She said the reason for this sudden urge to put her affairs in order was because Ray Lamphere was threatening to kill her and burn down her farmhouse. She told Leliter that she was in mortal fear of the insanely jealous Lamphere. The whole thing took a matter of minutes, and was drawn up and signed before she left the lawyer's office.

That very night the new hired hand, Joe Maxon, said goodnight to the family and went to bed. In the middle of the night, he was awakened by the loud crackling of a fire. Shaking the cobwebs from his mind, he rose slowly, then realized that the entire house was engulfed in flames. He shouted at the top of his lungs to wake Belle and the children, then staggered toward the window, and jumped from the second storey, wearing only his underwear.

The next morning, as the charred rubble cooled, the remains of Belle's three children, Lucy, Myrtle, and Phillip, together with the headless body of a woman, were found in the cellar, having fallen through the floor.

Because of the veiled threats made by Lamphere, and the well-known feud that existed between him and Mrs. Gunness, he immediately came under suspicion. A youngster swore he had not only seen Lamphere near the farmhouse on the night of the fire, but had actually spoken to him. Ray was arrested, and Belle's lawyer came forward and told of her accusations against the accused man. In due course, Lamphere was charged with the murder of Belle Gunness.

Neighbors who had known Belle for years were asked to identify the headless corpse. At the time of the fire Belle was estimated to weight 280 lbs.—not an easy figure to mistake. All her neighbors said the burnt corpse was too short and far too light to be Mrs. Gunness. This rather startling development threw an entirely new light on the macabre affair. For starters, who was the burned, headless corpse? If the corpse wasn't Mrs. Gunness then where was she? To further confuse an already confusing situation, Mr. Antone Olson heard about the fire and rushed down to the farm to find his Jennie. She too was nowhere to be found, although neighbors said that some time previously Belle had mentioned that she had gone to California to continue her schooling.

The authorities searched everywhere for the missing head, but try as they might, they couldn't find it. Then Mr. Asle Helgelein showed up, looking for his brother. He didn't even know there had been a fire, but he had a deep suspicion that his brother had met with foul play at the hands of the woman he had come to Indiana to marry. Asle noticed that the Gunness' yard was uneven, and that patches of earth in the yard were of different colors. Maxon, the hired hand, volunteered that there had been slight depressions in the ground, and Mrs. Gunness had told him to bring earth from an adjoining field to even it off. Asle wasn't taking any offhanded answers, and urged the police to dig in these areas. The very first hole they dug uncovered the corpse of Andrew Helgelein, whose brother had the unfortunate experience of staring down at it as it was unearthed. He positively identified the body, and the digging started in earnest.

The next hole produced the body of Jennie Olson, who hadn't gone to California at all. Three more bodies were uncovered before darkness fell on the eerie scene and the diggers had to stop for the night. The next day, May 4, 1908, four more bodies were dug out of the farmyard, and on the third day another body was uncovered. The bodies were in various stages of decomposition, and some were never to be identified. Others were positively identified as John Moo, and Bud Budsberg. Over and above these complete corpses police uncovered bits and pieces of other bodies that had no matching parts, leading them to believe that many more suitors had been put to death on the farm. With the discovery of these parts of human bodies, the police had to consider Belle's private abattoir in the basement. The implication was obvious—had Belle been butchering more than hogs?

Gossip comes a narrow second to farming as the principal occupation in the Hoosier State, and the murder farm was soon on everyone's lips. Crops lay unattended as men gathered to discuss the case, with the more curious driving out to the farm to peer at the now excavated farmyard. All the while they talked, exchanging information, telling stories, until one bit of gossip became so prominent that it took on the status of a distinct possibility.

The night the house burned, Belle had been seen heading for her farm in her buggy with a stout lady. Joe Maxon, who was in the house that night, said that he didn't see any stout lady, but added that it would have been possible for a woman to be in the house without his knowledge. The local speculation was that Belle had somehow arranged to bring a strange woman out to the farm, kill and decapitate her, set the house on fire, and take off, thinking that everyone would believe she had perished in the fire. She had come up with a stout lady, but she couldn't quite duplicate her own massive poundage.

By now the weird case was on the front page of every newspaper in the U.S. and, because of its doubtful aspects, it gave rise to theory and speculation. Everyone had a story to tell about Belle or one of the victims. Dr. Ira P. Norton read about the case and volunteered the information that he had once done dental work for Belle, and could identify his own work if the authorities could produce it. This appeared to be a hopeless task, as the police felt that a fire hot enough to destroy a head would certainly melt gold caps and change porcelain beyond recognition. The doctor explained that this was not so, and that if his dental work could be found, it would be easy to identify. The police looked at the rubble of the burned farmhouse and realized they had a mammoth task before them.

Into a case already loaded down with strange and interesting characters came the most colorful of all, Louis Schultz. He had heard about the missing old dental work in the rubble of the fire. Louis was an experienced gold miner just back from the Yukon, and told the police that if they would build him a sluice box, he would sluice the entire farmhouse and if there was any gold in the rubble he would find it, using the same methods he had used in the Yukon.

The scheme seemed practical enough. In due course the sluice box was set up in the farmyard with running water piped over from the barn, and Louis set to work.

The sluice box manned by Louis in the yard received almost as much publicity as the crimes themselves. Crowds poured out to the farm to take in the spectacle of a sourdough mining gold on an Indiana farm. They cheered Louis on, and rising to the occasion, he waved and joked with the crowd. Christened Klondike Louis by the press, he was always good for a colorful quote, and because of him and the eeriness of the scene, on a good day the crowd surrounding the farm swelled to 5,000. You could even place a friendly wager as to whether or not Louis would strike gold.

Then it happened. After four days on the job, and after washing tons of mud and debris through his sluice box, Schultz came up with a bridgework containing two lower bicuspids capped with gold and four porcelain teeth. Louis was proclaimed a hero, and the teeth were rushed to Dr. Norton for examination. He positively identified the work as his own, and the teeth as belonging to Belle Gunness.

This lent considerable weight to the assumption that Belle's head had been completely burned by the fire and only dental work had survived. Ray Lamphere stood trial for Belle's murder. The evidence against him was strong; he had argued bitterly with Belle and had been seen near the house on the night of the fire. There was just one thing—the jury didn't believe that Mrs. Gunness was dead. Lamphere was acquitted, but was tried for arson and convicted. After hearing all the evidence, the jurors came to the conclusion that Belle was alive but that Lamphere had burned down the farmhouse. Lamphere was suffering from tuberculosis, and died in Michigan City Prison in December 1909.

Before he died, he told two different versions of his life with Belle and particularly what happened on the night the house burned down. The first version was told to a friend in prison who came forward after Ray's death. Ray told him that the whole thing was a setup—Belle did not die in the fire. She had advertised for a housekeeper and had culled the applicants, trying to find one as large as herself. With pressure mounting from Andrew Helgelein, she had to settle for the stoutest woman she could find, but one still far short of her massive structure. After drugging her, Belle cut off her head, and Ray and Belle buried it in quicklime in the nearby swamp. Belle had dressed the stranger in some of her own clothing to further aid in the identification; then she had killed her three children, leaving Ray to light the fire. Ray claimed that he never actually killed anyone himself, but had aided Belle in any way she asked in getting rid of the bodies. She had killed her own children because they knew too much of the strange goings on. He said there had been 28 more murders committed on the farm that were never uncovered. Belle butchered the bodies in her basement, feeding the small parts to the hogs and burying the larger pieces in quicklime in the swamp.

Upon hearing the story of the hogs' unorthodox eating habits, the man who purchased them in La Porte was reported to have remarked: "They were still the best damn hogs in the county."

Lamphere said that Belle had sneaked up behind Mr. Gunness and split open his head with an axe. She then placed his body under the shelf that held the sausage grinder and dropped it on his head. A little girl in La Porte remembered a conversation she had with Belle's daughter Myrtle who told her, "Mama brained Papa with an axe. Don't tell a soul."

Lamphere died shortly after telling his friend these details about the crime. After he had passed away, Reverend E.A. Schnell, the prison minister, told of Lamphere's confession of his part in the crimes. This version differs in many details from that given to his friend. Lamphere told the minister that on the night of the fire he had chloroformed the three Gunness children and set fire to the house. He said he was completely captivated by Belle and would comply with anything she desired. But whatever the major variations, the two stories were the same in one important detail—he swore that Belle had not died in the fire.

Readers can pick their own version of what took place that last night on the farm, but whichever they choose they must consider Belle's bridgework found in the debris of the burned-out farmhouse. Is it within the realm of possibility that

Belle, operating in a mad frenzy, with her three children dead beside her, could have taken a pair of pliers and torn the permanent bridgework from her own mouth? Dentists have recorded instances where lumberjacks and others working in isolation have suffered from terrible toothaches and have pulled out several of their own teeth. A 280-lb. woman who had disposed of a possible 42 human beings might not find the act as appalling as it appears to us.

Belle Gunness has not been seen or heard of since the night of April 27, 1908, when her house burned to the ground.

H.H. HOLMES

HERMAN Webster Mudgett was born in 1860 to a respected family in the tiny New England community of Gilmanton where his father had been postmaster for over twenty-five years. Though young Herman early showed a vicious streak— neighbors of the Mudgetts were to recall seeing him setting a cat on fire—he had many redeeming features, not the least of which was his keen intelligence.

His teachers remembered him as a bright, alert scholar. After his graduation with honors from Gilmanton Academy, he eloped with a farmer's daughter from the nearby village of London, and paid his tuition at the University of Vermont, at Burlington, from a small inheritance his wife had just received. He transferred to the University of Michigan at Ann Arbor, where his wife gave birth to a son.

Mudgett started his criminal activities while still at university. He and another student concocted a scheme whereby Mudgett took out an insurance policy on his friend's life in the amount of $12,500. The friend promptly disappeared, leaving the way clear for Mudgett to steal a corpse from the dissecting room of the university, positively identify it as his missing friend, and collect the insurance. Shortly after the successful completion of this scheme, he qualified as a doctor of medicine and abandoned his wife and infant son. Mrs. Mudgett returned to Gilmanton, never to lay eyes on her husband again.

The doctor, now a tall, good-looking 24-year-old with all the qualifications to be a legitimate success, struck out on his own. With his fashionable walrus moustache and his luminous brown eyes, he was a distinguished-looking gentleman. And when he was decked out in his bowler hat, tweed suit and shiny shoes, Herman held more than a little attraction for the opposite sex.

For six years he wandered through Minnesota and New York, making a dishonest dollar wherever he could. The fact that he could have made a fine living at his own profession apparently didn't enter his mind. Records show that in St. Paul he was appointed receiver of a bankrupt store. He filled the store with merchandise purchased on credit, sold off the stock at cost price or less, and took off with the proceeds.

In 1885, he reappeared in Wilmette, a suburb of Chicago, as an inventor, using the name Henry H. Holmes for the first time. He met a dark-haired beauty named Myrtle Z. Belknap, who was not only a looker, but also had a father who was one of the wealthiest residents of Wilmette. Holmes married her without going through the annoying formalities of a divorce from his first wife. He succeeded in getting enough money out of Myrtle's daddy to build a house, and then started forging Mr. Belknap's name on cheques. Though the family was furious, they decided to sidestep a scandal and not to prosecute the scoundrel, for he still held a fascination for his wife, who stood beside him no matter what sort of scrapes he managed to get into.

Next, Holmes answered an advertisement in the local newspaper requiring a chemist for a store owned by a Mrs. Holden on the corner of 63rd Street and Wallace, in Englewood, another suburb of Chicago. Mrs. Holden, who had been recently widowed, was thrilled to have such a highly qualified and handsome man apply for the position, and gave him the job without any qualms whatsoever. Almost at once she became disillusioned with her new employee and confided to close friends that she suspected him of theft from her store. Early in 1890, Mrs. Holden suddenly disappeared without mentioning anything to friends, except to Holmes, who claimed she had told him she was taking a long holiday in California. Then he soothed her acquaintances by telling them that she had sold the store to him and was staying on the west coast. It seems that no one was interested enough in Mrs. Holden to delve deeper into her disappearance, and she was never seen again.

In the meantime, with his knowledge of medicine, Holmes was making the business prosper. He had a few sidelines, such as his own patent medicines which he sold at enormous profits, and things were going so well that by 1892 he figured there was nothing further to be gained from the Belknap family, so he left his wife and moved into rooms above his store. Then he commenced the construction of a monstrous building directly across the street. It was three storeys high, measured 50 by 162 feet and contained more than 90 rooms. On the main floor Holmes opened a jewelry store, restaurant and drugstore. The false turrets gave the whole structure a somewhat medieval appearance, and the ugly pile soon came to be known as Holmes' Castle.

Ostensibly Holmes built the structure to accommodate the huge crowds which were expected for the Chicago World's Fair in 1893, and the third floor of the castle was divided into apartments for this purpose; but the second floor had winding staircases, connecting hallways, trapdoors, and asbestos-lined rooms, some of them equipped with gas jets. Holmes had his own comfortable quarters on the second floor; inside his closet were valves that controlled the flow of gas to the various rooms. From his bedroom Holmes could gas a victim, turn a switch that controlled a trapdoor and plunge the body down a chute to the basement. The basement was equipped with a dissecting table, medical instruments, a crematorium, a huge vat of corrosive acid and two further vats of quicklime.

Into this veritable murder castle came Mr. Icilius Conner, his wife Julia, his sister Gertie, and his eight-year-old daughter Pearl. Conner was a jeweler by trade and was looking for ways to get into business. Holmes obliged by making a part of his drugstore available to him for the sale of jewelry, and by hiring Julia as his personal bookkeeper. The Conners were an extremely handsome family, particularly Julia, and it wasn't long before the cunning doctor had alienated her from her husband, and she had in effect become his mistress. Holmes let it leak to Conner that his wife had been sharing his bed, and Conner left Chicago in disgust. Mrs. Conner and her daughter Pearl were to live with Holmes for the next two years. During these two years, Holmes took a trip to Texas, where he stayed for over six months, engaging in his usual activities of thieving and swindling before returning to Chicago.

In 1893, the doctor received a visit from an acquaintance he had met during his stay down south. Her name was Minnie Williams, and her greatest claim to fame was the fact that she and her sister Nannie jointly owned property valued at $50,000 in Fort Worth, Texas. She was a welcome guest to the castle, and it wasn't long before she was Holmes' mistress. Coinciding with her coronation as queen of the castle, Julia Conner and her daughter disappeared.

Holmes and his new flame lived together for a full year, and it was during this year that more visitors started to enter the death castle than were seen to leave it. It is difficult to believe that Minnie could have lived there at this time without having some guilty knowledge of what was going on. Holmes was easier to figure; if ever there was a born criminal it was Henry H. Holmes. He was motivated by lust and greed, not necessarily in that order, and seems never to have even considered leading an honest life.

The list of his known victims is a long one. Years earlier, while serving a three-month jail sentence in St. Louis, Holmes had met fellow inmates Benjamin F. Pietzel, a small time con artist, and a rather well-known train robber, Marion Hedgepeth. Pietzel was soon to be released to join his wife and five children, but Hedgepeth was awaiting transfer to a penitentiary and a lengthy sentence. Pietzel now showed up in Chicago and looked up his friend Holmes. He kept telling Holmes about a beautiful young girl he had met in Dwight, Illinois. Her name was Emeline Cigrand, and she had made a lasting impression on Pietzel, who told Holmes she was the most beautiful girl he had ever seen. Finally, at Pietzel's urging, Holmes corresponded with the girl and offered her a job at a salary far above the average. She couldn't resist the temptation, came to Chicago, entered the castle, and was never seen again. Her boyfriend, Robert E. Phelps, inquired about her at the castle, was invited in, and never left. Holmes was later to confess to Emeline's death, describing in detail how he kept her in a soundproof room for the sole purpose of having sexual relations with her. He claimed he didn't want to kill her, but Minnie got jealous and he had to do it. The boyfriend, Holmes said, was just too nosy to live.

Nannie Williams, Minnie's sister, came to visit. Holmes made love to her, got her to sign over half the property in Fort Worth, and killed her, in that order. He told friends of Minnie's that her sister had returned to Texas.

Now we enter the even stranger period in the saga of Henry H. Holmes. In the fall of 1893, he left his friend Ben Pietzel in charge of his various businesses and took a trip with Minnie to Denver. Using the alias of Howard, he married a Georgianna Yoke of Richmond, Indiana, without Minnie's knowledge. He spent many weeks in Denver living alternately with the two women, neither of whom knew of the other's existence. Even after Georgianna returned to Indiana, Holmes visited her on many occasions during the next two years and seemed to have become quite attached to her. She lived to testify at his trial and was the only person to speak highly of him.

Before Christmas 1893, Minnie made the same mistake as her sister Nannie; she signed away her half of the Fort Worth property and promptly disappeared. Later Holmes was to show the police where to find her skeleton and her sister's, in the cellar of the castle.

How was Holmes able to build a structure that was obviously custom-designed for murder? Firstly, he personally supervised the entire construction, from the cellar to the top floor. Then he kept the same crew of workmen for only a few days before he discharged them. A new crew would start, often entirely unaware of what had transpired before they appeared on the job. In this way, no one saw the master plan or knew that the cumulative effect of their labors was a bona fide murder castle.

When he had been in jail with Pietzel and Hedgepeth years earlier, Holmes told them that he had figured out a foolproof way of defrauding an insurance company. He said he needed a really smart lawyer to pull it off. Hedgepeth gave Holmes the name of his lawyer, Jeptha D. Howe of St. Louis, and received in return a promise of $500 after the scheme was successfully completed. Holmes kept this plan under wraps for a few years, and then took it out of mothballs in the early summer of 1894.

The scheme was the same one that Holmes had used so successfully in university. Pietzel was to have his wife take out insurance on his life, and then he was to drop out of sight, while Holmes was to come up with a corpse which would be identified as that of Pietzel. Mrs. Pietzel would collect the insurance and the partners would divide the spoils. Everyone agreed that the plan had some merit. Pietzel took out a policy amounting to $10,000. Then he went to Philadelphia and set up a shop as a patent attorney, using the name B.F. Perry. Within a month his body was found on the floor of his office, badly burned, particularly around the face. The police investigating the accident found a broken bottle of benzine on the office floor.

The preliminary assumption was that an explosion had taken place, causing the accident. Then an autopsy was performed and the death was found to have been caused by chloroform. Jeptha D. Howe reappeared on the scene and informed the authorities that the dead man was Ben Pietzel, and as Mrs. Pietzel's attorney, he was representing her in asking for any insurance money that was due his client. Pietzel's good friend Holmes arrived and also identified the body. The insurance money was paid off to Mrs. Pietzel; it was later dividied up, with Howe getting $2,500, Mrs. Pietzel $500, and Holmes receiving the balance.

Holmes, the arch-criminal, had really murdered his friend Pietzel. The corpse was no stranger to him, but he managed to deceive Howe and Mrs. Pietzel, who throughout the con thought that Pietzel was in hiding. Howe returned to St. Louis assuming that the scheme was a complete success and that Mrs. Pietzel would be joining Mr. Pietzel in a few months and that everyone would be happy. He visited his client Hedgepeth in prison and mentioned how well the scheme had worked. Hedgepeth was furious, as he had been promised $500 by Holmes and never received a cent. Hedgepeth called the warden and told the whole story. The warden called the insurance company, who in turn called in the Pinkerton Detective Agency to investigate the case. When Hedgepeth told the story he naturally repeated it as he had heard it from Howe; that it was a stranger's body that was found on the office floor, not Pietzel's. It didn't take long for the Pinkertons to realize that there was more than simple fraud involved, and they called in the police.

By this time Holmes had fled, and he proved to be an elusive quarry. He had talked Mrs. Pietzel into meeting him in Detroit. She took two of her children with her, while Holmes took the other three, Alice, Nellie and Howard. He told her they would all meet with Mr. Pietzel in Detroit in two weeks' time. Holmes arrived before the allotted time and placed the three Pietzel children in a boarding house while he scampered to Richmond, Indiana, returning with the lady who really thought she was his wife, Georgianna Yoke.

Holmes set up three different groups while in Detroit. One consisted of the three Pietzel children, another consisted of Mrs. Pietzel and the other two children, while a third contingent was made up solely of Georgianna. Holmes would join any of the three groups, who at no time knew of the others' presence in the city.

Finally he took all three households on the road, and it is a measure of his cunning that he managed to stay ahead of the police for two months. They finally caught up with Holmes in Boston on November 17, 1894. The other two detachments were accounted for when gullible Georgianna, who was innocent of any wrongdoing, was located by the police in Indiana where Holmes had stashed her, and Mrs. Pietzel and her two children were discovered living in Burlington, Vermont, waiting for the reunion with her husband that was never to come.

Only Nellie, Howard, and Alice Pietzel, the three children who were travelling with Holmes, could not be found by the police, and Holmes steadfastly refused to give them any information concerning the three children.

The interior of Holmes' murder castle was now exposed, and the police realized they were dealing with one of the most hideous monsters who ever lived. The search was on for the three children; the trail led from Detroit to Toronto to Cincinnati to Indianapolis, throughout the midwest and back into Canada. Finally, at 16 Vincent Street in Toronto, the authorities found a house that had been rented to a man with two little girls.

The police found out that the man had borrowed a spade to dig a hole, supposedly to store potatoes. They were able to find the neighbor whose spade had been used, and he loaned the same spade to the police. They dug up the same hole, and in it found the pathetic bodies of Nellie and Alice Pietzel. In an upstairs bedroom of the house they found a trunk with a rubber tube leading from it to a gas outlet. Diabolical Holmes had enticed the girls to enter the trunk and had asphyxiated them. The discovery now accounted for all the family, except Howard.

While questioning neighbors in the area of 16 Vincent Street, the police found one who had talked to the two girls. This neighbor remembered the girls had mentioned their little brother lived in Indianapolis. The investigation moved to Indianapolis, where 900 houses were searched, and finally, in the suburb of Irvington, police found the house in which Holmes had lived for a week. It has been vacant since Holmes left, and the charred remains of Howard Pietzel's body were found in a stove in the kitchen.

Holmes made a full confession while in jail, but as it is sprinkled with proven lies, it does not give an accurate account of his atrocities. While it seems that he operated basically for gain, when his castle was dismantled it was discovered that he had a rack which he used to try to stretch people, believing that he could make them permanently taller.

On October 28, 1895 Holmes was tried for the murder of Ben Pietzel. It was one of the most widely publicized trials of the last century. Every detail was reported in the press, for nothing quite like it had ever been perpetrated in the U.S. before. The jury was out for two and a half hours, but later a member of the jury was to state that the verdict was decided in one minute with a show of hands. They stayed out because it was a capital case, but no one wavered from their unanimous one-minute verdict.

While his appeals were being heard, Holmes embraced the Roman Catholic Church. All of his appeals failed, and on May 7, 1896, accompanied by two priests, Holmes mounted the scaffold at Moyanensing Prison. He made a short speech to the assembled onlookers, but saved his last words for the gentleman who adjusted the noose around his neck.

"Make it quick," he said.

H.H. Holmes, one of the most notorious murderers who ever lived, would have been 36 had he lived nine more days.

CARL ISAACS

THE good folks of Seminole County, Georgia, gathered around the tombstones in the graveyard and prayed for the Alday family.

It has been over 21 years since animals, in the guise of human beings, killed six members of the old respected Georgia family. No one has yet paid the supreme penalty for the massacre, although the leader of the gang of killers, Carl Isaacs, says that if he is ever released from prison he will kill again.

After an adolescence marked with criminal activity, Carl found himself confined to Yoke Crest Inc., a minimum security institution for youthful offenders in Harrisburg, Pennsylvania.

A short time earlier, he and his younger brother were in a minor car accident. A woman, 58-year-old Anne Merrill Elder, had given them a lift to the closest service station. She identified Carl as the youth who had burglarized her neighborhood.

Carl couldn't get the thought of Mrs. Elder out of his mind. On January 14, 1973, after a stay of only one week, he walked away from the institution. It didn't take long for him to wreak his revenge. Within days he had stolen a car and had found Mrs. Elder's home. He lay in wait for her and shot her dead. Eleven days after the senseless murder, Carl was apprehended in his hometown of Baltimore while burglarizing a house.

Carl was surprised that he was wanted only for burglary. The police didn't think a 19-year-old punk could have any connection to the murder of Mrs. Elder. Carl pleaded guilty to the robbery charges and was sentenced to four years imprisonment in the Maryland State Penitentiary.

In the spring of the same year, Carl was successful in obtaining a transfer to a minimum security institution, Poplar Hill. He had heard that his half-brother, 26-year-old Wayne Coleman, was serving time there. No sooner were the boys reunited than they were planning to escape. It required little effort. Together with Wayne's friend, George Dungee, they crawled through a bathroom window to freedom.

Robbing and collecting firearms as they travelled, the three escapees made their way to Baltimore, where they picked up Carl's 15-year-old brother, Billy. The four stole a 1965 Buick and headed for McConnellsburg, Pa. Carl called the foursome the Isaacs Gang and compared himself to John Dilinger and Billy the Kid.

The gang had car trouble in the country east of Baltimore. They stole a truck parked in a farmyard, but two miles down the road the truck chugged to a stop. It was high school student Richard Miller's misfortune to witness the theft. He watched as the four strangers made off with his neighbor's truck. Richard decided to follow the thieves in his new Chevy. He worked part time in a service station and knew very well that Lawrence Schoolby's truck wouldn't go far. When the truck stopped, so did Richard.

He approached the truck and stood transfixed when he saw two weapons pointed directly at his head. Richard Miller was driven to a wooded area where Wayne Coleman shot him dead.

The gang, now firmly committed to theft and murder as a way of existing, continued on their aimless journey. They drove to Seminole County, Georgia, where their lives were to become entwined with those of the Alday family.

If ever two groups of individuals were diametrically opposite, it was the Isaacs gang and the hard-working, well-respected Aldays. The family name is one of the oldest in that part of Georgia. All 7,500 citizens either worked or played with some member of the well-liked clan.

Ned Alday, 62, left most of the farm labor to his sons. He and his wife, Ernestine, led a contented life on their 525-acre spread. True, it wasn't an exciting life, but it was one of enjoyment in one's family. The Aldays had nine children, five daughters and four sons. Three of the boys worked on the farm. Jimmy, 25 and unmarried, lived in the farmhouse with his parents. Shuggie, 32, and his wife Barbara, 27, lived in a house trailer parked in the farmyard. Jerry, 35, and his wife Mary, 26, had another trailer parked about a half mile away. The fourth son, Norman, was in the U.S. Army, stationed in Munich, Germany.

On May 14, 1973, the Isaacs gang was down to its last 15¢. The looting of a house trailer netted $2, good enough for a six pack of beer. An isolated farmhouse yielded over $100. It seemed so easy. Out here in the Georgia countryside, most farmers didn't even lock their doors. Carl figured the Isaacs gang had easy pickings among the yokels.

Jerry Alday rose early. He joined his brother, Jimmy, and together they went to work in the fields. Jerry's wife, Mary, jumped into her 1970 Chevy Impala and headed for her job at the Dept. of Family and Children's Services. The Aldays' trailer was vacant. Mary didn't even bother to lock the door.

Carl Isaacs spotted the Aldays' empty trailer. It looked like child's play. Still driving Richard Miller's Chevy, they parked in the driveway. Within minutes the gang was looting the trailer.

Jerry Alday and his father, Ned had occasion to drive past the trailer during the course of their farm work. They noticed the green Chevy with Pennsylvania plates parked nearby and decided to investigate. They were spotted by the armed men inside.

The four men pointed weapons and led father and son into the trailer. The farmers where stripped of rings and watches. Then the gang members discussed who was going to have the pleasure of the kill. George Dungee actually begged, "Can I have one?" Despite his plea, it was Carl Isaacs who escorted Jerry Alday into a bedroom, forced him to lie on a bed and emptied his pistol into the side of the helpless man's head. Wayne Coleman shot Ned Alday dead with a .380 automatic. Carl Isaacs laughed uncontrollably as each man was murdered.

The noise of the shots had hardly subsided when Billy Isaacs sighted a truck pulling up to the trailer. Shuggie and his uncle Aubrey had seen the green Chevy and the family jeep parked beside the trailer. They told jokes to each other as they drove up to take a look.

The laughter stopped when the two men found themselves staring into the barrels of Billy's and Carl's handguns. Once inside, the captives were stripped of all valuables. Carl and Wayne then had a short discussion over who should do the killing. It was decided that Carl would kill Aubrey Alday. The young, gun wielding bandit led his older captive to a bedroom where he shot him dead. Meanwhile, Billy and Wayne forced Shuggie Alday into another room. He, too was shot dead.

Four members of the Alday clan lay dead in the trailer, but the slaughter wasn't over. Mary Alday drove up to her trailer after a day's work at the office. The terrified woman was held captive as still another Alday drove up to the trailer on a tractor. It was Jimmy, the youngest of the Alday boys. He opened the door of his brother's trailer to stare directly into the barrel of a gun. Once inside, Jimmy was made to lie on a sofa. Carl shot him in the head.

Mary Alday was sodomized, raped and driven a few miles into woods, where she too was shot in the head. George Dungee did the killing. It was his turn.

The Isaacs gang abandoned Richard Miller's car and drove away in Mary Alday's Chevy. That night, the bodies of the six Aldays were discovered. The citizens of Seminole County were stunned at the extent of the tragedy. Who were the madmen who descended from nowhere to mercilessly kill six of their own?

The Isaacs gang was soon identified from fingerprints found on Richard Miller's car. Their pictures appeared on television screens across the nation. In the meantime, they were making a desperate attempt to reach Baltimore, where George and Billy thought they might find refuge. But it was not to be. West Virginia State Patrol officers spotted the fugitives. All four were taken into custody when they made a wild dash to escape by foot.

Returned to Donalsonville, Georgia, the accused killers stood trial. Billy turned state's evidence and was not prosecuted for any of the murders. In exchange for his testimony he was charged only with armed robbery. For this crime he received a 40-year prison sentence. A year later he was returned to Pennsylvania and stood trial for the murder of Richard Miller. Found guilty, he was sentenced to 100 years imprisonment.

While the other killers were spending time in the Donalsonville jail, friends of the Alday family asked surviving members if they would approve of a lynching. The Aldays refused, expressing the opinion that there had been enough killing.

Carl Isaacs, Wayne Coleman and George Dungee were found guilty of six counts of murder and were sentenced to death. The men were transferred to Georgia State Prison to await their execution. Innumerable appeals followed.

Twelve years after the massacre, the U.S. Court of Appeals ruled that the accused could not have received a fair trial in Donalsonville. Despite the fact that the men had confessed, the court threw out the initial guilty verdict.

The men who killed the Aldays, although convicted and sentenced so many years ago, still languish in prison while their case again goes through the courts.

JOHN JOUBERT

IT is a fact of life that there are predators out there stalking and killing innocent citizens. When they are apprehended, we are amazed that they do not look like monsters. The Ted Bundys and Jeffrey Dahmers of the world have the appearance of the average man on the street. This is the story of one such monster in disguise.

John Joubert was the product of a broken home. He and his sister were raised by their mother. John was a smallish boy who kept to himself during his school years. His main activity centred around the Boy Scout movement, which he would later say gave him a feeling of belonging.

As a teenager in Portland, Maine, John, who had never had a girlfriend, began to experience deep urges to hurt defenseless strangers. He fantasized as to how it would feel to actually attack someone. The urges grew stronger, until John decided to act out his fantasy in real life.

In the winter of 1979, he stopped an eight-year-old boy on the street and clutched him by the throat. The little boy struggled and broke free. John let him go. It had been an exhilarating experience, but he considered it a failure. He would try again. A month later, he stopped another eight-year-old—a girl this time. John struck up a conversation with the youngster but, for reasons unknown even to himself, he let her go without even initiating an attack. John was disappointed at not following through.

John rode past nine-year-old Sarah Canty on his bicycle. As she bent over, he thrust a pencil into her back. Sarah ran into her home crying. The pencil had not penetrated more than a quarter of an inch into her back and her wound soon healed. Although she described the boy on the 10-speed bike to the police, the culprit was never found.

It amazed John that his attacks had been accomplished with such ease. The youngsters were so vulnerable. They stopped and talked to him without question. It also occurred to John that if he was careful, he might never be apprehended. To his way of thinking, the police were incompetent stupid oafs. Next time he would use a knife.

On March 24, 1980, nine-year-old Michael Witham sloshed through the snow on his way home. John struck up a conversation with the little boy. As the youngster looked away, John slashed his throat. Michael was able to run home as blood poured from his neck. The wound would take 12 stitches to close.

John had discovered a new thrill. His crime was featured in the newspapers and on the radio. Commentators wondered what kind of person would slash a little boy's throat. For the first time John realized that the notoriety of his crime brought with it the danger of being caught. It bothered him. Two years would pass before he felt compelled to attack again.

After John finished high school, he tried his hand at college. It didn't work out. At age 18, he found himself at loose ends, wondering what to do with the rest of his life. Sometimes the urge to attack would come over him. On Aug. 22, 1982, he prowled the streets on his 10-speed bike, looking for a victim. He found one in 11-year-old Ricky Stetson, all 60 pounds of him. Ricky was jogging when John rode up on his bike. Next morning, his body was found by a passerby. Ricky had been stabbed in the chest and bitten about his calves.

John Joubert had killed for the first time. He experienced no remorse or sorrow for what he had done, only exhilaration and relief.

John joined the U.S. Air Force, completed training as a radar technician and was posted to Offutt Air Force Base in Bellevue, Nebraska. Judy and Leonard Eberle lived right beside the Air Force base. On September 18, 1983, their 13-year-old son Danny went out on his paper route as he did every day. It was Danny's misfortune to cross paths with a monster.

By now, John Joubert was driving a 1979 Nova. In an instant, he clamped one hand over the boy's mouth while his other hand held a knife to Danny's throat. Danny was forced into the trunk of the Nova, driven to a secluded area and stabbed four times in the chest. John bit the dead boy's legs before dragging his body into a field adjoining the road. The experience left him hungry. It was almost morning. John drove to a restaurant and ate a hearty breakfast.

When Danny failed to return home from his paper route, his parents pinpointed the last paper he had delivered. They searched the area and found their son's bike leaning against a fence. Days later, Danny's stabbed and bitten body was found in the field.

Airman John Joubert was ecstatic. He was acting out his fantasies and enjoying every minute of the kill and the aftermath. Murder is news and John revelled at being in the news. He would kill again within three months.

On December 2, 1983, Chris Walden, 12, left his home for the few minutes walk to the Pawnee Elementary School he attended. John forced the boy into his Nova and drove away. Beside an isolated dirt road some distance from town, John choked and stabbed Chris until he was dead.

The monster returned to the air force base and, as if by magic, was transformed into mild-mannered, pleasant Airman John Joubert. He soaked up every detail of the latest infamous murder. Now there was more talk than ever about the killings. It was difficult not to connect the Eberle and Walden murders. The victims were so young, the killings so senseless.

Certainly Barbara and Warren Weaver were well aware of the madman in their midst. They warned their young son of the potential danger, never dreaming that it would be Barbara who would cross the monster's path.

On January 11, 1984, just a little over a month after Chris Walden's murder, Barbara was at work as a preschool instructor at the Aldersgate United Methodist Church. At about 8:15 a.m. she noticed a Chevy Citation circling the church. Barbara paid little attention until the vehicle stopped in front of the church. A young man came to the door. It was bitterly cold out, but Barbara's instinct told her to open the door only a crack. She wondered if this could be the man who killed children. That's what made her decide to memorize the Citation's license plate—59-L5154.

The man shivered in the cold. He asked, "Can I use your phone?" Barbara lied, "There's no phone here." Suddenly the man growled, "Get back inside or I'll kill you!" Barbara threw open the door and raced outside past the stranger. She ran, fell, cut her hand on the icy road, but made it to the nearby home of Pastor David Kelly.

Nancy Kelly called police. Barbara was able to give them the licence number of the Chevy Citation. It didn't take long to trace the vehicle to a car dealership. Airman John Joubert had been given a loaner while his Nova was being repaired.

Less than two hours after Barbara Weaver's harrowing ordeal, John was located in his room at the air force base. It was over. When questioned about the threat to Barbara, he confessed to killing little boys.

John stood trial for the murders of Danny Eberle and Chris Walden. He was found guilty of both murders and sentenced to die in the electric chair. Since then he has been returned to Maine, where he was found guilty of murdering Ricky Stetson.

Psychological tests revealed that John Joubert has an IQ of 123, considered to be in the superior range. He is presently on Death Row in Nebraska State Prison.

STEVE JUDY

THE clean-cut 12-year-old with the wide grin explained that he was a Boy Scout and was selling cookies door to door. The lady of the house smiled and beckoned for the youngster to enter. When the lad innocently inquired if her husband was at home, the woman replied that he was at work.

Steve Judy flashed a jackknife, held it to the terrified woman's throat and forced her into a bedroom. Once there, he stabbed her over and over again. Then he raped the hapless woman. When the blade of his knife snapped in her sternum, he ran to the kitchen looking for another weapon. The woman, bleeding profusely, staggered to a bureau to fetch a small hatchet her husband kept there.

Steve returned just as the woman found the hatchet. He grabbed it and swung wildly, severing the woman's left index finger and splitting her head open.

This remarkable woman underwent brain surgery and survived the attack. Steve was quickly apprehended and incarcerated in a mental institution for juveniles. After spending only nine months in the institution, he was released into the care of foster parents.

Steve continued to be in and out of trouble for the next nine years. His most serious brush with the law occurred when he beat and almost killed a woman in a Chicago suburb. Only the intervention of passers-by saved the woman's life. The 20-year-old was sent away for another of his many short stints in prison. In March 1977, he was paroled after serving only 20 months. A month after his release, Steve robbed a woman and spent another year in prison.

On April 28, 1979, two men searching for wild mushrooms along White Lick Creek outside Indianapolis, Indiana, stumbled across several articles of women's clothing near the bank of the creek. As they followed the trail of clothing, they came upon the nude body of a woman. Her legs rested on the creek bank, while the rest of her body was submerged.

Within minutes, the area was swarming with Indiana State Troopers, who went about securing the crime scene. Det. Sgt. Jerry Conner interviewed the two men who had found the body and then proceeded to walk downstream from the location where the body had been discovered. Later, he would say he was look-ing for any other clothing belonging to the dead woman. What he found was far different. Conner took about 100 paces when he came across the body of a little girl tangled in the weeds in the creek.

Officials were still absorbing this horrendous discovery when detectives, who had continued to walk downstream, came across another child's body. The small boy had washed up on a sandy outcropping. Police scanned the area. From where they stood beside the little boy's body, they were able to see the body of yet another child. What monster had snuffed out the lives of four indi-viduals and what reason could anyone have for killing three children, all under six years of age?

A preliminary examination of the bodies revealed that the woman had been raped and strangled. The children had no marks of violence on their bodies. All three had drowned in the swirling waters of White Lick Creek.

From a bankbook found at the scene, the woman was identified as Terry Chasteen. The three little victims were her children. Terry regularly drove her children to a baby sitter's before continuing on to work at a local grocery store. She hadn't shown up for work that day.

Terry had a boyfriend who was genuinely shocked to learn of her death. He cooperated fully with investigating officers and it was he who was asked to offi-cially identify the bodies. On the way to the mortuary, he shouted out to accom-panying police, "That's Terry's car!" By blind luck, the victim's distinctive bright red vehicle had been found.

Terry's boyfriend later identified her body and those of her three children, Misty Ann, 5; Stephen Michael, 4; and Mark Lewis, 2. Terry was only 22 years old at the time of her death and was divorced from the children's father, who was in the U.S. Navy.

Police solicited the public's assistance. They asked anyone who had been near Highway 67 and White Lick Creek that morning to contact the Indiana State Police. Scores of calls were received. One caller reported that he and his young son had driven across the bridge over White Lick Creek before 8 a.m. They had noticed a distinctively painted red and silver pickup truck parked down an access road.

Police put out a bulletin to adjoining states describing the conspicuous vehicle. But it wasn't necessary. Once again, by coincidence, the truck was located. The same man who had spotted the red and silver pickup called police the day after the murder. His young son had seen the vehicle parked near a neighborhood construction site.

Police quickly learned that the truck belonged to Steve Judy, who was well known to Indianapolis police. Steve was taken into custody and questioned. It had taken less than 36 hours to home in on their chief suspect.

Initially, Steve, on the advice of his lawyer, wouldn't talk about the crime. Authorities went about building a case against the vicious young criminal. Tests proved that Steve's blood type was compatible with semen stains found on Terry's clothing. Threads taken from Steve's clothing matched threads from Terry's blouse. Casts of tire tracks lifted from the murder scene were the same as the tire tracks of Steve's pickup truck.

Steve Judy testified toward the end of his trial. From the witness stand he related how he stopped Terry Chasteen. It was simple. He pointed to her tire, indicating that she was having a flat. When she stopped, he pulled up and offered assistance. At the same time, he offered to look under the hood of her car. That's when he ripped out the ignition coil. When the car wouldn't start, he offered to give Terry and her children a lift.

They travelled a short while before Steve pulled off the road and parked near White Lick Creek. In an obvious attempt to save her children, Terry didn't resist. She was forced to walk down to the creek. Steve told the children to go downstream and play. He then commanded Terry to remove her clothing. She complied in silence and was raped. Suddenly, she screamed hysterically. Steve ripped away a piece of her clothing and stuffed it in her mouth before strangling his helpless victim.

The children ran toward their mother's screams. One by one, Steve picked them up and threw them in the creek, where they drowned. Steve Judy begged the court to execute him.

Sitting in the courtroom was a woman who would later testify against the accused man. The witness had no index finger on her left hand. She was the woman who had survived the vicious attack on her life nine years earlier.

On March 8, 1981, Steve Judy's wish was granted. He was executed in Indiana's electric chair.

EDMUND KEMPER

SOME time ago I travelled to the tiny village of Bovingdon, England, to research the unbelievable case of Graham Young. Young poisoned his own family in 1963, when he was only 14 years old. Released from Broadmoor nine years later he proceeded to poison his colleagues at his place of employment in Bovingdon. After causing two deaths and many bouts of illness, he was taken into custody. In 1972 he was tried for murder, convicted, and is presently in prison.

The Young case received worldwide publicity, as it went to the very heart of major social questions the western world had been grappling with for years. Should our judicial system emphasize rehabilitation or punishment? Does capital punishment ultimately save lives?

At the time, I believed that the bizarre case of the obsessive poisoner who had fooled psychiatrists and lawyers into releasing him to kill again was an isolated incident. I was wrong.

At approximately the same time another young man, age 15, was following the same path as Graham Young. The methods of killing were different, but the dates, the motives, and even the mental ability of the two murderers are so similar they stretch coincidence to the limit.

The other boy's name is Edmund Kemper. This is his story.

Edmund was born on December 19, 1948 in Burbank, California. His father was a huge man, towering six feet, eight inches, while his mother, Clarnell, stood an even six-feet. The Kempers had three children—Susan, the oldest; Edmund, and Allyn. Edmund's parents argued incessantly. The more heated of these arguments usually culminated with Mr. Kemper leaving home for long periods of time.

There is no evidence that either parent ever physically abused their son. Edmund, as the only boy in the house, may have felt some rejection by his mother, who probably identified him with her husband. Eventually, in 1957, Mr. Kemper left his wife and never returned. Clarnell was to go to work to support her three children. She would marry twice again in a futile attempt to find companionship and a father for her children.

In the meantime, Clarnell moved to Helena, Montana, where she obtained employment as a secretary with the First National Bank. She made a new home for her three children, but Edmund was miserable. He longed for his father, and visited him at every opportunity at his new home in Los Angeles. Mr. Kemper had remarried. Edmund may not have been the most welcome of guests with the new Mrs. Kemper.

At the age of 10, Edmund, who was a tall, big-boned boy, began exhibiting some strange traits. He enjoyed taking the arms, legs and heads off his younger sister's dolls. When he was only 13 years old, Edmund shot a dog belonging to another boy who lived nearby. Young Kemper had been well schooled in the use of firearms by his father, who prided himself in having been a member of the Special Service during World War II. After the incident with the dog, neighboring children mocked and made fun of Edmund. From then on Edmund Kemper had no close contact with anyone other than his mother. Their relationship was strange in many ways. Edmund always brought his troubles to his mother, who seemed concerned, but their discussions usually ended in shouting matches, with one or the other storming out of the house.

Shortly after Edmund killed the dog, he cut the head off the family pet, a Siamese cat. This time he was terrified at what he had done, and quickly buried the cat in his backyard.

In September 1962, Edmund went to live with his father in Los Angeles. He was ecstatic. For a few months he led a happy, normal existence. At Christmas, Mr. Kemper visited his parents on their farm at North Fork, California.

Most 15-year-old boys would look forward to a visit with grandparents down on the farm. Not Edmund. He suspected his family of subterfuge. For the first time in his life Edmund's instincts were correct. His father left him on the farm and returned to Los Angeles. Edmund felt rejected, cast aside, and, above all, bored. His grandparents meant well, but they were old and set in their ways.

Grandfather Edmund Kemper was 72 and retired. He still did some farming on his eight-acre spread. Maude Kemper, at 66, spent her spare time writing juvenile stories. Being something of an artist, she illustrated her own work. All of this was an idyllic situation for the elderly couple, but was utterly boring for

15-year-old Edmund. His grandfather detected the unrest in the young lad and tried to help. He presented Edmund with a rifle to shoot gophers and rabbits. At school in the nearby town of Tollhouse, Edmund did well, making from C-plus to B-minus in all his subjects.

The school term ended and Edmund went to Helena to visit his mother and her third husband. In two weeks he was back on the farm with his grandparents. There was a marked change in Edmund's behavior. He now appeared even more withdrawn and sullen. The change was so evident that his grandfather wrote to Edmund's father especially to tell him that the visit with his mother had not done the boy any good.

Later, Edmund was to reveal that his feelings towards his grandparents vacillated from gratefulness for what they were doing for him to resentment. Edmund resented the fact that his grandparents often mentioned how much it was costing them for his room and board. Sometimes his grandmother reminded him of his mother who Edmund felt was the most domineering woman in the world.

Occasionally, deep in thought, Edmund would stare off into space. The weird habit bothered his grandmother. She always shouted at him to bring him out of his reverie. Maude Kemper had no way of knowing that her grandson was fantasizing about murdering her.

On August 27, 1963, Edmund was sitting at the kitchen table proofreading one of his grandmother's stories. Slowly he began to stare off into space. As usual his grandmother shouted at him, bringing him back to reality. Edmund then nonchalantly mentioned that he was going out to shoot some rabbits. He picked up his .22-rifle and went out on the porch. Edmund raised his .22 and took careful aim at the back of his grandmother's head. The bullet travelled through the screen door and into his grandmother's skull. Did Edmund Kemper feel remorse at what he had done? Was he terrified at the consequences? Edmund raised the gun and twice more shot his grandmother in the back. He then dragged the body into the elderly couple's bedroom. Just then a car chugged up the driveway. It was his grandfather. Edmund raised the rifle until the back of the old man's head was in his sight. He squeezed the trigger ever so gently just as his father had taught him. His grandfather fell to the ground never knowing what had killed him.

Edmund went to the telephone and called his mother. His first words to her were "Grandma's dead and so is Grandpa." His mother, understandably shaken, composed herself enough to get the story of the killing from her son. She pleaded with him to call the police. Edmund put down the phone and minding his mother like a good boy should, he called the sheriff's office.

When questioned by police Edmund had a hard time explaining his motive. He had often thought of killing his grandmother, because at times she had annoyed him. His grandfather was another story. Edmund had performed a mercy killing. You see, had the old man discovered his wife's body, it was quite possible he would have had a fatal heart attack. Edmund had mercifully spared his grandfather a great deal of grief.

Psychiatrists who examined Edmund discovered two things. Their subject had an I.Q. of 136, indicating superior intelligence and they felt he was a paranoid schizophrenic. Still only 15 years old, Edmund was declared insane. On December 6, 1964, the ominous doors of Atascadero State Hospital closed behind him. Ironically, half-way around the world in England, 15-year-old Graham Young had already been in Broadmoor for over a year. Both boys would gain their freedom to kill again.

Once in the huge hospital which specialized in sex offenders, Edmund appeared to make a complete adjustment. He responded to treatment exceptionally well. So well, in fact, that eventually Edmund worked in a psychology lab testing other patients. Even in the confines of the institution he led something of a double life. To all outward appearances he was the well adjusted mental patient making an extraordinary recovery. His other life consisted of delving into every detail of sexual perversion garnered from fellow inmates. Edmund's curiosity knew no limits. He wanted to know it all.

After five years at Atascadero, Edmund was enrolled in a community college, where he earned straight A's. In the meantime his mother, now Clarnell Strandberg, had moved to Santa Cruz, where she worked at the University of California as a secretary. Clarnell made one close friend, Sara Hallett, while employed at the university. The previous five years had been most pleasant for Clarnell. She didn't have to worry about or argue with her son Edmund.

Now the lumbering six foot, nine inch giant was paroled to his mother. Edmund worked at menial tasks, saved his money and bought a car. He coerced his mother into getting him a University of California sticker for his vehicle, ostensibly so he could park on the campus.

Edmund had a plan. California law had a unique loophole, which Edmund proposed to use to his advantage. On his lawyer's advice he was examined by two different psychiatrists. Both doctors gave him glowing positive reports. Their recommendations were interspersed with words such as "normal," "adjusted" and "no danger to society." These two reports were placed before a superior court judge, who then ruled that Edmund's juvenile record be sealed forever. This meant that Edmund could apply for any job without having to reveal his previous record. He could serve on a jury, or join the army. Why, Edmund could even legally purchase guns.

Edmund Kemper had killed both his grandparents at 15. Now the slate was clean. He had fooled all the experts. Edmund had what amounted to a licence to kill again.

It wasn't long before Edmund and Clarnell were taking part in their monumental shouting matches. Edmund drifted from job to job, never approaching a task which would tax his intellectual abilities. He drank some beer at local hangouts and cruised around in his Ford. For no apparent reason, he purchased a few knives and guns and stashed them in the trunk of his car.

The university campus was located a little way from Santa Cruz.

Most students lived in the town and hitchhiked to the campus. During the day and early evening it was customary to see both male and female students catching lifts to class. One day Edmund got up enough nerve to stop for a girl hitchhiker. He noticed that the girl glanced at the University of California sticker on his car before jumping in. It was easy.

After that initial triumph, Edmund not only picked up girls near the campus, but roamed all over the state picking up female hitchhikers. He didn't do anything to the girls, just talked. For two years the young giant spent his every spare moment giving lifts to young girls.

Edmund fantasized about possessing a girl. Later he was to state that possession to him meant not only sexual possession, but a type of total ownership that only death could bring.

On Sunday, May 7, 1972, Edmund Kemper was hunting—hunting for a human victim. He found two. Near Berkeley he picked up two Fresno State

College coeds. The two friends, Anita and Mary Ann, were hitching a ride to Stanford University. From the time they stepped into Edmund's car they were never seen again.

Edmund pulled a 9-mm Browning automatic from under the seat of the Ford Galaxie. Anita and Mary Ann were terrified. Edmund found a deserted rural road. Both girls knew they were about to be raped. Mary Ann tried to talk Edmund out of it, but without success. Edmund sized up the two girls, who didn't seem to be overimpressed with what he thought were his daring actions.

Finally Edmund told them he would drive them to his mother's house, but in the meantime Anita would have to be placed in the trunk. All the while Edmund had made up his mind to kill both his captives. With no choice in the matter, Mary Ann allowed herself to be handcuffed. Anita, looking in to the barrel of the Browning automatic, was led to the trunk. She got in. In the front seat of the car the insane giant stabbed the 105-lb. girl repeatedly until she was dead. He then opened the trunk and proceeded to stab Anita until she lay still in death.

Edmund drove home with the two bodies in his car. First he washed up, then returned to his vehicle and carried Mary Ann's body to his room. Fully aware of his actions, and without panic or remorse, Edmund dissected his victim. He returned to the car for the second body and repeated his insane ritual. Wrapping the sections of human remains in plastic bags, Edmund drove into the Santa Cruz mountains and buried the two girls. Their heads were thrown over a ravine. Edmund drove home and fondled the girls' wallets.

Four months later, on September 14, a 15-year-old dance student named Aiko disappeared. Edmund had raped, suffocated and decapitated his victim.

In the months which followed three more girls, Cynthia, Alice and Rosalind, were murdered by Edmund Kemper. Parts of the various bodies were found. Some were identified, others were not. Investigating officials knew they were dealing with one killer, but had no idea who he was or why the mad killer struck in such a vicious manner. They also knew they were dealing with a necrophiliac and cannibal.

On Easter weekend, 1973, Edmund decided to kill his mother. The idea so excited him that he couldn't sleep. He tossed and turned in bed until he gave into the uncontrollable urge which boiled within. At a little after 5 a.m., armed with a knife and claw hammer, he entered his mother's bedroom and, without saying a word, bludgeoned her to death. He then decapitated his mother. Later Edmund was to tell police that the whole thing took less than a minute. Edmund placed his mother's body in a closet, cleaned up the bedroom and left to have a few beers at a local hangout.

Somewhere in the dark recesses of his mind Edmund felt that he had to create a reason for his mother's disappearance. She was not the type of woman to leave her job and home without good reason. Edmund thought about the problem all day. As he drove home the solution came to him. If his mother's best friend, Sara Hallett, dropped out of sight at the same time, it would be logical to assume that the two women had gone away together.

At around five that evening Edmund returned home and opened a can of beer. The phone rang. Edmund picked up the receiver. It was Sara Hallett asking for his mother. Edmund explained that his mother was out, but had asked him to invite Sara to dinner that evening. Sara was delighted to accept. A few hours later the unsuspecting woman walked into hell. Edmund throttled her to death, breaking her neck in the process. He placed her body in the closet with that of his mother.

On Easter Sunday, Edmund awoke and decided to flee. He drove his car east to Reno, Nevada, where he rented another vehicle from Hertz. Carefully he transferred what amounted to an arsenal to the rented car. He drove for 18 hours without stopping.

When he arrived in Pueblo, Colorado, Edmund made up his mind to call Lieutenant Charles Scherer, who he knew was in charge of the investigation of the missing girls. When the long distance call was received in Santa Cruz, Lt. Scherer was not on duty. Edmund had a hard time explaining just who he was and that this was no crank call. He was told to call back. When one of the most despicable monsters who ever lived called back at 1 a.m., he was told that Lt. Scherer would not be on duty until 9 a.m. He was informed that the police were not supposed to accept collect calls. The officer hung up.

At 5 in the morning Edmund tried for the third time. This time he contacted a policeman who was familiar with his case. He kept Edmund on the line until the Pueblo police took him into custody while he was still speaking on the phone. Edmund hardly had time to tell the police to go to his home where they would find the bodies of his mother and Sara Hallett.

When taken into custody, big Edmund Kemper directed police to gravesites which had not yet been uncovered. Police were astounded to learn that the monster they were seeking was this intelligent, lucid giant. Edmund resorted to his photographic memory to recount every detail of the eight lives he had snuffed out. He claimed that his reason for surrendering was to get the whole thing off his chest. To psychiatrists he suggested that possible repressed fears and anxieties had driven him to kill. None of this was new to Edmund. He had been through it all before when he had killed his grandparents.

Edmund Kemper stood trial for murder. He was found to be sane and guilty of eight counts of murder in the first degree. Edmund Kemper is now confined to a maximum security prison at Folsom.

JOHN LIST

JOHN List planned it all in meticulous detail. He called the children's school advising them that his three children would not be attending class for some time. He cancelled newspaper, milk and mail deliveries. You see, John List had decided to disappear. First, he would kill his entire family.

Quiet, religious John was 45 years old in 1971 when everything seemed to turn sour in his life. He simply couldn't continue to make payments on the two mortgages he had placed on his huge, 18-room mansion at 431 Hillside Ave. in fashionable Westfield, New Jersey. His accountancy salary didn't come close to covering his reserved but comfortable lifestyle.

Wife Helen was a disappointment. She adamantly refused to attend church regularly. His daughter Patricia even talked about going into the acting profession. John's rather fanatical religious beliefs were definitely not being adhered to by his family.

There were choices. He could declare himself bankrupt or seek assistance from welfare agencies, but John couldn't bear to think of the shame and disgrace that these avenues held for him and his family. After all, he was a highly-respected accountant who had once been vice president of a bank. He had taught Sunday school at the Lutheran church, which he attended regularly. No, in John's mind there was only one proper thing to do and that was to send his entire family to heaven.

Calmly, John went about the details of his plan. It was November 9, 1971. He loaded his 9 mm pistol and his .22 calibre revolver. John shot his wife Helen in the back and dragged her body to the ballroom. He then made his way up to the third floor and shot his 85-year-old mother, Alma.

John wanted to move the body down to the ballroom, but it was too heavy. He decided to place his mother's corpse in a closet, but found the dead weight difficult to manipulate. James Moran, who was then chief of police of Westfield, says, "When we went upstairs, we found Alma List's body halfway in a closet. We figured that whoever killed her gave up trying to get her in."

John drove to Westfield High School, where he picked up his 16-year-old daughter Patricia. He killed her with a single shot in the back. Patricia's body was carried to the ballroom and placed on a sleeping bag beside the body of her mother. Frederick, 13, was picked up from his after-school job. Once in the house, he too was shot in the back and placed on a sleeping bag in the ballroom. John List, Jr., 15, arrived home from soccer practice. He had a few moments of awareness before he was shot nine times from both of his father's weapons. His body was placed in a row beside those of his mother, sister and brother. The killing was over. There was no one left.

The diabolical mass murderer cleaned the blood-spattered kitchen to the best of his ability. He stood amidst the bodies of his family and prayed for their deliverance. Then he sat down and wrote a letter to his pastor, the Rev. Eugene A. Rehwinkel. Pertinent excerpts of this letter follow.

"Dear Pastor Rehwinkel:

"I am sorry to add this additional burden to your work. I know that what has been done is wrong from all that I have been taught and that any reasons that I might give will not make it right. But you are the one person that I know that while not condoning this will at least possibly understand why I felt that I had to do this.

"1. I wasn't earning anywhere near enough to support us. Everything I tried seemed to fall to pieces. True, we could have gone bankrupt and maybe gone on welfare.

"2. But that brings me to my next point. Knowing the type of location that one would have to live in, plus the environment for the children, plus the effect on them knowing they were on welfare was just more than I thought they could and should endure. I know they were willing to cut back, but this involved a lot more than that.

"3. With Pat being so determined to get into acting I was also fearful as to what that might do to her continuing to be Christian. I'm sure it wouldn't have helped.

"4. Also, with Helen not going to church I knew that this would harm the children eventually in their attendance. I had continued to hope that she would begin to come to church soon. But when I mentioned to her that Mr. Jutze wanted to pay her an elder's call, she just blew up and said she wanted her name taken off the church rolls. Again this could only have an adverse result for the children's continued attendance.

"So that is the sum of it. If any one of these had been the condition, we might have pulled through but this was just too much. At least I'm certain that all have gone to heaven now. If things had gone on who knows if this would be the case.

"Of course, Mother got involved because doing what I did to my family would have been a tremendous shock to her at this age. Therefore, knowing that she is also a Christian I felt it best that she be relieved of the troubles of this world that would have hit her.

"After it was all over I said some prayers for them all—from the hymn book. That was the least I could do.

"One other thing. It may seem cowardly to have always shot from behind, but I didn't want any of them to know even at the last second that I had to do this to them.

"John got hurt more because he seemed to struggle longer. The rest were immediately out of pain. John didn't consciously feel anything either.

"Please remember me in your prayers. I will need them whether or not the government does its duty as it sees it. I'm only concerned with making my peace with God and of this I am assured because of Christ dying even for me.

"P.S. Mother is in the hallway in the attic—3rd floor. She was too heavy to move.
"John."

John turned on some lights, locked the doors of his home and drove away. A month passed. Light bulbs burned out. Neighbors, who later confessed they hadn't known the Lists very well, became suspicious. Finally, they called police.

Chief James Moran spoke to me from his home, "I've handled scores of murders over the years, but nothing like this. We forced the back door and walked through some rooms to the ballroom. The smell was terrible and there they were, four bodies all neatly placed in a row. They were blackened and partially decomposed. I will never forget the sight."

Police found John List's car at Kennedy Airport on December 7, two days after the discovery of the bodies of his family. But John wasn't found or traced. Moran says, "We didn't have the remotest idea where he had gone. He had no real friends and no one really knew the man."

John's past was ordinary in every way—strict religious parents, high school, university, a stint in the army during World War II and, later on, service in the Korean War. As the admitted perpetrator of New Jersey's most infamous crime, he was sought on three continents. All tips and clues led nowhere. John List had apparently committed the perfect murder, not once, but five times.

After the murders, John made his way to Denver, Colorado, where he changed his name to Robert P. Clark. For a while he eked out a living as a cook, but in 1977 gravitated to his original profession of accountancy. Soon he was earning $400 per week. He met his second wife, Delores, at a Lutheran Church gathering. The quiet, introverted Robert was a good and devoted husband.

In 1985, a friend showed Delores Clark a newspaper account of an old New Jersey murder. The photo of John List which accompanied the article bore an eerie resemblance to her husband Robert. Delores dismissed the whole thing as ridiculous.

In 1988, the Clarks moved to Richmond, Virginia. Robert Clark attended Lutheran services, puttered in his garden, watched TV and melted into the woodwork. But modern technology caught up with List. The old unsolved New Jersey murders were televised on the syndicated program, America's Most Wanted. Forensic sculptor Frank Bender, working from 18-year-old photos of List, produced a model of the wanted man's head. Bender ingeniously created an uncanny likeness of John List, aged 18 years.

Sure enough, the same neighbor who had shown the newspaper account to Delores Clark three years earlier, recognized the sculpted head. She had a relative call the program.

John List was traced to an accounting firm in Richmond. Robert Clark denied being the wanted man, but a fingerprint check of old army records on file in Washington proved that he was indeed John List.

In May 1990, 64-year-old John List stood trial for murder, almost two decades after he had eliminated his entire family. He was found guilty of all five murders and was sentenced to five consecutive life terms in prison. When the judge passed sentence on List, the courtroom broke out in applause.

HENRY LEE LUCAS

Is Henry Lee Lucas one of the greatest con artists and liars the world has ever known or is he the world's most prolific serial killer?

Henry will always be remembered as the man who, on various occasions, claimed to have murdered 150 people, then 300 people, and at the height of his "confession period," 600 during an eight-year spree of robbery, rape and murder.

To lay credence to Henry's claims, in many of the killings he had an accomplice, one Otis Toole, who was easily located to corroborate Henry's wild stories. Otis was on Death Row in Stark, Florida.

Henry's early life makes Dickens' poor houses seem like resorts in comparison. He was brought up by a mother who was a prostitute and an alcoholic father. His father had lost both his legs in a railroad accident. The Lucas family lived in the backwoods of Virginia, where Henry's mother took relish in performing the sex act with her customers in front of her young son.

At age seven, Henry suffered a severe eye injury which resulted in the loss of his left eye. It was replaced with a glass eye which, to this day, gives him a somewhat sinister appearance.

In 1960, Henry stabbed his mother to death. He was found guilty of murder in the second degree and was sentenced to 20 to 40 years imprisonment. On August 22, 1975, after spending 15 years behind bars, he was released. Henry tried married life, but that didn't work out. He took off and it was during this transient period that Henry met Otis Toole.

Otis was a big mean transvestite who took a liking to Henry and brought him home to live with his mother. It was here that Henry met Otis' niece Becky, 12, and his nephew Frank, 9. The unlikely foursome drove throughout the States in Henry's dilapidated Olds. Sometimes, they scavenged for empty pop bottles along the highway. Desperate for gas money, Henry often sold his blood.

The foursome broke up. Becky and Henry ended up at a sort of mission for the destitute near Wichita Falls, Texas. After spending some time there, Becky disappeared. An elderly widow, Kate Rich, who lived nearby, also disappeared.

Henry was a suspect in the Rich disappearance and was picked up by the local sheriff.

It was while incarcerated that Henry got his bright idea. He decided to "confess" to hundreds of murders throughout the States and Canada. He now says he started confessing because he was being tortured in jail.

First he confessed to killing Becky Powell and Kate Rich, but he didn't stop there. He began confessing to other murders, abetted by investigating officers who often talked about the crime en route to murder scenes, revealing many details about the victim's clothing, personal characteristics and date of the murder. Most times, Henry seemed confused about the exact location, but a few times the officers actually pointed out the crime scene. On these occasions, the media reported that Henry had related details about the crime which only the murderer could know.

Sometimes Henry would travel by helicopter to the crime scene. At the height of his confession period, it was tough to get an interview with Henry. When I phoned the Georgetown Jail around that time, Sheriff Jim Boutwell told me, "Henry is away visiting a crime site today."

One can't help but believe that in Henry's world eating restaurant food and travelling in air conditioned vehicles was far better than sitting in the Georgetown Jail.

Could the sham sustain itself?

Two things assisted Lucas in his role as the self-confessed super serial killer of all time. One of his confessions was given directly to Sheriff Boutwell, who became convinced that Henry was the killer of an unidentified young girl found in Williamson County, Texas. As a result of his convictions, Boutwell applied for and received funding from the Dept. of Public Safety to establish a Henry Lee Lucas Homicide Task Force. From that time, Henry was flying high.

The air-conditioned vehicles couldn't wait to take their star killer on his macabre missions. Law enforcement officers flocked to the Georgetown Jail.

To cap his unbelievable confessions, Henry implicated his old buddy, Otis Toole, comfortably ensconced on Death Row in the Stark, Florida penitentiary. When told of Henry's confessions and that he was being implicated in them all, Otis figured he had nothing to lose. He confirmed every single murder. Otis went a bit further. He volunteered that the reason Becky Powell was never found was simple enough. He had eaten her.

It couldn't go on forever. Responsible journalists delved into details of Henry's confessions. They found that Henry had claimed that he and Otis had murdered people in 1978. There is strong evidence the two men hadn't met until 1979.

Then there was the Adam Walsh case.

Adam, the six-year-old son of John Walsh, was kidnapped from a Florida shopping centre and murdered in 1981. While a desperate search was underway for Adam, Otis Toole confessed to his murder. Otis said that the body would never be found because he had eaten the child.

Adam's body was eventually found, which didn't add to the credibility of Lucas' corroborating witness. John Walsh went on to spearhead changes in the laws of several states, so that missing children could be more easily traced. He is presently host of the highly-rated TV program, America's Most Wanted.

In hindsight, it is rather improbable that Henry and Otis, travelling with two youngsters, roamed the country robbing, raping, mutilating and killing as many as three victims every week.

Finally, even Henry grew tired of the deception, supposedly because the gruesome pictures he constantly had to view made him sick. He turned full circle, claiming that he hadn't murdered anyone, except, of course, his mother. Once again, Otis agreed. It had all been a hoax.

In 1986, Texas Attorney General Jim Mattox issued a comprehensive report on the Lucas affair. In essence, the report states that Henry's confessions concerning Becky Powell and Kate Rich appear authentic. All the rest are extremely doubtful. The report castigates the Texas Rangers for perpetuating the deception by insisting that Henry had killed hundreds of people.

Did he kill three or three hundred? Despite the irrefutable evidence that Henry and his pal hoodwinked law enforcement officers from all over the States, there are those who still believe he is the most prolific mass murderer the world has ever seen.

Otis Toole has had his death sentence commuted to life imprisonment.

As for Henry, he claims he is finally telling the truth. He never killed anyone, except his mother.

Henry had a close call in 1990. Tried and convicted of one of his many confessed murders, he was scheduled to be put to death on December 3. Two days before the sentence was to be carried out, a state appeals court indefinitely delayed his execution.

THE MAD BUTCHER OF KINGSBURY RUN

MANY believe that serial killers are a recent phenomenon. Nothing could be further from the truth. Serial killers, the most heinous of all criminals, have always been out there, preying on the unwary.

On September 5, 1934, a man walking on Euclid Beach, about eight miles from downtown Cleveland, stumbled across a young woman's nude body partially buried in the sand. The girl had been decapitated. Her description was checked against reported missing persons, but she has never been identified.

At the time, police had no idea that they were dealing with the first in a series of murders, which would later be called the Kingsbury Run murders, named after the rather ugly ancient creek bed running through the heart of Cleveland.

A year later, on September 23, 1935, the bodies of two men were found at the foot of East 49th St. and Kingsbury Run. Both bodies were nude, headless, and had had their penises removed. The heads were recovered separately, buried some distance from the bodies. Several clues were found at the murder site—a blue jacket, a shirt, cap, flashlight and some rope. All were sent to a police laboratory for analysis.

Attempts to trace these items failed. To some it appeared that the clues had been left by the killer as red herrings to frustrate investigators. A fingerprint check identified one of the bodies as Edward Andrassy. The other was never identified.

Edward's past was thoroughly investigated in the hope that something would be uncovered which would lead police to the murderer. Edward had been a transvestite who frequented local bars. He sometimes posed as a doctor and had been arrested for examining female patients. Four days before his decapitated body was found, he had left his rooming house at 8 p.m. and had not been seen alive after that time.

Two things puzzled police. A type of preservative had been used on the remains of the headless body found on Euclid Beach. The same preservative had been applied to the unidentified man found more recently. Another connecting link was the skill with which all heads had been removed. Was it possible that a madman was loose, systematically killing and decapitating both male and female victims?

Four months after the two bodies were found, a woman reported that a basket of meat had been left in the alley behind 2315 East 20th St. The basket proved to contain the right arm, lower torso and thighs of a woman. Thirteen days later the legs and left arm of the woman were found behind a derelict building on Orange Ave. The head of this victim was never found, but a fingerprint check identified her as Mrs. Florence Polillo, a 42-year-old alcoholic prostitute.

Florence had walked out on her husband 13 years earlier. Andrew Polillo travelled from Buffalo to identify the various parts of his long lost wife's body. Weeks were spent delving into Florence's past, but all efforts failed to uncover her killer.

The Mad Butcher of Kingsbury Run, as he was now called, struck three more times in the same year. On June 5, 1936, two young boys found a human male head wrapped in a pair of men's pants. Next day, a railroad worker found the matching torso. Once again, a degree of skill had been utilized to separate head from body. Police were still attempting to identify this latest victim when, two months later, another decapitated body was found. This time, the head was only 15 feet from the body and the crime scene indicated that the murder had taken place where the body had been found. Why had the Mad Butcher changed his pattern of delivering bodies to selected locations?

On September 10, beside a hobo jungle on Kingsbury Run, a man's torso was found bobbing in a stagnant pool. The body had been emasculated with the same surgical skill as previous victims. The head was never found.

One can only imagine the effect this series of strange murders had on the general population of Cleveland. The Mad Butcher of Kingsbury Run was the main topic of conversation in the community. Visitors shunned the city. Vagrants and hobos travelled in groups. The city of Cleveland was held in the grip of fear.

The Mad Butcher took a holiday from his macabre profession until February 23, 1937, when a female body turned up on the beach close to where victim

number one had been found. As the arms and head were never recovered, identification proved to be impossible.

A coroner's report issued after this latest murder pointed out the similar conditions of the various victims' bodies: "It is the peculiar dissection of the bodies
which groups these cases together. All show that the heads were severed from
the bodies through the intervertebral disc by means of a sharp knife. Cases four,
seven and eight, showed further that the bodies were cleanly dismembered at the
shoulder and hip joints, apparently by a series of cuts around the flexure of the
joints and then by a strong twist, wrenching the head out of the joint cavity and
cutting the capsule.

"The torsos were further sectioned through the abdomen, the knife being
carried in cases four and seven through the intervertebral discs. Case number
four was further mutilated by disarticulating the knee joints roughly, frac-
turing the mid portion of the bones of the lower legs and slashing the abdomen
down through the pubic bones. All the skin edges, muscles, blood vessels and
cartilages were cut cleanly.

"The procedure followed by these cases suggests to us that the dissection
was done either by a highly intelligent lay person or, as is more likely, by a person with some knowledge of anatomy, such as a doctor, a medical student, nurse,
orderly, butcher, hunter or veterinary surgeon."

The bodies kept turning up bearing the Mad Butcher's unique signature. On
July 6, 1937, portions of a man's body were pulled out of the Cuyahoga River.
During the remainder of 1937-1938, four more bodies were found near Kingsbury Run. On August 16, 1938, the last murder took place and the nightmare
that had haunted Cleveland came to an abrupt end.

From time to time, suspects were arrested, but all were released when they
proved to be innocent. Special police units were formed to track down the
butcher, but these too failed. Many deranged men confessed to the serial killings.
These confessions proved to be false.

In January 1939, Cleveland's Chief of Police George Matowitz received the
following letter, which is believed to be authentic. It was postmarked Los Angeles, California: "You can rest easy now as I have come out to sunny California
for the winter. I felt bad operating on those people, but science must advance. I
shall astound the medical profession, a man with only a D.C.

"What did their lives mean in comparison to hundreds of sick and disease-twisted bodies. Just laboratory guinea pigs found on any public street. No one missed them when I failed. My last case was successful. I know now the feeling of Pasteur, Thoreau, and other pioneers.

"Right now I have a volunteer who will absolutely prove my theory. They call me mad and a butcher, but the truth will out.

"I have failed but once here. The body has not been found and never will be, but the head minus the features, is buried on Century Blvd., between Western and Crenshaw. I feel it my duty to dispose of the bodies as I do. It is God's will not to let them suffer. (Signed) X."

The Mad Butcher of Kingsbury Run was never heard of again. The series of killings which took place in Cleveland has never been solved.

CHARLES MANSON

OVER 25 years have passed since that night when the rage within Charlie Manson's soul was unleashed inside the home of director Roman Polanski and his pregnant wife, movie actress Sharon Tate.

When small time thief and pseudo folk singer Charlie Manson was paroled from Terminal Island in San Pedro, California in 1967, no one was aware that the 5-foot-2 misfit with the magnetic personality would commit crimes so horrible they are remembered over 25 years later.

There was Charlie, 32, free at last, after serving almost seven years in prison. It was the era of love and peace, peace and love; homeless girls wandered the country in search of a meaning to life. LSD helped. It was an era custom-made for Charlie Manson, with his guitar and charismatic personality.

Gravitating to San Francisco, Charlie's inner circle of sub-culture followers grew in number. Mary Brunner, Lynette (Squeaky) Fromme and Patricia Krenwinkel became known as 'Charlie's girls.' They slept, travelled, stole and begged together. They purchased an old bus and scoured the countryside. They were like family.

New recruits joined the Manson family. Susan Atkins, a 19-year-old hellion, came aboard. Robert Beausoleil, a 20-year-old actor, who sometimes lived with Gary Hinman, became a Manson follower. Diane Lake, 14, who was later renamed Snake because of her distinctive movements during intercourse, joined the family in their nomadic existence. Tex Watson was an avid Manson disciple. Later, Tex would prove to be a valuable and loyal member of the family.

Growth in the family was not derived solely from outsiders. Some of the girls became pregnant. Susan Atkins had a child. Mary Brunner gave birth to Charlie's baby.

In 1968, Charlie and his followers made their headquarters at the Spahn movie ranch, a dilapidated group of buildings near Los Angeles. The sect had evolved from love and peace to Satanism, hate and revenge. Charlie would send out groups of his followers to change the world, make it a better place in which to live.

In July 1969, Gary Hinman had a falling out with Charlie. Although Gary had always allowed members of Charlie's family to crash at his house, he was never a committed member of the sect. When Gary, who reputedly had money hidden in his house, steadfastly refused to devote himself to Charlie and his children, he signed his own death warrant.

Robert Beausoleil and a couple of the girls paid Hinman a visit. Gary wouldn't give them the time of day. Charlie showed up and, in a fit of rage, stabbed Hinman in the head with a sword, almost severing his ear. Then he left. Beausoleil and the girls bound Hinman with rope. When they phoned Charlie for instructions, they were told to kill their captive.

Hinman was stabbed twice in the chest and died on his living room floor from loss of blood. Charlie's girls wrote "Political Piggy" on the wall in Hinman's blood, after which they returned to the Spahn ranch and sang songs. Within two weeks, police had matched a fingerprint in Hinman's home to Robert Beausoleil. He was picked up and charged with murder.

On the night of August 8 and early morning of August 9, 1969, Charlie's followers went on a mission. They were well-equipped. Inside their vehicle they had placed a pair of bolt cutters and a quantity of nylon rope. Linda Kasabian, Susan Atkins and Patricia Krenwinkel jumped in. Tex Watson drove. Charlie instructed: "Leave a sign. You girls know what to do. Something witchy." On the way, Tex told the girls they were going to kill everyone in a house once owned by Doris Day's son, Terry Melcher.

Tex drove up to 10050 Cielo Drive, then leased by director Roman Polanski. Polanski was on a roll. His movies in the '60s included Repulsion and The Fearless Vampire Killers, as well as the runaway hit, Rosemary's Baby. On this night, he was in Europe.

His wife, actress Sharon Tate, 8-1/2 months pregnant, was at home entertaining friends: coffee heiress Abigail Folger, hairstylist Jay Sebring and Voityck Frykowski.

It was Steve Parent's misfortune to have picked that particular night to visit the Polanskis' caretaker, Bill Garretson, in a separate dwelling on the estate. Steve was in his car, just about to pull away, when he spotted Tex Watson.

According to later testimony, Steve said, "Hey, what are you doing here?" Tex thrust his .22-calibre revolver into the open driver's window. As Steve said, "Please don't hurt me," Tex pulled the trigger five times. He probably thought he had killed the caretaker. Inside his house, Bill Garretson heard nothing. He would not hear a sound the rest of the night.

Once inside Polanski's house, Tex accosted Frykowski. He shouted, "I'm the devil! I'm here to do the devil's business!" The girls were instructed to secure Frykowski with nylon rope. Abigail Folger was found reading in bed in her room. Sharon Tate was lying in bed in another room. Jay Sebring, fully clothed, sat on the bed talking to Sharon. All the occupants of the house were gathered together in the living room.

It was killing time. Jay Sebring was shot by Tex for suggesting that the gang should allow Sharon to sit down. After all, she was pregnant. While Sebring lay on the floor, unconscious, Tex kicked him in the head.

Abigail and Sharon were tied around the neck with nylon cord. One end of the cord was tossed over a beam. Susan Atkins pulled the rope taut. Abigail and Sharon had to stand straight up or strangle. Tex announced that they were all about to die. He ordered Susan to kill. She complied, stabbing Voityck Frykowski repeatedly. When Frykowski continued to struggle, Tex clubbed the wounded man with his gun and shot him. Frykowski made it outside before being killed on the lawn. Later, 51 separate stab wounds were found on his body.

Sharon and Abigail frantically struggled to free themselves. Abigail was successful. She ran to the back door. Patricia Krenwinkel stabbed at her wildly, but Abigail warded off the blows, her hands and arms now horribly cut. Tex spotted the melee. He ran over and cut Abigail's throat and abdomen.

Outside the house, Linda Kasabian stood watch. She observed Steve Parent's body in his vehicle. She saw Frykowski stagger out, screaming for help. It certainly was an action-filled night. Linda wondered how much money would be taken from such a nice home. Inside, the killing continued. Sharon Tate, unattended for a few moments, freed herself. She started toward her front door, but was seen by Patricia Krenwinkel. Patricia solicitously assisted Sharon to a chair. Then Susan Atkins held her, while Tex Watson stabbed her to death. The three members of Charlie's family took turns stabbing the body.

It was quiet. Tex decorated the bodies with nylon rope. Susan wrote the word "PIG" in blood on the door. Only 30 minutes had elapsed. It was so very quiet. Everyone was dead. Sharon's black kitten meowed forlornly amidst the silent bodies.

Charlie would be delighted. As they drove, the family members changed out of their bloody clothing. Blood soaked garments and knives were tossed out of the car. Tex's revolver was thrown into a ravine.

Back at the Spahn ranch, the children of evil reported to Satan. He was pleased. They were tired. Everyone slept well.

Next morning, the scene of death was discovered. Horror swept Los Angeles. America—and ultimately the entire world—was made aware of the ritual-type massacre that had taken place in exclusive Benedict Canyon.

Charlie and his children were ecstatic at the publicity his crime was receiving. It had been a commendable job, but messy. That very night they would do it all again, but Satan himself would lead the way.

Linda Kasabian drove the '59 Ford to the home of grocery chain store owner Leno LaBianca, 44, at 3301 Waverly Dr. His wife, Rosemary, 38, was in bed when Charlie Manson appeared in the living room waving a sword at her husband. Charlie tied the LaBiancas standing up back to back.

Charlie walked out of the house. His family, waiting in the car, was ready for action. It was killing time again.

Tex Watson, Leslie Van Houten and Patricia Krenwinkel were given their instructions. After the job was completed, they were to hitchhike back to the ranch. Linda Kasabian and Charlie sped off.

The killing squad did their work efficiently. They led Rosemary into the bedroom, where they stabbed her to death. Leno was killed in the living room. Neither victim panicked until the very end. Tex carved the word WAR on Leno LaBianca's chest. Using the dead man's blood, they wrote DEATH TO PIGS on the walls. On the refrigerator door, Patricia wrote HEALTER SKEALTER. The killing squad then bathed and raided the fridge. Killing was hard work, but it was worth it. The LaBiancas' house was quiet. The family left.

Rosemary's children by a previous marriage called on the house of death and the second night of horror was made known to the world. The ritualistic aspects of the two killing sprees linked them forever. They became known as the Tate-LaBianca murders.

As the days turned into weeks without the killers being apprehended, famous movie actors such as Warren Beatty, Peter Sellers and Yul Brynner established a reward of $25,000 for the apprehension and conviction of the killers.

Weeks turned into months. The family kept busy. They stole gasoline and robbed indiscriminately. One man, Shorty Shea, 40, somehow found out details of the Tate-LaBianca killings. Charlie's clan, led by Steve Grogan, tortured, killed and buried Shorty in the desert.

By the end of September, members of the Manson family were being rounded up for minor crimes. Many were in and out of jail on various charges. Fingerprints recovered at murder scenes were checked against suspects. Snitches were placed in cells. A myriad of evidence pointed to the family as perpetrators of the Tate-LaBianca murders. Finally, the family's leader was taken into custody.

The world was shocked. These suspects were young girls from middle class American families. They likened their leader to Jesus Christ and displayed no remorse for what they had done. Tex Watson was a high school track star from Texas. Leslie Van Houten had been a small town high school princess. Yet these same young people had stabbed a pregnant woman and stuck a fork in the stomach of a man they had just killed.

Somewhere in the deep recesses of his mind, Charlie Manson believed that the blacks of the world would rise against the whites. He would be the catalyst, the trigger that would change the world. Instead, his madness was directly responsible for nine known deaths.

The Manson Family received various prison sentences for their part in the summer of horror. Their leader was sentenced to death on eight counts of first degree murder, but his sentence was commuted to life imprisonment during the short time when the state of California abolished capital punishment.

Now, 25 years later, Charlie, Squeaky Fromme, Robert Beausoleil, Susan Atkins and Patricia Krenwinkel are still in prison. Leslie Van Houten has obtained a university degree in psychology and literature and is still serving her time. Tex Watson remains in prison, where he has sired three children via conjugal visits.

Linda Kasabian, who testified for the state in return for immunity from prosecution, is now living in New Hampshire. Diane Lake, who also testified for the state, is believed to be working for a large corporation in California.

LUIS MONGE

ALMOST everyone is familiar with the saga of Gary Mark Gilmore and his execution before a Utah firing squad on January 17, 1977. With Gilmore's death capital punishment returned to the United States after an absence of nine years, seven months, and 14 days.

Gilmore's execution grasped the notorious mantle of "last man to be executed in the United States" from a far less known murderer. Unlike Gilmore, Luis Jose Monge was not an habitual criminal. In fact, for all but a very short period of his life, Monge was a good husband and an ideal father. Yet his crime was a horrible and disgusting one.

After the death of his parents when he was 11, Luis was sent from his native Puerto Rico to Brooklyn, N.Y., where he was raised by assorted relatives. He left school after completing Grade 10 and took a series of jobs until he was 22, when he joined the Army Air Corps. While stationed at Lowrey Air Force Base near Denver, Colorado, Luis met Dolores Mitla. The young couple married in 1944.

Luis received his discharge and became a successful insurance salesman. He always wanted a large closely knit family. Dolores agreed. By 1961 Luis and Dolores were the proud parents of seven boys and two girls.

Luis Monge was a happy, rather handsome middle-aged man who loved his wife and children. His home, while not lavishly furnished, was more than adequate. No one could honestly say that the large family went without any of the necessities of life.

Luis was somewhat of an athlete and loved to coach his children at various sports. The large family almost made up a team. Luis enjoyed playing baseball and football with his boys and table tennis and volleyball with the girls. When he wasn't actively participating in sports with his family, Luis sang in his church choir. He attended mass regularly.

Despite his outward appearance of tranquility and contentment, Luis was a troubled man. Unknown to the members of his family he had developed a deep rooted sexual attraction for one of his own daughters. Seven-year-old Janet loved her father. She loved to be kissed and hugged, but sometimes her father invented special games just for her. The child became afraid and told her mother.

Dolores was appalled upon hearing of Janet's suspicions. She couldn't believe her ears. She faced her husband with the dreadful accusation. Luis quickly told his wife of his problem. Crying in shame he swore that he would be able to control himself and would never again touch his child in an improper manner. Dolores believed Luis, but warned him that if such an incident ever occurred again she would leave him.

Years passed and Luis was able to control his unhealthy sexual urges. In April 1961, Luis Monge dropped out of sight. Dolores reported him missing. As suddenly as he disappeared he reappeared two months later. He had been in New Orleans and told his family that he had suffered from amnesia. They accepted his explanation, and soon life was as it always had been. Luis was once more the loving husband and father. Once again the family played sports together and partook of formal Sunday dinners.

But Luis had lied to his family. His unnatural feelings towards his daughter had resurfaced. Rather than succumb to these feelings he had run away. Now, two months later, he had overcome his strange infatuation toward his daughter. It was safe to return home.

By 1963 Luis' family had increased. He now had 10 children, with an eleventh due that August. The oldest was 18.

On Friday, June 28, 1963, the Monge family were sleeping peacefully in their beds. All except Luis. The urge to touch his daughter Janet overtook the tormented man. Janet, now 13, was no longer the child her father fondled years before. She lay sleeping in an upstairs bedroom with her 16-year-old sister, Anna. As if in a trance, Luis climbed the stairs and entered the girls' bedroom. He sat on the edge of the bed. Slowly his hands reached under the bedclothes. Luis Monge, loving husband, and devoted father to 10 children, was in a state of sexual excitement.

Suddenly Anna sat bolt upright in bed. She shouted, "What are you doing?" Luis tried to placate Anna, but she wouldn't listen. He fled from the room.

Luis Monge paced the floor of his living room. In a single moment he had lost the love of his family. His wife would have nothing more to do with him. He had run away once, but that was no answer this time. It was too late. His family would hate him. Outsiders would learn of his shame.

Luis Monge, loving husband and devoted father, decided to kill his entire family and himself as well.

He picked up a large poker and slowly entered his wife's bedroom. Dolores didn't move as several blows rained down on her head. Then, acting in a deliberate manner, Luis picked up his stiletto and stabbed his 11-month-old baby to death. He neatly placed the body of the baby beside his wife.

Thomas, 4, was the next to die. He too was placed in bed with his mother and baby sister. Freddie, 6, his father's favorite, was clubbed to death with the poker and placed with the other bodies.

Luis had intended to kill all his family and then kill himself with carbon monoxide in his garage. Later, he couldn't explain what made him stop. Possibly the whimpering of his favorite child, Freddie, brought him to his senses. Whatever the reason, Luis picked up the telephone and called the police: "I just killed my wife and three of my kids. You'd better come over before I kill somebody else."

Within minutes police arrived and were greeted by the macabre sight of the four bodies neatly arranged in bed. Taken to a police station, Luis revealed many of the facts that are related here. Psychiatric examination indicated that he was legally sane. Throughout his questioning by police and psychiatrists, Luis insisted that he wanted to die for his crimes as fast as possible, and not bring further shame and disgrace to his family.

All seven of Luis Monge's surviving children, accompanied by an uncle and aunt, visited their father before he stood trial. Each one in turn embraced their father and told him that they forgave him for what he had done. They reasoned that their father was suffering from a mental illness. Later, the family was allowed to have Sunday dinner with Luis. It was like old times. Luis held court as his loving family showed their respect for the head of the house.

Eventually Monge was found guilty and sentenced to death. On March 20, 1964, he was transferred to Death Row in Colorado State Prison, where he lingered for three months. On June 2, Luis Monge was escorted to the gas chamber by Warden Wayne Patterson. Meanwhile, in Denver, Gov. Love remained near his telephone. He had promised to grant a last-minute reprieve if Monge requested it. As Luis entered the gas chamber, he glanced at the telephone, but he didn't hesitate.

At precisely 8:04 p.m. sodium cyanide pellets were dropped into receptacles containing acid. Luis Monge breathed deeply and slumped into unconsciousness.

It would be nine years before Gary Gilmore would defiantly utter his last words, "Let's do it." Luis Monge was no longer the last man to be executed in the United States.

WAYNE NANCE

MISSOULA, Montana is in the heart of Big Sky Country, where the Marlboro man mounts his trusty steed and gallops off into the fading sunset. It was also the home of Wayne Nance, serial killer extraordinaire.

Wayne was born in 1955 to Charlene and George Nance. Charlene worked as a waitress, while George was employed as a trucker. The family lived in a trailer park just outside town.

As a small boy, Wayne was often in minor scrapes, but excelled in school. Sometimes he displayed a hair trigger temper and occasionally fought with his school chums. Still, no one gave a second thought to his often unwarranted outbreaks. Other little boys have temper tantrums. They don't turn out to be serial killers.

Wayne sailed through grade school. In high school he displayed a deep interest in Satanism, which was a popular topic with many teenagers in the '70s. Other than belaboring the subject with schoolmates, Wayne didn't make waves.

Donna and Harvey Pounds were poor, hardworking and religious. Donna worked part-time at the Christian Book Store in Missoula. Harvey was employed in the shoe department at Yandt's Men's Store, but his real interest was religion. He was a deacon of the Bethel Baptist Church and had just been appointed pastor of a church in nearby Stevensville. The Pounds had three children; a son, Kenny, in the army, and two daughters, Karen, 20, and Kathy, 12, living at home with their parents. All were excited at their father's appointment.

The anticipation of a new beginning was to change forever on April 11, 1974. Karen and Harvey were at work. Kathy was in school. Donna was home alone.

The intruder was wearing rubber gloves. He had found Harvey's .22 calibre Luger and encountered Donna in the master bedroom. The man had come prepared. From his black gym bag he extracted lengths of clothesline, which he used to tie Donna's arms and legs to the posts of her bed. After raping the defenceless woman, he untied her and led her down to the family's unfinished basement. Donna was forced to crawl under the stairwell. Her attacker retied her arms and legs. Then he coolly shot her five times in the back of the head.

Harvey came home from work, discovered his wife's body and called police. A bloodstained surgical glove found behind the Pounds' home, along with the cords dangling from the bedposts, were removed for laboratory analysis.

Wayne Nance was a neighbor of the Pounds. He knew where Harvey kept his .22 Luger. When a witness claimed to have seen someone who looked like Wayne near the Pounds' home on the day of the killing, Wayne was questioned. He denied any connection with the crime, stating that he hadn't been feeling well that day and had stayed home from school. He was alone all day.

Detectives searched his home and discovered a black gym bag and a bloodstained pair of underwear, which had recently been washed. The bloodstain, although identified as human, could not be classified. No matching clothesline cord was found in the house.

Wayne was a serious suspect, but nothing of a concrete nature was found to connect him with the murder. When detectives learned that Harvey may have been involved with another woman, he too fell under suspicion, but again authorities met a blank wall. There was no direct evidence connecting either man with the crime. Both took polygraph tests. Harvey's results were inconclusive. Wayne's indicated that he was telling the truth and had no guilty knowledge of the crime.

Two months after Donna Pounds' murder, Wayne graduated from high school. A few days later, he joined the navy. When he was charged with possession of marijuana for the second time, he was given a general discharge. After having served two years, Wayne moved back into the trailer in Missoula with his parents. For a while, he kicked around town, but soon took a night job as a bouncer at a western bar known as The Cabin. By day, he worked at Conlin's Furniture Store as delivery and set-up man for their products.

It should be pointed out that Wayne was well liked. Sure, some folks called him weird, with his odd collection of knives and all, but generally speaking, as the years sped by, no one took much notice of Wayne Nance.

Many employees of The Cabin were pleased when Wayne started to date a girl named Robin, who just happened to be passing through town. In time, Robin moved in with Wayne and his father. Unfortunately, Wayne's mother had been killed in a car accident while under the influence of alcohol. According to Wayne, on September 28, 1984, Robin left town after being his woman for the best part of the summer.

Almost three months later, on the afternoon of Christmas Eve, a wildlife photographer tramping through the woods outside Missoula spotted a human foot sticking out of the earth. An autopsy indicated that the unidentified female had been dead for approximately three months. No one had been reported missing from Missoula during that time span. Much later, this body was identified as Robin.

On December 12, 1985, Mike and Teresa Shook and their three children— Matt, 7, Luke, 4, and Megan, 2—had finished their evening meal when someone knocked at the front door and entered their house, barking out commands. By the time the intruder left, Mike Shook lay stabbed to death on the floor. Teresa was raped and stabbed in the chest. She, too, was dead. The killer then set the house on fire. Miraculously, the fire didn't spread and the three children were found by a friend the next morning, unconscious and in critical condition from smoke inhalation. All three would survive.

Down at Conlin's Furniture, Wayne was considered the best delivery man in their employ. He was obliging to all the salesladies and in particular, the store manager, Kris Wells. Wayne had a crush on Kris and she knew it. She went out of her way not to encourage his flattery. She even discussed Wayne's infatuation with her husband Doug. They agreed that it was harmless. They were wrong.

On a brisk fall night in September 1986, Kris and Doug returned to their home around midnight. After Kris retired for the night, Doug thought he spotted someone outside. He went out and discovered Wayne Nance. Incredulous, Doug asked him what he was doing there. Wayne explained that he had been driving by the house and thought he had spotted a prowler. He suggested Doug get a flashlight and take a look. As Doug turned to enter his home, he was struck a severe blow on the back of his head. Bleeding profusely, Doug fell to the floor and saw Wayne, wild-eyed, lunging in his direction. Doug was able to rise and struggle with his attacker. From the bedroom, Kris heard the commotion. She rushed to Doug's side in time to see Wayne pull a revolver out of his pocket. He shouted, "Get back. I've got a gun!"

Kris backed off. Doug sank to the floor. Although weak, he didn't lose consciousness. Kris begged Wayne to tell them why he was doing this. He said that he wanted money to get out of town. Wayne forced Kris to tie her husband's hands and feet. He then tied her hands behind her back and carried her down the hall to the bedroom. Once there, he tied her hands to the bedframe and returned to Doug.

Wayne untied Doug's legs and forced him down into the basement. He struck Doug on the back of the head and tied him by the neck to a post. He then left to check up on Kris. He soon returned. Doug, barely conscious, was horrified when Wayne straddled his legs and slowly stuck an eight-inch knife into his chest just below the heart. Doug Wells thought he was about to die but, despite the beating, loss of blood and the stab wound, he did not lose consciousness. He watched as Wayne removed the knife from his chest.

When Wayne went upstairs once again to check on Kris, Doug managed to free himself and locate his own Savage 250 rifle. He staggered upstairs and made a noise, knowing it would attract Wayne. As his adversary appeared in the hallway, Doug fired. The slug ripped through Wayne's side, but the fallen man was able to crawl on his hands and knees. Doug swung his rifle, striking Wayne on the head and back over and over again until he finally shattered the rifle's wooden stock. Wayne was able to get out his own revolver. Doug swung his rifle at the revolver just as Wayne fired, deflecting the shot directly into Wayne's head. Wayne fired again. This time, the bullet struck Doug in the leg just above the knee. Despite this added wound, Doug rained blow after blow on Wayne's head until Wayne was nothing more than a bloody hulk cowering in a corner. Doug disarmed Wayne and told the now-freed Kris to call 911. He lay down on the bed, convinced he was about to die.

Both men were rushed to hospital. Wayne died soon after he arrived. Courageous Doug Wells miraculously survived.

I have related here the four murders officially attributed to Wayne Nance. Several other unsolved murders, which took place around Missoula during the many years Wayne lived in the area, are believed to have been perpetrated by him.

Because Kris and Doug Wells experienced the horror of being attacked by a serial killer, they often attend sessions at Quantico, Virginia, where the FBI maintains a Behaviorial Science Unit studying serial killers.

CHARLES NG

MARK Twain immortalized Calaveras County with his humorous tale of a frog who refused to jump because its stomach was full of buckshot. The Celebrated Jumping Frog of Calaveras County has delighted readers for over 100 years. The famed author had no way of knowing that the isolated area 250 kms. northeast of San Francisco would make headlines around the world in 1985 as the scene of a series of the most horrendous crimes ever committed in the United States.

No one paid much attention to the odd couple who lived together on a ranch outside the tiny town of Wilseyville. One was a big man with a bushy beard, who liked to strut around in army fatigues. He explained away the cinder block bunker on the three-acre ranch as being a survival capsule in case of nuclear attack. Leonard Lake didn't even cause any raised eyebrows in Calaveras County. Neither did his slight, 25-year-old Chinese friend, Charles Ng, who hardly spoke to anyone.

Lake, a former U.S. Marine, had served a stretch in Vietnam, but didn't see any action. In the summer of 1982, he met Ng, whose background was far different. Ng was born and educated in Hong Kong and later attended a private school in England. After graduation in 1977, he returned to Hong Kong, where he worked for a short while as a teacher. A year later, he travelled to San Francisco and attended Notre Dame College. In 1979, he left Notre Dame to join the U.S. Marines.

Ng orchestrated a robbery of firearms from a Marine armory and was sentenced to 14 years imprisonment. This sentence was later reduced to three years. In 1982, he was released from prison and teamed up with Leonard Lake. It was to be an unholy alliance.

On Sunday, June 2, 1985, in San Francisco, a slight Chinese man walked out of a lumberyard hardware store without paying for a $75 vice. A clerk alerted Officer Daniel Wright, who happened to be close by. Wright immediately spotted the man putting the vice in the trunk of his Honda Prelude. At the same time, the young man spotted the police officer and took off on foot with Wright in pursuit. Wright was unable to catch his man. When he returned to the car, he was met by a bearded man, who identified himself as Robin Stapley.

It's all a mistake, Stapley said. He thought I had paid for it. Wright peered in the trunk of the car. Spotting a tote bag, he inquired as to its contents. Stapley said, "I don't know. It must belong to that young fellow who was with me."

Wright opened the bag and found a .22 calibre automatic pistol equipped with a silencer. He informed Stapley that silencers were illegal and that he would have to accompany him to the police station. Stapley readily consented. At the station he claimed to have no connection with the silencer. He said he didn't know his companion, Charles Ng, that well, but had planned to hire him to do some work around his ranch.

Abruptly, Stapley asked for a glass of water. He gulped down a pill with the water. Within a few seconds, he collapsed. Police officers were sure their suspect had suffered a heart attack. Rushed to hospital, Stapley was found to be brain dead and was placed on a life support machine. A few days later, he was removed from the machine and died.

A police check revealed that one Robin Stapley had been reported missing five months earlier. Since then, his pickup and camper had been in a slight accident, having collided with a tractor. The accident had been reported. A Chinese man was driving the missing Stapley pickup truck.

Police now did a computer check on the Honda Prelude. It belonged to Paul Cosner, a San Francisco used car dealer, who had been reported missing seven months earlier when he went out with the Honda to deliver it to a customer. Meanwhile, a fingerprint check on the man on the life support system in the hospital proved that he was not Robin Stapley, but Leonard Lake.

A check with the National Crime Information Computer revealed that Leonard Lake had jumped bail. He had been charged with burglary, possession of explosives and illegal automatic weapons, and had been hiding out in his isolated Calaveras County ranch since 1982. Apparently Ng had been his companion since that time.

Police realized that they were not dealing with a simple case of shoplifting, but quite possibly a series of killings. Lake and Ng were now directly connected to two missing persons: Robin Stapley and Paul Cosner. There would be more.

Equipped with search warrants, police drove to the Lake ranch. They observed what appeared to be an average clapboard house. Adjacent to the house was Lake's survival bunker. Inside the house, officers found handcuffs and chains. In the bedroom, they observed eye bolts screwed into the ceiling.

Officer Irene Brunn spotted a new VCR in a corner. She had recently investigated the disappearance of a family in San Francisco. Deborah and Harvey Dubs and their 16-month-old son had simply vanished. Neighbors had noticed a young Chinese man removing furniture from the Dubs' apartment. Among the missing items was a VCR. Officer Brunn had been able to locate the store which had sold the VCR and to obtain the serial numbers. It was the machine found in Lake's home.

Meanwhile, outside the house on a hillside, police officers made gruesome discoveries. Tiny particles of bone and baby teeth were found on the ground. The door to the bunker was forced open. Water, canned goods and firearms were scattered about. A trap door led underground. Enlarged photos of several girls in various stages of undress lined the walls. A filing cabinet held video cassettes. It is from these cassettes that we know the diabolical nature of the alleged killers and the fate of their hapless victims.

One of the cassettes depicts Deborah Dubs bound on a chair. Another shows Kathleen Allen, 18, who had disappeared from a supermarket in 1985, being forced to disrobe and ordered to do anything Lake desired. On the same tape, Brenda O'Connor, who disappeared with her husband Lonny and their infant son, is handcuffed and bound in chains. She is begging for the welfare of her baby and is told by the two men that they have given the baby away. Then, one of the men, whom police say is Charles Ng, cuts off her bra when she refuses the order to undress.

While a total of 60 officers gathered evidence of the mass slaughter of men, women and children, an all-points bulletin was issued for Charles Ng. He had become one of the most wanted men in the world, sought by the FBI, Scotland Yard, Interpol and the RCMP.

More horrors were uncovered. Two 500-page diaries belonging to Lake were found on the property. In them, he described torture, rape and murder. He also philosophically commented that females were nothing more than sex slaves meant to succumb to his every desire.

During the search for fragments of bodies, investigators learned that Ng's one friend, Michael Sean Carroll, and his girlfriend, had been missing for a month, and Carroll's driver's licence was found in Lake's house.

The gruesome search continued. Several missing persons were positively identified as having met their deaths at the Lake ranch. In all, it is believed that at least 25 murders took place there.

Where was the only living person who had allegedly taken part in the slaughter? Where was Charles Ng?

In the weeks following the horrible discoveries near Wilseyville, Ng made his way to Detroit, crossing the border into Windsor. From there he travelled to Chatham, then to Sudbury, and on to Calgary, Alberta.

On a pleasant July day, a month after Ng ran from Officer Wright in San Francisco, security officers George Forrester and Sean Doyle spotted a man shoplifting in a Calgary Hudson's Bay store. When accosted, Ng pulled a .22 calibre pistol from his belt. Two shots were fired. Doyle was superficially wounded in the hand, but the men succeeded in disarming the shoplifter. Ng was quickly identified as he was carrying his authentic driver's licence on his person.

Ng was tried and convicted of assault, robbery and illegal use of a firearm, all charges pertaining to offences which took place in Calgary. He was sentenced to four-and-a-half years imprisonment.

Ironically, Ng, who faces several murder charges in the U.S., is protected from extradition by Canadian law, which stipulates that because there is no death penalty in Canada, the prisoner may not be extradited to a state where the death penalty exists, unless the requesting state provides assurances that the death penalty will not be implemented.

Since California has the death penalty, this left a suspected mass murderer in a Canadian prison, affording him the right to fight extradition upon release from prison and to avoid standing trial for murder.

Despite the legal ramifications, Ng was returned to California. He has been tried, convicted and sentenced to death.

JOEL RIFKIN

WHEN we conjure up thoughts of the modern serial killer, we picture a derelict wandering the countryside, stealing, raping and killing at random. Many serial killers fit this mold, but the man known as the Long Island Serial Killer was quite different.

Joel Rifkin was brought up in a middle class neighbourhood, had loving parents and a better than average education. Something went drastically wrong. Joel, his mother Jeanne and his sister Jan, lived together at 1492 Garden St. in East Meadow, Long Island. They were a close-knit family. Jeanne mourned her late husband Ben, who had succumbed to prostate cancer some years before Joel began his diabolical exploits.

Back in 1959, when the Rifkins learned they couldn't have children, they adopted newborn Joel. Three years later they adopted Jan. Shortly after Jan's adoption, they moved to Garden St. in East Meadow, where, for all intents and purposes, the children were raised in a middle class environment. Jeanne, whose hobby was gardening, soon found that Joel shared her interest. It wasn't unusual to see mother and son laboring over their showplace garden on sunny summer afternoons. Jeanne had high hopes for her son, whose IQ tested at 129. He would be a doctor or a judge. Joel would one day make the Rifkin family proud.

When the apple of his mother's eye started high school, it was evident that he wasn't a personality kid. There was nothing you could put your finger on. Joel just wasn't well liked. In addition, he was skinny and awkward. Other kids soon learned that they could tease Joel and make him the brunt of their practical jokes without fear of reprisal. Despite his unhappy social life, Joel graduated from East Meadow High in 1977 with better than average marks.

Now watch their son soar, thought Jeanne and Ben Rifkin. For a short while it appeared that Jeanne's aspirations for her son would bear fruit. Joel enrolled in State University at Brockport, but two years later he dropped out and moved back home with his parents. Joel tried a local college. He lasted only a few years before abandoning his studies to pursue menial jobs at minimum wages. None of these jobs had any permanence. Joel was a ship without a rudder. Jeanne couldn't fathom her son. Maybe he just needed more time to settle down than other boys. Soon Joel would find his niche, just you wait and see.

Joel aspired to be a writer, but didn't write much. He tried his hand at photography, but soon lost interest. He drifted from job to job. In time, Jeanne stopped cleaning his room or making his bed. She agreed with him when he explained that a man required some privacy. Joel's room was his alone, off limits to other members of the family.

Ben Rifkin, respected volunteer of many community charities and services, committed suicide by taking an overdose rather than linger through the last weeks of his painful illness. Ben left a note, asking his Jeanne to forgive him. He was 68. It was February 20, 1987. His son Joel was 28 years old.

Unknown to members of his family, Joel had, since high school days, sought out the favors of prostitutes. He would drive into Manhattan in his mother's Toyota and cruise the streets for hours. Joel was fussy. He preferred petite girls. From $30 to $50 changed hands and willing girls performed their skills in Mrs. Rifkin's car. The money he spent on women left Joel perpetually broke. After all, he seldom worked at any job that brought in more than the minimum wage.

The summer after his father's death, Joel brought joy to his mother's heart when he announced that he planned to be a landscaper. He had a natural talent for the work and intended to further his education, this time in a field he really enjoyed. He enrolled in the agricultural program at State University at Farmingdale. Initially, as with most things, Joel did well and actually obtained a job which lasted almost a year as a result of his specialized studies in horticulture. Running true to form, by the spring of 1989, Joel had lost interest and left both school and his position. He placated his mother by assuring her that it was now time for him to go into the landscaping business on his own. Jeanne helped him purchase a 1978 Chevy van and a trailer.

Because of his rather impressive credentials, Joel was successful in obtaining several contracts to take care of local estates. The future looked bright for a time, but it didn't take long before Joel was neglecting lawns, showing up late for appointments or not showing up at all. Soon, contracts were cancelled. Coincidental with his business failure, Joel neglected his personal appearance. He wore dirty clothing and let his unkempt hair grow long.

It is difficult to pinpoint what drove Joel Rifkin to murder. For years he had been denied a normal social life. Worse still, he had often been ridiculed by fellow students and later by colleagues. Shunned by girls, he had sought out prostitutes to satisfy his sexual urges. But it wasn't enough.

Little is known of Joel's first two victims. Their bodies have never been found. Joel has told police that he picked up two prostitutes, one in 1989 and one in 1990, and had sex with each before strangling them. He dissected their bodies and disposed of the body parts in New York Harbor and in the ocean off New Jersey. Years later, he couldn't remember the exact locations.

Joel purchased two old Mazda pickups for his almost non-existent landscaping business. No one, not even his family, took much notice of Joel's coming and going. After all, that's what landscapers do; they travel from job to job. No one pays much attention. Joel even rented space to store his trailer and other equipment. Whether he planned it or not, he now had adequate transportation to move bodies, a place to store them and an occupation which allowed him freedom of movement without being conspicuous.

In May 1991, Joel picked up Barbara Jacobs. Barbara, 32, was a well-known prostitute with a drug problem. She worked hard on Manhattan's Lower East Side to earn the money to support her habit. The petite Barbara fit the pattern of Joel's victims. Her body was found in a garbage bag near the Hudson River on July 14, 1991.

Whatever brake mechanism had restrained Joel Rifkin in the past was now out of control. It was 31-year-old Yun Lee's misfortune to be spotted by Joel as she was walking the streets, looking to turn a trick. A few words of conversation and the tiny prostitute made a deal. Her body was found on September 23, 1991, squeezed into a steamer trunk floating down the Harlem River.

Unlike Joel's previously known victims, Mary Ellen DeLuca had never been arrested, although she was a known drug user. Mary Ellen left her home in Valley Stream periodically to live on the streets of New York, but she always returned to her parents' home. On September 1, 1991, she left their residence and never returned. Somewhere along the way, she crossed paths with Joel Rifkin. On October 1, Mary Ellen's body was found by a man searching through a dump near West Point, the famed military academy. The body was not identified until much later when Joel was arrested. Ironically, Mary Ellen's parents continued the search for their missing daughter long after she had been found and buried.

Joel Rifkin had become a killing machine, yet he was able to function in society without any discernible change in his personality. Both his mother and sister had no hint that the young man living under the same roof was spending his nights prowling the streets of New York seeking out a certain type of prostitute. His method was simple, his supply of victims plentiful and the time to perform his strangulations was unlimited. After his killings, Joel would park his Mazda outside 1492 Garden St. and carry a trophy from his latest victim's body into his bedroom. Items such as a piece of jewelry or a garment would serve to remind Joel of that particular night's work. Like many other serial killers, Joel was a trophy collector.

Around this time in his career, Joel found that it wasn't always convenient to dispose of a body immediately after a kill. Sometimes he stored bodies at his rented space and disposed of them later. This method proved to be tedious. Joel decided to try something new. He purchased four 55-gallon steel drums.

Around Christmastime, Joel picked up a prostitute, strangled her and placed her body in one of his drums. The last he saw of the drum, it was floating down the Harlem River. This particular victim has never been found. The innovative disposal method proved so satisfactory that Joel decided to make use of all his drums. It wasn't until May 13, 1992 that a sanitation worker sighted a steel drum floating in a creek in Brooklyn. A skeletal leg was sticking out of the drum. This unfortunate girl has never been identified.

In January 1992, Joel used his third drum. Twenty-eight-year-old, four-foot 11-inch Lorraine Orvieto had gone down the pike from college graduate and successful businesswoman to confirmed crack cocaine user. She gravitated to prostitution to support her habit. Lorraine had always kept in touch with her middle-class family, but just before Christmas 1991, the phone calls stopped. In July 1992, a fisherman came across a steel drum with Lorraine's skeleton inside.

Around the same time that Lorraine Orvieto was murdered, Joel claimed another victim, Maryann Hollomon, 39. Her body was found in a steel drum off Coney Island. Joel had used up his fourth and last drum.

One must remember that while bodies were floating in steel drums and others were scattered and hidden in woods and bushes, Joel was functioning as a somewhat erratic landscape gardener. No one even mildly suspected him of wrongdoing, nor was anyone aware that a serial killer was at large. Several of the bodies had not been recovered. Some of the girls were listed as missing. Given their addiction to dope and their profession, there was the distinct possibility, if not probability, that they had moved out of the greater New York area.

Iris Sanchez, 25, was strangled and shoved under a mattress near John F. Kennedy International Airport. Her body lay there undiscovered for over a year. Anna Lopez, 33, the mother of three children, was murdered on May 25, 1992. Her body was transported upstate to Putham County and deposited in woods off Interstate 84. Unlike some of the other victims, Anna's body was found within 24 hours by a trucker who entered the woods to relieve himself. Although she was a prostitute and heavy drug user, Anna had always kept in touch with her family and her children. When she failed to contact them, they were sure she had met with foul play. A month and a half later, Anna's family learned of the unidentified woman found in Putham County. At last they knew the fate which had befallen their missing daughter.

As the summer of 1992 drew to a close, Joel killed again. The body, which Joel later admitted cutting into several pieces, has never been identified. It was recovered from a suitcase floating in the East River. Joel also claims to have killed another young woman at this time, but police have as yet been unable to locate the body.

In the fall of 1992, Joel picked up and murdered Mary Catherine Williams, a 31-year-old former cheerleader from the University of North Carolina. Life hadn't been easy for Catherine. Shortly after leaving university, she married, but the marriage had lasted only a few years. Catherine headed for the Big Apple to pursue an acting career. The frustration of being out of work most of the time drove her to cocaine. When the money ran out, she turned to prostitution, and that's how she met up with Joel Rifkin. Catherine's decomposed body was found in Westchester two months later. She was buried as an unidentified Jane Doe in a pauper's grave. Catherine was the only victim Joel couldn't remember killing.

Leah Evens was the daughter of a Manhattan Civil Court judge and a graduate of Sara Lawrence College. Upon graduation, Leah had difficulty finding employment. Like many other young women in similar circumstances, she took a job as a waitress in Manhattan. Leah and a colleague lived together for a few years and had two children, Julian and Eve, before he walked out on the relationship. Leah became despondent and sought to relieve her depression with the use of drugs. Before long she was hooked on crack and was forced to turn to prostitution. On a few occasions, she was arrested for soliciting.

On February 27, 1993, Joel Rifkin paid Leah $40 for sex. Then he strangled her and transported her body in his Mazda pickup over 60 miles to Northampton. Joel buried Leah's body in a shallow grave, which was only discovered three months later when wild vegetable pickers spotted a hand sticking out of the earth. It wasn't until Joel Rifkin was apprehended that authorities learned how Leah Evens had ended up buried in the lonely field.

The murder of Jenny Soto, a 23-year-old prostitute, was indelibly etched in Joel's mind. She didn't die easily. Joel would later state that Jenny struggled ferociously for her life. When her body was found, her fingernails were broken. Underneath some of them was the skin of Joel Rifkin. He had dumped her body in the Bronx at the edge of the Harlem River.

Although Joel's memory of events has in the main been fairly accurate, it has not always been completely reliable. He claims to have murdered Julie Blackbird, 31, who was plying the oldest profession on the streets of New York when she encountered Joel. He has been unsuccessful in leading authorities to her body.

It was a pleasant warm night in June 1993, when Joel cruised New York's Allen St. in his mother's Toyota looking for another victim. He spotted 22-year-old Tiffany Bresciani, who needed a fix badly. Tiffany had left her folks back in Louisiana in 1987 to make her mark as a dancer. Seven years later, she was selling her body to obtain money for drugs. Joel Rifkin paid her $40 for sex before strangling her in his mother's car. He drove the body back to East Meadow, lugged it into the garage and placed it in a wheelbarrow, where it was to remain all weekend in the midsummer heat. In the wee hours of Monday morning, June 28, as his mother and sister slept, Joel transferred the body, which by now was giving off a putrid odor, into the covered bed of his Mazda pickup. Joel pulled out of the driveway and made his way to the Southern State Parkway. He was travelling at the speed limit when he caught the attention of a patrol car. The Mazda's rear licence plate was missing.

Police officers flashed their red light and attempted to pull the Mazda over to the side of the road. Much to their surprise, the driver seemed to ignore them. The officers tried their siren. Still the stubborn driver didn't respond. He neither increased nor decreased his speed. Frustrated, the police activated their loudspeaker, "Pull over to the side of the road!" When they failed to get a reaction, the officers requested backup. Their quarry didn't attempt to get away. He simply wasn't obeying police commands. Soon there were three patrol cars following the driver of the Mazda pickup.

Suddenly, the driver of the pickup stepped on the gas and swung off the main road in an attempt to pull away from the officers on side roads. The ploy didn't work. The Mazda veered out of control and hit a utility pole.

By now, six police cars had joined the chase. The officers approached the Mazda. Inside, Joel wasn't hurt, nor was he armed. They searched him for drugs, but found none. The more experienced officers recognized the pungent odor permeating the area around the Mazda as that of a dead body. Their suspicions were confirmed when they pulled back a blue tarp and gazed at the partially decomposed corpse of Tiffany Bresciani.

Joel was arrested and taken into custody. He answered questions calmly and lucidly. Yes, he was a landscaper who was temporarily without clients. Yes, he had been riding around with a body which he had planned to drop off at some secluded spot. Rather nonchalantly, Joel informed the officers that he had murdered a total of 17 or 18 women over the past few years. He related the horror stories as if he were reciting a nursery rhyme. Emotionless, he informed the amazed police that all his victims had been prostitutes with whom he had had sex before strangling them.

Once he started talking, Joel cooperated fully with police. He directed them to several bodies which had not been found at the time of his arrest. A search of his room uncovered the trophies which proved that his recital of murder was accurate in most details. Items such as Leah Evens' driving licence and employee identification card were found in his room. Police discovered Catherine Williams' credit cards, pictures of Jenny Soto's boyfriend, as well as credit cards belonging to Anna Lopez. And so it went. Joel had surrounded himself with bits of clothing, jewelry and other mementos belonging to his victims.

In his wake, Joel left grieving families to mourn the loss of their loved ones. The insignificant Joel Rifkin, now referred to in the press as the Long Island Serial Killer, gained a degree of infamy by becoming New York State's most prolific mass murderer. He has been found guilty of murder and is currently serving several life sentences in prison.

DANNY ROLLING

SONJA Larson really wanted to live on campus, but all the dorms at the sprawling University of Florida campus in Gainesville were occupied. The 18-year-old education student settled for an apartment at the Williamsburg Village Apartments just a few minutes walk from the university.

Sonja's roommate, architecture student Christina Powell, 17, drove down from Jacksonville. Both girls were looking forward to the next semester. They were exuberant young women, who tragically had only hours to live. Another girl was to join them in a few days to share the apartment. Her delay in arriving saved her life.

Unknown to all, an evil presence was about to descend on the university, an evil so repulsive that officers who have investigated hundreds of homicides over careers which have spanned decades were to state that they had never witnessed a crime scene to equal the horror of the one which greeted them when they entered the girls' apartment.

On Thursday, August 23, 1990, Sonja phoned home to let her father know she had arrived safely in Gainesville. Three days later, on Sunday, Christina Powell's sister and brother knocked on the apartment door, but received no response. They summoned a policeman, who entered the building with the aid of a janitor. When the officer opened the door he was repulsed by the putrid odor of decaying flesh. The sight before him repelled his senses. He closed the door abruptly, barring Christina's brother and sister from entering.

The bodies of the two girls were nude and posed in such a way as to set a macabre scene. The killer had not had sex with either victim, but had extensively mutilated their bodies. Both girls had been stabbed to death, most probably on the previous Thursday night or early Friday morning.

The university community was reeling from the horrendous murders on Monday when Christa Hoyt, an 18-year-old student, failed to report at her part-time job. Christa was the overnight clerk at the Alachua County sheriff's office. She was interested in crime and planned on a career as a crime lab technician.

When she didn't show up by 1 a.m. for her midnight shift, her superior had a deputy check her off-campus apartment. Christa lived alone since her roommate had moved out just a week earlier.

The deputy entered the apartment and was chilled to the bone by the posed scene before him. Christa had been decapitated and her head had been placed on a shelf.

Tracy Paules was a 23-year-old political science student, who had been out of town that weekend, visiting with her boyfriend's parents. She arrived back at the Gatorwood Apartments in Gainesville on Sunday night. She and the rest of the 34,000-student population were well aware of the double murder. But Tracy didn't have the concern of other girls living alone. She shared her apartment with Manny Taboada, a six-foot, two-inch, 200-pound fellow student. Tracy and Manny were not romantically involved, but were good friends.

On Monday, Tracy talked to several friends about the murders. By Monday afternoon, the news of the third victim had become common knowledge. Tracy was worried, but she did have big Manny for protection. On Monday night, a friend became concerned when Tracy didn't answer her phone. Next morning, a janitor, using a pass key, entered the apartment. He found Tracy and Manny. Both had been stabbed to death while they slept.

Detectives ascertained that all five victims were most probably killed during a 72-hour time span. The killer had lingered in the three apartments. In the case of Christa Hoyt, he had stripped her of her clothing, bound her with duct tape and stabbed her to death. Her body had been horribly mutilated after death.

The killer then went about cleaning the body with a germicide. The absence of blood at such a violent crime scene was unusual and gave an eerie appearance to the stage setting the killer obviously took some time to create. Detectives believe that the murderer would have been unable to clean the floor of blood stains. They feel he must have used some sort of drop cloth, which has never been found.

Investigators are reluctant to reveal details of the crimes, but it is known that the diabolical killer used mirrors to heighten the horror for the first people to come across the staged settings he had constructed.

The murderer of the five students had taken the time to obliterate his finger-prints from anything he had touched in all three apartments. This attention to detail was unusual and was frustrating to detectives. He had virtually cleaned the apartments of all clues which could be used to trace his identity.

An attempt was made to connect the four female victims. All were attractive brunettes who were excellent students, but other than attending university, they had nothing else in common. The occupants of the three apartments did not know each other.

Fear gripped Gainesville, as law enforcement agencies stepped up the hunt for the killer. Initially, part-time University of Florida student Ed Humphrey was a major suspect. A few days after the series of murders, Humphrey was picked up after he had severely beaten his 79-year-old grandmother. Ed had known Tracy Paules and had lived close to her apartment. He turned out to be a madman, but he wasn't the Gainesville serial killer. Humphrey is presently confined to a state mental institution and is no longer considered a suspect in the case.

Stymied in obtaining a speedy solution to the murders, police proceeded to employ routine and time consuming methods of investigation. It was this plodding which brought Danny Rolling to their attention.

Danny was a big man who had served time in three states, as well as an Alabama mental institution. Three months before the Gainesville murders, he had shot his father, retired police officer Lt. James Rolling, in the head. Father and son had argued. Danny had wrested a gun from his father and, after shooting him in the head, had kicked the fallen man. He then shot his father in the stomach. Lt. Rolling survived. That same night, Danny held up a couple he knew in Shreveport, Louisiana, relieving them of $30 and some food.

Danny made his way to Florida. On September 7, only 10 days after the student murders, he held up a Winn-Dixie supermarket in Ocala. Police were called and a car chase ensued, in which Danny wrecked the stolen Mustang he was driving. The desperate man was taken into custody. A Colt revolver and ammunition were recovered from the vehicle.

Police had no idea that Rolling was in any way connected with the Gainesville murders. In a routine manner they were obtaining hair samples and blood from prisoners arrested since the murders. Although authorities are not revealing details, it is believed that DNA "fingerprinting" has placed Rolling in the Gainesville victims' apartments.

Danny Rolling has been found guilty of the attempted murder of his father and of several other crimes he committed both before and after the Gainesville tragedy. He is serving a life sentence for these crimes in Florida State Penitentiary.

Since being incarcerated, Rolling has confessed to the murders of the five Gainesville students and has been sentenced to death. He currently resides on Florida's Death Row.

ARTHUR SHAWCROSS

ARTHUR Shawcross was a Vietnam veteran with a problem. Upon returning to civilian life he was in and out of trouble, serving some time in prison.

In 1972, Art and his wife Penny resided in Watertown, New York. On the afternoon of June 4, 11-year-old Jack Blake followed Art wherever he went. Art took shortcuts through remote fields, but still, according to Art, the youngster followed him. Finally, Art lost his temper and struck the boy a vicious blow to the head. Jack fell to the ground. Art walked away. Three days later he returned to the scene and covered the boy's body with leaves and debris.

Three months later, Art was fishing when eight-year-old Karen Ann Hill strolled up to the river bank. The strange urges which motivated his evil deeds came to the fore once more. Karen Ann was raped and strangled. Art covered her body with stones and mud. But this time was different. He had been seen with the little girl.

Questioned by police in the presence of a public defender, Art was able to cop a plea. In return for his confession and revealing the location of the bodies, he was allowed to plead guilty to manslaughter in the case of Jack Blake. He was never formally charged with any crime concerning Karen Ann Hill.

Art was sentenced to the relatively light term of 25 years imprisonment. The enraged community was assured that without his cooperation the cases might never have been solved. At any rate, Art Shawcross would be out of circulation for a long long time.

Fifteen years passed. In March 1987, Art was paroled. The community of Watertown adamantly insisted that he not be paroled to their town. Art agreed. He didn't want to go to a place where he was thought of as a monster.

Art was paroled with a stringent reporting schedule and other tight restrictions to the city of Binghamton. While Art was in prison, his wife divorced him and he became a pen pal of Rose Walley. Rose visited the prison and, upon Art's release, the pair married.

When Binghamton police were advised of Art's presence, they often called on him while investigating criminal cases. Art requested a move, which was granted. The couple moved to Rose's home town of Delhi. When news got out that a double killer, who had somehow been released from prison, was in their town, the police and the public made it clear he wasn't welcome.

From Delhi they moved to Fleischmanns and from there to Elmira. No one wanted Art Shawcross.

Finally the authorities settled on Rochester. Surely, in a larger community, Art would remain anonymous. He obtained a job with Brognia Brothers, making salads which were distributed to schools and other institutions.

Despite being married, he acquired a girlfriend, Clara Neal, and often borrowed her Dodge to take long drives by himself. Rose knew of his attachment to Clara, but didn't seem to mind. She also tolerated Art's solitary fishing.

What no one knew, except those girls who were selling their bodies along Lake Ave., was that Art was a frequent visitor to Rochester's red light district.

In February 1988, Dorothy Blackburn was picked up by Art. They drove to an isolated area and parked. Buyer and seller dickered over price. When a price was agreed upon, sexual intercourse took place.

According to Art, during the lovemaking, Dorothy bit him. He retaliated by biting back. Art claimed that right then and there he decided to kill his companion.

He tied Dorothy's arms and legs and drove to one of his favorite fishing holes. Once there, he strangled her and dumped her body over the bridge spanning Salmon Creek. It had been almost 16 years since Art had last killed. He liked the feeling. After it was all over, he put the entire episode behind him. In time, ice formed over the creek. Dorothy Blackburn ceased to exist.

When spring arrived in upper New York state, the ice covering Salmon Creek melted. A hunter discovered Dorothy's fully-clothed body.

In light of future events, it seems inconceivable that Rochester police had not been informed by parole authorities that there was a child killer in their city.

By merely driving a vehicle Art was in violation of his parole. By having a drink in a public place he could be returned to prison. Since they didn't know that such a man lived among them, Rochester police never routinely questioned Art when they investigated Dorothy's murder.

Art became well known in Rochester's red light district. Anna Steffen met

Art in a bar on Lake Ave. They drove to a secluded area and proceeded to argue over Art's inability to perform. He strangled the girl beside the Genesee River and let her body slide into the water.

Eventually, Anna's body was discovered. Art did not enter the sphere of the investigation into her death.

Art's third victim was not a prostitute. She was a girlfriend of sorts—58-year-old Dorothy Keller. Dorothy often visited Art and Rose, but Rose had no idea that the pair was making love at every opportunity.

In June 1989, while fishing, and after they had had intercourse, Art accused Dorothy of stealing his money. She denied the accusation and threatened to tell Rose of their relationship.

Art broke the hapless woman's neck with a piece of wood and then hid the body in bushes. Months later, Art visited the body, which had decomposed in the summer heat and was now nothing more than bones.

Six months after the murder, Dorothy's body was found by fishermen. Once again, Art Shawcross was not questioned. In fact, police did not connect this murder to the two previous killings.

In 1989, the death toll climbed. Patty Ives and Frances Brown brought his total to five.

When June Stotts became victim number six, news reports of a serial killer on the loose emanated from Rochester. Like the Green River killer, he preyed on prostitutes and operated in one general area. Many victims were dumped in and about the Genesee River.

Marie Welch braced herself against the brisk November wind swirling along Lake Ave. She felt herself fortunate when Art picked her up. Art made love to Marie and then killed her.

Darlene Trippi was Art's last victim of 1989. Art claimed she had to die when she laughed at his inability to perform. He stripped her body and deposited her clothing in a Salvation Army box.

Liz Gibson was killed because she accidentally broke the gear shift of Clara Neal's car.

June Cicero, victim number 10, laughed at Art, as had so many previous victims. For this, she too had to die.

It is beyond belief that this man roamed the district where prostitutes plied their trade without being seen picking up any of the women who were later reported missing. Art Shawcross, child killer, parolee, operated with immunity—an invisible killing man.

On January 3, 1990, Art drove out to Salmon Creek, parking only scant yards from where he had dumped June Cicero's body. He brought along his lunch. From his position on the bridge, he could just make out the form of the body enveloped in ice under the bridge. Art didn't notice the State Police helicopter as it swooped down the river. From the helicopter, police spotted the form of a body and the man in the car on the bridge.

As soon as Art sighted the helicopter, he drove away, but the vehicle was followed and Art was taken into custody. When questioned by police, he confessed to the most horrid series of murders in New York State's history. While in custody he confessed to an 11th murder, that of Felicia Stephens.

Art was tried for 10 of the 11 murders he confessed to having committed. His attorneys entered a plea of insanity but a New York jury thought otherwise.

Shawcross, now 46, was found guilty of 10 counts of first-degree murder. He was sentenced to 10 life terms to run consecutively with no possibility of parole for 25 years on each. He will be eligible for parole in 250 years.

GENE SIMMONS

MURDER takes no holidays. The most horrendous mass murder ever to take place over the Christmas season occurred in Dover, Arkansas in 1987.

The first signs that retired U.S. Air Force Sgt. Gene Simmons led a strange life came to light years before when he was charged with sexually molesting his 16-year-old daughter, Sheila.

The Simmons family lived in Cloudcroft, New Mexico. When Sheila told her brother that their father had been sexually attacking her, he told friends, who in turn told their parents. Concerned parents informed school officials, who related the facts to police.

Eventually, an arrest warrant was issued for Simmons, but before it could be served, the entire family moved away. Sheila was pregnant with her father's child and later gave birth to a daughter. After a year of unsuccessfully attempting to locate Simmons, police dropped the charges against him.

May Novak, Gene's mother-in-law, begged her daughter to leave Gene. Rebecca Simmons simply couldn't. With a house full of children, how would she survive?

The family surfaced in Dover, Arkansas. Although retired from the Air Force, Gene worked at several jobs around Russellville over the years. In November 1986, Gene left his job at Woodline Motor Freight and took a part-time job with Sinclair Mini-Mart until December 18, 1987. He quit on that day, claiming that his wages were far too low.

When Gene Simmons, 47, walked into a law office in Russellville shortly after Christmas, no one had any idea that a few days earlier he had killed his entire family. Kathy Kendrick, 24, a legal secretary, had once worked at Woodline Motor Freight. She had repulsed Gene's advances over a year earlier. Because of this or some other imagined grievance, Gene calmly shot her four times through the head.

He then moved on to the Taylor Oil Co., where he accidentally met James Chaffin. Without hesitation, he shot the 33-year-old Chaffin dead on a loading dock. Gene proceeded into the oil company offices and shot Russell Taylor, 38, the proprietor of the firm. Russell would survive the killing spree. Gene had at one time worked for Taylor and no doubt felt he had some score to settle.

A madman was on the prowl, settling imagined ills. Gene proceeded to Sinclair Mini-Mart. Without hesitation, he shot store manager David Salyer, 38, and employee Roberta Woolery, 46. Both would survive the senseless attack.

The shooting wasn't over. Gene made his way to Woodline Motor Freight. He shot and wounded 35-year-old Joyce Butts. Today, Joyce still has nightmares about the traumatic experience. She vividly remembers waking up 10 days after the shooting and being told that surgeons had successfully removed a bullet which had lodged near her heart.

Ten minutes after this last shooting, the building was surrounded by police. Gene gave up without incident, turning over two .22 calibre handguns to police.

Authorities proceeded to the Simmons' home. The Christmas tree was gaily decorated. Wrapped presents were under the tree. No Christmas presents had been opened for the very good reason that all the occupants of the house had been dead since before Christmas. Five victims were found in the house and were identified as one of Gene's daughters, his son, their respective spouses and one grandchild. All were still wearing overcoats, indicating to police that they were killed soon after they arrived bearing Christmas gifts.

Freshly dug earth was observed close to the Simmons home. There, in a 1.5-metre deep grave were the bodies of Gene's wife, four of their children, ages 7 to 17, and two grandchildren.

The horror story continues. In the trunks of two old abandoned vehicles near the Simmons house, two bodies were found. These tiny bodies had been wrapped in plastic garbage bags. They were later identified as Gene's grandchildren.

Ironically, after the last body was recovered and the killer behind bars, a letter written by Simmons' wife to her daughter shortly before her death was made public. In the letter, 46-year-old Rebecca Simmons wrote, "I am a prisoner and the kids are too. I don't want to live the rest of my life with Dad." She went on to say, "Dad has had me like a prisoner."

Rebecca revealed her life of isolation and fear in her dilapidated rural home. Her husband wouldn't allow her to have a telephone. He censored all mail and kept neighbors away. Rebecca attempted to explain, "You have to remember I've never had a job since I've been married, or before that either. I know I have to start somewhere. It would all be so much easier if it was just me."

Rebecca's attempt to escape the maniacal clutches of her husband came too late. Too late for Rebecca, 13 members of her family and two respected citizens of Russellville, Arkansas.

Gene was tried for the murders of Kathy Kendrick and James Chaffin. The Arkansas jury deliberated only one and a half hours before finding him guilty.

Believed to be the most prolific family mass murderer in U.S. criminal history, Robert Gene Simmons was executed by lethal injection in Arkansas State Prison.

WAYNE WILLIAMS

SELDOM has a city, its inhabitants and its officials come under such critical scrutiny as Atlanta, Georgia did between 1979 and 1981. Someone was systematically murdering the city's black children. As the number of victims grew, the case became known around the world as the Atlanta Child Murders.

On July 28, 1979, a woman pushed back shrubs and rubbish along Campbellton Rd. in Atlanta. She was looking for returnable bottles. The unwary woman recoiled in horror at the sight of a human leg sticking out of the foliage. Police were soon on the scene. They were in for a surprise. Barely one hundred yards from the first body, they uncovered a second victim. The boys were identified as Edward Hope Smith, and Alfred Evans, both 14.

In itself, two teenaged boys found shot to death on the same day in the same place was unusual. But there was more to come. Much more.

Six weeks after the bodies of Edward and Alfred were found, another 14-year-old boy disappeared. Milton Harvey had one possession he loved above all others and that was his bicycle. It was found abandoned along a dusty road. Investigators discovered that Milton had skipped school on the day of his disappearance because he was embarrassed to wear his worn-out tattered shoes. Three weeks later, his decomposed body was found in a dump in the Atlanta suburb of East Point, not far from where the first two bodies had been discovered.

Little Yusef Bell, 9, was running an errand for a neighbor when he dropped out of sight. His body was found by a vagrant in the heart of Atlanta. Four children had been murdered. All were poor and all were black.

In retrospect, the Atlanta police have been criticized for not intensifying their efforts to apprehend an obvious madman who, for some perverted reason, was killing black boys. Would more effort have been put into the investigation if the victims had been white?

The story soon drifted out of the local area. These killings were different from anything which had preceded them. The murders continued.

The Christmas season of 1979 passed without incident. The following

March, 12-year-old Angel Lanier was found dead. She had been raped and strangled with an electrical cord. A pair of panties not belonging to the dead child had been stuffed down her throat. Angel's murder was a departure from the killer's usual pattern. For the first time, he had murdered a female, and for the first time, sex was involved in the killing.

A week later, 10-year-old Jeffrey Mathius left his home to pick up a pack of cigarettes for his mother. He was never seen alive again. Jeffrey's skeletal remains would be found months later.

Camille Bell, little Yusef Bell's mother, probably did more than anyone to bring the series of murders to the public's attention. She gave statements to journalists, accusing police of laxity in apprehending the killer. She insisted that one person was responsible and had to be apprehended before he killed again. Mrs. Bell's concern was well-founded. The killings continued, but now the terror which had enveloped Atlanta was being reported by the world press. Strange details concerning the murders became public knowledge. Some of the victims had been washed after they were killed.

Eric Middlebrooks, 14, was stabbed and beaten to death. Christopher Richardson, 11, disappeared on his way to a swimming pool. His skeleton was found eight months later. La Tonya Wilson, 7; Arron Wynche, 10; and Anthony Carter, 9, were murdered in quick succession.

The effect on Atlanta was devastating. Racial tension ran high. Rumors spread throughout Georgia. Some claimed a white man had taken it upon himself to wipe out black children. Others said the killings were not the work of one individual, but a diabolical scheme initiated by the Ku Klux Klan to kill black children so they would not grow up to propagate their race.

The city of Atlanta is reported to have spent a quarter of a million dollars a month conducting the extensive investigation. Funds poured in from the public and from private interested parties. Frank Sinatra and Sammy Davis, Jr., headlined a benefit concert at Atlanta's Civic Centre, raising $250,000 for the investigation. Schoolchildren and the public in general staged fund raisers. Actor Burt Reynolds contributed $10,000. Atlanta's first black mayor, Maynard Jackson, announced that the city had instituted a reward of $100,000 for the apprehension and conviction of the killer. Several corporations, with the help of heavyweight boxing champion Muhammad Ali upped the reward to half a million dollars.

Still, the litany of murder continued: Earl Lee Terrell, 11; Clifford Jones, 13; Darron Glass, 10; Charles Stephens, 12; Aaron Jackson, 9; Patrick Rogers, 16; Lubie Geter, 14; Terry Pugh, 15; Patrick Balazar, 11; and Curtis Walker, 13—all under 16 years of age, all from underprivileged backgrounds and all black. By now, the list numbered 21 victims. Many thought the number to be far greater, claiming that other missing youngsters had fallen to the madman, but their bodies had not been found.

Ronald Reagan became president of the United States. He immediately allotted $1.5 million to help defray the cost of the investigation, as well as ordering the Federal Justice Department to assist in the case. That month, Jo Jo Bell, 15, and Timothy Hill, 13, were murdered by the Atlanta Child Killer.

On March 30 and 31, 1981, the bodies of Eddie Duncan and Larry Rogers were plucked from the Chattahoochee River. These two victims were a departure from the now well-patterned category of victim. Both were 21 years old and both were mentally retarded.

The task force solely devoted to apprehending the killer had interviewed and released scores of suspects during the course of their investigations. One such man was Wayne Williams, a rather unlikely suspect. Williams was a bright young man, who lived with his parents, both retired school teachers, on Penelope Rd. in north-west Atlanta.

As a high school student, Williams had constructed and operated his own radio station in the basement of his parents' home. Currently, he was active as a freelance newspaper photographer, media consultant and music producer. It was this latter activity which first connected him to the child killing case. Involved in promoting musicians, Williams had flyers printed outlining his credentials in this field. These flyers had been found on, or in the possession of, four of the victims.

Was it possible that Williams had lured victims with promises of recording dates and stardom? Williams also had access to the city's streets. He often roamed the streets in his station wagon, ostensibly looking for the opportunity to take saleable photographs. Williams often showed up at accidents and fires. He was well-known to police.

While Williams was being investigated, the bodies of Mike McIntosh, 23, and Jimmy Payne, 21, were pulled from the Chattahoochee in the same week in April.

That same month, John Porter, 28, was found stabbed to death on the streets of Atlanta. In May, William Barrett, was discovered strangled to death in a ditch.

On May 22, 1981, three Atlanta police officers and an FBI agent were on stakeout duty at the South Cobb Drive Bridge over the Chattahoochee River. Suddenly, there was a splash in the water. The police saw automobile lights on the bridge. As the car sped away, they radioed another member of the stakeout team in a vehicle.

The chase was on. The car, a green station wagon, drove away, stopped, turned, and reversed its course, driving back over the South Cobb Drive Bridge. A second police car joined the chase. Two miles down the road, the station wagon was stopped by police. The driver was Wayne Williams. He was taken into custody, questioned and released. However, he was kept under close surveillance while the FBI dragged the river for a body. Two days later they recovered the body of 24-year-old Nathaniel Cater. Two weeks later, Williams was taken into custody and charged with Cater's murder, as well as that of Jimmy Payne.

Williams' murder trial lasted nine weeks. Prosecution attorneys produced microscopic fibres and dog hairs taken from the Williams' residence and car, which matched fibres found on victims. It was the state's theory that Williams hated his own race and killed so that they wouldn't become parents. It was also believed that he exulted in the challenge of outwitting the combined police forces attempting to solve the case.

Williams testified in his own defence. He claimed he was on the bridge at 2:45 a.m. looking for a female vocalist he wished to interview before she auditioned later that day. He swore he hadn't killed anyone, nor had he any knowledge of the murders.

A jury of eight black and four white citizens found Williams guilty of two counts of murder. He received two life sentences to run consecutively. After the sentencing, police announced that Williams was responsible for over 20 other murders, but it would serve no purpose to have him stand trial on those charges.

Not everyone is convinced of Williams' guilt. In 1987, an attempt to reopen the case, led by the mothers of several of the victims, was quashed. They believe that a ring of pornographic profiteers used the children before killing them.

Wayne Williams is presently serving his sentences at the Georgia State Correctional Centre in Jackson.

AILEEN WUORNOS

THE woman waved her thumb in the air and struck an appealing pose as cars sped along one of Florida's sun drenched highways. Those who failed to stop had no way of knowing that they had just prolonged their lives. Others weren't as fortunate. They stopped and picked up 34-year-old Aileen Wuornos.

Aileen is unique. She is the only female serial killer in the United States. The phenomenon of taking three or more lives at different times in different locations has been strictly male dominated. All that changed when Aileen took up the killing profession.

Initially, Florida police had no idea that a serial killer was in their midst. The discovery of video store owner Richard Mallory's body in December 1989, was thought to be an isolated incident. Mallory's blood-stained Cadillac had been found a mile away two weeks before the gruesome discovery of his body.

I spoke to investigator Larry Horzepa of the Volusia County Sheriff's Office. He had no idea of the hornet's nest he was about to open when he was assigned the Mallory case. All that summer of 1990, Larry kept getting teletypes from other law enforcement offices in central Florida concerning murdered men. There was a striking similarity between the victims. They were all white middle-aged men who had been travelling alone. Their bodies had been found in wooded areas off main roads and all had been shot with small-calibre handguns.

The number of murders mounted. The occupations of the victims varied. There was a construction worker, truck driver, sausage company delivery man, missionary, retired police officer and a Florida state employee among the seven victims eventually attributed to Aileen.

Det. Horzepa says, "When we established that the bodies found in several counties were the handiwork of one individual, we joined forces with law officers in the other counties." A year after Richard Mallory's body was found, police received a break in the case.

Witnesses had seen two women running from a Pontiac Sunbird after they had crashed the vehicle through a fence. The damaged car belonged to Peter

Siems, a missionary who had been missing since earlier that summer. With good descriptions of the two women, police released composite drawings to three tabloid TV shows. Citizens' tips pointed to one Tyria Moore, a domestic who had worked at a local hotel. The other woman turned out to be Aileen Wuornos.

Detectives found that Aileen had a long criminal record, which included disorderly conduct, armed robbery and prostitution. She was the constant companion of Tyria, whom she referred to as her wife. Authorities soon found out that the pair were lesbian lovers, who hung around rough tough bars in the Daytona area. Police staked out several such bars for two weeks. Sure enough, Aileen showed up at the Last Resort, a bar frequented by bikers. She was quietly taken into custody.

Aileen's lover Tyria had left her job and was picked up in Pennsylvania. Despite their relationship, it was believed that she had nothing to do with the murders. According to Larry Horzepa, "Moore had a full-time job at a hotel and worked a 40-hour week. They were lesbian lovers, but Aileen hitch-hiked alone and met Moore after working hours."

Moore broke up with Aileen because she feared for her own life. She told authorities that on one occasion Aileen had told her, "I killed a guy today."

Aileen confessed to the murders of seven men who had picked her up while she was hitchhiking on the highway. She told a heart-rending story about her youth, claiming that she was sexually abused as a child, pregnant at 13, and was actively selling her body by the time she was 15. She also stated that she had attempted suicide on six different occasions.

Aileen's uncle Barry, who would eventually travel to Florida to testify against his niece, disputed Aileen's claims of an abused childhood. He testified that Aileen came from an average home.

Det. Larry Horzepa obtained a search warrant for storage space Aileen had rented. Among her personal belongings he found several items she had taken from her victims, such as a police officer's badge, an alarm clock and fishing equipment. In some instances, she gave away items taken from her victims. No doubt she sold some of her loot, but robbery was not her primary motive.

Throughout her interrogation, Aileen absolved her lover of any complicity in the murders, adamantly stating that she had acted alone. She said that she sometimes posed as a woman in distress and at other times as exactly what she was—a prostitute looking for a customer. On some days she had turned as many as a dozen tricks and had never harmed any of her clients. She had only killed those men who had become physical with her or hadn't wanted to pay her. In her own words, she told Horzepa, "All I wanted was to get my money for sex."

Some of the tales told by Aileen about her early home life have been confirmed. She did become pregnant at the age of 13 and was sent to a home for unwed mothers. Her baby was taken away from her at birth. At the same time, her family received word that her father, a convicted child molester, had hanged himself in prison. From the age of 15, Aileen was on her own, making her living from prostitution.

Det. Horzepa, who was the first to question Aileen and was the first to hear her litany of death-dealing drives, finds it difficult to be sympathetic towards the multiple killer. He claims that Aileen went "from prostitution to murder for the cash the men carried on their person."

Recently, Aileen stood trial for the murder of Richard Mallory, the first of a series of murder trials she faces in the near future. She was found guilty and sentenced to death in the electric chair.

At her trial, Aileen took the witness stand in her own defence. She testified that she had killed her victims in self-defence. Det. Horzepa scoffs at this. "Some self-defence!" he says, "Several of the men were shot as many as four times in the back."

Aileen Wuornos awaits her second trial while residing on Death Row in Florida.

ZODIAC KILLINGS

IN all the history of crime, no killer has ever written as many letters to newspapers and authorities as the infamous California murderer known as the Zodiac.

On December 20, 1988, David Faraday, a 17-year-old Vallejo High School student drove his father's 1980 Rambler into a secluded side road overlooking Lake Herman Reservoir. Beside him in the passenger seat was pretty 18-year-old Betty Lou Jensen. It was the young couple's first date. It would be their last.

David and Betty Lou had only been parked in the well-known lovers' lane for a matter of minutes when a man appeared at the side of the Rambler and ordered them out of the car. When they hesitated, he fired two shots through the car window. Once the youngsters were outside the vehicle, the gunman placed the barrel of his .22 calibre pistol behind David's right ear and fired. Betty Lou ran for her life, but it was no use. She took five slugs in her back and died where she fell.

Twenty minutes after the attack on the two students, a woman driving past the lane noticed them sprawled on the ground. She drove into Benicia, where she informed police. They arrived on the scene to find David Faraday still breathing. He died on the way to hospital.

Seven months passed before the killer struck again. Michael Mageau, 19, and Darlene Ferrin, 22, drove into the parking lot of the Blue Rock Springs Golf Course. This time, the gunman walked to the side of the vehicle and sprayed the unwary couple through an open window. Michael managed to stagger out of the car before falling to the pavement. Miraculously, although critically wounded, he would survive the attack. Darlene died in an ambulance while being rushed to a nearby hospital.

Thirty minutes after the couple was found in the parking lot, police received a phone call. A male voice declared, "I want to report a double murder. If you will go one mile east on Columbus Parkway to the public park, you will find the kids in a brown car. They were shot with an 8 millimeter Luger. I also killed those kids last year. Goodbye."

Police verified the facts mentioned in the phone call and were convinced the call was authentic. They knew they were dealing with a weirdo who preyed on couples in parked cars. He didn't rob his victims, nor were the attacks of a sexual nature. In fact, he gave no hint as to his motive, but authorities knew the man was cunning. No clues were left behind to identify him.

A month later, the three major newspapers in the San Francisco area received letters revealing details of the two attacks which only the killer could know. In addition, each paper received one third of a complicated cryptogram with the killer's demand that it be published on the front page of their newspaper. The cryptogram, which was made up of Greek and English letters, as well as triangles and circles, was turned over to U.S. Naval Intelligence where experts were given the task of decoding it.

A week later, the experts had not deciphered the killer's correspondence, but two high school teachers from Salinas were successful. Donald Hardin and his wife Betty managed to decode the message. Here is the letter as it was translated. Note the mistakes in spelling and other errors.

"I like killing people because it is so much fun it is more fun than killing wild game in the forrest because man is the most hongertue (dangerous) animal of all to kill something give eryetheyo a thrilling experience it is even better than getting your rocks off with a girl the best part of it I athae when I die I will be reborn in paradise and all the I have killed will become my slaves I will not give you my name because you will trs to sloi down or atop my collecting of slaves for my afterlife ebeo riet emeth hpiti."

The last four words of the message have no meaning to anyone to this day.

In the weeks which followed, the man with the strange urge to prove he was the killer wrote several letters to newspapers. For the first time he began his correspondence with the phrase, "This is the Zodiac speaking." The name stuck and forever after he has been known as the Zodiac.

On September 27, 1989, Zodiac struck again. Cecilia Shepard, 22, and Bryan Hartnell, 20, were attending Pacific Union College close to Vallejo. Bryan drove his Volkswagen to a pleasant spot beside Lake Berryessa to have a picnic. He and Cecilia were sitting beside the shore that evening when a man suddenly emerged from the brush. He wore a black hood which covered his entire head and carried a pistol in one hand and a knife in the other. The intruder had Cecilia tie Bryan's hands and feet. He himself bound Cecilia.

The hooded man uttered the terrifying statement, "I'm going to have to stab you people."

Bryan replied, "Well, then, stab me first."

Zodiac obliged. He plunged his dagger into Bryan's back six times and then proceeded to inflict ten stab wounds to Cecilia's back and four more to her chest.

When a fisherman found the two young people on the shore, they were still alive. Cecilia died in hospital two days after the attack, but Bryan survived and was able to tell authorities of his experience. As usual, Zodiac wanted credit. An hour after the attack, he called the Napa police, "I want to report a murder. They are two miles north of park headquarters. They were in a white Volkswagen Karmann Ghia. I'm the one that did it."

Two weeks later, Zodiac was at it again. Paul Stine was studying toward his doctorate degree at San Francisco State College. To finance his education, he drove a yellow cab at night. Paul picked up a fare in downtown San Francisco. Unfortunately, his passenger was Zodiac. The madman produced a nine-millimeter pistol and shot Paul directly in the temple, killing the 29-year-old student instantly. Before leaving the cab, Zodiac tore away a piece of Paul's shirttail. Three days later, the San Francisco Chronicle received a letter detailing Paul Stine's murder. As proof that the letter was authentic, Zodiac enclosed a small piece of his victim's bloody shirt.

Zodiac had deviated from murdering young couples. He was clever enough not to become a pattern killer. Ballistic tests proved that he had used a different weapon for each murder. His letters continued to arrive at the Chronicle building in San Francisco, some in English and some in cryptogram form. Several cryptograms were unsolvable, leading authorities to believe Zodiac was mocking them or simply having fun at their expense.

As time went by, other unsolved murders dating back to 1986 were attributed to Zodiac. If there was any doubt, Zodiac himself kept police informed by mail. He added postscripts to his letters. The last one received had the ominous notation: Me 37 SFPD 0.

Because Zodiac wasn't above writing provable untruths in his letters, it is difficult to know if his claim of 37 victims is a fact or an exaggeration.

The Zodiac killings and the unusual correspondence stopped as suddenly as they had begun. Police believe that a thrill killer such as Zodiac would never stop killing of his own volition. Many feel he must have died or been incarcerated in an institution where letter writing would be too risky.

Zodiac has never been identified and his known murders have remained unsolved to this day.

CLINT BANKSTON

MOST murderers are not very clever. On occasion, more by luck than design, they manage to avoid detection. Sometimes, as if they want to be apprehended, they kill again.

This is the story of one such teenager who took innocent lives and, in the end, left a trail a cub scout could follow.

Clint Bankston was only 16 years old, but he was an adult in every sense of the word. He was attending school in Athens, Georgia, when the senseless murders took place.

It all began on Saturday, April 25, 1988. Neighbors of Rachel and William Sutton couldn't understand why the elderly couple didn't answer their phone. When they knocked on the Suttons' door, they received no response. The neighbors had good reason to be concerned. You see, Rachel was 78 years old, while William had seen 82 summers come and go. Both were employed as professors at the University of Georgia.

Police were notified. It was necessary for them to gain access to the home through a window. The sight which greeted the officers was not a pleasant one. William's body was lying on the hall floor beside the door to the dining room. He was draped over a laundry bag which held the body of his wife.

The crime scene was strange in many ways. A dining room rug had been thrown over the Suttons' bodies by the killer, who had attempted to clean up blood with a sponge mop which was found in the kitchen. It was impossible to ascertain if anything had been taken from the house. William's wallet was found intact in his pants pocket.

The couple's two vehicles, a Buick and a Chevrolet, were still in their garage. In the trunk of the Chevy, investigators found bloodstained clothing and a bloody dishpan. The trunk of the Buick contained bloodstained rugs and women's clothing, as well as a butcher knife, which proved to be one of the murder weapons.

An autopsy indicated Rachel Sutton had been stabbed six times, while

William had been stabbed 11 times with the butcher knife. In addition, the killer had stabbed William twice with a decorative African spear which had been on display in the dining room.

What type of human predator had descended on this inoffensive elderly couple and snuffed out their lives for no apparent reason? The Suttons had no known enemies. Members of the academic community were interrogated without result. During the investigation, it was learned that the Suttons owned a dozen properties in and around Athens. Tenants were questioned, but it appeared no one had any reason to cause the Suttons harm, let alone kill them. Despite the array of clues and fingerprints recovered from the crime scene, police could not come up with the identity of the murderer.

Four months passed. On August 15, 1988, the killer struck again. Ann Morris left her home in Athens to visit a friend, Sally Nathanson. When friends of both women couldn't reach them by phone, police were dispatched to Sally's residence. On the lawn near the front door lay the body of 63-year-old Ann Morris. Inside, police found the bodies of Sally Nathanson and her daughter, Helen.

In reconstructing the crime, investigators felt the intruder had killed Sally first, then barged into the dining room where Helen was eating breakfast. Detectives found food on the dining room table, partially eaten. Both women had been sexually assaulted. Male hair and semen were found on both bodies. Ann Morris had no doubt arrived at the front door just as the killer was exiting the residence. All three women had been killed with what police felt was a small axe or hatchet.

Each of the three victims had owned an automobile. Only two were parked in the driveway. Sally Nathanson's 1984 Dodge Diplomat was missing. The Dodge's licence number was immediately issued to all police, who felt they would find the car abandoned. Surely the killer would rid himself of the incriminating Dodge within minutes of making good his escape.

It didn't work out that way.

Officer Kirk Graham couldn't believe his good fortune as he drove past a Moreland Ave. home in East Athens. There, in the driveway, was Sally Nathanson's Dodge Diplomat. Officer Graham notified homicide of his find and proceeded to knock on the front door of the house beside the wanted vehicle. Sixteen-year-old Clint Bankston answered the door. He handed over the keys of the Dodge to Officer Graham. Clint claimed a friend, Chris Ward, had loaned him the vehicle.

A few hours later, Clint changed his story. He told his interrogators he had found the car abandoned. When keys to Sally Nathanson's home were found in his shirt pocket, Clint lost his composure, but still contended his friend Chris Ward had committed the crimes. Clint admitted he had been in the Nathanson home with Ward. To gain favor with detectives, he led them to a wooded area, where they recovered a blood-spattered hatchet, a pair of women's slippers and a bloody man's shirt.

Once Clint felt police believed his friend Ward was responsible for the three murders which had taken place in the Nathanson home, he broached the subject of the Sutton murders. He also attributed these two murders to the mysterious Chris Ward.

Detectives felt it was time to pick up Ward. That task proved to be a difficult one. Clint led police to his friend's house. No Chris Ward lived there. Three more times, the accused killer led authorities on wild goose chases to locate Ward. After a week of searching, it was apparent Ward was a figment of Clint's imagination. In time he confessed to a psychiatrist that Chris was a fictional character he invented to take the blame for the five murders.

Meanwhile, police had built a formidable case against their suspect. Fingerprints taken from the Sutton and Nathanson homes proved to be Clint's. It was his hair that was found on the bodies of Sally and Helen Nathanson. Of course, all of this incriminating evidence was only matched to Clint after he was located, which might never have happened had he not been dull enough to park his victim's automobile in the driveway of his own home.

Clint Bankston was found guilty of multiple murder and received five sentences of life imprisonment.

As I said at the outset, most murderers are not very clever.

BECK & FERNANDEZ

NINETEEN-forty-seven was not a good year for Martha Beck. Her husband had just divorced her and to make matters worse, she lost her job as a nurse at a home for crippled children in Pensacola, Florida. Fate had left her with two children; one sired by her former husband and the other the result of a tryst with a bus driver.

Martha had been willing to marry the bus driver, but unfortunately he had an aversion to settling down, particularly with Martha. You might call it an absolute phobia, because the bus driver took a step which assured him that no marriage could take place. Rather than marry Martha, he committed suicide.

You see, Martha was not a raving beauty. She was of average height, but that is about all that was average about her. Tipping the scales at 203 lb., Martha had an array of chins and extra slabs of blubber that she wasn't even using. She was inclined to wear bright red lipstick, and overindulged her ample face with layers of rouge, which gave her an overstuffed, ghostlike appearance.

Martha had those normal urges which ladies sometimes have and longed for the company of a man. Facing the fact that she was not a cutie she joined a lonely hearts club. Before long she received a letter, which read:

Dear Martha,

I hope you will allow me the liberty of addressing you by your Christian name. To tell the truth, I don't quite know how to begin this letter to you, because I must confess, this is the first letter of this sort that I have ever written.

Would you like to know a little about me? I am 31 and I've been told I'm not a bad looking fellow. I am in the importing business from Spain, my mother country. I live alone here in this apartment, which is much too large for a bachelor, but I hope some day to share it with a wife.

Why did I choose you for my debut friendship letter? Because you are a nurse, and therefore I know you have a full heart with a great capacity for comfort and love.

Your friend,
Raymond Fernandez

Martha didn't know it, but Raymond Fernandez was having a busy year as well. He was a swindler and killer who worked the lonely hearts clubs. Once Raymond met, seduced, and got his hands on a lady's available funds, he disappeared leaving the poor women dabbling at their bloodshot eyes with the corner of a handkerchief. When absolutely necessary, he killed his victims.

Raymond had just returned from Spain where he had gone vacationing with a Jane Thompson. Jane unfortunately, didn't come back to the U.S. It seems she met with a car accident in La Linea, Spain. Fernandez had all the documentation concerning her death. He even had her last will and testament. Naturally it left the contents of her apartment to none other than Raymond Fernandez.

At Raymond's invitation, Martha went to visit him in New York. Raymond, always frugal, had moved right into the late Jane Thompson's apartment. My, my, what a surprise Raymond had when he threw open his front door and there stood the overstuffed, over-rouged, over-lipsticked Martha. Raymond gulped and said, "Come on in."

Fernandez was repulsed at the sight of Martha, but she thought he was an absolute heartbreaker. She fell madly in love with Raymond at that very first meeting. Not one to let grass grow under her bed, she let Raymond have his way with her the very first time they laid eyes on each other. Raymond, in his experienced way, checked out Martha's assets, and all things considered, decided to give Martha what they used to call the cold shoulder. Martha would have none of it. In desperation, Raymond decided to tell her the truth, namely, that she was falling for a con artist and killer. You can imagine his surprise when Martha professed undying love for him in spite of his wayward habits. She even went so far as to suggest that they should become a team. She would pose as his sister, and instill confidence into the ladies he proposed to fleece.

Raymond warmed up to the idea and the partnership was formed. From the very beginning the Spaniard and the fat lady were a perfect combination.

Raymond would correspond with lonely ladies, mostly widows, through several lonely hearts clubs. Once contact was established, usually instigated by the ladies themselves, Raymond and Martha would show up at the mark's house. The unsuspecting victim would be impressed with Raymond and appreciate his honorable intentions of lugging his sister along with him. After they got their scheme rolling, the odd couple averaged one fleecing a month.

There was one fly in the ointment. Martha was almost driven crazy with jealousy. She couldn't stand the thought that her Raymond had to caress and make love to other women. Raymond assured her that it was just part of his chosen profession and that it meant nothing personal.

Business is business, as the saying goes, and the partnership continued on its merry way. One incident is worthy of note. Raymond and Martha had made contact with a 66-year-old widow, Janet Fay of Albany, New York. After Raymond had seduced her and gotten his hands on Mrs. Fay's life savings of $6,000, Martha wanted to leave her high and dry. It appeared to Martha that Ray was lingering a little too long after the money was safely in his hands.

In a jealous rage, Martha hit Mrs. Fay over the head with a hammer. Ray finished the job by strangling her with a scarf. Martha was later to state that she and Ray made love on the floor beside the body of their victim.

The following day Fernandez bought a trunk and placed the body of Mrs. Fay inside. He then managed to store the body at a friend's house for a few days. Raymond and Martha located a house for rent at 149th St., Ozone Park, Queen's and took it on a trial basis for one month. They dug a hole in the basement, placed Mrs. Fay's body inside, and cemented the floor over. They remained in the house for four days until the cement had dried. Then the odd couple moved out, informing the real estate agent that the house was unsuitable. In this way they effectively disposed of Mrs. Fay's body.

Out of sight out of mind—the strange pair went on their merry way. Six weeks later they made contact with a widow from the suburb of Grand Rapids, Michigan. Mrs. Delphine Downing had lost her husband two years previously. She was leading a lonely existence, raising her three-year-old daughter Rainelle by herself.

Soon Raymond and Martha visited Mrs. Downing at her invitation. In his usual charming way, Raymond made friends with little Rainelle. Then following his regular script and drawing on his vast experience, he seduced the lonely Mrs. Downing. She became so enthralled with her lover and his large sister that she invited them both to move in with her and Rainelle. Raymond added to his role of lover and took on the extra responsibility of financial advisor. He and Mrs. Downing soon contemplated wedding bells. Raymond got busy converting her worldly assets to his name in anticipation of their impending marriage.

It appeared that Mrs. Downing could be the source of future concern for Raymond and Martha, so one fine day Raymond shot her in the head. Rainelle kept crying, and as a result made Martha nervous. Martha cured her nervousness by strangling the child. That same night Raymond dug a hole in the cellar. Here he placed the two bodies and poured cement into the hole. To relax after a hard evening's work, Raymond and Martha took in a movie.

The next morning, when neighbors couldn't get a satisfactory answer as to Mrs. Downing's whereabouts, they didn't hesitate to call the police. The authorities just couldn't believe that a woman who had lived in the same house for years would leave with her daughter, and not tell her future husband where she was going. They decided to search the house, and lo and behold they discovered that damp patch of cement in the basement.

Once the bodies of Mrs. Downing and Rainelle were uncovered, both Raymond and Martha poured out the whole horror story. They led police to the exact location in Queen's where the body of Mrs. Fay was buried under cement in the basement. As the house was now rented to new tenants, we can only speculate how they felt when informed that there was a body in their basement.

The authorities decided to extradite the pair from Michigan to New York State and charged them with murder. Michigan had abolished capital punishment while New York still retained the ultimate penalty.

Both were found guilty. On March 9, 1951, in the company of a Roman Catholic priest, Raymond was executed in the electric chair in Sing Sing Prison. Twelve minutes later Martha joined him.

THE BENDER FAMILY

THERE have been some nasty families down through the years. I don't mean yours or mine, but those families who slayed together and stayed together.

One of the vilest little domesticated groups to kill together were the Benders of Kansas. Pop Bender was originally from Germany, and was around 60 years old when he settled in the Sunflower state. Ma Bender was a tough-looking doll about 10 years Pop's junior. The hard rock couple had two children. John Jr. was a strapping, dull 27-year-old, while daughter Kate was 25. Kate was a looker with an hourglass figure, who attracted members of the opposite sex like honey attracts bees.

In 1871, the Benders moved into a dilapidated house in Labette County, halfway between the small railroad crossroads of Thayer and the tiny town of Cherryvale. Old man Bender divided his 16 by 20-ft. home into two parts. One half was used as living quarters for the Bender clan, while the other half was used as a store and what could charitably be called a restaurant. The two sections were divided by a canvas partition.

Situated on the main road, and with Kate as a build-up attraction, the Bender establishment, despite its humble appearance, did a thriving business. During the daylight hours horsemen stopped for groceries. At dusk travellers stopped for a hotel meal, and were later put up on cots to spend the night.

If one was to believe rumors which circulated through the Kansas prairies, one would be forced to come to the conclusion that Kate did more for the tired strangers than wait on tables. Other than the oldest profession, Kate had another vocation, which to us unsuspecting souls appears to be diametrically opposite to her horizontal activities. Are you ready? She was a spiritualist who claimed to heal the ill. When thusly employed, she billed herself as Professor Miss Kate Bender. When the mood moved her, she also gave lectures on spiritualism.

From 1871 to 1873, using Kate and apparently good food as bait, the Bender family started killing people. Kate would seat the travellers with their backs to the canvas partition. Choosing only those who looked prosperous, Pop

Bender and Junior would wait for an opportune moment to bring a sledgehammer down on the unsuspecting victim's head. The only thing left for the Bender family to do was slide the body under the canvas to effectively remove it from the public eating area and into the privacy of their living quarters. Here they would combine their talents to trap and rob the victims. Then the body would be dropped through a trap door in the floor into a pit. Later the family would pick a few quiet moments under the Kansas sky to plant the strangers in an adjoining pasture.

For almost two years this simple, diabolical little drama was enacted time and time again. Like most foolproof schemes, something happened to cramp the Benders' style. In the spring of 1873, Dr. William York was returning home from visiting his brother, a colonel in the army. His route took him past the Bender establishment. He had mentioned to his brother that he would be stopping over at the Bender place. When Doc York mounted his trusty steed for the trip, he waved goodbye to his brother. The doctor then rode into the sunset, never to be heard from again.

Well, folks, Col. York went looking for his brother and ended up at—you guessed it—the Benders' friendly inn. The Bender group offered to look for the missing doctor. Remember, this all took place in 1873 when travelling was sometimes hindered by outlaws, not the least of whom was that well-known chap Jesse James. Anyway, Col. York was satisfied with the Benders and rode off to continue his search for his brother elsewhere.

The Benders figured that with guys like the colonel showing up, it was time to leave the scene. Neighbors first noticed that the house was deserted on May 5, 1873. Soon after, who should show up but Col. York, still looking for his lost brother. The colonel, accompanied by other men, discovered the murder pit under the trap door. It was encrusted with blood. The colonel stood looking out over the Benders' property and noticed several indentations in the pasture.

The men started to dig and ironically, the very first grave contained the body of Dr. York. The back of his head was crushed and his throat had been cut. In all, eight bodies were taken from the Benders' pasture, including that of a little girl who was unlucky enough to be travelling with her father. During the 18 months in which they operated, the family killed eight innocent people, averaging a victim every 10 weeks.

Later, men were to come forward with little tales of how angry Kate used to become when they chose not to sit at the table with their backs to the canvas. Their random choice of seating arrangements saved their lives.

Just like in the movies, a posse was formed to find the Benders. When members of the posse returned they were extremely grim and close mouthed. Later one of the Benders' wagons was found riddled with bullet holes which gave rise to the rumor that the posse had lynched the Bender family and decided not to talk about it.

You may choose to believe that the Benders got clean away. For 50 years off and on people believed they spotted members of the family. In 1899, the case again received a measure of notoriety when two women were extradited from Detroit in the belief that they were Kate and her mother. When they arrived in Kansas there was a great deal of difficulty in identifying the pair and they were eventually released.

If you're ever down Kansas way, you can drop into the Bender Museum in Cherryvale and see first-hand relics of the Bender clan and their crimes. You will notice a canvas partition dividing the room. While the gentle folks running the museum are hospitable enough, I might suggest that you don't sit with your back to the canvas.

BICKERSTAFF & DAVIS

DONNA and Fred Bickerstaff were well aware that their 17-year-old daughter Teresa was a bad seed. She skipped school so often that her teachers gave up on her. During her last school year, she spent time in a drug rehab institution. Three years earlier she had run away from home and had hitchhiked to California, prostituting herself for drinks, drugs and rides. Yes, by the time she was 17, the slight, attractive teenager knew the ins and outs of existing by her wits.

The Bickerstaffs lived in an attractive home in rural Harrisville, Ohio, located about 40 miles from Cleveland, where Fred worked for Alcoa Aluminum. Besides Teresa, the Bickerstaffs had two other children; Fred Jr., 14, and Ken, 13. Unlike their wild reckless sister, the two boys were average teenagers.

When Teresa was around the house, there was usually some domestic disaster brewing. The latest turmoil resulted when she brought home a 21-year-old unemployed man from Cleveland. Fred and Donna disliked Eric Davis from the moment they laid eyes on him. The more they discouraged the budding romance, the more Teresa seemed attracted to Eric. On one occasion, Fred ordered the boy off his property and forbade him ever to return.

On August 28, 1980, Fred Bickerstaff's concern over his troubled daughter took a back seat to the major tragedy which befell his family. While Fred was at work, fire raged through his home. When the heat subsided, firemen found the bodies of 38-year-old Donna Bickerstaff and her two sons. They were told that Teresa had been home the night before when Fred Sr. had left for work in Cleveland. Renewed efforts were made to locate Teresa's body, without success.

When neighbors informed police that the Bickerstaffs' second car, a Datsun, was nowhere to be seen, the search for Teresa took a more ominous turn. Detectives soon learned that the missing teenager was not your average daughter. They found out she was a drug abuser, part-time prostitute, and had previously run away from the parental nest.

Autopsies on the three bodies revealed that they had been shot with a .357 calibre Ruger. Donna and Ken had been shot in the head. In addition, Ken had been stabbed ten times in the chest. The shot to the head had killed Donna instantly, but Ken had survived two shots to the head and the multiple stab wounds for the few minutes it took for him to succumb to smoke inhalation. Fred Jr. had been shot in the shoulder, chest and head, as well as being stabbed once in the stomach.

To add to the evolving horror story, the state fire marshall's office informed investigating officers that the fire had been set by an arsonist who had used gasoline, evidence of which was found throughout the house. A $10,000 reward was offered for the apprehension of the killer or killers. Meanwhile, a nation-wide search was instituted for the Bickerstaffs' missing Datsun and their daughter, although there was no proof of any connection between Teresa and the murders. There was no proof, but there was grave suspicion.

On October 3, 1980, over a month after the murders, U.S. Custom officials at Detroit stopped a Datsun entering the U.S. from Windsor, Ont. Inside the vehicle, inspectors found guns and knives. After extensive questioning, the occupants admitted that they were Teresa Bickerstaff and her boyfriend Eric Davis.

Teresa confessed that she had killed her mother and brothers. She told detectives that Eric had come to her house in the wee hours of the morning to take her away. Upstairs, her family was asleep. Eric picked up Fred's .357 Ruger and found a box of cartridges. He loaded the weapon and gave it to Teresa, who proceeded upstairs to pack a suitcase. Her mother woke up and called out. Teresa went into the bedroom. An argument erupted immediately, whereupon Teresa shot her mother dead.

Ken was awakened by the shot and ran into the room. He met the same fate as his mother. Fred Jr. ran toward Teresa, cursing at her as he took in the sight of his dead mother sprawled on the bed. Teresa fired twice and her brother fell to the floor. Then the cold-blooded teenager calmly shot both her brothers one more time. Her terrible recital neglected to mention any details concerning the stab wounds found on her brother's bodies.

Eric admitted that he had been in the house. He claimed the killings had not been planned. He was there to steal the Datsun and run away with Teresa. When everything went crazy and Teresa started shooting her family, he had attempted to get her out of the house. After getting Teresa outside, he admitted that he had thrown a five-gallon gas can into the house and had lit it with a match. His statement also didn't account for the stab wounds found on the two bodies and conflicted with the fire marshall's report that the gasoline had been spread throughout the house.

Eric and Teresa made their way to Canada, gaining entry into the country at Niagara Falls on the day after the murders. In Canada, Eric found work as a welder, but when he lost his job the couple decided to flee to Mexico. That's when they were apprehended in Detroit.

On April 22, 1981, Eric stood trial for the three murders. Defence counsel painted Eric as a young man with the best of intentions, who had been caught up in a web of circumstances he couldn't control. Eric's lawyer claimed that his client had broken Teresa of her drug habit and had attempted to have her return to her home to live with her parents. He had also tried to become friends with her parents, but they were abusive and rejected his overtures. Unable to gain parental consent, the couple planned to run away together. Eric claimed he was an innocent bystander when Teresa went berserk and started her shooting spree. He admitted to the theft of the Datsun and setting the house on fire.

The prosecution attorney revealed that Eric had earlier instructed Teresa to gather up the guns in the house. He contended that at least one of the victims had been killed by smoke inhalation, a direct result of Eric having set fire to the house and that he was equally guilty of the other two deaths as they had occurred during the commission of a robbery. The jury agreed. After deliberating for two days, they found Eric guilty of the three murders and a number of lesser charges. He was eventually sentenced to three life terms on the murder charges and three terms of 25 years each on three robbery charges. In addition, he received a sentence of five to 25 years for arson. All sentences were to run concurrently, except for the last, which would start after the other sentences had been served.

At her trial, Teresa changed her story completely, stating that she had initially confessed to the shooting to protect Eric. Now she claimed it was Eric who had killed her mother and brothers. No one believed her. She was found guilty of the three murders and received three concurrent life sentences.

Teresa Bickerstaff has been incarcerated in the Marysville Reformatory for Women since her conviction.

JERRY BRUDOS

JERRY Brudos didn't smoke or drink. His I.Q. was well above average. He was a skilled electronics technician, as well as a qualified electrician. Jerry was a big man, standing an even six-feet and weighing a solid 180 pounds. When he was 23, an acquaintance introduced him to his first real girlfriend, 17-year-old Ralphine Leone.

In 1962, Jerry and Ralphine wed. That same year Ralphine gave birth to a daughter, Therese. In 1967 their second child, Brian, was born. The Brudos family lived in a pleasant little house on Center St. in Salem, Oregon.

To the outside world, Jerry appeared to be a quiet, happy family man. To Ralphine he was a considerate, sensitive husband. Unknown to Ralphine, there were two incidents in her husband's past which may have served as warning signals had she been aware of their existence.

When Jerry was 17, he became frustrated when a date repulsed his sexual advances. Enraged, he beat the girl badly with his fists. As a result, Jerry was committed to the Oregon State Mental Hospital in Salem. The terms of his commitment allowed him to attend high school during the day. Nine months later he was released to his parents.

The other incident occurred after Jerry graduated from high school and joined the U.S. Army. Stationed at Fort Gordon, Georgia, Jerry fantasized that a woman entered his barracks each night and went to bed with him. Each night he beat her unmercifully. The dreams were so real that Jerry sought out army psychiatrists. When they heard his story, the recommended that he be discharged as not being fit for military service.

What no one knew, not his high school teachers, not the mental health people in Salem, not the army psychiatrists, and certainly not his wife, was that Jerry Brudos had been stealing ladies' underwear and high-heels for years. Initially, underclothing was taken from clotheslines, but Jerry was not above entering houses while the occupants slept, in order to steal items to satisfy his fetish.

Behind his home in Salem, Jerry had a garage. He outfitted the garage with an intercom connected to the house. When Ralphine wanted him for meals, she called on the intercom. There was a hard and fast rule. Ralphine was never to enter the garage. Jerry told her he developed pictures there, and didn't want sunlight pouring in unexpectedly. Men do have hobbies. Even when her husband moved the family freezer into the garage, Ralphine put up with the inconvenience.

Jerry Brudos was a time bomb ready to explode. He paraded around in women's underclothing and high-heels in the privacy of his own garage. Sometimes he took pictures of himself in the stolen clothing, but the games had become less stimulating. True, he had talked Ralphine into posing in the nude, but she did so reluctantly. No, there was no other way. He had to have his very own woman in order to act out his fantasies.

An encyclopedia saleslady knocked on Jerry Brudos' door on January 26, 1968. Faking interest in purchasing books, Jerry had no trouble enticing her into the basement of his home. Once there, he hit her over the head with a plant. Then he choked her to death.

Jerry was happier than he had ever been in his life. He had his very own model. For hours he dressed and undressed the body in his collection of women's underwear. Slowly the realization came to him. His new friend would have to leave. But surely there was something he could keep.

Jerry took a saw and cut off the left foot of his victim. It would serve him well in the weeks to follow as a form for his high-heeled shoe collection. He placed the foot in the freezer for safekeeping. Jerry tied an engine block to the body. At 2 a.m., displaying unusual strength, he tossed his macabre cargo into the Willamette River. Days later, he weighed down the foot and threw it into the river as well.

Jerry loved the game and could hardly wait for his next victim. Jan Susan Whitney was a 23-year-old University of Oregon student. On November 26, 1968, Jan disappeared while driving her old Rambler from Eugene to McMinnville. It had been Jan's misfortune to have car trouble. It had been her fatal misfortune to encounter a monster posing as a good Samaritan. Jerry told her he could repair her car, but first he had to go into Salem to get his tools.

Jan jumped in Jerry's car and ended up in his garage in Salem. He throttled her with a leather strap. Jerry had outfitted his garage for just such an occasion.

He now had the proper photographic equipment. A pulley system had been installed and a hook inserted in the ceiling. The body could be raised to a standing position. Jerry dressed and undressed his victim. To add to his many perversions, he had now become a necrophiliac.

Jerry left the body hanging there in the garage when he and his wife took a trip to Portland. While they were away, a stranger drove into the side of the garage. When Jerry came home he found a card from the police department in his mailbox. It had been a close call. Police inspected the damage. Jerry repaired the garage. The body inside had not been detected. Later, Jerry weighed it down with scrap iron and threw it in the river.

Pre-med honor student Karen Sprinker, 19, was plucked off the streets of Salem four months after Jan Whitney met her terrible fate. Her car was recovered, but gave no clue as to the owner's whereabouts.

Jerry had forced the hapless girl to his garage with a toy gun. Once there, he took pictures before strangling his victim. He then indulged in his fantasies, weighed down the body with a cylinder head and tossed it into the Long Tom River.

A month later, on April 23, 1969, Linda Dawn Salee, 22, became Jerry's fourth victim. After work, Linda had driven her Volkswagen to a shopping centre, where she purchased a birthday gift for her boyfriend. Jerry pointed his gun at Linda's head just as she was about to enter her parked car. She ended up in Jerry's garage. She too was subjected to the madness that was Jerry Brudos. That night he threw her body into the Long Tom River.

Eighteen days later, a fisherman discovered Linda Salee's body. Her killer had been careless and had thrown her into a shallow section of the river. A car's transmission had been tied to the body with nylon cord and a copper wire.

While diving for other clues, police discovered another body, that of Karen Sprinker. The macabre details made the front pages of the nation's newspapers. No one was more interested than Jerry Brudos.

Despite his madness, Jerry was an intelligent, cunning adversary. He read about the bodies, but was sure he had covered his tracks and would not be apprehended. He had no intention of curtailing his bizarre activities.

In fact, Jerry had hit upon a new scheme. He discovered that by phoning the university and asking for a common female name, he could get a girl to the phone. In this way he sometimes enticed girls to meet him for coffee. So far none had appealed to him. By interviewing Oregon State co-eds, detectives learned of the man who attempted to get blind dates.

Finally, they found one girl who had met him for coffee in her dormitory's cafeteria. When interviewed, this young girl stated that the man had kept talking about the two murder victims taken from the river. Police instructed the girl to stall her caller if he ever phoned again. Sure enough, she heard from him again. She told him it would take her some time to dry her hair. In the meantime, she called police. Detectives greeted Jerry Brudos.

A search of Jerry's garage turned up his vast array of women's underclothing and high-heels. Police also discovered photos of the dead girls, as well as one shot which revealed Jerry's image in a mirror. In the same photo was a picture of one of his victims.

Once in custody, Jerry made a full confession. Seven psychiatrists conducted extensive tests. Their conclusions were unanimous. Jerry Brudos had killed in a planned and premeditated manner. He was judged to be sane.

Jerry Brudos pleaded guilty to three counts of first degree murder and was sentenced to three consecutive life sentences in Oregon State Penitentiary.

Ralphine Brudos obtained a court order forbidding her children to visit their father in prison. In 1970, she obtained a divorce.

Officials of the Oregon State Prison in Salem advise me that Brudos has made a "good institutional adjustment." Initially, as a high-profile inmate whose crimes were committed against women, he was the subject of abuse by other prisoners. One inmate made an unsuccessful attempt to stab him. The Oregon State Parole has decreed that he will never be paroled.

JUDI BUENOANO

WHEN Ana Lou Weltey was 17 years old, she gave birth to a son, Michael. Ana couldn't pinpoint the father of her baby with any degree of certainty.

Never mind. A year later, in 1962, she met Jimmy Goodyear. A whirlwind romance ensued, culminating with the young couple's marriage. Jimmy adopted Michael. Four years later, Ana gave birth to their second child, a daughter. Jimmy was elated. The family settled nicely in Orlando, Florida.

The Vietnam War interrupted the Goodyears' life, as it did so many American families. Jimmy served in Vietnam, returning home in 1971. He was one of the more fortunate servicemen who returned unscathed by enemy bullets or the ravages of disease. Yet he was no sooner back in the Sunshine State and comfortably employed with a large company that he suddenly took ill.

On September 16, after being rushed to hospital, Jimmy died. The official cause of death was listed as kidney failure. Ana was beside herself with grief. We can only assume the $70,000 insurance money she collected served to alleviate her sorrow to some extent.

A few years passed before Ana met Bobby Joe Morris. Bobby Joe was smitten. When he moved from Florida to Trinidad, Colorado, he took Ana and her children along. All went well until the winter of 1978, when Bobby Joe took ill. He retched, bent over with abdominal pains and in general felt lousy. Doctors said he had an inflamed pancreas and kept him in hospital for three weeks. Much improved, he returned home to Ana's loving care. Two days later he was rushed back to hospital, suffering from severe nausea. He lingered for 48 hours before he lapsed into a coma and died. Death was attributed to liver failure. Distraught Ana cashed in insurance policies totalling $77,000.

Ana was becoming well known in insurance company circles. Every time the name Goodyear popped up, the companies knew it would cost them. As a result, Ana was having difficulty purchasing insurance. To dispense with embarrassing questions, she had her name legally changed to Judi Buenoano.

In 1979, when Michael was 18 years old, he joined the U.S. Army. He spent his first leave with his mother. On his very first night back home under his mother's protective wing, he became ill. Judi took him to the hospital, where his severe nausea cleared up within a day. Upon his release from hospital, his condition progressed from bad to worse. In two months time, he was so ill that he was outfitted with a prosthetic device on his right arm and cumbersome metal braces on both legs. The U.S. Army transferred Michael from hospital to hospital in an effort to find the source of his serious ailment. Finally, when Michael's condition stabilized somewhat, he went back home to his mother.

One day after Michael's return home, Judi had a great idea. She would take Michael and her daughter on a canoe trip on the East River north of Pensacola. The outing didn't go well. A fisherman spotted Judi and Michael struggling in the water. He manoeuvred his boat beside the thrashing pair and managed to pull them out of the water. It was too late for Michael. He had drowned. Judi, as usual, had the foresight to insure her son for a whopping $180,000, which was paid immediately. The tragedy was officially labelled an accident.

Never one to let grass grow under her feet, Judi latched onto a new boyfriend. When he took seriously ill, he told authorities that he had been given some vitamin capsules by his girlfriend, Judi Buenoano. He had some left. These were turned over to authorities at the state crime laboratory for testing. The capsules had been emptied of their original contents and had been filled with poisonous paraformaldehyde.

Judi was taken into custody and charged with the attempted murder of her boyfriend. She was also charged with the murder of her son Michael. Now that Judi's past life was being reviewed, the previous deaths returned to haunt her. Bobby Joe Morris' body was exhumed and found to be laced with arsenic. Remember hubby Jimmy Goodyear? He had been dead for 13 years. Now his body was exhumed and arsenic was found in his hair and fingernails.

Judi was tried for Michael's murder. The prosecution based its case on the premise that she had planned the drowning. The prosthetic apparatus Michael wore on his legs weighed 50 pounds. The entire idea of taking him on a canoe trip was foolhardy. The fisherman who pulled mother and son from the water stated that initially he thought the pair was playing in the water. It didn't appear to him that Judi was attempting to pull her son out of the river. Her motive was clear enough. Judi collected insurance money, as she did from all the other deaths.

After deliberating only six hours, the jury found Judi guilty of first-degree murder. She was sentenced to life imprisonment with no possibility of parole for 25 years. Just as the verdict was announced, she was charged with the attempted murder of her current boyfriend. The old adage that it never rains but it pours was never more true than in Judi's case. She was also charged with the murder of Jimmy Goodyear.

At the trial concerning Judi's current boyfriend, the capsules containing paraformaldehyde were introduced by the prosecution. It took the jury only 40 minutes to find Judi guilty of attempted murder. She was sentenced to 10 years imprisonment to run concurrently with her life sentence.

Before her trial Judi had booked an around-the-world cruise for herself and her daughter. Instead, she entered prison, where it was expected she'd be a guest of the state for 25 years.

COLUMBOS & DE LUCA

THE bodies were discovered by accident. Police found Frank Columbos' stolen Thunderbird stripped to its frame in Chicago's South Side. Now they were bringing the bad news to Frank in his comfortable suburban Elk Grove Village home. But no news would be delivered on this day in May 1976. Everyone in the Columbos home was dead.

Frank had been bludgeoned about the head with a heavy blunt instrument, stabbed repeatedly and shot four times. His body was found clad only in trousers and socks. His killer or killers had butted out cigarettes on his chest.

Mary Columbos' body was lying in a hallway a few feet from that of her husband. She had been similarly attacked and shot. Upstairs, police came across the body of 13-year-old Michael Columbos. Like his parents, he had been hit over the head, stabbed and shot. A bloodstained bowling trophy had probably been the weapon used by the attacker to strike each of the victims on the head.

Mercifully, pretty 19-year-old Patty Columbos had not been at home when the attack occurred. Two years previously, Patty had had a dispute with her parents. She was madly in love with a married man, 37-year-old Frank De Luca, the proud father of five little De Lucas. When Patty's parents forbade her to see him, she moved out of the family home and into an apartment with Frank. At the time of the murders, it was thought that this move had saved her life.

The perpetrators of the slaughter had apparently ransacked the house, but had taken precious little. They had left money, jewelry and portable appliances untouched.

Initially, rumors that the murders resembled Mafia execution style killings circulated among the police, as well as the curious in the neighborhood. However, investigators could turn up no organized crime connection to Frank Columbos. He was what he appeared to be—a family man who had worked for years in middle management for Western Auto, an automobile accessory chain.

Detectives attempted to seek out any enemies Frank might have had, but apparently he and Mary led a quiet life, except when it came to Patty. Their slim, beautiful daughter was a handful. At the age of 16, she began dating Frank De Luca, whom she met while working as a clerk in the cosmetic department at a Walgreen Drug Store where he was the pharmacist manager. Patty outraged her parents by quitting school to work in the drugstore full-time. The family had fought bitterly when she moved in with Frank. He, in turn, had left his wife and five children for the shapely teenager.

On one occasion, Patty's father attacked De Luca with an unloaded rifle, knocking out several of his teeth. Yes, there was no love lost between Patty, her boyfriend, and her parents. To add to the tension, Columbos had altered his will, leaving his son Michael the bulk of his estate, amounting to several hundred thousand dollars, and cutting Patty off with a measly $5,000. Significantly, if Michael died, Patty would become the sole beneficiary of the estate.

Patty felt that her parents were the cause of all her troubles, both emotional and financial. She decided to murder her entire family. In true Chicago style, she went about looking for a hit man. She found two. Lanny Mitchell, a 24-year-old clerk, and Roman Sobezynski, a 34-year-old employee of Cook County. They agreed to kill her parents and brother for $50,000 and sexual favors on demand. There was one thing wrong with the entire scheme. The two men, who were posing as tough professional killers, had no intention of killing anyone. When Patty offered them sex as part payment, they decided to string her along. They delayed her for months, all the while keeping trysts with her at various motels. Five months passed before the men tired of the game and stopped returning her phone calls.

Now that the Columbos family had been murdered, friends approached police, informing them of Patty's relationship with her parents. Patty herself had confided to a girlfriend that she was attempting to have her parents murdered by professional assassins. After the killings, this girlfriend told her father, who marched his daughter down to a police station.

That's how police were to learn that Patty Columbos had actually attempted to hire hit men to kill her parents and her brother. They were even provided with the names of the hit men. Mitchell and Sobezynski were picked up and questioned. They admitted that they had strung along an attractive, promiscuous girl for sex, but claimed they had had nothing to do with the murders.

Upon being questioned, Patty admitted that she had tried to hire Mitchell and Sobezynski, but had changed her mind. When she had attempted to call off the hit, she had been unable to contact them. She further stated that De Luca had been unaware of her plans. Patty wasn't believed. She was arrested and charged with triple murder. De Luca was similarly charged.

While both accused were in jail awaiting their murder trials, Clifford Childs, a 29-year-old cellmate of De Luca's, informed authorities that De Luca was arranging for him to make bail. He had offered to pay Childs several thousand dollars to kill two witnesses who were prepared to testify against him. Childs also told investigators that De Luca had given him intimate details of the triple murders, admitting that he was actually involved in the shootings.

In one of Chicago's most sensational murder trials in years, the prosecution stated that Patty had tried to hire contract killers to murder her family. When that failed, she and Frank De Luca had done the job themselves. The defence claimed that Patty had tried to call off the killers, but had failed. It was the hit men who had committed the murders, not Patty and De Luca.

Unfortunately for the defendants, they were extremely loose-mouthed immediately after the murders and had confided in several people, including Patty's girlfriend, fellow employees at Walgreens, and a former lover of De Luca's, who swore that Frank had bragged of his involvement. None of these witnesses had anything to gain by giving their damaging evidence. Some of them were provided with police protection, so fearful were they that De Luca would arrange to have them killed rather than allow them to testify.

The Illinois jury took only two hours to find both defendants guilty of three counts of murder, conspiracy and solicitation to commit murder. Each was sentenced to a total of from 200 to 300 years on the murder charges. In addition, Patty Columbos was sentenced to 20 to 50 years imprisonment for solicitation to commit murder. Frank De Luca was sentenced to 10 to 50 years for the same crime. One can only assume the lovers will not walk the streets of Chicago for some time to come.

FAYE & RAY COPELAND

THERE are 130 hard-working farmers who call Mooresville, Missouri home. Among them were Faye and Ray Copeland, maybe the hardest-working couple in that northwestern section of the "Show Me" state.

The Copeland children left the farm while still in their teens. No doubt they were happy to leave the back-breaking labor and stern discipline meted out by their father. In the mid-1980s, Ray had seen 75 summers come and go, while Faye was a work-worn 69 years old.

Despite their advanced years, the Copelands worked harder than many couples half their age. Faye was up before dawn feeding cattle and preparing breakfast for Ray. Then off she went down the road to her part-time job as housekeeper at the Holiday Motel. Ray toiled on the farm all day when he wasn't busy attending cattle auctions. Over and above working the farm, the Copelands were very active purchasing cattle at auction and apparently selling them at substantial profits.

The Copelands had a secret. They would hire strangers as cattle buyers. Usually these men were ecstatic to gain a position with the Copelands. Ray treated them decently enough for awhile. He even took them to area banks and saw to it that they opened accounts, ostensibly to have a place to deposit their paycheques and facilitate the purchase of cattle.

For the first few months, each buyer would successfully bid on small quantities of cattle and pay the auctioneer with his own cheque. Under Ray's direction, when the time was ripe, the buyer would make a large purchase. Ray would have the cattle presold in various counties of Missouri. Nothing suspicious there. The hay hit the fan when Ray's hired cattle buyer's last cheque bounced and the bank attempted to contact him. Surprise! He was nowhere to be found. On those occasions when Ray was questioned, he claimed he had no idea as to the whereabouts of his buyers. These strangers would work for awhile before moving on. The bank was left holding the bag and that, for all intents and purposes, was that.

And now, folks, I'll let you in on a little secret. The two elderly Copelands killed their cattle buyers by shooting them in the head and burying them in lone-some graves on nearby farmland. This substantially decreased their labor costs and effectively brought the cost of their latest cattle purchase to zero.

In a few short years, Dennis Murphy, John Freeman, Wayne Warner, Jimmy Harvey and Paul Cowart disappeared off the face of the earth. In hindsight, we wonder why no one became suspicious. There were some reasons. Ray took his buyers to different banks, so that no one institution got taken more than once. He often recruited inexperienced, rootless men from the Victory Mission in nearby Chillacothe.

Of course, some eyebrows were raised. A neighbor, Bonnie Thompson, thought it strange that young men would appear at the farm in Ray's pickup truck and would drop out of sight in a few short months. She reported the odd goings-on to the sheriff's office. In addition, the number of complaints received from banks concerning rubber cheques had one thing in common. In every case, the passer of the cheque had some connection with the Copelands.

Meanwhile, Ray and Faye were in the market for a new cattle buyer. On July 25, 1989, Ray recruited Jack McCormick at the Victory Mission. Jack was a bit different from the other cattle buyers. For one thing, he was a 60-year-old who had drifted halfway across the United States. He had worked farms, knew his cattle and loved vodka. Jack could also smell a rat when he saw one, but couldn't resist the $20,000 per annum he was offered. The job seemed a cinch. He was to accompany Ray to auctions and do the bidding, because Ray claimed his sight and hearing didn't allow him to follow the auctioneer.

It all sounded great, but Jack was suspicious from the very first day. Per-sonalized cheques arrived in the mail. Ray asked him to sign a few just in case he couldn't make it to auction. Worldly-wise Jack pieced together the whole scheme. After attending a few auctions, he was in fear for his life. When Ray instructed him to purchase 40 head of cattle, he bought only three because he knew he only had enough money in his account to cover the much smaller pur-chase. Ray was furious. Jack got out of town in a hurry. He drank his way to Nebraska, where he sobered up long enough to call local authorities and tell them of his suspicions. They, in turn, relayed the information to Missouri.

The sheriff decided to obtain a warrant to search the Copeland farm. Earth-moving equipment rumbled down the county roads. Bonnie Thompson now told her story in detail. Others came forward, advising police Ray had often been seen in isolated areas of little-used or abandoned farms. When police were directed to a barn in Ludlow owned by Neil Bryan, they hit paydirt. There, in the barn, under a light covering of earth, police found the decomposed bodies of Paul Cowart, John Freeman and Jim Harvey. A few days later, Wayne Warner's body was found under bales of hay on another farm.

Farmer Joe Adams remembered the day Ray asked his permission to dump trash down an old abandoned well on his property. Sure enough, the well yielded the body of Dennis Murphy. In removing the body, witnesses were aghast when Dennis' head broke away from his body. Ray and Faye Copeland, who looked as if they had stepped out of a photo depicting rural America, were arrested and charged with multiple murder.

Faye was the first of the unholy duo to stand trial. Her lawyer attempted to paint her as the submissive partner in a dominant/submissive marriage. Her adult son and daughter testified their mother had always followed their father's wishes and demands without question.

The state contended Faye had knowledge of the murders and was a willing accomplice. They produced a list of the victims' names in Faye's handwriting, as well as much of the murdered men's belongings, found on the Copeland farm.

The jury deliberated for only three hours before finding Faye guilty of all five murders. She was sentenced to death.

Ray followed his wife to trial. When a bullet taken from the skull of one of the victims was proven to have been fired from Ray's .22 Marlin rifle, he too was found guilty and was sentenced to death.

The husband and wife team was the first such pair to receive the death sentence since the resumption of the death penalty in the U.S. While incarcerated in Potosi Prison, Ray suffered a stroke and died. Faye Copeland still resides in the Missouri Correctional Facility for Women in Chillacothe. She has the unenviable distinction of the being the oldest woman on Death Row in the United States.

JUAN CORONA

STRANGE and unusual murders are remembered for many reasons, but nothing makes violent crime more newsworthy than a large number of victims. Few have surpassed the killing spree of Juan Corona, a transplanted Mexican who made his living as a labor contractor near Yuma City in northern California.

One of Corona's clients was Goro Kagehiro, who owned and operated a successful peach orchard. Kagehiro took pride in his orchard, which he had nurtured for 21 years. As he walked along the straight lines of peach trees, he mused to himself that Corona's seven-man crew was doing a good pruning job. When he came across a large hole between the trees, he couldn't help but wonder why such a hole had been dug. It was big—three-feet deep, over two feet wide and about six feet in length. He would inquire about it later. In the meantime there was work to be done.

That evening, Goro made a point to check on the hole in his orchard. He was surprised to find that it was filled in. That night, he couldn't get the incident out of his mind. Next morning, he decided to inform the sheriff's office. A deputy was dispatched to the peach orchard. Goro and the deputy figured someone had buried garbage on his property. The two men turned over the soil covering the hole. Within five minutes they uncovered a human foot. On that Thursday morning of May 20, 1971, they had no way of knowing they had discovered the first of 25 bodies that were to establish the record for the largest number of murder victims attributed to one person in the U.S. up to that time.

Police knew the murder victim. He was Kenneth Whitacre, one of the thousands of transient laborers who follow California's vegetable and fruit harvests. Many work a few days or weeks, stock up on cheap wine and move on to the next town. Whitacre had been stabbed in the chest and had been struck with five vicious blows to the head, which the coroner thought might have been inflicted by a machete.

For four days, police investigated Whitacre's murder. In the course of their inquiries, they came in contact with labor contractor Juan Corona, who was rather well-known in the area. Corona provided the labor for many of the ranches in the lush fruit belt, including Goro Kagehiro's orchard.

On the fourth day after Whitacre's body was found, a worker on the huge Sullivan ranch nearby noticed an indentation in the ground. Because of the recent murder, he immediately became suspicious and reported his find to police. Sure enough, the body of another transient laborer was found buried on the Sullivan ranch. The unfortunate man had been stabbed in the chest and slashed about the head with a machete. Due to the similarities of the victims and the identical wounds on the two bodies, detectives felt that they were looking for one killer.

Once again, the name Juan Corona entered the investigation. He had also contracted labor for the Sullivan ranch. Police learned that months earlier, Juan had been involved in an altercation in a restaurant where he reportedly wielded a machete. Witnesses said he had a hair-trigger temper.

And so Juan Corona became an early suspect in the case, but other matters occupied investigators. The Sullivan ranch stretched for miles along the Feather River. Could there be more bodies? Police searched for graves in the orchard. Several suspicious indentations in the earth were uncovered. All contained bodies of transient workers. During the ensuing days, a further 23 bodies were found, making a total of 25 victims. Each had been killed in the same manner.

News of the multiple murders flashed around the world. The most prolific mass murderer in U.S. history had killed in wholesale lots in the lush agricultural section of California. Apparently no one had inquired after the missing men. They were lost souls, who had led a life without friends or family. Later, most were identified as men with troubled pasts made tolerable by alcohol. Many had long jail records for vagrancy and drunkenness. Several have never been identified.

Juan Corona's past was investigated. It was learned that he had spent some time in a mental institution 15 years earlier. Juan had immigrated from Mexico and, by the sweat of his brow, had succeeded in building a lucrative business as a labor contractor. In California's agricultural belt, ranchers don't look for and hire their own part-time labor. They employ the services of a labor contractor. Juan was known to the laborers and ranchers alike as an honest, reliable broker. He prospered, but now the married father of four children was in serious trouble.

Juan's truck and home were searched. Police confiscated a bloodstained machete. They also found a ledger containing nine of the victims' names on a list of 34 transient workers. A plaster impression of a tire track found near one of the graves matched one taken from Corona's pickup truck. Witnesses volunteered that they had seen Corona in the little-travelled area where most of the bodies were found.

Juan Corona was arrested and charged with 25 murders. The entire case against him was circumstantial. The prosecution was criticized for the manner in which they presented their case. Despite these flaws, Juan was found guilty of all the murders and received 25 sentences of life imprisonment. It was specified that the sentences were to run consecutively. So sure was Corona's lawyer that his client could not be convicted on the available evidence that he called no defence witnesses. He was wrong.

A successful appeal was launched, enabling Corona to stand trial for a second time after he had served 11 years in prison. This second trial lasted seven months and cost the state of California in excess of $5 million. Juan was not the same man. The years had taken their toll. He had suffered three heart attacks while serving his time. In addition, he had lost an eye when he had been attacked by a fellow prisoner.

The prosecution produced one new witness, a Mexican official, Jesus Rodriquez Novarro, who had visited Juan in 1978 between the two trials. In a private interview, Corona told Novarro, 'Yes, I did it, but I am a sick man and a sick man cannot be judged by the same standards as other men.' Once more, the accused man was found guilty and again received 25 sentences of life imprisonment.

TONY COSTA

TONY Costa was an exceptional gardener. He planted only two crops: marijuana and female bodies.

Aside from his horticultural pursuits, Tony made a precarious living as a part-time carpenter in and around Provincetown, Massachusetts. In 1969, Provincetown, located on the northern tip of Cape Cod, was a home away from home for hundreds of youths who felt that the drug scene took precedence over that dull but necessary activity known as work.

Tony married young. He was a high school student when he met 14-year-old Avis, who quickly became Mrs. Costa. In the succeeding years Avis gave birth to three children, while Tony chafed under the responsibility of providing for a family.

Tony entered the drug scene with a vengeance. He was rarely without his supply of pills. In fact, he kept such a large supply on hand that he secreted it in some woods near Truro, a few miles down the road from Provincetown.

Tony spent less and less time at home, until finally he and Avis were divorced. Free to play the field, Tony was often in the company of girls who were either visiting Provincetown or were among the hordes of youths who made the hippie resort town their home.

In January 1969, Pat Walsh and Mary Anne Wysocki were reported missing. The two girls had left Providence, Rhode Island, to spend the weekend in Provincetown, but had not returned. Police traced the girls' last known movements. On Friday, January 24, Pat and Mary Anne had checked into a guest house owned by Mrs. Patricia Morton. They had paid $24 in advance for two nights' lodging.

The girls left on Saturday morning. When questioned by police, Mrs. Morton said that she had seen a note from a permanent resident, Tony Costa, pinned to the girls' door. He had asked them for a lift to Truro. He, too, had not been seen by Mrs. Morton after Friday night. It appeared to the police that the girls had given Tony a lift in Pat's light blue 1968 Volkswagen on Saturday morning and had not been heard of since.

When Provincetown police checked with Truro's two-man police force, they learned that a light blue Volkswagen had been reported parked by the woods near Truro. The Truro police informed them that when they had checked out the parked car, they found a note on the windshield. It said, "Engine trouble, will return." They now returned to the South Truro woods and found that the Volkswagen was gone.

Upon examining the wooded area beyond the road, police found torn insurance documents and sales slips in the name of Patricia Walsh. There was the very real possibility that the two friends had wandered away from their car and become lost in the woods. Exposed to the frigid January weather, they could easily have frozen to death.

Next morning, one hundred men searched the wooded area. Three hours after the search began, a slight depression in the ground was detected by the searchers. The men dug and soon uncovered a human foot. Further digging revealed a leg and two arms. Police believed they had recovered the dismembered remains of Pat Walsh but they were mistaken.

Returning to Mrs. Morton's guest house, detectives found that Tony Costa had left his personal belongings in his room. Obviously, he had departed in a hurry. His mother thought that he had gone to Boston. His ex-wife Avis had no idea as to his whereabouts.

Provincetown police were surprised to receive a phone call from Tony. He called from Burlington, Vermont. His mother had informed him of the body found in the Truro woods and of the two missing girls. He was calling to clear up matters. According to Tony, he had met the girls at a Provincetown bar. Pat wanted an abortion and was going to meet a man named Russell, who would accompany her and Mary Anne to Los Angeles, where she would undergo the operation. The last Tony saw of the girls, they were heading down the road towards Hyannis.

Tony returned to Provincetown driving Pat Walsh's Volkswagen. He now told police a different story. He said that he knew the two missing girls from the previous summer. They had purchased dope from him and skipped without paying. When he spotted them in Provincetown, he bought the Volkswagen from Pat for $900, paying $300 cash and deducting $600 Pat owed him. This was the first of many stories Tony was to tell officials to account for his possession of Pat Walsh's Volkswagen.

It was while interrogating Tony's acquaintances that police stumbled upon Tony's horticultural bent. Somewhere in the Truro woods he maintained a marijuana garden and had often taken girls into the woods when he watered his plants. Tony also kept his cache of drugs close by, but none of his girlfriends had actually seen the drugs.

One girl, Marsha Mowery, was willing to lead police to Tony's garden. In freezing rain they passed by the open grave where the remnants of the still unidentified body had been uncovered. Walking along a partially obscured trail through the woods they came to a clearing. This was the site of Tony Costa's marijuana garden.

Six weeks had passed since Pat Walsh and Mary Anne Wysocki had left Mrs. Morton's guest house. On March 5, the two girls' bodies were discovered in shallow graves near Tony's garden. Both had been viciously attacked with a knife, horribly mutilated and sexually ravished. Several organs had been removed from the bodies. Clothing found in the graves identified the victims. Dental charts verified the identification. An autopsy indicated that the two girls had been shot with a .22-calibre weapon.

While removing the remains of the two girls, police uncovered another body. The dissected sections of this female body were in an advanced state of decomposition and had obviously been buried for a much longer period of time. A fingerprint check of missing girls identified the body as that of Sydney Monzon, who had been reported missing the previous May 28.

By tracing a ring found on the very first corpse, detectives were able to identify 17-year-old Susan Perry. She had at one time lived with Tony Costa and was last seen in his company.

Tony was taken into custody, but steadfastly denied any guilt in any of the four deaths. He claimed that he was being harassed and persecuted because of his involvement in the Provincetown drug scene.

Tony twisted and elaborated on his original story to cover all the circumstances concerning the murders already known by the investigating officers. He vehemently swore that his brother had loaned him the $300 he required to complete the purchase of Pat Walsh's car. At first Tony's brother verified this story, but as the case developed he admitted that he had lied to protect his brother.

Tony had a handwritten bill of sale for the Volkswagen signed by Pat Walsh.

FBI handwriting experts stated that Pat's signature was in Tony's disguised handwriting.

Gradually, Tony opened up. Initially, he would only admit to being on the scene while a friend killed the girls and dissected the bodies. Slowly, he gravitated to helping his friend mutilate the bodies. Finally, he admitted to the killings.

Tony Costa was examined by psychiatrists and adjudged to be legally sane. He was also considered to be a psychopath, caring only for the fulfillment of his immediate needs with no thoughts or feelings for others. In short, a monster.

Tony was tried, found guilty on two charges of murder and sentenced to two life terms in prison with no possibility of parole. On May 12, 1974, Tony Costa fastened his leather belt over the upper bars of his cell at the Massachusetts Correctional Institute at Walpole and hanged himself. He was 29 years old.

RICHARD COTTINGHAM

RICHARD Cottingham was employed for over a decade with Blue Cross and Blue Shield of Greater New York. He was a valued and highly regarded member of the company's large computer staff.

Richard and his wife Janet lived in a pleasant three-bedroom home in Lodi, New Jersey. They had three children: two boys, Blair and Scott, and a daughter, Jenny. Richard commuted to New York each day. Because of the nature of his employment, he had the option of reporting to work at any hour convenient to him. He normally worked from 4 p.m. to 11 p.m.

Among his colleagues, Richard Cottingham was a regular guy. Janet was the first to become aware that her husband was not what he appeared to be to the outside world.

In 1976, after Jenny's birth, 28-year-old Richard refused to have sexual intercourse with his wife. As a result, she gravitated to spending more and more time with her own friends. Richard, in turn, spent most of his time at home in his own private room. After work, he rarely drove directly home. Indeed, it was common for Richard to arrive home at dawn with the smell of alcohol on his breath. Sometimes he stayed away for several days.

One day, Richard inadvertently left his private room unlocked. Janet walked in. She was amazed to find an assortment of ladies' used underclothing and cheap jewelry scattered about the room.

No, Richard Cottingham was not normal. He was clever and cunning, but far from normal. For years he had led a double life, committing abnormal criminal acts which had not been attributed to one man.

On December 16, 1977, the body of 26-year-old nurse Maryann Carr was found in the parking lot of the Quality Inn in Hackensack, New Jersey. Maryann, who had been married only 15 months, had been handcuffed hand and foot before being strangled to death. Despite an intensive investigation, her murder went unsolved.

Two years later, New York firemen were called to the Travel Inn Motor

Lodge on West 42nd St. The blaze was localized in Room 417. Firemen had no trouble extinguishing the flames which originated from a double bed. When the smoke cleared, even the hard-nosed New York firemen recoiled in horror. There, on the bed, were the bodies of two nude, partially burned females. They were headless and their hands had been removed.

The investigation into the gruesome murders revealed that both girls had been prostitutes. Lighter fluid had been sprinkled over their bodies and ignited. New York detectives surmised that the strange mutilations had a purpose. With no heads, there were no teeth to check against dental records. With no hands, there were no fingerprints to compare. It would be six weeks before one of the girls would be identified. The identify of the other girl has never been established.

The man who had checked into Room 417 at the Travel Inn had given his name as Carl Wilson of Merlin, N.J. Both his name and the name of the town were fictitious. The room was clean. No fingerprints, no cigarette butts, nothing that would lead to the identity of the killer. He had checked in on Wednesday evening, November 29, and for four days was rarely seen by hotel staff. The "Do not disturb" sign hung from the doorknob of 417 for almost all of those four days.

After weeks of tedious legwork, detectives identified one of the victims as Deedeh Goodarzi. Jackie, as she was known, plied her trade in Atlantic City and New York City. The beautiful five-foot six-inch Kuwait native had left Atlantic City to attend a meeting with her pimp in New York during the last week of November. She never kept the appointment. Instead, she ended up in Room 417. It has never been ascertained whether a headless corpse greeted her when she entered the room or whether she was the first of the two to die. For the time being, the Times Square Torso Murders, as they came to be known, remained unsolved.

Valorie Street found Miami too hot for comfort. She had been arrested for prostitution several times. Once more on the street, she decided to try the Big Apple. Valorie arrived in New York City on May 1, 1980. Four days later, using the name Shelly Dudley, she signed herself into the Quality Inn Motel in New Jersey. Valorie was assigned Room 132. Her nude body was found under the bed. She had been handcuffed, bitten, beaten and raped.

Twenty-five-year-old prostitute Jean Mary Ann Reyner's body was found in the Hotel Seville on May 15, 1980. She had been stabbed to death and her breasts had been removed. The police had only a composite drawing of the fictional Carl Wilson to work on, provided by employees of the Travel Inn Hotel off Times Square.

Three days later, on May 18, 1980, Leslie Ann O'Dell, 18, arrived in New York by bus from Washington, D.C. Alone in the big city, without money or friends, Leslie was approached by a friendly man who bought her breakfast. The man explained that he could put her in touch with another man who would see to it that she made plenty of money. Within 24 hours Leslie was walking the New York streets under the protection of a pimp.

Leslie, on her fourth night as a New York streetwalker, was motioned over to a blue and silver Chevy Caprice. The man, who called himself Tommy, suggested a drink at a bar in New Jersey. Leslie was happy to comply. Tommy proved to be a pleasant companion. He even seemed interested in her problems.

They left the bar and dropped into a restaurant for a bite to eat. Over coffee they negotiated, finally agreeing to the fee of $100 for a half hour of Leslie's time. Dawn was breaking when they pulled up to the Quality Inn Motel in Hasbrouck Heights, the very same motel where Valorie Street had been murdered. Tommy paid $27.77 in advance for the keys to Room 117.

Soon they were in bed. Without warning, the now wild-eyed Tommy pulled a knife from his attache case. He quickly fastened handcuffs about the helpless girl's wrists. Gruffly Tommy ordered, "You have to take it. The other girls did. You're a whore and you have to be punished."

For the next three hours, Leslie endured sexual perversions and torture rarely equalled in the annals of crime. Her attacker threatened her with a pistol if she screamed. Leslie bit her lips until blood ran down her chin as she muffled her cries of pain.

At one point, while being whipped, she fell to the floor beside Tommy's gun, which he had put down so that he could wield his whip to better advantage. Leslie picked up the gun. Tommy advanced towards her with his knife. Leslie, who had never before held a firearm, pulled the trigger again and again. Nothing happened. The gun jammed. Figuring she was about to die, she screamed at the top of her lungs.

It was 9 a.m. A maid doing her rounds heard Leslie scream and called the front desk. Todd Radner, the assistant manger, called police. Together with head housekeeper Paula De Matthews, Radner headed for Room 117. Inside, the man known as Tommy had clamped a hand over Leslie's mouth. Radner knocked on the door.

Under instructions Leslie, leaving the chain intact, opened the door. Her eyes were black and blue, her cheeks swollen. "Everything is okay. I have no clothes on. I can't open the door." As she talked, Leslie attempted to signal that she was in trouble. Radner and De Matthews walked away.

Just then a police car arrived. Tommy saw the car pull up. He frantically dressed and gathered up his implements of torture. As he ran down the hall, Leslie hollered, "Stop him, stop him! He tried to kill me!"

Tommy, carrying a small calibre weapon, unknowingly ran directly toward Patrolman Stan Melowic. The police officer raised his shotgun and commanded, "Hold it right there and don't move!"

The hunt for the madman who had raped, mutilated and murdered prostitutes for years had come to an end. Tommy was identified as computer expert Richard Cottingham. Costume jewelry and bits of clothing found in his home enabled detectives to link him with the previous killings, as well as several vicious rapes that they had thought were perpetrated by several different men.

After a series of trials in New Jersey and New York, Cottingham was convicted of assault, kidnapping, rape and murder. His accumulated sentences total 250 years in Trenton State Prison, where he is currently incarcerated.

ANNIE CRAWFORD

SOME families have no luck.

Take the Crawford family of New Orleans, for example. In June 1910, Mary Agnes, the elder of a seemingly inexhaustible supply of daughters, suddenly became ill and just as suddenly died. A few weeks later Walter, the head of the family, passed away with hardly a whimper. Would you believe that 13 days after his untimely demise, his ever-loving wife also departed this cruel world?

Surviving daughters Elise, Gertrude and Annie moved in with an aunt and uncle, Mary and Robert Crawford, on St. Peter St. Elise was a pleasant-looking secretary employed with the railroad. Gertrude, 19, was the youngest member of the family. She too was an attractive young woman. Annie, the eldest surviving sister was 28, and presumably had never been kissed. Annie's forehead was too wide and her eyes seemed to be placed much too far apart. They resembled two little green peas. Her hair, which should have been blonde, was a dirty yellow, which she accentuated by having it done up in a huge ball at the back of her head. You could say that Annie was not attractive.

Annie had been working for six years at the New Orleans Sanitarium, but was unemployed when the series of tragic events befell her family. Soon she emerged as the dominant sister, demanding obedience from Elise and Gertie. In all fairness, she seemed to have their best interests at heart.

The three sisters had barely adjusted to living with their aunt and uncle when Elise suddenly took ill. She seemed to be constantly vomiting. It got so bad that one day she couldn't go to work and was confined to bed. Fortunately, Annie took charge. She consulted with the family physician, Dr. Marion H. McGuire, who prescribed capsules of calomel and soda for his patient.

Annie rushed down to the corner drugstore to purchase the medicine. Later that same night she summoned Mrs. Crawford to inform her that Elise appeared to be much worse. Mrs. Crawford took one look at Elise, who was in a coma, and agreed. Annie phoned Dr. McGuire, who arrive a short time later. After conducting some preliminary tests he decided the best thing for his patient would be to get her on her feet. The treatment apparently worked. Slowly Elise came around.

The next day, a Tuesday, Elise seemed to be much better, and the following day she was up and around. On Friday she suffered a relapse and again was confined to bed. That evening Annie brought her sick sister some tea. Elise complained to Gertie that the tea tasted bitter and refused to take it. Finally, Gertie brewed another cup, which Elise drank.

Then a strange conversation took place between the two younger sisters. Elise took off her rings and locket and presented them to Gertie. Despite Gertie's objections, Elise forced the jewelry upon her stating: "I won't need them any more."

Later that night Elise began breathing with great difficulty. Her aunt was most concerned. Remembering the doctor had once before brought Elise around by keeping the poor girl moving, Mrs. Crawford tried to get Elise on her feet. She was shocked when Annie exclaimed: "Why don't you let her alone and let her sleep?" Mrs. Crawford looked at Annie. For the first time the thought entered her head—was it possible that Annie was responsible for Elise's illness?

While these thoughts were dancing through Mrs. Crawford's head Annie made an appearance with a steaming cup of tea for dear Aunt Mary. Mrs. Crawford threw the teacup to the floor. At this precise moment Dr. McGuire made his entrance, ordered an ambulance, and thus the tense moment between aunt and niece passed. Next morning Elise died.

That Sunday Elise was buried, but not before a curious coroner had extracted two containers of liquid from her stomach and bladder. Upon examination the liquid was found to contain three grains of morphine.

The entire family was taken to police headquarters where the chronological events leading up to Elise's death were related to the police. It was revealed that Annie had placed a small insurance policy on Elise's life amounting to $132. Elise's funeral had cost more then the insurance payoff. After the questioning only Annie was detained by the authorities. Despite vehemently denying giving her sister the morphine, Annie was charged with murder. While confined in jailed she admitted to being a morphine addict who was accustomed to stashing it around the house. She also admitted she may have giver her sister morphine tablets instead of calomel and soda by mistake.

Authorities delved into Annie's history, with special emphasis on her family's unfortunate inability to live to a ripe old age. It was discovered that when Annie's sister Mary Agnes and her parents had died, a different doctor had been summoned on each occasion. Annie was always the one doing the summoning. Each doctor had mildly suspected poisoning, but had dismissed the suspicions from their minds.

Elise Crawford's body was exhumed. An autopsy was performed and revealed she had died of opiate poisoning. Annie was charged with her sister's murder.

It was felt at that in there was nothing to be gained by exhuming the bodies of Annie's parents or her sister Mary Agnes. After more than a year, if any morphine had been administered to them it would have decomposed.

There matters stood. Annie was tried for Elise's murder and admitted she may have given her sister morphine tablets by mistake. Circumstantial evidence weighed heavily against her but without a confession murder was difficult to prove. Annie stated time and again during her trial that she had no motive for killing Elise and to even suggest she was responsible for the deaths of other members of her family was preposterous.

The prosecuting attorney's could only state that it was possible Annie had pure hatred for her entire family. That was motive enough for them. Defence attorneys put forward the strong argument that Elise might very well have committed suicide.

The jury deliberated all night before reporting they were hopelessly deadlocked. The presiding judge declared a mistrial. Annie was released from custody and left for Texas the same day. Many believe that one of the cleverest and most diabolical killers in U.S. history walked out of the New Orleans courtroom that day in 1912, having successfully killed her mother, father and two sisters.

HARRY DE LA ROCHE JR.

HARRY and Mary Jane De La Roche were justifiably proud of their home and the lifestyle they had carved out for themselves. This was middle-class America, the way it should be.

Harry and Mary Jane lived in the New York City suburban town of Montvale, New Jersey. Most of Montvale's 8,000 citizens were interested in the high school football team and Little League baseball. With three sons, Harry Jr., 18, Ronnie, 15, and the always smiling Eric, 12, the De La Roches were no exception. Encouraged by their father, the boys took part in sports. Ronnie was an exceptional athlete. All three were introduced to guns at an early age by their father. They practised at a rifle range located a short distance from their comfortable home.

In 1976, when six-foot, three-inch Harry Jr. graduated from high school, the family was thrilled to learn that he had been accepted by The Citadel, a liberal arts military college in Charleston, South Carolina.

Harry Jr. was the first to leave the De La Roche nest. His parents wished him well. Harry Sr., a Ford Motor Co. employee, had always emphasized the need of a good education. His son would be an officer some day. The strict discipline, which Harry had stressed in his relationship with all three sons, would stand young Harry in good stead now that he had chosen a career in the military. Even his familiarity with guns would be an asset.

Photographs of Harry Jr. in his snappy cadet uniform were sent home during those first few months. The family couldn't wait until November, when Harry would be coming home for Thanksgiving. Many of the De La Roches' friends in town shared the family's pride in Harry.

Finally, November rolled around. Harry didn't talk much about his life at The Citadel, but his parents let him know how very pleased they were with him. Unknown to the De La Roches, Harry had made up his mind not to return to The Citadel. He knew the news would be devastating to his parents, particularly his father. Harry decided that he wouldn't break the news to them until after Thanksgiving dinner.

The meal was a culinary and social success. The boys' grandparents joined in the celebration. The three De La Roche boys wolfed down turkey and all the trimmings. Harry was in turmoil. He couldn't get up the courage to break the news to his family of his decision to leave The Citadel. The gnawing thought that sooner or later his mother and father had to be told preyed on his mind. He thought of little less.

While Harry Jr. struggled with his dilemma, his brother Ronnie also faced potential problems. Ronnie was actively using drugs. He kept a stash under his bed and was delighted to show it to his older brother. Harry admonished Ronnie, warning him that if their father ever found out about his involvement with drugs, there would be hell to pay.

And so the middle-class American family had flaws, invisible to the outsider, but flaws nevertheless. The oldest son, a disgruntled student, was fearful of being a failure in his ambitious father's eyes. The middle son was involved with drugs. Above all, gun enthusiast Harry Sr. had the ever-present instruments of death in his home.

Three days after Thanksgiving, Harry Jr. drove his 1970 Falcon downtown and blurted to Officer Carol Olsen, "Quick come to my house! I have just found my parents and younger brother dead and my middle brother is missing!" It was 4 a.m. Olsen rushed to the De La Roche home and took in a scene of wanton carnage. One bed held the bloody body of Mary Jane De La Roche. Harry Sr. lay dead in another bed. Eric's body was on the floor. All had been shot.

Other officers were quickly at the scene. Harry Jr. was questioned. He related that he had come home and discovered the three murdered members of his family and that his younger brother Ronnie was missing.

Meanwhile, police swarmed over the De La Roche home. Around noon the next day, two officers made their way upstairs leading to the attic, where they opened a metal locker. Stuffed inside, under Christmas decorations, was the body of Ronnie De La Roche. Like his parents and brother, he had been shot to death.

Shortly after the body was discovered, detectives found the murder weapon, a .22-calibre pistol. It was wrapped in a blood-soaked rag and had been placed in a basement drawer. In Harry Jr.'s room, police found a Citadel t-shirt and a pair of long underwear. Both were bloodstained. Harry Jr. was subjected to a lie detector test, which indicated that he was not telling the truth concerning the murders.

That same day, Harry confessed. It was a cold-blooded confession, describing in detail how in a few minutes he had annihilated his entire family. He revealed that he had removed his clothes except for the t-shirt and long underwear. He desperately thought of his dilemma. He simply would not return to a life he hated in Charleston. Yet, he couldn't tell his parents of this decision. He approached his parents' room several times, but each time returned to his own room without saying a word.

Finally, he made his way to their room and said, "I can't go back." At the same time, he closed his eyes and pulled the trigger of the .22-calibre pistol he clutched in his hand. He then turned the weapon from his father to his mother. Operating in a frenzy, he entered Ronnie's room and turned on the lights. According to Harry, Ronnie opened his eyes and was shot dead.

In his twin bed, Eric stirred. He too was shot. But Eric wasn't dead. when Harry returned to his own room, he heard noises coming from his brothers' bedroom. He went back to find Eric attempting to speak and get out of bed. Harry put his hand over his brother's eyes and said, "Eric, go to sleep, go to sleep. It's just a dream." Eric, if he heard at all, paid no heed. He managed to get up. Harry pistol-whipped him until he was dead.

In an attempt to divert blame from himself to Ronnie, he lugged Ronnie's body up to the attic and hid it in the locker. Noticing blood on Ronnie's bed, he had the presence of mind to realize that he would have to account for it. He transferred his father's body to Ronnie's bed. Harry then hid the gun, placed his two pieces of bloody clothing in his drawer, took a shower and raced downtown to tell officer Olsen that someone had killed Eric and his parents and that Ronnie was missing.

Harry De La Roche was charged with four counts of first-degree murder. He later recanted his confession, claiming that his brother Ronnie had been caught with drugs by their father. Ronnie had killed the family. Harry, in turn, had killed Ronnie. Harry's story was not believed.

On January 26, 1978, after deliberating six and a half hours, the New Jersey jury reached a verdict. They found Harry De La Roche guilty on the four murder charges. He was sentenced to four terms of life imprisonment to run concurrently.

Because the sentences were not to run consecutively, Harry was first eligible for parole in 1987. However, at that time he was denied parole. He currently resides at New Jersey's Garden State Prison.

ALBERT FISH

CANNIBALISM! The word itself screams out from the page as no other word in the English language. Incidents of human flesh being consumed by fellow humans to sustain life are well recorded. Marooned sailors, bush pilots, and surviving victims of plane crashes have all forced themselves to eat human flesh in order to survive. North American Indians and some African tribes ate portions of their fallen enemies as an act of respect, in the belief that they would acquire some of the admirable qualities of their former foes.

Those cases where cannibalism is practised for the sheer perverted pleasure of the act are much rarer. In the 20th century, the case most often referred to as an example of pure cannibalism is the bizarre saga of Albert Fish.

"Young man, 18 years old, wishes position in the country for the summer." The ad appeared in the Situations Wanted column of a New York City newspaper on Monday, May 21, 1928. Edward Budd was to regret placing the ad for the rest of his life.

The Budd family lived in West 15th St. apartment house in what was then the edge of New York City. Edward Budd, Sr., and his wife, Delia, had four children, the oldest being Edward Jr., and the youngest Grace, 12. Ed Budd had made up his mind. This summer he would escape from the city heat and noise. He placed the ad for summer employment in the newspaper.

Two days after the advertisement appeared an elderly, respectable looking man arrived at the Budd's door. He explained to Mrs. Budd that he had a large vegetable garden operation near Farmingdale, Long Island, and could use help over the summer months. Edward was enthusiastic. A deal was struck then and there. The elderly gentleman, who had introduced himself as Frank Howard, would pick Edward up the following Thursday or Sunday. The Budds invited Howard to come early on Sunday and have dinner with them. The old man promised to try. Later in the week, the Budd family received a telegram advising them that Howard would arrive early on Sunday.

Sure enough, Mr. Howard arrived the following Sunday and broke bread with the Budds. He said grace and proved to be a charming conversationalist. At the conclusion of the meal he informed his hosts that he had a surprise. His sister, who lived in New York, was having a birthday party for her daughter, who just happened to be Grace Budd's age. He was planning on attending and would take Grace along if it was all right with her mother. When they returned he and Ed could then leave for the country. Mrs. Budd was at first apprehensive, but with exuberant coaxing by her daughter, she finally consented. Hand-in-hand, little Grace and one of the worst monsters who ever lived strolled out of the apartment and, in Grace's case, into oblivion.

By subway, Frank Howard led Grace to Westchester County near Irvington. There, in a ram-shackle house called Wisteria Cottage, the old man choked the life from the little girl. He then dissected his victim and wrapped a portion of the body in his bandanna. Frank Howard left the house of death and proceeded to his rented room. Next day he ate the portion of meat that had once been Grace Budd. Every few days the old man would return to Wisteria Cottage. Each time he left with a parcel, which he later consumed. Nine days after the murder he made his final trip. What remained of Grace Budd was thrown out of a window into a weed-infested back yard.

Grace was reported missing. The case, considered to be a kidnapping perpetrated by an old man, presented only one clue. The missing person's bureau of the New York City Police Force was able to trace the telegram sent to the Budd family. This provided them with a sample of the kidnapper's handwriting, but nothing further turned up.

Years went by, and the little girl's disappearance was all but forgotten. From time to time the Budd family received crank notes and letters, which they routinely turned over to the police.

Six years after the kidnapping, one of these letters, thought to be from a crank, proved to have been written by the same hand which had written the old telegram to the Budds. The contents of the unsigned letter described Grace Budd's fate in detail.

Police were able to trace the writing paper to a type used by an organization known as The Private Chauffeurs Benevolent Association. A janitor for this organization admitted taking some of the stationery to his rooming house for his personal use. He told police that he had left some in his room at 200 East 52nd St. when he had moved out.

The police proceeded to Room 11 at the janitor's former address. The land-lady gave the police a description of the occupant of Room 11. There was no question about it—the occupant was Frank Howard, who had abducted Grace Budd almost six years previously.

The landlady informed police that Number 11 was often vacant for most of the month, but her tenant, known to her as Albert Fish, always returned to pick up a cheque sent to him by a son in North Carolina. This time when Fish returned to his room, police were waiting for him.

The mild-mannered old man readily confessed to the abduction. His story was one of perversion, which had begun at the age of five, when he discovered that he enjoyed pain after being spanked by a teacher. Brought up in an orphan-age, he later married and had several children. His wife always considered him strange, but lived with him for 20 years before leaving him. His grown children later testified that their father often thought he was Christ, and from time to time would disappear without an explanation.

Police uncovered the skull and some bones of Grace Budd, which had lain where they had been thrown so many years before. In the same weeds, they found a rusty knife and cleaver.

Fish was examined extensively by both psychiatrists and police. It was dis-covered that he had visited various communities in the northeastern U.S. at the exact time when young children had been murdered. Fish denied any knowledge of these crimes, but admitted to leading a life of molesting children, while he wandered from one job to another, usually as a house painter.

In a case as weird as any ever recorded, there was still more to come. While X-raying Fish, doctors found 29 metal needles in various parts of his body. Some were as large as those used to repair canvas. All had been inserted by Fish to cause pain. Doctors stated that some of the needles had been in his body for as long as seven years.

When Fish related his life story to doctors, he revealed that over the years he had been in several mental institutions for short periods of time. On each occasion he had been released as harmless.

Albert Fish stood trial for the murder of Grace Budd on March 11, 1935 in

White Plains, N.Y. Despite the efforts put forward by his defence counsel, pleading that his client was insane, the jury deliberated only a few hours before finding Fish guilty of murder.

Just before being transferred to Sing Sing, Fish confessed to four additional murders of small children.

As the end drew near, Fish told the guards that he was delighted at the chance of experiencing the ultimate thrill of being put to death. Albert Fish was electrocuted on January 16, 1936.

HARVEY GLATMAN

HARVEY Glatman was a specialist. He robbed only women.

In 1945, Harvey spent a year in the Canon City, Colorado prison for a series of armed robberies perpetrated against women. Shortly after his release, he was apprehended for stealing purses from women as they walked along dimly-lit streets. This time he spent five years in Sing Sing, before being paroled to his mother's loving care in Denver.

In 1957, Harvey migrated to Los Angeles, where the strange desire he had bottled up in his psyche came to the surface. Nondescript, owlish Harvey, with the oversized ears, shell-rimmed glasses and large nose, did not take L.A. by storm. You see, Harvey, at age 30, was a virgin. He had tried to become acquainted with members of the opposite sex in the past, but had always been rejected. Swinging Los Angeles would be different. Besides, Harvey had a plan.

Using the alias Johnny Glynn and posing as a professional photographer, Harvey had no trouble making contact with model Judy Dull. Judy, a beautiful blonde, was only 19, but had already been married and divorced. She lived in a rather plush apartment at 1302 Sweetzer Ave. with two equally beautiful models.

Harvey met all three girls, explaining that he had an assignment for one of them. It was to pose for the cover of a detective magazine and would involve some nude shots. He thought Judy Dull was exactly the type. A fee was established. The shooting would take place in the girls' apartment. Harvey explained that his studio was undergoing renovations.

On August 1, 1957, Harvey pulled up in his black Dodge bearing Colorado plates. He told the girls that there was a slight change of plans. He had been able to borrow the well-equipped studio of a friend. He wouldn't have to use their apartment after all. One of the girls mentioned that Judy had appointments for later that same afternoon. Could she have a telephone number where Judy could be reached? Without hesitation, Harvey jotted down a number on a piece of paper and passed it over.

Judy and Harvey sped away. They drove to a dreary building on Melrose

Ave. Judy, carrying her model's suitcase, briskly walked to a second floor apartment. She was no doubt reassured by the tripods, lights and other photographic equipment already set up. Harvey took several shots of Judy fully clothed before asking her to take off her blouse. He took more photographs. Then he suggested she slip out of her skirt.

Harvey approached Judy with a five-foot piece of white sash cord. Initially, Judy objected, but Harvey calmly explained that he had to tie her up for a few shots in order to fulfil his obligations to the detective magazine. Reluctantly, Judy allowed her hands and feet to be tied and a gag to be placed over her mouth. Harvey took more pictures. He then produced a gun and informed Judy that was going to release the gag and untie her hands and feet. If she didn't comply with his every wish, he would shoot her in the head.

Once free of the gag, Judy pleaded for her life. She tearfully explained that she and her husband were in the midst of a divorce. She was about to receive custody of their little girl. She promised to keep Harvey's secret. She just wanted to be spared. Weird Harvey raped the terror-stricken girl and forced her to watch TV with him. Every so often, Judy pleaded to be released, but Harvey was deep in thought.

Finally he agreed. He would drive out to the desert, take a few more photographs and then set her free. The pair drove for hours into the San Jacinto mountains. Harvey stated, "Just a few quick shots. Then we'll go back to the highway and you're on your own. Sorry we had to come so far, but there wasn't any other way, Judy."

Harvey was lying. He realized that Judy knew his address, knew he had Colorado plates on his Dodge and could describe him in far more detail than her roommates. Harvey once more tied Judy's hands and feet and gagged the hapless girl. He took another piece of rope and wrapped it around Judy's neck. In minutes the girl was dead. There, on the lonely desert, Harvey dug a shallow grave with his hands for Judy Dull.

Judy's roommates went to the police with the phone number given to them by photographer Johnny Glynn. It proved to be a bogus number.

Seven months later, posing as plumber George Williams, Harvey joined a lonely hearts club and managed a blind date with 24-year-old Shirley Ann Bridgeford. Shirley, who had recently been divorced, had two small sons and lived with her mother. To "mix with new friends," she answered a lonely hearts club ad. It was Shirley's misfortune to answer an ad extolling the virtues of Harvey Glatman. As soon as Shirley entered his car, Harvey pulled out his gun. He drove into the desert and took a series of photographs before raping and killing his victim.

Shirley's mother reported her daughter missing to police. A quick check with the lonely hearts club revealed that plumber George Williams had given a fictitious name and address.

Two months later Harvey, posing as Mr. Johnson, called a nude modelling service. He required a model for an hour or two, and was put in touch with Ruth Rita Mercado, who had her own studio. A date was set and Harvey showed up in his beat-up Dodge.

On this occasion, he didn't waste time. Ruth opened the door and stared into the barrel of Harvey's trusty black automatic. In minutes, she was tied, gagged and helpless. Harvey took his pictures. At gunpoint, he untied his quarry and led her to the Dodge. They sped into the desert. The usual outdoor pictures were taken. Ruth was raped and then murdered in the usual hideous manner with the rope draped around her neck. Acquaintances reported Ruth Mercado's disappearance to police.

Harvey was confident. After all, hadn't he had his way with three lovely women and no one had the slightest idea why they had disappeared? In fact, no one even knew they were dead.

Harvey was referred to model Lorraine Vigil by another model. Lorraine was newly arrived in Hollywood from San Francisco and was eager for work. Harvey called at Lorraine's apartment. During the drive to his non-existent studio, Lorraine sized up her companion. He didn't seem right. She couldn't quite categorize her anxiety, but this strange man just didn't act like a professional photographer. When she realized her silent companion was leaving the city far behind, she knew her instincts were correct.

Lorraine didn't have long to wait. Harvey braked the car, pulled out his gun and told her he would kill her unless she complied with his every desire. Lorraine replied, "All right, just please don't hurt me." When Harvey took out his rope, Lorraine pleaded not to be tied up. She promised over and over that she would obey his every wish. Lorraine knew intuitively that she was in a life and death situation. The previous three victims possibly felt they would be spared. Lorraine knew better. This man was going to kill her.

Without warning, she pushed Harvey's gun aside. The two desperately struggled for possession of the weapon. The gun went off, but only slightly seared Lorraine's thigh. She moaned and slumped against him, feigning death. Harvey stared at the gun in a stupor. Slowly, Lorraine inched her hand toward the door handle on Harvey's side of the car. She moved the handle mechanism until she knew the door was ajar. Then, with all her strength, she shoved Harvey out the door.

The force of her thrust landed her on top of the gunman. Desperately, she fought to get control of the gun. Her teeth clamped down on Harvey's gun hand. With a yelp, he let go. Lorraine pounced on the gun, picked it up, pointed it and fired it at Harvey. The gun jammed. As Harvey crouched like an animal, about to attack Lorraine, the courageous girl had one stroke of incredible good luck that day.

Tom Mulligan of the California Highway Patrol drove up on his motorcycle at that moment. Instantly realizing what was taking place, he barked at Harvey, "You stay right were you are!"

Harvey confessed in detail to his crimes and led police to the three lonely graves in the desert. On August 18, 1959, Harvey Glatman was quietly strapped into the gas chamber in San Diego and put to death.

JOHN GILBERT GRAHAM

A few years ago John Wayne Gacy paid the ultimate price for murdering 33 young men and boys, thereby becoming the most prolific mass murderer in U.S. criminal history. Twenty-five years earlier another citizen of the U.S., John Gilbert Graham, actually murdered a larger number than Gacy. Only a technicality deprived this earlier day monster from being the all-time champ.

John first saw the light of day in 1932 in Denver, Colorado. His father passed away when he was only five years old. Left destitute, Jack's mother Daisy had little choice but to place her son in an orphanage, where he remained for six years. In 1943, Mrs. Graham remarried a wealthy rancher, John Earl King and brought her 11-year-old-son to his new home. For a while he was joined by his sister, who later moved to Alaska.

Jack was not a contented child. While he got high marks, he never really showed any interest in school work. He is mainly remembered for an explosive temper, which could flare up at the slightest provocation. When Jack didn't get his way he ran away from home. At the age of 16 he lied about his age to join the Coast Guard. Nine months later his deception was uncovered and he was dismissed from the service.

Jack returned to Denver and found a job, but quickly succeeded in getting into trouble. He stole several of his company's blank cheques, forged the name of one of the company's directors, and cashed $4,200 of the bogus paper. With the proceeds he travelled to Texas, where he became a bootlegger. He was apprehended, and after serving a few months in jail was returned to Colorado to face forgery charges. Daisy King stepped in and made restitution in the amount of $2,500, with the firm promise that her son would pay off the balance of $1,700 in instalments.

Jack secured work in a garage, married pretty Gloria Elson, and for a while seemed to settle down. The attractive young couple promptly had two children. Daisy doted over her grandchildren.

In 1954, tragedy once again entered Daisy King's life. Her husband Earl died. This time Daisy was left with a comfortable fortune. She decided that her wayward son would reform if given a proper opportunity. Daisy presented Jack with a new home. She would live with her son and daughter-in-law, but the house was in his name. Daisy had also found a drive-in restaurant, which she purchased for $5,000, and asked Jack to run it. No son could ask more of a mother.

But things just didn't work out. Jack always seemed to be short of cash at the end of the day. Daisy couldn't understand how an intelligent 23-year-old man could not manage to balance his cash with his cash register tapes. Mother and son began to argue over the operation of the restaurant. To relieve the tension, Daisy decided to visit her daughter in Alaska. During October 1955 she bought Christmas presents to take north.

On November 1, Jack and Gloria, accompanied by their two children, drove Daisy to the airport. Daisy was catching Flight 629 for the first leg of her trip to Alaska. There was a slight delay at the weigh-in counter when it was discovered that her luggage was in excess of the allowable weight of 66 pounds. She was over by 37 pounds. When an attendant was told that one suitcase contained Christmas presents, he suggested that those items could be mailed a lot cheaper than the $27 he had to charge. Jack would hear none of it. He talked his mother into paying the $27.

It is to be remembered that there were no security measures at airports 40 years ago, but insurance was available from vending machines. Jack sauntered over to the machines and popped in quarters. You could buy $6,250 protection for a quarter. Jack bought several policies totalling $87,500. His mother joked with him as she signed the policies.

Daisy hugged her grandchildren, kissed her daughter-in-law, and clasped her son to her bosom. Flight 629 took off. Before the Graham family was out of the airport word was received that the DC6 had exploded in mid-air. There were no survivors. A total of 44 men, women, and children had perished. Among them was Mrs. Daisy King.

The FBI lab in Washington quickly ascertained that the plane had been blown up by dynamite. Traces of sodium nitrate and sodium carbonate were found in the gaping torn metal believed to be the location in the baggage compartment.

Authorities could not locate the baggage of one Daisy King, leading them to believe that her luggage may have contained the dynamite. They did find Daisy's handbag, which had been carried aboard the ill-fated plane. It was then they found newspaper clippings concerning her son, Jack Graham, who four years earlier had been sought by Denver police as a forgery suspect. FBI agents dug into Jack Graham's life and discovered that he had a penchant for getting into trouble with the law.

Nine days after the disaster, FBI agents knocked on Jack's door. He denied any knowledge of the crime. A search of his home uncovered a roll of wire used in connecting up dynamite. Agents also discovered gaily wrapped Christmas presents. Had Jack, unknown to his mother, substituted a dynamite bomb in place of the presents?

After three hours of questioning, Jack Graham calmly changed his story and confessed to perpetrating the horrendous crime. He told the FBI of actually working as an apprentice electrician for ten days so that he could manufacture the bomb without blowing himself up. He had bought 25 sticks of dynamite and all the accessories to construct the bomb. Later clerks in hardware stores identified him as the purchaser of these supplies.

Jack Graham stood trial for the murder of his mother only, thereby escaping the historical notoriety of becoming the greatest convicted mass murder in U.S. history. After deliberating only an hour and a half, a jury found him guilty of murder in the first degree.

Graham was one of the coolest men ever to be executed. A few days before his death he reminded a guard, "if any mail comes for me after next month you can readdress it to hell."

On January 11, 1957, he calmly entered Colorado's gas chamber, inhaled deeply, lost consciousness, and was pronounced dead twelve minutes later.

WILLIAM HEIRENS

THE city of Chicago has long been familiar with violent death. The citizens of that community take a gangland killing as casually as we take our morning coffee. It takes a bizarre and baffling case to arouse public interest. Here is such a case.

On June 3, 1945, Mrs. Josephine Alice Ross was found dead in her apartment. Her body had horrible knife wounds about the head and neck. The jugular vein had been cut, allowing her to bleed to death. A nylon stocking and skirt were wrapped around her neck. The bed she lay on was completely soaked in blood. The investigating officers knew immediately that this was no ordinary crime when they discovered that the body had been washed clean of blood and adhesive tape had been applied to the cuts and abrasions. Mrs. Ross had not been sexually attacked, but her murderer had lingered in the apartment and had meticulously wiped the entire apartment clean of fingerprints.

For the next five months, police investigated several attacks on women in the general area of the University of Chicago. Some were shootings and some were beatings, and all could have ended in tragedy but for the fact that the attacker was either interrupted or was successfully fought off by the women.

Then on December 10, the murderer struck again. Frances Brown's nude body was found draped in a kneeling position over the bathtub of her apartment. She had been stabbed repeatedly in the head and neck, and had been shot as well. Again the murderer had taken great care in washing the body. He had also stayed in the apartment long enough to wash every piece of furniture free of fingerprints. This time he missed one lone print—the right index finger. An attempt to trace him through this print failed.

Overshadowing all other evidence in the Brown case was an actual message left by the killer. On a wall in the living room, written in lipstick, were the words:

For heavens
sake catch me

Before I kill more
I cannot control myself

The similarity of the two murders as well as the several other attacks on women convinced the police that they were looking for one sick man. On the morning of January 7 they were to find out just how sick.

A little six-year-old girl, Suzanne Degnan, had been abducted from the first-floor bedroom of her two-storey home. Her father found a ransom note on her bed.

Get $20,000
Reddy &
Waite
For word
do not notify
FBI or
police
Bills in 5's and 10's

One fingerprint was found on the note. It was the print of the left little finger. A check of police files again proved fruitless, as no match could be found.

A search was started for Suzanne in the immediate vicinity of her home. An officer noticed that a sewer lid looked as if it had been recently pried loose. He lifted the lid and peered into the sewer. There floating on the surface was a human head. A search of other sewers revealed the rest of pathetic little Suzanne's body. She had been abducted and dismembered on the same night.

In scouring the neighborhood for any clues to the killer's identity the police found an apartment building close by where Suzanne had been dismembered. The basement, like many of the buildings in that area, was equipped with a washbasin for the tenants. Here the police found bloody rags, and not a great deal more. It was estimated that the killer had spent over two hours cleaning the washroom. Again despite an all-out effort by the police, there was a vacuum of concrete clues to the wave of wanton killings. Months dragged by, and then in a completely unrelated incident, the police found their killer.

A young man was interrupted as he was ransacking an apartment. He dashed out of the building, and into an adjoining building at 1320 Farrell Ave. He stopped at the back door of an apartment occupied by Mrs. Frances Willett, and asked for a drink of water. He picked the wrong door. Mrs. Willett was the wife of a policeman. She sensed something wrong and told him to sit down on her porch. She then hooked the door from the inside and pretended to get the water. Instead she called the police.

In the meantime, an off-duty policeman, Abner Cunningham, was coming home from the beach wearing swimming trunks and a t-shirt. He saw the youth dash out of one building and into another. Cunningham started a door-to-door search of the second building.

The police, responding to Mrs. Willett's call, arrived at the back of her building. She called out, "He's up here on the back porch!"

Det. Tiffin P. Constant started up after him. As he looked up the stairs he saw a young man pointing a gun at him. He was pulling the trigger but the gun failed to fire. The detective caught up with the youth and they started to fight and roll on the porch. Officer Cunningham heard the noise and started up the stairs. As he did so he picked up three flower pots. When he reached the pair, he hesitated for a minute, not knowing which was the fugitive. Det. Constant sensed the hesitation. He screamed, "That's him!" Cunningham brought the flower pots down on the young man's head with all his might. The fight was over.

The young man was William Heirens, a 17-year-old University of Chicago student. William was a clean-cut, good-looking boy, weighing 155 pounds and standing five-feet, 10-inches. In a routine check of the boy's room at the university, police found two suitcases. They contained several pistols, $1,800 in War Bonds, and a surgical kit. Upon checking Heirens' fingerprints, it was found that the print of his left little finger matched the print found on the Degnan ransom note.

In one fell swoop, the William Heirens case was transformed from that of a prowler to one receiving world-wide publicity as a mass killer.

At first the young student would say nothing, and for a while there was some question as to whether the flower pot had resulted in permanent damage to his brain. A thorough examination proved these suspicions to be unfounded, and gradually young Heirens started to talk. He claimed he was dominated by another person, whom he referred to as George. George, he said, did the bad things, while he, William tried to stop him.

In the end though, William Heirens took the responsibility for his crimes. He confessed in detail to the three killings, and to an estimated 300 robberies. He led police to various caches of loot throughout Chicago. Thousands of dollars in bonds and cash were recovered. Heirens never spent more than five dollars a week on himself. He went to the three murder locations, and while the officers watched, he reenacted every horrible detail of his crimes.

The authorities were baffled on one point-what was his motive?

Heirens revealed that while ordinary people received sexual satisfaction from a relationship with a member of the opposite sex, he received this same satisfaction only by breaking into and robbing a house or apartment. He would get this sexual urge that had to be satisfied. He never molested or interfered in any way with the three women he killed. In each case, he panicked when they made too much noise.

Heirens stood trial and pleaded guilty to three indictments of murder, and 26 of assault with intent to kill, burglary, and robbery. He received three life sentences to run consecutively, and a one year to life sentence for the 26 non-murder charges to follow the three life sentences.

He was committed to Statesville Penitentiary at Joliet, Ill., but has since been transferred to the Vienna Correctional Facility in Vienna, Ill., where he is to this day.

HICKOCK & SMITH

PERRY Smith met Dick Hickock while both were nonpaying guests of the State of Kansas. They were cellmates at Kansas State Penitentiary in Lansing.

Dick was a high school graduate with an above average I.Q. His parents, who lived on a small farm, had high hopes for their athletic son. Dick had received offers of baseball and football scholarships, but even with assistance he felt that attending university would place too great a financial burden on his parents. He took a mechanic's course instead and worked off and on in garages. At the age of 19, he married a 16-year-old girl, but the marriage didn't last. Dick played around with another girl. When she became pregnant, he divorced his wife and married for the second time. This marriage fared no better than the first.

Good looking, pleasant Dick Hickock had no trouble passing bad cheques. Even his victims admitted that he could charm the birds out of the trees. When he wasn't passing rubber cheques, he was stealing, and when he wasn't doing either he was in prison serving time. That's how Dick met Perry Smith.

While cellmates at Kansas State Penitentiary, Dick and Perry became good friends. Dick had an obsession. A fellow inmate, Floyd Wells, had told him that years before he had worked for a wealthy farmer named Clutter in Holcomb, Kansas. The Clutter farm was rather isolated and easy pickings for anyone with brains. Wells claimed that Herb Clutter was known to keep large quantities of cash in a safe in his home. When Wells helped with the crops on the Clutter spread the occupants of the house were Herb Clutter, his wife Bonnie, a son Kenyon, and a daughter Nancy.

Dick constantly repeated the story to Perry. The two men arranged to get in touch with each other once they were paroled. On July 6, 1959, Perry Smith walked out of the Kansas State Pen. Five weeks later Dick Hickock was paroled. The two friends met as they had promised and agreed to rob Herb Clutter. Wells had provided the pair with details of how to reach the Clutter farm. Dick had one stipulation. There would be no witnesses. Perry agreed.

Herb Clutter had worked hard all his life. At 48 he was lean, suntanned, and tough as leather. As a young man he had majored in agriculture at Kansas State University. Soon after graduation he had purchased a piece of land. His wife Bonnie was of some concern. She suffered from bouts of depression and from time to time had been admitted to rest homes. Nancy, at 16, was an outgoing, good-looking young girl who planned on attending university. It was Herb's hope that Kenyon, 15, would some day run the ranch.

The Clutter home was a sprawling, ranch style, modern dwelling with every convenience. Herb did have one idiosyncrasy. He didn't believe in keeping money around his house. In fact, he hardly ever carried more than a few dollars with him. Everyone in Holcomb knew that Herb Clutter always paid by cheque.

In the early morning hours of November 15, 1959, the two small-time hoodlums, Dick Hickock and Perry Smith, drove up to the Clutter ranch. Equipped with adhesive tape, rope, a shotgun, and a knife, the two desperate men had little difficulty gaining entrance to the house. The side door was unlocked. Quietly they made their way to Herb Clutter's panelled office. Try as they might, they couldn't find the safe which was supposedly located there. Herb Clutter woke up and was herded into his office. He explained that he didn't keep any appreciable amount of money in his home. He offered the two men the few dollars he had in his pocket.

Frail, nervous Bonnie Clutter was the next member of the family to be awakened that night. She confirmed that there was no money in the house. Herb Clutter and his wife were locked in a bathroom, while Perry and Dick went looking for Nancy and Kenyon Clutter.

Now the whole Clutter family was gathered together. Herb Clutter's hands were tied and, while Dick stood guard over the remaining three members of the family, Herb was marched down to the basement of his home. Here Perry forced Herb to lie down while he tied his feet. One by one each member of the Clutter family was tied hand and foot. Kenyon was taken down to a separate room in the basement. The two women were taken to their bedrooms and placed on their beds.

Without blinking an eye Perry Smith slit Herb Clutter's throat. Then he shot the dying man at point blank range in the head. One by one each member of the Clutter family was annihilated. Later in the car the two men counted their take: Under $40 in cash, a pair of binoculars, and a transistor radio. Four mutilated corpses were all that was left of a hard-working, loving family.

Next morning the bodies of the Clutter family were found. Law enforcement officials were amazed at the viciousness of the senseless attack.

Dick and Perry were disappointed at the meagreness of their score, but it was too late. They read about the murders in the newspaper, but later admitted they felt no sorrow or remorse at what they had done. Their minds contained only two thoughts – to survive and to have some fun. Dick managed to pass enough bad cheques in one day to finance their getaway to Mexico. Once there Dick became disillusioned, and as the money ran out the pair made their way back to the U.S.

The Clutter massacre was considered to be one of the most vicious crimes ever perpetrated in the state of Kansas. News of the murders remained on the front pages of the area's newspapers for several days. Floyd Wells heard of the murders on the radio in the penitentiary and immediately became the one person in the world who knew the identity of the killers. He couldn't believe that Dick Hickock had actually taken him seriously and tried to rob Herb Clutter. Prisons are full of desperate men trying to impress each other. Men brag, rumors of the big score pass the lonely months and years. Such haphazard information is rarely acted upon once the prisoner is on the outside. Dick Hickock was an exception.

Tempted by a newspaper's offer of $1,000 reward, Wells went to the authorities with his story. He was believed. As soon as the police knew who they were looking for, Dick Hickock and Perry Smith became the most wanted men in 10 states. Ironically they made their way back to Kansas City, where Hickock passed several bad cheques. This time the men decided to make their way to Miami for the Christmas season. Unbelievably Hickock used his own name while passing the phony cheques. A storekeeper became suspicious when Dick purchased a TV set. He had the presence of mind to jot down Hickock's license number.

After a short stay at a sleazy hotel in Miami, the wandering killers decided to move on through New Mexico, Arizona, and on to Las Vegas. On the last day of 1959 two Las Vegas police officers in their patrol car spotted a Kansas licence number which was on their hot list. They edged the stolen car over to the curb. It was the end of the road for Dick Hickock and Perry Smith.

Both men later had conflicting stories of the exact events which had taken place inside the Clutter home on that fateful night. Both were sure of one thing. They admitted being the murderers.

Dick and Perry were tried and found guilty. They survived three execution dates on Death Row, before being hanged on April 14, 1965.

RAY JACKSON

ANNETTE Stewart was fed up with her job and, as a result, had an interview lined up for the following Monday morning. She had no way of knowing that she wouldn't live through the weekend.

On the pleasant Friday night of September 16, 1989, Annette dropped into a bar in downtown Kansas City, Missouri. The work week was over and she figured she deserved a few minutes to relax with a tall cool one.

As 33-year-old Annette was leaving the bar, a young man struck up a conversation with her. Together they walked along the city's Gillham Park. Suddenly, the young man clutched Annette by the throat and dragged her into some nearby bushes. When she went limp, he carefully removed her clothing. Annette didn't utter a sound. She was dead.

As quickly as he had struck, the young man disappeared into the darkness. Next morning, a businessman discovered Annette's nude body and called police. The murder of Annette Stewart, although tragic, was considered to be another routine big-city homicide, if homicide can ever be called routine. Her death would take on far more sinister connotations four days later.

On September 20, the nude body of 22-year-old Kimberly Creer was found in Gillham Park, about four blocks from where Annette Stewart had been strangled. As at the previous crime scene, Kimberly's clothing had been spread around the body, but nothing had been torn or ripped. Both women had been strangled. It appeared that Kimberly may have screamed for help as her killer carefully wrapped her brassiere across her mouth and around her head to prevent her from shouting.

While there was no direct proof that the killings were connected, investigators suspected the two similar murders committed in the same area only four days apart had been the work of the same perpetrator.

On October 23, the body of 22-year-old Teresa Williams was found adjacent to Gillham Park. She had been manually strangled and her clothes had been removed. For the first time, the dreaded words serial killer were used to describe the murderer who was stalking women in and around the park. He had taken three lives, yet no one had seen him, nor had he left any traceable clue to his identity. None of his three victims had known each other.

Seven days later, the Gillham Park strangler struck again—36-year-old Janice Berryman's body was found in the same condition as the previous three victims.

November and the Christmas holiday season came and went. It was as if the madman, who had struck terror into the hearts of the citizens of Kansas City, had taken a vacation or moved out of the area.

On January 18, 1990, with the discovery of 23-year-old Tonya Ward's body, investigators knew the killer was still in their midst. All the tell-tale signs were there. Tonya had been strangled, her body stripped of clothing. Nothing had been torn or ripped.

Winter gave way to spring. Maybe the urge to kill had left the murderer, but such was not the case. On April 6, Michelle Mitchell was strangled in Gillham Park. Only hours before her body was discovered by a passerby, Michelle, her girlfriend and two men were stopped by police. When drugs were found in their vehicle, one of the men was arrested. Michelle and her girlfriend were released.

Michelle's girlfriend was traced through the licence number of the vehicle. She told investigators that after their run-in with the police, she and Michelle had given a lift to another man. She had let this man and Michelle out of the car after he helped pay for some gasoline. With the help of a police artist, Michelle's friend was able to provide enough details to come up with what she felt was an extremely good likeness of the possible suspect.

The artist's sketch was widely distributed on TV and in the local newspapers. Tips poured in to police headquarters. One woman told how she was attacked and dragged into bushes in Gillham Park. Her attacker was intent on strangling her, but just as she was losing consciousness a man walking his dog came upon the scene and her assailant ran away. She thought the man in the composite sketch was the same man.

Now police had two witnesses who could identify the strangler, but still had no name to go with the picture. One lead appeared promising. A woman called police. Although she didn't know the name of the man in the newspaper sketch, she said she was a neighbor of his and could point out his house.

Following up on this tip, police picked up 22-year-old Ray Jackson. He bore a stunning resemblance to the sketch featured in the newspapers. Within minutes, Jackson was confessing to the string of Gillham Park murders. He described in detail how he had struck up conversations with the women and had pounced upon them just as he had gained their confidence. He was very strong and, struggle as they might, once he had clamped his hands around their throats, they had no chance of escape.

His last victim, Michelle Mitchell, had managed to scratch his arms. Jackson proudly displayed the scratches to his interrogators. She was the only one of the six women who had been able to fight back. Jackson also admitted that he had attacked the woman who had escaped when the man with the dog stumbled upon them.

Michelle's girlfriend and the surviving woman positively identified Ray Jackson from a police lineup.

In December 1991, Jackson's lawyers and the prosecution came to terms regarding a plea bargain agreement. In exchange for Jackson's guilty plea to all six murders, as well as an aggravated assault charge, the prosecution did not request the death penalty. Jackson was sentenced to six terms of life imprisonment for the murders and a further term of life imprisonment for the aggravated assault. The sentences are to run consecutively.

It is interesting to note that Ray Jackson had never been in any trouble in his entire life before he went on his killing spree.

FRITZ KLENNER

SUSIE Newsome had all the credentials of the proverbial southern belle. She was good looking in that delicate way which girls from the southern U.S. seem to inherit at birth. Her family was respectable, upper-middle class. Susie hailed from Charlotte, North Carolina, so it was only natural that she attend Wake Forest University. It was there in her junior year that she met and fell in love with Tom Lynch, a pre-dental student.

In 1970, Susie and Tom were married. While I would like to report that the wedding was a gala affair enjoyed by all, such was not quite the case. Susie and her mother-in-law, Delores Lynch, got into a tiff over one of the wedding party's dresses. It was a matter soon forgotten by everyone but Susie. She was one to hold a grudge. Would you believe years and years?

After spending the next four years at the University of Kentucky, where he obtained his dental degree, Tom joined the navy. He and Susie moved to Beaufort, S.C. Susie proceeded, in the succeeding two years, to give birth to two sons, John and Jim. Now I would be amiss not to inform you that while these happy events were unfolding, Susie was decidedly cold to her mother-in-law. To give you an idea, Delores didn't see her grandson Jim until he was a full year old.

Tom received his discharge from the navy and decided to practise dentistry in Albuquerque, New Mexico. Our Susie didn't like the heat. She didn't like the food. She didn't like Albuquerque, period. She was inclined to blame Tom for the town's perceived deficiencies. Susie stood the place for an argumentative three years before she piled the two boys into her Audi and took off. She didn't stop until she hit the comforting confines of North Carolina. Only then did she call the understandably worried Tom, advising him that she would not be returning. Not ever.

The once devoted couple formally separated. Susie obtained custody of the two boys. She busied herself becoming reacquainted with old friends. One fine day, she visited her doctor, Fred Klenner, who just happened to be her uncle. His son Fritz had been assisting him around the office. It was in this way that he and Susie got to know each other.

Fritz had an interesting history. Back in 1970, he had flunked out of the University of Mississippi's pre-med school. He returned to his father's office, where he passed his time wearing a white jacket with a stethoscope conspicuously sticking out of his pocket. Dad was disappointed, but was given some cause for hope when his rather weird son informed him that he had been accepted at Duke Medical School in Durham, N.C.

Fritz rented an apartment near the campus. As far as anyone was concerned, he was only a smidgen away from becoming a doctor. It was all a sham. For years, Fritz spent his days frequenting gun shops and biker hangouts. Even they thought he was a couple of cards short of a full deck. One of his so-called friends decided to check up on him. It didn't take more than a telephone call to the university to verify that there was no one remotely resembling Fritz enrolled at Duke.

When the sham was exposed, Fritz returned to being an almost doctor, assisting his father. In 1984, Dr. Klenner died and left Fritz $25,000, which he used to buy guns and survivalist paraphernalia.

This, then, was Susie's new companion. For some unknown reason, she didn't find Fritz that strange at all. In fact, she was very attracted to her first cousin. Friends attempted to have her reconcile with her husband, but Susie wouldn't hear of it. For his part, Tom obtained a divorce and married his dental assistant, Kathy Anderson. Tom's only contact with his former wife were his constant efforts to be allowed to spend more time with his two sons. Slowly, Susie was losing the friendship of her entire family. Her mother and brother Rob didn't approve of Fritz. Her mother-in-law hated her and any spark that Tom may have felt for her had been long extinguished. Let's face it, Susie had weird Fritz and that's about all she had.

On July 24, 1984, Delores Lynch was found murdered in her home in Kentucky. She had been shot in the face. The body of her daughter Janie was located in an upstairs bedroom. She too had been shot in the head. Nothing had been taken from the house and no clues to the killer's identity were uncovered. Back in Albuquerque, Tom was devastated to learn of the murders of his mother and sister.

Susie was not disturbed by her mother-in-law's untimely demise. In March 1985, Fritz moved in with her. Susie's main aim in life was to prevent her ex from having access to their two sons. To add insult to injury, her own parents felt that Tom should be allowed more time with the boys.

On May 18, 1985, police were called to the home of Susie's parents. They found her father's body in the hallway. Bob Newsome had been shot in the head, arm and stomach. Susie's mother Florence had been stabbed to death and her grandmother had been shot through the temple. Expensive jewelry and cash lying around the house had not been touched.

When Tom Lynch heard that his former wife's mother, father and grandmother had been murdered in North Carolina, it was just too much. After all, only a year earlier, Susie's mother-in-law and sister-in-law had been murdered in similar fashion in Kentucky. He informed police of his suspicions. Sweet Susie was questioned. Yes, it was true. A horrible coincidence had taken place. Perhaps that evil husband of hers was behind it all.

Police conducted an extensive investigation, attempting to connect the two sets of killings. Naturally they learned of Susie's close relationship with her first cousin Fritz. He was questioned and came up with an alibi. On the day of the murder, he had been with Ian Perkins, a student friend. Ian was interrogated. He admitted knowing Fritz and considered him quite a guy. According to Ian, Fritz had told him that he was a CIA agent. On occasion Fritz claimed that he was a hit man for the agency.

Rather than providing Fritz with an alibi for the night of the murders, Ian's story tended to incriminate him. He told police that on the night in question he had driven Fritz to within a mile of the Newsome home and had let him out. Fritz had been equipped with two guns and a bayonet. Ostensibly, he was going to rub out a drug dealer under instructions from the CIA. Fritz returned to the pickup point sometime later and told Ian that the job had been successful. After hearing Ian's incriminating statement, it was decided to keep a close surveillance on Fritz and Susie.

On June 3, Fritz, who sensed the heat was on, pulled up in front of Susie's apartment. Police watched as he loaded his Chevy Blazer with survivalist equipment. Susie, her two sons and the family's two dogs, jumped in. Fritz took off with the police in pursuit. All pretense of secretive surveillance was out the window. Fritz fired one of his weapons and wounded a pursuing police officer. Finally, he sighted a roadblock and pulled up. In seconds, the Chevy Blazer and all its occupants blew up. Fritz had set a bomb under the vehicle. When he felt he was trapped, he set off the device. Every living thing in the Chevy was blown apart.

In all, nine individuals had lost their lives. Many believe that one man, Fritz Klenner, was solely responsible for all eight murders. Others feel that Susie may have had guilty knowledge in the first five killings. The most popular theory is that Fritz acted independently in all the murders in some misguided belief that he was acting on Susie's behalf.

DANNY LA PLANTE

IT would be a blessing if murder and its vile ramifications would respect the Christmas season, but such is not the case. In December, when decent citizens enjoy the spirit of giving and goodwill, there are those among us who prey on their fellow human beings with scant regard for the holy season.

The community of Townsend, Massachusetts, is tucked away about 90 km northwest of Boston close to the New Hampshire border. If ever there was a peaceful rural American town, well removed from violent crime, it was Townsend. The 7,000 individuals who lived and worked there did so with a degree of confidence that violence was something to be read about in the Boston newspapers. The God-fearing folks of Townsend were concerned with church affairs, local politics and good old-fashioned gossip. That is, until December 1987, when Townsend lost its innocence.

Lawyer Andrew Gustafson drove through the crisp late winter afternoon toward his Cape Cod style home. It had been an ordinary day at the office. As he drew closer, he anticipated the children's usual enthusiastic greeting. William, five, and Abigail, seven, were the apples of Andrew's eye. He considered himself fortunate to have such a fine family. Of course, there was Priscilla, his 33-year-old wife, who took good care of all three of her charges. Anyone who was acquainted with Andrew knew he worshipped his wife. Yes, that day in December 1987, Andrew Gustafson was looking forward to arriving home to his family.

The house was in darkness. Funny thing for this time in the evening, he thought to himself.

Andrew walked into a scene which no husband and father should ever have to witness. No one responded to his shouts. He made his way to the bedroom, where he gazed in horror and disbelief at Priscilla's body lying on the bedroom floor. She had been shot in the head. Dazed, Andrew dreaded what might have befallen his children. His worst fears were realized. First, in one bathtub and then in another, he came across the bodies of the two children he had anticipated playing with only a few short moments earlier.

Police were at the scene in minutes. State and federal authorities were called in to assist town police in tracking down the triple murderer. Detectives went about establishing the time of death. They learned that William and Priscilla had been alive and well at 1 p.m. when Priscilla had picked up William at his babysitter's. Abigail had been driven home from the Spalding Memorial School, getting off her school bus at 3:30 p.m. Because Andrew had reported the murders at 5:20 p.m., it was theorized that Abigail's murder took place between 3:30 p.m. and 5:20 p.m., while William and Priscilla could have been murdered any time after 1 p.m.

An autopsy revealed that Priscilla had been raped, although she was clothed in a shirt and slacks when found. She had been shot with a .22-calibre weapon. The two children had been strangled and placed in the water-filled bathtubs after death. For some unknown reason, the killer had opened a bottle of beer but had left it unconsumed on the kitchen table.

In Townsend, most of the citizens know each other. Among them were the usual share of bad seeds. One young man who had been in jail years before was questioned and released. Another had robbed a convenience store a year before the murders. He too was questioned and exonerated. Most folks figured the perpetrator of such a crime had to be a stranger. Police picked up the few drifters who had stopped over in Townsend, but all proved to have alibis.

Probably the most notorious young man in town was 17-year-old Danny La Plante. On one side of the ledger, Danny was an average student at St. Bernard High School. He was a star on the school track team and on the football squad. But Danny was a loner and had been in trouble of one kind or another most of his life.

A year earlier, Danny, who lived on Elm St. close to the Gustafson residence, had entered his girlfriend's home in nearby Pepperell, wearing a mask. He had chased the four occupants of the house from room to room. When he tired of the game, he had smeared mayonnaise and ketchup over the walls. That little caper cost Danny a few weeks in a state department of youth services facility. Now, Danny La Plante, because of his reputation, was the prime suspect in a far more serious crime than the wild spree in his girlfriend's house.

Word of the police suspicions spread throughout the community. Danny's relatives were questioned. His brother-in-law stated that on the fateful day,

Danny had attended a birthday party for his six-year-old niece. He had played extensively with the child earlier that afternoon. It was inconceivable for anyone who had been at the party to believe that Danny could have been capable of leaving such an event and of immediately murdering three people.

Investigating officers had no concrete evidence against Danny, but decided to bring him in for questioning. Directly after his interrogation, Danny fled from the police station and ran into an extensive wooded area between his home and the Gustafsons'. His guilty actions precipitated a manhunt the likes of which the good folks of Townsend had never seen before. As the search party proceeded through the woods, they found various items discarded by the suspect. The first item was a torn pillow case. Close by were two spent .22-calibre casings. Further on, they came across a yellow glove.

Eventually, the investigators arrived at the La Plante home. A search of the residence uncovered a .22-calibre casing, which eventually proved to have been fired from the same weapon which took the life of Priscilla Gustafson. A match to the yellow glove picked up in the woods was also found.

While the La Plante home was being searched, desperate Danny broke into a home in Pepperell, kidnapped the female occupant and took off in her Volkswagen van. The terrified woman managed to escape unharmed. Minutes later, Danny was stopped and taken into custody. Back at the scene of the abduction, he had opened a bottle of wine but had not consumed any of its contents.

In reconstructing the crimes, investigating detectives believed that William was the first to be murdered so that he would not be a witness to the rape and murder of his mother. After the rape, Priscilla was allowed to dress. She hurriedly put on a shirt and slacks before being shot. It was Abigail's misfortune to return home from school before Danny left. She met the same fate as her little brother.

In October 1988, Danny La Plante stood trial for the three murders. He was found guilty and received three life sentences to run consecutively. In passing sentence, the presiding judge stipulated that he never be set free. Today, Danny La Plante is serving his sentence at Concord State Prison.

BOBBY JOE LONG

BOBBY Joe Long felt all his problems were caused by his accident, but he had other problems as well.

Bobby Joe was born in Tampa, Florida into a poverty-stricken family. His mother divorced his father when he was only two years old. Louella Long brought up her son to the best of her ability, maintaining a single room in a motel. She made her living as a waitress. Louella worked nights. Bobby Joe attended school during the day. Sometimes Louella entertained men in the motel room which was her home.

At age 11, Bobby Joe experienced the strangest phenomenon. He started to grow breasts. The boy was shattered. The breasts became so large that other boys teased him. He attempted to hide his deformity, but as time passed it was impossible. Louella had seen the same strange growth in male members of her family before and knew what to do. Although she could ill afford it, she took her son to a doctor, who surgically removed the breasts.

Bobby Joe met Cindy Jean Guthrie when he was 14 years old. He dated her for seven years before they married. Cindy's outstanding feature was her startling resemblance to Louella.

Bobby Joe enlisted in the U.S. army. He was already an electrician and took courses to expand his knowledge in preparation for the day he would reenter civilian life. Unfortunately, six months after his army career began, he met with an accident while driving his motorcycle. Bobby Joe fractured his skull and spent months in hospital before receiving his discharge from the army. He was never the same man after the accident.

The boy Cindy knew as placid and easy going was now an explosive individual who demanded sex several times a day. His work habits were unstable. He drifted from job to job, usually being fired for harassing female employees. By 1980, he was actively trolling for females to relieve his abnormal sexual appetite. Bobby Joe was well aware of his unnatural urges. He even realized that during periods of a full moon his need for sex became unbearable. Yet he seemed helpless to control his desires.

In 1981, Bobby Joe was charged with rape and found guilty. However, he was able to obtain a new trial on the grounds that the girl involved had consented to intercourse. At his second trial, he was acquitted.

While Bobby Joe was hoodwinking the authorities, he was carrying out a series of rapes. He would gain entry into women's homes by scanning classified ads in newspapers. After learning when the woman was home alone, he would pay a visit. A task force was formed to hunt down the man known as the Classified Ad Rapist.

In 1983, Bobby Joe graduated to murder. His first victim was Ngyuen Thi Long, who by coincidence had the same last name as her killer. Ngyuen was a saloon dancer and prostitute, who picked up Bobby Joe on North Nebraska Ave. in North Tampa. He drove outside the city, where he raped and strangled the helpless girl. Next day, Bobby Joe slept for 14 hours. When he awoke, he could hardly remember the incident. He wasn't totally convinced that he had taken a human life until he purchased the local newspaper and read about it on the front page. He had no remorse for the victim or her grieving family. Bobby Joe knew in his heart that he would rape and kill again.

When the urge overcame Bobby Joe, he knew where to hunt for victims. The prostitutes of North Tampa were his prey. Unwittingly, they solicited his business and sped away to their deaths. Although Bobby Joe had no remorse for the prostitutes, he was ashamed of what he was doing. He attempted to put an end to his murderous spree and even thought about suicide, but couldn't get up the nerve to do the trick. After he had killed eight prostitutes, he realized that his fame was spreading.

Bobby Joe was aware that the police were canvassing and cruising along the strip which provided him with his girls. Their efforts seemed childish. He would later state that he could have left North Tampa at any time to avoid capture. By now the rapist/murderer consciously wanted to be apprehended. Cindy had divorced him and remarried. He had nothing to live for and existed only to satisfy his uncontrollable urge to have sex. It had to stop.

After his eighth murder, Bobby Joe spotted a young girl on a bicycle. She had just finished her shift at a doughnut shop and was driving home late at night. Bobby Joe hid in some nearby bushes. As the girl sped by, he pulled her off her bicycle. This girl was different; she was not a prostitute. Bobby Joe was moved and, for the first time in his murderous career, felt some remorse for his captive. He loosely blindfolded the terrified girl.

Bobby Joe drove around for 24 hours talking to the girl, who managed to get brief glimpses of her abductor through the blindfold. He raped his victim, but eventually drove her back to the spot where he had pulled her from the bicycle and set her free. The experienced killer must have known that this young girl would be able to identify him and his vehicle. Was this Bobby Joe's way of letting himself be apprehended? He has always claimed this to be the case.

Two days later there was a full moon. Despite his wish to be captured, Bobby Joe's need for sex was too strong. He went on the prowl for a female. His ninth and final murder victim was Kim Swan. Bobby Joe came to Kim's aid when he noticed she was having car trouble at the side of the road. Once she was in his car, he attacked her. Although she fought fiercely, she was finally overpowered. Bobby Joe drove the unconscious girl to a secluded area, where he raped and strangled her.

A few days later, the police traced Bobby Joe, mainly from information given to them by the 17-year-old survivor. He was arrested and confessed to all his murders without much prompting.

At Bobby Joe's trial, his lawyers leaned heavily on the head trauma he had suffered years earlier in his motorcycle accident. Despite this factor, he was found guilty and was sentenced to death. Bobby Joe Long presently resides on Death Row in the Union Correctional Institute, Raiford, Florida.

BLANCHE TAYLOR MOORE

BLANCHE Kiser was your average pleasant Southern girl, who spoke in that friendly North Carolina drawl that we northerners find so fascinating. Blanche, a minister's daughter, had been raised to follow the word and fear the Lord. She worked as a checkout clerk at Krogers, one of the large grocery chains in the southern U.S.

At 18, Blanche married James Taylor, a local Alamance County man. James, an antique dealer, was 26, but those who knew the couple considered Blanche to be the more mature of the two. The years passed and the Taylors had two daughters.

It is unfortunate to report that as the Taylor marriage approached the 20-year mark, James's health gradually deteriorated. Nothing you could put your finger on, mind you, he just complained of not feeling well. Obviously, his complaints were well founded. On October 2, 1973, he died in his bed. Doctors attributed his death to a massive heart attack.

In times of crisis, you can always tell who your true friends are. Blanche was fortunate in having Ray Reid at her side as she went through the trauma of her husband's death. Blanche and Ray had known each other for years, but only became close when they were co-workers at Krogers, where Ray was manager.

About two years before the death of James, Ray and his wife Linda, who had two sons, were divorced. That was just about the time James began to complain about not feeling well. Blanche had comforted Ray during his divorce. It was only fitting when James died for Ray to be at Blanche's side. They prayed together and they went to bed together, not necessarily in that order.

During moments when the two friends were, shall we say, comforting each other, Blanche let Ray know that she and her daughters were in dire straits financially. James had left a pile of debts. In the following few years, Ray admired Blanche, some say to the extent of $10,000 in loans and outright gifts.

Despite Ray's attention and generosity, Blanche's feelings for him gradually cooled. Oh, she still prayed for his salvation and delivered piping hot dinners to his home, but their gymnastic machinations became fewer and fewer. You see,

Blanche had met Reverend Dwight Moore, pastor of the United Church of Christ in nearby Columbia. The reverend was infatuated with Blanche. After all, she displayed those qualities near and dear to his religious heart. She prayed a lot and was forever performing kind acts for those in need.

Blanche's friend Ray Reid took ill around the time that Blanche and Rev. Dwight became an item. Blanche spent a lot of time visiting Ray. When he was in hospital, she saw to it that he had a generous supply of her outstanding rice pudding. Kind, gentle Blanche was popular with the nurses who attended Ray. She brought them sandwiches, which they sometimes ate while Blanche fed Ray his rice pudding.

While in hospital, Ray instructed his two sons that Blanche was to be the executor of his will should anything happen to him. They agreed that the angel of mercy was entitled to one-third of their father's estate.

Blanche was a busy girl. What with visiting Ray, romancing Dwight and attending church regularly, she had scant time to run routine errands. That's why she asked Rev. Dwight to pick up some poisonous Anti-Ant powder down at Ken's Quickie Mart, where she had previously purchased a supply. Nasty ants had infested her home again. Dwight was more than happy to oblige.

As summer gave way to the fall of 1986, Ray's condition worsened dramatically. Doctors agreed that he was close to death and they were right. On October 7, Ray, age 50, went to his great reward.

Medical authorities, who had always been mystified as to the cause of Ray's illness, suggested an autopsy. Blanche, the executor of the deceased's will, would not give her permission, claiming that Ray would not have approved. The pain of losing her dear friend was soothed somewhat by her inheritance of $45,000, one-third of Ray's estate.

During the next few years, Blanche and Dwight were inseparable. In 1989, they married. While they were on their honeymoon, Dwight took ill with severe stomach cramps. The happy couple were forced to return home to North Carolina.

Dwight visited a doctor, who found it difficult to pinpoint the cause of his discomfort, but there was no denying the seriousness of the problem. Dwight was in such extreme pain he was admitted to Memorial Hospital in Chapel Hill. In time, he was transferred to the intensive care unit.

Dwight's condition didn't improve. His body was distorted in agony as he

periodically lost consciousness. Blanche was a rock. She ministered to her seriously ill husband day and night, while doctors frantically performed test after test
in an attempt to discover the cause of his strange illness. They informed the distraught Blanche that they were helpless and death was imminent.

As the end drew near, attending physicians were shocked to receive the
results of urine tests indicating that their patient had been poisoned by arsenic.
In fact, the readings indicated that Dwight had the highest concentration of
arsenic ever found in a still-living human.

Doctors questioned Blanche. Had her husband come in contact with arsenic
used around their home? Blanche could only tell them that he puttered around
the garden. She didn't know whether he used arsenic or not. It was decided to
notify police of the strange illness which had befallen the popular pastor.

Investigators questioned Blanche. She could add nothing to what they
already knew. They interrogated Dwight in his hospital bed. The pastor was
recovering from the brink of death, but it was a slow, painful recovery. He
searched his memory of the day when he first had stomach trouble, but could add
nothing that would help the investigation. He did casually recall that years earlier a friend of his wife's named Ray Reid had died suddenly. Come to think of
it, so had her husband, James Taylor, back in 1973.

Records were checked. Nurses who had attended Ray were interviewed.
Blanche's habit of bringing tasty rice pudding to Ray was of particular interest.
Blanche was questioned again. Despite the irrefutable fact that she had fed Ray
in hospital, she steadfastly professed that she had never brought food to
the institution.

On June 13, 1989, Ray Reid's body was exhumed from Pine Hill Cemetery
in Burlington. It was laced with arsenic. Three weeks later, James Taylor's body
was exhumed.

It too contained large amounts of arsenic.

On July 18, Blanche was arrested and charged with Ray Reid's murder.
There was grave suspicion that over the years she had sent others to their deaths,
including her own father, Parker Kiser, whose death had been attributed to a
heart attack. When his body was exhumed, small amounts of arsenic were found
to be present. The same results were obtained when Blanche's former mother-
in-law, Isla Taylor, was exhumed.

In the end, Blanche was tried only for the death of Ray Reid. She was found guilty and sentenced to death. Today, Blanche Taylor Moore resides on Death Row in North Carolina Women's Prison. She is a model prisoner and reads the good book several times each day.

Rev. Dwight Moore has obtained a divorce and is now pastor of a small con-gregation in Virginia. He is trying to start life a new after his narrow escape at the hands of his devoted wife.

JUDITH & ALVIN NEELEY

HE called her "Lady Sundance." She called him "Nightrider." There were those who called Judith and Alvin Neeley the most sadistic, cold-blooded killers who ever roamed the highways and byways of the United States.

Judith claims she was sexually abused as a child. She ran away from home at the age of 15 to marry Alvin. If ever there was an unholy union, it was the Neeleys. Although Alvin was 26 when he met Judith, many believe she was the dominant personality.

The Neeleys lived by their wits, wandering through Tennessee, Alabama and Georgia, pulling off small thefts and passing bad cheques. In 1980, they attempted to graduate to armed robbery and were quickly apprehended. Alvin spent several months in jail, while Judith was placed in the Youth Development Centre in Rome, Georgia, where she gave birth to twins.

Two years later, Judith and Alvin were free once more. Alvin took a job at a garage and promptly absconded with the company's weekend receipts. With the proceeds of the theft, he purchased a Ford Granada for himself and a Dodge Charger for Judith. Equipped with CB radios and .38-calibre revolvers, they transformed themselves into Lady Sundance and Nightrider. It is difficult to pinpoint when the evil pair made the transition from dangerous punks to sadistic murderers, but transform they did.

In September 1982, Lisa Millican, 13, a ward of the Ethel Harpst Home for neglected children, was taken on a trip to a shopping mall in nearby Rome. Seven girls and six boys made the trip. Once at the mall, they were told to stay in groups and meet at a prearranged location for the return trip home at 8 p.m. Lisa didn't show up. Counsellors and children searched the mall, but Lisa was nowhere to be found. Police were notified.

Hours before she was reported missing, Lisa met a young woman, who struck up a conversation with her. The lady told Lisa that she was new in town and very lonely. Little Lisa, a solitary, lonely child herself, knew just how the lady felt. She accepted a drive in the country in the stranger's Dodge Charger.

Once in the car, Judith Neeley's voice crackled over the airwaves, "This is Lady Sundance. Do you read me?" Nightrider read his accomplice only too well.

It is not necessary to detail the horrible fate which befell little Lisa Millican. It is enough to know that she was moved from motel to motel and sexually abused in every way imaginable. Judith was later to state that after a couple of days the little girl complied with every indignity in order to please her tormentors and avoid being killed.

For some diabolical reason known only to the perpetrators themselves, they decided to kill the child by injecting Drano and Liquid Plumber into her veins. Judith later told investigators that the caustic substances were used for no other reason than to satisfy her curiosity. Detective theorized that the killers were trying to give the murder the appearance of an overdose.

Even as killers of a helpless child, Judith and Alvin were inept. Judith couldn't find the youngster's vein. The searing substance was injected intramuscularly. The pain must have been excruciating, but not fatal. Lisa was spirited away to remote Little River Canyon and again injected with cleaning fluid. Judith was disappointed. The child didn't die. She was then dragged to the lip of a 100-foot deep canyon. There, Judith drew her .38 revolver and shot the child in the back. She listened as Lisa Millican's body plunged to the jagged rocks below. Alvin watched from a few feet away.

Judith wanted more than sex, more than murder. She wanted the thrill of the hunt. She called police and told them where they could find the missing Lisa Millican's body. Because of the nature of the terrain, the child's mutilated body was not recovered until the next day.

Police studied the tape recording of the woman who called and told them where to find Lisa's body. They knew they were listening to the voice of a murderer, but no leads to the killer's identity were uncovered until some days after the body was found.

Not far from Rome, a man was shot in the back. The Neeleys had struck again. Twenty-six-year-old John Hancock and his fiancée, Janice Chatman, were strolling down Shorter St. in Rome. A Dodge Charger with Tennessee plates pulled up beside the young couple. The driver explained that she had just arrived in the area and was very lonely. If they wanted a ride into the countryside, they were welcome to hop in. John and Janice had nothing better to do. They were happy to accept. Once they were inside the car, Lady Sundance told them that a friend of hers would join them with a cooler of beer. In minutes, Nightrider appeared in his Ford Granada. The two automobiles pulled into a secluded wooded lane.

Judith placed her .38-calibre pistol directly between John Hancock's eyes. She then marched him into the woods. Without warning, Hancock heard the loud report of the gun going off. At the same time, he felt a searing pain in his back. John fell to the ground, feigning death, but was conscious and well aware that the slightest movement meant a second shot and most probably death. Alvin Neeley called into the woods for his wife. Judith left the fallen Hancock where he lay. The pair sped in their vehicles with the terrified Janice Chatman.

A few minutes later, John Hancock was able to stagger to the road and wave down a passing motorist. In hospital, police played the tape of the woman who had called in the whereabouts of Lisa Millican's body. John believed his abductor's voice and the voice on the tape were one and the same. The hunt was on for the two vehicles, but the identities of Lady Sundance and Nightrider were still unknown.

The connecting information came from the Youth Development Centre in Rome, where Judith Neeley had once been confined. Someone had called the home and threatened to kill members of the staff in retaliation for abuses received while the caller had lived there. The recipient of the call listened to the taped call from Lisa Millican's killer. It was his opinion that the same woman had made both calls.

Detectives began the dogged work of checking every girl who had been released from the institution in the previous two years. By the process of elimination, they came up with six suspects. John Hancock was shown the six photographs. He picked out Judith Neeley's photo as the woman who had shot him.

The identification was too late for Janice Chatman. She had been taken to a motel immediately after John Hancock was shot. She was handcuffed naked to a bed and sexually abused all night. Early in the morning, Judith and Alvin drove their hapless victim to a lonely area of Chattanooga County and shot her in the head and back.

The wanton pair found themselves short of money. Reverting to their old method of raising money fast, they decided to pass a few worthless cheques in

Murfreesboro, Tenn. They were caught within hours and quickly identified as the suspected murderers of little Lisa Millican and the abductors of Janice Chatman. Alvin couldn't wait to ingratiate himself with police. He drew maps indicating where Janice Chatman's body could be found. Alvin's maps were authentic. Janice's body was speedily recovered.

Eventually, Alvin Neeley pleaded guilty to the murder of Janice Chatman. He received one life sentence for aggravated assault and a second life sentence for murder. He is presently serving these sentences in a Georgia prison.

Judith Neeley was charged with the murder of Lisa Millican. She was found guilty and sentenced to death. While in jail, Judith gave birth to her third child.

Today, Judith Neeley is one of only two women under sentence of death in the State of Alabama. She is presently on Death Row in the Julia Tutiwiller Correctional Institute in Wetumpka, Ala. The assistant warden of the institution, Mrs. Shirlie Lobmiller, informs me, "Judith has adjusted well to the institution while her sentence is being appealed."

In compliance with a state law, her cell is checked every 30 minutes night and day. Judith has access to TV and enjoys soap operas and religious programs. Each morning, at 6:30 a.m., she is moved to a shower by a guard, but is allowed her privacy in the shower for five to seven minutes. Her mornings are spent in handicrafts. Lunch is served from 10:30 to 11:00, after which Judith takes a nap. She keeps herself clean and well-groomed, although she is compelled to wear a plain white dress.

After supper Judith watches TV. Lights are automatically turned off at 10:00 p.m. except for a solitary safety bulb, which casts a dim glow while the prisoner sleeps. She adds, "You would never think Judith is the same person who committed the horrible crimes attributed to her."

Lisa Millican and Janice Chatman are not here to voice their opinions.

ALFERD PACKER

To normal folk the practice of cannibalism is downright disgusting. After all, the consumption of a fellow human is not compatible with pleasant dining nor does it do anything for one's digestive system.

Despite the repulsive nature of cannibalism, the subject does hold a certain fascination. Usually it is associated with another crime, such as murder. Rarely do we humans kill each other for the sole purpose of a good nourishing meal. All of which brings us to the subject of Alferd G. Packer.

In the fall of 1873, Alferd, together with 19 inexperienced prospectors, trudged from Salt Lake City deep into Colorado's San Juan Mountains searching for gold. Alferd had some knowledge of the area, but his fellow travellers were strangers to each other and to the region.

The party had no success in their quest for the elusive yellow metal. For weeks they searched until, with little left in the way of supplies, they stumbled, half starved, into the Indian camp of Chief Ouray. The chief not only fed the ragtag group, but provided them with enough food to continue their prospecting venture.

A problem arose. Ten of the men wanted to give up the hunt for gold and return to Salt Lake City. Their close brush with death had given them their fill of the prospecting game. After many arguments, these 10 men decided to return to Salt Lake City.

Alferd, who had headed the faction wanting to continue prospecting, became the unofficial leader of the party. He led the remaining men to Los Pinos and beyond, figuring that the rumors of gold strikes up the Gunnison River would at last bring riches to himself and his group. After trudging along the river for weeks, supplies grew dangerously low. Four men elected to return to Los Pinos and on to Denver. Alferd and the remaining five men left the river bank for the treacherous mountains. Their names are worthy of mention, mainly because no one ever saw Swan, Bell, Miller, Noon and Humphrey alive again.

In February, Alferd made his way out of the frigid cold back to Los Pinos.

He looked terrible and was practically in rags. Someone thrust a bottle of whisky into his gnarled fingers. Alferd greedily consumed huge gulps from the flask. When he was offered food, Alferd said that he wasn't that hungry; the booze would do just fine, thank you.

Alferd had a story to tell. He said that he had become ill and that his five companions had left him in the mountains to die. Instead of dying, he had recovered and miraculously had made his way to Los Pinos. He figured that the lure of gold had affected the good judgment of his companions. No doubt they had starved to death in the unforgiving mountains.

Alferd stayed at Los Pinos recuperating for 10 days. He had an abundance of money which allowed him to stay well oiled most of the time. In due course, fit as a fiddle, he left and made his way to Saguache. Word of his remarkable feat had preceded him, along with the nasty rumor that he had a lot of money for a man who had started out broke. Then there was the unmentionable insinuation that he was extremely well nourished for a man who had spent so many weeks in the wilderness.

On April 2, 1874, two of Chief Ouray's men arrived in camp with the distressing news that they had found strips of frozen meat from white human beings in the snow just outside the camp. When faced with the gruesome evidence, Alferd broke down and confessed. He claimed that supplies had run out. The men were desperate. One day, when he returned to the group after collecting firewood, he found that Swan had been killed by a blow to the head. The four remaining men were in the process of cooking portions of his body and dividing up the $2,000 removed from the dead man's pockets.

Assorted parts of Swan lasted only a few days. The men eyed each other suspiciously. Little intrigues and cliques developed. Who would be the next to go? Answer—Miller. When he wasn't looking, one of the men split his head open with a hatchet. In time, Humphrey and Noon were killed, roasted and eaten as well. Alferd claimed that he and Bell agreed that they wouldn't attack each other, but would remain together even if it meant starving to death. Despite the agreement, Bell went out of his mind and attempted to club Alferd with the butt of his rifle. Alferd overpowered his adversary and killed him with his trusty hatchet.

Our boy wasn't telling the absolute truth. We know that for a fact, because early in June artist John A. Randolph, while traipsing through the mountains doing sketches for Harper's Magazine, came across the bodies of the five men. Noon, Humphreys, Swan and Bell had been shot in the back of their heads. Miller's body, sans head, was found some distance from the others. The head was found nearby and showed evidence of having been hacked with a hatchet. Now for the bad part. Strips of flesh had been removed from the chest areas of each body.

Shortly after the bodies were discovered, Alferd escaped from custody. For nine years he led an exemplary life in Salt Lake City under the name of John Schwartze. It's quite possible he would have remained at large forever had he not had the misfortune to run into one of the original members of his ill-fated prospecting trip on the streets of Salt Lake City.

Alferd was immediately arrested and brought to trial on April 3, 1883. He claimed that he had killed only Bell and that was done in self-defence. Part of his statement is startling: "When I came to Los Pinos, I threw away the strips of flesh I had left and I confess I did so reluctantly, as I had grown fond of human flesh."

No one believed Alferd's story and he was found guilty on five counts of murder. His lawyers managed to obtain a new trial on a technicality. This time he was more fortunate, being convicted of five counts of manslaughter. In 1885, 12 years after the murders, Alferd was sentenced to a total of 40 years imprisonment. He served 16 years in prison before being paroled in 1901. Alferd died of natural causes in Denver on April 24, 1907.

You may be interested to know that Alferd's name will live on. Students at the University of Colorado in Boulder have named their cafeteria The Alferd G. Packer Grill. They commemorate his dubious deeds each spring with an Alferd G. Packer Day. One of the major events on that special day is the students' raw meat eating contest.

JESSE POMEROY

I am often asked if wanton mass murder is a recent phenomenon. Are the Mansons, Sutcliffes and Olsons the products of modern society? The truth is, the strange mental processes which motivate these modern-day monsters have always been with us.

Probably the most reprehensible mass murderer of the nineteenth century was the American teenager, Jesse Pomeroy.

Jesse's family owned a retail store in Boston and was relatively well off. The Pomeroys knew they had a troubled youngster from the very beginning. When he was only nine, Jesse displayed an aggressive attitude towards other children and took delight in making life miserable for neighborhood dogs and cats.

A brooding, introverted youngster, Jesse was cursed with grotesque features. One of his eyes was covered with a white film, the result of a cataract. There was an unsightly twist to his upper lip which gave him the appearance of wearing a perpetual snarl. Altogether, Jesse was a repulsive-looking character who, because of his innate meanness, was shunned by other youngsters.

In 1881, when Jesse was 14, several children between the ages of seven and ten were reported missing in Boston. A short time later their bodies were discovered in fields and garbage dumps. Other hapless victims were found nailed to the doorways of buildings on dark, deserted streets. Some were discovered tied to posts.

In all, the murders of 27 young boys and girls were attributed to the unknown killer. A wave of hysteria and shock, similar to that which was to envelop Atlanta, Georgia, a hundred years later, swept through Boston. Despite the concentrated efforts of the police, no clue to the identity of the murderer was immediately uncovered.

Twelve-year-old Albert Pratt's father had hired an armed bodyguard to accompany his son home from school. This precaution had received some publicity and eventually came to the attention of the killer.

Mr. Pratt received an unsigned letter in the mail telling him that his son would be the next to die. A few days after this letter was delivered Harry Pomeroy, Jesse's younger brother, knocked on the door of Albert Pratt's classroom and told teacher William Barnes that Albert's father was outside and wanted to see his son. Mr. Barnes excused Albert from the classroom. Two days later Albert's mutilated body was found in a field outside the city.

Questioned by police, Harry Pomeroy would only say that a tall man in a blue suit had requested that he pass along the message. The next strange incident to take place in a case fraught with the unbelievable occurred when one potential victim escaped the clutches of the monster.

Nine-year-old Willie Barton was playing near a field when a big boy grabbed him and tried to take off his clothes. Willie wrenched free of the bigger boy's grasp and ran away.

Because Harry Pomeroy was already connected with the case, police thought that young Willie might be able to identify his assailant at Harry's school. Willie shrieked in horror when he spotted not Harry, but Jesse Pomeroy. The white eye, snarling lip, and coarse features couldn't be missed.

Instead of denying his guilt, Jesse readily confessed to all the murders. He seemed to relish the spotlight, was defiant, and swore, "I shan't be hanged. I'll fool you all again!"

At his trial, Jesse discussed his case intelligently with lawyers and the judge. At other times he swore he would kill all those who testified against him, as well as the members of the jury.

Jesse was found guilty, but insane. Unbelievably, one year later he was released from an asylum as cured. His release didn't go unnoticed by the general public. A great many petitions were forwarded to Governor Groves of Massachusetts demanding that Jesse be kept in jail. Both the governor and the presiding judge at Jesse's trial were convinced that he was cured.

A year passed. Jesse stayed close to home. There was a real fear that relatives of his victims might take matters into their own hands and kill him.

Eventually, other matters captured the public's interest. Soon Jesse Pomeroy was out of the spotlight, but not for long. One day his parents left him in charge of their store. A little girl, Alice Curran, entered the Pomeroys' store and was never seen again.

Police naturally questioned Jesse, but he vehemently denied having had anything to do with the disappearance, claiming that he was being harassed because of his past. Other children disappeared. Fields and marshes were searched, but no bodies were found.

At the rear of Pomeroys' store there was a large refuse dump. That summer neighbors claimed that an offensive odor was emanating from the refuse. The city ordered Mr. Pomeroy to remove the dump. Buried in the refuse, authorities uncovered the bodies of twelve children. As the bodies were removed Jesse watched in the yard, smiling. He was enjoying the sight.

Such a furor accompanied this second group of killings that Governor Groves, who had authorized Jesse's release, was forced to resign.

Once more Jesse confessed in detail to all the murders. He was his cocky, defiant self and swore he would seek vengeance on all who were against him.

Jesse was tried and found guilty of murder in the first degree. While a mob outside the courthouse shouted, "Lynch him!" Jesse was sentenced to death by hanging. However, there were those who thought that Jesse must certainly be insane and should not hang. They worked frantically to save him. Finally his sentence was commuted to solitary confinement for life.

Jesse Pomeroy entered prison at the age of 17 and immediately began planning to escape. It wasn't an easy task. He was watched constantly while in solitary confinement. Cunning Jesse was a model prisoner, conforming to all the rules, and spending much of his time reading. Soon he was receiving small privileges.

His mother visited him and tried to help her wicked son to escape. Once she brought him a large meat pie for Thanksgiving. At the last moment guards found some small tools baked in the pie. On another occasion Jesse complained of back trouble and asked permission to have his mother bring him an armchair. Guards found tools and hacksaws hidden in the stuffing of the chair. After this last incident Mrs. Pomeroy was not allowed to bring her son gifts.

Jesse continued to try. His next scheme took three years. He found out that the prison was heated by gas, and that a gas pipe ran directly behind his cell wall. Jesse decided to get through the wall in some way, tap the gas line, and fill his cell with gas. He would then light a match and blow the place up. He didn't seem to care if he blew himself up in the process.

Jesse talked his keepers into providing him with a few simple tools, ostensibly to work on inventing a pencil sharpener. Every night for three years Jesse scraped at the cement which held his granite block cell together. The scrapings were then kneaded into his bread, which he ate.

Finally, he broke through and made a hole in the pipe, allowing the gas to fill his cell. He had secreted away one match months before. He lit the match. The whole area exploded. Two prisoners in adjoining cells were killed. Jesse was blown through the cell door. He was found alive, but badly injured.

Jesse recovered. This time he was watched day and night in a special escape-proof cell in Charleston Prison. It was as close to living in hell as you get on earth. Years passed, Jesse was forgotten. Many assumed he had died.

In 1924, an old man, sick, frail, but still defiant, was transferred from prison to Bridgewater State Farm. Jesse Pomeroy, the "White-Eyed Boy Murderer of Boston" had served forty years in solitary confinement. Special security was provided at Bridgewater to prevent Jesse from escaping. He remained there until the day he died.

MICHAEL ROSS

As I drove down the main street of Jewett City, Connecticut, Al Schumanski was busy at his Amoco Gas station pumping air into the rear tire of a little boy's bicycle. Hendel's Furniture Store didn't have a single customer despite the big mattress sale signs in their front window. Clair LaPointe sold gas and cigarettes at Chucky's Country store.

"Visited Toronto years ago," Al Schumanski told me. "Is the Spaghetti Factory still there? Great place. Haven't been back for years." The little boy pedalled away toward the town square where East Main and North Main intersect. It's dry and hot in the David Hale Fanning Park where three large stones list the names of every soldier in the vicinity who served in World Wars I and II and the Korean War. There is no memorial for those who served in Vietnam.

This is small town New England, the heart and soul of the U.S. The tiny Connecticut towns are reminiscent of Norman Rockwell paintings: Danielson, Brooklyn, Canterbury, Plainfield, Jewett City, Lisbon, Griswold, Preston. They run into each other, similar, neat, sun drenched, off the beaten path. No real need to lock a door at night. Most neighbors have known each other for a lifetime. Violence and its ugly ramifications belong in Boston and New York, not in these pleasant, quaint towns.

Police Chief Thurston Fields knows pretty well every one of Jewett City's 4000 inhabitants. His five-man police force keeps the peace with the aid of two patrol cars. Chief Fields assures me, "There has never been a murder in Jewett City in the 11 years I've been chief and I can't remember one before that."

On January 5, 1982, the small community of Brooklyn, Conn. was shocked when Tammy Williams, 17, disappeared. Hundreds of acres of brush and swamp in the area along Route 6 were searched. Tracking dogs were used. Five hundred volunteers searched the rough terrain. No trace of Tammy was found.

On June 15, 1982, Debbie Taylor and her husband James of Jewett City ran out of gas near Danielson. Debbie walked down the highway looking for a service station, while James walked in the opposite direction. Debbie never returned. Next day she was reported missing. Four and a half months later, Debbie's body was found in a Canterbury cornfield. Her skull had been crushed.

No doubt a sex-crazed stranger had lured Debbie into his car. It was horrible. It was shocking. But after all, it was an isolated incident.

Over a year passed. Most people forgot about Debbie Taylor's fate. Most forgot about the missing Tammy Williams, but not Tammy's father. He frequented flea markets, bazaars and other public gatherings, inquiring about his missing daughter. He never turned up a clue.

On November 16, 1983, Robin Stavinsky disappeared off the streets of Norwich. The attractive high school student and state discus champion had a date that day, but never kept it. A week later a jogger found her body in a wooded area on the outskirts of Norwich on Thames Hospital property. Robin had been strangled to death.

Two girls murdered and one missing in two years. Were they unrelated or were the murders the work of one deranged individual? Rumors spread throughout the Connecticut towns.

Leslie Shelly, 14, and April Brunais, 15, were last seen walking on the streets of Jewett City. When they failed to return to their respective homes on April 22, 1984, they were thought to be runaways. The two friends had run away once before for one day. This time they apparently left for good.

Seven weeks later Wendy Baribeault, 17, left her Lisbon home on Round Hill Court to make a purchase at Chucky's Country Store. She left a message for her parents telling them where she was going.

Police Chief Fields and I measured off the distance between Wendy's home and the Country Store. It is exactly 1.6 miles. Somewhere in that short distance Wendy Baribeault disappeared. Wendy was immediately reported missing. A massive search of the area uncovered her body two days later. She had been sexually attacked.

The killer's luck had run out when he murdered Wendy Baribeault. This time an alert citizen informed police that she had seen Wendy walking along the road. A man in a blue 1983 Toyota seemed to be following her. Police checked over 2,000 vehicles with the State Department of Motor Vehicles. By elimination they came up with Michael Ross, 24, a man who had attacked a woman in Ohio years before.

At that time Ross pretended to run out of gas in front of a house he had picked at random. He asked to use the telephone. Once inside, he attacked the lone woman occupant. Ross had picked the wrong woman. She was an off-duty police officer who was an expert in ju jitsu. He managed to get away, but was arrested a short time later.

Michael Ross was arraigned in Ohio, but allowed to return to his Brooklyn, Conn. home when his parents posted a $1,000 bond. He received psychological evaluation for two months before being brought back to Ohio, where he served four and half months in jail. He was released on December 22, 1982 to spend Christmas with his parents in Connecticut.

Michael Ross was arrested and charged with the murder of Wendy Baribeault. Connecticut detectives are reluctant to discuss details, but the fact remains that almost immediately after Ross' arrest, they recovered the bodies of Tammy Williams, Leslie Shelley and April Brunais in woods beside local roads. Ross has been charged with felony murder in the deaths of all six girls. Felony murder carries the death sentence in Connecticut.

Born in Brooklyn, Michael Ross lived most of his life in eastern Connecticut. In 1977 he graduated as an honors student from nearby Killingly High School. His teachers remember him as a keen student, who was quiet and well-behaved. In 1981 he graduated from Cornell University with a major in agricultural economics.

He lived in Jewett City in a large green and white house at 158 North Main St. His girlfriend, Debbie Wallace, divorced mother of three children, lived there with him. She refused to believe that Michael could be responsible for the brutal murders of six women. Neighbors also find it difficult to believe that the polite, well-dressed, friendly young man could be a killer.

While living in Jewett City, Ross was employed with the Prudential Insurance Co. of America as a district agent and registered representative. An official of the insurance company has stated that of the 26,000 agents employed across the U.S. by the company, nothing like Michael Ross has ever happened before.

The hamlet of Brooklyn, Conn., population 900, was incorporated in 1796. A large statue of Major General Israel Putnam, a hero of the War of Independence, adorns its main thoroughfare. A little further up the road Michael Ross' family owns and operates one of the largest businesses in town, a poultry and egg factory.

It is here that Michael grew up, an unobtrusive boy who worked hard at his father's business. His parents refuse to discuss their son since his arrest. Some of the townspeople can't believe that their town may have spawned a serial killer.

Carol Kovacs, an employee of the New England Centre for Contemporary Art, remembers well hearing the devastating news that an acquaintance had been arrested for the alleged murder of six girls. Carol knew Tammy Williams, one of the victims. She intersperses her emotions with such words as "unbelievable," "dumbfounded," and "shocked" when discussing the arrest of Michael Ross.

Connecticut police inquired about Michael Ross' activities in other locations. While he was attending Cornell University in Ithaca, New York, 25-year-old Vietnamese student Drung Ngoc Tu was murdered. Her body was found at the bottom of a gorge. Miss Tu was majoring in agricultural economics and lived one block from the Alpha Zeta fraternity house. Michael Ross lived at the fraternity house at the time of her murder.

But Ross' connection with Miss Tu was dropped when he was found guilty of murdering Tammy Williams and Debbie Taylor. For these murders he was sentenced to life imprisonment.

On July 6, 1987 Michael Ross was found guilty of the murders of Robin Stavinsky, Leslie Shelley, April Brunais and Wendy Baribeault. He has been sentenced to death in Connecticut's electric chair.

RAMON SALCIDO

RAMON Salcido was born in Los Mochis, Mexico, but as he grew up his heart was in glamorous California to the north. While still a teenager, Ramon dreamed of getting into the U.S., making a fortune and returning to Mexico as a millionaire. It wasn't that he didn't have a good life in his native country. His parents were upper middle class and were more than willing to provide their son with every advantage.

In 1980, Ramon smuggled himself across the border into California and made his way to the wine country near Fresco, where he quickly gained employment with one of the many vineyards in the area. Ramon was an attractive young man with a steady job, but it bothered him that he was an illegal immigrant.

To correct this situation, Ramon married a local girl, obtained his green card and became a legal resident of the U.S. The couple had one child, a daughter, but the marriage didn't work out and Ramon split. He travelled to the famed Napa/Sonoma wine country, where he again had no difficulty catching on with one of the local vineyards.

One day, quite by chance, in Santa Rosa, Ramon met Angela Richards. To say Angela was attractive would be an understatement. The 19-year-old was a beautiful young girl, certainly the most beautiful creature Ramon had ever met. It didn't matter that he couldn't speak a word of English and she couldn't speak a word of Spanish; there was an electricity between the two young people. But there were problems. Angela's parents were very strict. She had never been on a date before meeting Ramon. In order to see her lover, it was necessary for Angela to climb out of her bedroom window at night while the family slept. Angela and Ramon made love in the back seat of Ramon's old Ford LTD.

When Angela became pregnant, there was no way out but to inform her parents. Furious at their daughter's predicament, and distasteful as Ramon appeared to be, they insisted that the couple marry. An uneasy peace prevailed between Ramon and his in-laws. Inwardly, the Richards didn't like Ramon and he burned inside at their reluctance to accept him as a true member of the family.

As the years passed, the Salcidos had three daughters. Ramon was steadily employed at a winery, while Angela augmented the family income by working as a seamstress. Perhaps life would have unfolded peacefully in its normal way had not other factors come into play. Ramon had never told Angela that he had been married and, more importantly, that he had never been divorced from his first wife.

In 1989, Ramon's first wife was successful in locating him. She obtained a court order forcing him to pay her $511 a month, as well as $5,807 to the Social Service Department of Fresno County to repay sums turned over by that agency to her. Angela was devastated. As if this wasn't enough, she had other reasons not to be enthralled with her husband. Angela's exceptional beauty had recently come to the attention of two modelling agencies, who seriously felt she might have a lucrative career in television commercials. Ramon wouldn't hear of his wife straying from their home. He became unreasonably jealous, often following her when she went grocery shopping.

By March 1989, Ramon was under extreme pressure, all of it his own doing. He constantly argued and fought with his wife, truly believing that every man she met was a bona fide threat to their marriage. On the night of April 13, Ramon visited his favorite bar. As he gulped beer and wine, he grew despondent. Life held no hope, only disgrace and failure. Ramon drove home to his duplex on Baines Ave. in Boyes Hot Springs. Angela wasn't in, but the three girls lay peacefully asleep in their beds.

Ramon loaded the children, Sofia, 4, Carmina, 3, and Teresa, 2, into his LTD. He drove to a landfill site at the edge of town and there committed one of the most gruesome murders ever perpetrated. He slit the children's throats and tossed them over an embankment. Sofia and Teresa bled to death where they came to rest. Carmina landed on her head and was rendered unconscious.

Ramon drove to his in-laws' home in nearby Cotati. Marion Richards must have put up a courageous struggle, but was no match for the powerful Ramon. He viciously cut her throat. Angela's two sisters, 12-year-old Ruth and eight-year-old Maria, met the same fate. At work, Bob Richards had no way of knowing that his son-in-law had entered his home and killed his wife and two daughters.

Ramon wasn't through. When he returned to his own home, Angela was there, unaware of the havoc and death her husband had meted out that night. There is evidence that Angela raced from room to room in an attempt to escape his intense rage. There would be no escape. She was beaten and then shot to death.

The deranged man's mind turned to those men whom he believed were attracted to his wife. He drove to the Grand Cru vineyards, where he met one of his imagined adversaries, 35-year-old Tracy Toovey, just inside the vineyard gates. Toovey was attempting to get out of his old Volkswagen Carmen Ghia when he was mowed down by six well-aimed bullets in the face from Ramon's .22 revolver.

It was exactly 8:18 on the morning of April 14 when police were called to the scene of a shooting. Ken Butti, a foreman at the Grand Cru winery, had been shot in the shoulder. Ken informed police that Ramon Salcido had driven up to his home in his old LTD. When Ken got up to greet him, he was amazed to see Ramon aiming a .22 at him. Ramon fired and wounded him in the shoulder. Ken's wife, who was standing nearby, screamed. Ramon fired at her, but the gun either misfired or was empty. Ken had no idea why Ramon, whom he knew well, had shot him. He told police that at one time Ramon had been a valued employee at Grand Cru, but in recent months his work had deteriorated. Rumor had it that Ramon was experiencing financial and marital difficulties.

The hunt was on for Ramon Salcido. Although investigators were unaware of the other crimes Ramon had committed during the preceding hours, they realized they were after a man with a gun who had wounded one man and, only by luck, had missed wounding or killing Mrs. Butti.

Within hours, police came across the body of Tracy Toovey.

Other officers were dispatched to Ramon's home, where they found Angela's bullet-riddled body. Great concern was felt for the three Salcido children, who were nowhere to be found. That same morning, officers learned of the animosity between Ramon and his in-laws. Detectives drove to the Richards' home, where they found a body in each of three rooms.

On Saturday, over three days after the murder spree began, a young man walking along the edge of a quarry bordering a county dump came across the bodies of two little girls lying on their backs. He ran to the quarry supervisor's office and summoned police. Meanwhile, the young man and the supervisor returned to the crime scene. They were amazed to find a third little girl, Carmina

Salcido, in a sitting position, staring straight ahead. She was alive. Carmina couldn't answer the men's questions. She simply stared into space, sitting there in her blood encrusted nightgown. Within minutes, she was being rushed to hospital.

A massive manhunt, both in United States and Mexico, was on for Ramon Salcido, now charged with seven murders and three attempted murders. The wanted man made his way to his hometown in Mexico, where his own relatives turned him in to the authorities. He was immediately returned to the U.S.

Ramon was tried in Redwood City, Calif. He was found guilty of six counts of first-degree murder, one count of second-degree murder and two counts of attempted murder. In the courtroom, when the death sentence was passed, sat Bob Richards. In one night of horror his son-in-law had murdered his wife, his three daughters and two of his three grandchildren.

Little Carmina Salcido underwent a tracheostomy and had a tube inserted into her windpipe to ease her breathing until her neck wound healed. She was unable to talk for some time, but her voice has since returned and she has long since been released from hospital. Bob Richards says that his granddaughter has received over 15,000 cards and letters from well wishers all over the world.

LYDIA SHERMAN

I drove through the lush Connecticut countryside towards the small town of Derby. It is difficult to imagine that this peaceful community tucked away on the side of a hill along the Housatonic River was once the home of one of the most prolific female mass murderers in the history of the U.S. It was here that Lydia Sherman ended her career of dispensing arsenic with a degree of abandonment rarely experienced before or since.

Lydia's infamous history can be traced back to 1847, when she married a policeman, Edward Struck, in New York City. The marriage was to last for seventeen years, during which Lydia gave birth to six handsome children: Lydia, Anne Eliza, William, George, Edward, and Mary Ann.

After such a lengthy period of marital bliss, an incident occurred on the streets of New York that was to have far reaching effects on the Struck family. Edward was abruptly dismissed from the Metropolitan Police Force. Evidently there was some question concerning Struck's reaction under pressure. It was reported that he hurriedly left the scene of a disturbance, leaving a citizen to disarm a madman in a saloon.

Lydia was not only furious—she was embarrassed and ashamed. She began making excuses for her husband. He was ill, he was insane—anything that came to mind.

Meanwhile, Lydia had to face the practical problem of feeding her children. Lydia obtained a position as a nurse to Dr. L.A. Rodenstein. It was while employed with Dr. Rodenstein that Lydia first became acquainted with arsenic and its lethal qualities.

One glorious day in May 1864, Lydia dropped into a Harlem drug store and purchased a quantity of arsenic. She explained to the druggist that her apartment was "alive with rats." What better way to rid herself of the wee beasties than a good dose of arsenic? The deadly powder cost her ten cents.

That night Lydia cooked up a batch of warm oatmeal for Edward. It didn't agree with him at all. Within hours he was confined to bed. Lydia was concerned.

She nursed him all night, attempting to relieve his agony with assorted medicines. She even endeavored to bolster his strength with more oatmeal, but Edward had lost his appetite.

In the morning Edward was in such bad shape that Lydia called in a neighboring physician, Dr. N. Hustead. At this point in Lydia's saga it is rather strange that no one wondered why she did didn't summon her employer, Dr. Rodenstein, but at the time no one gave it a second thought.

At any rate, it was too late for Edward. He died in agony before Dr. Hustead arrived at his bedside. Lydia was overcome with grief at her loss. The good doctor could scarcely stand the way she carried on. She suggested that "consumption" carried poor Edward away." Dr. Hustead agreed, and signed the death certificate accordingly.

Once Lydia got the hang of the poisoning business, there was no stopping her. In the following months she proceeded to annihilate all six of her own children. July 5 seems to have been a red-letter day—on that day she killed three of her offspring.

By the time the second anniversary of Edward's demise rolled around, the entire family was dead and buried. Lydia was clever enough to employ various doctors, all of whom attributed the rash of deaths to natural causes.

Only one man was suspicious. Reverend Mr. Payson of the Harlem Presbyterian Church, who had watched Lydia, the eldest Struck daughter, die in agony, couldn't get certain evil thoughts out of his mind. Several days after young Lydia's death he passed his suspicions along to the district attorney's office. The D.A. failed to act.

Through an acquaintance, Lydia secured a position in Stratford, Connecticut, as nurse and housekeeper to a Mrs. Curtiss. There seems little doubt that Mrs. Curtiss was ripe for one of Lydia's little white powders, but the old lady proved to be a crusty, intelligent New Englander who wouldn't be bamboozled. Lydia let it be known around Stratford that she was available for employment elsewhere if the opportunity presented itself.

Eight uneventful months passed. One day, while grocery shopping in John Fairchild's store, Lydia was told by Mr. Fairchild that an old gentleman named Dennis Hurlbut of Corum, Connecticut had just lost his wife and was looking for a housekeeper. When Lydia learned that Hurlbut was over seventy-five years old and was reputed to be wealthy, she required no further encouragement.

Lydia dashed over to Corum, now known as Shelton. Harlbut, who was approaching senility, expected an old lady with whom to argue away his remaining years. The old dog was smitten the moment he laid eyes on attractive, trim, 44-year-old Lydia.

Within a week Hurlbut proposed. The odd couple married on November 22, 1868. Lydia played the industrious housekeeper and loving wife to the hilt. Three months after the knot was tied, Hurlbut made his will.

Eleven months later Lydia, complete in widow's garb, buried her second husband. Old Hurlbut's demise left Lydia a wealthy woman by 1870 standards. She became the sole owner of her late husband's farm, as well as cash amounting to $10,000.

Today, 125 years since the murder, you can still find the record of the unsuspecting Hurlbut's death in the registry of births, deaths, and marriages, at the Shelton Town Hall. Under cause of death is the ominous notation—arsenic poisoning.

Lydia always seemed to be in the right place at the right time when it came to members of the opposite sex. This time, Mr. William Thomas, who delivered the mail to Lydia's farm, told the brand new widow that a man named Nelson Sherman of Derby had just lost his wife and was left with four children. He was in dire need of a housekeeper. Lydia indicated that she was interested, even though her true love, old Hurlbut, was scarcely two months removed from this mortal coil.

A meeting was arranged. Nelson Sherman, who held down a good job with a Derby tack manufacturer, was delighted at the prospect of having good-looking Lydia as his housekeeper, and who knows, maybe even much more.

He explained to Lydia that he had an infant son and three other children at home. Besides his offspring, he was stuck with his deceased wife's mother, Mrs. Mary Jones. His mother-in-law simply didn't get along with his children, and things were going from bad to worse. His 14-year-old daughter Ada and Mrs. Jones were at each other's throats constantly. Horatio, 18, Nattie, four, and Frank, the nine-month-old baby, rounded out the household.

In the ensuing months Nelson wooed the widow Hurlbut. This time, with old Hurlbut's coin rattling in her pockets, Lydia was in no particular rush to wed.

However, when she felt the time was right, she once more let herself be led to the altar.

On September 2, 1870, Lydia became Mrs. Nelson Sherman. Things did not proceed smoothly from the very first day. The mother-in-law proved to be an ornery old woman, who relished arguing with young Ada. Baby Frank was a handful. Slowly it dawned on Lydia that by marrying Nelson Sherman she had bitten off more than she could chew.

One day, completely frustrated at the direction of events were taking in his household, Nelson blurted out that he wished baby Frank were dead. Then his dear old mother-in-law would have no further reason for staying on.

The cool waters of the Housatonic River flowed gently past the Shermans' white house the day Lydia heard this very practical suggestion. Her ears perked up. A twinkle came to her eye. Did someone suggest a death in the family might be beneficial?

Lydia strained to hear. Yes, she was positive—there were rats scurrying about in the attic. She must fetch some arsenic and get rid of the nasty little devils.

Quick as a wink, Frank became ill. He simply couldn't hold anything in his stomach. Small wonder. Lydia had laced the baby's milk with arsenic. To put it in her own words, "I was full of trouble, and not knowing what to do, I put some arsenic in his milk."

Mother-in-law Mary Jones grew alarmed and sent for Dr. A. Beardsley, the family physician who lived a few doors away from the Shermans. Dr. Beardsley arrived at the house in the morning, took one look at Frank, and declared that the child was suffering from colic. The doctor gave the sick child several medicines. By late afternoon the baby appeared to be recovering slowly. Lydia put a stop to all that. When the doctor left, she gave little Frank some of her own medicine. Frank was dead by 11 o'clock that night.

Around this time it is quite possible that Nelson Sherman had some inkling that he had married a monster. Always a man who liked his whisky, Nelson took to the bottle with a vengeance. Rarely did he show up at the tack factory where he was employed. In fact, at this juncture in his life, Nelson was pretty well in the sauce all the time. He had good reason.

During the holiday season of 1870 a heavy snowfall descended on the peaceful little village of Derby. Sleighs pulled by proud horses, gaily decorated with Christmas bells, dashed through the centre of the town. No one was aware that in their tranquil community dwelt a mass murderer who poisoned without feeling or remorse. Lydia had by now chalked up nine victims.

That Christmas, Nelson's daughter Ada was busy helping the Rev. Morton decorate the tree down at the Congregational Church. Unaccountably, Ada became so ill that Rev. Morton sent her home. Lydia felt that Ada had partaken of too much candy, but Rev. Morton thought the matter much more serious.

He was so concerned that he showed up at the Sherman residence later that afternoon with Dr. Beardsley, the same doctor who had unsuccessfully treated Ada's brother Frank. Dr. Beardsley prescribed brandy for his patient. Ada lived through the night.

Lydia was later to state, "I felt so bad I was tempted to do as I had done before. I had some arsenic in the house and I mixed some in her tea and give it to her twice. She died the next morning."

After the death of his second child, Nelson Sherman stayed drunk all the time. Things were not going well for Lydia, who was financing Nelson's drunken sprees in New Haven. But to every cloud there is a silver lining. Nelson's mother-in-law moved out.

Lydia's joy at seeing Mary Jones depart was diluted by Nelson's unquenchable thirst. Now a confirmed drunk, he no longer shared her bed. In short, he became an absolute bore.

One fine day in April, Lydia hitched up her wagon and together with five-year-old Nattie, drove over to the village of Birmingham. She pulled in front of the Birmingham Drug Store and walked inside with Nattie. Mr. Peck, the proprietor, waited on Lydia, who stated, "We are overrun with rats. What is best to kill them?"

Mr. Peck suggested several patent poisons, but in the end added that, "Arsenic is cheaper and just as good." Lydia chose arsenic.

When Lydia returned home Nelson was away in New Haven, dissipating $300 he had received from selling the family piano. Lydia waited for her husband's return for several days before dispatching Horatio, the eldest son, to bring his father back to Derby. After much saloon searching, Horatio located his father and brought him back.

Nelson immediately had an attack of stomach cramps. Lydia was up to her old tricks. "I had about a pint of brandy in the house, and I put some arsenic in it. That night he drank some of the brandy, and the next morning he was very sick."

For the next few days Nelson continued to suffer. Dr. Beardsley was called in. He attributed Nelson's trouble to his excessive drinking. The patient grew weaker. Dr. Beardsley brought in a colleague, Dr. Pinny, but Nelson continued to deteriorate. Nelson lasted a week before expiring.

It was now all too much for Dr. Beardsley. He had been the attending physician at three Sherman deaths. Despite the grieving wife, despite the alcoholic husband, something was wrong. All three deaths had been accompanied by similar symptoms—dry mouth, nausea, vomiting, stomach pain, faintness, and great thirst, all symptoms compatible with arsenic poisoning.

Dr. Beardsley actually was bold enough to ask Lydia if she had given her husband arsenic. Lydia was aghast. Heavens no, she replied. The concerned doctor then asked for permission to perform an autopsy. Lydia consented.

On Saturday, the day after Nelson's death, his liver and stomach were rattling along the New Haven railroad, on the way to Yale University to be examined. The next day the bodies of Ada and Frank Sherman, as well as Dennis Hurlbut, were exhumed. Their vital organs were sent to Yale as well.

On Monday, before the results of the tests for arsenic were returned to Derby, Lydia took off for New Brunswick, New Jersey, where detectives took her into custody. She was returned to Derby, and later transferred to New Haven, to stand trial for the murder of Nelson Sherman. Meanwhile, doctors had examined the vital organs of Nelson, Ada, and Frank Sherman, as well as those of Dennis Hurlbut. All were laced with arsenic.

Lydia Sherman's trial for murder began on April 16, 1872. Throughout the several months of her incarceration at Derby, she steadfastly maintained her innocence. Her case captured the imagination of the entire country. It was a rare day that curious onlookers and reporters didn't hover about the Derby jail, hoping for a glimpse of the "Birmingham Borgia."

Lydia's trial lasted ten days and concluded with her being found guilty of murder in the second degree and being sentenced to life imprisonment. While in jail awaiting her lawyer's attempts to obtain a new trial, Lydia dramatically confessed in detail to killing six of her own children, her three husbands, and the two Sherman children. In all, eleven murders.

Despite her admissions, she did not give detailed motives for her horrible crimes. Students of the Sherman case believe Lydia did away with Dennis Hurlbut, her second husband, to gain his wealth. In her confession, she mentioned that she killed several of the children so they would be "better off."

Lydia was imprisoned in the Connecticut State Prison for five and a half years, until her death on May 16, 1878.

CHARLES STARKWEATHER

WANTON murder is impossible to anticipate. There is very little defence against it. The difference between a traffic light turning red or green can place an innocent victim in the sight of a deranged sniper. You can cross the paths of desperate men during the commission of a robbery through no fault of your own.

When innocent people become the victims of such a murderer, the public has a natural abhorrence to the crime. We can all relate to being in the wrong place at the wrong time.

On Tuesday, January 27, 1958, Charlie Starkweather, 19, visited the home of his 14-year-old girlfriend, Caril Fugate. It was a blustery grey day in Lincoln, Nebraska. Charlie had brought along his .22 rifle. He and Caril's stepfather, Marion Bartlett, had a date to go hunting. As soon as Charlie entered the house, Caril's mother, Velda, started telling Charlie that she didn't want him around the house any more. A heated argument erupted and Velda slapped Charlie in the face. Charlie retaliated by slapping his girlfriend's mother.

Finally, Mr. Bartlett couldn't take any more. He came at Charlie. Without any more provocation than that, Charlie Starkweather raised his .22 and calmly shot Marion Bartlett in the head. Mrs. Bartlett grabbed a knife and advanced towards Charlie. The rifle was raised a second time and Charlie shot her, again with a bullet to the head. Two-and-a-half-year-old Betty Jean Bartlett started to cry. Starkweather beat her to death with the butt of his rifle.

The house became silent. Everyone but Caril and Charlie was dead. Charlie carried Mr. Bartlett's body out to a chicken coop at the rear of the house. He dragged Mrs. Bartlett's body to an outhouse. Little Betty Jean was placed in a cardboard box and put beside her mother. Charlie cleaned the blood off the floor, and unbelievably, he and Caril settled down to watching television for a few hours. Then Charlie went out to use a phone. He called Mr. Bartlett's employer and told him that Bartlett had the flu and wouldn't be in to work for a few days. Upon returning to the house he had intercourse with Caril. Later, he was to state that he had sex with Caril every day and twice on Sunday.

The young couple stayed on in the house. In the normal course of events, people started to arrive at the front door. Caril didn't answer some callers and they went away. The more persistent were told through the door that everyone had the flu and the doctor had ordered the house placed under quarantine. For six days the two teenagers stayed in the house after the killings. Finally Caril's elderly grandmother, sensing that something was wrong, went to the police, who investigated and discovered the three bodies. Caril and Charlie had left just before the police arrived. Starkweather took Bartlett's .410 shotgun with him.

They hadn't travelled far when Charlie's car got stuck near August Meyers' farm. Charlie, who knew Meyers, walked up to the house and asked for help in getting his car out of a ditch. The farmer went into the house for his overcoat. When he came back out, according to Charlie, he had a gun. Without hesitation, Starkweather shot him in the head. They got the car out of the ditch and drove away, but it wasn't long before they were stuck again. This time young Robert Jensen and his girlfriend, Carol King, stopped to see if they could help in any way. Charlie and Caril pulled their guns on the surprised pair. They had the terrified couple drive to a deserted school a few miles from Bennet, Nebraska. Starkweather led the pair to a storm cellar, shot young Jensen in the head, raped and stabbed Carol King, and shot her in the head as well.

That night Starkweather and Fugate spent the night in the Jensen car. The next day they walked into the home of wealthy Laver Ward in Lincoln, Nebraska. A maid opened the door to the young couple. It was to be her last day of life. Mrs. Ward came downstairs in her nightclothes. Later, on some pretext, she got permission from Starkweather to go upstairs to dress. Charlie waited for her for 40 minutes, and then went upstairs to investigate. He claimed later that Mrs. Ward was waiting for him with a rifle. He overpowered her and stabbed her to death in minutes.

At 6:30 in the evening Mr. Ward arrived home. He immediately sized up the situation and instinctively knew his only chance was to attack Starkweather. He lunged at Charlie with an electric iron. Starkweather shot him in the head, and as he spun around, he was again shot in the back. The maid was taken upstairs, tied and gagged. She was found dead of suffocation.

Charlie and Caril left the house and headed for Wyoming. They decided to change cars about 10 miles outside of Douglas, Wyoming. They hailed a passing motorist, salesman Merle Collison. In order to gain possession of his car Charlie shot him nine times.

Then Charlie's luck ran out.

As soon as he killed Collison, another motorist stopped, thinking the two vehicles were having difficulties. The driver, Joe Sprinkle, got out of his car. Charlie levelled a revolver at him and said, "Raise your hands, help me release the emergency brake or I'll kill you."

Out of the corner of his eye Sprinkle saw the body of Merle Collison lying on the floor of the car. He lunged for the rifle and wrestled it away from Charlie. Later he was to state that he knew instinctively that to lose this tug of war meant death. Unarmed, Charlie dashed for his car. Strictly by coincidence, Deputy Sheriff Bill Romer drove up. Caril, who had been in the dead man's car, ran to the deputy. Starkweather roared away in Collison's vehicle. The sheriff used his radio and a car driven by Douglas Police Chief Robert Ainslie took up the chase. He fired some shots at the fleeing vehicle. One bullet went through the rear window of Starkweather's car. Charlie pulled up and dashed out of the car screaming that he was bleeding. A sliver of glass from the broken window had nicked his ear.

Immediately after his capture Charlie Starkweather started to talk. He confessed to one other murder that had taken place seven weeks before his murderous spree began. It involved a gas station robbery where the owner was taken into the woods and shot to death. In all, 11 people fell to the deadly impulses of Starkweather, the last 10 in the space of two weeks.

From the beginning Charlie insisted that Caril was a hostage and had nothing to do with the actual killings. Caril also professed to be terrified of Charlie, and thought she would become a victim at any time during the killing orgy. Later Charlie, who made seven different confessions, changed his story and implicated his girlfriend, stating that she was a willing lover and accomplice.

When they placed Charlie in the electric chair on June 25, 1959, his last request was to task the guards to tighten the leather straps holding his chest and arms.

Caril's main defence was based on the fact that she was a hostage. The prosecution attorney pointed out the many times she was armed or alone and could have run away during the deadly two weeks.

In the end, she received a sentence of life imprisonment. Imprisoned at the age of 14, Caril spent more than half her life in prison. She was twice denied parole. However, she had her sentence of life imprisonment commuted. Caril has since been granted parole.

HOWARD STEWART

HOWARD Stewart couldn't stand the thought of his wife Brenda sleeping with another man. It didn't matter that he and Brenda were separated. In fact, folks around Corsicana, Texas, never could fathom why Brenda married Howard in the first place.

To say that 37-year-old Howard was not well liked around town would be an understatement. The man wore a perpetual scowl and had the reputation of blowing his cool at the least provocation.

In the summer of 1987, Howard shaved his head and outfitted himself with military camouflage clothing and combat boots. He became something of a character around Corsicana, a town of 30,000 solid Texans.

Folks shook their heads when he took to wearing a .22 automatic with a 50-bullet clip strapped to his leg. About the only living creatures Howard acted civilly towards were his two pet bulldogs. Behind his back, people called him Rambo.

In hindsight, Howard Stewart was a bomb waiting to explode. When he lost his job at Hulcher Services Inc., he had time to think. He had a lot to think about. First there was Brenda and her new boyfriend, Edward Persons.

The thought of her making love to that stranger drove him mad. Then there was Dennis Wade, his former supervisor who had fired him. It wasn't fair for a man to lose his job and his wife. Howard was relegated to living alone with his two bulldogs. No, it wasn't fair.

On September 9, Howard Stewart decided he had to get away from Corsicana to pull himself together. He boarded a bus and spent a week with relatives in Lebanon, Missouri. The change of scenery didn't help. A rage burned within Howard, a rage that could not be extinguished. Slowly, he donned his camouflage garb, taking special care to strap his .22 automatic to his leg. He told his relatives that he was hitchhiking back to Corsicana.

George Brewer, 43, and his wife Carol, 36, left their mobile home in their white Chevy van. It was their misfortune to pick up Howard Stewart who was hitchhiking back to Texas. Both George and Carol were shot in the head by Howard. The double murder first came to the attention of the authorities when the Brewers' abandoned van was found by a sheriff's deputy. The interior of the vehicle was drenched in blood. A search of the area uncovered George's body, but Carol was nowhere to be found.

Almost simultaneously with the discovery of George's body, police received a missing person's report filed by Mrs. Steve Vestal. Her husband had been scheduled to meet her at the church in nearby Phillipsburg for choir practice. When Steve failed to show up, his wife grew worried and called police.

The few days in September 1987 were fast becoming the busiest and strangest in the history of peaceful Laclede County, Missouri. Instead of locking up a few locals for being inebriated, police found themselves with one murder, possibly a second one, and a third person missing. The activity didn't abate.

Volunteers searched for Carol Brewer's body. A man in a truck spotted some clothing in a ditch about a mile and a half from where her husband's body had been recovered. What he thought was clothing turned out to be Carol's body. She too had been shot in the head.

Ten miles down the road in Lebanon, a woman noticed blood dripping from a truck onto the pavement of a parking lot. She peered into the vehicle. Slumped on the floor of the truck was the body of Steve Vestal, a bullet hole through his head.

Police were stymied. Ballistic checks on the .22 calibre slugs indicated that all three victims had been shot with the same weapon. A bloody shoeprint found beside George Brewer's body matched one found on Steve Vestal's jacket, but an investigation into the backgrounds of the victims indicated that the Brewers had not been acquainted with Steve Vestal. Money and jewelry had not been taken from any of the victims. Who would kill three individuals without any apparent motive?

Authorities had no idea of the existence of Howard Stewart. He had managed to hitchhike back to Texas without casting any suspicion on himself. Back in Corsicana, Howard told a friend that he had wasted three people in Missouri. The friend laughed. What could you expect from a guy who dressed like Rambo?

Howard Stewart wasn't finished killing. A week after his murderous spree in

Missouri, he woke up in a rage and struck out at what he may have loved most of all. He shot his two bulldogs and let the bodies lie in his van where they had fallen.

Howard drove to the location of his former employment, Hulcher Services Inc. By chance, the first man he met was Dennis Wade, the very man who had fired him weeks earlier. In front of a witness, he poured ten slugs into Wade and left the premises without uttering a word.

Howard drove across town and walked into the Seventh Avenue Steak House where his estranged wife Brenda worked as a waitress. He fired three shots into the ceiling before the assistant manager told him his wife wasn't scheduled to report for work until three that afternoon. As if his entrance had been of no importance, Howard thanked the man for the information and calmly walked out of the restaurant.

The assistant manager firmly believed that Brenda's life was in danger. He phoned Brenda and told her that he believed Howard was on his way to her house with nothing good on his mind. Then he called police. Brenda took the warning seriously, but felt that she could handle Howard. She was wrong.

Within minutes, Howard was storming through Brenda's house. Edward Persons was in bed when Howard entered, guns blazing. Edward was shot dead where he lay. Brenda raced to the bathroom and locked the door.

Howard sprayed the door with bullets and knocked it in. He found Brenda cowering with fear in a corner. Without hesitation, Howard fired and Brenda died instantly.

No doubt Howard heard the police sirens approaching. As they drew near, he placed his .22 automatic to his temple and pulled the trigger.

The killing was over. Six innocent individuals had been murdered and the man who dressed like Rambo had taken his own life.

MARY BETH TINNING

CAN a woman murder eight of her nine children over a period of 14 years and go undetected? That's what the 70,000 citizens of the factory city of Schenectady, N.Y. are asking themselves.

Mary Beth Tinning, 44, was born in the area back in the war years when the local General Electric plants employed 45,000 workers churning out strategic war materials. That large figure has steadily declined, and today 12,000 are gainfully employed at G.E., still the largest industry by far in Schenectady. The town, adjacent to Albany, has seen better days.

Joe Tinning worked at General Electric as a systems analyst. He and Mary Beth had moved frequently over the years. No one gave it much thought. The area around Albany, the state capital, is surrounded by villages and towns. It is difficult to ascertain where one stops and the next one begins. There was one thing different about the Tinnings. They suffered tragic misfortune with their children—all nine of them.

On January 3, 1972, the Tinnings' new baby Jennifer, died while still in hospital. She was eight days old. Jennifer is the only Tinning death not considered to be suspicious. Seventeen days later, on January 20, two-year-old Joseph died. Understandably, the Tinnings were devastated. But there was more to come. On March 2, 1972, four-year-old Barbara died.

What a horrible experience for any family to endure. In two months less a day all three Tinning children were dead. Their deaths were attributed to natural causes. Those who knew the Tinnings offered their sympathy. It happens. There was little anyone could do.

Nine months later, Mary Beth gave birth to a son, Timothy. On December 10, 1973, 14 days after his birth, Timothy died. The cause of death noted on the death certificate is SIDS (Sudden Infant Death Syndrome). In its purest sense, SIDS is not a cause of death. It really means that the cause of death is unknown.

With Timothy's death occurring so soon after being taken home from hospital, rumors spread among the Tinnings' few acquaintances. Was it possible that there was something wrong with the Tinnings' genes, some imperfection which caused their offspring to die suddenly?

Just under two years after this tragedy, five-month-old Nathan died. When Nathan died on September 2, 1975, various individuals in official capacities, such as doctors and social service workers, became somewhat suspicious. However, it must be pointed out that the same doctors and social workers were not necessarily involved in all the deaths. Autopsies were performed on all the Tinning children. The results were always the same. Death was attributed to natural causes.

Dr. Robert Sullivan, the Schenectady County Medical Examiner, admitted that when Nathan died, he was aware of the earlier deaths. Nathan's death was thoroughly investigated, but no evidence of foul play was found. Dr. Sullivan revealed, "The parents were doing nothing wrong. They were initiating examinations into the deaths of the children."

Joe Tinning had a responsible position at the G.E. plant. He is an avid bowler. Over the years, Mary Beth often worked as a waitress to supplement the family's income. Sometimes she served as a volunteer ambulance driver. There was absolutely nothing to distinguish the Tinnings from their neighbors.

Absolutely nothing except the inexplicable deaths of their children.

After Nathan's death, three and half years passed before Mary Beth gave birth to another child, a daughter, Mary Frances. The beat continued. Mary Frances died at age three and a half months.

Ten months later, Mary Beth had a little boy, Jonathan. He died three months later, on March 24, 1980. That same year, the Tinnings adopted a son, Michael. He died a year after Jonathan, on March 2, 1981.

Michael's death put an end to the theory that some kind of black genetic evil was at work causing the strange deaths of the Tinning children. After all, he was adopted. An autopsy was performed. The official cause of death was listed as viral pneumonia. Now, suspicions ran rampant. Although there was no proof of any wrongdoing, pediatricians and social workers advised police that should any further Tinning children die, a forensic pathologist should be called in immediately.

Eight children were dead. It seems unbelievable that, despite an extensive investigation into some of the deaths, nothing more than dark suspicions were cast in Mrs. Tinning's direction. The bodies of Timothy and Nathan were exhumed, but nothing new was found.

Over three years passed. Mary Beth became pregnant for the eighth time. She gave birth to Tami Lynn, who died four months later, on December 20, 1985. This ninth death initiated a massive investigation. I have been unable to unearth just what, if anything, investigating officers uncovered. Evidently, a tip concerning Tami's death came from someone attached to the Schenectady County Social Services Department's Child Protective Unit.

On February 4, 1986, Mary Beth was picked up by detectives and taken to the nearby State Police Headquarters at Loudonville. Under intensive questioning, which lasted a total of 10 hours, Mary Beth admitted killing three of her children: Timothy, Nathan and Tami.

She was duly arrested, lodged in jail and charged with two counts of second degree murder concerning Tami's death. More specifically, she was charged with one count of "having intentionally caused her daughter's death by smothering her with a pillow," and in the other count, "with showing depraved indifference to human life by engaging in conduct which caused Tami Lynne's death."

Joe Tinning was not suspected of the crimes.

The maximum penalty for second degree murder in New York state is life imprisonment. The minimum penalty is from 15 to 25 years.

On March 19, after spending a month and a half in jail, Mary Beth Tinning was released on $100,000 bail. She immediately instituted court proceedings to have her confession deemed inadmissible evidence at her impending murder trial.

Mary Beth professed that her constitutional rights had been violated when the confessions were obtained. The suppression hearing into this charge was concluded in April. As a result, the details of what was said on the night Mary Beth confessed to detectives, can now be made public.

The first statement, given in narrative from, describes how Mary Beth smothered Timothy, Nathan and Tami, "With a pillow, because I'm not a good mother. I'm not a good mother because of the other children." She also said, "I did not do anything to Jennifer, Joseph, Barbara, Michael, Mary Frances or Jonathan."

In a second question and answer session with detectives, Mary Beth gave more details of Tami's death. She arrived home that night, five days before Christmas in 1985, at about 8:35 p.m., after being out shopping with a friend.

Her mother-in-law and father-in-law had been babysitting four-month-old Tami. They, as well as her friend, left at about 9:30 pm. Mary Beth sat in a recliner chair with Tami on her lap. After a while she put the baby to bed.

Mary Beth related, "I tried to give her a bottle, but she didn't want it. She fussed and cried for about a half hour. She finally went to sleep. I then went to bed." Joe came home at 11 p.m. They chatted for a few moments.

"I was about to doze off when Tami woke up and started to cry. I got up and went to the crib and tried to do something with her to get her to stop crying. I finally used the pillow from my bed and put it over head. I did it until she stopped crying." Mary Beth went on, "When I finally lifted the pillow off Tami, she wasn't moving. I put the pillow on the couch and then screamed for Joe and he woke up and I told Joe Tami wasn't breathing."

It was this chilling recital that Mary Beth attempted to suppress. However, a county court judge ruled that her statements would be admissible at her upcoming murder trial. He also ruled that they had been given willingly and voluntarily.

On July 19, 1987, Mary Beth Tinning was found guilty of second degree murder in the case of her infant daughter Tami. She was sentenced to 25 years to life imprisonment.

GEORGE KENT WALLACE

SOME criminals never reveal the reasons for their perverse and violent actions. Quite possibly they don't know the deep-seated trigger mechanism which activates their aberrant behavior. Such a criminal was George Kent Wallace.

The series of strange murders began on the evening of February 17, 1987, when 15-year-old Bill Domer was sent to the grocery store by his parents to purchase snacks. The Fort Smith, Arkansas lad never returned home. Five days later, his body was found by small boys playing near a pond adjacent to Leard Cemetery, just yards over the state line in Oklahoma. Bill's fully clothed body was lying face down in seven inches of water. He had been shot twice in the back. Despite the best efforts of the police, months and years passed without any concrete clues being uncovered which would lead to the killer.

Four years later, on November 11, 1990, Mark McLaughlin, 14, left his home in nearby Van Buren to pick up a loaf of bread at the neighborhood grocery store. He was last seen riding his bicycle towards the store. Next morning, a fisherman found Mark's body in the same pond where Bill Domer had been found years earlier. Like Bill, Mark had been shot in the back. He also had bruises on his buttocks, which pathologists felt were the result of a beating.

Only 12 days after the tragic death of Mark McLaughlin, another boy, Alonzo Cadeiz, attended a basketball game at Westark Community College in Fort Smith. After the game, friends saw him riding away on his bicycle. Alonzo was never seen alive again.

Two weeks passed. Authorities were frantically attempting to get a handle on the individual who was preying on Fort Smith boys when Chris Ferguson, 18, another Westark Community College student, finished his work at a grocery store in Van Buren. Chris jumped in his pickup and was about to drive away when a four-door 1981 Chevrolet pulled up behind him. A well-dressed man approached Chris and flashed ID indicating he was a police officer. The man in the dark blue suit asked for Chris' driver's licence before ordering him to get out of his vehicle and lock the doors. Chris complied.

The officer placed handcuffs on Chris' wrists and fastened leg irons around his ankles. He then led Chris into his Chevrolet. Chris studied the interior of the vehicle, noting there was no police radio or anything else to identify the car as a police vehicle. As they drove along, he grew suspicious. When he asked why he was being treated in this manner, the man told him he was a strong suspect in a grocery store robbery in Booneville.

The Chevy pulled off the road. The well-dressed man climbed into the back seat, pulled down Chris' pants and inflicted a severe beating to his buttocks with a stick, which Chris thought might have been a broom handle. Chris, who stood five-feet, two-inches tall and weighed barely 120 pounds, cringed in pain. Finally, his assailant tired and pulled up Chris' pants. He forced the hapless youth to walk ahead of him through the woods. Chris was well aware of the two younger boys who had been murdered. He was sure this man was no police officer, but the mad killer the police were seeking. As they trudged through the woods, the strain proved to be too much. Chris whirled and shouted, "Are you going to shoot me?" The man opened his suit coat, indicating he wasn't carrying a gun. His captive was ordered to keep walking.

Without warning, Chris felt the poker-hot sting of a knife being plunged into his back over and over again. Instinctively he felt the best thing he could do was play dead. He fell to the ground, attempted to hold his breath and let his body go limp. Chris' attacker undid his handcuffs and leg irons before trying to remove his pants. Chris decided to act. He jumped to his feet and ran for his life. The man ran after the terrified teenager, but Chris made it to the parked Chevrolet, praying the key would be in the ignition. As luck would have it, the key was there. Chris roared away, leaning on the horn all the way to attract attention. He stopped at the first house, where the occupants called police.

Chris was rushed to hospital. He had been stabbed five times in the back and once in the arm. Although he had lost a lot of blood, he survived. Meanwhile, police had no difficulty picking up George Kent Wallace trudging along the highway.

Wallace, a part-time truck driver, also ran a mail-order business in Fort Smith. Since arriving in the community, he had served a year in jail for forging bogus figures on credit cards used by his mail-order customers. Wallace also had a prison record before settling in Fort Smith. Back in 1966, he had been convicted of abducting a police officer. For this offence, he was sentenced to 15 years imprisonment, but was released after serving nine years.

Shortly after his release, Wallace was convicted of kidnapping and assault with a deadly weapon. For this infraction, he received a sentence of eight to 10 years, but was paroled after serving only three years. Significantly, the kidnapping charges for which Wallace was convicted involved the paddling of his victims across their buttocks.

In addition, Arkansas authorities learned that Wallace had been suspected but never charged in the abduction and murder of two young boys in the Winston-Salem area. These two homicides were still unsolved.

The dates of all the attacks and murders coincided with dates when Wallace was not in prison. All the paraphernalia used during Chris Ferguson's ordeal was recovered. Police were able to locate handcuffs, leg irons, flashlights and the ID Wallace had used to pose as a police officer.

On December 20, 1990, with George Wallace safely behind bars, the body of Alonzo Cadeiz was discovered in a nearby gas well drilling pond. Alonzo had been stabbed in the back and beaten across the buttocks.

Wallace was charged with attempted first-degree murder and kidnapping in the Chris Ferguson case. He confessed to this crime and also the murders of Bill Domer and Mark McLaughlin, relating in detail the abduction, beating and murder of both boys. He refused to discuss his own youth or how he had developed the weird perversion of spanking young boys and then killing them.

A myriad of charges were eventually brought against Wallace. He received a 60-year sentence for the abduction and attempted murder of Chris Ferguson. For the Domer and McLaughlin murders, Wallace was sentenced to death. Because these bodies were found across the Oklahoma State line, George Kent Wallace currently resides with 125 other inmates on Death Row in McAlester, Oklahoma.

Chris Ferguson, by escaping the clutches of this madman, is believed to have saved many lives. He has received several civic rewards for his actions.

DAVID WOOD

AUTHORITIES were sure they knew the identity of the rapist killer, but couldn't quite prove it.

Marjorie Knox, 14, of Chaparrel, New Mexico, shouted over her shoulder to her parents that she was going to the convenience store at the corner of her Byrum St. home to purchase a soft drink. That was on September 14, 1987. Marjorie never made it to the store and has never been seen since.

Six months later, on March 7, 1988, Melissa Alaniz, 13, of nearby El Paso, Texas, told her mother she would be back in time for dinner. She was going out to play with some other kids down the street. Melissa has never been seen again.

The heat of summer descended on the dry desert country just north of the Mexican border. It was quite possible that there was no connection between the disappearances of the two girls, although a parent of each girl was employed with Rockwell International, the giant aerospace company.

The terror which came with the knowledge that a serial killer could be in their midst accelerated on June 2, when Desiree Wheatley, 15, went missing. Desiree left her parents' El Paso apartment to purchase an ice cream. She never returned. An investigation into her disappearance uncovered the fact that the young girl had chatted with some friends on the street after she left home. One youngster saw her talking to a man who had pulled up in a pickup truck. When she looked again, both the truck and Desiree were gone.

Panic spread throughout the area, when only three days after Desiree's disappearance, Karen Baker, 20, simply vanished off the streets of El Paso as she walked to visit a friend.

Whoever was plucking girls off the streets sped up the frequency of the abductions. The third girl to disappear that June was Cheryl Vasquez-Dismukes, 19, who didn't return after leaving her apartment to purchase a pack of cigarettes.

The citizens of El Paso and surrounding communities were terrified. They purchased weapons and locks, although there was no evidence that the killer had ever entered a home to abduct a victim. Detectives knew precious little about the man, who seemed to operate like a phantom in broad daylight. They felt he might be driving a pickup truck and he could have black hair. It was theorized that because the victims had not cried out, they might have been acquainted with the abductor.

The reign of terror continued. Maria Casio, 24, who had travelled from Addison, Texas to visit friends in El Paso, disappeared after she left her friends' home. A month later, two water company employees came across her body in a shallow grave in the desert at the edge of the city.

Police were quickly at the scene, searching the area for clues. Instead of clues, they found another body, that of Karen Baker, 20, who had been missing since the previous June. Both women had been strangled to death. From their partially nude bodies and the position of their clothing, it was ascertained that they had been raped before being killed.

Two weeks later, hikers, aware of the rash of disappearances, came across a patch of disturbed earth which looked suspiciously like a grave. They brushed away the earth, revealing the body of Desiree Wheatley, the little girl who had left her parents' home to buy an ice cream. Near Desiree's body, police uncovered the body of yet another victim, Angelica Frausto, 17, who had been reported missing on September 6.

An investigation into the backgrounds of the victims uncovered several connecting links between the girls. Some of the girls had attended the same high school. Three of the victims' parents were employed at Rockwell International and two of the girls, Wheatley and Knox, had known each other. Police felt that the connecting links could be nothing more than coincidence. Unable to overlook any possibility, this tangent of the investigation was vigorously pursued.

Police received the first break in the case when two rather unsavory women came forward with their stories. Both had been previously charged with prostitution and drug-related crimes. They felt compelled to tell their stories for the good of the community, although they realized, because of their records, that they might not be believed. One woman, whose name has not been made public, told of getting into a pickup truck on an El Paso street. The driver pulled out a knife and drove into the desert, making his intentions clear to the terrified prostitute. Convinced that she would be killed, the woman jumped from the moving vehicle. She was unhurt, except for cuts and bruises, and managed to hitchhike back to El Paso.

Next day she told her best friend of her ordeal. As she did so, her friend confessed that she too had experienced a similar incident. A man picked her up and pulled out a gun. He drove her into the desert, threw her a shovel and ordered her to start digging. She was convinced she was digging her own grave, when both she and her abductor heard strangers approaching. The man ordered her back into the truck and drove into the city, where he raped her. Then, inexplicably, he let her go.

Both women said they were reluctant to tell their stories, but felt they might be the only ones who could identify the serial killer suspect. The description they gave police fit a known sex criminal, 30-year-old David Wood. Wood had once been convicted of raping a 13-year-old girl and later, a 19-year-old. For those crimes, he received two 20 year sentences, but was paroled in January 1987, after serving seven years in prison. He was released eight months before the rash of disappearances in El Paso.

Wood was placed in a police lineup. Both women positively identified him as the man who had abducted them. Wood was charged with kidnapping and rape. He claimed that he was totally innocent and was not the serial killer.

Police had little to directly tie Wood to the series of murders. He claimed, "I am a lover, not a killer." Wood has been tried for the abduction of the two prostitutes and the rape of one of them and has been found guilty of sexual assault. The Texas jury took only 40 minutes to reach their verdict.

David Wood has been sentenced to 50 years imprisonment, the maximum sentence allowed by law. With his arrest and incarceration, the rash of murders in and around El Paso came to an abrupt end.

PART 3

U.S. DOCTORS

DR. JOHN WEBSTER 1849

THE medical profession has an unenviable record in the murky environs where murder abounds. Many a doctor has taken time off from healing and curing to maim and kill.

Dr. John White Webster was a professor of medicine at Harvard University, Cambridge, Mass. He was also the author of several books on the subject of chemistry. The professor had one failing. He tended to live well beyond his means, which isn't that difficult to do if your salary is $1,200 per year. Even in 1849, that was not a princely sum. Besides living high off the hog, the doctor had a wife and three daughters.

To complement his income, Prof. Webster sold tickets to his chemistry lectures. But it really wasn't enough. The professor liked to throw parties and entertain friends just as if he could afford it.

From time to time, Prof. Webster found himself in such dire financial straits that he was forced to borrow money from an affluent colleague, Dr. George Parkman. Dr. Parkman had loaned Webster $400 some seven years earlier. The loan was secured by a promissory note and a mortgage on some of the professor's personal property.

When Prof. Webster had difficulty paying off the note, Dr. Parkman came to his aid once again. The doctor, with some other men, loaned the professor a further $2,432. This loan was secured by a mortgage on all of Webster's personal property, including a valuable mineral collection.

Nothing seemed to alleviate Webster's financial woes. He approached Dr. Parkman's brother-in-law, Robert Shaw, gave him a hard-luck story and succeeded in selling him his mineral collection for $1,200. By chance, Parkman and Shaw were discussing Webster and his tight financial situation when the subject of the mineral collection came up. Dr. Parkman was furious to find out that Webster had sold an item on which he held the mortgage. In the weeks that followed, Dr. Parkman put real heat on Webster, threatening legal action if the professor failed to ante up.

On a Friday in November 1849, Dr. Parkman had an appointment to meet Prof. Webster in his laboratory. Dr. Parkman arrived at 1:45 p.m. No one could remember ever seeing him again.

Two days after Dr. Parkman disappeared, Prof. Webster paid a visit to his colleague's brother's home. Rev. Parkman was somewhat surprised to see Webster. The professor told the minister that he had met with Dr. Parkman the previous Friday and had paid him $483 against the money he owed. He said that the doctor had rushed out of his laboratory and apparently no one had seen him since that time.

A man of Dr. Parkman's stature doesn't go missing every day. His disappearance was the talk of the university campus, if not all of Boston. By paying a visit to the missing man's brother , Prof. Webster lent credence to those who believed that the doctor had been attacked, robbed and quite possibly murdered. It was these rumors which came to the attention of a man named Littlefield, who was the janitor of the building housing Prof. Webster's laboratory.

Littlefield decided to make a thorough search of the premises. He had found it strange that the professor had double locked his vault-like laboratory, which was situated below his living quarters. The lab contained a huge furnace.

Using a crowbar, Littlefield worked at breaking through the wall of the lab. His wife stood guard in case Webster showed up. It was slow going, taking the better part of a night. Finally, he broke through and poked his torch inside. "I held my light forward and the first thing which I saw was the pelvis of a man and two parts of a leg. The water was running down on these remains from the sink. I knew it was no place for these things."

University officials and the police were notified. Dr. Webster was taken into custody. Here was a distinguished man of letters incarcerated for taking the life of an equally distinguished colleague. Dr. Webster was a Master of Arts, a medical doctor, a member of the American Academy of Arts and Sciences. The list was as long as your arm. In custody, he was near collapse.

Dr. Webster's trial captured headlines throughout North America. To facilitate the thousands who wished to attend, the courtroom was cleared every 15 minutes so that a new group of spectators could gain entrance. In this way, thousands could later claim they had attended the famous murder trial of Prof. Webster. The trial itself lasted 11 days.

Janitor Littlefield was one of the main witnesses for the prosecution. He explained that Dr. Webster's lab was more of a vault where body parts were delivered from the dissecting room. They were burned in Webster's furnace. On the evening of Dr. Parkman's disappearance, Littlefield had seen him walking towards Webster's flat, but had not seen him enter.

During the next few days, while scores of officials were searching for the missing Dr. Parkman, the professor had locked himself in his vault for hours on end. Fires were kept burning in the furnace and water could be heard steadily running in the vault. The vault gave up several human body parts and fragments of teeth were found in the furnace.

Defence counsel attempted to raise doubts over the body parts, claiming that they were not those of the good doctor. It was further claimed that even if the human remains were those of Dr. Parkman, it was quite possible that someone else had placed the parts in the vault to incriminate Prof. Webster. Defence counsel even suggested that Littlefield himself had as much opportunity to do away with the doctor as did Webster.

In the end, the trial hinged on whether or not the body parts were indeed Dr. Parkman's mortal remains. This was proven without a doubt when false teeth found in the furnace were produced in evidence. Dr. Nathan Keep, a friend of both Parkman and Webster, had retained the molds he had made when fitting Dr. Parkman's teeth. The teeth found in the furnace fit the molds exactly. Dr. Keep cried as he gave evidence, fully aware that he was sealing the fate of a good friend.

The evidence, totally circumstantial, for no one had seen the two men together, was now in. The jury retired for only three hours before returning with a verdict of guilty.

Prof. Webster was given the opportunity to make a statement. Following is a pertinent portion of that statement: "Repeating in the most solemn and positive manner, and under the fullest sense of my responsibility as a man and as a Christian, that I am wholly innocent of this charge, to the truth of which the Searcher of all hearts is a witness."

The statement was heart rending and caused many a tear to flow. It was a pack of lies.

Some weeks later, Webster withdrew his courtroom statement and wrote out a detailed confession. He told how Parkman had approached him in a gruff manner demanding, "Have you got the money?" Webster replied, "No, doctor." He went on to state that he had attempted to explain his position but was constantly interrupted and called a liar and a scoundrel. When Parkman waved mortgage papers in his face, he couldn't control himself. He picked up the closest weapon at hand, a piece of wood, and brought in down full force on Parkman's head. The doctor didn't move. He was dead.

According to his own statement, Webster never gave a thought to calling for assistance. He immediately thought of disposing of the body to avoid being suspected. Webster dragged the body into an adjacent room and removed the doctor's clothing and the contents of his pockets. Both were burned in the furnace. The body was dismembered in the sink while the water kept running, moving blood down the drain.

Prof. Webster pleaded for his life, claiming that he had acted in a fit of anger. He also apologized to Littlefield for having his lawyer cast suspicion in the janitor's direction. His confession did nothing to save his life, but it did provide us with certain insights. Respectable professional men who have never committed a violent act in their lives are capable of murder. They can also lie eloquently from the witness stand.

Dr. John White Webster was hanged for the murder of Dr. George Parkman on the last Friday in August 1850.

DR. ROBERT BUCHANAN 1891

DOCTORS should really stay out of the murder business and stick to healing. Don't get me wrong, as a class of killer, men of medicine can be extremely adept at sending the unsuspecting to the great hereafter, but for some reason, at the conclusion of the dastardly deed, they are prone to act in a downright stupid manner.

Dr. Robert Buchanan left Halifax, N.S. to set up his office in New York City. He and wife Helen settled at 267 West 11th St., where he gradually built up a rather lucrative practice.

Bob was not the robust swashbuckling type. He was a short man with a rather sad countenance set off by a scraggly moustache. He did have two outstanding traits. He loved the ladies and had a thirst that could only be quenched in the many saloons which dotted his neighborhood.

After living in New York for four years, Doc Bob was a regular patron at a saloon owned by Richard Macomber. He got to know Macomber and another regular, William Doria, extremely well. The three men downed many a slug of rotgut during the cold New York nights. Boys will be boys.

One night in 1890 the three friends ventured to Newark to visit a house of ill fame owned and operated by the partnership of madam Anna Sutherland and elderly janitor James Smith.

Can we take a moment here to describe Anna Sutherland? Just as the doctor's wife Helen was an attractive woman, Anna was not. She was fat, I mean really big. She wore excessive makeup and dyed her hair a hideous shade of red. Unfortunately, she had a distinctive and prominent wart on her nose. Doc Bob was not yet 30; Anna was twice the good doctor's age.

When Doc Bob's two buddies tired of their periodic sojourns to Newark, the doctor continued to visit Anna. Soon he was taking care of her minor medical ills. Quite unexpectedly, Doc Bob informed his friends that he was divorcing Helen. He swore he was through with marriage. The divorce was granted on November 12, 1891. Exactly 14 days later, Anna Sutherland made out a will, leaving everything she owned to her future husband or, if she died single, to her dear friend, Dr. Bob Buchanan. Three days after she made out her will, Anna married Bob. Helen moved back to Halifax. Bob relocated his practice in Anna's brothel on Halsey St. in Newark.

Medicine and prostitution do not as a rule mix well. Male patients would often be accosted by Anna at the doctor's front door. She would inquire as to their preferences in a sex partner. This did nothing to enhance Doc Bob's medical practice. To make matters worse, James Smith, Anna's partner in the prostitution business, was extremely jealous of the doctor, whom he considered an interloper. After all, James had proposed more than once to Anna and had been turned down every time.

Folks, the marriage didn't work, but Doc Bob hung on until well into 1892. There is little doubt that the doctor put his plan into action in March of that year when he purchased a single ticket to Edinburgh to further his medical studies. The ticket was for travel on April 25. When Anna heard that she wasn't included in the trip, she threatened to cut him out of her will. On April 21, Doc Bob told his buddies down at the saloon that dear Anna had become too ill to travel and that he had cancelled the trip.

On April 22, Dr. B.C. McIntyre was called in to minister to Anna. The doctor found Mrs. Buchanan raving and near hysteria. She complained that her throat was contracting. When his patient lapsed into a coma, Dr. McIntyre called in Dr. H.P. Watson for a second opinion. Next day, after an illness of only 26 hours, Anna died with both doctors in attendance. Death was attributed to a cerebral hemmorhage.

Dr. Bob displayed no sorrow at the loss of his wife. In fact, he was elated. Anna had left him a cool $50,000, an absolute fortune in those days. Bob took off for Halifax, but before he left he hired a private detective to guard his late wife's grave. That was a stupid thing to do.

Lurking in the reeds, observing everything through his beady eyes, was Anna's old partner, James Smith. That sterling gentleman smelled a rat and high-tailed it to the coroner's office with his suspicions. The coroner listened, but upon learning that two reputable doctors had been at Anna's bedside throughout her illness, dismissed Smith as a troublemaker.

A reporter for the old New York World overheard the conversation and decided to look into Anna's untimely death. He dropped into Doc Bob's favorite watering hole and learned of the doctor's aborted trip to Scotland. He checked with the steamship company and learned that Bob had cancelled his passage and had obtained a refund on April 11, over a week before his wife had taken ill.

The reporter, now hot to trot, also learned that Doc Bob and his cronies had often discussed a current New York murder case which involved morphine. Doc Bob had expressed the opinion that he could administer a lethal dose of morphine which would never be detected. When the reporter learned that the doctor had remarried his first wife Helen in Halifax, he knew he was tracking down a diabolical killer.

The New York World put its case to the coroner who agreed to exhume Mrs. Buchanan's body. An autopsy revealed the presence of a residue of morphine, indicating that Anna had been given enough morphine to kill her. When the dead woman's eyes were checked for telltale contractions of the pupils (even after death an obvious symptom of morphine poisoning), doctors were shocked to note that there was no contraction.

The district attorney's office was convinced that Doc Bob had found a method of concealing this symptom. Someone in the DA's office remembered that, as a little boy, he had been given drops of belladonna to enlarge his pupils for an eye examination. Anna's eyeballs were tested for belladonna. Sure enough, they tested positive. When a nurse who had attended Anna before the two physicians arrived at the house recalled that Doc Bob had given his wife eye drops for no apparent reason, the doctor was arrested and taken into custody.

On March 20, 1893, Doc Bob stood trial for the murder of his wife. The evidence against him was entirely circumstantial. A strange demonstration took place in the courtroom. A cat was poisoned with morphine. Belladonna was dropped into the cat's eyes, which served to disguise the contraction of its pupils.

On April 26, the New York jury deliberated for 28 hours before returning a verdict of guilty of murder in the first degree. Dr. Robert Buchanan lingered on Sing Sing's Death Row for two years. On July 2, 1895, he was executed in the electric chair.

DR. HENRY MEYER 1894

YEARS ago groups of ambitious men sat around grog shops in London, England, betting on whether or not the latest explorer to the new world would make it back to England. From these humble beginnings sprang what we know today as the insurance business. Almost as quickly as the insurance industry developed, another group of cunning individuals developed schemes to defraud the insurance companies.

None was more cunning that Dr. Henry C. Meyer of Chicago. The good doctor had been in and out of trouble all of his adult life, having had the misfortune of having his first two wives die under mysterious circumstances. Was the man of medicine discouraged? Not on your life. He appeared before the altar for the third time in 1888 with a blue-eyed, rosy-cheeked young thing of 20, who sported long braids down to her waist. The doctor was 38.

Dr. Meyer had an unprofitable back-street practice and was struggling to make ends meet, when a patient, Ludwig Brandt, strolled into his office. Ludwig was to change Dr. Meyer's life forever.

Ludwig was in the insurance business. His conversation about claims and big payoffs simply fascinated Dr. Meyer. It seemed that a man with an over-abundance of grey matter between his ears would have no trouble at all parting those wealthy insurance companies from some of their cash. A few months after their initial meeting the two men decided to defraud Ludwig's own company.

Ludwig had no trouble obtaining insurance on a non-existent person. Dr. Meyer then produced a cadaver. Mrs. Meyer, posing as the cadaver's sister, would collect the insurance money. The scheme lacked sophistication, was amateurish, and fell apart when the examining physician made the startling discovery that the cadaver had been dead for some days rather than a few minutes.

To every cloud there is a silver lining. Dr. Meyer and Brandt met small time swindlers August Wimmers and Gaustave Baum while serving time in jail. The four men became personal friends and planned on combining their devious talents once out of jail. Before they could join forces, Baum was caught on an individual caper and was stashed away in a Cincinnati cooler for two years.

Dr. Meyer had a scheme. He explained to Brandt and Wimmers that using Baum's identity, Brandt would marry Dr. Meyer's cute young wife Marie. A short time after the marriage Baum (even though you and I know he really is Brandt, let's call him Baum from here on in) would purchase life insurance with his everloving wife Marie as the beneficiary. Baum would then be fed poisonous antimony over a prolonged period of time, causing him to become seriously ill. A regular doctor would attend Baum throughout his illness. At the last moment Dr. Meyer would restore Baum to health, substitute a fresh body somewhat similar to Baum in appearance and call in a new doctor. The new doctor would examine the body, and after being urged to consult with the regular attending physician by Marie, he would find out that Baum had been ill and under a physician's care for some months. Under those conditions he should sign the death certificate without hesitation.

Baum married Marie. He then took out $3,500 life insurance with Mutual Life, $3,000 with Washington Life, $1,000 with Aetna, and another $1,000 with New York Life. In all $8,500, a princely sum in the Gay '90s.

Baum, accompanied by Wimmers, moved to New York City and rented a flat at 320 East 13th St. The first night at supper Wimmers suggested that there was no time like the present to start the poison flowing. Dr. Meyer had provided him with a supply of antimony and suggested that it would be most palatable with a sweet desert. Baum turned chicken. After all, it was fine for everyone to be so enthusiastic, but it was he alone who was to become seriously ill.

The next day Baum again found some lame excuse not to take his poison. Wimmers had no recourse but to call Dr. Meyer and inform him that Baum was behaving like a stubborn child who refused to take his medicine.

Dr. Meyer and Marie whipped over to the Big Apple from Chicago to straighten matters out. Dr. Meyer pleaded, begged, and beseeched Baum to take his poison like a good boy, but nothing worked. Finally Marie assured Baum that she and Dr. Meyer would stay right there in the flat with him to ensure that nothing went wrong.

Each evening Baum was given small doses of antimony. He became unpleasantly ill. Young Dr. S.B. Minden, who had a general practice nearby, was picked to be the attending physician. Dr. Minden was mildly puzzled by Baum's condition. He prescribed some medicine or other and left with the warning that if the patient should become worse, Wimmers should call him again. As the weeks drifted into months, Dr. Minden made several visits to Baum, whom the doctor now considered to be chronically ill.

Baum was going through hell. He felt that the time had come for him to get well and have a nice fresh body take his place. Dr. Meyer assured him that as soon as the time was ripe, he would run down to the morgue, identify some young stiff as his long lost cousin and claim the body. We will never know if Dr. Meyer ever even entertained the thought of substituting a body for Baum. What we do know is that on March 26, 1892, Baum was given a massive dose of arsenic and died in Dr. Meyer's arms. There was no need to find a substitute body now. Baum's would do nicely.

Dr. Minden was called immediately. His patient was dead and duly buried without incident, if you choose to ignore the wailing and carrying on of the spurious Mrs. Baum at graveside. Marie put on quite a show, particularly as she was several months pregnant with what everyone thought was her dead husband's child. Of course we know it was the child of that devil, Dr. Meyer.

The grieving widow went around to the insurance companies and collected the gang's ill gotten gains. Meyers, Wimmers, and Marie set up housekeeping in Toledo. They took in a rather dull, good-looking young girl named Mary Neiss while Marie awaited the blessed event. It wasn't long before Dr. Meyer wanted to pull off the insurance fraud once again. He cautiously approached Mary, who thought it was a great idea. This time the doctor explained that he would become Dr. Hugo Wayler. Mary would be Mrs. Wayler, and would be fed the poison.

It is conceivable that Meyer might have pulled off the entire scheme successfully for the second time, had it not been for the intervention of true love. What the doctor didn't know was that August Wimmers and Mary Neiss were seeing each other on the sly. Wimmers told Mary that the last time the scheme was pulled, Baum died. To make sure that didn't happen to Mary, Wimmers and Mary eloped.

Dr. Meyer was fit to be tied. It was getting so you couldn't trust anyone. As soon as Marie gave birth, the Meyers moved to Detroit in real fear that Wimmers might tell all to the authorities. It took Wimmers a full year, but he did seek out the doctor with blackmail in mind. Finding the medic living in poverty, he dropped the idea. Like Ford, he had a better idea. He went to one of the defrauded insurance companies and made a deal. For $500 he would reveal Dr. Meyer's address. The insurance company took up Wimmers' proposition and that's how Dr. Meyer and the again pregnant Marie were taken into custody.

Marie gave birth to her baby while in jail. The baby died in jail. Marie was never tried for her part in her husband's murderous ways. She died many years later of natural causes.

Dr. Meyer's murder trial began on December 5, 1893, and was a complicated and sensational one in many ways. It was revealed that Baum was alive and well, a fact which caused the prosecution no end of aggravation until they proved that the murder victim was Brandt, posing as Baum.

In the end evil Dr. Meyer was convicted of murder in the second degree and sentenced to life imprisonment. He remained in Sing Sing from 1894 to 1914, a total of 20 years, before being paroled.

DR. J. HERMAN FEIST 1905

IT is unusual for a man to stand trial for murder when it is uncertain where and when the crime took place, or if a murder was committed at all. Strange as it first appears, these circumstances did occur back in 1905 in Nashville, Tennessee.

Oscar Mangrum, 35, was the not too bright owner of a barber shop down Nashville way. His wife of nine years, the former Rosa Mason, was an attractive woman of 33 when our little tale of intrigue and possible mayhem took place. The couple had no children.

They had a room and board arrangement at Mrs. Cullom's comfortable establishment on Sixth Ave.

Rosa was quite unlike her husband in many ways. Oscar was an introvert; Rosa had a bubbly, outgoing personality. Where he was content, she was ambitious. To fulfil her energetic nature, Rosa threw herself into working for philanthropic organizations, often heading up charitable fund-raising drives in cities other than Nashville. It was not unusual for Rosa to travel alone to New Orleans, St. Louis and Chicago. She was extremely successful and grew financially independent of her husband. In fact, Rosa sported several diamond rings which were far beyond what the average barber could afford in 1905.

The Mangrums had a friend, their family physician, J. Herman Feist. It was an open secret among their acquaintances that handsome Dr. Feist had more than a professional interest in pretty Rosa. She, in turn, appeared to encourage the attention. Oscar wasn't exactly unaware of what was taking place behind his back. He spoke to Rosa. She seemed to take the matter lightly, but promised to cool it if her friendship with the doctor was a source of embarrassment to her husband.

There matters stood until December 14, 1905. For several days Rosa had been planning a business trip to Chicago. She would leave on the 8 p.m. train and arrive in Chicago the next morning. Rosa mentioned to her brother, J.H. Mason, a cashier at the First National Bank, that she had obtained an upper berth for the trip. Her sister, Mrs. Logan Trousdale, thought she was working too hard and should slow down.

It was a Saturday night, a busy one down at the barber shop. Rosa told Oscar it wasn't necessary for him to accompany her to the station. She caught a hack and promised to call him the next day when she arrived at her destination. Oscar was never to see his wife alive again.

When Rosa failed to call him, Oscar phoned the Hotel Newberry in Chicago. His wife had not been there for several months. Distraught and somewhat suspicious, Oscar called his brother-in-law at the bank. He was informed that Rosa had withdrawn her entire savings, the substantial sum of $1,433.62, the day before she left for Chicago. Oscar searched his rooms at Mrs. Cullom's and discovered that Rosa had taken all her jewelry and a trunk of clothing. The thought occurred to him that his wife might have left him for good. Oscar, naturally enough, thought of Dr. Feist, but that worthy gentleman was still in Nashville, attending to his practice as usual.

Weeks passed. Oscar approached Dr. Feist, imploring the doctor to tell him anything he knew about his missing wife. Feist swore he knew nothing. When Rosa's sister spoke to the doctor, she received the same answer.

On January 26, 43 days after Rosa left for Chicago, steamboat pilot George Spence found her body floating in the Ohio River, near Cairo, Ill. Oscar read about the unidentified body in the newspaper and rushed to Cairo. He positively identified his Rosa.

An autopsy served only to add to the mystery. Doctors agreed that the dead woman had been in the water for a lengthy period of time. They could not, however, ascertain when death had occurred, nor could they find the cause of death. The dead woman had not drowned. There were no marks on her body. Her internal organs were healthy.

Had she met with an accident? Had she committed suicide or had she been murdered? If murder had taken place, where was the foul deed committed? The location on the Ohio River, where the body was recovered, was 265 miles from Nashville. Rosa's money and jewels were not found on her body.

The dead woman's movements were traced. The hack driver, who picked her up in Nashville, was located. He swore he dropped her off at the railway station. Rosa's trunk was recovered from the train depot in Chicago, where it had rested since December 15, the day after she disappeared. It seemed that Rosa had checked her trunk and boarded the train for Chicago.

In Nashville, nasty rumors circulated about Dr. Feist's relationship with Rosa. He was seen in Nashville each day in December, but there were those who believed the doctor could have robbed and murdered Rosa at night. Maybe poison was used. The doctor could have thrown Rosa into the river without ever leaving Nashville during daylight hours. Many came forward with information that they had seen Dr. Feist and Rosa in compromising circumstances. It was all only gossip before, but now the relationship took on far more serious connotations.

Based on these innuendoes and rumors, Dr. Feist was arrested and charged with Rosa's murder. His trial was the most sensational to take place in the Southern U.S. in years.

During his trial, evidence was produced indicating that Dr. Feist had never had more than $159 on deposit in his bank at any one time. He had often borrowed money from Rosa. While it was never established what the doctor did with his substantial income, many believed he bet heavily on the horses.

Other doctors occupying the Wilcox Building, where Dr. Feist had his practice, swore that they had seen Rosa and the doctor embrace on several occasions. One had even warned Feist to be more discreet. As the trial progressed, there was little doubt that hanky panky had taken place between the doctor and Rosa, but hanky panky does not a murder case make. There was more.

E.H. Mitchell, a livery stable owner, stated that he received a call from a Dr. S.A. Bean at approximately 8:30 p.m. on December 14. The doctor asked that a rig be delivered to him at the Wilcox Building. Mitchell complied and met Dr. Bean. Next day, he again met Dr. Bean when he picked up his rig, which was mud-splattered inside and out. There was no Dr. Bean listed in Nashville. Mitchell swore that the man he met was Dr. Feist. The defence produced a myriad of witnesses who swore that Mitchell was a habitual liar.

Five passengers had boarded the sleeper car on the night of December 14. Rosa supposedly had Upper 7. Understandably, neither the Pullman conductor nor the porter could remember anything about the passengers. The prosecution insisted that Rosa had checked her trunk through to Chicago, but had not boarded the train. On some ruse or other, Dr. Feist had enticed her into his rented rig and later that night robbed, killed and tossed her into the river. They claimed the body had floated the 265 miles to where it was found.

Defence counsel believed Rosa had boarded the train and, for some reason known only to herself, disembarked at Evansville, Ill. Here she was murdered for her possessions and thrown into the Ohio River, where she was later found.

The presiding judge reminded the jury that there was really no proof that Rosa Mangrum had been murdered. If she had been murdered, there was no proof that the crime had taken place in the jurisdiction in which the trial was being held. Despite these warnings, Dr. Feist was found guilty of murder.

Dr. Feist appealed. It took a full year for the appeal to reach the state Supreme Court. That august body declared that murder had not been proven and reversed the jury's decision. Dr. Feist was not tried again. He immediately left Nashville and never returned.

Was Dr. Feist innocent or guilty? Would a man of his intelligence hire a rig from a man who could later identify him? Very unlikely.

Then again, there are those suspicious souls who relish the convoluted. They claim the wily doctor, deeply in debt, talked Rosa into withdrawing all her money. He had her pack her clothing on the pretence that they were running away together. She purchased a single ticket. To allay suspicion, he told her he would buy his own ticket. At the last minute, after the trunk was checked, he talked her out of taking the train. He then killed her and submerged her body on one of the rivers around Nashville. The doctor had over a month and a half to lug the body the 265 miles to where it was found.

Of course, we will never know whether Dr. Feist was guilty or not. He died without telling a soul.

DR. WALTER WILKINS 1906

HUSBANDS who hasten the departure of their wives should exhibit some sign of physical or emotional anguish. Wailing at the moon, uncontrollable flailing, or even simple tears are recommended. Never, but never, nonchalantly decide to take the dog for a walk. Strangely enough, Dr. Walter Keene Wilkins of Long Beach, N.Y. did just that.

Dr. Wilkins was a kindly appearing gentleman, who sported a fine display of muttonchop whiskers, as was the fashion in 1906. At 67 years of age, he was somewhat older than his dear wife Julia.

One chilly February evening the police of tiny Long Beach received a call from Max Mayer, a neighbor of the Wilkins'. Upon investigating the call, they found Dr. Wilkins bending over his wife's prostrate form in front of their home. He was washing blood from Julia's horribly battered face. The poor woman was rushed to the hospital by ambulance, where two hours later she died. It took some effort to notify the distraught husband. He was busy walking the two family dogs who, incidentally, answered to the rather prosaic names of Duke and Duchess. I might add, but only in passing, that the Wilkins owned a parrot and a monkey, whose names fortunately have been lost to posterity.

Dr. Wilkins had quite a story to tell. He and his wife arrived home from shopping. As they approached their house on Olive St., the doctor thought there was someone inside. He entered alone, advising his wife to stay outside. Suddenly, he was struck a vicious blow to the head. Luckily, he was wearing a derby hat at the time, which no doubt cushioned the blow. Nonetheless, he was jumped upon by at least three men, but managed somehow to scream a warning to his wife, who in turn yelled for help.

One of the doctor's attackers dashed past his fallen form and obviously hit Julia repeatedly over the head until she lay dying on the sidewalk. Slowly the doctor regained consciousness. He ran to his neighbor's home and raised the alarm. Then he returned to help his wife as best he could.

Robbery had obviously been the motive. The doctor had been robbed of his wallet and diamond stickpin. The house had been ransacked as well. It appeared that three assailants had taken part in the attack. Three glasses and a bottle of the doctor's good brandy were found on the kitchen table. It appeared as if three men were having a drink when the doctor entered the house.

Outside in the yard, the police found a half-inch lead pipe wrapped in cloth. It was surmised that this was the weapon used on Dr. Wilkins. A broken machinist's hammer, held together with wire and wrapped in newspaper, was found beside the unfortunate Mrs. Wilkins.

Now, all of this business of hammers and pipes caused a tremendous amount of excitement around the tiny community of Long Beach. A great deal of pressure was put on the police to come up with the killer. Despite what appeared to be a galaxy of clues, the authorities were hard put to produce a bona fide suspect. In a kind of desperation born of frustration, they decided to look into the benevolent Dr. Wilkins' past. Well, folks, they found out a thing or two.

At the relatively tender age of 35, Wilkins had married one Miss Grace Mansfield. Now Grace wasn't a knockout, but she did have a father who indulged his new son-in-law to the extent of an allowance of $150 a month. When Wilkins failed to make any attempt to support Mrs. W., she divorced him and returned to being just plain Grace.

In 1893, Dr. Wilkins again entered the holy state of matrimony. This time he wed Suzanne Kirkland, a widow who owned a few rooming houses. The new Mrs. Wilkins fell downstairs one day. During her convalescence from this unfortunate accident she became depressed and nervous. The doctor prescribed ice cold baths. In fact, he filled the tub with ice. Suzanne stepped in and dropped dead. There was no question about it; Dr. Wilkins had a poor track record when it came to wives.

The most recent Mrs. Wilkins had managed to stay married and alive for a full 13 years, but disturbing facts were fast coming to light. Julia had also been married before and had about $100,000 in her name. Dr. Wilkins, it appears, had a fat zero in his name. So much for motive.

The string which had been used to tie newspaper around the murder weapon was traced to a butcher shop where the doctor had purchased the family meat for years. The wire used to repair the mechanic's hammer came from a roll of wire found in the Wilkins' home. It became downright embarrassing when Julia's false teeth were found in the house after the doctor had stated explicitly that his wife never entered the house on the evening she was killed. When it was discovered that the doctor had taken a bloodstained suit to a dry cleaning establishment on the day after the murder, it was just too much. He was arrested and charged.

On June 5, Dr. Wilkins' murder trial began. It immediately became apparent that the evidence against him was overwhelming. When it was revealed that his diamond stickpin, supposedly taken during the course of the robbery, was found in his overcoat, his goose, so to speak, was cooked. The good doctor was found guilty.

The day after the verdict was delivered, Dr. Wilkins managed to hang himself with a piece of rope from a shower fixture. The doctor, who seemed to have a flair for the dramatic, didn't disappoint, even in death. He left three letters. One provided for Duke, Duchess, the parrot and the monkey. Another revealed that he preferred death to life in Sing Sing, and the third left his lawyer $50 to pay for his cremation.

DR. ARTHUR WAITE 1917

IT is seldom in the annals of crime that a man can first be suspected, then arrested and finally stand trial for murder without ever taking the entire matter seriously. One man went through the entire ordeal, laughing and joking to the end.

Dr. Arthur Warren Waite was born in Grand Rapids, Mich. in 1887. He took his dental surgeon's degree in Glasgow, Scotland, and practised in South Africa before returning to the United States at the age of 28. Dr. Waite married Clara Peck, the daughter of a Grand Rapids millionaire in September 1915. Then he set up practice in New York City and at the same time did pure research at the Cornell Medical School. He played a good game of tennis, led an active social life, and all in all appeared to be a man who had everything.

There was one thing though; you see, the doctor decided to kill all his relatives.

Mrs. John E. Peck was Art's mother-in-law. Her daughter and the charming dentist were married for three months when she decided to visit the couple over the Christmas holidays. She arrived a healthy, robust woman. By January 30, she was dead. A doctor certified that she had died of kidney disease.

Art informed Clara that her mother had confided in him during her brief illness that she wished to be cremated. Clara thought it strange that her mother had never mentioned this to her, but gave her consent to the request.

After his wife's funeral, Mr. Peck came to visit with his daughter and son-in-law. He was dead by March 12. Again, the doctor called it kidney disease and the body was to be cremated. Apparently Mr. Peck had confided this wish to Arthur and no one else. Dr. Art made all the arrangements. He had the body embalmed, and then it was to be shipped to Grand Rapids to allow the rest of the family to pay their last respects. Finally the remains were to be forwarded to Detroit for cremation.

Everything went according to plan, until the party accompanying the body met the rest of the family in Grand Rapids. Here, Clara's brother Percy, who never got along with Art, acted very hostile to the dentist. He had received an anonymous letter telling him not to allow his father's body to be cremated. Percy decided to take over all the details concerning his father's body. Arthur and Clara returned to New York.

Meanwhile, Percy gave the order to have an autopsy performed on his father. Then at his urging the authorities started to look more closely into Arthur's background. They found that as a student, Arthur had stolen money, and later in South Africa had tried to marry a wealthy lady whose father had him chased out of the country. Then the story broke that charming, considerate Art was having an affair with a married singer named Margaret Horton. We begrudgingly have to give him a certain amount of credit. It isn't easy to get married, kill your mother-in-law and father-in-law, and carry on with a mistress, all within a period of five months.

The floss that broke the dentist's drill was when five grains of arsenic were found in Mr. Peck's body. This was too much even for Art; he took some poison and when the police went to arrest him, they found him almost dead. He survived and stood trial for double murder.

It was during the trial that Dr. Waite distinguished himself. For starters, despite pleading not guilty, he never once denied killing his in-laws. In fact, he described the whole thing in detail. He even cracked jokes to the jury while he recounted the sordid affair.

In his own words, he said: "I started poisoning her from the very first meal after she arrived. I gave her six assorted tubes of pneumonia, diphtheria and influenza germs in her food. When she finally became ill and took to her bed, I ground up 12 five-grain Veronal and gave her that, too, last thing at night." Art woke up in the middle of the night, found his mother-in-law dead, and went back to sleep. He had ready access to the germs from his research work at the medical school.

Art went on to tell how Mr. Peck didn't die easy. He tried several types of poisons on him, but nothing seemed to work. He went through his supply of germs, then tried chloroform, and finally in desperation he held a pillow over his father-in-law's nose and mouth until he was dead.

The obliging dentist volunteered that he tried to kill his wife's aunt, Catherine Peck, by giving her ground glass in her food when she had visited at Christmas. He only spared her because he switched his attention to his mother-in-law, who seemed to be easier to finish.

In his jocular way the dentist explained that, if he had more time, he would have also poisoned his wife. Art thought this so humorous that he laughed out loud while giving his statement from the witness stand.

He wasn't all fun and games. It was learned that behind the scenes he had attempted to bribe two members of the jury. He also had paid an embalmer to put arsenic in an embalming fluid sampler, so that when the police tested it they would find arsenic, thereby explaining its presence in Mr. Peck's body.

The doctor said his motive for the double murder was to inherit his in-laws' fortune. He even joked that he had done his wife a favor by speeding up her inheritance. His mistress, Margaret Horton, testified that Arthur actually told her that he killed his wife's parents. He said he planned on going to an asylum for a short time as an imbecile.

Dr. Waite was found guilty. He carried off his charade to the bitter end, requesting that he be put to death at the earliest possible date. On May 24, 1917 he arose, ate a hearty breakfast and read a book of John Keats' poems. He then joked with his guards as he walked calmly into the execution chamber and was put to death in the electric chair.

DR. WILMER HADLEY 1918

WILMER Amos Hadley pursued religion, medicine and members of the opposite sex with unequal vigor. He was always partial to women.

Wilmer was a good ol' boy from Friendswood, Texas. At 20 years of age, he heeded the call, venturing to Wichita, Kansas to study theology. Wilmer's ecclesiastical career lasted two years. One night he ventured into the town's small but active red light district, where he discovered the joys of the flesh. He dropped the religious game like a hot potato. Instead, he took up with a local belle, Bertha Lollar, and ended up marrying the girl.

Now divested of any clerical restraints, Wilmer went home with his new wife. He finagled a job in his father's large dry goods store, but found the cloth of his dad's store no more fulfilling than the cloth of his previous calling. He decided to take up the noble profession of medicine. To further this pursuit, he enrolled in Galveston State University.

Bertha, staunch lass that she was, took a job in order to help pay the cost of her husband's education. She even found time to present him with a bouncing baby boy.

On June 2, 1911, our Wilmer graduated with honors. He divorced Bertha and started his new life by hanging up his shingle in the town of Dickinson, Texas.

It didn't take long for Wilmer to have the largest practice in town. Not only was he a better than average sawbones, he also had an extremely soothing bedside manner with women. Those ladies who were disappointed with their work-weary husbands' performance, were invigorated and thrilled to consent to the doctor's unique treatment.

Dr. Hadley appeared to have everything—a thriving practice, the respect of his neighbors, and a bevy of local beauties more than willing to share his bed. But the good doctor wanted wealth—I mean real wealth. He looked around and homed in on the millionaires from Dallas and Galveston who spent their summer months on ranches near Dickinson.

One fine day the gods smiled down on lascivious Wilmer. He was asked to minister to a young morsel named Sue Kathleen Tinsley, the guest of Commodore E.M. Hartrick. Sue had a bad sunburn. She also had everything else in all the right places. The doctor cultivated the romance and reaped the harvest.

On October 13, 1913, Wilmer and Sue were married. Sue's sister paid for the shindig, which sort of surprised Wilmer. When he questioned his new bride, he discovered for the first time that her once rich daddy had lost his entire fortune. Wilmer flipped, but there was very little he could do other than bide his time. Demonstrating the patience of Job, the man of medicine kept his eyes open for his next try at the brass ring.

Wilmer figured that Colorado, with its wealthy silver miners, should be ripe for picking. Besides, the miners' wives should be sufficiently neglected to be susceptible to a large dose of his particular cure-all. Wilmer and Sue settled in Eagle County. The doctor had figured correctly. He soon owned a thriving private hospital, chock-full of women with an assortment of minor ailments and some with no ailments at all. It didn't matter to Wilmer. He cured what ailed each and every one.

Rumors of the doctor's peccadilloes spread throughout the county. A few robust silver millionaires got together with the idea that the district would be a far better place without the virile doctor. Wilmer didn't have to be told twice. He sold the hospital and headed for Red Cliff, Colo., where he was hired to run a hospital owned by Empire Zinc. The job came with the usual perks for Wilmer—nurses.

But a man of Wilmer's greed can only live on love for a limited period of time. He still wanted a wealthy wife. Maybe doctoring in the service would put him in touch with a rich Southern belle. Wilmer joined the army and was assigned to Debarkation Hospital No. 52 at Westhampton, Virginia.

As luck would have it, he met nurse Cheryl Johnson, who was everything a red-blooded southern peach should be, without the pit. This time, Wilmer didn't take any chances. He consulted Dun and Bradstreet. Sure enough, Cheryl's daddy was a financial heavyweight. Wilmer commenced his campaign with the flair of a Patton and the attention to detail of an Eisenhower. It only took three dates before Cheryl was enjoying the doctor's physical attributes. There was talk of marriage. Serious talk. Daddy and Mummy Johnson consented.

Almost forgotten was everloving wife Sue. Cheryl knew that her true love was married, but firmly believed that Sue was in California finalizing her divorce. Nothing could be further from the truth. At this crucial juncture in his campaign, Wilmer received a call from Richmond. Sue was on her way for a visit. Wilmer did a neat bit of footwork. He rented a furnished room, met and made passionate love to his wife, and then formulated intricate plans to kill her.

It was a momentous day, November 11, 1918, the day the armistice was signed ending World War I. Wilmer took Sue for a boat ride on the James River. He brought along a bottle of whisky, liberally laced with a drug which would render his wife unconscious. Once this was accomplished, it would be a simple matter to dump her overboard. A tragic accident, a drowning. Why, Wilmer could see the headlines: Doctor Makes Heroic Attempt to Save Wife.

He offered Sue a drink. It was cold that November afternoon out on the river. Sue took a healthy gulp, swayed and keeled over. Wilmer was just about to dump her overboard when he absently felt for a pulse, as doctors sometimes do. He was shocked. Sue was dead. As any fan of Agatha knows, if a person is dead before being submerged in water, there will be no water in the lungs. That's a prerequisite to drowning. Wilmer had to improvise. He tied Sue up with a rope and the boat's anchor. Then he dropped the whole bundle overboard.

Wilmer went ashore and faked checking his wife out of the furnished room, explaining that she was moving into larger quarters with him. He packed her belongings in a trunk, which he shipped to Atlanta, to be held there until he called.

Details, details—they were cumbersome. But in a few hours they were completed, enabling the murderous doctor to keep his date with wealthy Cheryl that very night.

A few days later, Wilmer wrote to Sue's sister, advising her that Sue had become seriously ill on a cruise to Puerto Rico. Unfortunately, she had died of natural causes. It had been tragic.

On December 5, Dr. Hadley received his discharge from the army. He told Cheryl he had to travel to Texas to prepare their new home and make arrangements to practise there. Cunning Wilmer travelled via Atlanta, where he picked up Sue's trunk. While he was in Atlanta, Sue's body was discovered, caught in some bushes at the edge of the James River.

It was a month and a half after the murder and the body was badly decomposed. However, the woman who had rented the furnished room to Dr. Hadley, identified some of the clothing found on the body as belonging to Mrs. Hadley. Sue's sister was called in. She identified her sister's ring. The hunt for the missing husband had just started when the coroner announced that Sue Hadley was a possible murder victim.

Wilmer felt the heat. He stayed one step ahead of the law for two years before being tracked down by Pinkerton detectives in August 1921. He was bedded down with two young Mexican girls in San Juan County, New Mexico when he was taken into custody.

Brought back to Richmond, Wilmer confessed to killing Sue. He added the little white lie that she was having an affair with one of his friends. His story didn't hold much water. At the time the friend was accused of having the affair, he was serving overseas in France with the armed forces.

Wilmer was tried and found guilty of his wife's murder. On October 27, 1921, Dr. Wilmer Hadley was executed in the electric chair in Richmond, Va.

DR. THOMAS YOUNG 1925

IT is difficult to apprehend a murderer when no crime is known to have been committed.

Grace Hunt hailed from a well-known California family. When she met and married Patrick Grogan in 1909, her happiness seemed assured. After all, Pat Grogan had made a fortune in the olive trade and was a bona fide millionaire. Grace and Pat had one son, Charles.

As the years drifted by, Grace and her husband agreed to disagree. When Charles was 10, she and Patrick were divorced. The divorce was a civilized affair. Grace was given custody of Charles and a cool half million dollars to soothe any hurts and to keep the wolf from the door.

There were wolves of a far different kind at Grace's door. She was an attractive young woman with oodles of cash, just waiting for the right swain to come a-calling.

Two years later, when Patrick died, leaving the balance of his estate to his son, with Grace sole administratrix, she became an extremely attractive catch indeed. After Patrick had been duly planted, Grace became a regular in Los Angeles' social circles. Many a young stud with one eye on Grace's figure and the other on the figures in her bank book courted the widow with a vengeance. One such suitor emerged with the prize.

Dr. Thomas Young was a newly turned out dentist who had decided to establish his practice among the socially prominent of Los Angeles. He fixed his sights on Grace like the lead hound pursuing the fox. Initially, Grace rejected the dentist, but eventually his persistence paid off.

In the winter of 1923, Grace became Mrs. Thomas Young. For two years, Dr. Young's practice flourished, as did his marriage to Grace. The attractive couple were seen in the best restaurants and were asked to the most prestigious parties. The Youngs were definitely leading the good life in Lotusland.

And then it happened. On February 22, 1925, Dr. Young contacted Los

Angeles police, informing them that his wife Grace had disappeared. The dentist told his story.

Twenty-four hours earlier, he and Grace had left their Beverley Glen cottage for dinner in Venice. They had a few drinks, enjoyed dinner and were about to leave the restaurant when they happened to bump into a woman he knew. It was nothing more than a chance meeting, but afterwards Grace flew into a jealous rage. According to Young, this was not an isolated incident. Grace was insanely jealous. Embarrassed, he hustled his wife out to their car.

While driving back to Los Angeles, Grace was beside herself with rage. During the trip, she took a swing at her husband and broke his glasses. Eventually, she quieted down and even apologized for causing a scene. The Youngs made up and decided to drop into Los Angeles' Hotel Biltmore to dance and have a few drinks.

Grace excused herself in the lobby of the hotel and made her way to the powder room. As far as her husband knew, no one had seen her since that moment. Dr. Young added that Grace was carrying $150,000 in negotiable securities and all her jewelry. In total, Grace was lugging around a quarter of a million dollars on her person. Young's statement begged the question—why would a woman carry a fortune in her purse? Dr. Young told police he thought his wife may have been afraid that their cottage in Beverley Glen was susceptible to being burglarized.

The unusual disappearance made front page headlines. It's not often that a socially prominent woman disappears carrying a fortune in her purse.

A few weeks after the disappearance, Grace's friends began to receive letters, apparently in Grace's handwriting. The letters were postmarked from towns and cities within 500 miles of Los Angeles. In these letters, Grace informed friends that she was tired of the incessant arguments with her husband. She planned to get away from it all for a while in Europe.

It all seemed so perfect, except for one thing. Anyone who knew Grace realized that she would write or contact her son, Charles, if she were leaving her home for any prolonged period of time. Grace's father, Earl R. Hunt, was not satisfied with the way the investigation was being conducted. He hired the famed Burns Detective Agency to find out what had happened to his daughter. Dr.

Young hired another detective agency to locate his wife. In all, there were now three different organizations searching for Grace Young.

Months passed. The investigation wound down. Dr. Young and Charles spent a lot of time together at their cottage. Gradually, Young started to live a normal life again. He even threw a few parties for friends.

Early that summer, the Burns Detective Agency came up with the disconcerting information that Dr. Young's secretary had been seen wearing one of Grace's rings. When questioned, the secretary said Young had showed up at work one day with the ring. She had worn it for a day or so and had returned it to him. For the first time, it was discovered that Dr. Young had lied. He had told police that his wife had taken all her jewelry with her. The Burns boys shared their information with the authorities.

A meeting was held. It was decided that the various organizations conducting inquiries into Grace Young's disappearance share their information. It seems everyone had found out something which incriminated Dr. Young.

Since his mother's disappearance, Charles Grogan had changed his will, which had previously left everything to his mother. His new will made his stepfather sole beneficiary.

Witnesses were located who swore Grace had been carrying a tiny purse on the night she disappeared. It could not possibly have held all her jewelry as well as negotiable securities. The Burns Agency had unearthed the hitherto unknown fact that Young had been married twice before.

Police were successful in obtaining a search warrant to go over the Beverley Glen cottage during Young's absence. They found a three carat diamond ring.

Dr. Young was questioned. When he was shown the ring, he was as cool as a cucumber, claiming that Grace often placed various pieces of her jewelry in the side pockets of their automobile. He had found the ring in the car and had placed it with his personal papers in the cottage. Dr. Young apologized for not informing police that he had found the ring.

Everyone concerned was now sure that Young was lying, but they had absolutely no proof that he had committed any crime. In fact, they had no positive proof that any crime had been committed at all.

On June 14, 1925, Young was brought to police headquarters for another round of questioning. Worn to a frazzle by the constant harassment, he broke down and revealed what had happened to Grace. He blurted out that she had accidentally struck her head and had fallen into a cistern at their cottage.

Police rushed out to the cottage. In the cistern, under a thin layer of concrete, they uncovered the body of Grace Young. A piece of rubber tubing was in her mouth. Dr. Young changed his story. He now told police that after an argument in the hotel, he had taken his wife to his office, where he had given her enough Scotch to render her unconscious. He then drove to the cottage and put her to bed. He administered a gas called sommonoform (used by dentists during that era) through a rubber tube until Grace was dead. Then he threw her body into the cistern.

The very next day, he had Charles mix the cement which was to cover Grace's body. Young told police, "I had covered the body with newspapers and I thought it would be a great joke on the boy to have him unknowingly cover his mother's body with cement."

Dr. Young went on to state that he had killed Grace to get rid of her and obtain her fortune. He revealed that he was planning to kill his stepson Charles and place him in the cistern as well.

Dr. Young's murder trial was in its tenth day when he was found dead in his cell. He had managed to strangle himself with a piece of wire.

DR. THOMAS DREHER 1927

COME on down Louisiana way to swamp land, where Cajuns still love to pot 'gators and wash down their jambalaya with a good swig of rotgut bourbon. That's where Ada and Jim Le Boeuf were born, lived, and died.

Ada, an attractive southern girl, was only 18 when she married Jim in 1907. A big, gruff, quiet man, Jim was easily brought to the boiling point. No one messed around with Jim Le Boeuf. Ada liked that quality, which brought respect from other men. She would eventually grow to fear it.

Jim, who had little formal education, started out as a laborer, but ended up as the manager of the Morgan City Power Plant. For a man with his limited ability, he did rather well for himself. He and Ada had a fine home in Morgan City, their own automobile, life insurance, and four children.

On the surface their marriage appeared to be loving and stable. Below this veneer lay the seeds of discontent. As each year went by Ada slipped further and further into drudgery. She washed, she cleaned, she cooked. She was a good mother, a good wife. But she was still a young woman and desperately longed for something better.

The gruff male quality she had so admired in Jim gradually became boring and even despised. Jim was extremely jealous and his constant suspicions only added to Ada's dislike of her husband and her life. In short, Ada was in a rut. Jim's life was in direct contrast to Ada's. He loved to hunt and fish and spent all his spare time at these activities. Sometimes he would be gone for days with his closest friend, Dr. Thomas E. Dreher and the doctor's rather crude friend, Jim Beadle.

Dr. Dreher had established his practice over 25 years before and was one of the town's leading citizens. He was a married man, with a son studying medicine at Tulane University. A good doctor, Dreher never pressed his patients for payment and often accepted whatever they could afford. Everyone in town loved Dr. Dreher.

Now and then someone might remark that Jim Beadle didn't appear to be a suitable companion for the doctor, but others realized Beadle was an expert shot and there was no one better at handling a small boat. The doctor paid Jim Beadle for his services as a loyal guide.

Morgan City had little to offer the bored Ada Le Boeuf in the way of diversion. Perhaps it was inevitable that she and her husband's best friend, Dr. Dreher, would get together. The opportunities were plentiful. Dreher was the Le Boeufs' family physician. He often visited their home socially and professionally. Ada and the doctor became lovers.

As the years passed there were many in the close-knit community who knew very well that Dr. Dreher was bedding down with his best friend's wife. Of course, Jim Le Boeuf had no idea of his wife's infidelity until someone sent a note to Mrs. Dreher. Poor, timid Mrs. Dreher, who really doesn't enter our story as anything other than a victim of circumstances, paid a visit to Jim Le Boeuf.

Jim saw red. While he couldn't prove the serious accusations that Ada vehemently denied, he managed to make his wife's life miserable. Jim swore that if he ever got even a smidgen of proof, he would kill both his best friend and his wife. Ada didn't doubt it for a minute. Jim didn't go fishing or hunting with the doctor and Jim Beadle any more.

In 1927 the Mississippi overflowed its banks, resulting in one of the worst floods on record. Morgan City was hard hit. Only two streets escaped the flood waters. Still, the citizens of Morgan City were accustomed to coping with floods. Soon their boats could be seen darting up one street and down another. Life went on.

Naturally, with Jim's strong suspicions, coupled with the flood, Ada's and Dr. Dreher's opportunities for romance diminished. Ada had one confidante, a Mrs. Noah Hebert, who could be trusted to deliver messages to the doctor.

On July 1, 1927, Ada sent her lover a message. It read: "Jim and me will go boat riding on the lake tonight. I talked to him and I believe he will treat you friendly. So meet me tonight and fix this up friendly and we will be friends. I am tired of living this way hearing Jim say he is going to kill both of us. As ever, Ada."

The note sounds almost innocent, but later there were those who claimed that the language was purposely guarded and that the note was in reality Jim Le Boeuf's death warrant. That night Dr. Dreher and his friend, Jim Beadle, stepped into their green pirogue, a canoe-like boat, and paddled silently into the night.

Ada and Jim hitched two boats to their car and drove over to Ada's sister's home for supper. They would go for a boat ride after they dined. It was a beautiful night. When they went boating the Le Boeufs always used two boats. Ada was an excellent oarswoman.

After supper the pirogues were taken down from the car. Ada's sister's home was almost surrounded by flood waters. The two boats were launched into a nearby street. Ada suggested they row over a route known to them both, which would lead to Lake Palourde.

The pirogues made their way into the dark night. Slowly houses disappeared from view. The muddy swamp water glistened in the moonlight. The trees hung heavy with Spanish moss. Wild flowers peeked out from the decayed branches of long dead trees. It was a night made for murder. Ada carefully led her husband to his death.

The Le Boeufs paddled silently. Gradually they discerned the outline of two men in a boat directly in their path. One of the men shouted, "Is that you, Jim?" "Yes, who's that?" Jim replied.

A shotgun flashed twice, the noise of the reports roaring across the water. Ada turned quickly and rowed away. Jim Le Boeuf would torment her no more. He lay dead in his boat.

Quickly, two 65-pound railway angle irons were tied to the body. A knife glistened and in an instant the dead man's stomach was slit open. The body was dumped overboard, the boat sunk, and the two shadowy figures rowed away.

Next morning Ada told her children that she and their father had had a terrible quarrel the night before and he had left. No doubt he would be back when he cooled off.

Six days later some men were hunting alligators on Lake Palourde. They found Jim Le Boeuf's body lying face down under a few inches of water. The heavily weighted body had been prevented from sinking by a small submerged tree.

Ada immediately came under suspicion. She was questioned for three hours before telling police officers that she and Jim had come across two strangers while out boating. It was too dark to identify them. She saw a flash, saw her husband fall, and then panicking, rowed away. She had not told the truth before because she knew her lover would be suspected.

Dr. Dreher was questioned. When informed of Ada's statement, he too admitted being at the scene of the crime, but claimed that Jim Beadle had committed the murder out of loyalty to him. The third member of the unholy trio, Jim Beadle, also admitted being at the scene, but claimed Dr. Dreher had orchestrated the killing and had fired the fatal shots.

All three suspects were arrested and stood trial for the murder of Jim Le Boeuf on July 25, 1927. The murder, because of its eerie setting and the fact that most of the evidence against the accused had come from their own mouths, became a national sensation. The defence offered little in the way of rebuttal.

All three were found guilty. Jim Beadle was sentenced to life imprisonment. Dr. Thomas Dreher, the best-liked man in Morgan City, and Ada Le Boeuf paid for their crime on the gallows.

DR. FRANK LOOMIS 1927

EVERYONE who ever met Grace Loomis liked her very much. Yet I know for a fact that there was an exception. That person hit Grace flush in the face three times with a blunt instrument, killing her instantly.

We know the exact time the fatal blows were struck. At precisely 9:06 on the night of February 22, 1927, a Detroit telephone operator, diligent Doris McClure, plugged in a telephone line and heard a woman's blood-curdling, terror filled scream. Abruptly the scream stopped. The operator then heard a terse male voice say, "Never mind." The line went dead. Diligent Doris didn't call police, but made a note of the time—9:06.

At 9:06 p.m. Tom Blockson and Ethel Bell were walking in the street close to Frank and Grace Loomis' home. They heard a loud shriek coming from the house, followed by a windowpane shattering. They thought Dr. Loomis was treating a patient and didn't call police. Tom and Ethel never did explain what type of pain they thought shattered windows.

The cause of all the commotion at the Loomis residence became clear at 9:45. That's when Dr. Frank Loomis ran from his home and summoned his neighbor, Mrs. Mildred Twark, with the unoriginal but nevertheless informative phrase, "My wife has been murdered!"

The doctor and Mildred returned to the Loomis home. Unlike glamorous Hollywood corpses, poor Grace lay in the sun parlor with one leg drawn under her, her neck twisted, and both arms spread out. The upper portion of her body was covered with blood. All in all a horrible sight.

The sun parlor was spattered with blood, reaching to the ceiling. Several pieces of furniture were in odd positions and had obviously been pushed aside during the brief struggle Grace had put up for life.

At Mildred Twark's urging, Dr. Frank checked on his children. Upstairs, Ralph, eight, and Jeanette, five, were fast asleep. The doctor then ran the one block to summon police.

The first officer at the scene asked Dr. Frank, "Did you move anything?", to which the doctor answered, "Yes, and the coroner won't like that. I know this looks bad for me." The officer did a double take.

Senior officials arrived to take Dr. Frank's statement. He told them that he arrived home before 9 o'clock. He talked to his wife briefly, telling her that he was going to take a walk. This was not unusual for the doctor, who was in the habit of taking health walks at every opportunity. Before he left he gave his wife $100 to go shopping for children's clothing the next day.

It was drizzling out. The doctor put on his rubbers and left at exactly 8 o'clock. He outlined his route for detectives and stated that he had arrived back home at 9:45 to find his wife's battered body sprawled in a pool of blood. He had run to her side, put his head to her heart, and at one point attempted to move her to a divan, but gave up. Grace weighed 165 lbs.

It may be noted that the doctor's story accounted for his bloodstained suit-coat, vest and pants. The doctor added his personal theory that maybe a peeping Tom had seen him pass over the $100 to his wife and had killed her six minutes after he left the house. The money was nowhere to be found.

Within 48 hours homicide detectives had pieced together a series of facts which simply didn't jibe with Dr. Frank's theory. For starters, isn't it a bit unusual to take a walk in the rain? Walking slowly, a policeman covered the route taken by the doctor in 34 minutes.

An examination of the Loomis furnace uncovered two pearl shirt buttons. Dr. Frank had been asked to turn over the clothing he had been wearing on the night of the crime. Everything was blood splattered, except for his spotless white shirt. Did the doctor take off his blood-saturated shirt and burn it in the furnace, account-ing for the two pearl buttons found there? Police thought so. They also found a fence with two by four stakes attached to fence wire rolled into a coil in the Loomis basement. One of the two by four stakes was missing, which led detectives to believe that the doctor may very well have burned the murder weapon.

Dr. Frank was taken into custody. Investigating officers were sure that the doctor, who was known to have a violent temper, had killed his wife during an argument. If he had not gone for a walk at all, he would have had plenty of time to set up all the physical evidence to fit his story and dispose of the murder weapon in the furnace before dashing over to Mildred Twark's house at 9:45.

Counteracting police theories was the fact that Frank and Grace were a happily married couple. The doctor was a devoted family man with an unblemished reputation. Then there was the little matter of motive. There was absolutely none. Despite police suspicions, Dr. Frank was released from custody.

That isn't to say Frank was home free. Not by a long shot. Detectives followed the doctor in the hope that he would lead them to the motive for killing his wife. Once released, Dr. Frank attended to his most pressing problem first. He buried Grace. After disposing of this pedestrian inconvenience, he led police to one of the oldest motives in the distressing history of murder—the other woman.

Her name was never made public, but we do know juicy tidbits about her. She was not the type of lady one would think would appeal to Dr. Frank. The object of his affection hung around shady bars and loved partying. The doctor visited her every day before his wife's un-timely demise. The lady in question would say no more than that she was a good friend and patient of the kindly doctor.

Now equipped with a motive, police arrested Dr. Frank and charged him with his wife's murder. As there was no evidence of premeditation, it was felt that there was no hope of convicting the doctor of first degree murder. At his trial the jury never got to hear that the doctor was having an affair while his wife was alive. No one knows to this day why the unsavory lady wasn't called to testify.

Prosecution attorneys felt that Dr. Frank would crack on the witness stand; the state would accept a manslaughter plea and everyone would be happy. It didn't turn out that way. The doctor was found not guilty.

Dr. Frank was never the same man after his acquittal. He sent his children to their grandparents in Brooklyn, Mich., and concentrated full time on his lady friend. The doctor was completely at his love's mercy. When things went well, which wasn't too often, he was ecstatic. When he had a lovers' quarrel he sank into the depths of depression. His practice suffered until it was nonexistent. He moved frequently. Nothing mattered to him except his girlfriend.

On May 19, 1929, a year after his acquittal, he opened his office at one o'clock in the morning, had a few blasts of whisky, read the Bible, wrote a couple of letters professing his innocence, and hooked himself up to a gas stove. Dr. Frank Loomis was found dead at 8:30 that same morning.

DR. HAROLD GUILFOYLE 1928

GIVEN the right set of circumstances, even the most intimate little dinner parties have been known to deteriorate to bloody murder.

Come along with me now back to 1928. Together we will attend a dinner party thrown by Mrs. Harold Guilfoyle of Hartford, Conn. Mrs. Guilfoyle, together with her doctor husband, Harold, lived in a comfortable upstairs flat at 691 Maple Ave.

The dinner party was being held in honor of Claire Gaudet of New Haven. Claire had arrived in Hartford to attend to legal matters pertaining to her late father's will. That inconsiderate gentleman had died, leaving his estate of over half a million dollars to charity and three old cronies. Claire was attempting to have the will overthrown. She attended the dinner party with her five-year-old daughter, Patricia.

Claire, who was pretty as a picture, if somewhat overweight, had been carrying on a torrid affair with Dr. Guilfoyle for years. Harold was a rascal. There are those who say that he revealed every detail of his dalliances with Claire to his dear wife. Don't go away, our intimate little party warms up appreciably.

Also at the dinner party that night were Algernon Sidney Way, better known as Sid to his friends and his wife. You couldn't miss Sid in a crowd. He had only one arm and a withered side. Sid and Claire also had a little something going between them. Maximin Gaudet, Claire's everloving husband, was back in New Haven. Let's leave him there for now, but he does show up later on.

There you have the guest list—the Guilfoyles, the Ways, Claire Gaudet and little Patricia. Medium rare steaks were served with Idaho baked potatoes. The men puffed on Havanas as they sipped their Courvoisier. All the while both men cast anticipatory glances at the ever willing Claire while the two wives seethed with jealousy.

At 9:30 p.m. it was time for the guests to leave. As they prepared to leave, Sid Way suggested that he treat Patricia to an ice cream cone at the drugstore across the street. Patricia was thrilled at the offer, and away the pair went down the stairs and out the front door. Harold volunteered to give Claire and Patricia a lift to the station, where they were planning on catching the train back to New Haven. Mrs. Guilfoyle, spoilsport that she was, offered to go along as well.

Claire threw on her coat and left the apartment, followed by Harold. Mrs. Guilfoyle went into a bedroom to fetch her coat while Mrs. Way waited for her in the living room.

The loud report of three shots echoed from the downstairs hall. Mrs. Guilfoyle and Mrs. Way dashed out to the top of the stairs and stood dumbfounded as they gazed down at the scene below. Claire Gaudet was now a crumpled heap on the hall floor. Harold was staggering about the hall with blood gushing from a bullet wound in his head. A neighbor, Dr. F.L. Benton, was at the scene in minutes. He examined Claire and pronounced her to be near death.

Claire and Harold were removed to the Guilfoyle apartment. It was found that a bullet had entered Harold's skull just above the left eye and had exited just above the left temple. When able to speak, he could only say that he had had the impression that the attacker had left by the back door. In the dimly lit hall he was unable to distinguish whether the attacker had been a man or woman.

Just after the shooting, Sid Way appeared on the scene. He had left Patricia at the drugstore to eat her ice cream from a dish. The store was out of cones. He was lingering outside the front door waiting for the rest of the guests to come down when the shootings occurred. He told police that no one had come out the front door.

About an hour and a half after the shooting Maximin Gaudet arrived at the Guilfoyles. His story was simply that he had taken the train to Hartford with the intention of meeting his wife at the dinner party. He would then accompany her back to New Haven. As his train was late in arriving, he decided to eat in a restaurant and pick up Claire and Patricia later. Maximin Gaudet didn't seem surprised at his wife's predicament. He told police that considering his wife's lifestyle, it was to be expected.

The investigation continued into the wee hours of the morning. A search was conducted for the murder weapon in the hall and outside the building, but nothing turned up. Finally, the Guilfoyle's apartment was searched with more positive results. A pearl handled .38 calibre revolver was found in a chest of drawers in the living room. Three cartridges had been fired, and eventually this revolver proved to be the attacker's weapon. When questioned Guilfoyle verified that the gun was his. He usually kept it in either his car or in the chest of drawers where it was found. He couldn't say for sure where it was on the night of the shooting. Now it was obvious that the assailant was probably someone who had attended the dinner party that night and had returned the gun to the chest of drawers. At 10:30 the next morning Claire Gaudet died from her wounds.

There you have it. Six people attended a dinner party. One is dead and one is seriously wounded. That leaves four suspects. Let's eliminate five-year-old Patricia, but we had better add Maximin Gaudet. After all, he could have arrived earlier than he said, lurked in the hall and observed Way and Patricia leaving for ice cream. Did he wait for his wife and lover to walk down the steps before shooting them? Did he then make his way out the back door? Gaudet had a motive. He hated his wife and her lover for cheating on him.

Then again, maybe Gaudet was telling the truth. It could have been Way who, after leaving Patricia eating her ice cream, returned to the dimly lit hall, shot Claire and Harold, and then left the premises, only to rush in again a short time later. Did he realize Guilfoyle was winning the competition for Claire's affection and decide to kill them both?

Mrs. Guilfoyle and Mrs. Way? Well, it's difficult to suspect the two ladies. They would have to have been partners in the crime, but then again in the murder business nothing is impossible. They both hated Claire with a passion.

Who killed Claire Gaudet? Don't feel bad if you're having trouble with this one. The Hartford police gave up after five weeks and turned the case over to the county detective Edward J. Hickey.

Hickey decided that since there was a limited number of suspects he would try to locate the killer's position at the time of the murder by the location of the three bullets extracted from the wall. The first bullet struck Claire in the upper back and travelled downward through her body, lodging in the hall wall four feet from the floor. As the bullet was not deflected by bone, Hickey could place the assailant on the stairway behind Claire. The second bullet did not pass through human flesh. From its position in the wall the detective was able to state that this bullet was fired from the same position.

The third bullet was fired from a completely different position. At precisely five-feet, four-inches from the floor, it penetrated the wall horizontally. Guilfoyle was five-feet, eight-inches tall. The bullet was fired four inches lower than the crown of his skull and entered the wall exactly five-feet, four inches from the floor. The wound could have been self-inflicted.

When confronted with this theory, Guilfoyle confessed. Claire was tiring of him and he couldn't bear to lose her. He killed her just as Hickey had described and then turned the gun on himself, intending to commit suicide. In the confusion after the killing he had placed the gun back in the chest of drawers. When he found out everyone but him was suspected of the shooting, he decided to let matters take their own course.

Dr. Harold Guilfoyle was sentenced to life imprisonment in the Connecticut State Prison at Wethersfield. Detective Edward Hickey went on to become commissioner of the Connecticut State Police.

DR. JAMES SNOOK 1929

ALICE and Beatrice Bustin, two Ohio State University students, had reason to be concerned. Their roommate, Theora K. Hix, had left their room at the women's residence on campus at about 7 p.m. on a warm June evening in 1929. She never returned. Next day, with no word from Theora, the two sisters reported her absence to police.

When detectives read the missing persons report, they knew there was no need to search further for Theora Hix. Earlier that day her body had been found in deep grass behind a shooting range about five miles northwest of Columbus, Ohio.

The 24-year-old second year premedical student had been stabbed many times. She had also received several blows about the head, possibly inflicted by a ballpeen hammer. Her jugular vein and her carotid artery had been slashed. Strangely enough, three fingers on her right hand were crushed. The victim had not been sexually attacked.

Alice and Beatrice Bustin were questioned extensively, but could shed little light on their roommate's private life. Theora was a quiet girl who kept to herself. As far as they knew she had no boyfriends. However, they told detectives she had the habit of leaving their room each evening at about 5 p.m. and not returning until after 10 p.m. Knowing that Theora was a very private person, the Bustin sisters never inquired about her absences and Theora never volunteered any information.

An examination of the victim's body indicated that she had met her death sometime before a heavy rain had fallen on Thursday, the night before her body was found. The time of death was further narrowed by Constable John Guy, who was at the shooting range that Thursday evening.

Guy stated that up until 8 p.m. the shooting range was being used by two competing shooting teams. From 8 p.m. to 10 p.m. the range was deserted. At 10 p.m. Guy had concealed himself in an adjoining field in order to apprehend thieves who were stealing livestock from a nearby farm. Had the murder taken place after 10 p.m., Guy would have witnessed it.

Around 10:20 p.m., there was a heavy rain shower. Guy discontinued his surveillance. Since the victim had been killed before the rainfall, it was reasonable to assume that the murder had taken place between 8 and 10 p.m. on Thursday night.

Unknown to Theora's friends, she was keeping company with a man. This fact was revealed to authorities when a university instructor, after being promised anonymity, came forward with the information that he had often seen her driving with Dr. James Howard Snook in the doctor's blue Ford.

Dr. Snook was an unlikely suspect. The lean, balding, bespectacled 50-year-old Snook was a professor of veterinary medicine on the medical facility at Ohio State University. He was married and had an exemplary reputation.

Snook had an interesting hobby. He was an excellent pistol shot, having represented the U.S. at the 1920 Olympics. At one time he was a world champion, and on six occasions was U.S. champion.

When questioned, Snook remained aloof from his interrogators, answering all questions in a curt, brief manner. He immediately admitted having known Theora Hix for three years and volunteered that for some time he had assisted her in paying her university tuition. They often went for drives together in his car and she was an intelligent, interesting conversationalist. Dr. Snook assured detectives that there was nothing further to their relationship.

Columbus police were positive they had their man, but the good doctor was admitting nothing. Then the unexpected happened. Mrs. Smalley, an astute lady who rented furnished rooms on Hubbard Ave., saw photographs of Dr. Snook and Theora Hix in the local newspaper. She had quite a story to tell.

Four months earlier, on February 11, 1929, Dr. Snook had rented a room from Mrs. Smalley, supposedly for himself and his wife. The doctor arranged with Mrs. Smalley that his wife would do the day to day cleaning of the room, while she would give the place a good cleaning once a week. In the four months Dr. Snook and Theora occupied the room, Mrs. Smalley caught a glimpse of Theora only once. She remembered her as she was impressed by the age difference between the doctor and his wife.

Mrs. Smalley went on to state that on the Friday Theora's body was found behind the firing range, Dr. Snook told her he had to leave the city immediately. His wife would be staying until Sunday to wind up their affairs. While Mrs.

Smalley wished Dr. Snook good luck, Theora Hix's unidentified body lay in a Columbus funeral home.

Dr. Snook proved to be one cool cucumber. The first hint that his iron-like composure wasn't emotion free occurred when Mrs. Smalley was brought into his presence. Without hesitation she said, "Good evening, Mr. Snook." Snook replied, "Good evening, Mrs. Smalley."

It was story changing time. Dr. Snook admitted that he had set up the little love nest with Theora, but vehemently denied any involvement in her death.

Now hot on the trail, Columbus detectives discovered that Snook had taken a suit to a dry cleaning establishment on the day Theora's body was found. The suit was examined. There were bloodstains on the jacket sleeves and the knees of the trousers. The blood type was the same as Theora's.

While Mrs. Snook looked on helplessly, police raked through ashes taken from her furnace. They recovered bits of fabric, which they were able to prove came from pyjamas owned by the slain girl.

Snook weakened when faced with this overwhelming array of evidence and admitted killing his lover. It was a brief and skimpy confession, hinting that Theora had been a cocaine addict who had badgered him for money on a daily basis. However, an analysis of Theora's internal organs revealed no signs of her having been an addict.

On July 24, 1929, Dr. Snook stood trial for the murder of Theora Hix. Defence attorneys attempted to prove that his confessions had been obtained under duress and that the doctor was insane anyway. No one was buying.

Dr. Snook took the witness stand in his own defence. He told the court that he had attempted to break off his affair with Theora and return to his wife. He said Theora became incensed, cursing and striking him as he drove his car. He stopped, tried to calm her, but then in a rage rained blows to her head with a hammer. Again, no one was buying the doctor's story. The girl had been attacked with knife and hammer. Her jugular had been severed by the deliberate stroke of a knife. Dr. Snook did clear up one minor mystery. Theora had incurred the three crushed fingers when he accidentally slammed the car door on her hand.

Dr. James Howard Snook was found guilty of murder. On February 28, 1930, he was executed in the electric chair, courtesy of the State of Ohio.

DR. ALICE WYNEKOOP 1933

ONE of the most unusual and, at the same time, interesting individuals ever to stand accused of murder, has to be Dr. Alice Wynekoop. For one thing, Alice was old enough to know better. She was 63 in 1933 when she pulled the trigger.

Frank and Alice Wynekoop were medical doctors, who lived in a large, rambling custom-built home at 3406 W. Monroe St. in Chicago. During their happy years, the Wynekoops had three children. Walter, the eldest Wynekoop, became a successful businessman. He married, moved to the suburbs, and doesn't enter our story. The second child, Earle, was his mother's favorite from birth. Earle was no good. We'll get back to him later. Catherine, the youngest child, following in her parents' footsteps, became a respected medical doctor.

Unfortunately, Frank Wynekoop died before his children reached adulthood. It fell to his wife Alice to raise the children. She was quite a lady. Alice continued to practise medicine from her well-equipped office in the basement of her spacious home. Not only did she raise her children, she also found time away from her busy practice to work diligently for several charities.

While Catherine and Walter grew up to be honest, hard-working individuals who eventually moved out of the Monroe St. home, Earle was quite another kettle of fish. Earle was in his early twenties when he married 18-year-old Rheta Gardner of Indianapolis. Because Earle was unable to support himself, let alone a wife, Alice converted the third floor of her home into an apartment for the young couple. The mansion on Monroe had one other occupant, Enid Hennessey, a middle-aged schoolteacher who had roomed at the Wynekoops with her elderly father. When her father died, Enid stayed on.

Rheta was not happy. She had several fair to middling reasons. First of all, what young bride wants to live under the same roof with her mother-in-law? Then there was Earle's habit of spending a lot of time away from home. It was an open secret that he habitually played the field with other ladies. On top of all this, Rheta was a bit of a hypochondriac, forever complaining of a variety of aches and pains.

Things came to a head on the evening of November 21, 1933. At about 10 p.m., police were called to the Wynekoop home. Enid Hennessey and Alice met them at the door. Dr. Alice said, "Something terrible has happened; come on downstairs and I will show you."

Once downstairs, police were faced with the eerie sight of beautiful young Rheta Wynekoop lying on an operating table. Her nude body was wrapped in a thick blanket. The dead girl's clothing lay in a bundle beside the table. When the blanket was removed, a bullet hole was discovered in the girl's breast. Under a cloth on the operating table, police found a .32 calibre Smith and Wesson revolver. The girl's face appeared to be slightly burned.

Dr. Wynekoop said something about money and drugs being missing from the house. She thought robbers might be responsible. No one took the doctor's theory very seriously.

Naturally enough, police were anxious to chat with the deceased woman's husband. Earle was pursuing his latest attempt at making a living. He was on a train headed for the Grand Canyon, supposedly to take photographs. Notified of his wife's untimely demise, the grieving husband returned, a shapely brunette draped over his arm. When asked the identity of the lady, Earle told reporters that his little address book held the names of 50 more just like her. Earle suggested that some moron must have killed Rheta. He admitted that his marriage was a failure and volunteered that his wife was mentally ill. Earle didn't impress anyone.

When it became obvious that Earle the cad could not have killed his wife, police directed their attention to the victim's frail mother-in-law, Alice Wynekoop. Under intensive questioning, Dr. Alice confessed. She stated that Rheta had always been concerned about her health. She disrobed each day to weigh herself. Early on the afternoon of her death, the doctor had walked in on Rheta, who was sitting nude on the operating table. She had just weighed herself and was complaining of a severe pain in her side.

Dr. Wynekoop suggested that since Rheta had already disrobed, it was a convenient time for her to be examined. The doctor thought that a few drops of chloroform might ease the discomfort. Rheta breathed deeply from a chloroform-soaked sponge. Dr. Wynekoop inquired if her patient was still experiencing discomfort. She received no reply. Rheta wasn't breathing. Dr. Wynekoop tried artificial respiration without success. Rheta was dead.

Alice Wynekoop claimed that she panicked. It was a known fact that Rheta and Earle were not getting along, and that there was a great deal of ill-feeling between Alice and her daughter-in-law. Who would believe the freak death? There was a loaded revolver in the room. Holding it about six inches from the nude body, the doctor fired into the lifeless corpse.

Chicago detectives simply didn't believe Dr. Wynekoop's story. The doctor was arrested and charged with murder. Due to the accused's poor health, the trial was delayed several times. When it finally took place, things didn't go at all well for the good doctor.

From the witness stand, Enid Hennessey related details of the events of that fateful day. She had returned to the Wynekoop home about six that evening. Alice put pork chops on the stove for dinner. The two friends discussed literature. There was a place setting at the table for Rheta. Alice explained that Rheta had gone downtown at about three that afternoon and had not returned. That seemed strange to Enid. Rheta's coat and hat were hanging in full view.

After dinner, Enid and Alice chatted in the library. When Enid complained of hyperacidity, Alice volunteered to go down to her office to fetch some pills. It was then that the doctor discovered the body of her daughter-in-law.

Hold the phone! Something's wrong. According to Alice's own confession, Rheta was dead early in the afternoon. Did Alice calmly await her friend's return, cook up pork chops, chat about books, knowing all the while that Rheta lay dead in the basement? For shame!

The prosecution had a few other damaging tidbits. A post mortem indicated that Rheta had died as a result of the bullet wound. The body was exhumed. The burning about the face was caused by powder burns, not chloroform. In fact, Rheta's body held no traces of chloroform.

The prosecution proved through the evidence of several witnesses that Dr. Alice always thought that Earle had entered a poor marriage. Rheta was not good enough for her boy. To add frosting to the cake, she had recently insured Rheta's life.

An Illinois jury deliberated 14 hours before bringing in a guilty verdict. Dr. Wynekoop was sentenced to life imprisonment and was incarcerated in the Women's Reformatory at Dwight, Ill. After serving over 15 years, she was paroled in 1949 at age 78. Dr. Alice Wynekoop died two years after her release from prison.

DR. MERRILL JOSS 1941

DOCTORS Merrill and Laverne Joss were the most respected young couple in the town of Richmond, Maine. Not that much ever happened in Richmond, but all that changed on the evening of March 27, 1941.

That was the night the town's chief of police was called to Dr. Merrill Joss' impressive old colonial home. Dr. Joss met the chief at the door. To say he was distraught would be to understate the case.

"It's my wife," the doctor explained. "She's been attacked by a dope addict or at least that appears to be the case. A bearded stranger appeared at my door demanding narcotics. Naturally, I turned him away. A doctor's house is an easy target, you know."

When the chief asked for a description, the doctor quickly replied, "The man was about five-feet-eight, had shaggy unkempt hair, wore a beard and had a dark coat and cap."

The doctor went on to hurriedly explain that he had left the house to complete an errand and was as far as the railroad tracks when he heard his dog Trixie barking. He returned to the house to find his office burglarized. Alarmed for his wife's safety, he searched the house for her. When he noticed that the door leading off the kitchen into the cellar was open, he dashed downstairs to find his wife lying on the cellar floor, bludgeoned about the head.

All of this was blurted out to the chief as they made their way through the house and down the cellar stairs. The chief noted blood on the stairs, wall and the floor. There was Laverne Joss, unconscious. In minutes, Dr. Edwin Pratt joined Dr. Joss, peering over Laverne's still form. Dr. Pratt dressed the head wounds as best he could with some gauze. Joss said that he would drive his wife to the hospital. Pratt insisted that an ambulance be called immediately. There was a tense moment, but Pratt prevailed.

An ambulance sped away to hospital with Laverne, while a horde of detectives and citizens joined in an effort to apprehend the man described by Dr. Joss. In a community the size of Richmond, everyone knew the victim of the wild attack. Both she and her husband were beloved by their friends and neighbors. Both were on a first-name basis with many of the police officers now investigating the burglary and the assault on Laverne. That same night, Dr. Laverne Joss died of her wounds.

Dr. Merrill repeated his story to detectives in detail. Probably it was State Police Lieutenant Leon Shepard who first privately doubted his story. The seasoned detective had never heard of a dope addict knocking at a door and asking for drugs. Buying dope, stealing dope, yes; but walking up to a doctor's residence and simply asking for dope just didn't sit well.

As the extensive search for the shaggy stranger continued, detectives were provided with another piece of information concerning Merrill Joss. Evidently, when Laverne was brought into hospital, a blood transfusion was immediately ordered. Merrill objected, insisting upon a blood cross-matching. Laverne died before any transfusion was attempted. It was noted she had 27 head wounds and that her wedding ring was missing.

When Merrill was questioned about the ring, he confirmed that his wife always wore it and he had no idea how it had disappeared. Astute Lt. Shepard had his own theory. He got down on his hands and knees on the Joss' kitchen floor and, in true Columbo fashion, searched for the ring. Sure enough there, underneath the refrigerator, was Laverne's ring.

Now, hot to trot, Shepard examined the cellar. In nearly empty bins of vegetables, he found a watch belonging to Laverne. The wily detective reconstructed the crime in his mind.

Shepard dismissed Merrill's story as a fabrication to cover his own tracks. He theorized that Merrill and Laverne had not been getting along—possibly there was another woman. The pair had argued in the kitchen. Laverne had taken off her ring and had thrown it at her husband. The ring had lodged under the refrigerator.

Merrill had picked up something and struck out at his wife. She had slumped to the floor, unconscious. He then threw her down the cellar steps. As she tumbled down, her wrist hit the wall, flinging the watch into a bin of carrots. Merrill cleaned the blood off the kitchen floor, ransacked his own office and either hid or destroyed the murder weapon before calling police. Shepard's theory accounted for all the known facts, except the 27 wounds on Laverne's head.

Shepard continued his investigation. Laboratory technicians were brought into the house. From the kitchen floor, they extracted tiny cotton threads almost invisible to the naked eye. Elsewhere in the house, they found a cloth which proved to be of the same fibres as those taken from the floor. Someone had wiped the floor clean. Certainly, a dope addict wouldn't have stopped to clean the floor after throwing his victim down the stairs.

Lt. Shepard's suspicions had first been raised by the doctor's implausible story. Now, he checked out the doctor's friends and discovered that Merrill was keeping company with a winsome cook at a local eatery. Elizabeth Mayo was questioned and readily co-operated with police. It was true. She and the doctor were seeing each other on the side, so to speak. Merrill had talked of divorce, but Elizabeth had never thought he would go as far as killing his wife. She produced love letters written by Merrill only hours before his wife's death. That's called motive, folks.

Detectives made a moulage cast of Laverne's head. They then proceeded to make a cast of the crude cellar floor. They found that by placing the head cast against the cast of the rough floor, they could match the two. Eerily, the wounds on the head cast fit the rough edges of the floor. Laverne had received some of her wounds when she was thrown down the stairs onto the floor.

An examination of the steps uncovered a lone eyebrow hair and minute pieces of flesh. The eyebrow hair matched those taken from Laverne's skull. The impact of her head against the steps may have accounted for several of the head wounds.

The entire case against Merrill was circumstantial, but it added up the way Lt. Shepard figured at the beginning, while boy scouts and police were scouring three counties for a man who didn't exist.

Most of the community were gathered at the Methodist church for 37-year-old Laverne Joss' funeral. Merrill Joss was supported by a galaxy of friends as he dabbed at his eyes with a white handkerchief. As Merrill left the church, he was taken into custody by State Police Chief Henry Weaver. Charged with his wife's murder, he was incarcerated in the Sagadahoc County Jail.

A few weeks later, while awaiting trial, Merrill borrowed a razor blade from another inmate. He cut the skin of his right arm and, using his fingernail, raised an artery. He then cut the artery with the blade. A guard found him unconscious and immediately summoned a physician. He was rushed to hospital and given blood transfusions. Attending physicians managed to save his life.

On June 23, 1941, Dr. Merrill Joss stood trial for his wife's murder. The trial lasted 10 days. Prosecuting attorneys dramatically revealed the history of the Joss' marriage. Both had been married before and had become attracted to each other while working together in a hospital. They had divorced their respective spouses and married each other.

Merrill admitted from the witness stand that he and his wife had not been getting along and had discussed divorce. Although married for over five years, they had never lived as man and wife. Laverne had undergone an operation just before marrying him, which made normal sex impossible. Their married life had been more of a brother/sister relationship than one of husband and wife. He further stated that his wife had been aware of his love for Elizabeth Mayo. Their talk of divorce had been amicable.

Merrill Joss got off relatively easy. The jury evidently felt that the crime did not contain the necessary "malice aforethought" and so reduced their verdict to one of guilty of manslaughter.

On July 5, 1941, Dr. Merrill Joss was sentenced to not less than 10 years and not more than 20 years imprisonment in the State Prison at Thomaston, Maine.

DR. BOB RUTLEDGE 1951

GENTLEMEN who monkey around with other gentlemen's wives sometimes find themselves in all sorts of hot water. Occasionally the hot water becomes positively scalding.

It takes two to tango, but it takes three to triangle. Let's follow the three corners of our love triangle to the day all hell broke loose.

Bob Rutledge Jr. was born and raised in Houston, Texas. He always found schoolwork relatively easy, and from the very early grades he was considered college material. He breezed through high school and entered university as a pre-med student. While still an undergraduate Bob had a strange but pleasant experience.

In 1943, Bob met a U.S.O. singer, whose group was entertaining soldiers at Fort Des Moines. He married the girl. Four hours later she left town with her group. I can find no record of what the young couple did during their short four-hour marriage, and maybe it is just as well. Bob and his blushing bride were divorced two years later without ever seeing each other again.

Bob went on to graduate as a full-fledged medical doctor. He then joined the navy and served 15 months at a navy hospital in Boston. It was during his stint in the navy that he met Sydney. I should explain—Sydney was a girl, and quite a girl at that. She had long blonde hair, and a very well proportioned figure spread over a height of six feet. At 23, Syd was a looker. In 1946, Bob and Syd were married. A short time later Bob entered Children's Hospital in St. Louis to specialize in pediatrics, drawing down a cool $25 per week.

Syd, who was the daughter of a physician, was well aware of the long training period required to become a specialist. To pass the time and supplement their income, she obtained a job at the Emerson Co. as a mathematician. Working directly across from her desk was the third member of our triangle, Byron Hattman. Byron glanced up from his drafting table and took in all six feet of the voluptuous Syd.

Byron was a graduate engineer, having received his diploma from the

University of Pittsburgh. After a spell in the Marines, he had joined Emerson in St. Louis as an airplane instrument designer. Now 29 years old, Byron was a bachelor without a care in the world. He drove a big car, owned a sailboat, and loved to carry a substantial wad in his pocket.

Day after day Byron looked at the statuesque doctor's wife. In July the Emerson Co. had an outing, a cruise on the Mississippi River. As usual Dr. Rutledge was working at the hospital. Syd went on the cruise with a group of girls from work. For the first time, Hattman struck up a conversation. Soon the pair were enthusiastically discussing sailing. One thing led to another. Hattman invited Syd and some other girls to go sailing the following Saturday. Everyone accepted the invitation.

That weekend the girls had a great time on the boat. The next Saturday was another story. This time Hattman invited Syd to join him alone. Syd accepted and even told her husband of her innocent date. He approved.

The sailing session lasted until 6 p.m. During the trip Hattman impetuously told Syd that he didn't think it could be much fun being the neglected wife of a doctor. That afternoon Hattman made a date with Syd to have dinner. When Syd went home to change, she neglected to tell her husband about the dinner engagement.

We will never know for certain what took place that evening. It all depends on whom you choose to believe. Sydney was to forever state that she was viciously raped. Hattman always claimed she gave of herself willingly. Whatever happened that night, Syd did not mention a word of the evening's activities to her husband.

Poor Dr. Rutledge found out about his wife's having intercourse with another man in a most disturbing way. He overheard Hattman bragging about his conquest of Syd at another Emerson party—this time a day of golf at the Norwood Hills Country Club. Dr. Rutledge had the day off and decided to join his wife at the company function. Hattman didn't notice him changing his shoes when he was telling a group of employees of his romp in the hay with Syd.

This startling bit of information stuck in the doctor's craw for several weeks. Then he did something about it. He called Hattman on the phone, informing him that he knew what had happened. He issued a warning to Hattman to stay away from his wife. In passing, he also mentioned that it was quite possible Syd was pregnant. The doctor suggested that Hattman cough up $250 for the necessary abortion. Hattman replied tersely that he didn't much care if Syd was pregnant or not. He suggested that the doctor contact his lawyer for anything further. Some weeks later Hattman was advised that Syd wasn't pregnant after all. Nature had merely played one of her cruel little jokes.

Meanwhile Dr. Rutledge and his wife had a tête a tête concerning Hattman. It was then that Syd told him that Hattman had forced himself upon her. He decided to stick by his wife.

During the month of October and the remainder of that fall, the Emerson Co. subcontracted a large job to Collins Radio Co. in Cedar Rapids. Hattman was directly involved in this job and had to split his time between St. Louis and Cedar Rapids. Each Monday he would travel the 300 miles to Cedar Rapids, and check into the Roosevelt Hotel, where he stayed for two or three days.

On December 15, 1948 he never made the return trip. That morning a chambermaid, with the apt name of Carrie Chambers, found Byron Hattman dead on the floor of Room 729. Beside his head was a large bloodstain and an empty wallet. The room showed signs of a vicious struggle. Bloodstains covered all four walls. The victim had bruises about his face, broken ribs, and assorted cuts about the head. Later the coroner was to state that Hattman had been stabbed repeatedly in the chest. One of the thrusts had punctured his heart, causing death.

Hotel guest Eugene Pastock stated that he had heard a fight at about 5:45 p.m. the previous evening. He assumed it was a domestic squabble and never gave it another thought. Police, knowing nothing of the victim's private life, felt that Hattman had surprised a prowler.

Detectives called at the Collins factory where Hattman worked. Kenneth L. Ebershoff told them that Hattman had confided in him that he was having trouble with a Dr. Rutledge, because of the doctor's wife. Officials of the Emerson Co. also informed the police that Hattman didn't have an enemy in the world, except for a Dr. Rutledge, whose wife seemed to be having an affair with Hattman.

The police, now hearing the name Rutledge from two independent sources, decided to probe a little deeper into the activities of the good doctor. When they found out he had spent Monday night at the Montrose Hotel in Cedar Rapids, he became a prime suspect. Just as quickly Rutledge appeared to have an airtight alibi.

On the day of the murder, Tuesday, Dr. Rutledge had checked out of the Montrose early in the morning. The office manager of a garage, Mrs. Bee Nichols, stated that the doctor had brought his car into her garage that same morning to have a water pump repaired. He picked the car up before noon. Rutledge had been short of cash and told Mrs. Nichols he would send her the money through the mail. At 7:30 that evening Mrs. Nichols received a long distance call from Dr. Rutledge, apparently from St. Louis, confirming that he had just dropped her cheque in the mail. If this were so, he couldn't be the killer. It had been established that the murder had taken place in Cedar Rapids at 5:45 p.m. There was no way Dr. Rutledge could travel the 300 miles to St. Louis in one hour and forty five minutes.

Cedar Rapids detectives weren't taken in by the flimsy alibi. They filled the tank of their car with gas and took off for St. Louis. When the tank neared empty, about one hour and 45 minutes out of Cedar Rapids, they began canvassing gas stations. Sure enough, the police found the station where the doctor had not only purchased gas, but had made the long distance call to Mrs. Nichols, leading her to believe that he was calling from St. Louis.

When detectives went to pick up Dr. Rutledge, the ever faithful Sydney asked them to wait. The doctor was in the bathroom. During those few minutes Rutledge administered poison to himself and collapsed on the way to the police station. He survived, but while being washed in the hospital it was revealed that he had used large quantities of pancake makeup to hide the many superficial scratches he had obtained during his fierce struggle with Hattman.

The Rutledge murder trial was a sensation. The doctor and his wife held hands throughout the trial. Long queues formed each morning to catch the juicy details of the seduction of the doctor's wife. Much was made of the fact that Sydney could have left her job at Emerson at any time to escape Hattman's advances. She left the day his body was found in the hotel room.

Dr. Rutledge was found guilty and received a sentence of 70 years in prison. After serving only a year, he appealed and was released on $40,000 bail pending the results of his appeal. The Rutledges moved to Houston, Texas, where the doctor opened a clinic for the treatment of children.

On April 4, 1951, an Iowa court ruled that the doctor had received a fair trial. The next day Dr. Rutledge bought a long plastic hose. He drove his car to an isolated road about 15 miles from Houston where he attached the hose to his exhaust pipe and placed the other end inside the car. He then closed all the windows and turned on the gas. A drilling contractor found his body at 5:30 that evening.

In 1952, a court decision was made as to who would receive the proceeds of Dr. Rutledge's $10,000 insurance policy. While in the navy he had named his first wife of four hours as the beneficiary, and had neglected to change it after his marriage to Sydney. A judge decided to divide the $10,000. Ironically, Rutledge's wife of four hours received the bulk of the money.

DR. SAM SHEPPARD 1954

MAYOR Spencer Houk looked at the clock beside his bed, yawned, turned over and went back to sleep. The mayor had every right to be at peace with the world. It was going to be a beautiful summer's day in his town, Bay Ridges, a fashionable suburb of Cleveland.

It was 5:30 a.m., July 4, 1954. The phone on the mayor's night table rang. From that moment, nothing was ever quite the same in Bay Ridges. Dr. Sam Sheppard, who lived only a few houses down West Lake Rd., was on the other end of the line. He urged the mayor to come to his house immediately. The doctor sounded frantic. He said, "For God's sake, Spen, get over quick! I think they've killed Marilyn!"

Houk and his wife dashed over to the Sheppard residence. They found Dr. Sam sitting in his den, barechested. His trousers were wet and he was wearing a pair of loafers. He mumbled, "They killed Marilyn."

Mrs. Houk proceeded to the second floor. She peered into the Sheppards' bedroom and was shocked to see Marilyn Sheppard's body on the twin bed closest to the door. Mrs. Houk, a strong woman under the circumstances, felt for a pulse, but there was none. She went downstairs, told her husband what she had seen and called police.

From Sam Sheppard and other witnesses, police reconstructed the evening preceding the murder. Sam and Marilyn had visited with neighbors, the Aherns, earlier in the evening. After having cocktails, the Aherns and their children, together with the Sheppards, returned to the doctor's residence, where they had dinner. After dinner, they listened to a ballgame on the radio and watched T.V. Dr. Sam curled up on a couch and dozed off. Around 12:30, the Aherns left. The next thing anyone knew of events at the Sheppard residence was when Mayor Houk received the phone call from Sam.

When police questioned Sam that morning, it was noted that he had a bad bruise around one eye and complained of pain in his neck. His two brothers, Stephen and Richard, both doctors, whisked their brother to Bay View Hospital.

Back at the house, authorities examined the body and the premises. The bedroom was spattered with blood. Marilyn was lying on her back, with the upper portion of her body exposed. Her head was a mass of blood and the bed clothing was soaked. Later that same morning, Mayor Houk's son found a bag in some bushes leading to the beach while he was searching the grounds around the Sheppard home. Inside the bag were Sam Sheppard's wristwatch, a pocket chain and a ring.

Dr. Sheppard told his story. He claimed that Marilyn retired for the night and went upstairs alone. Someone was there in hiding. When Marilyn screamed, he raced upstairs and in the darkness received a blow to the head. Down he went, stunned, if not unconscious. Regaining his senses, he heard movement downstairs. He raced after his attacker and overtook him on the beach. Once again, he was struck down and rendered unconscious. Sometime later he regained consciousness and staggered inside the house. He made his way upstairs, observed his wife, and called his friend, Spencer Houk.

Dr. Sam's story seemed reasonable enough, but a strange thing happened in Cleveland. A mood swept over the city. Rumors spread that the neurosurgeon had orchestrated his wife's death and because of his wealth and influence, he would get away with murder. Evidence pointing to guilt was highlighted in the press, while evidence pointing to his innocence was overlooked.

Dr. Sheppard was taken into custody and charged with his wife's murder. On October 18, 1954, he stood trial. Because his brothers had tended to his wounds, they testified as to the seriousness of his injuries. Sam's claim that he had been twice knocked out in the course of two battles with his wife's killer was in the main substantiated by Sam's brothers. Such testimony was felt to be biased. Sam wore a neckbrace during the entire trial. Cleveland papers called it trickery.

An expert insinuated that the murder weapon may have been a medical instrument, the inference being that the doctor would have easy access to such an instrument. Maybe the most damaging evidence to Sam's cause was the appearance of his mistress, Susan Hayes. She testified that she had been intimate with Sam for over two years. Their most recent tryst had taken place only a month before the murder. No array of character witnesses swearing Sam was a loving, caring husband could overcome sexy Susan.

And so it went—no absolute proof, but a strong insinuation of guilt. In summing up, the prosecuting attorney left the jury with several questions. Why was Sam, a big, well-conditioned athlete, so easily knocked out? Why had he not turned on the light switch when he went upstairs to answer his wife's call for help? Why didn't he phone the police from his wife's bedroom? Why did he chase the prowler who had just slain his wife and overpowered him? If he had to chase the murderer, why didn't he pick up a weapon when several were handy?

The questions boomed across the courtroom and had a great effect on the jury, although upon close examination not one actually connected Dr. Sam to the murder. Sam Sheppard was convicted of murder in the second degree and sentenced to life imprisonment.

When prison gates closed behind the doctor, his brothers began a campaign to gain a second trial. Meanwhile, Dr. Sam stayed active in his own way.

For some reason, certain women are enamored of men convicted of murder. Ariane Tebbenjohanns, a glamorous, wealthy German divorcee, corresponded with Sam in prison. Eventually she flew over from Dusseldorf to meet her pen pal. The unlikely pair were soon married.

Steven and Richard Sheppard retained famed lawyer F. Lee Bailey to act on their brother's behalf. He succeeded in obtaining a new trial for his client based on the grounds that "prejudicial publicity" had deprived Dr. Sam of a fair trial 12 years earlier.

At his second trial for the murder of his wife, Dr. Sam was found not guilty. He was free at last, but life held little happiness. It took over a year to have his medical licence reinstated. Once again practising medicine, he soon was faced with so many negligence suits that insurance companies refused to provide him with coverage.

The love story with the German beauty came to an end. Ariane obtained a divorce. She claimed that Sam had threatened her with a knife.

Dr. Sam had always been a bodybuilding enthusiast. He turned to wrestling to support himself. A broken and lonely man, he married the 19-year-old daughter of a wrestling friend. Six months later, his health began to deteriorate. His young wife implored him to consult a doctor, but Sam refused.

On April 6, 1970, Dr. Sam Sheppard died of natural causes.

DR. BERNARD FINCH 1960

DR. Bernard Finch had everything any man could ever want. He had a big home, lovely wife, two children, a Swedish maid, a Cadillac, and a thriving practice. He also had a mistress.

In August 1956, an 18-year-old girl named Carole Tregoff was sent to the West Covina Medical Centre in West Covina, California to apply for a position as a receptionist. Carole was a tall, shapely redhead, in full bloom, so to speak.

Doctor Bernie took his time and it wasn't until the winter of 1957 that a cute little apartment was found and rented in the name of Mr. & Mrs. George Evans. Now, for well over a year Bernie and Carole "teamed up" pretty well every day at lunch, and sometimes before work in the morning. Carole had one embarrassing hurdle to get over. You see, she too was married. Her husband, Jimmy Pappa, was not aware of his wife's affair. Their marriage was on the rocks and he and Carole were living together without sharing the connubial couch. It seems Jimmy was the only one who wasn't aware of the torrid romance.

Certainly Barbara Finch knew that something was wrong. She also knew that if she let her husband have a divorce, she would become, under California law, legally entitled to only 50 per cent of his assets. If she could prove adultery, she would get a much larger settlement. Not one to let sleeping dogs lie, Barbara called Jimmy Pappa and told him about his wife. When Carole came home from work that day, Jimmy did the manly thing. He punched her in the mouth. Carole packed up her belongings, left the house and filed for divorce all in the same day.

Meanwhile back at the Finch residence, conditions became intolerable. In May 1959, the Finches were quarreling and fighting on a regular basis. On May 16, Bernie beat up Barbara. On May 20, Barbara filed for a divorce. On May 21, she sought a restraining order that forbade her husband to harm her. At the same time the order prevented him from using or disposing of any funds or property, and as of June 11 the restraining order was signed into the record. At this time Bernie was worth three quarters of a million dollars. Not only could he not touch a penny without Barbara's consent, but every cent of income went into their joint account.

This was the tense state of affairs that existed on the night of July 18, 1959 when Barbara Finch drove up the driveway of her West Covina home. Barbara had taken to carrying a .38 calibre revolver for protection. As she started to get out of her car, she saw her husband and Carole Tregoff walking toward her out of the shadows. Instinctively she reached for her gun and pointed it at the advancing pair. Bernie grabbed the gun and took it away from his wife. He then proceeded to attack Barbara. Her screams were heard by their Swedish maid, Marie Anne Lidholm, who came running to Mrs. Finch's aid. Dr. Finch was in an uncontrollable rage. He grabbed the woman and threw her against the garage wall with such force that an impression of her head was implanted in the stucco wall. Bernie fired a wild shot into the air, and then ordered Marie Anne and his wife into the car. Barbara, fearing for her life, went in one side of the car and out the other, and kept on going. Bernie took off after her. Marie Anne saw her chance and ran to the house to call the police. Later she was to testify that she was dialling the police number when she heard a shot. Bernie admitted firing the gun. He claimed that he was flinging the gun away when his finger caught on the trigger, accidentally discharging the weapon. Firing so haphazardly he proved to be a fantastic shot. The .38 calibre slug made its way through Barbara's back and into her heart.

All this time Carole was hiding in the bushes just out of sight of the action. Only after the police came and finished their investigation did Carole finally get away. She didn't know that Bernie had left or that Barbara was dead. The only living person the police found at the scene was Marie Anne, who had called them in the first place.

Next day, Dr. Finch was arrested and charged with murder. Later Carole was charged as well. At the trial the prosecution brought out the fact that Bernie and Carole had hired an assassin to do away with Mrs. Finch. His name was John Patrick Coady, and he fingered the accused pair from the witness stand. In fact, he received a total of $1,200 for the job that he had no intention of doing. He told a convincing story.

Over and above Coady's damaging evidence, the police had come up with an attache case at the scene of the crime. The case did not contain what your average kindly old doctor would call the essentials. Instead it held two 10-foot-long ropes, an eight-inch butcher knife, a bottle of Seconal, a hammer, a flashlight and a box of .38 calibre cartridges. The attache case was quickly dubbed the "murder kit" by the press.

It took three trials to get a jury to agree, but finally on March 27, 1961, Dr. Bernard Finch and Carole Tregoff were convicted of murder in the second degree. Both were sentenced to life imprisonment.

In 1969 Carole was paroled, and is now employed under an assumed name as a medical records clerk in a hospital in California. Dr. Finch was eventually paroled, and is again practising medicine.

DR. GEZA DE KAPLANY 1962

DR. Geza de Kaplany had interned at Milwaukee General Hospital in 1957. Later he specialized in anesthesiology at Harvard University, after which he taught at Yale University for a year. In 1961, he was chief medical resident at San Francisco's Franklin Hospital. Still later he accepted the post of staff anesthesiologist at Doctors' Hospital in San Jose, California.

At the age of 36 you might say Dr. de Kaplany was a high achiever. Even in the field of matrimony he hit the jackpot. In July of 1962 he married Hajna Piller, a model and former showgirl. She was gorgeous. Anyone who ever saw Hajna came away impressed by her beauty. Both had immigrated from Hungary to the U.S. while still single.

On the stifling hot night of August 28, 1962, about five weeks after their marriage, Dr. de Kaplany killed his wife. On the day of the crime, Mrs. de Kaplany visited her mother. She arrived home in the early evening and met her husband outside their apartment. They proceeded up to their apartment which was in a two-storey ranch style structure. The young couple commenced to make love on the bed. For no apparent reason Dr. de Kaplany jumped up from the bed. He had an entire torture kit with him. First he beat his wife with his fists. He then tied her hands behind her back with electric cord, and trussed up her feet in the same manner. To stifle her screams he placed tape over her mouth. Dr. de Kaplany slashed at Hajna's breast with a knife. He wasn't through. Calmly donning rubber gloves, he applied nitric acid all over her body.

Despite the fact that the doctor turned the hi-fi on full blast, Hajna's screams pierced the hot summer night, arousing the neighbors' interest. When the police and an ambulance arrived on the scene, they found the doctor pacing outside the apartment in a pair of Bermuda shorts and slippers. Hajna lay nude in agony on the bed, horribly burned over 60 per cent of her body. The officers and medical people had trouble breathing at the scene of the crime due to the nitric acid. Periodically they had to run out of the apartment to get a breath of fresh air.

Hajna lingered in agony for 33 days after the attack before she mercifully passed away on September 30. During the time the doctors struggled to keep her alive she made many statements to the police, but in the end she really could not say just why her husband had done such a terrible thing to her.

On Monday, January 7, 1963, Dr. de Kaplany stood trial for murder. During the trial he changed his plea from not guilty to guilty. Sanity meant the gas chamber, and insanity meant life imprisonment. The trial was a sensation and swayed back and forth on medical evidence attesting to Dr. de Kaplany's mental condition at the time of the murder.

The defence brought forward doctors who claimed he suffered from depression due to leaving an aged mother in Hungary. They said he suffered from paranoid schizophrenia. The prosecution countered with the actual torture paraphernalia which they lugged into court. It made an impressive display in front of the jury—surgical gloves, a quantity of surgical swabs, rolls of adhesive tape, electric cord, one pint of nitric acid, one pint of hydrochloric acid, one pint of sulphuric acid and two knives.

A sensation was caused at the trial when the defence put a young psychiatrist, Dr. A. Russell Lee on the stand. Dr. Lee claimed that de Kaplany suffered from multiple personality. He stated that de Kaplany had two people living in the same body. One was a kind and gentle doctor. The other was brutal and cruel. The brutal one went under the name of Pierre LaRoche. It seems de Kaplany heard some gossip about his wife being unfaithful to him. Instead of dealing with this rumor in a rational manner as de Kaplany would have done, he changed into the aggressive cruel Pierre, and tortured and killed his wife. De Kaplany would change his outward appearance and adopt the personality of Pierre LaRoche, for short periods of time.

Horrible pictures of poor Hajna were introduced as evidence, showing the agony in which she died. The jury could not believe that a man, sane in the legal sense, could perform such atrocities on his wife. They brought in a verdict of guilty. He was sentenced to life imprisonment.

When Dr. de Kaplany was taken away to San Quentin, a reporter asked him one final question as a guard assisted him into the prison van. "Have you any last statement, Doctor?"

"This is the end. I am dead," he replied.

DR. JOHN BRANION 1967

DR. John Branion Jr. owed a lot to his father. John Sr. was born into deep south Mississippi poverty, with all the ugly ramifications the location and social standing held for members of the black community at the turn of the century.

Despite all odds, John's father made his way north, attended the University of Chicago Law School and became a prominent attorney. He devoted his life to championing the causes of his people. His one son would never know the hard times he had endured.

John Jr., to the chagrin of his parents, was a mediocre student. His marks in school didn't warrant acceptance to any medical school in the U.S. Like many well-off families, the Branions found a medical school in Europe which would accept their son. John applied himself and returned home with his medical degree. He interned in Chicago, specialized in obstetrics and gynecology and set up a practice. Within a very short while, Dr. John Branion was a wealthy, respected physician.

To add to his lustre, John married into a prominent black family when he wed Donna Brown, the daughter of banker Sidney Brown. The influential, socially prominent Branions of Chicago had two children. Theirs was a success story that Hollywood writers would deem too perfect to be accepted by the public.

Surely there had to be a flaw in the perfect couple's life that begged to be uncovered, but such was not the case. Years passed. The Branions accumulated the trappings of wealth. Cars, designer clothing and a classy 10-room apartment were theirs to enjoy. In time, John acquired a substantial stable of racehorses. Oh, sure, there were some whispers of other women, but such whispers are the norm among the wealthy.

Shortly after 11:30 a.m. on December 22, 1967, Theresa Kentra, who lived in the same apartment complex as the Branions at 5054 S. Woodlawn Ave., heard several short reports she thought might have emanated from the Branions' apartment. She paused for a moment, but thought nothing more of the incident.

Accompanied by his four-year-old son, John drove up to his apartment. He told his son to wait in the car while he went inside. John opened the door, walked through the kitchen into a utility room and came across Donna's body lying on the floor. He ran out the back door of the first-floor apartment and called up to Dr. Helen Payne, who lived on the third floor. Dr. Payne and her brother William rushed downstairs. They were met by John, who pointed, "In there. It's Donna."

John hustled his son up to a third-floor apartment occupied by a relative. He returned to his own apartment as William Payne was calling police. In minutes, officers were at the scene. They were greeted by John, who told them, "I haven't touched her. As soon as I observed the lividity in her legs, I knew she was dead." Dr. Payne introduced herself to the officers, explained that she was a medical doctor, advised them that she had examined the body and confirmed that Mrs. Branion was dead. By now John had seated himself, covered his face with his hands and was quietly sobbing.

It was three days before Christmas. It seemed natural to suspect that some gun-happy thug had robbery in mind when he had entered the Branions' home. People have been murdered before for a few gaily wrapped Christmas presents under a tree. When homicide detectives arrived, they immediately checked for evidence of forced entry, but found none. The officers searched the house with John. Nothing was missing. They theorized that Donna Branion must have opened the door to her killer, whom she no doubt knew.

Crime lab technicians examined an electric iron cord they found beside the body. It appeared that Donna's killer had attempted to strangle her. When she put up a fierce struggle for her life, he started shooting. Four cartridge cases were found under the body.

An autopsy indicated that Donna had been shot seven times. Three of the bullets had gone through her hands as she raised them in a futile effort to ward off her attacker. Any of the other four bullets could have caused her death.

Dr. Branion was questioned by detectives. He told them that he left his office at 11:30 a.m. to pick up his four-year-old son, which took only five minutes. He then drove to East Fifty-Third St. to pick up Maxine Brown for lunch. Maxine, a relative of his wife's, couldn't make lunch because of an unexpected business appointment. John drove home and discovered his wife's body. He went on to tell investigators that upon entering his apartment he called out to his wife. When he didn't get a response, he felt something wasn't right. He told his son to wait in the hall while he continued on into the kitchen. When he turned on the light of the utility room, he was shocked to find his wife's body on the floor. John noticed the lividity present in her legs and realized she was dead. That's when he made his way outdoors and called Dr. Payne.

That was the doctor's story. It was concise and straightforward. A couple of things caught the attention of the detectives. There were a number of guns in the apartment's laundry room. When asked about the weapons, John told the investigators that he was a gun collector and owned about 25 guns. He kept his collection in the laundry room. John checked out the guns for the officers and assured them that none was missing, nor had any of the guns been recently fired.

The first day of the investigation into the tragic death of Donna Branion was fast drawing to a close. Detectives left the Branion residence. The next day, two days before Christmas, would bring further attempts to find out who had murdered the socially prominent doctor's wife. No doubt investigating officers would be interviewing Dr. Branion in the morning.

Surprise! Next day homicide detectives learned that early that morning John, his 13-year-old daughter and four-year-old son had taken off for a skiing vacation in Vail, Colorado.

Folks, that's not a natural reaction to suddenly losing a wife. No question about it, Dr. John Branion had managed to gain the full attention of the police.

Now that the doctor had managed to draw suspicion to himself, investigators delved into his lifestyle, checked out his friends and rechecked his statement. They learned that Theresa Kentra, who lived in the Branions' apartment building, heard several loud reports on the day of the murder a few minutes after 11:30 a.m. About 20 minutes later, she heard the doctor shouting to Dr. Helen Payne for assistance.

Joyce Kelly, a teacher at John's son's nursery school, stated that she had seen Dr. Branion enter the school between 11:45 and 11:50 a.m. and help his son on with his coat. This was in conflict with John's original statement to police in which he had said that his son had been waiting outside when he came to pick him up.

Tracing the doctor's every move on the day of the murder, detectives next drove to the office of Maxine Brown, who had been unable to keep her luncheon date with the doctor. Although she knew John well, that was the first time he had ever asked her out for lunch. Investigators felt that the good doctor had planned on having Maxine with him when he came across his wife's body. He had no way of knowing that an unexpected business appointment would make it impossible for Maxine to lunch with him and his son.

John had claimed that he had known immediately that his wife was dead because of the presence of lividity in her legs. Dr. Helen Payne told police this was impossible. She had examined Donna's body moments after John had found it and there had been no lividity evident at that time.

Little by little, John's statements were found to contain small discrepancies. Firearm experts reported that Donna had been killed with a Walther PPK pistol, the same type made famous by James Bond in the movies. An examination of John's guns turned up no such weapon. He swore he had never owned such a weapon. Detectives pressed on. They learned that the doctor had a girlfriend, his nurse, Shirley Hudson. She had accompanied him on his skiing trip to Vail. That little caper, detectives all agreed, takes a certain type of man. After all, Donna's body was being prepared for a post mortem while John, his mistress and the kiddies were off skiing in Colorado. Folks, in better circles, that is rarely done.

Dr. Branion was a busy little gynecologist. He had another lady on the line, Anicetra Souza, who admitted to being a good friend, but swore there was nothing of an intimate nature between her and John.

When detectives learned that John had asked his wife for a divorce and had been refused, they were sure they were on the right track. Now they set out to prove that Dr. Branion had had sufficient time to commit the murder by retracing his every move, starting at his office at Ida Mae Scott Hospital. They drove to his home, allowed time for the shooting, drove to Branion's son's nursery school, proceeded to Maxine Brown's office and then back to Branion's apartment. Investigators traced the route a half dozen times. Each time they gave the benefit of the doubt to the doctor. On every trip, they proved that he had plenty of time to commit the murder and show up at the times stated by various witnesses.

Although officers knew they had a strong circumstantial case, they desperately wanted to locate the murder weapon. Once again they searched the Branions' laundry room, which was more of a workshop, looking for any clue that would lead them to the Walther PPK. Sure enough, in the doctor's work bench, they found a box which had contained a new Walther. Since John had sworn he had never owned such a weapon, detectives had every reason to believe they had the right man.

Inside the box was a paper listing the serial number of the pistol and on the outside of the box the name of the importer, Joseph Galeff and Sons, New York City. They had sold the gun to Bell's Gun Shop in a Chicago suburb, where it had been purchased three months earlier by James Hooks, a good friend of none other than Dr. John Branion.

Hooks initially denied any knowledge of the weapon, but when he was shown a copy of the gun shop's invoice with his name on it, he admitted that he had bought the gun. He went on to tell the officers that he had given the gun to John Branion as a birthday present.

That was it. John was picked up at his office and charged with his wife's murder. An Illinois jury took only seven hours to find him guilty. The presiding judge sentenced him to not less that 20 years or more than 30 years imprisonment.

John appealed his conviction and, in an unusual move, was granted bail until his appeal could be heard. Bail was set at $5,000, which meant that only a $500 payment was required for him to gain his freedom. No question about it, strings were pulled to spring the murderous medic. The public was outraged, but despite the outcry, John walked.

Branion's next legal ploy came in the form of a petition for permission to move to Cheyenne, Wyoming. Once again, an exception was made and John was allowed to relocate. He packed up bag, baggage and nurse Shirley Hudson and headed west. Once there, he married Shirley. Then, in a whirlwind matrimonial merry-go-round he divorced Shirley and married Anicetra Souza. Remember her? She was the girlfriend who claimed her relationship with John had never been an intimate one. John wasn't through. He divorced Anicetra, remarried Shirley, divorced Shirley and remarried Anicetra. That comes to four marriages and three divorces in the two-year period he was appealing his conviction for murdering his first wife.

Finally, John's conviction was affirmed by the Illinois Supreme Court. He immediately flew the coop, forfeiting his bond and was charged with unlawful flight to avoid incarceration. Over the next few years, he kept one step ahead of the law.

In 1972, John was spotted in Khartoum in the Sudan. Now on Interpol's hot sheet, he was next traced to Uganda, where he worked for the Department of Health and later became personal physician to dictator Idi Amin.

When the mad dictator's reign collapsed, John fled and remained at large until Interpol learned that he was in Kuala Lampur, Malaysia. Once more, he managed to stay one step ahead of the law. He fled back to Uganda, but evidently that country had had enough of the evasive doctor. In 1983, Ugandan authorities advised the U.S. that they had their man under lock and key.

Chicago detectives flew to Entebbe and brought back the fugitive. On November 2, 1983, after a 12-year chase, John was back in a Chicago court-room. From there he was transported to the Illinois State Prison, where he served seven years. His sentence was commuted on August 7, 1990, when a tumor was discovered on his brain.

A month later, 64-year-old Dr. John Branion died in the University of Illinois Hospital.

DR. JOHN HILL 1969

WHEN blonde and beautiful Joan Robinson met John Hill, there were those who said that the young couple were made for each other. On the surface it appeared that way.

Joan was the only daughter of multi-millionaire oil man Ash Robinson. Ash had eyes for only two things in this world—money, and his daughter Joan. As a result she had her every desire fulfilled from the day she was born.

John Hill was brought up in a small southern Texas town, but had a bright future ahead of him as a plastic surgeon when he met Joan in 1957 in Houston. Within 15 years of their first meeting both would die violently.

Although Joan and John appeared to be happily married, it wasn't long before the deep-rooted differences in their backgrounds and interests rose to the surface. Joan, who at 27 had gone through two unsuccessful marriages, had a consuming interest in horses. From the age of five, when she first learned to ride, horses were to play a major role in her life. By the time she met John she was one of the leading horsewomen in the U.S.

John took no interest in his wife's equine pursuits. Other than his lucrative medical practice, he had an obsessive love of classical music. The doctor played several instruments, including the piano, at a near professional degree of excellence.

Later Ash Robinson would present his daughter and son-in-law with a beautiful new home. John went about indulging himself in the real passion of his life, music. He remodeled and equipped a ballroom-sized area of his home into a music room.

In 1960 the Hills had a son, Robert. This normally thrilling event only served to interrupt Joan's appearances at horse shows for a short while. Soon servants were tending to Robert. John apparently cared little for his new son, and continued building up his medical practice, while spending more and more time in his elaborate music room. Ash Robinson adored Robert and spent every moment he could with his grandson.

In August 1968 Joan and John visited a summer camp to pick up their son Robert. While there John met Ann Kurth, an attractive divorced mother of three sons, who was visiting her boys at the same camp. John became madly infatuated with Ann. The successful doctor pursued Ann with notes, flowers, and other expressions of undying love, until Ann began to appreciate the attentions paid to her by John Hill. Soon she was in love with the dashing, attentive doctor. When Ann broached the subject of Joan, she was assured that the Hill marriage was on the rocks and that John would soon obtain a divorce.

Quite out of character, John impetuously moved out of his home, leaving Joan only a brief note of explanation, and moved in with Ann. When John served Joan with divorce papers, Ash Robinson was furious. No one was going to treat his little girl in such a shoddy manner. Ash met his son-in-law and threatened him with ruin if he didn't reach a reconciliation with Joan. Ash had provided John with cars, a mansion, indulged his musical taste to the fullest, and assisted him in building up his medical practice. Influential Ash Robinson would see to it that the house of cards came tumbling down if John didn't return to his wife. The meeting between the two men resulted in John signing an agreement stating that he was sorry that he had acted irrationally and that he would give up everything Ash Robinson had provided if he did not return to the side of the everloving Joan.

John moved back with Joan.

In the light of future developments, the evening of March 9, 1969 holds a great deal of significance in the lives of Joan and John Hill. On that night the Hills were entertaining when John's telephone pager went off. He was called away and did not return until after 11 p.m. Upon his return he offered the guests pastries which he had brought with him. He insisted that his wife eat the one particular pastry which he set before her. Evenings later John was again interrupted while his wife was entertaining guests. Again he returned with pastries and insisted that his wife eat one in particular.

Within 48 hours Joan became dreadfully sick. John prescribed bed rest. Two days later Joan developed a raging fever. Frantically her maid called John to come home to tend to his wife. John arrived home and made arrangements for his wife's admittance to a small hospital. Eyebrows were raised when the desperately ill woman wasn't sent to the Texas Medical Center located less than 15 minutes from the Hill residence. Dr. Hill kept insisting his wife would be fine, and that her illness was of a minor nature. In the wee hours of the following morning, Joan Hill died in agony.

Ash Robinson took his daughter's sudden death very hard. It was incomprehensible to him that a healthy young woman could die so suddenly with her husband, a well known doctor, being readily available at all times.

Dr. John seemed to take Joan's death in stride. He continued his affair with Ann Kurth. Ash Robinson was convinced that his son-in-law had murdered Joan. He approached the district attorney with his suspicions, but was put off.

Less than three months after Joan's death, John married Ann Kurth. The marriage reinforced Ash Robinson's belief that John had killed Joan. Private investigations carried out by Ash Robinson uncovered the strange circumstances of the pastries being served by John to Joan and her friends.

Finally the D.A. impanelled a grand jury, but they failed to indict. Rumors were flying around Houston, when eight months after his marriage to Ann Kurth, John filed for divorce. When the divorce became final Ann Kurth went to the D.A. and talked of her marriage to John Hill. As a result of these revelations the grand jury was impanelled once again. This time one of the leading prosecution witnesses was none other than Ann Kurth. Miss Kurth stated that John had confessed to her that he had made up a horrible poison of human excrement and administered it to Joan, causing her sudden and fatal illness. She also told of her former husband's strange Jekyll and Hyde personality when, on two occasions, he turned on her with a syringe.

Dr. Hill was charged with the crime of murder by neglect. His trial commenced in March 1971. It was now two years since Joan Hill's death. Dr. Hill, who apparently didn't let any grass grow under his feet, now had another lady friend. Connie Loesby had one thing Joan and Ann didn't have. She had a genuine interest in music. John wanted to marry her, but heeded his lawyer's advice to wait until the conclusion of his trial.

Hill's trial proved to be one of the most sensational ever held in Houston. Ann Kurth was the acknowledged star of the piece. Wives are not allowed to testify against their husbands. However, as Ann was no longer married to John, she was allowed to testify, providing she limited her testimony to events which occurred before she legally became Mrs. John Hill.

Ann became emotional while giving testimony, and blurted out that John had told her in detail how he had killed Joan. This was inadmissible evidence and the judge ordered a mistrial.

Soon after the mistrial John married Connie Loesby and tried to begin a new life. It wasn't easy. The doctor's practice had quite naturally suffered but as the months went by the notorious Hill case was put on the back burner. That is, until one fateful day in September 1972.

The Hills had just arrived home by plane from a trip to the west coast. While John paid off the cabby, Connie walked to the front door of their home. Connie rang the doorbell and was shocked to be greeted by a man wearing a green Halloween mask. The stranger grabbed Connie by the neck, dragging her into the house. He said only, "This is a robbery."

By this time John was at his wife's side. As he grappled with the intruder Connie managed to break free and run towards a neighbor's home. While running she heard gunfire.

Police were on the scene in a matter of minutes. Dr. Hill had been shot in the shoulder, chest and right arm. His killer had grotesquely placed tape over his mouth, eyes and nose. The doctor's second trial for murder was scheduled to take place in two months, but someone had taken justice into his own hands.

Houston police were successful in tracing a young hood named Bobby Vandiver, who confessed that he, together with prostitute Marcia Mckittrick, had killed Dr. Hill. According to Vandiver he had accepted the contract killing from Lilla Paulis, a shady but influential acquaintance of Ash Robinson.

Vandiver and Mckittrick told all, but before Lilla Paulis came to trail, Vandiver was killed while attempting to escape from jail. Mckittrick turned state's evidence and revealed all the details of the killing. As a result Lilla Paulis was found guilty and sent to prison for life. To this day she has not verified that Ash Robinson was involved in the contract killing. Robinson has never been charged with any crime.

DR. CLAUDIUS GIESICK 1973

INTRICATE murder plots, disguised to look like accidents, oftimes go asunder. Occasionally, relatives smell a rat and assist police.

Stanley and Josephine Albanowski of Trenton, New Jersey, simply couldn't believe that their beautiful daughter, Patricia, had been a hit-and-run victim in New Orleans. They hired a lawyer, who contacted New Orleans police. The lawyer's inquiry was routinely turned over to Det. John Dillman, who responded by getting in touch with Patricia's mother.

Mrs. Albanowski informed the policeman that Patricia had moved from New Jersey to Dallas in November 1972. About two weeks before Christmas, her daughter met Dr. Claudius Giesick, who swept Patricia off her feet. Patricia had never received such attention from a man in her life.

Handsome, debonair Giesick showered gifts and attention on naive Patricia. As a token of his affection, he gave her a pair of St. Bernard puppies. On January 2, 1973, they were married. Dr. Giesick reportedly gave his wife a new Monte Carlo automobile for a wedding present. The happy couple took off for Miami, where they were to board a cruise ship for a trip throughout the Caribbean. Patricia was on Cloud 9.

Then, disaster struck. At first, the Albanowskis thought it was a minor setback. Their daughter phoned them from her motel room in New Orleans. She was alone in her room when she informed them that her car was in a repair shop. She had just walked some distance to pick up a pizza.

Nine hours later, Patricia's parents were told that their daughter was dead, the victim of a hit-and-run driver. Dr. Giesick was understandably beside himself with grief.

The doctor explained to investigating officers that he and his wife had gone for a midnight stroll. They were walking back to their car when Patricia and he raced across the street. They didn't see the vehicle approaching. Early next morning, Patricia died in hospital without regaining consciousness.

A few days later, the Albanowskis met their son-in-law for the first time at their daughter's funeral in New Jersey. The doctor was accompanied by a man who was introduced to them as his spiritual adviser, Rev. Sam Corey.

A couple of things bothered Josephine Albanowski. A few hours before the tragedy, Patricia had told her that her car was in a garage for repairs, yet the doctor said they were returning to their car when the hit-and-run took place. Why the discrepancy in stories? Mrs. Albanowski informed police that the doctor's first wife had also been a hit-and-run victim. On the phone, Patricia had mentioned that her life had been insured by her husband.

Det. Dillman did some poking around. He found out that Dr. Giesick had picked up the Monte Carlo from the repair shop eight hours before the death of his wife. Dillman looked up the officer who had taken the hit and run report. The officer had been sympathetic to the doctor, which was only natural. The poor man had just lost his wife on his honeymoon.

When the officer had asked where Dr. Giesick's own vehicle was, the doctor had pointed to an Olds Cutlass parked in the motel parking lot. The officer took the doctor's word and didn't bother to check. There didn't seem to be any point. Now Dillman wondered if the doctor had an ulterior motive in pointing to a motel patron's car.

It was also revealed that Dr. Giesick had paid his bill at the Ramada Inn with a credit card issued to Dr. Charles Guilliam. The motel's management assured the detective that this is often done. They merely checked to insure that the credit card was good.

More inquiries uncovered the fact that Dr. Giesick had taken out a $50,000 life insurance policy with Farmers Insurance Group of Houston, Texas. The policy had a double indemnity clause, doubling its value in case of Patricia's accidental death. It had been purchased five days after the wedding.

Dr. Giesick had attempted to collect on this policy the day after Patricia's fatal accident, but had been delayed until the insurance company completed their investigation. Later, Dillman would learn of another insurance policy, issued by Mutual of Omaha for $200,000 on Patricia's life.

Det. Dillman was now sure that Patricia Giesick had not met with an accident. He found out that Giesick lived in Dallas, but could not reach him on the telephone. Without benefit of interviewing his chief suspect, Dillman delved into the history of the dead girl and her husband. He learned that Patricia had worked for a couple of days in a body massage parlor. Naive Patricia didn't know the place was really one of several such parlors, which were fronts for a prostitution ring run by Rev. Sam Corey. It was Reverend Sam who officiated at Patricia's wedding and later accompanied her husband to her funeral in New Jersey.

You couldn't miss Reverend Sam. He weighed more than 350 pounds and stood no more than five feet nine inches. Among those who knew the Reverend Sam's real vocation, he was called the Massage Parlor King.

While the net of circumstantial evidence was slowly encircling Dr. Claudius Giesick, he was picked up for passing a bad cheque in Dallas. By the time Dillman arrived in Dallas to question his man, Giesick had been released on bail posted by Rev. Sam Corey.

Det. Dillman interviewed Rev. Corey, who admitted knowing Dr. Giesick for some time. He had had dinner with the Giesicks a few days before they left on their honeymoon. He claimed he had learned of the tragedy from Patricia's mother, who had phoned him while Patricia was unconscious in hospital. Dr. Giesick had called him a few hours later, advising him that his wife had died. He invited the doctor to stay at his house in Dallas. Giesick accepted his invitation and together they had flown to Trenton, N.J. for the funeral.

Dillman had no trouble checking Corey's story. The Albanowskis swore they had not called Corey and stated that the first time they had seen him was at their daughter's funeral.

Dillman proceeded to learn the address of Dr. Charles Guilliam, whose credit card had been used by Giesick to pay his bill upon checking out of the Ramada Inn after his wife's death. Mrs. Guilliam informed the detective that her husband was not at home. She appeared nervous. When asked about Giesick, she told the investigator that he was a business associate of her husband's.

While interrogating Mrs. Guilliam, Dillman noticed the two Guilliam children playing with a pair of St. Bernard puppies in the backyard. He well remembered that Giesick had given Patricia a pair of St. Bernards. Dillman was sure that Dr. Guilliam and Dr. Giesick were one and the same man.

Finally, Dr. Giesick was interviewed and confirmed that he had picked up the Monte Carlo hours before the accident. The vehicle was examined by police. Near the left front tire, technicians removed two hairs which matched hairs removed from Patricia's head.

There seemed little doubt that the scheming doctor, who lived two lives, one as Dr. Guilliam, a family man with two children and the other as Dr. Giesick, had, together with a con artist minister, orchestrated the hit and run death of an innocent girl from out of town. The motive, a whopping $300,000.

Dr. Giesick and Rev. Corey were picked up and charged with murder. Giesick made a deal in exchange for being allowed to plead guilty to manslaughter.

Dr. Giesick revealed the entire plot. He and Rev. Sam Corey hand-picked Patricia Albanowski. When Patricia found out what was expected of her in the massage parlor, she threatened to quit. The doctor swept her off her feet. On the night of her death, he conned her into taking a walk. Unknown to her, the Rev. Sam Corey was waiting for the pair to appear. He roared down the road with his car lights extinguished. Dr. Giesick tripped Patricia, sending her sprawling into the path of the car.

It took the jury only 20 minutes to find Rev. Sam Corey guilty of first-degree murder. He is now serving a life sentence in Louisiana State Penitentiary.

Claudius James Giesick was sentenced to 21 years imprisonment. On May 17, 1986, after serving 11 years in prison, he was released from custody.

Katherine (Guilliam) Giesick was not charged with any crime.

Det. John Dillman is no longer with the New Orleans Police Dept. A book, Unholy Matrimony, later made into a TV movie, describes in detail how the persistent work of a dedicated police officer brought two heinous criminals to justice.

DR. CHARLES FRIEDGOOD 1976

To all outward appearances Dr. Charles Friedgood had the world by the tail. A successful surgeon, he owned a large eighteen-room home in the affluent Kensington section of Long Island's North Shore. He was the father of a grown, well educated family, and above all was the husband of Sophie, his loving wife of 28 years.

It just wasn't that way at all. Dr. Friedgood, who was in his mid-50s, neglected his wife. He arrived home late for meals, sometimes by hours. No matter what the occasion Sophie never started a meal without him. She waited, and when he finally arrived, she argued, she screamed, and she bickered. To make matters more frustrating, Friedgood ignored his wife's outbursts, and never offered any excuses for his tardiness.

In 1967 Friedgood became infatuated with his Danish nurse, Harriet Larson. Although Harriet wasn't a beauty, she was attractive. Initially the doctor kept his relationship with Harriet a secret, but soon he was carrying on an open affair. For years his daughters, Toba, Esther, Beth, and Debbie had believed that Harriet was nothing more than a faithful employee. Gradually the truth became known to them. Typically, Sophie was the last member of the family to accept the fact that her husband was keeping another woman.

All semblance of secrecy crumbled when Harriet became pregnant. Early in 1972 she flew to Denmark, where she gave birth to a boy, who was named Heinrich after Dr. Friedgood's dead father. When she came back to the U.S., Friedgood set Harriet and Heinrich up in an apartment not far from his home. He paid her an allowance of $1,000 a month. Two years later Harriet found herself pregnant once more. Again she returned to her native country. This time she gave birth to a girl, Matte, with Friedgood at her side. He had told his wife that he was attending a medical convention in Arizona, when in reality he flew to Denmark.

When Harriet and the two children returned to the U.S., Friedgood obtained a larger apartment for his second family, again quite close to his home in

Kensington. He helped furnish it with older pieces from his own home that Sophie had discarded. Friedgood was under pressure from Harriet to obtain a divorce from Sophie. He convinced his mistress that because of financial difficulties incurred while he was purchasing a hotel, he had signed over everything he owned to Sophie, almost a million dollars in stocks, bonds, and cash. As soon as the deal cleared the courts, he would be free to marry, but in the meantime Sophie legally owned everything.

At the same time the doctor tried to explain away Harriet to his wife by telling her that he couldn't dismiss his nurse because she had been witness to several documents he had signed concerning the same financial deal.

As the Friedgood girls grew up they came to know and like their father's nurse. Sometimes they were puzzled when little Heinrich would hug their father and call him Papa. Later they realized that the child was named after their own grandfather, and that besides, he bore a striking resemblance to one of their brothers. One by one the Friedgood girls married. Each of their husbands eventually learned of the strange, rather open relationship their father-in-law had with his nurse. Occasionally one of his daughters would approach her father and beg him to explain his relationship with Harriet. Friedgood wouldn't hear of such scandalous talk. He assured them that it was nothing more than that of doctor-nurse. He was so convincing that sometimes his children believed him.

Naturally, Sophie, who over the years had been humiliated by her husband literally hundreds of times, fought back in the only way she knew. She screamed at him, "Go to your whore!", "Sneak away to your bitch!" Friedgood had the exasperating habit of calmly reading his newspaper during these tirades.

The tense relationship between Charles and Sophie Friedgood could not continue indefinitely. Things came to a head on June 17, 1975. That evening Charles and Sophie had a date to meet for dinner at Lundys Restaurant in Brooklyn. Sophie was in good spirits, having heard that Harriet was in Denmark. She arrived promptly at 6 p.m. Typically, Friedgood was late. Sophie sipped wine as she waited for him for over an hour.

After dinner, at approximately 8 p.m., the couple drove in separate cars to their accountant's home, where they were expected. They arrived at 8:30, stayed one hour, and then drove home. At 11 p.m. Esther called her parents from New Jersey. It was an exciting time for her. She and her husband had both just received their law degrees. Esther had a good chat with her mother and father. Moments later Charles and Sophie retired to their bedroom. They were alone in the big house.

We will never know exactly what happened in the Friedgood bedroom after 11 p.m. that night. Later, at Dr. Friedgood's trial, a medical examiner reconstructed the events as they must have unfolded.

Sophie and Charles undressed. Sophie lay in bed while Charles went to a filing cabinet in his study. From the top drawer of the filing cabinet he removed a long needle and syringe. He then filled the syringe with demerol.

Sophie, lying on her back in bed, had no way of knowing she had only moments to live. Charles pounced on his wife, firmly grasping one outstretched arm above her head. As Sophie struggled, Charles injected the demerol up under her armpit. The doctor then held his wife helpless for the ten or twelve minutes it took the demerol to take effect. Sophie screamed frantically. The big house was empty. There was no one to hear.

A few minutes passed. Sophie became drowsy. Her efforts grew weaker. Charles lifted his wife's other arm, and once more jabbed the needle under her armpit. Injections in her thigh and buttocks followed. She lay quiet, but was still breathing. Charles turned his wife's limp form over. He gave her one last injection between the ribs directly into the liver. Sophie stopped breathing.

Dr. Friedgood replaced the needle and syringe in the top drawer of his filing cabinet and returned to his bedroom. He went to sleep beside the lifeless body of the woman who had been his wife for so many years.

Next morning Dr. Friedgood went to work as usual. Lydia Fernandez showed up for work at the Friedgood residence as she did every day. She tidied up around the house, and found it a bit strange that Mrs. Friedgood had not left her a note telling her when she should be awakened. Later that day, at 1 p.m., Lydia found Sophie Friedgood dead in her bed.

Dr. Friedgood was notified of his wife's death. He hurried home. He told of Esther's call the night before, of going to sleep, of waking up, of Sophie kissing him goodbye. It was shocking. His wife must have had a stroke after he left her. Because Sophie had suffered a stroke years before, it was assumed that she had suffered another one.

In keeping with the Friedgood's religion, steps were quickly taken to have

Sophie buried in her hometown of Hazleton, Pennsylvania, the following day. Dr. Friedgood signed his wife's death certificate.

News of Sophie's death spread throughout Kensington. Something clicked in police chief Raymond Sickles' memory. While he didn't know the Friedgoods personally, he recalled that one of the Friedgood daughters had once frantically called him because her mother and father were having a terrible row. When one of his men arrived at the Friedgood residence they found nothing more than the usual family dispute. Sickles learned that Dr. Friedgood had signed his wife's death certificate. Although there was no law preventing a medical doctor from signing a spouse's death certificate, it was unusual. Normally another doctor would have been called upon to sign the certificate.

Sickles decided to inform the Nassau County Police of his suspicions. Officials felt that Dr. Friedgood's actions were so unusual that they consulted Dr. Leslie Lukash, the county medical examiner, who agreed that the funeral should be delayed long enough for an autopsy to be performed. Detective Thomas Palladino was dispatched to Hazleton to see to it that the burial did not take place as scheduled.

While he was mourning at the funeral chapel, Dr. Friedgood was first made aware that the police were concerned about the manner of his wife's death. Under threat that a court order would be obtained granting the autopsy, Dr. Friedgood gave his permission to proceed. He had no choice.

A post mortem was performed at St. Joseph's Hospital, while Detective Palladino looked on. Unbelievably, Dr. Friedgood insisted that he be allowed to observe his own wife's autopsy.

The autopsy revealed that at the time of death Sophie's stomach had been full. How could that be? The meal she had eaten the night before at 8 p.m. would have been digested long before 9 a.m. when the doctor left for work. Sophie must have died within six hours of having eaten the meal. Dr. Friedgood must have been lying when he stated his wife returned his parting kiss the morning after she consumed that meal. She was positively dead at that time.

Dark red bruises were found under the armpits, on the thigh, buttocks, and on the chest. Testing indicated that demerol had been injected in each bruised area. A lethal amount had been injected directly into the liver.

Detectives returned to Long Island hoping to find the needle and syringe in the Friedgood home. While detectives searched the first floor rooms, Dr. Friedgood was able to whisper to Esther, "Upstairs! File cabinet, bottle, syringe—top drawer."

Esther looked in her father's eyes. The surgeon held her stare. A father was to be obeyed and protected. Esther calmly strolled upstairs to her father's study. From the top drawer of the filing cabinet she extracted two bottles and a syringe and placed them in a paper bag. Trembling, she lifted up her dress and put the death kit inside her underpants.

Back downstairs Esther told her sister Toba her terrible secret. After the detectives left she showed her sister the contents of the paper bag. One of the bottles was marked demerol. The Friedgood children discussed their father's plight and his obvious guilt with their husbands that night. Meanwhile, Esther had hidden the syringe and bottles in an upstairs closet. She revealed their location only to her father. The death kit promptly disappeared from its hiding place.

A few days later Dr. Friedgood forged his wife's signature to documents dated prior to Sophie's death, giving him access to several of her safety deposit boxes. He forged authorization to sell several of her securities as well. In all, he gathered up $600,000 in cash, negotiable bonds, and jewelry. He then called his daughter Debbie and told her that his doctor had advised him to get away for a few days. No amount of questioning could get him to reveal his destination. Debbie's husband, realizing that his father-in-law's mistress was in Denmark, was convinced that Friedgood was about to skip. He called the police.

Teams of detectives manned the phones calling Kennedy Airport, canvassing overseas flights. There was no one named Friedgood, or anyone matching Friedgood's description flying to Denmark, but the airport computers did come up with a Friedgood flying to London.

Just as Dr. Friedgood's plane was about to take off, it was instructed to return to the terminal. Friedgood was taken off the plane. A search of his luggage revealed the $600,000 horde. Dr. Friedgood was arrested and charged with the murder of his wife. At his murder trial, his children testified against him. In January 1977 he was found guilty and received the maximum sentence possible —25 years to life imprisonment.

In 1978 New York State passed a law known as the Dr. Friedgood Bill, making it illegal for doctors to sign death certificates for relatives.

DR. LEWIS GRAHAM 1980

EVERY major city has at least one infamous domestic murder which becomes indelibly associated with that city. Who can forget the case of Charles Stuart of Boston, who killed his pregnant wife and then staged an attack on himself, or Toronto's Peter Demeter, who orchestrated his wife's murder while he was away from their home?

Shreveport, Louisiana, was the locale of one such crime. The murder took place on March 31, 1980 at 4:12 a.m.

Dr. Lewis Graham and his wife Kathy lived with their three children; David, 16, Eric, 12 and Katie, 8, at 2033 South Kirkwood Dr. in a fashionable section of Shreveport. Lewis had come into an inheritance which gave him an income of $100,000 a year. This was in addition to his substantial salary as a professor of biochemistry and a researcher at the Louisiana State University Medical Centre.

The Grahams were in the process of constructing a custom built home when, in a few short minutes, in the wee hours of a Monday morning, all their lives were to change forever.

Here's what happened according to Dr. Graham. He and his wife went to bed as usual on Sunday night. The children were asleep in their rooms. The first indication that anything was amiss occurred when Lewis thought he heard a scream, which was immediately cut off. At the same time he was thrown from his bed onto the floor. In the pitch blackness, he was picked up, jostled momentarily and thrown against the bedroom wall. He felt a burning sensation in his side.

Lewis fell to the floor, losing consciousness. He didn't know how much time elapsed before he regained consciousness, but when he woke up he turned on the bedroom light. There was Kathy with her head horribly crushed. A quick glance told Lewis that his wife was dead, but to make sure, he touched her body, which was clammy cold. He left the bedroom, locking the door behind him. Lewis claimed that he didn't want his children to see the terrible sight of their mother's body. He proceeded past his children's bedrooms down to the kitchen, where he located a telephone book and called police. He told police his house had been broken into, his wife was dead and he was hurt.

Lewis then called his neighbor, Carolyn Godwin, whose husband happened to be out of town. She called another neighbor, Jerry Siragusa, who rushed over to the Grahams' immediately. The children were awakened and taken across the street to Carolyn Godwin's home. Then the police arrived.

That was the story Dr. Graham told police minutes after he discovered his wife's body. It is substantially the same story he tells today.

Detectives descended on the Graham residence. Right from the outset, this was no ordinary crime. The Grahams had been married for 17 years. Lewis was a highly regarded professional with an IQ of 132. No hint of scandal had ever come close to touching any member of the family.

Immediately after police arrived at the scene, Lewis was taken by ambulance to hospital. He had a superficial knife wound in his side. The cut took only one stitch to close. Back at the Graham residence, police found pry marks at the back door. On the floor was a blood-smeared short-handled sledge hammer and a six-inch long hunting knife. Both items belonged to the family.

Initially it appeared that intruders had entered the house, picked up Lewis' knife and grabbed a sledge hammer from a closet before making their way upstairs. Kathy, a light sleeper, might have awakened, screamed and been struck a vicious blow with the sledge hammer. When she moved, she was struck again. Lewis, by his own statement, was dragged from the bed, stabbed and thrown across the room.

Lewis attracted suspicion to himself by his demeanor. He never shed a tear at any time over his wife's death. Carolyn Goodwin and Jerry Siragusa confirmed that he had not acted like someone who had just lost his wife. Detectives listened to Lewis' story over and over. It didn't sit well. After regaining consciousness, would a father walk by his children's rooms without looking in on them? After all, they too could have been attacked by the assailant or assailants. Lewis had no explanation for his illogical behavior.

Then there was that superficial wound. How fortunate. The knife blade only pierced the skin. Children who fall off bicycles and cut themselves often suffer worse injuries than the one supposedly inflicted by desperate men who had just killed a woman with a sledge hammer.

Detectives dug into every aspect of the 39-year-old biochemist's life. They discovered that he was in the midst of a prolonged affair with his lab assistant, Judith Carson. Judith was a married woman with two children. She explained to police that she and Lewis had worked together for years. He had told her that he and his wife were having marital difficulties. Apparently, over the years, Kathy's talkative, outgoing nature had gotten on Lewis' nerves. He had the reputation of being a quiet introvert.

Judith and Lewis worked together in the confined area of a laboratory. They never dated at night, nor did they ever spend a weekend together. About every two weeks, they would rent a motel room at noon hour. Police wondered if Lewis' love for Judith Carson was a motive for murder.

The case against Dr. Graham was totally circumstantial and far from airtight, but three months after the murder he was arrested and charged with killing his wife. He was released within an hour after posting a $200,000 bail bond.

On July 21, 1981, Dr. Lewis Graham stood trial for murder in one of the most publicized trials ever to take place in Louisiana. The details of the night Kathy Graham was killed with a sledge hammer were meticulously rehashed. Most damaging to the accused man was the evidence given by Prof. Herbert MacDonell, a criminologist whose specialty was bloodstain pattern analysis. He was the director of the Laboratory of Forensic Science in Corning, N.Y.

MacDonell had examined the T-shirt worn by Graham in bed on the night of the murder. He related to the jury that he had found hundreds of pinpoint blood spots on the back of the T-shirt. The blood was type A, Kathy Graham's blood type. According to the accused man's story of events which had taken place that night, it was literally impossible for him to have gotten those spots on the back of his shirt. MacDonell explained that the spots were entirely compatible with blood being cast off a sledge hammer being held by Graham as he lifted it over his head and struck his wife.

MacDonell also examined blood found on the front of the T-shirt. This blood was type O, Lewis' blood type. The stain formed a straight line of blood, probably made when the accused partially wiped blood from his own knife.

MacDonell's evidence had a profound effect on the jury. They returned a verdict of guilty of second-degree murder. The convicted man heard the judge's devastating words, "It is the judgment of this court, Lewis Graham, that you are hereby sentenced to life imprisonment at hard labor, without benefit of parole, probation or suspension of sentence."

Such are the vagaries of the justice system that the harsh sentence passed down by the judge would later be drastically altered. On February 3, 1988, outgoing governor Edwin Edwards commuted Graham's sentence to 25 years imprisonment. Nearly two years later, he became eligible for parole. On December 9, 1992, Dr. Lewis Graham was granted a parole and was set free after serving 11 years in prison.

DR. KEN TAYLOR 1984

WHEN Dr. Ken Taylor married for the third time, he would have to be placed in the high-risk category as far as faithful, long lasting husbands are concerned. The successful dentist, by his own admission, had always been a ladies' man.

Ken met wife number one when he was a 21-year-old dental student at Indiana University. He entered a naval program which provided him with a scholarship for his entire education. In return, upon graduation, he was compelled to serve several years in the navy.

When Mrs. Taylor became pregnant, Ken was not overjoyed. For one thing, he didn't like the responsibility of another mouth to feed. In addition, a new baby might curtail his favorite hobby, that of bedding down with anything in skirts. Ken picked a most inopportune time to leave his wife. It was in June 1974, in her ninth month.

The reason for the separation was a beautiful stewardess. In October, Ken's divorce became final. He married the stewardess in December. Fast worker, our Ken.

The marriage wasn't a successful one. One night, while wife number two was asleep in bed, Ken attacked her. He jumped on her and held a chloroform sponge over her mouth. The poor woman struggled and managed to roll off the bed, but Ken again pounced on her. Then, as suddenly as the attack had started, it abruptly stopped.

Ken begged for forgiveness. When his wife suggested he receive professional help, he agreed and placed himself in the care of a navy psychiatrist. The doctor believed that Ken was a maniac. He suggested that the police be called into the case and that the dentist be charged with attempted murder. Mrs. Taylor took the doctor's advice and Ken was charged.

Another navy doctor attributed Ken's action to his mixing alcohol and drugs. He felt that the violent incident was an isolated one. The charge of attempted murder was dropped. Ken received counselling and the Taylors' marriage seemed to get back on the rails.

In 1979, wife number two gave birth to a baby girl. Ken didn't exactly advertise the fact that he still took dope, drank excessively and slept with every dental assistant at the naval base.

In July 1980, Ken finished his navy service. He opened a dental clinic in Brooklyn, which prospered from the beginning. The practice was so lucrative that other dentists and hygienists were hired. One fine day, Teresa Benigno, a gorgeous young thing, applied for a job as a hygienist. Ken took one look at her figure, face and accessories and knew immediately that Teresa was for him. After a few months of his undivided attention, Teresa became Ken's lover.

Back home, wife number two noticed the tell-tale signs—the missed appointments, the lack of attention, the handkerchiefs smeared with lipstick. The marriage disintegrated and finally, in 1983, was dissolved.

On July 10, 1983, Teresa became wife number three. The happy couple honeymooned at a luxury resort in Acapulco. When Teresa's parents travelled to Kennedy Airport to pick up the newlyweds at the conclusion of their honeymoon, there was no sign of Ken or Teresa. Next day, Mr. Benigno called the Mexican resort and was amazed to learn that the Taylors had checked out three days earlier. A call to the American consular agent in Acapulco gleaned the information that Teresa had been seriously hurt and was in hospital. Dr. Taylor was in jail as the chief suspect in his wife's beating.

Within hours, Ken called his wife's family, explaining that robbers had attacked him and Teresa in their luxurious cottage. He had not been badly hurt and had just visited Teresa in hospital. His short stint in jail had been a farce. The Mexican police had insisted on a $500 bribe before releasing him.

Mr. Benigno and another daughter, Celeste, flew to Acapulco. They found Teresa in terrible shape. She had been badly beaten about the head and her throat had been slashed. She spoke to her father and couldn't tell him much about the attack, as she had not seen her assailants. Unfortunately, Mexican authorities had found cocaine in their room. That's why Ken had been taken into custody. Ken told his father-in-law that no charges had been laid against him. Two days later, the honeymooners were back in the United States. Teresa remained in hospital for another week. Slowly, she made a complete recovery.

The months which followed were the happiest of the Taylors' married life. When Teresa informed Ken that there would be an addition to the family, he appeared to be thrilled. Ken was ecstatic at little Philip's birth. But then his urge to play the field took over and once more Ken began leading a double life. There is some evidence that Teresa took to drugs during this time. Certainly the Taylors were willing drug users at private parties. Sometimes Ken admonished Teresa for being spaced out.

On November 12, 1984, Teresa failed to drop off Philip at her mother's on her way to work at Ken's clinic. Mrs. Benigno called Teresa at home, but received no reply. At about 10:30 a.m., Ken called. He told the family that Teresa had a bad drug problem. She had decided to go away by herself for a while to kick the habit. He had driven her to the airport in Newark and was taking baby Philip to his parents in Indiana. He explained that he couldn't care for the baby himself and didn't want to impose on his mother-in-law. He realized they would be worried and was calling from the road. He didn't know where Teresa was staying, but she had told him she'd be back in a few weeks.

The family couldn't help but think of the incident in Acapulco. Was it within the realm of possibility that Dr. Ken Taylor was some kind of maniac? They went over to Teresa's house and found such items as a half-baked cake and her keys. Unusual for a meticulous housekeeper, who never left the house without her keys. The Benignos reported their daughter missing to police. When Ken returned from the round trip to Indiana, he was questioned by the family and repeated the story he had told them on the phone.

Three days later, on November 15, Neil Griesemer was looking for beer cans along the highway at the bottom of Hawk Mountain in Pennsylvania when he spotted a sleeping bag beside the road. He pulled open the bag, exposing the body of a young woman. Mr. Benigno identified the body as that of his daughter, Teresa.

Dr. Ken Taylor was immediately suspected in his wife's murder. He told police of her movements on the night before she disappeared. According to Ken, Teresa had stayed up while he went to bed. He woke up at 4 a.m. Teresa was still up, spaced out on drugs. They had a long talk and she agreed that she had a drug problem. Later that same morning, at around 8 a.m., Teresa told him that she was going away to deal with her problem on her own. She preferred not to tell him where she was going. He drove her to the Newark Airport and never saw or heard from his wife until her body was found.

That was Ken's story, but police didn't believe it for a minute. When they found a bloodstained earring in the Taylors' garage which matched one found on Teresa's body, they were positive they had the right man. Faced with this incriminating evidence, Dr. Taylor broke down and confessed.

He told detectives that on the night in question he had come downstairs to find his wife strung out on drugs. But there was more. As he came down the stairs, he witnessed her sexually abusing their young son. Their eyes met. Teresa dashed into the sewing room, where the family's workout equipment was kept.

Ken placed the baby in a child seat. Teresa suddenly threw a five pound dumbbell at his head, striking him in the shoulder and sending him sprawling to the floor. She leapt on him like a wild animal. He clutched a bar and struck her on the head, at the same time pushing her off. Teresa rushed at him again. He swung the bar, striking her once more on the head. He could remember little else about the attack, but he did recall cleaning the house of blood, placing Teresa's body in the trunk of his car and dumping the body in Pennsylvania.

Dr. Taylor was arrested and charged with his wife's murder. His case was based on self-defence, but the jury didn't believe his story. Even if his story were true, Teresa was unarmed, so he couldn't have struck out in defence of his life.

Ken Taylor was found guilty of murder in the first degree and was sentenced to life imprisonment with no possibility of parole for 30 years. He is presently serving his sentence and has made four unsuccessful escape attempts since his incarceration.

DR. SAMSON DUBRIA 1991

DR. Samson Dubria was a rising young star at the Lyons Veterans Administration Hospital in Basking Ridge, New Jersey. The easygoing 28-year-old doctor was respected by both patients and staff. For as long as he could remember, he wanted only to be a doctor. While other young men enjoyed taking part in various sports and dating girls, Sam applied himself exclusively to his studies.

When Sam met 20-year-old Jennifer Klapper, all that changed. Sam was smitten. Unfortunately, Jennifer was not enamored with the young medic, although she respected him and appreciated his gentlemanly behavior. For the first time in his life, Sam made a concerted effort to ingratiate himself with a member of the opposite sex. To a degree he succeeded.

Over a period of months, Sam kept in contact with Jennifer. She made it perfectly clear that she already had a boyfriend and had no romantic interest in the doctor. Despite this rebuff, which would have discouraged a less persistent suitor, Sam continued to pursue Jennifer until he attained what at best could be called a platonic friendship with her. On several occasions, Jennifer invited him over to her home, where he met her parents. They too were duly impressed with Dr. Sam Dubria.

When Jennifer told her parents that Sam had suggested they vacation together, they told her to use her own judgment. The two would cross to the west coast, visit Sam's family in Los Angeles and continue on into Mexico. Jennifer liked the idea, but was perfectly blunt with Sam. She told him that she was thrilled with the opportunity to take an adventurous vacation, but wanted his assurance that sex was definitely not a part of the agenda. Sam agreed.

Off the pair travelled. They took in some of Los Angeles' tourist attractions and visited with Sam's parents. The doctor was a perfect gentleman and a delightful travelling companion at all times.

We now know that Sam secretly yearned for Jennifer, not in any platonic manner, but in a strictly sexual way. He wanted to possess her and meant to have her at some juncture on this vacation trip. He was just waiting for the opportune moment to present itself.

It was a steaming hot day in August 1991 when Sam suggested they stop at the All-Star Inn in Carlsbad on their way to the Mexican border. There would be plenty of time for Mexico in the morning. Sam looked at Jennifer in her skin-tight stretch pants and revealing blouse. It was time. He had come prepared. The chloroform was packed away in his luggage.

We will never know how Sam went about rendering Jennifer unconscious with his chloroform. She lay unconscious on the dingy motel room bed, while Sam ravished her in every way imaginable. It is quite possible that he didn't intend to kill Jennifer, but his intentions mattered little to her, for at some time during the orgy her heart stopped beating.

Dr. Sam Dubria fought an inner urge to panic. He attempted to remain calm and to avoid detection at all costs. Quickly, he replaced Jennifer's pants before calling 911 and shouting into the phone, "Come quick! My girlfriend—I think she is dead!"

Paramedics arrived at the motel to find the doctor attempting cardio-pulmonary resuscitation on the beautiful young girl on the bed. They rushed her to hospital, where she was pronounced dead on arrival. Sam was exhausted. Those who witnessed his distress had pangs of sympathy for the young man who had obviously fought so desperately to save his companion and had lost the battle.

No one suspected foul play. There were no marks on the body. The first minor mystery arose when a medical attendant who was preparing Jennifer's body for the post mortem noticed that her tight pants had been put on inside out. He mentioned the strange occurrence to his superior.

Dr. Sam returned to New Jersey. His colleagues sympathized with him. The entire affair had been a traumatic experience, but life goes on. Within weeks, he was his old quiet, confident self again.

In California, Dr. Leone Jariwala, who had performed the autopsy, was puzzled. Jennifer Klapper's heart, brain, lungs and all other organs had been perfectly normal at the time of death. Dr. Jariwala couldn't believe that a healthy 20-year-old woman could collapse and die in a hotel room with a physician present without their being some discernible cause of death. She meticulously checked and rechecked all organs which had been removed from the body. Blood samples were sent away for extensive and complicated toxicological testing.

It took two months, but finally Dr. Jariwala's persistence was justified. The tests indicated that Jennifer had been killed by chloroform. No wonder it had taken so much time to get to the truth. Authorities in California had never before encountered a case where chloroform had been used as a murder weapon.

Detectives flew to New Jersey, where they arrested Sam. So confident was the man of medicine that he waived extradition and accompanied the detectives back to California. Once there, he came up with a rather preposterous story. He told investigators that he and Jennifer had driven behind trucks transporting chemicals. The fumes had made him dizzy and no doubt had proved fatal to Jennifer. No one believed that one. When he was told there was evidence that Jennifer had taken part in intercourse immediately before or at the time of death, he quickly responded that their love-making had been consensual. Knowing that Jennifer had attached conditions before taking the trip, no one believed that one either.

In February 1993 Dr. Sam stood trial for Jennifer's murder. His ridiculous story of how Jennifer had come in contact with chloroform was dismissed by the court. Prosecuting attorneys proved that Jennifer had been drugged with a fatal dose of chloroform. The accused was the only one with her at the time and was the only one who could have administered the chloroform. In summing up, the presiding judge touched on the first hint that foul play had taken place. "It doesn't take much imagination. When taking the pants off, they are turned inside out and the sex act is accomplished. The pants are returned in haste and put on inside out."

Dr. Samson Dubria was convicted of murder, rape and administering an anesthetic during the commission of a felony. He was sentenced to life imprisonment, a term he is currently serving.

PART 4

CANADIAN MULTIPLE MURDERERS

FROM MULTIPLE MURDERERS AND MULTIPLE MURDERERS II

PART 4

ALLAN LEGERE

THIS is beautiful Miramichi country, tucked away off the beaten path in New Brunswick. Max Aitkin, who achieved fame and fortune as Lord Beaverbrook, was brought up in the north shore town of Newcastle. Ted Williams, the celebrated outfielder with the Boston Red Sox, was one of hundreds of sportsmen who sought out this small portion of paradise to fish the Miramichi River for the finest salmon in the world.

Well over 100 years ago, my grandmother and grandfather settled across the bridge from Newcastle in the adjoining town of Chatham. The young immigrants from Austria made Chatham their home for the rest of their lives. They had seven daughters and one son. One daughter, my elderly aunt Addie, still lives in the Chatham area. She was there through the seven months in 1989 when the reign of terror that was Allan Legere swept through the Miramichi.

As I sat in the kitchen of the homestead where my mother and my aunts played as children, it is difficult to imagine that an entire section of this province was caught in a grip of fear only a few short years ago. Back in 1989, as summer faded into fall and the leaves of the trees along the Miramichi burst forth in breathtaking hues of reds and golds, the entire nation would learn about a cruel killer, a man with an uncontrollable urge to mete out a terrible retribution upon innocent and vulnerable victims.

It all really began three years earlier, on June 21, 1986. John and Mary Glendenning finished the day's work in their general store in Black River Bridge, about 20 miles outside Chatham. They walked across the yard to their home, as they did most days. Although Black River Bridge is little more than a sprinkling of homes on a back road, the Glendennings, John, 66, and Mary, 61, had prospered over the 30 years they had been in business. Everyone in the region knew their store.

The Glendennings were reported to keep large sums of cash in their home. You wouldn't call it gossip. It was the sort of rumor that is harmless unless it is heard by the wrong types. Thirty-eight year old Allan Legere, Scott Curtis, 20, and Todd Matchett, 18, planned on stealing that money. Several different versions of what took place in the Glendenning home on that pleasant summer night have been told by the participants. There is no doubt about the outcome.

The three masked men crashed into the Glendenning home. By the time they left, John had been viciously beaten to death. Mary had been badly beaten, but survived the attack. The men made off with the Glendennings' safe containing some $45,000. The empty safe was later recovered.

The two younger men were well-known in the area as petty thieves. Legere, by far the most experienced criminal, was a professional break and enter man with a long police record dating back to his teens. The three men were soon traced, apprehended and speedily tried. Matchett and Curtis both pleaded guilty and received life sentences. Allan Legere went to trial, was found guilty of second degree murder and was sentenced to life imprisonment with no possibility of parole for 18 years.

The brutal murder and the ensuing trial caused a sensation along the Miramichi. Still, it was a local crime, a botched robbery. The perpetrators were behind bars. Life goes on. In time, Mary Glendenning recovered, although acquaintances tell me that even after this length of time she still suffers from the effects of the blows she received to her head.

On May 3, 1989, Allan Legere was escorted from the Atlantic Institution, a maximum security facility in Renous, N.B. to a Moncton hospital to have his ears checked. Although handcuffed and chained, Legere managed to shed the restraints, dash out of a bath-room past his guards and escape. Citizens along the Miramichi didn't know it at the time, but seven months of living in fear were about to begin. Twenty-five days later, they would learn of the rage within the soul of Allan Legere.

Annie Flam was a 75-year-old merchant in Chatham. She had been a fixture in her grocery store on Water St. longer than most people could remember. Annie lived with her sister-in-law Nina in a section of the premises attached to the store. Surely the two women deserved to be left alone to live out their lives in peace. But such was not to be the case.

On the night of May 28, Annie Flam was raped and beaten to death. Nina was likewise sexually assaulted and beaten. She survived the attack. The old Flam residence was set on fire. Nina, badly burned, managed to crawl downstairs, where she was rescued by a passer-by. She would later relate in vivid detail how the cruel man had entered their home and attacked them. Because the intruder had worn a balaclava, Nina was unable to describe his face.

Could Allan Legere have been responsible? It had been 25 days since his escape. Could he have made his way from Moncton back to his hometown? People remembered the Glendenning killing. There were similarities, yet it seemed too incredible. Why would a man facing years in prison if captured return to the area where he was born and was known by sight? There were reports of a shadowy figure being seen stealing food and slipping away into the woods. Allan Legere was certainly a suspect. Police poured into the area, but Legere, as if by magic, remained at large.

On October 13, the madman struck again, this time in Newcastle at the home of Linda and Donna Daughney on Mitchell St. The town fire station is on the corner of Mitchell and Jane Streets. It was a fireman who first spotted smoke emanating from an upstairs window of the Daughney residence. The fire was quickly extinguished before it could engulf the bodies of the two sisters. Linda, 41, and Donna, 45, had been sexually attacked and beaten to death. Police dogs and helicopters were used in the hunt for their murderer. There was little doubt they were looking for one man—Allan Legere, now a suspected serial killer.

Newsmen travel the globe to cover major fast-breaking stories. Rick Maclean, the 32-year-old editor of the Miramichi Leader, could walk the distance from his office to the Daughney home in under two minutes. It was a unique opportunity to cover the story, capture the fear of the community and get into the mind of Allan Legere.

Three years later, as we walked the short distance to the Daughney residence, Maclean explained that, in the towns and villages along the Miramichi, the average citizen had lived in a state of fear unlike anything they had ever experienced. Little else was discussed. Day after day, his paper featured the three recent murders with the built in anticipation that more would follow unless Legere was captured. At the time Maclean had no way of knowing that diagonally across the river from his office window, the killer would strike again.

Father James Smith was uncharacteristically late to conduct mass at the Nativity of the Blessed Virgin Mary Church. Parishioners gathered around the church, waiting for the 69-year-old priest to make his way across the yard from the rectory. Finally, someone peeked into the window of the rectory. Father

Smith had been beaten to death. But death had not come with any degree of speed. An examination of the murder scene and the post mortem revealed that the priest had been tortured. His face had been carved with a knife which hadn't penetrated more than a quarter of an inch. He had been repeatedly kicked so viciously that his entire rib cage had caved in.

Was no one safe from the madman who seemed fully capable of outwitting over 100 police officers? Jeeps sped up and down the Miramichi. Helicopters flew overhead, scanning the woods, while dogs led search parties through heavy brush. Many citizens installed floodlights in their backyards.

Father Smith's 1984 Olds Delta 88 was found abandoned near the train station 50 miles away in Bathurst. Authorities had correctly deduced that the fugitive had caught a train to Montreal. Perhaps he would never be apprehended. He might have been successful in crossing the border into the United States.

Allan Legere, now the most wanted man in the country, had checked into the Queen Elizabeth Hotel in Montreal. He was relaxing.

Seven days after Father Smith's murder, the urge to return to the Miramichi compelled Legere to take a train to St. John. It was a blustery cold night. Legere commandeered a taxi driven by Ron Gomke. As he stuck a sawed off .308 into Gomke's ribs, he announced, "I'm the one they're looking for. I'm Allan Legere."

The taxi driver did as he was told and headed for Moncton. Near that city's famed Magnetic Hill, Gomke, fighting the deteriorating road conditions, went off the highway into a ditch. Legere flagged down a passing motorist. By sheer coincidence, the driver happened to be Michelle Mercer, an RCMP officer on her way to her native province of Prince Edward Island.

Michelle stopped and offered Legere and Gomke a lift. Once they were headed for Moncton, the wanted man introduced himself and made Michelle aware of his .308. Although she was told to take the Chatham exit, weather conditions were so bad that Michelle missed the exit and ended up south of Moncton near Sussex.

Michelle Mercer's mind was racing. She pointed out to Legere that fuel would soon be a problem. He agreed and allowed her to pull into the Four Corners Irving gas station. Legere took the keys of the car and pumped gas into the vehicle. He then stepped the few feet inside to pay for his purchase.

Unknown to Legere, Michelle Mercer had a second set of keys. In a flash, she was speeding down the highway. Within minutes she located a phone and reported her experience. Roadblocks were immediately set up.

Legere cursed as the car vanished down the road, but he still had one more card to play. At the side of the gas station, he spotted Brian Golding working on his Mack flatbed tractor trailer. Never one to miss an opportunity to introduce himself, the wanted man said simply, "I'm Allan Legere. Let's get going." His rifle spoke volumes.

Near Newcastle, the big vehicle was spotted on a road never travelled by flatbeds. The police were notified and were soon directly behind Legere, lights flashing. Golding hit the brakes and jumped out. A few seconds elapsed before Legere stepped down from the cab of the truck. "I'm Allan Legere," he said.

The hunt was over.

Legere was charged with four counts of murder. He was positively linked to three of his victims through genetic fingerprinting, better known as DNA. This relatively new investigative tool was utilized by matching the genetic structure of Legere's hair and blood to that of semen samples found on his victims at the crime scenes. He was also identified as the man who had attempted to sell the Daughney sisters' jewelry in Montreal. In addition, he had left his bloody footprints in Father Smith's rectory.

Legere was found guilty of all four murders and sentenced to life imprisonment with no possibility of parole for 25 years. Since his conviction, he has been moved out of New Brunswick to the super maximum wing of the Ste Anne des Plaines prison outside Montreal.

Notorious Allan Legere will long be remembered along the Miramichi. Rick Maclean's book, Terror's End, is the definitive study of the drama which held an entire province in fear. Mary Glendenning often suffers from bad headaches as a result of the injuries she sustained from her beating. Nina Flam, who refuses to discuss her horrifying experience, moved to Halifax, but still comes back to visit the area she called home for so many years.

The Chatham business community has placed a globe in the new local library in memory of Annie Flam. Across from Father Smith's church, a home for the elderly has been renamed Father Smith's Manor.

As I left my Aunt Addie, she remarked, "I'm not afraid anymore." She could have been expressing the feelings of the entire Miramichi.

THE BLACK DONNELLYS

THEY came from County Tipperary in the mid-19th century to settle in a new land. Most made their way to Lucan, Ontario, about 14 miles north of London, to be with their own countrymen and to carve small farms out of the wilderness. It was a tempting proposition. Land could be purchased for a mere 13 shillings an acre. The new immigrants worked hard and they played hard.

One of their number was Jim Donnelly, a small, handsome man, who preceded his wife Johannah and son James to the new land. Two years after Jim's arrival, Johannah and her little son joined him in Lucan. A year later, Johannah gave birth to a second son, William, who was born with a club foot. In the years to follow, five more boys, John, Patrick, Michael, Robert, Thomas and a lone girl, Jenny, would bless the union.

Whatever reputation Jim Donnelly was to later attain, no one has ever claimed that he was a lazy man or that he lacked ambition. He settled on a piece of vacant land along the Roman Line, so called for the large number of Roman Catholics whose farms faced the road. The lot that Jim settled on belonged to John Grace. In 1855, Grace sold half the site to Michael Maher, who, in turn, leased it to Patrick Farrell.

Patrick Farrell wanted his land and therein lies the crunch. One must take sides when studying the saga of Jim Donnelly and his family. At every turn he could be painted either as a moody bully or a man justified in fighting for his rights and maintaining his principles. It is for the reader to decide.

The Irish had brought with them to the new world all the superstitions and feuds which had been passed down through generations back in Tipperary. Alliances were soon formed along the Roman Line. Neighbor fought neighbor. Disputes about land boundaries, livestock and rights of way were sometimes settled in court. More often, they were settled with fists outside Keefes Tavern, one of 12 watering holes which prospered in the small town.

Now Patrick Farrell wanted the land which he legally owned. There was Jim Donnelly. He and his wife, with the help of their small boys, had worked year after year, from dawn to dusk, clearing the land until it was a functioning farm. By all that was holy, it was his property. After all, others had squatted on land with little regard for legal formalities.

Farrell rode up to the Donnelly homestead. Jim came out of the barn, which still stands, 111 years later, grim witness to the events which were to follow. Farrell gave Jim an hour to get off his property. Words were exchanged. Blows were struck. Farrell towered over Jim and outweighed him by at least 40 pounds. Despite these inequalities, Jim is reported to have given Farrell a severe beating, as Johannah and the boys cheered him on.

Farrell took his case to court. The results of the court action didn't sit well with Jim Donnelly. Farrell was awarded the south 50 acres, while Jim was given legal title to the north 50.

The two men became blood enemies. Donnelly is said to have taken a pot shot at Farrell, who lived close by his farm. The shot missed, but Farrell was convinced that his enemy had attempted to kill him. He formally charged Jim with "felonious shooting." Just before New Year's 1856, Jim stood in the Goderich Courthouse and swore to keep the peace for one year and not to molest Patrick Farrell.

For the next two years, Farrell would claim that Jim was responsible for the string of misfortunes which befell his farm. Cows took ill and suddenly died. Farrell's barn mysteriously caught fire. Legend has it that it was Farrell who first coined the phrase `Black Donnellys.' As things turned out, he had good reason to be the originator of the derogatory description.

The second confrontation between Jim Donnelly and Patrick Farrell took place on June 27, 1857.

In pioneer days it was the custom to hold bees to clear land or raise a barn. The menfolk of the community donated their labor and animals to complete the work in record time. On that fateful hot day in June, several men were engaged at a logging bee on the small property of William Maloney. Some of the men brought jugs of whisky. Others relied on Maloney to provide the sauce for the day's labor. Pat Farrell was there. So was Jim Donnelly.

Oxen grunted and chains were pulled taut. Sweat stained men stripped to the waist. It was hard work, conducive to taking long deep slugs of whisky from Maloney's liberal supply.

According to reports of the events which transpired, it is certain that both Farrell and Jim were drinking that day. Most likely, Farrell was intoxicated. Each time the two men came close to each other, a nasty remark would pass between them. Jim and Pat teed off against each other, but were separated before any harm was done. Jim is reported to have taunted Farrell into continuing the fight. Big Pat grabbed the nearest weapon, a big handspike. The handspike, a three-foot-long piece of hardwood, was used as a lever to move large logs. It made a formidable weapon.

Within minutes, Farrell faced Jim, who had also picked up a handspike. Once again, cooler heads prevailed. The two adversaries were separated. It is reported that Pat fell to his knees, either from a push or from the effects of Maloney's whisky. At that precise moment, Jim raised his handspike and brought it down full force on Farrell's head. A few moments later, Patrick Farrell died. The logging bee came to an abrupt halt. Ashen-faced men looked at Jim Donnelly. Jim slowly left the scene and walked home.

Two days later, an inquest was held into Farrell's death. Jim Donnelly didn't show up, but the inquest jury managed just fine without his presence. They came to the conclusion that Jim had murdered Pat Farrell and a warrant was issued for his arrest.

Jim was nowhere to be found. He had fled, but not far. Tough Jim was hiding out in woods, which skirted the rear of all the farms along the Roman Line. Jim's older boys, James, 15, Will, 12, and John, 10, brought their father provisions. Sometimes Jim donned women's clothing and managed to work his distant fields while being sought by the law.

With the coming of winter and the severe windswept snows which swirled along the Roman Line, Jim had much more difficulty staying at large. Often he would spend the cold nights in a farmer's barn. There is some evidence that friends of the Donnellys allowed him to stay in their homes for short periods of time.

Still, life in hiding was no life at all. Johannah needed her man. Jim's children needed a father. On May 7, 1858, after being at large for a year, Jim Donnelly turned himself in to the local sheriff. Jim was tried, found guilty of murder and sentenced to hang.

Johannah Donnelly's nature wouldn't allow her to sit back while her husband's life was in jeopardy. She went about getting signatures on a petition for clemency. Some of the citizenry's hatred of Jim Donnelly was overcome by their sense of fairness. The death had taken place during a drunken brawl. Had Pat Farrell's wild swings connected with Jim's head, it would be Farrell who would be in the shadow of the hangman's noose.

Johannah wandered far afield to London and Goderich in search of men who knew her husband and regarded him quite differently than his enemies in Lucan. No less a personage than Attorney General John A. Macdonald, who would later become prime minister of Canada, commuted Jim's sentence from death to seven years imprisonment.

The cold iron gates of Kingston Penitentiary closed behind Jim Donnelly. Two months later, Johannah gave birth to Jenny, her only daughter.

One can only imagine the plight of Johannah Donnelly, with seven boys and a baby daughter to care for and a farm to run, living amongst many who hated the Donnelly clan with a passion. It is a tribute to this remarkable woman's resolve that she was successful in running and improving the farm during her husband's absence.

Seven years passed. Despite petitions, Jim served every day of his prison term. Now 48 years old, he returned to his family. His oldest son, Jim, was a young man of 23.

Jim Donnelly was back in town and life in Lucan would never be the same.

After Jim's return, every mishap which befell those who had testified at his trial seven years earlier was laid at the feet of the Donnelly family. The boys could scrap like hellions and there is no record of them ever losing a fight.

The Donnellys prospered. In the 1860s, they went into the stagecoach business. Will and young Jim discovered they had a knack for business. From all reports, their small line was the cleanest, most efficient of any in service in the area. Their competition, old Bob Hawkshaw, planned to retire. Will and Jim offered to purchase his line, but Hawkshaw sold out to John Flannigan. John was well liked and was confident that customers would patronize his stagecoach line rather than the Donnellys'. He was right.

Then, as if willed by the Devil himself, strange and unusual misfortunes befell Flannigan's stagecoach line. One day an axle broke, shaking up the passengers, severely damaging the coach and injuring a horse. Accident, maybe.

Sabotage, possibly. One of Flannigan's barns burned to the ground. Five days later, another Flannigan barn inexplicably caught fire. A stagecoach was burned beyond repair, but eight horses were rescued from the blazing building. It is even reported that on one occasion Flannigan found his horses with their tongues cut out.

Flannigan was understandably incensed at the Donnellys. Together with 17 men, who believed that the Donnellys had gone too far, he advanced toward the Donnelly farm. Will and James were preparing the stagecoach for the run to London. The unruly mob stopped in front of the Donnelly barn. Jim, Sr. and all seven sons looked at the mob and rolled up their sleeves. Jim, Sr. spoke first: "You gentlemen seem to be looking for trouble. If so, the boys and I will be pleased to oblige you."

Flannigan hesitated at the cockiness of Jim Donnelly. That hesitation was to cost him dearly. The eight Donnellys tore into the 18-member mob. Several witnesses observed the Donnelly boys as they clubbed and punched until their enemies lay prostrate on the ground or took flight. It was all over in 10 minutes, but the scene of the fearless family fighting against better than two to one odds remained indelibly etched in the minds of the witnesses, who never tired of telling the story of the epic battle.

To gain some perspective into the terror that was the Donnelly family, one has only to scan the criminal charges placed against them in the first three months of 1876. It is an impressive list of 33 charges, including assault, arson, wounding, robbing and shooting with intent.

Like all pioneer families, the Donnellys had their share of personal tragedies. Jim, Jr., is reported to have died of pneumonia. Like everything about the Donnellys, his death is shrouded in mystery. Some say he was shot to death and the shooting was kept secret by the family. Whatever the truth, he lies today in the country graveyard beside St. Patrick's Church. Later, brother Michael was stabbed to death in a barroom brawl. He is buried beside his older brother.

The feuds continued, fiercer and crueler than before. Word of the acts of terrorism and the law's inability to cope with the Black Donnellys slowly trickled to the outside world. Inside the tight pocket of pioneer Canada, desperate men had had enough. If the law couldn't tame the Donnellys, they would mete out their own brand of justice.

Jim Carroll was the catalyst which was required to ignite the local citizenry into action. Jim was born in the area, but had moved to the U.S., returning in 1878, at age 26. He was quickly made aware of the scourge known as the Black Donnellys. Big Jim let it be known that he had no fear of the Donnellys.

Robert Donnelly was hustled off to Kingston Penitentiary for taking a pot-shot at Constable Sam Everett. Everett was given a severe thrashing soon after Robert's conviction. He couldn't or wouldn't identify his attackers and, soon after, resigned his position.

Jim Carroll became a Lucan constable with the promise, "I will drive the Donnellys out of Lucan." In a way, he did just that.

On the night of February 3, 1880, grim-faced men met at the Cedar Swamp Schoolhouse. They called themselves the Biddulph Vigilance Committee. The stone schoolhouse had been the gathering place for socials and political meetings, but this was different. By lantern light, jugs of whisky were passed from man to man. Although the weather was not overly cold, the whisky was necessary for the task at hand.

Some say there were 31 men in attendance, some say over 40. It matters little. They walked down the road toward the home of Jim Donnelly. Other men joined them en route. Into the Donnelly home they marched. Patrick Grouchy Ryder was among their number. Grouchy's barn had been burned. After many postponements, Johannah and Jim, Sr., were to appear in Granton to answer to the charge of arson the next day.

Farming is a demanding occupation. Chores must be carried out and farm animals must be fed. To that end, the Donnellys had a neighboring youngster, 11-year-old Johnny O'Connor, sleeping over that night. Johnny was to take care of the animals the next day, while the Donnellys drove to Granton to appear in court. A niece, Bridget, was visiting from Ireland. Tom was at home with his parents.

Constable Jim Carroll led the group. He sighted Tom Donnelly asleep in a tiny bedroom off the kitchen. Jim snapped handcuffs on his wrist. Tom awoke with a start and cried out, "What the hell!" Carroll responded, "You're under arrest."

The noise woke up Johannah, who in turn woke up her niece Bridget. Jim, Sr., was sleeping with Johnny O'Connor. He pulled on his trousers and joined the rest in the kitchen. He saw his son in handcuffs, "What? Tom, are you hand-cuffed?" he asked.

"Yes," Tom replied. "He thinks he is smart." By candlelight, Jim, Sr., went back to the bedroom for his coat. Johnny O'Connor had been using the elder Donnelly's coat for a pillow. Now he held it out for Jim, who returned to the kitchen.

There, in the eerie glow of the candle, Johnny O'Connor's eyes met Jim Carroll's. Later, Johnny would state there was no way Carroll was unaware of his presence. In light of future events, it is a minor mystery that Johnny O'Connor's life was spared.

Did the men intend only to beat up the Donnelly clan? Bill Ryder, a great-great-great nephew of Grouchy Ryder, says, "I believe the intent was to rough up the Donnellys, but something went wrong and, once started, the mob got out of hand."

All but one of the inhabitants of the house that night were beaten and clubbed to death. Tom Donnelly fell. So did his parents and so did his cousin Bridget. Johnny O'Connor, trembling with fear, hid under a bed, where he could see a shovel being brought down time after time on a Donnelly skull.

The house was set ablaze and in moments the mob was gone. Johnny O'Connor escaped from the burning house and ran barefoot to a neighboring farm. The mob's work wasn't completed. Down the road they marched to the home of Will Donnelly. It was his brother John who answered the door. Silhou-etted in the light of the doorway, he was an easy target. John died moments after being shot. The mob thought it had killed the hated Will. Now the carnage came to an end. The men dispersed, leaving five members of the one family dead in their wake.

Next day, word of the tragedy spread. Initially, 13 men were held on suspi-cion. Of these, six were charged with murder—James Carroll, John Kennedy, Martin McLaughlin, Thomas Ryder, James Ryder and John Purtell. The six men were lodged in the jail behind the London courthouse.

On January 24, 1881, Jim Carroll stood trial for the murder of Johannah Donnelly for the second time. This time, he was found not guilty. Because the case against Carroll had been so strong, it was felt that it would be futile to try any of the remaining men. They were all released from custody. No one has ever been convicted of the five murders which took place in the wee hours of the morning of February 4, 1880.

In the years which followed the massacre of the Donnelly family, members of the Vigilance Committee were buried in the little graveyard beside St. Patrick's Church. Ironically, they rest forever beside the Donnelly family, victims of Canada's most infamous crime.

ALBERT GUAY

THREE times a week, a Quebec Airways flight left Montreal for Seven Islands, with stops at Quebec City and Baie Comeau. It was so punctual and reliable that people along the route used to set their watches by the roar of the engines.

On September 9, 1949, Patrick Simard was fishing for eels near his home at Sault-aux-Cochon, Quebec. He glanced up, idly following the flight of the Douglas DC-3 as it approached Cap Tourmente. Then he heard a loud explosion, and as he watched in horror the plane veered crazily to the left and went into a power dive, heading straight for the peak of Cap Tourmente. Simard ran through thick bush towards the crash; it took him an hour to get to the scene. Scattered among the wreckage of the aircraft were the remains of the passengers and their luggage. Surprisingly, there was no fire, but the ominous smell of leaking gasoline hung over the entire area. The propellers had been turned when the plane smashed vertically into the ground. There was no swath of torn trees, only the aircraft with its wings ripped off and its horribly mangled nose sticking into the earth.

The plane had held four crew members and 19 passengers. Simard checked to see if there were any survivors. Finding none, he started down the mountain for help. He met some men who were working on railway tracks nearby, and they took the news to St. Joachim, where it was relayed to Quebec City. Within hours Canadian Pacific Airlines, the parent company of Quebec Airways, had their investigating officials at the scene of the crash.

The left front luggage compartment showed signs of an explosion, and it was this explosion that had destroyed the control system of the aircraft, causing the disaster. They examined everything aboard the aircraft that could have caused an explosion. Items such as fire extinguishers and storage batteries were checked, but none of these was found to be the cause of the crash. The four crew members and 19 passengers had been killed instantly upon impact, but the lack of fire made identifying the bodies relatively easy, and the next of kin were quickly notified. Because of the explosion in the baggage compartment, the authorities concluded that they were dealing with a criminal case and not an accident.

On September 12, the entire matter was turned over to the RCMP. The Mounties were to be assisted by the Quebec Provincial Police and the Quebec City Police Force.

The left front compartment had been loaded in Montreal with cargo destined for Quebec City. It was completely emptied in Quebec City and reloaded with cargo destined for Baie Comeau. This was routine practice, and was employed to reduce unnecessary delay during the flight's many stops. The authorities realized that the explosive material must have been put into the left front baggage compartment at Ancienne Lorette Airport in Quebec City.

The passenger list of the ill-fated craft was closely scrutinized, as was the list of insurance policies taken out on the passengers' lives. A cursory check turned up nothing unusual, and the police decided to place all relatives of victims who boarded the plane in Quebec City under observation and to conduct an investigation into their private lives.

Undertaking the investigation from another direction, the police started with the plane on the ground in Quebec City and the left front baggage compartment empty. They questioned Willie Lamonde, the freight clerk who had been on duty on September 9, but he could recall nothing of significance except that several pieces of freight had been placed on the aircraft, in addition to the passengers' regular luggage. From company records the police were able to obtain the names of the senders and prospective receivers of all the air freight shipments, and they set about checking every name on the list. This approach bore fruit with the discovery of a 28-lb. parcel sent by Delphis Bouchard of St. Simeon, Quebec, to Alfred Plouffe, 180 Laval St., Baie Comeau. Neither sender nor addressee existed, so it seemed reasonable to assume that someone had walked up to Willie Lamonde with a bomb and shipped it air freight to Baie Comeau.

The police begged Willie to try to remember who had given him the parcel. Willie's memory was now jarred by names and addresses he could relate to, and he came up with a mental picture of the person who had given him the bomb. He said it was a fat woman who had come to the airport by cab. He remembered this because the cabbie had carried the parcel to the scale for the fat lady. The cost of shipping the 28-lb. parcel to Baie Comeau was $2.72, which she paid to

Willie, who gave her a receipt. The police started the tedious task of questioning every cabbie in Quebec City, and almost immediately they found the right man.

Paul Pelletier, who worked for the Yellow Cab Co., had picked up the fat lady on September 9 at the Palais Railroad Station. He described her as middle-aged and overweight, with dark hair and eyes. She didn't say one word to him on the trip to the airport, but because she was returning to the city with him, he had carried the parcel to the freight clerk. When they returned to the city she got out of his cab at the rear of the Chateau Frontenac Hotel, and Pelletier recalled seeing her walk toward Lower Town, the older section of the city.

Then, upon checking the relatives of victims, the police for the first time heard the name of Albert Guay, whose wife Rita had died in the crash. Albert had been fined $25 for causing a scene some months previously in a restaurant, where he had brandished a revolver at a waitress named Marie-Ange Robitaille. It was a small and relatively insignificant incident, but one that couldn't be overlooked by the authorities. The girl still worked at the restaurant and the police decided to question her about her relationship with Guay. The detectives confronted an attractive, shapely young girl who would have caused heads to turn anywhere.

Marie-Ange openly admitted knowing Albert Guay, and when asked if Guay had anything to do with a fat middle-aged woman, she immediately gave the police the name of Marguerite Pitre who lived at 49 Monseigneur Gauvreau St. The police stationed the cab driver outside Marguerite Pitre's house, so that when she came out he would be able to identify her. On September 20, a taxi drove up and Pelletier had a good look at Marguerite as she got in. He positively identified her as the lady he had driven to the airport on September 9. Marguerite had taken an overdose of sleeping pills, and the taxi had been summoned to rush her to Infant Jesus Hospital. The police decided to arrest her as soon as she was released.

Who was this strange woman? What circumstances tied her to the young waitress, Marie-Ange Robitaille? How was Albert Guay connected to the two women?

The tangled plot started to unfold. Albert Guay was born in 1917 to a working-class family. As a child, he liked games in which he played the part of a ship's captain or commander of great armies, and always had illusions of power and wealth. By the time he was 22, he was working in a war plant and selling watches as a sideline.

During the war he married the former Rita Morel, and when peace came he gravitated to the jewelry business as a full-time occupation, opening up a store in Seven Islands, Quebec. In 1948, he closed his store and opened a shop on St. Sauveur St., which he soon owned.

Guay was having a prolonged affair with Marie-Ange. It is almost certain that Rita Guay had knowledge of the affair, but being wise to the ways of men with wandering eyes, she figured Albert would have his fling, tire of the waitress, and return to her. Marie-Ange had lived in a room in Marguerite Pitre's house, and it was here that Albert Guay would come to make love to his mistress, with Marguerite's complicity. The heavy-set Marguerite, who always wore black, and as a result came to be known as The Raven, had met Guay during the war when they both worked in the same munitions plant. Another member of The Raven's family, her crippled brother Genereux Ruest, worked for Guay as a watch repair-man in his jewelry shop.

The Raven had come under Guay's influence when she started borrowing small amounts of money from him during the war. This led to more and more loans until finally she was compelled to comply his every wish. When first questioned, the Raven at first denied taking the bomb out to the airport, but when faced with the cab driver she confessed that she had delivered the explosives. Once started, the Raven continued to sing. She admitted getting in debt to Albert, until finally she owed him $600. He always demanded favors of her, and when Marie-Ange was only sixteen she had set the good-looking young girl up in her own apartment at his insistence.

The Raven claimed that Guay promised he would forget the debt if she would get him some dynamite, knowing that her neighbor had acquaintances in the construction business who had access to explosives. The Raven told her neighbor that if she could get her hands on some dynamite it would be her chance to get out of Albert's clutches once and for all. Guay had told the Raven that he needed the dynamite for a friend who was removing tree stumps. In the end the Raven succeeded in obtaining ten pounds of dynamite and 19 blasting caps.

On September 23, Albert Guay was arrested and taken into custody. He admitted everything except murder. Albert said he knew the Raven very well because she brought him leads for watch sales, and her crippled brother worked for him. He even admitted having the affair with Marie-Ange, but claimed it was over before the plane crash. Through it all he swore he loved his wife dearly, and that the Raven was a barefaced liar.

The police descended on Genereux Ruest's workshop to search it for any evidence that a bomb had been manufactured there. They found an insignificant piece of corrugated cardboard coated with black deposits. It was the only thing in the shop that looked unusual in any way. The cardboard was rushed to a Montreal laboratory for testing. In the lab, blasting caps were exploded using a piece of corrugated cardboard as a shield. The explosions left black deposits on the cardboard matching the ones on the cardboard taken from Ruest's workshop. The same tell-tale black deposits appeared on the inside of the left front luggage compartment of the downed aircraft.

Armed with this incriminating evidence, the authorities faced Ruest. Finally he confessed that he had constructed a time mechanism, and that he and Albert had experimented with setting it off. He claimed Albert had brought him all the materials for the bomb, and that he had no idea that Guay planned to use it for anything other than clearing stumps. He said he was afraid to volunteer the information earlier because he thought the police would believe he knew of Guay's intentions.

Meanwhile, Marie-Ange Robitaille added her chapter to the increasingly well-documented life and loves of Albert Guay. She said she had met Guay at a dance in 1947, when she was 16 years old. She thought he was a glamorous man-about-town in the jewelry business, and even though she knew he was married, it wasn't long before they were having sexual relations. Rita Guay had even complained to the girl's parents, but Marie-Ange moved out of her parents' home and into a spare room that the Raven provided. Several times she tried to break up with Guay, but each time he went after her and brought her back. There is little doubt that Marie-Ange was physically attracted to Guay, but in the end she could see no future with a married man. She had only seen Guay once after the crash. On the occasion he had begged her to come back to him, pleading that since his wife was now dead, no obstacles stood in their way. She told him the affair was over, and she now told police she knew nothing about the bomb.

Despite the incriminating statements of the Raven and her brother, Albert steadfastly maintained his innocence. On February 23, 1950, Albert Guay stood trial for murder. The jury took only 17 minutes to find him guilty, and he was sentenced to death by hanging. Once in Bordeaux Jail awaiting death, he made a full confession, implicating the Raven and her brother as willing accomplices. Both had been motivated by money he had promised them from a small insurance policy he had taken out on his wife's life, and both had been well aware that he planned to blow up the aircraft.

Albert Guay was hanged on January 12, 1951, and Genereux Ruest followed him to the gallows in 1952. The Raven was hanged in 1953.

DALE NELSON

MANSON, Bundy, Gacy, Dahmer—the names are synonymous with horrific acts perpetrated by evil men. Their exploits have been recounted in books, on TV and in movies. Yet one of Canada's most terrifying tales of wanton murder has gone relatively unnoticed by the country's media. The unspeakable deeds of Dale Nelson took place during the course of one night in Creston Valley, a rather isolated area in southeastern British Columbia.

Dale was in his early 30s back in 1970 when the crimes took place. A logger by profession, he lived with his wife, Annette, and their three children in a modest house along Corn Creek Rd. Dale was a good husband and a kind, caring father, except when he drank with his logging buddies in Creston. On those occasions, he would become aggressive, rowdy and unpredictable. Earlier that same year, Dale had gone into a deep depression and had made an unsuccessful attempt to take his own life. He underwent a psychiatric examination, after which he was returned to his family.

Dale's main hobby was hunting. He was an expert marksman in an area where hunting is the chief diversion from the back-breaking labor of the logging and farming industries. Everyone in the area knew Dale. Many were related to him. Sure, he had his moods and drank a bit, but there was nothing really wrong with Dale Nelson. When he was right, there was no finer fellow in the whole valley.

On September 4, 1970, Dale drove his blue Chevy into town. He picked up a six-pack of beer and a bottle of vodka at the liquor store and proceeded to the Kootenay Hotel, where he was well known. No one noticed anything unusual about Dale's behavior. He downed eight beers and chatted with friends, mostly about the upcoming hunting season.

After leaving the bar, Dale drove over to Maureen McKay's home to pick up his 7-mm bolt-action rifle, which he had previously loaned to her. He then made his way to Creston and purchased ammo for his rifle, as well as a further supply of booze from the liquor store. Even though he had been drinking on and off all day, Dale was in surprising control of his faculties. He strolled into Creston's King George Hotel and consumed another half dozen beers. Around 10:30 p.m., he was invited to one of the hotel rooms, where he and two friends drank more liquor.

The various people who crossed Dale's path that day had no way of knowing they would later be witnesses at a sensational murder trial. Clerks, drinking buddies and casual friends all thought Dale was in a good mood. He displayed no hint of what was to follow.

It was now past midnight. Ironically, the hunting season had opened moments earlier. Dale drove to the home of Shirley and Alex Wasyk. He knew that Alex was not at home, but had no way of knowing that one of the Wasyk children, Laurie, had accompanied her father. That left Shirley at home with daughters Debbie, 12, Charlene, eight, and Tracey, seven.

Debbie was alone in her bedroom when Dale Nelson came calling. She recognized his voice. After all, Dale was her cousin and often took her hunting. Suddenly, Debbie heard her mother scream, "No, Dale, don't!" The cry was followed by silence. Debbie sneaked out of her room to get a better view. She saw Dale lead Charlene into Tracey's bedroom, where her sister lay asleep. Debbie kept quiet and sneaked into her mother's room. She gasped when she saw her mother lying on the bed with her hands tied behind her back. A fire extinguisher lay close by. Trembling with fear, Debbie untied her mother's hands. When she heard Tracey scream, she picked up the fire extinguisher and dragged it to her room. She threw the extinguisher through the window and jumped out, just as she heard Dale at the bedroom door. Debbie ran to Maureen McKay's and hysterically blurted out her tale of terror. Maureen called the RCMP detachment in Creston.

The Mounties arrived at the Wasyk home to find that Shirley and Tracey had both been murdered. Shirley had been savagely beaten to death with the fire extinguisher. Tracey had been stabbed repeatedly. Charlene had been taken from the house, but had been set free. Dale's Chevy was still parked beside the house.

Fearing for the lives of Mrs. Nelson and other potential victims, the Mounties drove to the Nelson home and evacuated Annette and her children. In all, they were away from the Wasyk home for a total of 15 minutes. When they returned, they were stunned to find that Tracey's body was missing, along with

Dale's Chevy. Obviously, he had been hiding outside in the deep brush watching as the RCMP officers drove away.

Officers realized they were dealing with a man who had just taken two lives for no apparent reason. He was armed with a rifle, was a crack shot and was driving in pitch darkness through the countryside with Tracey's body.

Ray Phipps, 42, and his common-law wife, Isabelle St. Amand, 27, lived a few kilometres down the road in little more than a shack. Three of the children, Paul, 10, Cathy, eight, and Brian, seven, were Isabelle's by a previous marriage. Eighteen-month-old Roy was the child of Ray and Isabelle. It was Isabelle who called the RCMP detachment in West Creston. Among other disjointed phrases she whispered, "There's a man here with a gun!" The RCMP rushed to the Phipps home. They were too late.

Ray and Isabelle Phipps had both been shot in the head. The baby, Roy, had been shot as he lay in his crib. Paul and Brian had also been shot in the head. Eight-year-old Cathy was nowhere to be found, which the led the Mounties to surmise that Dale, who had taken seven lives in a few hours, had driven away with the little girl in his Chevy.

As dawn broke, Mounties from several neighboring detachments poured into Creston Valley. Systematic spot checks of houses in the area were conducted by the Mounties, who had no idea where Dale would strike next.

The following afternoon, Dale's vehicle was spotted from the air by the pilot of a Piper Cub engaged in the search. The unoccupied car was stuck in a ditch. Investigators found a bloodstained hammer on the front seat. The woods surrounding the Chevy bore grisly results. Parts of Tracey's body were discovered scattered throughout the immediate area.

Darkness fell on the valley with the monster still at large. Next day, the search intensified. Men stayed home from work. Rifles were taken down from racks. The hunting season was officially open, but the quarry on everyone's mind was Dale Nelson.

Late in the afternoon, Dale was located in the woods close to his own home. He offered no resistance. The question on everyone's mind was the fate of Cathy St. Amand. Without hesitation, Dale informed his captors that the girl was dead and pointed out the location of her body on a map. The RCMP found the child's body in the exact spot indicated by Dale.

From the time of his arrest, Dale underwent a series of psychiatric examinations. When he stood trial for the murders of Tracey Wasyk and Cathy St. Amand, there was only one question to be decided: Was Dale Nelson sane or insane? He had admitted committing all eight murders, but could give no reason other than his intoxication.

The B.C. jury found Dale sane and guilty. He was sentenced to life imprisonment.

Twenty-five years have elapsed since the madman ran amok through the peaceful countryside. Dale Merle Nelson has spent every one of those years in a B.C. prison. As you read this, he is still incarcerated. Should he ever be paroled, he will immediately be charged with the remaining six murders.

PART 5

ENGLISH MULTIPLE MURDERERS

FROM MULTIPLE MURDERERS AND MULTIPLE MURDERERS II

IAN BRADY & MYRA HINDLEY

THE story you are about to read involves two of the most reprehensible criminals who ever lived. The depths to which their depraved acts plummeted have not been equalled in modern times. If the retelling of this grisly true tale cautions just one parent to the dangers of allowing their children to accompany not only strange men, but strange women, then this effort will have been proven worthwhile.

At 12:40 p.m. on January 2, 1938, unwed Margaret Stewart gave birth to a son in Rotten Row Maternity Hospital, Glasgow, Scotland. For the first 12 years of his life foster parents brought up the lad as if he were their own child. Margaret, a waitress, visited her son Ian at every opportunity and contributed financially to his upbringing. In 1950, Margaret met Patrick Brady of Manchester. Recognizing her chance for happiness and escape from the slums of Glasgow, she married Patrick and moved to Manchester. Ian remained with his foster parents.

Ian was not your average child. There is evidence of his cruelty to animals while still in his preteens. He threw cats off five-storey buildings to prove that they didn't have nine lives. Once he crucified a frog and relished the sheer agony he caused the helpless creature. Between the ages of 12 and 15 he broke into several shops and houses, getting caught more often than not. Judges were lenient with the pale, lean lad who stood before them. Each time he was apprehended he was put on probation so that he could continue his schooling.

When Ian was 15, he left school and was promptly charged with nine counts of housebreaking. His foster parents gave up. They would have nothing more to do with the problem child. He was given one more chance by another lenient magistrate, and left Glasgow to live with his mother and stepfather in Manchester. He took his stepfather's last name, becoming Ian Brady.

Ian drank, couldn't keep a job and continued to break into houses. Apprehended again in the act, he finally met a magistrate who sentenced him to two years in Borstal. On June 9, 1958 Ian was released from prison, but nothing had changed. He sometimes worked in a Manchester fruit market, but still couldn't hold a steady job. In February 1959, Ian answered a newspaper ad for a clerical position. He got the job at Millwards Merchandise Ltd., a chemical supply company in West Gorton, Manchester. The job paid £12 a week. Ian kept to himself, opened the firm's mail and filed orders. At night he read about Adolph Hitler and the Marquis de Sade.

Myra Hindley was born in 1942 on Eaton St., Gorton, in the slums of Manchester. When she was four, her mother gave birth to a second daughter, Maureen. As the result of the overcrowding at Eaton St., Myra moved in with her grandmother a block down the street. She seldom saw her paratrooper father. Although her IQ was slightly above average, she was not a particularly good student. Myra left school while in her teens and drifted from job to job. Finally she managed to secure a position as a shorthand typist. The job paid £8.10 a week. It was with Millwards in West Gorton. Much of her typing was for a lean, pale, rather eccentric young man who fascinated Myra. His name was Ian Brady.

We will never know what catalyst was at work in the offices of Millwards which allowed two children of the slums to meet, become infatuated with each other and ultimately to become monsters living in the guise of human beings. The pair became inseparable. Myra purchased a mini-van, and since Ian didn't drive, it was she who chauffeured the pair to and from work.

Throughout the years Myra remained friendly with her younger sister Maureen, who joined Millwards in 1963. Now that the sisters were employed under the same roof, Myra confided to Maureen that she was having an affair with Ian Brady. When Myra and her grandmother moved to Wardle Brook Ave. in Hattesley, Ian moved in with them. The elderly grandmother kept to herself and never interfered with the machinations of Myra and her live-in boyfriend.

Slowly Ian's fascination with Nazi Germany began to rub off on Myra. She became enthralled with Irma Grese, the Beast of Belsen, and tried to emulate her heroine. Evenings were spent experimenting with sexual perversions, drinking cheap wine, and wandering the countryside outside Manchester in the mini-van. On their days off, Ian would indulge in his hobby, photography. Myra was a willing model, posing in the nude in every conceivable position or stance which Ian suggested.

Mrs. Sheila Kilbride gave her 12-year-old son John a peck on the cheek before he scampered off with a friend to attend the movies. The two lads left the movie theatre at 5 p.m. and wandered over to Ashton Market to see if they could perform some odd jobs for the tradesmen. It was getting late. John's friend caught a bus home. He last saw John talking to a friendly blonde lady. The lady was Myra Hindley.

Little John Kilbride never returned home. Police were notified and a comprehensive search followed. Months were to pass without the police uncovering anything approaching a clue as to what happened to the missing boy.

Ten-year-old Lesley Downey was excited this Boxing Day of 1964. Her mother had reluctantly given her permission to attend a fair being held only 200 yards from her home. Lesley was stepping out with neighborhood children. It all seemed so harmless. By 5 p.m., Mrs. Jean Downey became apprehensive when little Lesley failed to return home. She called on her neighbors and was startled to find out that the other children had been home for some time.

A mini-van parked ominously beside the fair grounds. Every so often the van circled the fair grounds, its occupants looking for a young girl. There's one! A little girl watched the bobbing painted heads of the wooden ponies on the merry go round. The mini-van came to an abrupt stop. A blonde woman approached the little girl and the pair began talking. It wasn't long before the blonde woman found out that the youngster had spent all her money. The blonde lady volunteered that she would be happy to pay for another ride and another after that. What 10-year-old child could resist such good fortune? Lesley Downey jumped on the wooden pony. Later she mentioned to the young lady that she'd better get home as her mother would begin to worry. The kind lady urged the child not to be concerned. She would personally give her a lift in her mini-van so she needn't be late after all. Lesley knew everything would be all right. Her mother had told her never to accept a ride with a strange man, but she had never said anything about a friendly, kind lady.

Lesley Downey jumped into the mini-van beside her friend Myra Hindley. In the shadows in the back seat, behind the unsuspecting child, lurked Ian Brady.

Lesley Downey was never seen again. A massive search was conducted by police which involved the questioning of 5,000 individuals and the distribution of 6,000 posters. Weeks turned into months, until gradually the investigation into the mystery of Lesley's disappearance wound down. Ten months after her ride in the mini-van her fate was to make headlines around the world.

When Myra's younger sister Maureen married David Smith, it seemed most natural for the two couples to become close friends. Especially so, since the Smiths moved into an apartment within walking distance of Myra and Ian. David Smith was not exactly lily white. He had been in several scrapes with the law and had an assault conviction on his record. David could never hold down a job for any period of time. He welcomed Ian's hospitality.

The two men were accustomed to staying up half the night drinking cheap wine, while Myra and Maureen went to bed. During one of these lengthy drinking bouts, Ian broached David with the idea that they rob a bank. He told David he had been planning such a caper for years. David seemed receptive, but Ian's scheme didn't progress beyond the planning stages.

The strange double life being led by Ian Brady and Myra Hindley erupted into violence and terror on the night of October 6, 1965. On that night, Myra's 77-year-old grandmother took a sleeping pill at 8:30 p.m. and retired for the night. Myra and Ian cruised the streets of Manchester in her mini-van. Myra parked the vehicle near Central Station while Ian took a stroll. He soon returned with 17-year-old Edward Evans. Edward was a homosexual who had gladly accepted an invitation to return to Ian's home for a drink.

Once back at Wardle Brook Ave., Ian and Edward engaged in conversation while Myra called on her brother-in-law, David Smith. She convinced David that Ian had some miniature bottles he wanted to give away. David was delighted to accompany Myra back to her home.

Myra and David lingered in the kitchen admiring the miniature bottles. Suddenly a blood-chilling scream ricocheted through the house. Myra screamed, "Dave, Dave, come and help Ian!" Smith ran from the kitchen into the living room and into hell.

The only light came from a television set. In its eerie glow David saw Edward Evans, whom he didn't know, lying half on the floor and half on a couch. Blood was cascading from Edward's head onto the floor. Ian Brady stood over the fallen youngster with a bloody hatchet in his hand. As David watched in terror, Ian brought the hatchet down on Edward's head time and time again. Edward tried to crawl away from his tormentor, but with each vicious blow his actions became weaker.

Ian interrupted his murderous frenzy to nonchalantly comment to no one in particular, "This one's taking a while to go." Then he attached an electric cord around his hapless victim's neck, and pulled until Edward Evans lay still in death.

Ian was soaked in blood. The room looked like a slaughterhouse. Myra's clothing had been splattered with blood as well. David Smith had been an audience of one to a murder which had been orchestrated just for him. Ian commented rather sheepishly, "It's the messiest one yet. Normally one blow is enough."

At Ian's urging Myra went about cleaning up the room. Ian then changed his clothing. Upstairs Myra's grandmother slept through it all. Ian solicited David's help in carrying the body upstairs to a bedroom. Myra then put on a pot of tea and while David inwardly shuddered, she and Ian gloated over their recent victim.

At about 3 o'clock in the morning David suggested that he should head home, and was surprised when his companions bade him goodnight and let him leave. For Smith the whole evening had been unreal. He felt he had lived through a nightmare.

David Smith ran all the way home. He was so terrified of Ian and Myra that he waited three hours before he dared to sneak out of the house in order to call the police.

When detectives arrived at 16 Wardle Brook Ave. they were let in by Myra. They had been told by Smith that the living room would be spotless. A search of the back bedroom revealed the horribly mutilated body of Edward Evans trussed up in a plastic bag. Taken to a police station, Ian confessed to murder and at every opportunity tried to implicate David Smith. Three bloodstained carpets and the murder weapon were carried away by the police from the murder house. Later, a post mortem revealed that Evans had been struck with 14 blows to the skull.

As police proceeded to interrogate Ian, and later Myra, it became obvious that neither of them had met Edward Evans before the night of the murder. What was their motive for luring the victim to their home to kill him? Was it possible, as it appeared to be, that the murderous pair had timed the first blow to coincide with David Smith's arrival so that he would be a witness to murder?

The house on Wardle Brook Ave. was practically dismantled in an attempt to discover further clues. The investigating officers were successful in their endeavors. They found Ian Brady's notes. On one page they came across the name John Kilbridge, the little boy who had been missing for almost two years. There was more. Police discovered that Ian had checked two suitcases at Manchester's Central Station. They were recovered and found to contain pornographic pictures of Myra, but more importantly there were weird photographs of the lonesome moors outside Manchester. Some of the photos showed Myra staring straight down at the moors, as if standing over a grave in mourning.

Police searched for and found the actual sites depicted in the photographs. They dug up the bodies of John Kilbride and little Lesley Downey.

The case was one of the most amazing murder cases ever uncovered. Christened the Murders on the Moors by the press, it received worldwide publicity. The trial took place at historic Chester Castle on April 19, 1966. Due to the nature of the evidence, it was felt that the two accused could very well be assassinated in the courtroom. When it came time for them to testify they were protected by four-inch thick bulletproof glass on three sides. The pornographic pictures, the photos of the gravesites of the two children, and Brady's diary left little doubt as to the guilt of the accused pair.

One piece of evidence was so horrifying that hardened homicide detectives left the courtroom when this particular evidence was presented. Myra and Ian had lured little Lesley Downey to their home and recorded on tape her agony as they sexually abused and tortured her to death. The tape, which also had Christmas carols as background music to the horror they were inflicting on a 10-year-old child, had been discovered intact by police.

The Moors jury took only two hours and 22 minutes to find Ian Brady guilty of three separate counts of murder. He received three life sentences, while Myra received two life sentences for the murder of Downey and Evans. She received a further seven years sentence for harboring Brady in the case of Kilbride.

Ironically, Ian Brady and Myra Hindley escaped the hangman's noose. A few months prior to their trial capital punishment had been abolished in England. They both remain in prison to this day.

JOHN GEORGE HAIGH

JOHN George Haigh was born in Stanford, Lincolnshire, on July 24, 1909. It was a difficult time for the family; John Sr. was an electrical engineer and had been out of work for several months. Being deeply religious (the family belonged to an austere sect known as the Plymouth Brethren) they were too proud to ask for help from friend or neighbor.

Their affairs took a turn for the better when Haigh Sr. obtained employment at the Lofthouse Colliery. He was to stay in their employ for the next 25 years, but the new job necessitated a move to Outwood, a small village near the city of Wakefield. Here they moved into a comfortable house that came with the job.

The Haighs have come under close scrutiny in hindsight, but nothing detrimental can be conjured up about them. John and Emily were a deeply religious couple, and no doubt the severity of their beliefs sometimes spilled over into the upbringing of their only son. Young George was brought up to respect authority in the puritanical atmosphere of their home. His parents were kind and loving to a point, but at the same time they were harsh and stern when it came to the qualities they and the Brethren deemed sacred. Qualities such as punctuality and obedience were deeply instilled in the young lad, and most probably he chafed at the bit under the strict rules.

When he became a teenager he mastered the organ and piano. His voice was better than average, and soon he was singing in the choir in Wakefield cathedral. The proud and pious Haighs delighted in listening to their John sing—a bizarre picture of domestic bliss in view of the grim events that were to befall the family in later years.

For the moment, time passed pleasantly enough for the respectable Haighs and their respectable son. In his last year at school, John won a prize for studies in divinity. He became very interested in automobiles and at the age of 18 got his first job as junior salesman at Appleyards, a car dealership in Wakefield. This position lasted about a year.

Something of a loner, Haigh had no close friends or social life. He was a strange fellow, but no worse than many blokes struggling to make a living. He was of average height, had a full crop of black hair, was always neatly dressed, and generally made a good impression on those he met.

For the next two years John moved from job to job and showed a distinct lack of interest in bettering himself. Then, when he was 21, he and a partner started a business, a combination advertising agency and real estate firm in Leeds. For a short while it prospered, but then the tiny company fell on hard times. In order to keep the business going, John tried to obtain funds under false pretences. He glibly misrepresented some buildings he was trying to sell, and obtained advances based on his misleading claims. The police picked him up, but because it was a first offence the charges were dismissed.

He then joined a combination car rental and insurance company, again based in Leeds, and again did very well at the outset. In fact, he was remembered as the ace of the staff. Then the bombshell fell. John was making up and signing fraudulent contracts, and had been doing so since joining the company. He had actually started up a dealership to perpetrate his frauds. He would sell a non-existent vehicle from his garage, and send the hire purchase contract to the company he represented. They in turn would send Haigh's garage a cheque, and of course Haigh would receive his commission from the company for bringing in the business. He had to keep meticulous records in order to make sure that all his fraudulent contracts were being paid each month, as it obviously wouldn't do to have someone trying to contact one of the false names and addresses which appeared on the contracts. One wonders if Haigh's penchant for forgery wasn't practice for bigger and better things that were to follow.

When his frauds were uncovered, his father made arrangements to pay the company the money that was missing and keep his son out of jail.

Haigh moved to Leeds, where he met, wooed and married Beatrice Hamer. He hadn't known the 21-year-old Beatrice very long and the wedding was not a gala affair, as John's parents didn't approve of the union and the bride's parents were not thrilled with John. The young couple exchanged vows, without benefit of parents at a registry office on July 6, 1934.

Fifteen months later John was again charged with fraud. Unbelievably, he had managed to secure employment with a branch of the same company from which he had previously been fired. He even used the fraudulent contract scheme again. This time he received 15 months in prison. While he was serving this sentence his wife gave birth to their baby. John was never to live with his wife again, nor was he ever to lay eyes on his child; he abandoned them without a thought for their welfare. He received three months off for good behavior, and was out after serving one year. His parents, who by now were feeling the disgrace of their son's petty crimes, still stood behind their only offspring. He swore that he was turning over a new leaf and, like parents everywhere, they believed him.

Haigh's father introduced him to a man who owned a dry cleaning plant in Leeds. John told the truth about his past, and because of his sincerity, got the job. As always, things went well at first and John soon became assistant manager. Then, following his previous pattern, he was found to be promising people jobs for small cash considerations. He was fired on the spot, and moved on to bigger and better things in London.

He got a job as manager of an amusement park in Tooting. For twelve months he worked diligently for the owner, William McSwan, and his son, Donald. Then Haigh got that old urge to take another short cut. He left the McSwans and somehow or other hit upon a novel get-rich-quick scheme.

He would find the name of a legitimate lawyer in one town, and set up a law office in another, using the legitimate lawyer's name. He would then write to a selected list of clients that he was winding up an estate. This fictional estate would have some stocks that would be offered at slightly less than the current market price. For a small deposit Haigh would hold the stock for the proposed buyer. After he had accumulated enough cheques, and just before his clients started to demand delivery of the stocks, Haigh would close shop and set up in another town under another name.

On November 24, 1937, the authorities caught up with him. This time he got four years in Dartmoor. He received time off for good behavior and was released in 1940. In the summer of '41, he sold some furniture that didn't belong to him, for which indiscretion he received 21 months in Lincoln Prison. Upon being released in 1943, John moved to Crawley, where, with the help of forged references and educational documents, he got a job with a light engineering firm owned by a Mr. Stevens.

Stevens was so taken with Haigh that he invited him to stay with his family, and John was quick to accept his offer. The Stevenses had two daughters. The younger of the two was usually underfoot, but Barbara was another story. She was an attractive young girl, and she and John became good friends. Barbara, like Haigh, loved good music, and the two of them spent many pleasant evenings discussing various compositions and composers. Sometimes Haigh played the piano while the entire family sat around and listened attentively.

John left the Stevens home and employ after six months, had some personal cards printed that read "J.G. Haigh, B.Sc., Technical Liaison Officer, Union Group Engineering," and started a light engineering firm on his own in London. At first he did rather well, and in 1944 he moved to Onslow Court Hotel in South Kensington. He had devised another get-rich-quick scheme, and this time it included murder.

One day, John bumped into young Donald McSwan on the street, and the two men struck up a conversation about the good old days when they had worked together in the amusement part in Tooting. Donald was a pleasant enough lad, somewhat taller and more extroverted than Haigh. In the course of making small talk with Haigh, he mentioned that he had sold his share of the amusement park and had invested his money in some property. No doubt Haigh's interest in his old friend blossomed with this information, and they got along so well that Donald invited John over to his home to have a meal with his elderly parents. Haigh accepted this invitation, and the McSwans were genuinely happy to see him again.

Donald and Haigh became chums. They would meet every so often for a meal or just to pass the time of day. There is no doubt that the friendship was being cultivated by Haigh for his own devious purposes and, on September 9, 1944, these purposes became clear enough. Haigh invited Donald over to his workshop at 70 Gloucester Road, sneaked up behind his chum and hit him over the head with a piece of pipe. He later claimed that it was only then that he thought of the perplexing problem of getting rid of the body. The idea of submerging it in sulphuric acid came to him the next morning. He had been using the acid to scale metal, and it was "mere coincidence" that two carboys of acid were at hand.

The next morning Haigh placed the body in a drum. He then had the rather difficult task of taking sulphuric acid out of a carboy and transferring it, with the aid of a pail, into the drum containing the body. It was a tough job, and several times the burning fumes were too much for him and he had to go out for fresh air. Slowly but surely the drum filled with sulphuric acid, completely immersing the body. Haigh was sure that he was removing both the body and all traces of the murder. What he didn't know is that certain parts of the human body, as well as foreign materials, take varying lengths of time to disintegrate. Gallstones may take a very long time to disappear completely, and human fat will remain for years. Haigh was later to refer to this fat as sludge, and it was this sludge that proved beyond a doubt that a human being had been disintegrated in his workshop.

Haigh left his gruesome deposit and travelled to Scotland. Here he forged a letter to the older McSwans in their son's handwriting, saying that he had skipped to Scotland in order to avoid being called into the service. Donald had mentioned his reluctance to enter the armed serves before, so the old couple had no reason to be suspicious.

Then Haigh came back to his workshop in Crawley and poured the now dissolved Donald down the drain. With commendable patience, he waited 20 months before he invited the elderly McSwans to 79 Gloucester Road, on a warm July day, and killed them both with vicious blows to the head.

Conscientious monster that he was, he had now outfitted himself with the tools of murder. He wore a mackintosh when he struck the fatal blows, in order to keep the blood off his clothes. He had also outfitted the workshop with a stirrup pump to transfer the sulphuric acid from the carboy into the drum. With two bodies on his hands, he now had two drums to fill, and had taken the precaution of wearing a gas mask to protect himself against the fumes.

Having disposed of their mortal remains, he equipped himself with forged power of attorney documents and ingeniously went about liquidating and transferring all the McSwans' assets to himself. They had two properties, a bank account, and some stocks.

When questioned about the missing couple, he would quickly produce personal letters in the McSwan's handwriting. These letters gave plausible excuses for their absence and assured anyone who inquired that they were fine. In order to make legal contracts, Haigh would produce the necessary forged documents demonstrating that his dear friends had empowered him to make transactions in their names. No one became suspicious. The McSwans were an unobtrusive lot who had never harmed anyone. It was just their bad luck that they crossed the path of our friend, John George. Haigh realized about £4,000 from the deaths of the three McSwans, and went home for Christmas, satisfied and now prosperous, to his mother and father.

Throughout all his activities Haigh was writing and seeing his old girlfriend, Barbara Stevens. He treated her with the utmost respect, and at no time was he anything but a perfect gentleman to her. A deep and lasting friendship developed between them. He confided many of his innermost thoughts to her, and a strong attachment grew between the couple. Dashing John was the greatest thing that had ever happened to Barbara. The well-groomed, mature charmer was very different from the awkward local lads her own age. They took in symphonies and plays, and had intellectual conversations on a variety of topics. This rather weird relationship got to the stage of discussing marriage, but of course we know that Haigh was already legally married.

Not once did Barbara ever suspect that her boyfriend was anything other than he seemed.

At this stage of his career, John had money in his pocket, a pretty girlfriend, and had successfully murdered three innocent people.

At about this time he decided to give up his shop at 79 Gloucester Road, the scene of his three murders, and take up a new location on Leopold Road in Crawley. He told the company he rented the premises from that he planned to conduct several experiments there.

In September 1947, Haigh answered an advertisement offering a house for sale at 22 Ladbroke Square, London. The home belonged to Dr. Archibald Henderson and his wife, Rose. Haigh didn't buy the house, but soon became a close friend of the handsome and wealthy Hendersons. For six months he cultivated their friendship and stored away all the personal bits and pieces of information he could. When he knew enough about the Hendersons, it would be time to kill them.

Haigh picked his spot. He waited until they were on vacation. Then one day he dropped in on them at the Metropole Hotel in Brighton, and suggested that the doctor might care to visit his "factory" in Crawley. It wasn't much of a drive, so the doctor accepted. As soon as they entered the storeroom, Haigh shot Dr. Henderson in the head from behind. His now familiar, macabre procedure was set into motion. The stirrup pump transferred the sulphuric acid from the carboy into the drum, and Haigh scurried about the small building in his gas mask, much like a busy chef overseeing a gourmet feast.

He then rushed back to Brighton and told Mrs. Henderson that her husband had suddenly been taken ill. On this pretext she accompanied him back to Crawley. Once in the storeroom he shot her in the back of the head and proceeded to dispose of her body in the same manner as that of her husband. Haigh had taken the liberty of stripping both bodies of a substantial amount of jewelry before placing them in the sulphuric acid, and he later sold the jewelry for £300.

A few days after these murders, on February 16, Haigh showed up at the Metropole Hotel in Brighton. He had a letter, apparently signed by Dr. Henderson, instructing the hotel to give him the Henderson's baggage. Haigh had studied the doctor's handwriting and forged the letter.

Mrs. Henderson's brother soon contacted Haigh regarding the whereabouts of his sister and brother-in-law. Haigh told him the couple had had a very serious disagreement in Brighton and had decided to go away by themselves to work out their marital difficulties. To facilitate their rush to privacy, Haigh told Mrs. Henderson's brother, he had loaned the couple £2500. He added that, if they didn't return in sixty days, the Hendersons were to give him their car and home. He showed the brother a document to this effect, apparently signed by the doctor.

The brother didn't like this story one bit, and insinuated that if he didn't hear from his sister soon, he would go to the police. Haigh dashed off a forged letter from Rose to her brother. Cunning devil that he was, he had learned and stored away very personal family matters. He even copied her style of writing. This letter substantiated Haigh's story, and set Rose Henderson's family at ease for the time being at least.

Haigh followed up with postcards and telegrams, and set up a fictitious situation that was extremely believable. Finally, he forged a 15-page letter from Rose to her brother, postmarked Glasgow, Scotland. In the letter, Rose explained that due to personal financial problems, she and the doctor were going to South Africa. The letter carefully stated that the brother should settle the £2,500 debt to their friend, John Haigh, and take his advice in clearing up all money matters.

Scotland Yard maintains that this letter, in the exact style and handwriting of Rose Henderson, is one of the most brilliant forgeries they have ever encountered.

Rose Henderson's family now considered Haigh a dear friend who had done many favors for the doctor. It is estimated from Haigh's bank statements that he realized over £7,000 from the Henderson murders, but within a year he had blown the money on high living, and was looking around for more people to kill.

The Onslow Court Hotel caters mainly to elderly ladies who have been left considerable incomes. Most of the ladies are there on a more or less permanent basis. They pass the time sitting on wicker chairs, sipping tea and recalling days gone by. John Haigh, a permanent resident himself, was popular with his more senior associates of the opposite sex. In fact, one might say that many of them doted on him.

Mrs. Durand-Deacon was typical of the residents at the Onslow Court. Grey-haired and matronly, she could have been typecast for the part. She and John Haigh sat at adjoining tables at breakfast and often passed the time of day. Sometimes Mrs. Durand-Deacon expressed an interest in Haigh's engineering business. In fact, Mrs. Durand-Deacon had the bright idea that she wanted to manufacture artificial fingernails. Haigh, who had the patience of Job and would wait until his victims almost begged to become entwined in his net, expressed keen interest in this. He thought it might be a good idea if she were to accompany him one day to his factory in Crawley.

On February 18, Haigh was having lunch at the Onslow Court when Mrs. Durand-Deacon suggested that it would be as good a day as any to visit the factory in Crawley. Haigh thought the day was just perfect. Mrs. Durand-Deacon told her good friend Mrs. Lane that she had an appointment with Haigh later that afternoon.

Haigh left the hotel heading for Leopold Road, carrying a hatbox, which, unknown to the occupants of the hotel, contained a revolver. He entered his workshop with Mrs. Durand-Deacon. Two sides of the main room had workbenches running the length of the walls, and three carboys of sulphuric acid took up much of the available space. By five-thirty that same afternoon Haigh had gone through the preliminary portion of his macabre routine. He had donned his mackintosh, shot Mrs. Deacon, and placed her body securely in the empty drum.

Then, exhibiting a quirk that most normal people have difficulty comprehending, John Haigh got hungry. He slipped over to Ye Olde Ancient Prior's Restaurant in the square in Crawley and had poached eggs on toast and tea. This brief respite is well documented, as he chatted with the owner of the restaurant.

Then, back to work. He donned rubber gloves and gas mask, started up the stirrup pump, poured in the sulphuric acid, and poor Mrs. Deacon was well on her way to disintegration in the drum.

Haigh was back in London by ten o'clock that night. When Mrs. Durand-Deacon didn't show up for dinner, her friend Mrs. Lane was mildly alarmed. When her friend didn't show up for breakfast, she approached Haigh for an explanation. He had a story ready. He told Mrs. Lane that he had an appointment to meet Mrs. Durand-Deacon in front of a store, but she didn't show up. He waited for her for over an hour, then decided that she must have been delayed or changed her mind, and went on without her.

He left the worried Mrs. Lane and went to Crawley to check on the disintegration of Mrs. Deacon and pay a visit to his girlfriend Barbara Stevens. Both Barbara and her mother were to state later that on this particular visit John looked ill and had a hoarse voice. The hoarseness of the voice we can attribute to too many acid fumes, and the peaked condition could be laid at the doorstep of the inquisitive and annoying Mrs. Lane back at the Onslow Court Hotel.

Haigh should have known better. Surely one of the first rules in the mass murderers' handbook should be never, never mess with little grey-haired ladies. If either the victim or a friend of the victim's falls into this category, the entire operation is invariably ruined. Ladies of this ilk simply tend to spoil everything.

But let's get back to it. For the first time, one of his victims was missed by someone who didn't accept his glib explanations. The next morning was Sunday, and Haigh knew he would have to face the troublesome Mrs. Lane at breakfast. He decided to be aggressive, and was the first to inquire as to the whereabouts of Mrs. Durand-Deacon. He suggested they go and report the missing woman to the police. Haigh offered a lift in his car, and Mrs. Lane accepted.

The police took a routine report from Mrs. Lane, and a woman sergeant was dispatched to the hotel to question all the guests, including Haigh, who had been one of the last residents to see the missing woman. The policewoman came away from the hotel with a nagging suspicion about this glib Haigh fellow. It bothered her so much she emphasized her suspicions in her report to her superior, Division Detective Inspector Shelley Symes. His first move was to check Haigh's record, and of course, he uncovered his lengthy criminal past. Inspector Symes decided to pay him a visit. On Monday Symes interviewed Haigh and was given substantially the same story as his sergeant had received. He obtained a picture of the missing woman and circulated it to the press.

The next day, Tuesday, Haigh checked the drum in Crawley, and discovered that the body had completely dissolved. He poured the liquid sludge out into the yard. On Wednesday Haigh was again questioned by the police. Again he gave the same story.

By Saturday, the police had located Haigh's landlord and decided to break the lock of the "factory" door. Inside they found a revolver and ammunition. They also found documents belonging to Mr. and Mrs. McSwan and their son, Donald. Further documents were found belonging to a Doctor Henderson and his wife, Rose. They also found a dry cleaning receipt for a Persian lamb coat. Mrs. Durand-Deacon was last seen wearing such a coat. When it was retrieved from the cleaners, the detectives found that there was a patch on the sleeve. Inspector Symes searched Mrs. Durand-Deacon's room at the Onslow Court Hotel, and inside a sewing basket he found the same material that was used to patch the coat. Because of the publicity the case was receiving in the press, a jeweler came forward with jewelry sold to him by Haigh. Mrs. Durand-Deacon's sister identified it as belonging to the missing woman.

The police picked up Haigh outside his hotel and took him to Chelsea Police Station. Inspector Symes produced the fur coat and jewelry, and asked Haigh for an explanation. Haigh was starting to give a cock-and-bull story to his adversary when Symes was called out of the office. Left alone with Detective Inspector Webb, for some reason Haigh started to talk. The conversation bears repeating here. Remember, at this point no one actually knew a murder had taken place.

Haigh said, "Well, if I told you the truth, you would not believe me; it sounds too fantastic. Mrs. Durand-Deacon no longer exists. She has disappeared completely and no trace of her can ever be found again."

"What has happened to her?" asked Webb.

"I have destroyed her with acid. You'll find the sludge which remains at

Leopold Road. I did the same with the Hendersons, and the McSwans. Every trace has gone. How can you prove murder if there is no body?"

Webb got Symes back in the office, and in front of Haigh told him what had transpired. Haigh interjected, "That's perfectly true, and it's a very long story and will take hours to tell."

Haigh spewed forth every detail of how he killed not only Mrs. Durand-Deacon, but the McSwans and the Hendersons. These former murders were unknown to the police. He elaborated on his diabolic behavior by adding the fact that he had made a tiny incision in each victim's throat. From this incision, he claimed, he extracted and drank a glass of blood.

The authorities converged on Haigh's factory once more. Now they knew what they were looking for, and they found all the paraphernalia of murder. On the ground outside the workshop there was a greasy area where the drums of sludge had been emptied. After a minute examination of the yard (it was all actually lifted up and taken to Scotland Yard) some gallstones and a plastic denture were found. The denture was identified as belonging to Mrs. Durand-Deacon by her dentist. She had also suffered from gallstones. Tiny particles of eroded bones were also found.

There was no doubt about it. Haigh was what he claimed to be—a monster. Realizing that his one chance to live was to appear insane, he maintained that he had killed for a glass of blood and not for material gain. Due to the rather large sums of money he diverted to himself, this reason proved hard to swallow. When questioned by psychiatrists he told about dreaming of Christ with open wounds bleeding into his mouth, and claimed that in this way he acquired the uncontrollable urge to drink blood. No one believed the blood theory. It was obvious that Haigh was trying to feign madness.

While awaiting trial he received a letter every day from his mother. Barbara Stevens wrote to him and visited him often. She was the one exception in his life—the only one he had ever treated decently. In his way, Haigh seemed to be genuinely fond of her. She in turn shared his affection, and remained loyal to him until the last.

On July 18, 1949, Haigh stood trial for murder of Mrs. Durand-Deacon. Huge crowds gathered outside the courthouse to catch a glimpse of the mass murderer. He pleaded not guilty. The defence tried to prove him insane, and the prosecution tried to prove him sane. The jurors obviously believed the prosecution. They took exactly 15 minutes to find him guilty.

Facing death by hanging, Haigh took great pains to bequeath his clothing to Madame Tussaud's Chamber of Horrors. There were certain stipulations. Vain to the end, he insisted that his wax image be kept in perfect condition, hair combed and pants pressed.

He was executed on August 10, 1949.

DENNIS NILSEN

IN 1942, pretty Betty Whyte of Fraserburgh, Scotland, married handsome Olav Nilsen. Their courtship had an aura of glamor. After all, it was wartime. Olav was stationed in Scotland with the Free Norwegian Forces. The couple, who would divorce in 1948, had three children: Olav, Dennis and Sylvia. No one knew then that quiet, well-behaved Dennis would become the most prolific mass murderer in the history of English crime.

Dennis joined the army in 1961, at the age of 16. He spent most of his army career in the Army Catering Corp., where he learned skills which were, in later years, to assist him in the most unusual way imaginable.

While in the service, Dennis discovered two things. He was sexually attracted to men. His comrades never learned of his secret desires, for Dennis was well aware of the ridicule heaped upon homosexuals by rough, tough army personnel. In fact, Dennis often led his colleagues in demeaning those men who appeared to be effeminate. Dennis also learned how to drink in the army. It was the one way he had of joining in, becoming one of the boys.

Eleven years later, Dennis was discharged from the army, having attained the rank of corporal. In 1972, he took a 16-week course at the Metropolitan Police Training School in North London and became a police officer. While serving with the police force, he was a practising homosexual. Unlike army life, Dennis found no camaraderie in the police force. At the end of their shifts his fellow officers went home to their families. A lonely, brooding man, Dennis left the force after one year.

For a while, Dennis was employed as a security guard, but found the work boring. Eventually, he obtained a position as clerical officer with the Department of Employment, where he would remain as a valued and conscientious employee for the next eight years.

In his spare time, Dennis picked up male companions at pubs, particularly the Wellington IV in Hampstead and the Salisbury in St. Martin's Lane. He took them to his room, but these encounters, though numerous, were of a passing nature. Dennis had no meaningful relationships, no real friends.

In 1975, Dennis received a bit of a windfall. His father whom he never knew, died in Norway, leaving him £1000. Around this time, Dennis met David Gallichan at a pub. He ended up taking the 20-year-old blond boy home with him. Next day, they decided to live together. Within days of paying one month's rent in advance, Dennis and David moved into a pleasant flat on the ground floor at 195 Melrose Ave. French windows opened onto a long garden at the rear of the flat.

The relationship provided a period of relative contentment for Dennis. He was a faithful lover, but the same could not be said of young Gallichan. It was Gallichan's promiscuity which precipitated the breakup. When both men began bringing home extracurricular lovers, the writing was on the wall. In 1977, the pair parted. Dennis Nilsen was devastated. About the only thing Dennis had left was his loyal mongrel bitch, Bleep. A year passed. He and Bleep spent the Christmas season of 1978 alone and lonely. Dennis spent Christmas Eve in a drunken stupor.

On December 30, Dennis picked up a lad at the Cricklewood Arms. They spent the night together at Dennis' flat on Melrose Ave. Next morning, Dennis looked at the nude, sleeping body beside him. How pleasant it would be to have a friend over New Year's. Silently, Dennis picked up his own necktie from the floor where he had dropped it the night before. He slid it under his new friend's neck and squeezed until the struggling boy went limp. Dennis noted that the boy was still breathing. He quickly filled a bucket of water and dunked the rasping boy's head into the water. After a few minutes, he was dead.

Years later, Dennis would relate that he bathed his victim in the bathtub, even washing his hair. The clean body was placed in the bed. Then Dennis went for a walk to clear his head. Slowly a plan formed in his tormented, twisted mind. He purchased a cooking pot, but put it away when he got home.

Dennis dressed the body in new clothing he had purchased for himself and laid it out on the floor. That day Dennis slept peacefully, getting up in the evening to watch TV. Next day he pried some floorboards from the living room and shoved his companion's body under the floor, after covering it with dirt from the garden.

A week later, Dennis retrieved the corpse, washed it once again in the bathtub and performed indignities to the body. It was then once again placed under the floorboards. Seven months later, the luckless youth's body was burned in the garden. Dennis had successfully obliterated his first victim. The body has never been identified.

After keeping a body for seven months and then disposing of it, Dennis was amazed at the ease of it all. No one seemed to miss the victim. Five months later, Dennis struck again. Ironically, his second victim was a Canadian on holidays in London.

It was Kenneth Ockendon's misfortune to meet Dennis the day he was to fly home to Toronto. Kenneth was having lunch when Dennis struck up a conversation with him. Later, the two men went sightseeing, before making their way to Dennis' flat for something to eat.

Back at the Central Hotel, Kenneth's baggage remained unclaimed. He never checked out. Dennis strangled Kenneth to death that same night. The Canadian tourist was reported missing. For a while, his mysterious disappearance was noted by the London papers, but he was never traced to civil servant Dennis Nilsen.

In the next few years, Dennis was to kill ten more young men. With the exception of his Canadian victim, none were missed. Most were wandering homosexuals. Dennis liked to wash the bodies and keep them around his flat, not only to satisfy his necrophilic desires, but also for their mere physical presence. He often dressed the bodies and propped them up on chairs to watch TV. On occasion he spoke to them and played them his favorite records. Only four of the 12 men killed at Melrose Ave. have been identified. Other than Ockendon, they are Martyn Duffey, Billy Sutherland and Malcolm Barlow.

Dennis was now killing at a rapid rate. To make room under the floorboards, he dissected some of his victims. Other victims were dissected and placed in suitcases, which were stored in an outside shed, together with various deodorants. Still, Dennis was having difficulty disposing of the bodies as fast as he was killing. At one point, in 1980, he had six bodies in various stages of dissection, both in the flat and outside in the shed.

In December 1980, Dennis built a huge bonfire beyond his garden in a vacant lot. A couple of old tires atop the fire served to disguise the odor. Dennis was housecleaning, destroying bodies.

Good thing, too. Dennis had never been a good tenant. In fact, he was a born complainer. As a result, he had often been asked to move by the agents acting for the owners of the building. In desperation, they located another apartment for their troublesome tenant and threw in £1000 as compensation for the inconvenience. It was an offer Dennis couldn't refuse. He moved into a self-contained attic flat at 23 Cranley Gardens. One can only imagine his feelings as the moving van pulled away from Melrose Ave. He had terminated 12 young lives and no one was the wiser.

Dennis Nilsen was not finished, but the business of disposing of bodies was not as easy as it had been at his previous dwelling. There was no garden, no floorboards and no shed. But Dennis was not to be denied. In the ten months between March 1982 and January 1983, he killed three more times. Each body was dissected. Individual parts were boiled in large pots on the kitchen stove. With flesh boiled away, the remaining bones were dumped in the garbage and taken away by the garbage collector.

Larger body parts, such as the skull and leg bones, were placed in bags, which were stored in a tea chest placed in the corner of the living room. A red cloth over the tea chest transformed the grave into an attractive table. Excess flesh, as well as some organs and hair, were flushed down the toilet. And that's how Dennis came to the attention of police.

The toilet clogged. Tenants complained and were told not to use the facilities until the trouble was repaired.

On Saturday, February 5, 1983, plumber Mike Welch showed up at 23 Cranley Gardens. Mike checked the pipes leading out of the house. There didn't seem to be any problem there. He checked outside the building, but couldn't correctly diagnose the difficulty. Mike advised one of the tenants to call an outfit named Dyno-rod. However, nothing could be done until after the weekend. Unknown to all, Dennis Nilsen was busy dissecting a body all that weekend.

On Tuesday, Michael Cattran, an engineer with Dyno-rod, arrived at 23 Cranley Gardens. He went down a 12-foot manhole outside the house and discovered the cause of the malfunction—strange looking pieces of flesh. Police were called.

When Dennis Nilsen returned home from work that night, Scotland Yard inspectors were waiting for him. He made no attempt to deny his guilt. When his flat was examined, plastic bags yielded two torsos, two boiled heads and four arms. The tea chest contained various bones.

Dennis Nilsen admitted to 15 murders. He was tried on six counts of murder and two counts of attempted murder. Dennis was found guilty of all charges. He received eight life sentences with a recommendation that he serve not less than 25 years.

MICHAEL RYAN

HUNGERFORD, England, a town of 4,000 inhabitants located about 100 km east of London, was an unlikely location for the worst mass murder in the annals of English criminal history. Not that much had ever happened in the quaint little market town.

Michael Ryan, 27, had an obsessive mother who doted on him. The 60-year-old Dorothy Ryan worked as a waitress and always saw to it that her Michael had a few bob for spending money. For her trouble, Michael often rewarded her with a slap across the face. Despite the abuse, Dorothy continued to cater to her son. After all, he was the man of the house now. His father had died of cancer two years earlier at the age of 80.

Michael quit school and drifted from one menial job to another. As a teenager, he displayed an extraordinary interest in guns. He belonged to two gun clubs and practised target shooting several times a week. Along with his passion for weapons, he favored the Rambo look and often wore army battle fatigues. He lied a lot, making up stories which everyone knew were blatant falsehoods. Michael loved to tell of his experiences as a paratrooper, dramatic tales, but all the product of his imagination.

No one will ever know what snapped in Michael Ryan's mind that summer day in 1987, but we do know the results all too well. It wasn't a spur of the moment thing. He planned his attack, assembled weapons, donned battle fatigues and even took target practice the day before the massacre.

Wednesday, August 19, 1987, started out as a normal market day in Hungerford. Stalls brimmed with fresh fruit and vegetables. The streets filled with shoppers. Susan Godfrey, got up early, gathered her two children, Hannah, 4, and James, 2, for what had been planned as a day in the country. The 32-year-old housewife left her home in nearby Reading and drove to Savernake Forest, a few miles outside Hungerford, where she found an ideal location for a picnic. Susan had no way of knowing that she was only minutes away from becoming the first victim of a madman intent on killing anyone he happened to meet.

In town, Michael slowly dressed in his U.S. Army fatigues. He fondled his Chinese copy of a Kalashnikov AK 47 assault rifle. In addition, he placed a 9 mm Beretta in his pocket along with hundreds of rounds of ammunition. In the trunk of his car he had stashed three other handguns. They rested beside his hunting knife, bandages, gas mask and flask of whiskey.

Michael Ryan had planned well. He drove his silver Vauxhall Astra to Savernake Forest, where he came upon Susan Godfrey and her children. For reasons known only to himself, he spared the children, but marched Susan into the woods some 100 meters distant. A volley of gunfire roared through the countryside. Michael shot Susan 15 times in the chest.

An hour later, the two Godfrey children were found wandering on the road. When taken to their grandmother's house, Hannah told her, "The man shot our mummie and he has taken the car keys and James and me can't drive the car so we are going home."

Michael had only begun his odyssey of terror. He drove toward Hungerford to Froxfield, where he pulled up to the gas pumps at the Golden Arrow garage. After filling his Vauxhall, he aimed his rifle at cashier Kakaub Dean and fired. The terrified woman dropped to the floor amidst a shower of broken glass. Michael walked through the door of the cashier's enclosure and pointed his rifle at the woman cowering on the floor. She could only whimper, "Please don't kill me!" She trembled in fear, eyes shut tight, as she heard the hammer of her attacker's rifle fall four times. The weapon had jammed, saving Kakaub's life.

Michael jumped in his car and drove away in the direction of Hungerford. Kakaub dialed 911. Police were already searching for Susan Godfrey's body in Savernake Forest. Other officers responded to Kakaub's call. Still others were dispatched from surrounding communities. A madman was shooting people.

Michael returned to his home at 4 South View to procure more ammunition. Constable Roger Brereton drove his patrol wagon down South View and recognized the killer about to pull away in his car. Brereton rammed Michael's Vauxhall. Michael responded by shooting the defenceless police officer dead.

Dorothy Ryan witnessed a portion of her son's wild rampage and begged him to put down his weapons. Michael shot and killed her before setting fire to the house. He then proceeded to shoot at houses on his own street. Several occupants were wounded. Two elderly residents, Roland and Sheila Mason, were getting ready to go out shopping. They were killed in their own home.

One of the wounded crawled to a phone and called a friend, 51-year-old George White. George jumped into his Toyota and rushed to South View. When he arrived at the scene, he was shot and killed instantly.

The carnage continued. Michael Ryan was literally shooting at anything that moved. Ken Clements was walking his dog and actually got to talk to the gunman before he too came under a barrage of gunfire.

Firemen arrived to fight the flames at 4 South View. They were spotted by Michael, who began shooting at them. The firefighters were forced to take cover. As a result, three additional houses caught fire and were destroyed.

The shooting continued. Michael made his way to Fairview Rd. Abdur Khan, a retired shopkeeper, and Douglas Wainwright, in town visiting his police officer son, were both shot dead. Michael stood in the street. As cars approached, he blasted the drivers. If he noticed any movement, he whirled and fired. The critically wounded lay where they fell. The less seriously hurt crawled away.

Eric Vardy, Francis Butler, Marcus Barnard, Jack Gibb and Sandra Hill had the misfortune to cross Michael's path. All were shot to death. Myrtle Gibb and Ian Playle both died of their wounds later in the hospital.

Around 3 p.m., the janitor of John O'Gaunt School, Michael's alma mater, called police to tell them that Michael Ryan was approaching the building. Within the hour the school was surrounded by police officers. Adjoining residences were evacuated. Because British police do not normally carry guns, there was a delay while weapons were brought in from a town 40 miles away. A helicopter hovered over the school. The drama unfolding in Hungerford was now being watched on TV in living rooms across the country.

Police cautiously approached the building and confirmed that their armed adversary was confined to the top floor. A negotiating team made contact with him. They were amazed at his calm demeanor. Michael expressed some remorse at having killed his mother.

At 7 p.m., a single shot echoed through the school. Michael Ryan had taken his own life. In his wake 16 people lay dead and 15 others were wounded. Surviving relatives of Michael Ryan had his body cremated and the ashes spread without a marker of any kind. No one felt that he deserved more.

PETER SUTCLIFFE

KATHLEEN and John Sutcliffe's six children grew up and one by one moved out of the family home. Their eldest son, Peter, was the last to leave 57 Cornwall Rd. in Bingley, England.

Peter was ambitious, more ambitious than the gang he ran with. They only thought of nights at the pub and birds to pick up. If a legit bird wasn't available, there were always the pros, who, for £5, would show a man a good, if hurried, time.

But Peter was different. He had met Sonia Szurma, the daughter of honest Czech immigrants. Sonia's parents were impressed with hard-working Peter, who over the years held jobs as a furnace operator, grave digger and lorry driver. On August 10, 1974, on Sonia's twenty-fourth birthday, she became Mrs. Peter Sutcliffe.

Six months after his marriage, Peter, always attempting to better himself, took a driving course at the Apex School of Driving, eventually earning a Class One licence. The Sutcliffes and the Szurmas were pleased. Handsome, pleasant Peter was making his way in the world. He soon obtained a good position as a lorry driver.

What the family didn't know, what the entire country didn't know, was that something deep in the recesses of Peter Sutcliffe's mind was changing and festering and smoldering. He was developing a hatred of women, a hatred so strong that for five and a half years the mere mention of the Yorkshire Ripper sent shivers up and down the spines, not only of women, but of men as well. With the possible exception of Myra Hindley and Ian Brady, no killer was ever more hated than the Yorkshire Ripper.

On July 4, 1975, Anna Rogulskyj couldn't go to sleep until she satisfied herself that her kitten was safe and sound. The kitten was missing, but Anna felt that her boyfriend must have taken it to his apartment just a five minute walk away. Even though it was 1 a.m., she decided to set her mind at ease and travel the few blocks.

A man lurking the shadows asked, "Do you fancy it?" There was no doubt in Anna's mind what the question implied. She threw an answer over her shoulder, "Not on your life!" She hurried on and soon arrived at her boyfriend's door, but no amount of knocking could get a response.

Apprehensively, Anna retraced her steps. Again, the whispered innuendo, "Do you fancy it?" Anna increased her pace. The man walked faster and caught up to her, raining three blows on her head with a ballpeen hammer. He then lifted her sweater and slashed at her midriff. A window opened, a head stuck out, "What's the matter?" The attacker ran away and the head tucked back in. The window closed.

An hour later, Anna was found on the sidewalk. Rushed to Leeds General Infirmary, she was given the last rites of the Catholic Church. A 12-hour operation saved her life. Anna spent months in hospital, and had to learn to speak and walk again. She was unable to describe her attacker. Peter Sutcliffe, the Yorkshire Ripper, the man who would terrorize a nation, had struck for the first time.

Five weeks later, Peter and a friend, Trevor Birdsall, were driving from pub to pub. Peter spotted Olive Smelt, a 46-year-old cleaning woman, who habitually spent Friday nights in a pub with a female friend. Now Olive was walking home and took a shortcut down an alley. Peter stopped the car and told Trevor he was going to try and have a go. He rushed into the alley, caught up with Olive and struck her twice on the head with a hammer. He tried to cut her body with a hacksaw, but gave up when a passing car came along. He returned to Trevor in the car.

Trevor asked what had happened. Peter would only say that he had been chatting with that woman. Next day, Trevor read of the strange attack on a woman where nothing had been stolen and no sexual attack attempted. He was positive that the victim was the woman Peter had followed down the alley. He said nothing, told no one. Beating up the wife or girlfriend was the norm in his crowd. The old lady survived, didn't she? Olive Smelt was unable to describe her attacker.

In the fall of 1975, Peter was hired as a driver for the Common Road Tyre Co. in Bradford. This broadened his scope. Peter came to know Leeds' inner city Chapeltown section with its teeming watering holes and tough prostitute population like the back of his hand.

Wilma McCann sold her body whenever she could for the going rate of £5. It was her misfortune to be picked up by Peter Sutcliffe. A deal was struck. Peter drove to a secluded spot and spread his coat on the grass. Wilma lay down. That's when he struck her a vicious blow to the head and stabbed her 14 times in the chest and lower abdomen. Next morning her body was found by a milkman.

As the Sutcliffe family celebrated Christmas that year, no one had any idea that obliging Peter had attempted to kill two women and had succeeded in killing a third. He gave presents to his parents, his aunts, his brothers and sisters and his wife.

On January 21 of the New Year he killed again. Prostitute Emily Jackson routinely picked up a client. After a short drive, Peter asked Emily to hold a flashlight while he raised the hood of his car. As the unsuspecting girl pointed the torch, Peter struck her twice on the back of her head with a hammer. In a frenzy he stabbed his hapless victim 52 times.

Peter didn't kill for the remainder of the year, but in February 1977, he struck again. Irene Richardson's body was found near a park. She had been hit over the head with a hammer, stabbed in the neck and chest and had been horribly slashed across the lower abdomen. The newspapers of the district for the first time coined the phrase "Yorkshire Ripper."

Leeds detectives realized from the nature and physical characteristics of the wounds, that all three women had been murdered by the same man. One hundred detectives worked on the Richardson murder without coming up with any concrete results. Policewomen, dressed as prostitutes, roamed Chapeltown but the elusive Ripper didn't show.

Tina Atkinson was dead drunk when she picked up Peter and took him to her flat. As she sat on the edge of her bed, he struck her with his ballpeen hammer, after which he stabbed her repeatedly, slashing her across the lower abdomen. Peter drove away and tossed the incriminating hammer from his car. Two days later a man found the hammer in Cottingley Bridge. He used it for three years before finding out it was a murder weapon.

Jayne MacDonald and her boyfriend left the dance at Hofbrauhaus early so they could have some fish and chips on the way home. They lingered too long. By the time they had eaten, Jayne had missed her last bus home. The pair parted. Jayne made her way down Chapeltown Rd. with the intention of calling a taxi.

Peter sneaked up behind her and struck her with his hammer. He dragged her off the street and performed his distinctive mutilations to the body.

Jayne was the Ripper's first murder victim who was not a prostitute. Whether this was a pertinent factor in the increased intensity of the Ripper investigation is not known. We do know that after Jayne's death, West Yorkshire's most famous detective, George Oldfield, was placed in charge of the investigation with one directive: Apprehend the Yorkshire Ripper.

Oldfield conducted a massive investigation. Four hundred citizens had been in the general area on the night of Jayne's murder. Three hundred and eighty were traced and cleared. One hundred and fifty two prostitutes were arrested. Over 3,500 statements were taken by police. None of these efforts produced one iota of useful information.

Late in the summer of 1977, Sonia and Peter Sutcliffe purchased a home at 6 Garden Lane, Heaton. With Sonia employed as a teacher and Peter on steady as a driver, the Sutcliffes were definitely on the way up. There was even talk of a baby.

Peter had other thoughts in mind. After being in his new home for only a week, he took off for Manchester's red light district. Jean Jordan jumped into Peter's red Corsair without hesitation. He passed over the usual £5 note and then parked behind a high hedge near municipal allotments as he was directed by Jean.

The hammer crashed against the girl's skull again and again. Peter dragged the body into the bushes, but a car arrived and he left before mutilating the body. In the days following the attack, Peter was perplexed that headlines were singularly devoid of any mention of the Ripper striking for the first time in Manchester.

He correctly figured that the body had not been discovered, but this wasn't the reason Peter decided to return to the scene of the crime. He realized that he had left a valuable clue behind. Peter had been paid in crisp, newly minted notes. The £5 note he had given Jean was one of these traceable notes. Peter had to get it back.

Eight days after the murder, he returned to find Jean's body exactly as he had left it. He stripped the body, examining every garment, but could not find the £5 note. Frantically, he searched for Jean's purse in vain. He stabbed the body again and again, as if to quell the frustration at not being able to retrieve the only clue he had ever left behind.

Next day Jean Jordan's body was found. Five days later, her purse, with the £5 intact, was turned over to police.

The Bank of England quickly confirmed that the note was one of a large supply distributed by Midland Bank of Shipley, located just outside Bradford. They had been distributed four days before the murder and had been placed in pay packets for various commercial firms in the area. The new bills had been used by 30 firms employing over 7,500 men.

One of the companies was T. and W.H. Clark Ltd., the trucking firm where Peter was at the time employed as a driver. A month after Jean Jordan was murdered, two detectives knocked at the door of Sonia and Peter Sutcliffe at 6 Garden Lane. Peter calmly told the officers that he was home on the evening of November 2 when Jean Jordan had been murdered. Sonia confirmed Peter's story. Peter had also been at home eight days later when the body had been mutilated. Once again, Sonia agreed. The officers left and reported nothing unusual to incriminate Pete Sutcliffe over the thousands of others being questioned.

Peter continued killing after spending another joyous Christmas season with his family and friends. In January 1978, he murdered prostitute Yvonne Pearson in his now familiar manner. Yvonne's body was not found for two months. On the last day of January, Helen and Rita Rytka, good-looking 18-year-old twin prostitutes, walked their regular beats. Helen was picked up by Peter.

The twins had an arrangement. After one completed her services, she would return to a certain location to check in with her sister. That way, through the course of the evening, they would see each other several times. On this night, Rita waited. Helen never returned. Her body was found three days later.

Someone had noticed a red Corsair in the vicinity where the body was found. Because Peter drove a red Corsair, he was once more visited by detectives. The obliging lorry driver explained that he was often in that area since he drove to work to pick up his lorry. Sonia confirmed that Peter hardly ever went out at night, which was true enough. He didn't go out often, but when he did, he killed women. Sometimes he would be gone only a half hour. The questioning detectives didn't know that Peter had already been interrogated by other officers concerning the £5 note. They left believing Peter's story. The two reports were never connected.

In May 1978, Peter cruised around with his friend Trevor. After dropping Trevor off at his home, he drove to Halifax and watched various people walking their dogs in a park. Finally, he spotted a young girl walking alone. He parked his car and accosted Josephine Whitaker, a 19-year-old clerk on her way home. Josephine was not a prostitute, but was simply in the wrong place at the wrong time.

Ten women had now been murdered at the hands of the Yorkshire Ripper. The police knew from saliva tests that the killer's blood belonged to group B, a rare type found in only six percent of the population. They knew precious little else.

George Oldfield received scores of letters from cranks, but firmly believed that one such letter was authentic. Tests on the envelope indicated that the sender was a group B secreter. Then, on June 20, 1979, the letter took a back seat to a tape recording received by Oldfield. The message on the tape was startlingly similar to letters written by the original Jack the Ripper 90 years earlier. George Oldfield was convinced that the tape was authentic.

Voice and dialect experts from the University of Leeds meticulously studied the tape and came to the conclusion that the voice had a "Geordie" accent, which is generally attributed to that area of northeast England immediately south of the Scottish border. Peter Sutcliffe did not have a Geordie accent. When a police directive was issued instructing officers to exclude anyone who didn't have a Geordie accent, Peter was off the hook.

The largest manhunt in the annals of British crime was now instituted. In all, over 150,000 individuals were questioned about the case. More than 22,000 statements were on file. The tape with the supposed Ripper's voice was played in public places, on the radio and even at soccer games. But nothing stopped Peter Sutcliffe.

In September 1979, Barbara Leach, a student at the University of Bradford, was slain in Peter's usual way. A short while later, while driving a Rover, Peter encountered 47-year-old Marguerite Walls in Farsley, a suburb of Leeds. Marguerite was strangled, a departure for the cunning Peter. He decided to throw the police off the trail by changing his tactics. He was right. Initially, the Walls murder was not attributed to the Yorkshire Ripper.

Peter's thirteenth and last victim was Jacqueline Hill of Headingly. She merely got off a bus and was followed by Peter until, in a darkened area, he struck her down with his hammer. She was his only victim in 1980.

On January 2, 1981, Peter took the precaution of taping old licence plates he had found in a junkyard over the plates on his Rover. He called Sonia and told her he'd be late. He then drove 30 miles to Sheffield, where he picked up prostitute Olivia Reivers. Peter parked in a dark area near a large stone building. Without warning, a police car pulled up. Sergeant Bob Ring and Const. Robert Hydes approached the Rover. Peter gave them a false name and told the officers he was merely parked with his girlfriend. Const. Hydes returned to his vehicle and checked out the plates with the national computer. The plates didn't belong to the Rover.

The officers returned to the car. After examining the Rover's licence plates, they found that they were taped over another set. The officers decided to take Peter and his girlfriend in for questioning. Olivia didn't realize it at the time, but the two officers had just saved her life.

Meanwhile, on the way to the police car, Peter asked if he could go around the corner of a building to relieve himself. He took the opportunity to throw his ballpeen hammer and knife behind a small storage tank.

At Hammerton Road police station Peter gave his correct name. He told police he had used the stolen plates because he was planning a robbery. He even told them he had been questioned as one of the individuals who had been paid with a new £5 note like the one found in Jean Jordan's purse. Peter was detained, but was still no more of a suspect than thousands of others who had been detained and questioned in the course of the massive investigation.

Next day, when Sgt. Bob Ring heard that the man he had brought in was being questioned by the Ripper squad, he decided to take another look at the spot where he had picked up Peter Sutcliffe. In particular, he searched the area where Peter had relieved himself. There, Bob Ring found a ballpeen hammer and a knife lying in a pile of leaves.

Word spread throughout the police hierarchy. This could be it. Inspector John Boyle conducted the questioning. He told the suspect he didn't believe his story. Early on in the questioning Boyle stated, "I think you are in serious trouble."

Peter replied rather cockily, "I think you have been leading up to it."

Boyle asked, "Leading up to what?"

"The Yorkshire Ripper," replied Peter.

"What about the Yorkshire Ripper?" the officer asked, hardly able to conceal his excitement.

The reply left little room for doubt. Peter said, "Well, it's me."

Peter Sutcliffe, 35, the man who had terrorized a country for five and a half years, confessed in detail to all his crimes. In May 1981, an English jury rejected his counsel's plea of insanity and found Peter guilty of 13 counts of murder. He was sentenced to life imprisonment and incarcerated at Parkhurst Prison on the Isle of Wight.

Since that time, due to mental deterioration and attacks on him by fellow inmates, he has been transferred to Broadmoor, an institution housing the criminally insane.

JEREMY BAMBER

NEVILLE and June Bamber had the world by the tail. They lived in a large home known as White House Farm in Essex, England. Neville, who stood six-feet four-inches, was a former magistrate and wartime fighter pilot. He had inherited an estate well in excess of $2 million, which enabled him and June to settle down to the genteel life which farming affords those who don't have to make a living at it.

Although the Bambers had just about everything, there was one blessing which had been denied them. They were unable to have children. In 1957, after 12 years of trying, they decided to adopt a newborn baby girl. They christened the infant, Sheila. Three years later, the Bambers adopted a second child, a boy, Jeremy.

It would be pleasant to relate that the two darlings were a joy to their parents. Little imagination is required to picture them frolicking about the farm, being kind to the animals, and later attaining superior grades at school. That just didn't happen. From earliest childhood, Jeremy got his jollies from torturing the domestic animals on the farm. Sister Sheila proved to be a handful from an early age as well. The child wouldn't obey her parents and seemed to relish getting into trouble.

As the two youngsters were growing up, they were sent to the best schools, where they distinguished themselves by their atrocious behavior. Jeremy picked on younger, smaller boys, while Sheila was borderline unmanageable.

When Sheila was 17, she talked her parents into allowing her to move out on her own to London. Generous Neville provided her with a $30,000 per year allowance to make ends meet. Nicely ensconced in a West End flat, the attractive Sheila soon obtained sporadic modelling jobs. She also married a boy from back home. In the following two years she had two miscarriages, gave birth to twins, Nicholas and Daniel, and divorced her husband.

Around this time, Sheila was heavily into marijuana and cocaine. As a result, she became paranoid, firmly believing that everyone in authority was her blood enemy. Sometimes she felt she was possessed by the devil. On more than one occasion, she ended up in St. Andrew's Hospital. Sheila was slowly going around the bend.

While sister Sheila was having her mental problems, Jeremy had turned into an obnoxious playboy. In 1984, Neville financed a cottage and farm for him at Goldhanger in an attempt to straighten him out. He had no way of knowing that his son had grown to hate him for no particular reason. But then again, Jeremy hated his entire family. He regarded his mother as a hindrance to his lifestyle and was jealous of Sheila and her $30,000 allowance. He considered the twins both-ersome little monsters who seemed always to be underfoot. No, Jeremy didn't care for his family. His main aim in life was to eat, drink and party with members of the opposite sex. He pursued these pastimes whenever he could slip away from the farm, which was often.

Jeremy loved to visit the closest town, Colchester, for fun and games. He took a part-time job in one of the pubs in order to be near the action. Often he had two or three girls on the string at the same time, but particularly favored one married local beauty who was 12 years his senior and the mother of two children. Sometimes Jeremy confided in his girlfriends, telling them that he would like to kill his parents. The method he would use would be simple enough. He would sedate them and then set the house on fire. Authorities would assume that Neville had dropped a cigarette. His two closest girlfriends told him to grow up and stop behaving like a child. Jeremy laughed.

In the wee hours of the morning of August 7, 1985, police received a call from Jeremy Bamber. He related that his sister had wiped out the entire family. Police rushed to White House Farm. They found Neville lying on the kitchen floor. He had been bludgeoned about the head and shot eight times in the head and neck. Sheila's six-year-old sons, Nicholas and Daniel, were found dead in their bed. Nicholas had been shot three times in the head, while Daniel had been shot five times in the back of the head while he slept. June Bamber's body was found beside her bed. She had apparently been sitting on the bed and had attempted to flee before she was shot seven times. Sheila lay dead in the same bed with a rifle and a bible at her side. It was tragically clear that mentally deranged Sheila had killed her family before taking her own life. In all, Sheila had discharged 23 shots in killing her entire family with the exception of Jeremy.

Fortunately, he had been out of the house at the time and so had escaped her wrath.

A few days later, the distraught Jeremy attended his family's funeral, but he wasn't one to mourn for long. Within days he was partying in London. He also slipped over to Amsterdam to replenish his supply of cocaine and marijuana. None of these actions were brought to the attention of the police. It took London's famed tabloid reporters to point out the rather simple fact that Sheila had been shot twice, once in the brain and once in the throat. Either shot would have been fatal. Sheila couldn't have killed herself twice.

Police decided to take another look. When they discovered that Sheila had been shot once with a gun equipped with a silencer and once without a silencer, they knew for certain that she hadn't killed herself. Other evidence came to light. Although the floors of the rooms where the family had been slaughtered were splattered with blood, Sheila's bare feet had been blood-free. It would have been impossible for her to have dashed about the house killing her family without getting blood on her feet. It also was difficult to believe that Sheila, who stood about five-and-a-half-feet tall, could have bludgeoned her six-foot-four-inch father before shooting him.

Although the police were now actively pursuing the theory that Sheila was a victim rather than a killer, it was left to one of the Bambers' relatives to find a silencer in a downstairs pantry. Everyone agreed that Sheila couldn't have put it there after being shot.

During the weeks in which the newspapers featured the gory details of the multiple murders, two of Jeremy's girlfriends kept their guilty knowledge to themselves. Jeremy had confided in them his desire to have his family dead. Not only did he hate them all, but upon their deaths, he alone stood to inherit the family fortune. Finally, unable to live with themselves, the two girls got together and went to the police.

Jeremy was taken into custody and charged with the murders of his mother, father, sister and two nephews. Tried in London's Old Bailey, he was found guilty of all five charges. Jeremy was sentenced to a minimum of 25 years to life on each count.

Jeremy Bamber will be eligible for parole in 2011. At that time, he will be 50 years old and will have spent exactly half his life behind prison bars.

REGINALD CHRISTIE

THE draw of Buckingham Palace was too much even for me, a man with a mission and an obsession all rolled into one. I checked into the Rubens Hotel on Buckingham Palace Road, and was relieved to see that the armchairs in the lobby were slightly frayed where thousands of elbows had rested in years gone by, and that the once-beautiful carpet had faded paths leading to doors, worn down by untold pairs of feet, scurrying to dine, scurrying to enter and scurrying to leave.

The year of my visit to England was 1972. I arose bright and early and briskly walked to the lift. Browning's line "Oh, to be in England now that April's there," came to mind. The lift descended ever so slowly to the lobby, and I dashed over to the hall porter.

I inquired of the young man, "Can you tell me how to get to 10 Rillington Place?"

"I never heard of that address myself, sir. Let me get a map," he replied.

I couldn't believe my ears – never heard of 10 Rillington Place! The lad must be pulling my leg. He returned with a street map of London.

"No sir," he said, "there doesn't seem to be a Rillington Place at all."

"But," I stammered, "everyone knows of 10 Rillington Place. It's Reg Christie's place—you know, the murderer."

"The name Christie does seem familiar. Let me get the manager, sir," the young man offered.

A tall balding man with a moustache looked down at me and said, "Yes?" in a manner, which seemed to demand an explanation.

"Have you ever heard of 10 Rillington Place?" I asked.

"Certainly, sir," he said.

This was more like it.

He took me aside, and in the confidential manner made famous by movie spies giving the secret password to enemy agents on street corners, he said, to me, "They changed the name, you know. It was so notorious after the murders, it was changed to Ruston Close. Nothing much there now, but I'll tell you how to get there."

One hour later, I was looking at the demolished houses that had once been Rillington Place. At last I was standing on the same ground as that most classical of all murderers, Reginald Christie.

Reggie was born in Halifax, England, in 1898, to normal parents.

There is nothing in his early life that can even vaguely be construed as a hint of what was to follow. He was a Boy Scout and eventually became an assistant group leader. In his teens he was a choirboy, and to many I am sure this activity will seem an admirable one, but the disproportionate number of choirboys who later in life go around killing people has always made me wonder.

Christie left school at the age of 15, and got his first job as a projectionist in a Halifax movie theatre. It was around this time that he induced a young lady to accompany him to a local lovers' lane for what was to be his first try at sex. Later the young lady, who was apparently a blabbermouth, told one of Christie's chums that Reggie couldn't get it up. From across the streets of Halifax came shouts of "Reggie no dick" and "Can't-make-it Christie." It seems that after this incident Reggie always felt inadequate around women, and while this experience may not have actually caused his inhibitions, it serves to illuminate the fact that he was never quite normal when it came to members of the opposite sex.

Christie enlisted in the army in September 1916, at the age of 18. He now stood five-feet, eight-inches tall, with blue eyes and reddish-blond hair atop a round, full ruddy face. The young soldier was a model rookie to everyone with whom he came in contact. We suspect that he gave an external impression of efficiency to his superiors and cheerfulness to his acquaintances, but inside smouldered a deep resentment for women. When he looked at the painted young girls flaunting themselves at the uniformed soldiers, we wonder if deep down he still heard the taunts of his chums a few years back.

In April 1918, Christie was sent to the front, and towards the end of June a German mustard gas shell knocked him unconscious. When he regained consciousness he discovered that he had lost his voice. Though he later claimed that he never said a word for over three years, in reality his muteness lasted only a few months and finally gave way to a low whisper. The army doctor diagnosed his affliction as functional aphonia, which means that the explosion scared the wits out of him and left him speechless.

Christie was discharged by the end of 1919, and returned to civilian life to pick up the pieces in Halifax. On May 10, 1920, he married a neighbor, Ethel Simpson Waddington. The young couple, both 22 years old, had known each other for some time. Ethel was a matronly individual, who did not stand out in any particularly memorable way.

Reggie, who now had a nondescript job as a clerk, moved into a new house with his bride. He did not have full use of his voice at this time, and it's fascinating to imagine the whispering Reggie explaining to frigid Ethel that he really wasn't that good at this sex business. We wonder who was more relieved, Reggie or Ethel.

To better his lot Christie changed jobs and became a postman. Almost immediately he started stealing postal orders, and almost immediately he got caught and received three months in jail. When he got out things went routinely enough, but in Reggie's eyes Halifax held no chance for advancement so he headed for London, leaving the wife with relatives in Sheffield.

Once in London, Reggie held a series of dull clerical positions. He took to breaking the law regularly, and just as regularly he received jail sentences for these indiscretions. In 1924, he received a three-month sentence, followed by six months, for two charges of larceny. In 1927, he was caught stealing and received nine months in jail. Two years later Reggie shacked up with a prostitute.

Like many men before him who couldn't hack it with normal women, he seemed to be in his element with prostitutes. No inhibitions here; his sex partners quite simply didn't give a damn one way or the other. One day he had a temper tantrum and hit a prostie over the head with a cricket bat, an indiscretion which earned him six months at hard labor for malicious wounding. In 1933, he got three months for stealing a car; it didn't help him that the owner of the vehicle happened to be a Roman Catholic priest.

After ten years of trying to get ahead of the game and finding nothing for this efforts except jail, Reggie decided to import the wife, who was still staying with those relatives in Sheffield. He wrote to Ethel from prison, and the pair reached a reconciliation during a visit at the jail. Coinciding with the reunion with his wife, Christie was released from prison and became a patient of Dr. Matthew Odess—

not that he had any major illness, but he lived in fear of recurring muteness and suffered from such ailments as nervousness and stomach trouble.

In 1938, the sickly Reg and Ethel moved their belongings into 10 Rillington Place. Situated in Notting Hill, Rillington Place was a dead-end street, coming to an abrupt stop at a factory wall. Number 10 was the last building on the left-hand side. Because of the light traffic, Rillington was an active, alive street. Children could play games and dogs could scamper in relative safety from the vehicles. Number 10 consisted of three flats, of which the Christies occupied the ground level. The whole structure was in a state of visible decay. Over the years everything had been painted many times, and was now sadly chipped and cracked; soot from the factory had rained down over the street, coating everything with a greasy deposit.

The flat above the Christies' was occupied by a partially blind old man named Kitchener, and the top flat was vacant. The three flats were connected by narrow stairs that started in the narrow passageway that let to the ground floor past the open door of Christie's flat. Reggie's front room had a bay window covered by curtains. In the evenings, he would part these curtains to watch the goings-on out in the street.

The passageway and stairs were common territory to the tenants of all three flats, but you were almost in the Christies' flat when you were coming and going. Their front room and back room were both only accessible through the passageway or hall. Behind these two main rooms, the Christies had a kitchen with an empty alcove that was used to store coal, and sometimes other things. Behind the kitchen was a wash-house that was mainly used as a storeroom, measuring four feet by four feet. Attached to this section of the house was a lavatory for the use of all the tenants.

The rest of the lot, measuring about twenty feet square, was to become famous as the garden. To gain a proper perspective of the Christie flat, one must try to realize that everything was undersized. Two people couldn't pass comfortably in the hall or on the stairs; the rooms were cramped and small. There was little in the way of comfort at 10 Rillington Place.

Shortly after moving into his new premises, Reggie joined the War Reserve Police. He was assigned to the Harrow Road Police Station, wore a crisp official uniform, and all in all cut a dashing figure. This was more like it. Reggie was a good, efficient cop, and quickly gained a reputation for being very strict with those who didn't obey the air raid regulations.

It was during this rather happy and contented time in Reggie's life that he met, quite by chance, a young lady named Ruth Fuerst. She was an Austrian student nurse who had found herself in England when the war broke out and decided to stay in England rather than return to Austria. When she met Reggie she was working in a munitions factory and living in a furnished room at 41 Oxford Gardens, in the same neighborhood as the Christies. This lonely 21-year-old, who spoke English with a slight accent, was a tall, pretty girl with brown hair and brown eyes. It wasn't long before she and Christie were seeing a great deal of each other.

In the middle of August 1943, Ruth visited Reggie at 10 Rillington Place. Though we only have Reggie's word for what took place that fateful afternoon, in this instance his account is probably accurate. Ethel was away visiting her relatives in Sheffield. While he was having intercourse with Ruth in the bedroom, Reggie strangled her with a piece of rope.

Pause and reflect on Reggie's state of mind then, as he lay spent, just having had intercourse (we must assume he enjoyed it) and having just strangled a naked woman (we can only assume that some perverted thrill was attached to his act) there was a knock on the door. The blood pounding in his temples, Reggie made himself presentable and answered. It was a telegraph-boy with a telegram. The message was from Mrs. Christie. She was returning home from Sheffield that evening with her brother.

Christie was frank about how he solved the problem: "I took her from the bedroom into the front room and put her under the floorboards. I had to do that because of my wife coming back."

A few hours later, Ethel and her brother, Henry Waddington, arrived. Ethel and Reggie slept in the bedroom and Henry slept in the front room, just a few feet from the remains of Ruth Fuerst. Next morning Henry went back to Sheffield, and in the afternoon Ethel went out visiting. At last Reggie retrieved the body from under the floorboards and removed it, and Ruth's clothing, to the wash-house. Then Reggie decided to do a little gardening – he dug a grave. That night, on the pretense of going to the lavatory, he moved Fuerst's body from the wash-house and put it in the hole he had dug. Next morning he tidied up, raking over the grave site and burning Ruth's clothes in a dustbin with some other rubbish.

In September, Ruth was reported missing to the police. No one pressed the matter. She had no relatives, no close friends. The bombs had claimed many victims who were not found for months, even years. Then again, she could be a young girl on the loose. She had probably taken a lover and gone away without telling anyone. No one gave her another thought, except Christie.

Let's let him tell it.

"Months later I was digging in the garden and I probably misjudged where it was or something like that. I found a skull and put it in the dustbin and covered it up. I dug a hole in the corner of the garden, and put the dustbin in the hole about eighteen inches down. The top of the dustbin was open, and I still used it to burn rubbish."

In December 1943, Christie got word that his application for employment at the Ultra Radio Works, Park Royal, Acton, had been accepted. He left the War Reserve Police, and early in the new year took up his new job. Ethel had gainful employment with a lightbulb factory, and again the Christies settled into that humdrum way of life so typical of many who have stubbed their toes on the ladder of success.

Reggie ate his lunch in the company canteen, and it was here that he met Muriel Amelia Eady, a respectable, 31-year-old spinster. Muriel had brown hair and eyes and was rather stout and short. Christie overhead that she had a steady boyfriend, so he asked Muriel to bring him over to 10 Rillington Place to have tea with himself and Ethel. A sort of friendship developed, and Muriel brought her boyfriend over to the Christie's on more than one occasion. In the course of idle conversation, Muriel complained of catarrh, and Reggie hold her he had an inhaling device that would ease her difficult breathing if she cared to try it.

One fine day in October 1944, Ethel was away visiting her brother in Sheffield when Muriel knocked on the door of 10 Rillington Place, wondering if the kind Mr. Christie would let her inhale some of his cure.

"Come right in," said Reggie. He had planned the whole thing for just such an occasion. His inhaling device consisted of a glass jar with a metal screw top that had two holes in it. The jar contained Friar's Balsam, and a rubber tube was inserted into one hole so that Muriel could breathe through the other end of the tube and inhale Friar's Balsam. Another tube was attached to the gas stove, with the other end of the tube inserted into the second hole on top of the glass jar.

Reggie sat Muriel in a chair so she wouldn't see what he was doing, and as she relaxed, she breathed deeply. Gas rushed into the jar and through the tube to Muriel's lungs, soon rendering her unconscious. Reggie carried her into the bedroom, placed her on the bed, took off her panties, had intercourse with her and strangled her. When it came to disposing of the body, this time he could afford to work more leisurely since Ethel wasn't rushing home. Muriel's body was taken out to the wash-house, and that night it was buried in the garden.

Miss Eady was reported missing by relatives, but no trace of her could be found. No suspicion was ever cast in Christie's direction.

The war ended and Christie changed jobs again. He obtained a position as a clerk in the savings bank at the post office. The years passed, and Reggie kept running to Dr. Odess with his minor ailments. Nothing of a serious nature was ever uncovered by the doctor. Perhaps Reggie used these visits to gain a brief respite from his boring existence at home.

A break in the monotony came when another tenant took up residence at 10 Rillington Place. At Easter 1948, Timothy Evans and his wife Beryl moved into the upper flat. Beryl was 19, three months pregnant, and quite pretty, while Tim was 24 and not too bright. He was employed as a van driver and could only read with great difficulty—though he was by no means a simpleton, and had definite ideas on world events as he saw them unfold around him. If his interpretations were erroneous, who are we to criticize? He spent many a night at the pub, and prided himself on his capacity for beer. He was also a compulsive liar, as everyone who ever came in contact with him was quick to point out.

Six months later Beryl gave birth to a little girl whom the Evans christened Geraldine. The cramped quarters, the lack of toilet facilities, the dirty diapers and the inadequate wages Tim brought home were all conducive to bickering. The bickering led to arguments, and the arguments led to screaming fights. What had started out for the young Evanses as a happy, carefree life together had deteriorated to the point where Tim was spending more and more time at the pub and Beryl was slaving away to keep some semblance of a home at 10 Rillington Place.

In the summer of 1949, Beryl found herself pregnant again, and resolved to try to bring on a miscarriage. She tried various pills and home remedies without success, before deciding to have an abortion. She told several people about this, including the Christies. By now the Evanses and the Christies were seeing each other quite often. Tim and Beryl liked the Christies, and the Christies seemed to take to the young couple living above them.

But seeing an attractive girl like Beryl on a daily basis must have played havoc with Reggie's perverted urges. Every time she entered the house, went up the stairs, or went to the lavatory, she had to pass a doorway leading to Reggie's rooms. Only he knew of the two ladies who had been resting comfortably for years in the garden. Later, Reggie was to say he never thought much about the two bodies. Once, while digging in the garden, a human femur popped to the surface. He nonchalantly used it to prop up the sagging fence bordering his property. The weatherbeaten bone was to remain exposed in this way for years.

In October and November, a series of seemingly common, everyday events started to unfold that were later to come under meticulous study. Mr. Kitchener's sight became so bad that he went to the hospital for an operation. He remained in the hospital for five weeks and was therefore absent from the scene during the crucial weeks that were to follow.

Toward the end of October, the landlord at 10 Rillington Place hired a firm of builders to carry out some repairs to the building. These men were in and around the house on and off for the next 15 days. During this time Beryl Evans told a friend that considerate Mr. Christie was going to perform an abortion on her, despite her husband's objections. The atmosphere between husband and wife was strained over the operation and over a sum of money that Tim had given her to make a payment on their furniture, but which Beryl had spent on something else.

On November 7, it started to rain early in the morning, so the builders, who were not actively engaged in working on the roof, knocked off for the day. When Evans came home from work, his wife told him that Christie would be performing the operation on the following morning. The Evanses argued about the abortion all that evening. Next morning, Tim went to work. The weather had cleared and the workmen were back doing their repairs at eight o'clock. Mrs. Christie went out. Beryl waited upstairs, preparing herself for her operation. Finally, Reggie appeared carrying a rubber tube, which he attached to an outlet on the side of the fireplace. He told Beryl that a few gulps of gas would make the operation less painful.

We do not know exactly what happened next, but it is very possible that Christie made an unmedical improper move, because at this moment she realized what was happening and started to struggle. Christie struck her several blows to the head and strangled her with his rope. He then turned off the gas and had intercourse with her remains.

There was a knock on the door. God, how scared Christie must have been! Remember the telegraph boy arriving at the exact moment he killed Ruth Fuerst? This time Reg didn't know what to do. A friend of Beryl's, Joan Vincent, was surprised to find the door to the flat closed. Beryl had never kept it closed before. She felt her friend was inside and didn't want to see her. Somewhat annoyed, she expressed her feelings through the closed door and left. Reg Christie breathed a sigh of relief.

All the while workmen were scurrying about on the ground floor, in the wash-house and the lavatory. Reggie moved Beryl's body to the bedroom and covered her with a quilt. When Tim came home from work Christie met him at the door and explained that the operation had been a failure, and that Beryl was dead. He showed Tim his wife's body laid out on the bed, explaining that she had poisoned herself by trying to induce a miscarriage and would have died in a few days had he not tried to abort her. Evans, a bit slow-witted, accepted this explanation and went about changing his baby's diapers and giving her something to eat.

Christie explained that he was in a jam for trying to do Beryl a favor, and needed Tim's help. He said that they would dispose of the body and this way no one would get in trouble. Evans, stunned, scared, and slow to comprehend, put himself in Christie's hands. The two men carried the body down to Mr. Kitchener's vacant flat. Evans inquired of Christie just what he planned to do with the body.

Christie replied, "I'll dispose of it down one of the drains." Both men went to bed in their own flats.

The next day the sun's rays couldn't break through the overcast, dreary sky as Tim Evans awoke in his flat and Reg Christie got dressed on the ground floor. It was Wednesday, November 8, and there was the important matter of an infant child to contend with. Evans and Christie met in the hall, and Christie told him not to worry, he would look after the baby for the day, maybe even make some inquiries about adoption. Tim went to work a troubled, confused man.

At eight o'clock the workmen arrived again and went about their tasks. By four in the afternoon they had finished, and stored their gear in the washroom for the night.

When Evans returned, Christie informed him that he had found a couple who would make a good home for Geraldine. Reggie told him to dress and feed the baby before leaving for work the next day, and when the couple came around for the child in the morning, he would let them in and give Geraldine to them. Christie told Evans that if he ever received any inquiries about Beryl and Geraldine, he was to say they were away on vacation.

On Thursday, November 10, Reggie strangled the child with a necktie and placed it beside its mother in Mr. Kitchener's flat. Evans got fired from his job that same day and arrived home by 5:30. Christie told him everything had gone well, the couple had come and picked up the baby. Christie, good friend that he was, had thought of everything—he had even arranged to sell Evans' furniture, so there would be nothing keeping Evans from leaving London.

On Friday, November 11, the workmen finished their repairs and cleaned out all their gear from the wash-house, leaving it bare. That evening Christie, knowing the workmen would not be returning, placed the bodies of Beryl and Geraldine in the wash-house.

By Sunday, Evans had sold the furniture (which he didn't own) and said goodbye to the Christies. He told them he was going to Bristol, but actually he caught a train at Paddington for Cardiff and Merthyr Vale to visit his uncle and aunt, Mr. and Mrs. Lynch. Tim said that he and his boss were touring the area for some vague business reason and had had car trouble in Cardiff. He was wondering if he couldn't stay with them until the car was repaired. In passing, he mentioned that his wife and baby were vacationing in Brighton. Evans stayed with the Lynches for the next six days. He acted perfectly normally, went shopping with Mrs. Lynch and to the pub with Mr. Lynch. Once he talked to his aunt about getting his daughter a Christmas present.

On November 23, Evans showed up on Christie's doorstep inquiring about his daughter. Christie replied that she was well and happy with her new parents, but that it was too early to see her. Disappointed, Evans returned to Merthyr Vale.

He had to make up more lies to pacify the Lynches, and told them a not-too-convincing tale to the effect that Beryl had left him and that he had left his daughter with friends.

On November 27, Mrs. Lynch wrote to Tim's mother saying that he was staying with them and that they felt something was wrong because they couldn't get a straight answer from him. Tim's mother wrote back that she hadn't seen Beryl or the baby for a month. Mrs. Lynch read this letter to Tim and accused him of lying to them. Evans, beside himself at being caught in his web of lies and childlike in his indecision and lack of planning, decided to go to the police.

He walked into the police station at Merthyr Vale and told the officer on duty, "I want to give myself up. I have disposed of my wife, put her down the drain."

The officer on duty took this statement from Evans:

"About the beginning of October my wife, Beryl Susan Evans, told me that she was expecting a baby. She told me that she was about three months gone. I said, 'If you are having a baby, well, you've had one, another won't make any difference.' She then told me she was going to make herself ill. Then she bought herself a syringe, and started syringing herself. Then she said that didn't work, and I said, 'I am glad it won't work.' Then she said she was going to buy some tablets. I don't know what tablets she bought, because she was always hiding them from me. She started to look very ill, and I told her to go and see a doctor, and she said she'd go when I was in work, but when I'd come home and asked her if she'd been, she'd always say she hadn't.

"On the Sunday morning, that would be the sixth of November, she told me that if she couldn't get rid of the baby, she'd kill herself and our other baby Geraldine. I told her she was talking silly. She never said no more about it then, but when I got up Monday morning to got to work she said she was going to see some woman to see if she could help her, and that if she wasn't in when I came home, she'd be up at her grandmother's. Who the woman was she didn't tell me.

"Then I went to work. I loaded up my van and went on my journey. About nine o'clock that morning I pulled up at a transport cafe between Ipswich and Colchester. I can't say exactly where it is, that's the nearest I can give. I went up to the counter and ordered a cup of tea and breakfast, and I sat down by the table with my cup of tea waiting for my breakfast to come up, and there was a man sitting by the table opposite me. He asked me if I had a cigarette I could give him. I gave him one and he started talking about married life.

"He said to me, 'You are looking pretty worried, is there anything on your mind?' Then I told him all about it. So he said, 'Don't let that worry you. I can give you something that can fix it.' So he said, 'Wait there a minute, I'll be back,' and he went outside. When he came back he handed me a little bottle that was wrapped in a brown paper. He said, 'Tell your wife to take it first thing in the morning before she has any tea, then to lay down on the bed for a couple of hours and that should do the job.' He never asked no money for it. I went up to the counter and paid my bill and carried on with my journey.

"After I finished my work I went home, that would be between seven and eight. When I got in the house I took off my overcoat and hung it on the peg behind the kitchen door. My wife asked me for a cigarette and I told her that there was one in my pocket, then she found this bottle in my pocket, and I told her all about it...

"I got up in the morning as usual at six o'clock to go to work. I made myself a cup of tea and made a feed for the baby. I told her then not to take that stuff when I went in and said 'Good morning' to her, and I went to work, that would be about half past six. I finished work and got home about half past six in the evening. I then noticed that there was no lights in the place. I let the gas and it started to go out, and I went into the bedroom to get a penny and I noticed my baby in the cot. I put the penny in the gas and went back in the bedroom and lit the gas in the bedroom. Then I saw my wife laying in bed. I spoke to her but she never answered me, so I went over and shook her, then I could see she wasn't breathing. Then I went and made some food for my baby. I fed my baby and I sat up all night.

"Between about one and two in the morning, I got my wife downstairs through the front door. I opened the drain outside my front door, that is No. 10 Rillington Place, and pushed her body head first into the drain. I closed the drain, then I went back in the house. I sat down by the fire smoking a cigarette.

"I never went to work the following day. I went and got my baby looked after. Then I went and told my governor where I worked that I was leaving. He asked me the reason, and I told him I had a better job elsewhere. I had my cards and money that afternoon, then I went to see a man about selling my furniture. The man came down and had a look at my furniture and he offered me £40 for it. So I accept the £40. He told me he wouldn't be able to collect the furniture until Monday morning.

"In the meantime, I went and told my mother that my wife and baby had gone for a holiday. I stopped in the flat till Monday. The van came Monday afternoon and cleared the stuff out. He paid me the money. Then I caught the five to one train from Paddington and I come down to Merthyl Vale and I've been down here ever since. That's the lot.

(Signed) T.J. Evans"

The Merthyr Vale police put in a call to the Notting Hill police, who in turn sent a car over to 10 Rillington Place. Sure enough, there was a manhole in front of Number 10. It took three men to open the lid, but the drain was empty; there was no body. When the Merthyr Vale police told Evans, poor Tim was flabbergasted—the body must be there. Christie said he was going to put it down the drain.

Caught in a lie again, he tried to brazen it out. The detective asked him who helped him lift the manhole cover. Tim said he lifted the lid himself, which was an impossibility. Six hours later he gave another statement. This time he told substantially what he believed to be true, that his wife died during an illegal operation. The police were again dispatched to 10 Rillington Place to make a thorough search, and this time they found the body of Beryl Evans behind some boards under the sink in the wash-house. Geraldine's body was found behind the door with the necktie still around her neck.

Evans was brought from Wales to London, and told of the gruesome find at 10 Rillington Place. He made a further statement telling how he had killed his wife and daughter. He gave plausible, exact details of how he tied the necktie around Geraldine's neck. He said he was happy to get the guilty knowledge off his chest. He kept up these pronouncements of guilt until he met with his lawyers, at which point he abruptly changed his story to put the blame on the shoulders of Reg Christie.

Did the lawyers tell him to cut out his lying and tell the truth? Evans' lies were designed to protect his friend Christie and make it appear as if he, Evans, was confessing to clear up a distasteful, unfortunate death that was unavoidable. Evans didn't start out confessing to murder. Read the words carefully. He only wanted to impart the knowledge that his wife's body was down the drain, not that he killed her. It isn't easy to have murdered your wife and still to have put her down a drain, but poor Evans managed to confess to both without doing either.

On January 11, 1950, Timothy Evans stood trial for the murder of his daughter in London's Old Bailey. Reg Christie, the respected former policeman and neighbor to the accused murderer, was the chief prosecution witness. Evans, begging to be believed, testified that he had found out about his daughter's death only after he had been told by the police. When he was informed of her death he didn't care what happened to him, and confessed, incriminating himself as a double murderer. He started off trying to protect Christie, but now he had to tell the truth to save his own life. He said time and again, "Christie did it," but no one believed him. He further said that the details of the murders had been given to him little by little by the police. They had mentioned that Beryl had been strangled by a rope and Geraldine by a necktie, so that when time came for his to give his statement, he repeated the details. The police denied these accusations.

Evans made a hesitant, unbelievable witness in the dock. Reg Christie's straightforward aloofness was impressive. Wounded serving his country in the First World War, Reg was treated with deference by the presiding judge, even being given a chair to make him more comfortable in the witness box. No one took Evans' irresponsible accusations against him seriously. The jury took only forty minutes to find Evans guilty. All appeals failed, and on March 9, 1950, Timothy Evans was hanged.

And so the Christies returned to 10 Rillington Place. Month after dreary month, Christie complained of minor ailments that necessitated continual visits to Dr. Odess. Black Jamaicans had rented the flat above him, and this increased his bad disposition. Mrs. Christie, too, couldn't stand the blacks coming and going all day long in her hall.

Reggie worked for two years as a clerk for British Road Services, and being back at work and away from home seems to have relieved his nervousness and minor ailments. Then in the spring of 1952, he became ill with fibrositis and was confined to hospital for three weeks. When his doctors decided his trouble was psychological rather than physical, he was released.

At this time, another real problem came to a head. He had abandoned sexual relations with his wife since Evans' execution. Not only that, but Ethel started to get on his nerves about being impotent. Did Reggie again hear those boys from the streets of Halifax shouting "Reggie no dick?" Did he lie beside Ethel night after night with his hands reaching to his ears as the boys' voices taunted him—"Can't-make-it Reggie?" He left his job, and was thrown together with his wife day and night.

On the morning of December 14, 1952, Reg took a stocking that was lying on a chair near his bed, leaned over and strangled Ethel. Her body was to lie in the bed for two or three days while Reggie decided what to do with it. Then he remembered—of course, the loose floor boards in the front room. He rolled back the linoleum, and under the floor she went. Christie covered the body with earth, put back the linoleum, and it was as if Ethel had gone away to Sheffield for another of her visits.

To neighbors and friends who inquired after her, and there were a few, it being Christmas time, Christie explained that she had gone to Sheffield and he was following her there later, as he had accepted a good job opportunity that had suddenly come up. Her friends thought it strange that Ethel didn't say goodbye, but passed it off as a rush trip and let it go at that.

Christmas and New Year's came and passed. Reggie, who by this time was sprinkling deodorant around the front room, made arrangements to sell all his furniture. He received only £12 for the lot. The used furniture buyer wouldn't even take some of the pieces, they were in such bad shape. Reggie stayed on in the flat a little while after the furniture had been removed.

It was now January, and Christie was alone. His wife lay under the floorboards in the front room, Fuerst and Eady were only skeletal remains resting in the garden, the Evanses, mother and child, were gone, and Timothy had met his end at the hangman's noose. Even the furniture was gone. In Reggie's solitude, his mind turned to the necrophiliac thrills that had almost faded from his memory.

On a night in the middle of January, at about eight o'clock, Christie went into the Westminster Arms, where he met a prostitute, Kathleen Maloney. He had met the 26-year-old Kathleen before, and within a short time the pair was seen leaving the Westminster Arms together. Kathleen was quite drunk, and Reggie was taking her home. She didn't require the finesse of deception; Reggie merely sat her down on his chair, attached the rubber tube to the gas, and placed the exposed end of the tube close to her mouth so she was bound to breathe in some of the fumes. Soon Kathleen became drowsy and Reggie strangled her with his piece of rope. He removed her undergarments and had intercourse with her right in the chair. Then he brewed himself a pot of tea and went to bed. When he got up in the morning Kathleen was still in the chair.

Christie pondered a moment—what to do with this corpse? He pulled away a small cupboard, revealing an alcove he knew was off the kitchen. He bundled the body in a blanket, pulled a pillowslip over the head, then hauled the corpse into the alcove, where he arranged it with the legs in the air against the wall. He then covered it with some ashes and earth, and put the cupboard back in place.

The perverse thrill of long ago was now fresh in Reggie's mind, and he wanted more. A few days later he picked up an Irish girl named Rita Nelson, a 25-year-old prostitute who had convictions for soliciting and drunkenness in Ireland. She ended up in Reggie's death chair inhaling gas, and she, too, was ravished after death and her body placed with Kathleen's in the alcove, resting on its neck and head, with the legs extended in the air, propped up against the wall.

About a month went by. Then, quite by chance, Christie met Hectorina Maclennan and her boyfriend, a truck driver named Baker, in a cafe. When Christie found out they were looking for a flat he offered to show them his, which he told them he was about to vacate. It was sheer aggravation for Christie when Hectorina brought Baker with her to inspect the flat. Since they had nowhere else to stay, Christie gave them sleeping privileges and they stayed for three days and nights.

On the fourth day Christie had had enough of Baker, and asked the couple to leave. Later the same day Reggie sought out the couple and invited Hectorina to visit him alone. He said he had something to tell her. Hectorina showed up at 10 Rillington Place, and Reggie poured a drink. In a terrible state of nervousness he was fumbling with his rubber tube, connecting it to the gas, when she became suspicious and got up to leave. Christie caught up with her and strangled her in the hall. He lugged her back to the kitchen, and thinking she was still alive, gave her an application of his infernal inhaling mechanism. He then had intercourse with her and put her body with the other two in the alcove.

Baker grew uneasy when Hectorina had still not returned from 10 Rillington Place at 5:30, and he dropped over to inquire. Christie said that he hadn't seen her, and offered a social cup of tea. Later that evening, when Baker went looking for his girlfriend, Christie accompanied him.

Reggie papered over the entrance to the alcove, and set about subletting his empty flat. On the premises, but not included in the inventory, were two skeletons still resting peacefully in the garden, Mrs. Christie under the floorboards in the front room, and the three bodies upside down in the alcove. Not on the premises, but certainly the responsibility of Mr. Christie, was the entire Evans family. Nine bodies in all.

While sauntering down Ladbroke Grove on March 13, Christie met a Mrs. Reilly who was looking at advertisements showing flats for rent. Christie, who never had any difficulty striking up a conversation, told Mrs. Reilly that he had a vacant flat. She was delighted, and with her husband went to inspect the flat.

On March 16, her husband gave Christie £7.13s for three months' rent in advance. Four days later the Reillys moved in, and after borrowing a suitcase from Mr. Reilly, Christie left 10 Rillington Place forever. That very evening the landlord showed up, and was amazed to find the Reillys living there. He informed them that Christie was several months behind with his rent, and that while they could stay the night, they would have to leave in the morning. The Reillys left the next day, unaware that they had spent the night at close quarters with six assorted corpses.

The landlord gave permission to use the vacant Christie kitchen to Beresford Brown, who was occupying one of the Evans' rooms upstairs. He used the kitchen for the next few days and started to tidy up the place. On March 24, he decided to put up a shelf to hold a radio. He was tapping to find a solid wall, but he kept getting a hollow sound from the alcove that Christie had thoughtfully wallpapered over. He tore off a piece of paper, pointed his flashlight into the alcove, and found himself a place in every book ever written about infamous murders. There, in the alcove, with their legs in the air, were the bodies of Kathleen Maloney, Rita Nelson and Hectorina Maclennan.

Scotland Yard descended on 10 Rillington Place, and the three bodies were meticulously removed from the alcove, being photographed at every stage of their removal. Someone noticed that the boards in the front room were very loose, and in due course a fourth body was removed from under the floor.

Old London Town has provided us with some weird murders, and the men who investigate them tend to become blase with the passage of time. But even for them, four bodies in one house on one night was not a routine evening. The word went out—the police would like to question John Reginald Halliday Christie. The days passed and Christie's description was everywhere. The news reached new heights of sensationalism when Fuerst's and Eady's skeletons were discovered in the garden.

Where was the elusive Christie? Not really elusive at all—he was wandering the streets of London. On March 31, Police Constable Thomas Ledger saw a man near Putney Bridge. Constable Ledger asked him a few questions and ascertained that the man was Christie. Reggie was taken into custody.

From the beginning, Reggie confessed to all the murders, except that of little Geraldine Evans.

Christie was charged with murdering his wife, and appeared, ironically enough, in Number One Court of the very court where he had been the chief prosecution witness against Evans nearly four years earlier. Christie's lawyers never for a moment denied his guilt; they pleaded that he was quite mad.

On July 15, 1953, Christie was hanged for his crimes. In January 1966, Timothy Evans was granted a posthumous free pardon by the Queen.

FRED DEEMING

FRED Deeming was a boisterous, free-spending, fun-seeking fellow. He loved to dress in tweed from his head to his toes. Fred could usually be found in the local hotel regaling fellow patrons with his tales of humorous and sometimes dangerous exploits around the world. Sucking on his ornately carved meerschaum, with a mug of stout before him on the bar, Fred kept the good citizens of Rainhill, England, amused all through the summer of 1892.

Rainhill was a fitting stage for Fred and his stories. Located in Lancashire, not far from Liverpool, his audience had no way of knowing that their drinking companion, whom they knew as Albert Williams, was really an ex-con who had been convicted of robbery, extortion, arson, bigamy, fraud, and embezzlement.

Williams, as he called himself, was of average height, sported a moustache, and was of medium build. One day he just showed up, ostensibly to purchase a home for a Colonel Brooks, whom he claimed was planning to retire in Rainhill. Williams explained that both he and the colonel had recently returned to England from Australia. He neglected to point out that in reality he had a wife and four children stashed away in Birkenhead, living with one of his brothers.

Albert, fast worker that he was, noted a rather plain but well-turned-out lass clerking at a stationery store close by his hotel. Emily Mather, who lived with her widowed mother, was attracted to the tweed-bedecked Albert. Within two weeks Al had proposed to Emily. Nothing like this had ever happened to her before. Would she marry Al? You bet your life she would. Quick like a bunny, the pair became engaged.

In the meantime Al went about securing a home for the fictional Colonel Brooks. He rented a semi-detached, seven-room house known as Dinham Villa, with the stipulation that after the colonel occupied the house for six months the lease could be renewed. Al made one small request of the owner. It seems that Colonel Brooks had a chronic phobia about uneven floors. Al noticed that the kitchen floor was definitely uneven. Did the landlord have any objections to Al's cementing over the floor? With an eye to having a floor replaced at no expense, the owner of Dinham Villa consented to the renovations. Al immediately ordered copious quantities of cement. Later it became obvious that cement was positively Al's favorite manufactured product.

Down at the hotel Al passed the summer evenings pleasantly enough. He informed his drinking companions that his sister and her four children were planning a short visit. Fortunately, he explained, they would be able to stay at Dinham Villa as the colonel did not plan to take occupancy of the place for some time yet.

A short time later the townsfolk noted a middle-aged lady and her four offspring dashing about Dinham Villa. No doubt Al's sister and her children had arrived. Strangely enough, all five occupants of the house didn't venture far from the backyard. As Al explained it, it was all quite logical. His sister and her children would be joining her husband in California in a few days. They simply wanted to spend as much time with Al as possible before moving on. Six days after arriving, they apparently left the quiet and comfort of Dinham Villa, for they were never seen again. Once the relatives departed, Al went about laying a new cement floor. He supervised the workmen himself. In a few days the job was completed.

Al, who was chock full of schemes and ideas, informed his dear Emily and her mother that he had accepted an attractive job in Melbourne, Australia. He and Emily would sail in November, but first they would marry. On September 22, the vows were duly exchanged. Six weeks later the newlyweds bid farewell to the good folk of Rainhill and departed for Melbourne. Mrs. Mather was never to see her daughter again.

The Williamses landed in Windsor, a suburb of Melbourne. Emily was somewhat puzzled as to why her husband insisted that they use the name Mr. and Mrs. Droven. However, times were different before the turn of the century. It was not Emily's place to question her husband. If he said their name was to be Droven, then Droven it would be.

At this time Emily's letters to her mother indicated that she was having the adventure of her life. In all of them she praised her husband. Then according to neighbors, the love affair between the Drovens seemed to cool. Actually, it turned to ice water. Sometimes, late into the night, it was obvious that they were not throwing kisses at one another. Neighbors figured that it sounded more like chairs and dishes.

On December 24, a particularly loud piercing scream emanated from the Droven residence. Later, the only unusual occurrence noted by neighbors was a rather large delivery of cement to the Droven domicile. On January 5, Mr. Droven left for Sydney and informed the owners of the dwelling that he was vacating the premises. They proceeded to list the property with a rental agency, which immediately commenced to show it to prospective tenants.

As time wore on these potential tenants complained about the decidedly repugnant odor evident as soon as they entered the house. The rental agency people were inclined to agree. They called in the police to locate the cause of the offensive smell.

In the bedroom fireplace, under freshly poured cement, the police found Emily's body. Her head had been smashed in with a blunt instrument and her throat had been slashed. On a table in the bedroom was a Bible. Inside the cover was the name of the previous owner, Mrs. E. Mather, Rainhill, England.

While the police searched for the elusive Mr. Droven they also began tracing his trail back to Rainhill. Mrs. Mather sadly confirmed that the murdered woman was no doubt her daughter. She also informed police that while Droven, whom she knew as Williams, had lived in Rainhill, he had redone the floor of Dinham Villa with cement. Not only that, but a woman and four children had stayed in the house.

Dinham Villa, which was still vacant, was searched by police, who tore up the kitchen floor. The bodies of a woman and four children were recovered. All except a baby had had their throats cut. The infant had been strangled. The victims were identified as Deeming's wife and children.

Now Deeming's murderous activities occupied the front pages of newspapers on two continents. Indeed, most of the English-speaking world awaited his capture. All of this activity seems not to have bothered Deeming at all. Posing as Baron Swanston, he met a cute little number named Kate Rounsfell on the boat from Melbourne to Sydney. By the time the sweet-talking Baron disembarked, he and Kate, believe it or not, were unofficially engaged.

The pair made their way to Bathurst, where Kate introduced her fiancé to her parents. They were duly impressed. Making some excuse or other the Baron left Kate and her family and made his way to Southern Cross.

He wired Kate enough money so that she could join him. En route to her lover she was informed that the police had picked up her Baron as a suspected multiple murderer. Kate turned right around and went back to her parents. For the rest of her life she knew that she had come within a whisker of ending up under some cement floor.

Deeming was transported from Perth to Sydney, to Adelaide, to Melbourne. Everywhere the prisoner was taken, huge crowds formed to catch a glimpse of the infamous murderer.

At his trial Deeming's attorneys attempted to prove that he was insane, but their efforts were futile. A jury brought in a verdict of guilty with a rider that, in their opinion, the prisoner was sane and knew the difference between right and wrong.

When asked if he had anything to say before sentence was passed, Deeming surprised the court by speaking for over an hour, claiming that he certainly was insane because he didn't even remember killing his wife and children back in Rainhill, England.

Deeming was hanged in Australia for the murder of Emily Mather. Had he managed to evade punishment for this crime, he would have been extradited to England to stand trail for the murder of his family.

The memorabilia of Deeming's crimes have gradually been obliterated. For years his wax image was displayed in Madame Tussaud's Chamber of Horrors in London, England. In more recent years, new monsters have taken his place in infamy. Dinham Villa, where five innocent people were murdered, was a sore reminder of the Deeming case. The owner of the property had it demolished, giving strict instruction that not one brick remain.

ARTHUR DEVEREUX

To look at Arthur Devereux, you'd never think he was one of the most cold-hearted fathers who ever drew breath. At the same time, weird Art loved one of his sons more than life itself.

Art wasn't tough to take in the looks department. He was a tall, slim charmer who could talk the birds out of the trees. One fine day in 1898, when he was displaying his charm, as well as his physical attributes, Art met Beatrice Gregory. Beatrice and her mom were vacationing in Hastings, England. Beatrice, who felt life was passing her by, took one look at Art and fell madly in love. Even her mom had to admit that on the surface Art appeared to be the genuine article. The attractive young couple were married after knowing each other for only a few months.

The marriage didn't go well. Charming Art turned out to be decidedly disinterested in his new wife. Well, that's not exactly true. He was attentive enough to put Beatrice in the family way only a few months after the minister had assisted in tying the knot.

Little Stanley's arrival was a joyous occasion, but it did tax the family's already stretched income, which was derived solely from Art's efforts as a chemist's assistant. Art did what he could. He changed jobs, moved to London. Nothing seemed to alleviate the financial pressure.

Art blamed Beatrice for all the family's problems. He yelled at her, insulted her and was an absolute boor. Strangely enough, while he grew to hate Beatrice, he was extremely fond of little Stanley. Nothing was too good for his son. Eventually, Art's world revolved around the boy.

Timing is everything. Of necessity, Beatrice had to inform her husband, that due to a lunar miscalculation, she was pregnant again. Art threw a tantrum, but that didn't prevent Beatrice, after the prescribed nine months, from presenting Art with a newborn babe. Make that babes. Beatrice had twins.

Human behavior is a strange phenomenon. Just as Art doted on Stanley, Beatrice had eyes only for the twins. The split in parental affection did nothing to cement the Devereux marriage. As the months turned into years, Art grew not only to hate his wife, but also the twins. In his warped mind, he felt if he had only to fend for himself and Stanley, everything would be fine. His income would do nicely. It just wasn't adequate to support five individuals.

Art was a man with a problem. He thought and thought and finally formed a diabolical plot. He purchased a large trunk, which he placed in the middle of the living room. Beatrice, in that annoying low voice of hers, inquired why, with money so scarce, they needed a big trunk. Art informed her he planned to store some useless articles that were hanging around the house. The explanation seemed to satisfy Beatrice.

Next day, Art brought home a bottle of tonic for Beatrice and the twins. She had complained all three were feeling poorly. Art volunteered to bring home a sure cure for what ailed them. The sure cure was laced with fatal quantities of morphine. Beatrice and the twins took liberal doses of the deadly concoction. Art placed all three bodies in the large trunk.

Next morning, Art made a substantial breakfast for himself and Stanley before venturing forth to make arrangements for the trunk to be picked up and placed in long-term storage. Art moved out of his flat and took new lodgings in London. He left his job and got another. He enrolled Stanley in a private school. Life was going to be perfect. He and Stanley were on the threshold of a new beginning.

If it weren't for Art's mother-in-law, it is quite possible Art might have pulled off the perfect triple murder. Mrs. Gregory had remained close to her daughter throughout her marriage, although in recent years, because of Art's vile temper and gross behavior, she hadn't visited as often as she once did. Now, all of a sudden, she couldn't locate her daughter's entire family. It took Mrs. Gregory several weeks to trace Art. She was dumbfounded to discover that Beatrice and the twins were not with him. Art appeared ill at ease when interrogated by the not-so-calm Mrs. Gregory. He told her some cock-and-bull story about Beatrice and the twins being away in the country on vacation. When pressed, Art refused to give Mrs. Gregory their address.

Mrs. Gregory, who may have had police blood coursing through her veins, made not-so-discreet inquiries around her daughter's former neighborhood. No one could remember anything unusual, except for an extremely large trunk being removed from the Devereux flat just before Art moved out. Mrs. Gregory tracked down the moving company, dashed down to their facilities and demanded in no uncertain terms that the trunk be opened. We all know what was found inside.

Meanwhile, Art knew his mother-in-law only too well. He realized she would trace the trunk, and he was right. By the time Inspector. Pollard of Scotland Yard knocked on Art's front door, he was gone. Art made his way to Coventry, where he obtained a job at his profession of chemist's assistant. The inspector knew his quarry would have to seek employment to support himself and Stanley. He advised all chemists to report any recent applicants for a position. In this way, Art was located working in Coventry.

When Pollard showed up at Art's place of employment and introduced himself, the wanted man volunteered this rather unfortunate statement: "I don't know anything about a trunk." The inspector knew he was in the right place.

Art was tried for the murder of his wife and two children in London's Old Bailey. He claimed Beatrice had killed the kids and then committed suicide. He realized no one would believe he wasn't the killer. He admitted he had purchased the trunk and placed the bodies inside. It was a fanciful story, believed by no one. The Crown produced telegrams proving Art had applied for a new job before Beatrice's death. One telegram stated he was a widower with one child.

When Arthur Devereux was sentenced to death in the Old Bailey, Mrs. Gregory sat in court clutching the hand of her seven-year-old grandson, Stanley. He was all she had. The man in the prisoner's box had killed the rest of her family.

Arthur Devereux, who left something to be desired as a father, was hanged on August 15, 1905 at Pentonville Prison.

JACK THE RIPPER

JACK the Ripper holds a fascination for criminologists and the general public that has not diminished for over 100 years.

He appeared in the East End of a turbulent London, England in 1888. The Whitechapel District of London was the last stop on the road down for the derelicts of the nation, and indeed a great portion of Europe. It is estimated that 15,000 men, women, and children did not have a roof over their heads. Workhouses held over 128,000 souls. There were 80,000 prostitutes plying the oldest profession throughout London. Large ethnic groups from the continent who could neither read nor write English tried to eke out a living.

Gin was the cheapest alcoholic beverage, and it was consumed in great quantities in the pubs that dotted the area. Beds were sold several times in one night. Crime in general and murder in particular ran wild in Whitechapel.

Jack the Ripper was the tip of the iceberg. The horror, audacity and method of his killings were so terrible that they brought the plight of the general population of the worst slums in the world to the attention of the authorities.

Mary Ann Nicholls was a 42-year-old prostitute. She had five front teeth missing. Dental care did not rank high on Mary Nicholls' list of priorities. On the night of August 31, 1888, she passed her old friend Nelly Holland. Nelly was later to say that Mary was so drunk she could hardly walk.

In the darkness of Bucks Row just off Whitechapel, a hand clamped over Mary's mouth from behind. A razor sharp knife held in Jack's other hand made a wide arc, starting under the left ear and ending across the throat under the right ear. The rip was so vicious it nearly decapitated the victim. His work not finished, the Ripper plunged his knife into the lower part of the abdomen and cut upward and to the right. Again the knife was plunged into the body, and from the lower abdomen the cut proceeded up the centre of the body to the breastbone. The two slashes just described became the trademark of Jack the Ripper.

Eight days later, Annie Chapman was walking the streets at two o'clock in the morning. She couldn't raise the two pennies for a bed for the rest of the night.

Annie was 47, and suffered from consumption. Her body was found next morning behind a house on Hanbury Street. The throat cut, the body laid open were plainly in evidence, but there was much more. The body was disembowelled and the womb had been removed. The intestines had been lifted out of the body and placed on the shoulder of the corpse. The doctors examining the body suggested that some of the incisions indicated knowledge of formal medical training.

On September 30, the Ripper struck again, twice on the same night. Louis Diemschultz drove his horse into a yard at 40 Berners Street. The horse shied and Diemschultz noticed what he thought was a bag of something lying against a wall. What he found was the remains of Elizabeth Stride. Only the throat had been cut. There was no mutilation. The Ripper had been interrupted in his work. It is believed that he may have still been at the scene, and was the cause of the horse shying as it did. Certainly he made a hurried exit out the back yard. A few minutes later Catherine Eddowes fell into his grasp. He mutilated her in the style of Annie Chapman. Poor Catherine Eddowes was, like her fellow victims, a middle-aged alcoholic prostitute. A man she was currently living with identified the body.

A German immigrant came forward and said he had seen Eddowes with a man shortly before she was killed. He described her escort as a man of about 30, well-dressed, fair complexion, moustache, medium build and about five-feet, eight-inches tall. The description fit thousands of men in London. Then the police released this letter they had received just before the double killing:

Dear Boss,
I keep on hearing the police have caught me, but they won't fix me just yet. I have laughed when they looked so clever and talk about being on the right track. The joke about Leather Apron gave me real fits.

I am down on whores and I shan't quit ripping them till I do get buckled. Grand work, the last job was. I gave the lady no time to squeal. How can they catch me now? I love my work and want to start again. You will soon hear of me and my funny little games.

I saved some of the proper red stuff in a ginger beer bottle over the last job, to write with, but it went thick like glue and I can't use it. Red ink is fit enough I hope. Ha! Ha!

The next job I do I shall clip the lady's ears off. Keep this letter back till I do a bit more work, then give it out straight. My knife is nice and sharp. I want to get to work right away if I get a chance. Good luck.

Yours truly
Jack the Ripper

Don't mind me giving the trade name, wasn't good enough to post this before I got all the red ink off my hands curse it. No luck yet they say I am a doctor now. ha ha

A few hours after the double murder the police received this postcard:

I was not kidding dear old Boss when I gave you the tip. You'll hear about Saucy Jack's work tomorrow. Double event this time. Number one squealed a bit. Couldn't finish straight off. Had no time to get ears for police. Thanks for keeping last letter back till I got to work again.

Jack the Ripper

The police considered both the letter and card to be genuine.

A Whitechapel Vigilante Committee was formed and was now actively engaged patrolling the streets late at night. The chairman of the committee, a Mr. George Lusk, received a letter enclosed in a box.

It read:

Mr. Lusk
Sir I send you half the Kidney I took from one woman presarved it for you, other piece I fried and ate it was very nice. I may send you the bloody knife that took it out if you only wate a while longer.

Signed Catch me when you can

This letter too is considered to be genuine. The kidney that had been enclosed with the letter had been removed from a human body not more than two weeks previously. It was in an advanced state of Bright's Disease. Eddowes was suffering from Bright's Disease, and her kidney had been removed by her killer.

Mary Kelly was the last to die at the hands of Jack the Ripper. She was a heavy drinker and a prostitute. Unlike the previous victims she was attractive, and only 25 years old. She even had her own room at 13 Miller's Court. Mary was on the skids but had not made the complete trip. On Thursday night, November 8, she picked up a customer and took him to her room. For the first time Jack the Ripper had no fear of discovery or interruption. He had reached the pinnacle of wanton mutilation and savagery in his treatment of Mary Kelly. Her body was hacked beyond recognition. The police officers who witnessed the scene at 13 Miller's Court were never to forget the sight that greeted them on November 9 when the body was discovered. Mary Kelly had been three months pregnant.

On Wednesday Nov. 21, the police received this letter:

Dear Boss.

It is no use for you to look for me in London because I'm not there. Don't trouble yourself about me until I return, which will not be very long. I like the work too well to leave it alone. Oh, it was a jolly job the last one. I had plenty of time to do it properly in Ha, ha, ha! The next lot I mean to do with Vengeance, cut of their head and arms. You think it is a man with a black moustache. Ha, ha, ha! When I have done another one you can try and catch me again. So goodbye dear Boss, till I return.

Yours,
Jack the Ripper

Jack the Ripper was never heard from again. It was generally agreed by the police in 1888 that while there were murders before the outbreak and some after it that were similar in nature, it is only those described here that are attributed to the one person. There were five in all, starting on the night of August 31, and abruptly ending 70 days later in the early morning hours of November 9.

Who committed these horrible crimes? There have been many theories.

Dr. Neill Cream is erroneously believed to be Jack the Ripper by many students of the case. He was born in 1850 in Glasgow, Scotland and immigrated to Canada in 1863. At the age of 26, he received his medical degree from McGill University in Montreal. In 1881, he was found guilty of poisoning a friend in Chicago and was sentenced to life imprisonment in Joliet, Illinois, but was out in 10 years. He appears on the London scene in October of 1891, where he started killing prostitutes by poisoning them. He would write letters to newspapers keeping the unsolved cases alive. In this way he brought suspicion to himself, and was finally tried and found guilty. He was hung on November 15, 1892. On the scaffold Dr. Cream's last words were "I am Jack the —."

It is unfortunate that positive documentation exists proving beyond a doubt that Dr. Cream was confined to Joliet Prison in Illinois during the 10 weeks Jack was committing his murders in London.

The Duke of Clarence was Queen Victoria's grandson, and was in a direct line to the throne of England. In 1970, Dr. Thomas Stowell wrote an article claiming that the Duke was Jack the Ripper. It seems the Duke was quite a ladies' man. The story goes that he contracted syphilis in his early twenties. As a result he was under the care of a doctor, Sir William Gull. The good doctor tried to restrain the Duke, but after the Kelly murder he knew he had to have him confined to a mental home.

Queen Victoria was accustomed to consulting a spiritualist named Lees. It is said that Lees saw the face of the murderer in his dreams. One day while travelling on a bus he saw the man who had appeared in his dreams sitting beside him. He followed this man off the bus to the home of Sir William Gull. Dr. Stowell's theory received wide publicity, and it is disheartening to report that there is documentary proof that Clarence was at Sadringham from November 3-12, 1888, and could not have killed Mary Kelly in London.

And so the theories go, from a Jewish butcher, to a medical student, to a secret agent of the Russian Czar.

There is only one theory and one man who fits all the known facts.

During the course of research for a television program in 1959, Lady Aberconway was interviewed. She was the elderly daughter of Sir Melville Macnaghten, who was Assistant Chief Constable of Scotland Yard in 1889, only a few months after the killings. Surprisingly, after all these years, Lady

Aberconway produced her father's notes. Here was a direct link to the man who had actually hunted Jack the Ripper. From these notes we learn what the police believed at the time of the hunt.

Montague J. Druitt was born on August 15, 1857. His father was a doctor and the entire family was highly respected. Young Druitt whizzed through school and ended up with a B.A. degree from Oxford University in 1880. On March 30, 1885 he received his law degree. It seems that he was unsuccessful in his practise of law, and in 1888 he was teaching at a private school and living in rooms at Kings Bench Walk. On December 31, 1888, M.J. Druitt's body was recovered from the Thames, his pockets full of stones. He had leaped to his death on December 4, twenty five days after the last Ripper murder.

Shortly before the first Ripper murder, Druitt's mother became insane, and Druitt thought he was going mad. He left a suicide note expressing his fear. The Macnaghten notes reveal the fact that all police agencies as well as vigilante committees were given the word to stop looking for the Ripper after Druitt's body was found. The police kept all information from the general public in order to save the respected Druitt family from unnecessary embarrassment.

The eyewitness reports fit Druitt. The idea that he was a gentleman fit Druitt's station in life. The Ripper's letters have been analyzed by experts, and they believe they were written by an educated man disguising his handwriting and using poor grammar to throw the police off the track. Would a real illiterate write the word "knif" or would "nife" be more natural?

It has always been believed that the Ripper had medical knowledge, or at least medical instruments. Druitt's father, uncle and cousin were all doctors, so he had ready access to medical instruments and could easily have picked up some knowledge from attending post mortems with his father. Druitt also lived in the centre of the area where the killings took place. This would give him the knowledge that the killer obviously had of the general area. It also gave him a place to go immediately after each killing.

Dr. Peter Druitt lives in Christchurch, New Zealand. He is the great grandson of Robert Druitt, Montague's uncle. He says that having Jack the Ripper as a possible ancestor is most enjoyable, and really livens up his otherwise dull family tree.

DOROTHEA WADDINGHAM

DOROTHEA Nancy Waddingham despised working on the family farm located about six miles north of Nottingham, England. She was thrilled when, at age 23, she secured a job at the Burton-on-Trent Workhouse Infirmary. It was here that she obtained her nursing experience, although she never did become a registered nurse. Nurse Waddingham, as she came to be known, was destined to go down in criminal history as one of England's most notorious female killers.

After two years working at the infirmary, Dorothea met Thomas Leech. In 1925, they married. Tommy wasn't that great a catch. He was more than twice Dorothea's age, didn't have two coins to rub together and was sickly. Dorothea spent most of her time working and looking after her husband. During the course of their marriage, Tommy was well enough to sire three children; Edwin, Alan and Mary.

After eight years of this less than ideal existence, Tommy introduced his wife to a friend, Ronald Sullivan. A short time later, generous Tommy invited Ron to move in with him and his family. Tommy didn't care that his wife was planning to make a nursing home out of their modest dwelling on Haydn Rd. in Nottingham. He did co-operate in his own fashion by dying of natural causes. Ron Sullivan stayed on with Dorothea and the kids. Soon after Tommy's demise, Dorothea and her menagerie relocated to 32 Devon Dr., where she went about attempting to build up a nursing home business.

One fine day in 1935, an official of the County Nursing Association called at the house on Devon Dr. Miss Blagg was constantly looking for adequate accommodation for the chronically ill. She approached Dorothea about two prospective clients—elderly Mrs. Baguley and her daughter, Ada. Mrs. Baguley was a feeble 90-year-old. Ada, 50, suffered from paralysis sclerosis and was grossly overweight. Both women had reached the stage in their lives where they couldn't look after themselves. Miss Blagg struck a deal with Nurse Wadding-ham and the pair moved into her nursing home. They accepted the arrangement on a trial basis for a month, stipulating that they would stay on if the accommodations and medical attention met their standards.

Three weeks later, Ada and her mother informed Miss Blagg that they were more than pleased with the home and planned to remain there. Several acquaintances visited in the following months and found both women cheerful and content. One touch of sadness befell the home when the only other patient, a Mrs. Kemp, died. In her final days her doctor prescribed morphia tablets, which were to play a large part in events to follow.

Life went on. Nurse Waddingham soon realized that the Baguleys required much more care than she had anticipated, although they were pleasant and obviously happy living at her home. Ada was not without funds. She often stated that these funds were a guarantee that she and her mother would not have to end their days in what was then called a poorhouse. The few thousand pounds and some property had been left to her dear mother. A cousin, Fred Gilbert, was executor and trustee of their wills.

Fred held a very special place in Ada's heart. Some 20 years earlier, they had been engaged to marry. The onset of Ada's illness postponed the wedding until finally, with the spreading of her disease, both knew they would never marry. Fred remained a close friend of Ada's and visited her often.

Some four months after Ada and her mother moved into the nursing home, Ada made a new will, leaving her entire estate to Nurse Waddingham in exchange for accommodation for herself and her mother for the rest of their lives. Ada's lawyer attempted to talk her out of such a will, pointing out that if anything unforeseen happened to Nurse Waddingham, she might find herself and her mother in a precarious position. Ada insisted, but did allow her lawyer to add Ron Sullivan to the will as an equal recipient of her estate.

Six days after this document was signed, Mrs. Baguley died and was buried at Caunton Church. All the participants in our drama attended the sad affair. Fred Gilbert guided Ada's wheelchair into the churchyard. When it was over, Ada returned to the nursing home. Months passed. Ada's good friends in the area continued to visit her at the home. On September 10, 1935, an old friend spent some time with Ada in the garden. The next day, around 9 a.m., Ron Sullivan called for medical assistance. Dr. Manfield arrived after 12 a.m. to find Ada dead. He attributed death to cerebral hemmorhage due to cardiovascular degeneration. Ada's body was scheduled to be cremated according to her wishes.

The first suspicion regarding Ada's death was raised when a crematorium official received a note allegedly written in advance by the deceased. It read: "It is my last wish that my relatives not know of my death." The unusual request prompted Dr. Cyril Banks, Medical Officer of Health for Nottingham, to institute an investigation into Ada's death.

A post-mortem examination was conducted. The results indicated that Dr. Manfield's stated cause of death had been wrong. Ada had died from morphine poisoning. It was found in her stomach, spleen, kidneys, liver and heart. There was no doubt Ada had been poisoned and grave suspicion that Mrs. Baguley might also have been poisoned. Her body was exhumed. Once again, morphine was evident.

The day after this last distasteful fact was made public, Fred Gilbert committed suicide. It is believed Fred had become depressed at the untimely deaths and may have felt had he married Ada, both mother and daughter would still be alive.

Once the conditions of Ada's will became known, Nurse Waddingham was immediately suspected of double murder. She was arrested and stood trial for murder. Prosecution attorneys leaned heavily on the fact that morphine tablets were in the home after Mrs. Kemp died. Doctors testified that at no time had they prescribed morphine for Ada or her mother.

Dorothea Waddingham was found guilty of murder. She was hanged on April 16, 1936 at Winson Green Prison in Birmingham.

GRAHAM YOUNG

As I drove into the peaceful village of Bovingdon, it was early in the morning. The fog was lifting from the rolling English countryside. I couldn't help but think of Graham Young driving up to work over these very same roads, his mind contemplating how much antimony he would administer to his fellow employees. Would Diana Smart get enough to send her home for a few days? Would Peter Buck be back today? If so, it just might be his turn for a dose.

But the Graham Young story doesn't start in this quaint English village. It begins in Honeyport Lane Maternity Hospital, North London, on September 7, 1947; for that was the day Graham was born.

Molly Young didn't have an easy pregnancy. She had pleurisy while carrying Graham, and although her new son grew to be a healthy baby, it was discovered that Molly had contracted tuberculosis. She died two days before Christmas when Graham was three months old.

Fred Young, a machine setter by trade, was beside himself with grief at the loss of his wife. He decided to keep his little family as close to him as possible without the benefit of a mother. Fred had one other child, a daughter, Winnifred, who was eight-years-old at the time of her mother's death. Winnie and her father went to live with Fred's mother at Links Rd., while Graham moved in with an aunt and uncle at 768 North Circular Rd. in the Neasdon section of North London. The two addresses were not that far apart, and the little family managed to get together each weekend.

Three years later, Fred Young met another lady named Molly. At the age of 33, Fred calculated that he could still have a chance for a happy and contented life with a new wife and his two children. He married Molly, purchased the house at 768 North Circular Rd., and moved in with Winnie and three-year-old Graham.

As Graham grew up it was noted that he wasn't a joiner. He read incessantly. Other than playing with his sister and a cousin, he kept pretty much to himself. Throughout his early years in school, he was considered to be well above average in his studies. His stepmother, Molly, doted on Graham, who appeared to return her love with genuine affection.

At the age of nine, Graham Young was experimenting with varnish and nail polish. He was not doing anything malicious with these substances, but experimenting with them to ascertain the qualities inherent in various products. For a nine-year-old child, many would think this advanced element of curiosity in Graham's makeup to be a very admirable trait.When Molly found acid and ether in Graham's room, she rightly felt that her son's interest had become abnormal for a child his age. Upon being questioned, Graham told his mother that he had found the substances in garbage thrown out by the local drugstore. Later she found books on witchcraft and the Nazi party in Graham's room.

By the time Graham was 12, his teachers believed that he had an outstanding future in the field of chemistry. Unknown to them, he was poisoning rats and performing autopsies on their bodies. His family was continually amazed at his advanced knowledge of chemicals. They could show Graham a detergent or waxing agent and he would rhyme off the chemicals which made up the product and what interaction was involved to make the substances perform as advertised.

At the age of 13, Graham knew the exact quantities of various poisons which could prove to be fatal. He also knew the effects of administering small quantities of certain poisons over a prolonged period of time. In fact, Graham was now an expert on the subject of poison. While everyone thought him a quiet little boy, no one knew the extent of his weird obsession.

In April 1961, Graham gave a cock-and-bull story to the chemist in his neighborhood, and managed to purchase 25 grams of antimony. He signed the poison book with the fictitious name M.E. Evans, and gave a phony address. Out of his allowance received from his father, and with money from odd jobs performed at a local cafe, Graham continued to purchase quantities of antimony.

His closest school chum, Chris Williams, remembers that Graham often showed him a vial of poison. Chris thought it was a great joke, somewhat akin to the country boy showing his pet frog to his buddies.

Once the boys had a falling out, as little boys often do. A few days later Chris had severe stomach pains. He had to leave school for the day. All through the spring and summer of 1961, Chris suffered from severe stomach pains which were often accompanied by vomiting. Later he realized that his discomfort always followed those occasions when he and Graham skipped school together. On those days Graham was in the habit of sharing his sandwiches with Chris.

Chris' stomach pains and headaches became so bad that he was forced to visit his family doctor, Dr. Lancelot Wills. The doctor couldn't find anything specifically wrong with Chris, but thought his head-aches were migraines.

One day, while cleaning Graham's room, Molly found a bottle of antimony. She had no idea what it was, but clearly understood the skull and crossbones on the label. She told Fred of her discovery. They both faced Graham and forbade him to have such dangerous substances in the house. Molly then went around to the chemist shop named on the bottle, and, in no uncertain terms, told the chemist never to sell Graham any dangerous materials. Unknown to his parents, Graham merely changed chemists.

It wasn't long after this incident that Molly Young began suffering from an upset stomach. She felt weak and lethargic. She often discussed her illness with Graham. It was his custom to have tea with his mother every day after school. Finally, Molly became so ill, she was taken to hospital, where she made a speedy recovery. Her illness was thought to be an ulcer. Poison was never suspected.

It is interesting to note that once antimony has passed through the body, no trace can be detected. Molly's recovery was to be temporary.

One day Winnie, now an attractive 22-year-old girl with a steady boyfriend, collapsed outside a cinema. She, too, was having periodic spells of abdominal pain accompanied by vomiting. This most recent attack set Winnie thinking. Why hadn't it occurred to her before? Her kid brother with his silly chemistry experiments. No doubt he had used the family dishes to perform the experiments. Some toxic substance might have adhered to a cup, causing Molly and her to become ill. She decided to speak to her father.

Fred Young didn't believe that Graham would bring poison into the house after being told to keep the terrible stuff away. Nevertheless, Fred gave Graham a real tongue lashing.

Soon Fred came down with a severe case of cramps. He never complained much, because at the same time his wife Molly became seriously ill. This time she had a complete new set of symptoms. She woke up on Easter Saturday, 1962, with a sensation of pins and needles in her hands and feet. Graham was concerned and solicitous towards his stepmother. It was decided to rush Molly to the hospital.

Once in the hospital Molly said to one of the doctors, "I hope you're not going to be long about this, because I've got my husband's dinner to get." Within minutes of making this frivolous remark, Molly Young, aged 38, was dead. For about a year, Graham had been feeding Molly antimony and observing the results. On the evening before Molly died, Graham had laced a trifle with twenty grains of thallium. It was this massive dose which caused her death. Graham probably didn't know it, but he had just become the first person in England ever to commit murder by the administration of deadly, tasteless, odorless thallium.

A post mortem failed to reveal the true cause of death. The following Thursday, Molly was cremated. Graham Young, at the age of 14, had committed the perfect murder. When mourners gathered at the family residence to pay their respects, Graham doctored a sandwich with a small quantity of antimony. One of his mother's relatives became violently ill. Graham was just having a little fun.

A few days after his wife's funeral, Fred Young suffered a series of stomach pains accompanied by violent bouts of vomiting. Finally his daughter Winnie forced him to see their family physician, Dr. Wills. The doctor could find no reason for the illness, but was startled when, at the conclusion of the examination, Fred collapsed on the office floor. He was rushed to Willisden General Hospital, where Molly had died less than two weeks before.

After spending two days in hospital, often comforted by his son who visited him constantly, Fred Young began to feel better. Graham seemed to enjoy himself around the hospital, amazing doctors by his knowledge of things medical. Fred was taken home, but in a few days his pains became so severe that Winnie rushed her father back to the hospital.

That same night doctors were surprised when extensive tests confirmed that Fred was suffering from antimony poisoning.

We must pause here to keep in mind that Graham was a quiet, studious youngster of 14. It was difficult for his family to accept the facts as we are able to do from the benefit of hindsight. Graham's father was the first to actually believe that his son had been administering poison to the entire family for more than a year. Doctors told him that one more dose of antimony would have proven fatal. Fred Young recovered, but has a permanently damaged liver as a result of his son's handiwork. He also lives today with the realization that Graham was responsible for his stepmother's death.

While Fred Young lingered in hospital with his dark suspicions, direct action came from another source. Graham's chemistry teacher, Mr. Hughes, heard of Mr. Young being rushed to hospital so soon after his wife's death. Lately, Mr. Hughes had wondered about Graham's lack of interest in his chemistry experiments. It appeared that the boy was obsessed with experiments using poisons, and recording data derived from his experiments in a notebook. Mr. Hughes decided to stay late at school and search Graham's desk. He found several bottles of poison.

Recalling Chris Williams' illness, Mr. Hughes felt the whole thing was just too much. He contacted the headmaster of the school and together they went to see Dr. Wills. The three men exchanged notes and, for the first time, the magnitude of Graham's poisonous endeavors came to light.

They arranged for a psychiatrist, posing as a guidance counsellor, to consult with Graham. Graham loved to display his knowledge of pharmacology and had a learned discussion with the psychiatrist, who was amazed at the lad's understanding of the subject. He went straight to the police with his suspicions.

Next day, Detective Inspector Edward Crabbe searched Graham's room. He found quantities of antimony, thallium, digitalis, iodine, atropine, and barium chloride. When Graham was searched, police found a vial of antimony, as well as two bottles of thallium, in his shirt. Later he referred to the vial of antimony as his little friend. Taken to jail the following morning, Graham revealed his entire career as a poisoner to the police.

Graham Young was unique. Obviously his age alone set him apart from most killers, but, above all, the fact that he lacked any motive made his crimes different. He did not dislike the people he poisoned. They were given poison specifically because they were close at hand and could be observed. Graham was experimenting, much as a scientist does with guinea pigs.

On July 5, 1962, Graham was tried in London's Old Bailey, one of the youngest ever to appear in the famous old court. He was charged with poisoning his father, his sister, and his schoolchum, Chris Williams. The charge of murdering his stepmother was not pressed. Her ashes were scattered, and it was believed nothing could be gained by bringing further charges against such a young boy.

Dr. Christopher Fysh, a psychiatrist attached to the Ashford Remand Centre, where Graham had been housed awaiting his trial, told of his conclusions after having extensive conversations with Graham. He quoted Graham as telling him, "I am missing my antimony. I am missing the power it gives me." The doctor elaborated on Graham's knowledge of drugs, and stated that on several occasions Graham had corrected him in minor areas when the properties of various drugs were discussed. Dr. Fysh suggested that Graham was obsessed with the sense of power his poisons gave him. In the doctor's opinion, given the chance, Graham would continue to experiment on humans. Dr. Fysh thought Graham should be confined to a maximum security hospital. As a result, he was sentenced to Broadmoor for a period of 15 years.

In July 1962, the gates of the ominous old brick structure closed behind 14-year-old Graham Young. He was one of the youngest patients ever to be admitted, but not the youngest. That distinction belonged to Bill Giles, who died there at the age of 87. He had been convicted of setting fire to a hayrick at the age of 10 in 1885. Giles had spent 77 years in Broadmoor, and coincidentally died three months before Graham was admitted.

About a month after Graham arrived at Broadmoor, an incident occurred which, all things considered, gives one room for thought.

John Berridge was a 23-year-old patient who had killed his parents. Quite suddenly one day he went into convulsions, collapsed and died. A post mortem revealed that his death was due to cyanide poisoning. The inquiry which followed established that no cyanide was kept at Broadmoor. However, the investigation also revealed that laurel bushes, from which an expert could extract cyanide, grew adjacent to the institution.

Several patients immediately confessed to poisoning Berridge. Among those confessing was Graham Young. He was the only one who could explain in detail the process involved in extracting cyanide from laurel bushes. The authorities chose not to believe any of the confessions. They leaned towards the theory that somehow the poison was smuggled into the institution. The Berridge case remains unsolved to this day.

At first Graham Young, the lad from the reputable suburb of North London, had difficulty adjusting to the maximum security institution. But as the years went by, he seemed to respond to psychiatric treatment. Dr. Edgar Udwin held high hopes for a complete recovery and early release for his young patient.

Meanwhile, Graham's family regarded his poisonous ways as mental illness. His sister Winnie, cousins, aunts, and uncles all felt that Graham had been sick and was now on the road to recovery. His father Fred had a difficult time accepting this live and let live view. He could forgive Graham for almost everything, but he could never forget that his own son had studied and apparently enjoyed the death of his poor wife Molly.

After consulting with Winnie, it was decided by Dr. Udwin that Graham be released for one week in November 1970. During the eight years of Graham's incarceration at Broadmoor, Winnie had married and was now the mother of a baby girl. She and her husband decided, in conjunction with Dr. Udwin, that no precautions against poison be taken during the week of Graham's visit.

Winnie now lived in a fashionable suburb of Hemel Hempstead, a city of 85,000, located about 30 miles north of London. Graham visited for the week, and the experiment was a huge success. With his doctor's consent and his family's urging, he visited at Christmas time for another week and was a delight to have in the house.

On February 4, 1971, 23-year-old Graham was released from Broadmoor. He was sent directly to Slough to the government resettlement centre for 13 weeks, training as a stockboy and shipper.

Nearing the completion of his course, on April 24, 1971, Graham performed two tasks which were to have far reaching effects. He applied for a job as a store-keeper at John Hadland Photographic Instrumentation Ltd., Bovingdon, Hertfordshire. Then he went to the centre of London, walked into a drugstore, and purchased 25 grams of antimony.

It was a stroke of luck when Graham's application for employment was accepted at Hadland's in Bovingdon, a quaint rural village only three miles from Hemel Hempstead.

Graham would have the steadying influence of a member of his family, but would still live and work in an independent environment. He took a room at 20 Maynards Rd. in Hemel Hempstead. His landlord, Mohammed Saddiq, a native of Pakistan, had no idea a murderer and former inmate of Broadmoor was his new roomer. At the time Mr. Saddiq didn't speak one word of English.

Seven years later, when I knocked on the door of 29 Maynards Rd., Mr. Saddiq well remembered his infamous tenant. He led me up the stairs to the room Graham had occupied. He pointed out the windowsill where Graham had stocked enough poison to kill scores of people. There, in a corner, was the bed under which Graham kept his diary of death. Mr. Saddiq assured me that his star roomer never ate at his home, nor had he ever entered his kitchen. Seven years before, Mr. Saddiq had considered himself fortunate to have such a quiet, well behaved roomer in his home.

I drove the three miles to the village of Bovingdon, and met with a director of Hadland's, Terry Johnson. Mr. Johnson explained how Graham Young became an employee of the firm. Young answered an advertisement and was granted an interview. He was highly recommended by the training school, having just completed a course in storekeeping, the exact position the firm was attempting to fill.

He accounted for the previous nine years by telling Mr. Foster of Hadland's that he'd had a nervous breakdown upon the death of his mother, but was now completely cured. Before hiring Graham, Mr. Foster checked out his story.

The government training centre got in touch with Dr. Udwin, the psychiatrist who was instrumental in securing Graham's release from Broadmoor. He obligingly sent along a letter confirming that Young was normal and competent in every way. At no time was Hadland's informed that Young had been a patient at Broadmoor, or that he had been convicted of being a poisoner.

On May 10, 1971, Graham went to work. He became assistant storekeeper at a salary of £24 a week. The one hundred employees at Hadland's are a friendly, cheerful group. Mr. Johnson, who showed me the premises, was called Terry by everyone we met. Hadland's exports expensive industrial photographic equipment all over the world. The firm received some measure of satisfaction from its mention in Guinness Book of World Records. They have produced a camera which takes 600 million pictures a second.

The men in the storeroom welcomed Graham in his new position. Within days he had gained the reputation of being a bit quiet, but certainly a nice enough bloke. His boss, Bob Egle, was 59 years old and looking forward to retirement. Bob had been married 39 years. He found out that his new assistant loved to hear of his wartime experiences, especially his evacuation from Dunkirk.

Fred Biggs was 60 and a senior employee in the Works in Progress Department. The two older men liked Graham Young.

Jethro Batt worked side-by-side with Graham in the stores. Each day after work Jethro would give Graham a lift the three miles back to Hemel Hempstead.

Twice a day May Bartlett wheeled a tea wagon down the long hall to the stores area. Members of the staff would then fetch their tea from the wagon. That is, before Graham came to work at Hadland's. Soon it became customary for Graham to pick up the tea from the wagon and distribute it to his fellow employees in the stores.

About a month after Graham started working at Hadland's, his boss Bob Egle became ill. He took a few days off work, but the pains in his stomach persisted. On June 18, he and his wife took a week's vacation at Great Yarmouth. The time off seemed to work wonders. Bob appeared so much better when he returned.

Two days before Bob was due back, Graham had travelled to London and purchased 25 grams of thallium. Within 24 hours of stating that he was feeling just great again after his vacation, Bob Egle took terribly ill at work. He went home, complaining of numbness in his fingers. Later he began to stagger. By morning the weight of the sheets on his bed caused him excruciating pain.

On successive days Bob Egle was transferred from West Herts Hospital in Hemel Hempstead to the intensive care unit at St. Albans City Hospital. He lingered in great pain for eight days before dying.

Back at Hadland's, everyone was concerned about the well-liked boss of the stores passing away so suddenly. None seemed to take it any harder than the new man, Graham Young.

A post mortem was performed on Bob Egle. Death was attributed to bronco-pneumonia in conjunction with polyneuritis. The following Monday, several members of the staff indicated a desire to attend Egle's funeral. It was decided that the managing director, Mr. Geoffrey Foster, would attend representing management, while Graham Young would represent the staff. The two men travelled together to the funeral. Foster remembers being surprised at Young's intimate knowledge of the medical diagnosis surrounding Egle's death.

Diana Smart, a fill-in employee in the stores section at Hadland's, didn't feel well all that summer. Nothing severe, but she was in enough discomfort to force her to go home several days during that July and August.

In September, Peter Buck, the import export manager, noticed that he always felt queasy after tea time. A few weeks later Diana Smart's attacks became more severe. Around this time Jethro Batt also became ill. One day he accepted a cup of tea from Graham and then gave him a lift to Hemel Hempstead. Next day Batt couldn't raise himself out of bed. Pains racked his stomach and chest. In the ensuing days his hair began to fall out in large tufts. He suffered hallucinations and became so distressed that he wanted to kill himself. Batt was admitted to hospital. Unknown to him or his doctors, the fact that he was removed from Graham Young and his poisonous ways saved his life. He gradually recovered.

In the meantime, David Tilson experienced violent stomach pains accompanied by vomiting. He was rushed to St. Albans Hospital, where he too started to lose his hair. After a short while, he began to recover and was discharged.

It seems that everyone at Hadland's had taken ill. By now the death of Bob Egle had the entire staff on edge. Could the outbreak of the strange undiagnosed illness be the same thing that killed Bob?

On a weekend early in November, the stores department at Hadland's was sorely understaffed. Bob Egle was dead. Both Tilson and Batt were off sick. Fred Biggs and his wife came in on a weekend to help Graham Young catch up. Graham made tea that Saturday for Biggs. Next morning Fred could hardly move. He would never return to work. Twenty days later Fred Biggs was dead.

By now, as one can well imagine, rumors were running rampant through the Hadland's plant. For some time previous to the current outbreak of sickness in the area, a virus had on occasion swept through Bovingdon, causing stomach complaints. These outbreaks were often blamed on the Bovingdon Bug.

To quell the rumors and suspicions of the employees, the management of Hadland's decided to call in Dr. Robert Hynd, Medical Officer of Health for the Hemel Hempstead area. Dr. Hynd inspected the plant and could find no cause for the wave of illness. Despite the doctor's statement that the cause of the illness didn't originate in the plant, rumors still persisted. They ranged from toxic chemicals being used in the manufacturing processes to medieval curses. After Fred Biggs died, some men even considered leaving Hadland's.

Management took another stab at coming up with the solution to the riddle. They called in the local general practitioner, Dr. Iain Anderson, to have an informal, morale-boosting chat with the employees.

Everyone had gathered in the cafeteria to hear Dr. Anderson. He explained that the authorities had ruled out radiation. They also checked out thallium, which was sometimes used in the manufacture of index lenses such as those manufactured at Hadland's. However, Hadland's did not keep thallium on the premises, so this agent had been dismissed as a possible cause of the sickness. The doctor leaned heavily toward a particularly strong strain of the Bovingdon Bug as being at the bottom of all the trouble. He assured the employees that the authorities were doing everything possible to isolate the cause of the dreadful sickness.

At the conclusion of his talk, the doctor inquired if there were any questions. Dr. Anderson was amazed when one employee, Graham Young, posed complicated questions regarding heavy metal poisoning and its effects. The doctor had a hard time getting the young man to sit down. The meeting was hastily brought to a close.

Dr. Anderson later made it a point to find Young and pursue the subject of poison. Again, he was dumbfounded at Young's detailed knowledge. Who was Graham Young, anyhow? Dr. Anderson and the chairman of the board, John Hadland, discussed the matter. Hadland called in the authorities, who checked Young's record at Scotland Yard. It revealed that he had been released just six months earlier from Broadmoor, where he had been sentenced for poisoning.

In Graham's room at 29 Maynards Rd., police uncovered his diary, detailing the dates and quantities of poison he had administered to Hadland employees. Graham Young had been playing God. He chose that some should die, while others should live. All were observed during their illness.

Young confessed to all his crimes, and to this day has never shown any remorse for the suffering he caused. All tests and examinations have indicated that he has above average intelligence, and is, in the legal sense, perfectly sane.

Young received several sentences of life imprisonment for his crimes. His victims, some of whom still live and work in the Hemel Hempstead area, want to forget Graham Young.

As I prepared to leave the Hadland's plant with its airy, cheery atmosphere, I asked director Terry Johnson, who had lived through the terror which was Graham Young, how in a sentence he would describe what went on there.

He answered without hesitation: "It was unbelievable."

PART 6

MURDEROUS DOCTORS FROM AROUND THE WORLD

DR. WILLIAM KING 1858

TODAY, the town of Brighton, Ontario is off the beaten path. Located about 100 miles east of Toronto, only a green sign on a superhighway indicates the exit to the peaceful little town.

Years ago, before the Macdonald-Cartier Freeway was built between Toronto and Montreal, Canada's two largest cities, it was necessary to travel through Brighton. In horse and buggy days the town was a main stopover. It was here, back in 1858, that murder so very foul took place, a murder which would capture the attention of the entire country.

William Henry King was born in 1833 on a farm just outside Brighton in the township of Sophiasburg. His parents moved to Brighton, where young William spent his formative years. At the age of five, he was sent off to school, where he displayed a remarkable aptitude to learn and absorb. We must remember that we are delving back into a time when schooling was not always available, even to those who were recognized as gifted children. William's main activity as he grew up was helping out on the farm which, in a few short years, became relatively prosperous.

The young man with the driving ambition was pleasant and charming. He stood five feet eleven inches tall and sported a lush growth of sandy whiskers, which was in keeping with the style of the times.

At the age of 18, William attended normal school in Toronto. Each summer he returned home to work on the family farm. During one of these summers, he started to date Sarah Ann Lawson. Ann, as she was known, left quite a bit to be desired in the looks department. She wore a perpetual frown, which gave her a rather stern appearance. Her personality was diametrically opposite to what one would describe as warm.

The powers that be have a way of evening things out. Ann's father was loaded. John M. Lawson owned a large, prosperous farm and was widely respected throughout the area. Can't you just hear the ladies of Brighton gossiping in the general store over a bolt of gingham—"That handsome King boy is after the Lawson money."

On January 31, 1855, William and Ann were married. While he continued his studies, his dutiful wife took in boarders to help defray the cost of his education. In Toronto, William obtained a first class teacher's certificate. He returned to Brighton, where he taught for a few months before obtaining a position as a third class teacher at Hamilton Central School.

About a year after their marriage, Ann gave birth to a daughter, who was sickly from the day she was born. The child lived for only a little more than a month. It was around this time that a rather ugly rumor circulated about the King marriage. The good folks of Brighton whispered that William mistreated his wife. The rumors were given some credence when Ann did what so many other women have done before and since. She went home to mother.

William's driving ambition would not be stifled. He threw himself into a new career, that of medicine. With his father- in- law's financial assistance, he enrolled in Philadelphia's Homeopathy Medical College. Meanwhile, Ann remained under her parents' roof in Brighton. William stayed in Philadelphia for three years, returning home each summer to teach in local schools between college semesters. During one semester, he wrote his wife several letters accusing her of infidelity, a totally bogus accusation. Anne showed the letters to her father, who was so upset he took them to his lawyer. When William apologized, his father-in-law agreed to return the letters. The wily Mr. Lawson took the precaution of copying the strange missives.

In 1858, William King returned to his home town. He was now a bona fide doctor, having graduated from the Homeopathy Medical College, Pennsylvania Medical University and the Eclectic Medical College.

Dr. King hung out his shingle. Right from the beginning, his practice prospered. And why not? Here was a local boy who had displayed the fortitude and determination to better himself. Besides, William dressed well, was always nicely groomed and had a delightful bedside manner. He and Ann reconciled. Everything was coming up roses, until that fall of 1858. Actually, it was exactly September 23 when the bloom came off the rose and love flew out the window, for on that day William King first laid eyes on Melinda Freeland Vandervoort.

It wasn't that the good doctor had eyes only for Melinda. Nothing could be further from the truth. He had simultaneously made advances to a patient, Dorcas Garrett, of nearby Murray. That was a mistake. Dorcas, a Quaker, was just not that type of woman. William had sent her a letter expressing undying love. He insinuated that his dear wife was not long for this world and added that Dorcas should acquaint herself with the niceties of life befitting a doctor's wife.

As I said, Dorcas wasn't having any. She replied in no uncertain terms that she was dismissing him as her physician and at the same time demanded an apology. She threatened to expose him if he made any further advances. William apologized.

Melinda was another kettle of fish. She responded to the doctor's letter by sending him a photograph with an accompanying letter containing such titillating lines as "You have unlinked the tender chord of affection until you have an alarming influence over my girlish nature," and, "One smile from your countenance can inspire a depth of veneration in my bosom never felt by me for any individual."

William had struck paydirt. The pair corresponded. It didn't matter one iota that Ann King was two months pregnant. Her husband wrote Melinda that she was very ill and could die at any moment. If Melinda would just wait for another year, she would become the second Mrs. King. When these letters were written, Ann was in perfect health.

Four days after William wrote Melinda concerning his wife's condition, Ann took ill. She vomited continuously, suffered excruciating pains in her stomach and complained of a burning sensation in her throat. During the initial stages of his wife's illness, William provided her sole medical care. He told Ann's family that she was suffering from ulcerations of the womb and that everything possible was being done. So concerned was William that he rarely left his wife's bedside. For three weeks, William labored over his patient. Some days she seemed to rally, but always slipped back into bouts of vomiting and retching. During the few times Ann was lucid, she implored her husband to stop giving her that hideous white powder five times a day. She complained that it "burned like fire" in her mouth.

Finally, as Ann grew weaker, William succumbed to Mr. Lawson's urging and sought a second medical opinion. Dr. A. E. Fife was told by William that the patient was pregnant and had ulcerations of the womb. The doctor was not asked, nor did he request, to examine Ann. He prescribed ipecacuanha and camphor to alleviate the vomiting.

Nothing seemed to help Ann King. Once again, Mr. Lawson begged his son-in-law to bring in additional medical assistance. Dr. P. Gross was given the same information as Dr. Fife. He too prescribed something to help stem the insistent vomiting.

Who knows what thoughts raced through Ann's mind as she lay there in agony? Certainly she was aware that her husband was carrying on with the rather notorious 20-year-old Melinda Vandervoort. No doubt word drifted back to her of her husband's house calls to rural areas with the ever present Melinda at his side. Sometimes, Melinda actually cared for Ann in the doctor's absence.

On November 4, 1858, Ann died. Dr. King was beside himself with grief. In fact, he carried on so much that witnesses were in fear for his life. The man convulsed, grew crimson in the face and required medical assistance.

Ann's parents never did like their son-in-law. Now that the worst had happened, they decided to find out once and for all if their suspicions were based on fact. While William was out of the house, Mrs. Lawson searched the premises. She came up with a photo of Melinda Vandervoort, along with incriminating letters from Melinda written to William insinuating how convenient it would be to have Ann out of the way.

On Sunday, November 7, Ann was buried. Dr. King was disconsolate. The following day, Ann's brother Clinton went to the county coroner with an array of incriminating evidence. He lugged along the accusatory letters his father had copied, as well as letters from Melinda to William and the letter written by William to Dorcas Garrett. As soon as she had heard of Ann's death, Dorcas had turned it over to Ann's brother.

The Lawsons demanded an inquest into their daughter's death and informed William that an autopsy was to be performed. He was furious, but not so distraught that he didn't proceed directly to Sidney and the everloving arms of Melinda Vandervoort.

Once the ball started to roll, there was no stopping it. A coroner's jury was hastily convened and Ann's body exhumed. An autopsy revealed that there was no ulceration of the womb. The stomach and its contents were removed for analysis.

Meanwhile William, no doubt realizing what the autopsy would reveal, had a meeting with Melinda at her home in Sidney. While at the Vandervoorts,

William met Melinda's father for the first time. He told both father and daughter that he and Melinda were in trouble due to his wife's death. He would be arrested and so would Melinda. He implored Mr. Vandervoort for permission to flee with Melinda to Cape Vincent in New York state, where Melinda's aunt lived. William was lying, as he wasn't being sought by the law just yet, but the ploy worked. Mr. Vandervoort allowed his daughter to flee with Dr. King.

A warrant was soon issued for William's arrest. He was apprehended, brought back to Canada, charged with murder and lodged in jail. Melinda, who had made her way to Cleveland, Ohio, returned to Brighton three weeks later. On April 4, 1859, Dr. William King stood trial for the murder of his wife. Farmers travelled to the trial by horse and buggy. Those who couldn't get a lift walked to the tiny Cobourg courthouse where the trial was held. It was estimated that 1500 people attempted to attend the proceedings, but only a fraction of that number gained admittance. King gave the appearance of tolerating the entire distasteful affair.

The Crown went about building its formidable case. The accused man had opportunity and motive. He had predicted his wife's death while she was still in good health and had invented a nonexistent illness to ward off other doctors and to account for her death. Professor Henry Croft of Toronto's University College testified that he had examined the deceased's stomach. It was found to contain 11 grains of arsenic. The liver contained small quantities of arsenic as well. This was vital evidence, as explained by Prof. Croft from the witness stand: "Arsenic cannot be put into the liver after death." Defence counsel's main thrust was that arsenic could have been placed in the stomach after death.

Ann's mother took the witness stand and tearfully related that she had watched William mix a white powder with water and administer it to her daughter. Most of the time Ann vomited and retched after each dose. She did admit under cross-examination that, on occasion, Ann's condition had appeared to improve slightly.

Melinda Vandervoort was called to testify. She accounted for her involvement with Dr. King with a few well chosen answers. In response to what everyone was thinking, she replied, "I never had any improper intercourse with Dr. King." Melinda gave the following explanation for replying to suggestive letters she had received from the doctor, as well as sending him her photograph.

Melinda said, "Mrs. King asked me to send the likeness to her. I directed the likeness to Dr. King. I thought that when I got the letter, it was written for amusement. I sent him this letter in answer for amusement."

No one really believed Melinda. After receiving Melinda's photograph, William dashed off a reply to his "Sweet little lump of good nature." In part, he wrote, "Could I indulge in the hope that those winning and genial smiles would ever be found in my possession, all troubles would then cease. It is a perfect infatuation to me. Can you keep from sacrificing yourself upon the hymeneal altar for the next year? I wish so."

Melinda responded with such tasty tidbits as, "Since I first had the pleasure of an introduction, my heart is constantly with you, and I'm not contented a moment. O could I forever be with you; I think I should be happy, for indeed I enjoyed myself to excess during my stay in your presence though suppose now I must eradicate such thoughts from my mind; for you are married, and my destiny must be to love and not share your interesting society."

The defence paraded an impressive array of doctors who testified to Dr. King's high moral standards, as well as his medical knowledge and skill. The defence made much of the fact that there was opportunity for arsenic to have been placed in the stomach contents after death. This was vehemently refuted by the Crown.

The jury retired to deliberate their verdict. When they had difficulty reaching a decision in a few hours, they were sequestered overnight. Promptly at 10 a.m., before a crowded but dead silent courtroom, the clerk of the court asked the question on everyone's mind, "How say you gentlemen, is the prisoner guilty or not guilty?" The foreman of the jury replied, "Guilty, with a strong recommendation to mercy."

On Saturday, April 9, Dr. King was once again led into the Cobourg courtroom for sentencing. When asked if he had anything to say before being sentenced, he replied, "I have this much to say, that upon my solemn oath I am not guilty of the charge laid against me. I have no doubt of this; my conscience is perfectly clear upon this point." The presiding judge then sentenced King to be hanged on June 9, 1859. Dr. King wept as he was led away to await his date with the hangman.

While in prison, William confessed to his spiritual advisor, Rev.

Vanderburg, that he was guilty of having murdered his wife. Then, quite unlike most killers, he wrote out his confession in detail. Following are excerpts from his written statement:

"Having sinned against society as well as God I feel it my duty to confess my guilt to society with deep humiliation and sincere repentance and ask forgiveness for all my offences against my fellow men."

"My present unfortunate position is the result of an unhappy marriage."

In explanation of his motive, Dr. King wrote: "Miss Vandervoort and myself were greatly enamored of each other. Actions speak louder than words, and I knew that she loved me, and that I could not help loving her in return. She was both lovely and loving. I looked upon her with all her personal charms, and attracting graces and virtues, her attainments and literary acquirements, her mild and affectionate disposition, her genial smiles and affable manners, her good character and winning ways, and while she perfectly reciprocated all my affections, it was as impossible for me not to love her as it would be to fly to the moon.

"Here then, I had found the object of my affections and the next thing was to get possession of that precious gem I had found, but there presented one obstacle in the way—my wife. It was only now that I allowed the thoughts to enter my mind of doing anything to shorten her life."

William further rationalized his actions by writing, "The law may compel man and wife to live together, but I defy it to compel them to love each other. Oh! how lamentable beyond description that so much misery and unhappiness should arise from unhappy marriages."

William refuted the experts' theories that his wife had died from the cumulative results of arsenic poisoning. He claimed he had given her chloroform. In describing his wife's last moments after she had fallen into a deep coma, he wrote: "Now I would have given worlds to have brought her to. I tried everything but could not succeed. O! what an awful feeling I then felt. How I repented, but, alas, it was too late. I just began to realize what had been done. Oh! the bitter pangs that I experienced cannot be imagined. The Devil had led me headlong into difficulty, but now came the remorse of conscience. Oh! how sharp, how pungent! I felt like death, and thought I would die."

Dr. King wasn't above passing out some free advice, "The way to avoid trouble is not to get in. Better far, not to marry at all than to do so to your sorrow.

To those who are married my parting advice is to pray to God for grace to guard you against all manner of temptation. Love your wives if you can possibly do so and use them kindly and affectionately if you can; but both men and women have their proper spheres in this life and sometimes they get united and there is no harmony in the family circle; if you cannot love your wives my advice to you is to separate, for you will either do one of two things; viz: be tempted to commit a crime perhaps that was the most foreign to your mind before, and that may force you first into jail, then in the criminal box to be put on trial for your life and have the sentence of death passed on you and thence face the halter and die a violent ignominious death amid a congregated multitude and go to a premature grave, or, you will be compelled to live a life of torture and drag out a miserable existence."

June 9, 1859 rolled around all too soon for Dr. King. He arose at 4 a.m. and ate a hearty breakfast. He then spent some time in prayer with Rev. Vanderburg. Several doctors who were close friends of the condemned man visited the jail to pay their respects. The solemn procession of jailers and spiritual advisors made its way to the scaffold. A crowd, estimated to be as high as 10,000, had trudged by foot and buggy to take in the spectacle. The public hanging took place without incident and the crowd dispersed.

Melinda Vandervoort took up with a new beau in Cleveland, but soon tired of him in favor of a gentleman from Montreal. Evidently, he left her high and dry in Montreal, after which she returned to Brighton, where she lived for many years, an object of scorn to many of the residents who knew her story. She drank heavily and is reported to have died in the late 1890s, penniless and alone, in an asylum in Toronto.

DR. EDMUND POMMERAIS 1863

I have always been a firm believer that one day a year should be set aside for mothers-in-law. Despite common belief, mothers-in-law, as a class, can be a fine group of ladies. Unfortunately, as individuals, they can be extremely annoying. What's even more exasperating, they are usually correct in their opinions.

Let's go back a few years across the big pond to meet Madame Dubizy and her future son-in-law, Edmund Pommerais, of Paris, France.

We'll start with Edmund, just for fun.

Ed was a tall, handsome lad of 24 when he arrived on the Parisian scene in 1860. Like many freshly turned out doctors, our boy thought it would be commendable to heal those on the bottom rung of the economic ladder. Before you could say syringe, Dr. Pommerais had a huge practice of non-paying, poor, sick patients.

This would have been just fine if the doctor hadn't had such expensive tastes. Ed was somewhat of a dandy when it came to clothing. He also maintained a lavishly furnished apartment and, in general, threw money around like it was going out of style. As his debts rose, so did his longing for female companionship. Just when the doctor felt those old biological urges, who should come strolling into his clinic but Madame Seraphine de Pauw. The poorly dressed but attractive lady had a husband in dire need of Dr. Pommerais' skill. Ed was more than willing to take on yet one more impoverished patient. Sadly, I must relate that despite the doctor's loving care, Mr. de Pauw was carried away to his great reward after several months.

Now, Madame de Pauw was ten years older than the doctor. Besides, she was encumbered with three small children, but as we all know, love or sex or whatever is blind. Madame de Pauw became Ed's mistress. Although deeply in debt, Ed managed to provide for her and the children.

Nothing wrong with all that, you might say, but darn it all, the bills kept mounting up. Ed was desperately in debt when, quite by chance, he met Madame Dubizy, who came complete with charming daughter. Ed did a double take.

Dubizy was an old battle-axe, but the daughter was built like one of those sexy manikins on display at Galleries Lafayette.

When Ed found out that the Dubizy clan was loaded with francs, he decided to woo and wed Dubizy the younger. Despite the madame's open dislike for our Ed, he managed to court and finally marry her young daughter.

That's when Madame Dubizy showed her true colors. She fixed up her daughter's wealth so that Ed could not get his hands on any of it. That is, as long as Madame Dubizy lived. Ed made a mental note that it might not be that long.

Ed was a busy boy. Of necessity, he had to break the news of his marriage to Seraphine de Pauw and let her know that their private horizontal arrangements would have to undergo something of an adjustment. Seraphine sobbed, but Ed assured her he would send her enough cash to keep the wolf from the door. Let's give Ed his due—he sent a few francs for a couple of months. Then he quit. Out of sight, out of mind.

Ed was putting out fires as fast as they broke out, but there was one blaze he couldn't quell. Those enormous debts kept piling up. Since he insisted that his wife have the best clothing and jewelry, his marriage, rather than alleviating his precarious position, only served to add to it.

That's when he decided to kill his mother-in-law. It wasn't that difficult. One evening Ed and the wife had dear Mama over for dinner. Ed liberally laced her favorite wine with poison. An hour after quaffing back half a litre, Mama felt ill. Not to worry. After all, her son-in-law was a doctor. Ed stayed with his stricken mother-in-law until dawn. Then he broke the sad news to his wife. Mama had departed this mortal coil.

Solicitous Ed comforted his wife, made all the funeral arrangements and signed the death certificate. He then got his grubby little paws on his mother-in-law's estate. The total amount conveniently wiped out Ed's enormous debts. Mama's death couldn't have been more timely.

Ed continued on his merry way. He gambled heavily on the stock market and lived lavishly. It was only a matter of months before he was once again over his head in debt. He attempted to borrow money through legitimate channels, but no bank would take a chance on him. Desperately, he tried money lenders, but they too wouldn't have any part of a man so deeply in the red.

At this juncture in Ed's life, who should write him a letter but Seraphine de

Pauw. Seraphine could tear your heart out. She and her children lived in a hovel and were literally starving to death. She apologized for bothering Ed, but if there was anything he could do, it sure would be appreciated. Ed dropped in on his old flame. The situation was just as Seraphine had outlined in her letter. Ed produced 20 francs for food and became an instant hero to Seraphine and the children.

In the following days, Ed once more entered his old girlfriend's life. The flame, which had diminished over the years, once more burned brightly. Seraphine figured her lover was loaded. Quite the opposite was true. Ed was dead broke and was delicately perched on the edge of bankruptcy and ruin. He did, however, have a diabolical plan.

He persuaded Seraphine, now completely under his influence, to take out a large insurance policy on her life. The face value was the equivalent of $150,000, a magnificent sum in the mid-nineteenth century. Ed would pay the first year's premium. Seraphine would then fake illness and call in her doctor, namely Edmund Pommerais. Ed would inform the insurance boys that their policy holder would be occupying a plot at the local cemetery within 12 months. Cunning Ed told Seraphine that the insurance company would offer her a cash settlement in order to avoid paying off the higher amount on her death. Ed explained that once they got their hands on the settlement money, they would be able to continue their relationship in style.

Seraphine de Pauw looked at the handsome young doctor who had re-entered her life like Prince Charming. She would do anything he asked. When Ed explained that he might have to give her some nasty medicine, which would make her feel slightly ill for a few days, she understood. After all, another doctor might be called in and it would be necessary to deceive him. Naturally, Ed was the beneficiary on the policy. To be on the safe side, he had Seraphine sign a will leaving everything to him. The poor woman had no idea what she was signing.

Ed's diabolical plot was put into motion. He scraped up the money to pay the first year's premium. Seraphine purchased the life insurance policy. After waiting a few months, she pretended to faint in front of neighbors in her tenement building. The rumor spread that she was in failing health. Finally, after one particular fainting spell, a neighbor called the doctor. Quick as a bunny, Ed was on the scene. He gave his patient some medicine, which contained small quantities of poison.

In the following days, neighbors visited. No question about it, Seraphine was seriously ill. Each day, Dr. Pommerais made a house call. Nothing seemed to help.

While Seraphine suffered, she firmly believed that her discomfort would soon be over and yield her a fortune. During a visit from her sister, Madame Ritter, Seraphine confided that her sickness was a sham. She told her sister the entire scheme. The story was so convincing, Madame Ritter believed it and told no one.

On November 17, 1863, Seraphine de Pauw died in agony. A neighbor called Dr. Pommerais. The doctor was at his lover's side during her final moments.

Ed wasn't a patient man. He was just itching to get his hands on that insurance money. He waited a week. On the day after Seraphine's funeral, he applied for the payoff. The insurance company acknowledged the claim and were about to issue a cheque, when who should show up but Madame Ritter with her unusual story.

Well, folks, the fat was in the fire. Seraphine de Pauw's body was exhumed and found to contain large quantities of digitaline. Ed was arrested and taken into custody. Madame Dubizy's body was also exhumed, but the exact cause of death could not be found. It didn't matter much.

Ed stood accused of murder. At his trial, Madame Ritter's story was enough to convince the jury that Ed had indeed murdered Seraphine de Pauw.

Dr. Edmund Pommerais was executed for his crime. He vehemently protested his innocence to the end. No one believed him.

DR. EDWARD PRITCHARD 1865

DR. Edward Pritchard married Miss Mary Jane Taylor in 1850 and, after accepting various medical posts, settled down to his own private practice in Glasgow, Scotland.

Now Dr. Pritchard was a tall, sensitive, attractive man, with a full flowing beard. He was extremely popular with his patients, but when it came to female patients, there were gossips who spread the word. It seems the good doctor performed extensive examinations on attractive ladies, when perhaps a more cursory examination would have sufficed. The doctor loved to spend money and loved to have a good time. He was a real charmer. However, this charm did not carry over to his professional colleagues. They frowned on the low standard of medicine he practised, and his private life.

All went well at home until May of 1863, when unaccountably a fire broke out in the servants' quarters of the Pritchard home. Mrs. Pritchard and another servant were out of town at the time. When firemen put out the blaze, the body of a young servant girl was found burned to death in her bed. She had made no attempt to leave the bed. It was one of those minor mysteries that occurs in every large city. While a few suspicious glances were tossed the doctor's way, nothing was ever done about it.

The experience was so distasteful the family moved to Clarence Place, and then things started to happen. The new home was four storeys high. The doctor and his wife lived in apparent harmony with four of their five children. The oldest lived with her grandparents in Edinburgh. The Pritchards had two servants, the cook, Catherine Lattimer, and Mary M'leod, a maid who was hired to replace the poor unfortunate servant who was burned in her bed.

Mary herself got burned in bed, after a fashion. You see, she and the doctor had arrived at an understanding that was not exactly the normal master-servant relationship. Mary became pregnant. Edward hastily performed an operation on Mary which had the desired effect of producing a miscarriage. After a brief recovery period, Mary and Dr. Pritchard continued their illicit relationship.

In October 1864, Mrs. Pritchard, who was always a robust healthy woman, started to suffer from headaches and stomach cramps. It got so bad, her husband confined her to bed. Her mother, Mrs. Taylor, wrote from Edinburgh that her daughter should visit with her to regain her health. At first the doctor wouldn't hear of being parted from his wife. Finally he yielded under pressure, and Mrs. Pritchard went to her mother's home. Here her health improved dramatically and rapidly.

On December 22, Mrs. Pritchard came home to be with her family for Christmas. Almost immediately, she became ill again. She was vomiting after every meal. She became so violently ill that late in January, Dr. Pritchard wrote his wife's cousin, one Dr. Cowan, in Edinburgh, to come and visit Mrs. Pritchard. On February 7, Dr. Cowan arrived and applied a mustard poultice to his cousin. Upon his return to Edinburgh he urged Mrs. Taylor to go to Glasgow to attend her daughter. In the meantime, Mrs. Pritchard had her worst attack to date. Despite her husband, who stood at her bedside, she implored the cook to fetch Dr. Gairdner, who lived close by. When he arrived he was told by Dr. Pritchard that Dr. Cowan had given his wife stimulants. Dr. Gairdner suggested this be stopped immediately. He prescribed a simple diet, and next day he was advised that Mrs. Pritchard was much better. Despite this reassurance, Dr. Gairdner became apprehensive about the entire matter. He remembered that Mrs. Pritchard's brother was also a doctor. They had attended college together. He wrote Dr. Taylor, who in turn wrote to his brother-in-law and suggested that it might be best if his sister visited him. Dr. Pritchard wouldn't hear of being parted from his dear wife.

In the meantime Mrs. Taylor came to Glasgow to be with her daughter. She found her continuously vomiting and suffering from severe cramps. Within a week Mrs. Taylor started to feel ill. On the night of February 16, she became so violently sick she was placed in bed with her daughter. Dr. Pritchard called another neighbor who was also a man of medicine, Dr. James Patterson.

If you are keeping score, this is the fourth doctor called in to treat one or the other of the two very sick ladies. Not counting Dr. Pritchard's ministrations, the total medical treatment up to this time was one mustard poultice, applied to Mrs. Pritchard. However, one must keep in mind that all the doctors were dealing with another doctor, who was the husband and son-in-law of the patients.

When Dr. Patterson entered the house, he was greeted by Dr. Pritchard and given the usual misleading symptoms. Upon examining Mrs. Taylor, Dr. Patterson expressed the opinion that she was under the influence of dope, probably opium, and was dying of opiate poisoning. He said there was nothing he could do. At 11:30 p.m. he left the house. At 1 a.m. he received a call to return but refused, saying that death was inevitable. Mrs. Taylor passed away a few minutes after 1 a.m. Dr. Pritchard signed the death certificate "paralysis 12 hours. Apoplexy one hour."

Dr. Pritchard continued to supervise everything consumed by his wife who deteriorated rapidly. Finally on Friday, March 17, after four months of excruciating pain, attended by her husband and Dr. Patterson, Mrs. Pritchard passed away. During her final hours Patterson asked Pritchard to make up a simple sleeping draught, but Pritchard replied that he kept no drugs in the house.

Dr. Pritchard was again called upon to sign a death certificate. This time he wrote "gastric fever, two months."

On Monday, March 20, Mr. William Hart, who held a post roughly equivalent to that of our coroner, received an anonymous letter. In substance it told of the two deaths and suggested foul play may have been involved. When the doctor arrived back in Glasgow from his wife's funeral in Edinburgh, he was detained by the police. Routine investigation revealed his relationship with Mary M'Leod. To make matters worse it was revealed that poor Mrs. Pritchard had stumbled on her husband and Mary in sundry compromising positions. She had long before decided to sidestep a scandal, and put up with her promiscuous husband and maid. The bodies of Mrs. Pritchard and her mother were exhumed, and found to be full of poison.

Edward Pritchard was arrested and stood trial for murder on Monday, July 3, 1865. While his trial caused a sensation, it provided no duelling match between prosecution and defence attorneys. There was really no defence. For a man who professed to have no drugs in his home, his two suppliers provided a list of drugs purchased by the physician during his victims' illness. They included enough poison to do away with half of dear old Glasgow.

Through it all the doctor remained a charming, polite scoundrel. He was found guilty and sentenced to hang. Before he was led to the scaffold in the presence of an Episcopalian minister, he confessed to both murders "in the way brought out in the evidence." Monster that he was, he kept his charming charade to the very end. Head erect, with a bold, almost marching step, he was hanged before a huge crowd on July 28, 1865.

Handsome Edward had the distinction to be the last person to be publicly executed in Glasgow.

DR. PHILIP CROSS 1887

DR. Philip Cross surveyed his domain from his fine old home in Dripson, Ireland. The doctor had recently retired from the British Army after serving for many years in India. Now in the winter of 1886 the old man could look forward to many peaceful, if not somewhat boring, years with his wife, Laura, his children, at his retirement estate known as Shandy Hill.

It was not a future that promised much excitement, but many men work a lifetime for just such twilight years of contentment. The doctor was a gruff, introverted man who apparently tolerated the matronly Mrs. Cross as long as she conveniently stayed out of his way. Then again, the British Army does develop character.

When twenty-one-year-old Effie Skinner joined the staff of Shandy Hill as governess to the Cross children the doctor paid little attention. It is hard to believe the doctor ignored the new governess, for Effie was a peach. Her complexion was unblemished, and when she smiled, two pink dimples appeared on each cheek.

It is unclear exactly when the kindly doctor did take notice of this breath of spring. A smile, a touch, a hidden kiss, who knows? At first the embarrassed Effie rejected the doctor's advances. But old Dr. Phil slowly won Effie to his side both literally and figuratively. Stolen kisses in the hall of Shandy Hill led to more basic acts behind closed doors. Dr. Cross and Effie became lovers.

As was inevitable, Mrs. Cross found out about her husband's dalliance with the hired help. Laura could have become indignant, but instead, she decided to let bygones be bygones. After all, Phil had never before acted in this unfaithful manner. Mrs. Cross did the practical thing. She gave Effie her notice. This may not appear to be a major calamity today, but an unemployed governess without references before the turn of the century could end up begging on the street.

To the rescue came Dr. Cross. Effie was understandably grateful for any help. The doctor's proposition was simple enough. He would provide the necessary cash for a flat in Dublin and would visit his paramour at every opportunity. Effie became Dr. Cross' mistress.

This new and convenient arrangement went along famously for several months. There was just one thing. The spry old doctor was in love with Effie and wanted to be with her all the time. Meanwhile, back home at Shandy Hill, Mrs. Cross began to suffer from the most annoying stomach cramps. Sometimes her distress was so severe as to bring on attacks of vomiting. Phil ministered to his wife for several weeks before bringing in Dr. Godfrey, a cousin and friend of the family, for another opinion. Phil explained to his colleague that Laura was suffering from a slight attack of typhoid fever. Dr. Godfrey examined Mrs. Cross and quickly concurred with the older and more experienced doctor. After all, who would detect typhoid fever if not a former military doctor who had spent years in India?

On May 24, 1887, when the local clergyman Rev. Mr. Hayes called to pay his respects to the ill Mrs. Cross, he was told by the kindly doctor that she had just dropped off to sleep. A most distressing week passed for Mrs. Cross. She suffered greatly from nausea and vomiting. On June 2, the maid, Mary Buckley, was awakened by the frantic doctor. Mrs. Cross had mercifully passed away.

Dr. Cross signed the death certificate without delay. Mrs. Cross was laid to rest two days later. The brief ceremony, conducted at graveside at the ungodly hour of 6 a.m., was thought by some good citizens of Dripson to be decidedly odd. It mattered not what the Dripsonites thought, for Dr. Cross was off to his true love.

Like a man possessed, he gathered up Effie in Dublin and sped to London, where the older gentleman and the 21-year-old governess became man and wife. Dr. Phil and Effie tiptoed through the English countryside on their honeymoon. Back in Ireland news reached Dripson that the doctor had married the former governess, and only two weeks after Mrs. Cross had given up the ghost. A relative wrote Dr. Cross informing him that his friends and neighbors had not taken kindly to his actions. The doctor felt that he had better return to Shandy Hill for appearances' sake.

Once ensconced in his old home, the doctor kept a low profile. But nasty rumors failed to abate. There were those who remembered that Dr. Cross had tended to his wife in her final illness. Then there was the hasty funeral. Bad news travels fast. It wasn't long before Inspector Tyacke of the Royal Irish Constabulary heard the rumors.

The inspector spoke to the coroner, who felt there was enough monkey business taking place to order an inquest. In conjunction with the inquest Mrs. Cross' body was exhumed. An autopsy indicated that she had never had so much as a touch of typhoid fever. What she did have was a massive quantity of arsenic, accounting for the nausea and vomiting she suffered before death.

Dr. Phil was arrested and charged with the murder of his first wife. He didn't have a chance. The prosecution produced one of those chemists who have a habit of taking the witness stand and pointing at the accused. The motive—Effie—was there for all to see.

On January 10, 1888, Dr. Cross, whose hair, incidentally, had turned chalk white during his confinement, was hanged for the murder of his wife.

DR. NEILL CREAM 1890

THE 1920s have often been referred to as the golden age of sport. Babe Ruth was clouting home runs, while Jack Dempsey was clouting anyone who stood in his way.

In the murder business the period between 1880 and 1895 should be called the Golden Age of Mayhem. It gave rise to so many unusual murders. A chap known as Jack the Ripper was roaming the streets of London cutting up ladies of the night. On this side of the big pond, a God-fearing, church-going New England lady named Lizzie Borden was accused of chopping up her mummie and daddy with a hatchet.

With the murder stage being so crowded with nefarious players, it is no wonder that Dr. Neill Cream never gained the notoriety he so richly deserved.

Neill was born in Glasgow, Scotland in 1850. His family migrated to Canada when he was five. Nothing is known of his formative years other than that he applied himself diligently to his schoolwork and did exceedingly well throughout high school. He continued on to McGill University in Montreal, where he received his medical degree. He later took post graduate work in London and Edinburgh before returning to Canada.

For the next five years Neill Cream led an eventful, if somewhat jaded existence. He set up practice in various Canadian towns and cities, but was always forced to stay on the move. You see, Dr. Cream's medical standards were decidedly below the norm, particularly when he was examining female patients. In fact, it wasn't an uncommon sight to see a lady running out of Dr. Cream's office in a state of undress. Finally, he found the temperature so unbearably hot that he left Canada for Chicago, in order to have more freedom to practise his particular brand of medicine.

In 1881, Dr. Cream went too far. He gave a huge quantity of strychnine to a patient named Stott. It is believed that the motive was two fold. Stott had a pretty wife whom the doctor was examining all the time, although her neighbors later stated that this was very strange since she was never sick a day in her life. It is believed to this day that Mrs. Stott was involved with Cream in her husband's sudden demise. At the time of Stott's death, Cream was trying to place a large insurance policy on the unfortunate man's life, with himself as the beneficiary.

Stott's death at first was attributed to natural causes. Then Dr. Cream did an extraordinary thing, which he continued to do throughout his criminal career. He started writing letters. He wrote to both the coroner and the district attorney suggesting that Stott's body be exhumed. Finally, at the anonymous urging of Cream the body was disinterred. Upon examination, it was found to be chock full of strychnine.

Dr. Cream and Mrs. Stott took off, but were soon apprehended and indicted for murder. Mrs. Stott, cutie that she was, testified for the state. Charges against her were dropped. Dr. Cream was found guilty of second degree murder and was sentenced to life imprisonment. In 1881, the prison gates of Joliet closed behind the strange doctor, but his career was far from over. In 1891, after Cream had spent just under 10 years in prison, Gov. Fifer of Illinois commuted his sentence, and Neill Cream walked out of prison, a free man. The governor had made a horrendous error.

While he had been spending time in prison, Cream's father died, leaving him an inheritance of $16,000, a veritable fortune before the turn of the century. Dr. Cream picked up the cash and headed for England, arriving in London on October 1, 1891. Whether it was the London fog or whatever, Dr. Cream didn't waste any time pursuing his secondary occupation, that of poisoner.

A 19-year-old prostitute, Ellen Donworth, let herself be picked up by Cream. During the course of the evening her tall, austere looking friend, sporting a top hat, offered her a drink out of his flask. She took two long drags of the bottle and almost immediately began to suffer from convulsions. Her friend was nowhere to be found, but neighbors called a doctor, who rushed the girl to the hospital. She died en route. An autopsy revealed that Ellen had died of strychnine poisoning.

The police had no clues to the poisoner's identity, but never fear. Our Dr. Cream made sure that he received some of the recognition he craved. He wrote the coroner offering to reveal the killer's identity in return for £200,000. The letter was signed A. O'Brien. The coroner tried to set up a rendezvous, but O'Brien-Cream never showed up.

One week after the Donworth murder, another prostitute, Matilda Clover, was found in her room writhing in agony. Her client for the evening, a man who called himself Fred, had given her some pills. Before she died, she described Fred to a friend who lived in the same house. Fred was a tall, well-built man, who dressed in a cape and tall silk hat. For some reason, Matilda's death was thought to have been caused by alcoholism, but Cream would have none of it. He dashed off a note to a distinguished doctor, accusing him of poisoning Matilda with strychnine. The doctor took the letter to the police. Other distinguished people received letters accusing them of poisoning Matilda. Because of the veritable shower of letters, Matilda's body was exhumed. The cause of her death was attributed to strychnine. Scotland Yard now realized that a systematic killer was on the loose in London.

The winter months drifted by without any further murders at the hands of the mysterious poisoner, with an abnormal urge for revealing his crimes in letters. Later, when every move Cream made was reviewed, the reason he stopped poisoning prostitutes during the winter months became clear. He had taken a trip to Canada, where strangely enough, he had printed 500 circulars, a copy of which follows:

ELLEN DONWORTH'S DEATH
To the Guests of the Metropole Hotel. Ladies and Gentlemen:
    I hereby notify you that the person who poisoned Ellen Donworth on the 13th last October is today in the employ of the Metropole Hotel and that your lives are in danger as long as you remain in this Hotel. London April 1892.
Yours respectfully,
W.H. Murray

Dr. Cream never used the printed circulars, and no one knows to this day why he had them printed. They do serve to reveal Cream's perverted obsession with publicity of any kind.

With the coming of spring, and with Cream back in England, things started to percolate once again.

Emma Shrivell, an 18-year-old prostitute and her friend, Alice March, lived in a furnished flat near Waterloo Road. In the middle of the night their screams woke the landlady. Both girls were in great pain and were convulsing violently. During brief periods when their agony subsided, they told of having a distinguished gentleman as a supper guest earlier that evening. The gentleman wore a tall top hat, called himself Fred, and claimed he was a doctor. The girls let him talk them into taking some pills. Alice March died before reaching the hospital, while Emma Shrivell lingered for five hours before she too died.

Quite by chance a bobby walking his beat had seen the two girls let their guest out into the night. He was able to provide a full description. The publicity surrounding these two deaths brought forth other ladies who had managed to escape the clutches of the mysterious Fred.

Lou Harvey told of pretending to take the pills, but unknown to Fred she had thrown them away. Violet Beverley refused a drink offered to her by the obliging Fred. Both of these ladies gave detailed descriptions of their weird acquaintance to the police.

Then Dr. Cream, still craving notoriety, did the ultimate. He complained to Scotland Yard. Using the name Dr. Neill, he told them that the police were following him and harassing him with accusations that he was the killer of March and Shrivell. Neill told the Yard that he had nothing whatever to do with the crimes, claiming that a Dr. Harper was the real culprit.

It is difficult to understand exactly why Dr. Cream would furnish the police with information which would lead them to his doorstep. It wasn't long before the authorities discovered that Dr. Neill was really Dr. Cream. Several of the surviving ladies identified him as the elusive Fred. So did the bobby who had seen him leave March and Shrivell's flat the night they died.

Dr. Cream was 42 years old when he was adjudged to be legally sane and placed on trial for murder. On November 15, 1892 he was hanged for his crimes.

With death only seconds away Cream's sense of the dramatic was not to be denied. As the trap door sprung open he yelled, "I am Jack the R—." Reporters ran to their files, only to find out that Dr. Cream had been securely locked up in Joliet when Jack was operating in London.

Dr. Cream suffered his greatest indignity when more than 80 years after his execution, Madame Tussaud's wax museum in London announced they were removing his wax image from their Chamber of Horrors. It seems there was a decided lack of interest, and anyway he wasn't scary enough.

DR. ROBERT MacGREGOR 1912

YOU'VE already met Canada's most infamous medical murderer, Dr. Neill Cream, who took tremendous delight in poisoning unsuspecting ladies before the turn of the century. Less well known but every bit as wicked was London, Ontario's Dr. Robert MacGregor.

By the time he was 30, Dr. MacGregor had left London and set up practice in the village of Ubly in Huron County, Michigan. One January afternoon in 1909, Carrie Sparling, the 45-year-old wife of dairy farmer John Wesley Sparling, walked into the doctor's office with a distressing bit of dust in her left eye.

Although Carrie was the mother of four strapping sons, she had the appearance of a girl of 25. Dr. MacGregor took one look at the bad eye, coughed and said, "Kindly disrobe." The doctor started by staring at Carrie's toes and after several pauses on his way northward finally concentrated on the sore eye. Dr. MacGregor extracted the dust and told his patient that he would drop in on her the next time he was near her farm in Sanilac County, about an hour's buggy drive from Ubly.

Dr. MacGregor was a tall, attractive man. Carrie didn't exactly repulse his advances. The doctor did have a meek, rather ugly wife of his own, who was forgotten from the very day Carrie showed up with that bad eye.

A week after Carrie's visit, Dr. MacGregor travelled to the Sparling farm, where he met big husky, John Wesley Sparling and his four sons, Ray, 20, Scyrel, 21, Albert, 23, and Peter, 24.

The doctor thought it best to give Carrie a physical examination. One never knew what damage dust in the eye could inflict. Dr. MacGregor and Carrie were directed to the bedroom by trusting John Wesley. An hour later they emerged and advised Mr. Sparling, "Everything was just fine, even better than we had hoped."

From then on Carrie suffered from a series of minor ailments. The doctor came every second week or so and never failed to cure what ailed her.

After several months had passed, Dr. MacGregor confided to his best friend Xenophon A. Boomhower, who lived in the neighboring village of Bad Axe, that he suspected John Wesley Sparling had Bright's disease. A few months later John Wesley was confined to his bed. Despite Dr. MacGregor's care, the poor man was called to that great dairy farm in the sky.

The doctor, who was now considered a dear family friend by the four boys and something altogether different by Carrie, met with the Sparling family. He advised the boys to take out life insurance. Considering the untimely demise of their father, the four lads thought it good advice. By coincidence, the doctor's father was an insurance agent back in London. He sold them Sun Life of Canada policies.

A year later Dr. MacGregor informed his friend Boomhower that Pete Sparling had acute pancreatitis. Everyone was shocked. Poor Pete. He was laid to rest beside his dad less than a year after the elder Sparling had departed this mortal coil.

Distraught, Carrie decided to sell the farm and purchase a smaller one in Huron County, a stone's throw from Dr. MacGregor's office in Ubly. Coincidental with the Sparlings' move, good friend Xenophon Boomhower was appointed county prosecutor.

The wood was hardly stacked for the winter at the Sparlings' new farm when Albert took ill. The doctor explained to Boomhower that Albert had lifted a heavy piece of farm machinery and had suffered internal injuries. A few months later Albert joined Pete and John Wesley down at the family plot.

It was vacation time. Dr. MacGregor took his wife on a motoring trip throughout Ontario. While the doctor was away, Carrie bought a house in Ubly for investment purposes. It was only a few streets removed from Dr. MacGregor's office. When the MacGregors returned, Carrie suggested that they move out of their present home and rent from her. It seemed like a good idea, and that's how the MacGregors became tenants of Carrie Sparling.

Mrs. MacGregor took ill. Her husband suggested she return to Ontario to visit relatives and rest up. Mrs. MacGregor left the scene. She was no sooner gone than Carrie took to visiting the good doctor. Sometimes she stayed all day. When the fancy struck her she stayed all night. Tongues wagged, but the untimely death of Scyrel Sparling interrupted the gossip.

The death appeared to puzzle Dr. MacGregor. He suggested an autopsy, which he conducted with another doctor in attendance. It was a cursory affair. Dr. MacGregor took one look and said, "Well, well, cancer of the liver." The other doctor agreed without really taking part in the examination. Scyrel joined the other members of his family down at the eternal place of rest.

Shortly after Scyrel's tragic passing, a village busybody observed Carrie leaving the doctor's residence at dawn. She informed elderly John Sparling, an uncle of the late John Wesley, who waited until he spied Carrie enter Dr. Mac-Gregor's home. He then climbed up a ladder and peered into the bedroom. Land sakes! The rumors were true. There were Carrie and Dr. MacGregor, coupled.

Things got hot. Old John informed Prosecutor Boomhower, who secretly had Scyrel's body exhumed. Vital organs were sent to the University of Michigan. The university report stated that Scyrel's organs were laced with arsenic. Albert's body was also exhumed. It, too, contained arsenic.

When Dr. MacGregor told Boomhower that the one remaining Sparling son, Ray, had taken ill, he knew he had to take immediate action. Unknown to Carrie, he visited the bedridden Ray at the farm and told him the whole sordid story. He advised Ray to pretend to take Dr. MacGregor's medicine but to save it for analysis. The medicine proved to be laced with arsenic.

Dr. MacGregor was taken into custody and charged with Scyrel's murder. Carrie was charged with being an accomplice. During the trial, Prosecutor Boomhower forcefully pointed out that both Albert's and Scyrel's bodies had contained arsenic. Dr. MacGregor was found guilty and sentenced to life in Michigan State Prison. The charges against Carrie were dropped.

As soon as the prison gates closed behind him in 1912, Dr. MacGregor began a campaign of letter writing proclaiming his innocence. One such letter reached Gov. Woodbridge Fuller, who was appalled that testimony concerning Albert's poisoning had been admitted as evidence at a trial which concerned Scyrel's death only. The governor interviewed several members of the jury, who said they would not have found MacGregor guilty if the evidence concerning Albert's death had not been presented.

Gov. Fuller pardoned Dr. MacGregor after he had served four years in prison. Once outside, the doctor was the object of ridicule. Friendless, he applied for the position of physician at Michigan State Prison. The appointment was granted. Dr. MacGregor ministered to the prisoners for 12 years, never leaving the institution until he died within its grey walls in 1928.

DR. HERMAN SCHMITZ 1926

SENDING human parts through the mail is definitely in poor taste. In Canada, our criminals rarely use Canada Post, no doubt firmly believing that any alternate mode of delivery would be less tardy. Not so in Europe, where the mails have often been used to advantage.

On April Fool's Day of 1926, the chief of police of Vienna, Herr Weitzel, was somewhat taken aback when he opened a personally addressed small package which had arrived by mail. It contained a human finger.

The chief turned the distinctive digit over to his lab. No sooner had he finished his strudel break than the lab boys provided him with a full report. The finger was the first finger from a woman's right hand. It was slender, the nail being well manicured and polished. The finger was free of callouses and was quite possibly that of a middle-aged woman. It had been recently severed with surgical skill.

The string and paper used to wrap the package were in common use and proved impossible to trace. The parcel had been mailed in Vienna.

Weitzel rubbed his goatee and thought of the possibilities. Of course, the distasteful parcel could be the prank of a medical student or mortuary employee, but the chief couldn't take a chance. He had to assume a crime had been committed.

While the Vienna police were checking out missing persons and calling on mortuaries, Weitzel received another parcel. You guessed it, the package contained another human finger. It was the third finger from the same hand which had provided the previous finger. Examination of the nail indicated that it was polished with the same nail polish. Medical examination revealed a rather disconcerting fact. The finger had been amputated with surgical skill while the victim was alive.

A plain gold ring was on the finger when it arrived. The ring was made of 22 carat gold. Tiny scratches or indentations on the underside of the ring had been made by the corrosive action of a diluted acid. The acid had many commercial uses, but the one detectives homed in on was its use in the removal of tattoos.

In order to find out if the amputated finger had ever been tattooed, it was necessary to remove the top skin. Once this was done, doctors were able to make out the image of a snake wound around the finger in the exact location covered by the gold ring. There was little doubt in the minds of the investigators that the acid used to remove the tattoo had made the indentations in the ring. But what did it all mean? Maybe the snake held some significance at one time, but had been displaced by the ring.

Tattoo parlors were canvassed, but police were unsuccessful in locating the one where the snake had been applied and removed. The ring also proved impossible to trace.

The story was leaked to the press, which caused Vienna police no end of embarrassment. Was a killer on the loose who took great relish in taunting the entire police force? Above all, could the chief expect further fingers to show up in his mail?

A week passed. The mystery deepened when a female body sans head and two fingers from the right hand was found in a swamp outside Vienna. An examination of the torso shed no light on the identity of the middle-aged victim. However, it was noted that the two fingers had been removed with skill and the use of surgical instruments.

Police were able to make a plaster cast of a footprint found in soft mud near the torso. From the footprint, an anthropologist gave a description of the man who had made it. It was ascertained that he was over six feet tall, with broad shoulders and long arms.

Weitzel and his boys now had something to work with. They were looking for a tall doctor, most likely a surgeon. They came up with several in Vienna, but gradually all were eliminated. All except one.

Dr. Herman Schmitz was a surgeon who had a small practice, catering mainly to wealthy patients. A search of criminal records revealed that at one time Dr. Schmitz had been charged with malpractice, but had been found innocent by a jury. Despite the verdict, the doctor's practice had suffered. Eventually he gravitated to a small but lucrative practice. His patients obviously were unaware of his past.

A cursory investigation of Schmitz's family revealed that he had a wife and children. The children were of school age and Frau Schmitz seemed happy enough. That's what a cursory investigation indicated. An in-depth investigation uncovered the mistress. It was somewhat of a disappointment for the Vienna detectives to find out that she was alive and well. The victim had to be someone else.

Twenty-four-hour surveillance teams were put on the good doctor, the dear wife and the willing mistress. The doctor stayed clean. So did the wife. But the mistress unwittingly led police to paydirt.

Detectives found a dress shop where the doctor's mistress had a charge account. In those long ago days before credit cards, kept ladies had their bills forwarded to their gentlemen friends every month or so. Vienna police, now hot to trot, questioned the store manager. He told them that the doctor's current mistress was somewhat of a pain, unlike his previous mistress, Anna Stein. He explained that Anna had purchased far more dresses before the doctor had changed horses in midstream.

Police dashed over to Anna's apartment only to find that she had vacated the premises three weeks earlier. A survey of her regular haunts brought the same results. Anna Stein had disappeared. Police were pretty sure they knew the location of her torso and two fingers. However, they weren't sure about her head.

This puzzle was solved when they surreptitiously searched Dr. Schmitz's office. The found a small laboratory off the main office. There, reposing in a bucket of preservative solution was the head of Anna Stein. Dr. Schmitz was picked up and charged with the murder of his mistress.

A meticulous search of the doctor's office turned up pieces of Anna's clothing, which had been partially burned. The doctor's current mistress was somewhat distressed to discover that several pieces of jewelry which had been given to her by Schmitz had once belonged to the deceased.

Witnesses were located who stated that Anna had been furious with her lover when she found out she had been replaced in his affections by a younger woman. They had argued fiercely, but the charming doctor sweet talked Anna into bringing her belongings to his office under the pretence of taking a long holiday in Paris. Anna fell for the ruse. Instead of a trip to the City of Light, she was first made helpless by dope, had two fingers amputated and was then murdered.

Dr. Schmitz admitted to quarreling with his former mistress, but claimed she had thrown herself upon him and expired as a result of a heart attack.

Examination of the body proved beyond a doubt that Anna had not died of a heart attack. She had been administered a lethal injection of potassium cyanide. Police found a bottle of diluted acid used to remove the tattooed snake from the dead woman's finger. This had been done to hamper identification of the victim.

Dr. Schmitz's trial for murder promised to be a sensation. The Austrian press carried little else on its front pages. But the drama of a sensational murder trial was not to be. Dr. Schmitz attempted to escape from jail. He made his way to the roof of the building and tried to jump to an adjoining lower roof. He didn't make it. He died on the ground after confessing to the murder of Anna Stein.

Why did the doctor send those fingers to the chief of police? It is believed he never forgave police for their investigation of the malpractice charge brought against him years earlier. He sent the fingers through the mail in an attempt to make the police appear foolish and incompetent. Instead, he drew attention to himself, which eventually caused his death.

DR. BENJAMIN KNOWLES 1928

TODAY, the tiny country is known as the Republic of Ghana. Back in 1928, it was a small jewel in the crown of British colonies on the west coast of Africa called Ashanti.

The resident doctor in the town of Bekawi was Dr. Benjamin Knowles. The good doctor and his wife lived in apparent harmony until 4:30 p.m., on October 20, 1928. That was the day someone shot Mrs. Knowles directly in, for want of a better word, the buttocks.

The Knowles' houseboy heard the shot and rushed to the home of Mr. Thortref Margin, the district commissioner. Margin was greeted at the Knowles front door by the doctor, who assured him everything was all right. Margin continued on to take part in a scheduled tennis match.

When he returned from tennis, he learned the houseboy had called on him again, leaving the message, "Missie cry very much."

Next morning, Margin reported the incident to Knowles' superior, Dr. Gush. Knowles told him there had been an accident. He showed Dr. Gush black and blue bruises on his knees and shins where, he claimed, his wife had struck him with an Indian club.

Dr. Gush found Mrs. Knowles standing up in her bedroom. She told him she had been wounded and invited him to examine the wound in her left buttock. The bullet had travelled upward and exited out of the right side of her abdomen.

Mrs. Knowles told Gush that she had been examining her husband's .455 Webley revolver. She placed in on a chair and later sat on the weapon and accidentally discharged it while trying to remove the gun.

Gush had Mrs. Knowles removed to a hospital and three days after the shooting, she died. Her husband was charged with her murder as the police firmly believed she went to her death protecting him.

Two .455 calibre bullets were found in the Knowles cottage. Bullet number one was found by a houseboy on the eve of the shooting in a pool of blood in the bedroom. Bullet number two was found in a wardrobe. There was a scorched hole in mosquito netting draped over the Knowles' bed, and a hole in the wardrobe door.

A search of the home uncovered a loaded .455 Webley revolver with only one discharged cartridge shell. On November 13, 1928, Dr. Knowles' murder trial took place in Kumasi before a lone judge.

The prosecution claimed bullet number two was fired by Dr. Knowles as he lay in bed. They speculated it travelled through the mosquito netting, his wife's body and the wardrobe door, then fell to the base of the wardrobe. They further claimed the doctor attempted to treat his wife's wound, thereby keeping the shooting a secret.

Dr. Knowles stated bullet number two was fired by his wife weeks earlier to frighten him. Bullet number one, the one found in the pool of blood, was the bullet which accidentally killed his wife.

Defence lawyers stated they traced the trajectory of bullet number two. In order for Mrs. Knowles to have been shot by her husband, she would have to have been standing on a chair or Knowles would have to be lying on the floor, both rather farfetched possibilities.

The prosecution countered by stating the fatal shot could have been fired as Mrs. Knowles bent over. If this was the case, how did that other bullet find its way into the pool of blood on the floor?

The perplexing case was decided by the lone presiding judge, who found Dr. Knowles guilty and sentenced him to death. Dr. Knowles appealed. His conviction was set aside because the presiding judge had not considered manslaughter as an alternative charge to murder. The good doctor was freed and never tried again.

Dr. Knowles died of natural causes in 1933 and took the riddle of the extra bullet to his grave.

DR. PIERRE BOUGRAT 1929

WHEN it comes to murders based on affairs of the heart, it seems there is no one quite like the French. Frenchmen display a certain style and elan toward their amours which is difficult to duplicate.

Take Dr. Pierre Bougrat as a classic example. At 32, Doc had a terrific practice in Aix, France, a gorgeous wife and a big home. To the casual observer it appeared that the young doctor had the world by the tail, but as you and I know, outward appearances are sometimes deceiving. In the doctor's case his wife left a lot to be desired in the love making department. Truth is she simply did not want to perform frequently enough to suit her husband.

Pierre looked elsewhere for his kicks. He discovered that in Marseilles, only about 30 kilometres from Aix, there was an abundance of houses which were not homes. The doctor found out that he could change out of his respectable clothing into the sloppy garb of the waterfront district, and have a barrel of fun every night.

Things went along famously for about a year, or until the frigid wife, suspecting that all was not kosher, put a private eye on Pierre. The detective reported back to Mrs. B. that her husband had a reputation as a real stud among the brothels of Marseilles. Now it so happened that Mrs. B. had an elderly father who thought the sun rose and set on his son-in-law.

In order to save her father from the disgrace of Pierre's philandering, Mrs. B. struck a bargain with her husband. They would continue to live under the same roof, but in the evening they would have separate bedrooms. Pierre was never happier. That night he whistled while he, shall we say, worked down at the waterfront.

Another year went by. Then Mrs. B.'s father died and she no longer had any reason to stay under the same roof with Pierre. She pulled out bag and baggage, and presumably found another roof under which to stay. The doctor found himself the only occupant of his large home in Aix.

At this time in his career, the doctor met a prostitute named Andrea Audibert. It is not quite clear just what made Andrea different from all the other ladies of the night. Whatever, Andrea said try it, you'll like it; and for once in his life Pierre fell in love. He spent every evening with Andrea, partaking of her many charms. There was just one catch. Andrea was owned by a rough, tough, pimp named Marius. The doctor wanted Andrea to stop sharing her favors with utter strangers. He also found that studding around all night and doctoring all day was just too taxing on his constitution. He wanted to install Andrea as his housekeeper in his home in Aix. He decided to buy his true love's freedom from her pimp. The doctor was a bit shocked at the price of the merchandise. Marius wanted 9,000 francs, and Pierre had no choice; he promised Marius he would raise the money.

As luck would have it, one of the doctor's patients back in Aix was the paymaster of a local steel mill. Macques Rumebe visited the doctor each week for an injection. Over the years Rumebe and the doctor became familiar with each other's routine. It was an easy matter for the doctor to reschedule Rumebe's appointment to a day when the paymaster picked up the payroll from the bank and carried it to the mill. The doctor's office was situated between the bank and the mill. It was quite natural for Rumebe to pick up the payroll and drop into the doctor's office for his injection.

With a jaunty walk and a twinkle in his eye Rumebe entered Dr. Bougrat's office for his injection. He received a shot of arsenobenzol and was deader than a mackerel in a matter of minutes.

Rather unimaginatively, the doctor nailed Rumebe upright in a closet and sealed the door. Later he had some wallpaper hangers come in and paper over the whole thing.

Speedy Pierre scampered down to Marseilles, paid Marius 9,000 francs and returned to Aix with his new housekeeper, Andrea. In the meantime, Rumebe had been missed in a matter of hours. There were two schools of thought. He had either met with foul play, or had absconded with his company's payroll. Dr. Bougrat made sure which way the wind blew. He wrote to Rumebe's employer. In disguised handwriting he informed them that Rumebe had been leading a double life and had been carrying on a love affair with a prostitute in Marseilles.

In the routine investigation which followed, the police called on Dr. Bougrat to question him about his patient, Rumebe. The detective was shown into the house by Andrea. The officer couldn't get the nagging feeling out of his head that he had seen Andrea before. When he returned to the police station he spent several hours going through pictures of girls suspected of a variety of crimes. Sure enough, there she was, the Marseilles prostitute, Andrea Audibert.

With his curiosity now aroused, the detective started to track down the route by which a Marseilles prostitute became a doctor's housekeeper in Aix. It wasn't difficult to uncover that the doctor had paid the pimp Marius 9,000 francs on the day Rumebe disappeared. Had the doctor killed the paymaster in order to obtain the money to purchase Andrea's freedom? The detective was sure he was on the right track. Where could the doctor have disposed of the body so quickly before Rumebe was missed? The officer deduced that the body must be somewhere on the doctor's premises. He only had to find evidence of recent renovations and he was sure he would find the body. On his next visit to the doctor's house he was proved correct in every detail.

Dr. Bougrat was arrested and tried for murder. The cagey doctor admitted everything except murder. He claimed he had inadvertently given an overdose to his patient and that the entire affair had been a horrible accident. After he discovered his mistake he had panicked and nailed poor Rumebe up in the closet.

The intriguing story saved Pierre's neck from falling victim to Dr. Guillotine's diabolical machine. He was sentenced to life imprisonment on Devil's Island.

Pierre was sent to the infamous prison in 1929. He was soon recognized by both inmates and officials of the famous penal colony as an extremely capable physician. He became a trustee, and after serving almost six years, he was allowed a month's freedom in the town of St. Laurent du Maroni on the French Guinea mainland. Although he was still under a loose guard the situation was not escape proof.

The first thing Pierre did was to find a woman, and after six years who can blame him. Her name was Annette du Bois, and she turned out to be a real peach. After teaming up with Annette the doctor made up his mind never to return to Devil's Island. To make matters even better Annette had some loot of her own stashed away and she was willing to go anywhere with Pierre.

Annette and Pierre slipped aboard a Dutch freighter heading for Venezuela. The cagey medic had noted that Venezuela didn't have an extradition treaty with France. Sly fox that he was, he pulled it off. Once in Venezuela he found out that he could get a licence to practise medicine in Caracas.

Believe it or not, Pierre married Annette, and set up housekeeping in Cara-cas. In time he built up a lucrative medical practice and became a respected doc-tor once again. For nine years Dr. Bougrat practised medicine by day and faithfully returned to his wife's side by night.

In 1944 Dr. Bougrat, a man who had crammed a lot of living into his 53 years, died of a fever epidemic which he was helping to fight.

DR. MARCEL PETIOT 1930

RARELY has a more despicable character taken his place on the stage of criminal infamy than Dr. Marcel Petiot.

Petiot was born in the picturesque French town of Auxerre. He grew up to be a bright, handsome young man. In 1921 he obtained his medical degree and by 1924 had acquired a general practice in Villeneuve. His practice soon became the most prosperous in town. Dr. Petiot was so popular in the community that he was elected mayor in 1925. That same year, he married Georgette Lablais, the daughter of a wealthy Paris restaurant owner. A year later, their son Gerard was born.

In the years which followed Petiot had several brushes with the law. Once he was convicted of fixing an electrical meter, enabling him to obtain free light and power. He was found guilty of this charge, received a suspended sentence and was forced to resign as mayor. On another occasion, he was accused of stealing gasoline from a garage. The charge wasn't pressed.

In 1930, the good doctor was accused of a far more serious crime. A Mme. Debeuve was found strangled to death in a dairy she operated. The place had been robbed. Dr. Petiot had been seen near the dairy at the time of the crime and was strongly suspected of Mme. Debeuve's murder. He was never charged, but from the time of the murder rumors of his involvement spread throughout the town. By 1933 the rumors had become so intense that Petiot moved to Paris and opened a general practice at 66 Rue Caumartin.

Seven years after his arrival in Paris, Petiot purchased a 15-room villa in the Rue Le Sueur near the Arc de Triomphe. He supervised extensive alterations to the villa, including an oversize furnace and a high wall around the garden. To the curious, the doctor explained that he had opened a mental institution at Rue Le Sueur while retaining his home and general practice at Rue Caumartin.

One of Petiot's first patients at his new address was Denise Hotin. Denise had heard that the doctor would perform abortions. After her abortion, she returned to her home village, but for reasons of her own went back to Paris to see Dr. Petiot. No one saw Denise after that. A few inquiries were made from her village, but nothing of an official nature was done. Germany had invaded France and occupied Paris. It was wartime; anything could have happened.

Dr. Petiot let it be known that he would supply drugs to addicts from his new office. His illicit drug trade kept a steady stream of cash pouring in. One fine day, a pimp named van Bever caused a fuss when the doctor refused to sell him dope on credit. Van Bever threatened to tell police of the doctor's drug business. A short while later, van Bever simply disappeared off the face of the earth. His friends figured he had fallen into the hands of the German secret police.

In 1942, Dr. Petiot hatched a diabolical plot which was to place him in a category as one of the most despicable multiple murderers in a world that has far too many vile killers. Realizing that those of the Jewish faith were fleeing France in the face of increasing persecution at the hands of the Germans, the wily Dr. Petiot posed as a man who had the connections to pay off authorities and pave the way out of the country for those in danger.

His first customer was a neighbor, Joachim Gruschinov. In the strictest confidence, Dr. Petiot told his neighbor that he was a member of the Resistance and could get him out of the country for a price. He assured Gruschinov that not a penny went to the Resistance or to himself. The complete amount was used to pay off officials. Gruschinov gathered together all his valuables and delivered them to Dr. Petiot, who assured him they would be sent to South America in advance of his arrival.

Gruschinov kissed his wife goodbye and promised to send for her as soon as possible. He entered Dr. Petiot's surgery, never to be seen again. Next day, Dr. Petiot told Gruschinov's wife that her husband was on his way to South America.

Dr. Paul Braunberger paid one million francs for his safe passage out of the country. He too told his wife he would be sending for her after he settled in Spain. Dr. Braunberger was never heard of again.

M. and Mme. Kneller and their eight-year-old son walked into Dr. Petiot's surgery and disappeared off the face of the earth.

In 1943, Petiot had a narrow escape. Pierre Beretta, an escaped prisoner of war, had made arrangements to flee France with Petiot's help. When he was picked up by the Gestapo, he squealed on Petiot to save his own skin.

Dr. Petiot was taken into custody by the Gestapo. Scared sick, he decided to play his one trump card. He confessed to murder, but pointed out that all his victims had been Jewish. The Gestapo checked out the identities of his victims and, after detaining him for six months, set him free. Dr. Petiot had correctly read his adversaries. The Germans felt the sleazy doctor was doing their dirty work for them.

Dr. Petiot returned to his wife and his practice. Numerous men, women and children fell into his net. He made millions of francs during his two-year killing spree. Initially, Petiot dissolved bodies in lime, but when this material became difficult to procure, he dissected them and burned them in his large furnace. It wasn't that difficult. His unsuspecting victims placed themselves totally in his care. They trustingly accepted the anti-typhoid injection he gave them, never for an instant realizing that it was a deadly poison.

On March 11, 1944, Dr. Petiot's chimney caught fire. A neighbor, Mme. Marcais, observed flames shooting out of the chimney. The odor of the smoke was nauseating. She called police, who in turn called the fire department. Firemen broke into the large rambling villa and made their way into the furnace room. They stopped short. There on the floor around the furnace were the arms, legs, torsos and heads of Petiot's victims.

Police searched an adjoining garage, where they uncovered a vast array of clothing and personal effects. They also found Petiot's death book, complete with names and addresses. The death list was headed with the word "Escapes."

French detectives descended on Petiot's home on Rue Caumartin, but the bird had flown. He had deposited his wife and child in his home town of Auxerre and had returned to Paris, where he hid out in a friend's house. The gruesome discovery of the doctor's victims was front page news until June 6, when the Allied landing in Normandy took over the news. On August 24, Paris was liberated and Petiot and his horrible crimes were again reported by the country's press.

Word was received by the police that Petiot might have joined the Resistance using a false name. A sample of his handwriting was checked against the handwriting of members of the Resistance who had joined since June 6. It was a long shot, but it paid off. Petiot's handwriting was identified as that of a Capt. Witterwald. On November 2, 1944, the Resistance turned over the bogus captain to the police.

On March 18, 1946, Dr. Petiot stood trial for the murders of 27 individuals killed at Rue Le Sueur. Petiot swore he had been working on behalf of the

Resistance and that all his victims had been German soldiers and collaborators. His story didn't wash with the French jury. The sensational trial lasted 16 days, but the jury took only two hours to find Petiot guilty of 24 counts of murder.

In an attempt to save their client's life, defence attorneys appealed to the president of France for clemency. Their plea was rejected. On May 26, 1946, Dr. Marcel Petiot was put to death with the assistance of a contraption invented by another French doctor named Guillotine.

DR. BUCK RUXTON 1936

SUSAN Johnson did what many people do when they stroll over a country bridge. She absently looked down at the meandering stream below. Could that be a human arm protruding from some newspapers on the river bank? Susan, who was vacationing in Moffat, Scotland, hurriedly returned to her hotel room where she told her brother of her suspicions. He travelled the two miles to the bridge and confirmed his sister's gruesome find. Then he called the police.

What confronted the authorities on that pleasant September afternoon in 1935 was not a pretty sight. The newspapers held the dismembered portions of not one, but two, bodies. There were four individual bundles containing small segments of both bodies. The victims were adult females.

Within the next two days additional parts of the same two bodies were found in the general area of the original four bundles. Complete sections of the two bodies had been cut away in an obvious attempt to hinder identification.

To add an element of mystery to the already strange discovery of two separate dismembered and mutilated bodies, police found a Cyclops eye in one of the newspaper bundles. This phenomenon, known as Cyclopia, is the fusing together of two eyes, which appear as a single eye in the middle of the forehead. This malformation is extremely rare in humans, but does occur more frequently in pigs. In the case of humans, it is usually accompanied by other deformities which result in death a few hours after birth. The name, of course, is derived from a mythical race of one-eyed giants whose chief occupation in Greek mythology was the manufacture of thunderbolts for Zeus. The human Cyclops eye was a strange and puzzling oddity to discover along a peaceful meandering river in Scotland.

A heavy rainfall had taken place on September 19. It was ascertained that the bodies would have been washed away had they been deposited on the river bank before this date. Police began their investigation by checking out all women reported missing since September 19.

In this routine manner, investigating officers found out that Mary Jane

Rogerson, a nursemaid in the home of Dr. Buck Ruxton, had been reported missing weeks before Miss Johnson's gruesome discovery under the bridge. Police were also given to understand that Dr. Ruxton's wife had left him at approximately the same time. Mary Rogerson's mother identified several pieces of clothing found with the bodies as belonging to her daughter. She had sewn a patch into one of the garments herself.

Detectives were already well acquainted with Dr. Buck Ruxton. He had called on them several times in the previous three weeks to complain that his wife had left him, and that he wanted her found and returned. After the gruesome discovery he continued to call on the police, claiming that rumors were being spread connecting him with the bodies found under the bridge. Dr. Ruxton stated that the rumors were ruining his practice and must be stopped.

Police were not ready to act. Mrs. Ruxton had not been identified as a victim and, while Dr. Ruxton was strongly suspected of complicity in the murder, police found it prudent to wait until positive identification could be established. I must point out that visual examination of the bodies was ruled out as a method of identification. The mutilations to both bodies were so extensive that it was impossible to identify the bodies in this way.

Dr. Ruxton was born in Bombay, India. Thankfully he had his name changed from Bukhtyar Rustomji Ratanji Hakim to Buck Ruxton. He received his medical degree from the University of Bombay, and later specialized in surgery at the same university. He had maintained a comfortable home at 2 Dalton Square, Lancaster, since 1930, where he carried on a rather successful medical practice.

Mrs. Ruxton was the former Isabella Kerr. She had been married once before in 1919. After meeting Dr. Ruxton, she had her marriage dissolved, and married the doctor in 1928.

During the seven years of their marriage, Mrs. Ruxton and the doctor argued and fought incessantly. Dr. Ruxton was insanely jealous, and often unjustly accused her of having affairs with other men. Ruxton had a short temper and often struck his wife.

His diary reveals that they always kissed and made up. Theirs was an unhappy household.

The Ruxtons had three children, aged six, four, and two. Mary Rogerson, their nursemaid, was 20. Mary rarely left the Ruxton residence during the week.

Usually she spent her day off with her parents. She had never been late for an appointment, nor had she ever stayed out overnight without informing her family. Neither Mrs. Ruxton nor Mary were seen by anyone after September 14, 1935.

Three women, other than Mary, worked at the good doctor's home. Mrs. Agnes Oxley, a charwoman, worked at 2 Dalton Square every day of the week, except Saturday, starting at 7:10 a.m. Mrs. Elizabeth Curwen also showed up every day starting at 8:30 a.m. and staying until her work was completed. A third woman, Mrs. Mabel Smith, had only recently been hired on a part-time basis, working Monday through Thursday from 2 p.m. to 7 p.m. The work schedules of these women later proved to be of crucial importance.

On Friday, September 13, Mrs. Curwen was told by Dr. Ruxton not to return until the following Monday. On Sunday, the 15th, Mrs. Oxley was surprised to find Dr. Ruxton at her doorstep at 6:30 a.m., advising her not to come to work. He told her that Mrs. Ruxton and Mary had gone on a holiday to Edinburgh. Mrs. Smith was not due at Dalton Square until Monday.

Dr. Ruxton had managed to dismiss his three employees, leaving him alone in his home on Friday night, Saturday and Sunday.

All that weekend Ruxton scurried about. To everyone who met him he appeared agitated and nervous. As his car was in for repairs, he hired a vehicle and placed his children with friends.

When the charwomen reported for work the following week they found two upstairs bedrooms locked. The house had undergone many changes over the weekend. The walls along the stairway appeared to be blood splattered. Rugs had been taken up and thrown into the backyard. These, too, had large brown stains. The doctor magnanimously gave the rugs to Mrs. Oxley and Mrs. Curwen. He explained that he had severely cut his hand while opening a tin of fruit, accounting for the bloodstains on the wall and rug. He also told them that he was preparing the house to be redecorated. The ladies worked hard all that week cleaning up.

To everyone, even those who didn't inquire, Dr. Ruxton gave conflicting stories about his wife's and Mary's sudden departure. To some he stated that Mary was pregnant, and that his wife had gone away with her to attempt to terminate the pregnancy. He told others that the two women were on vacation. All week the charwomen cleaned and threw out rubbish. One of them later remembered a bloody piece of cotton wool which the doctor had her burn in the backyard, together with a bloody dress.

On September 19, at 7:30 a.m., Ruxton brought his car around to the back door of his home. As Mrs. Oxley worked out of sight in the kitchen, he made several trips upstairs and back down to his car. After he left, Mrs. Oxley, who was now joined by Mrs. Curwen, noticed that the two upstairs rooms, which had been locked for five days, were now open. The two ladies entered the rooms and remarked on the vile smell emanating from them.

Next day Dr. Ruxton mentioned the smell to the two women. He suggested they buy a bottle of eau de cologne. Mrs. Curwen bought the cologne and gave it to the doctor. Later on the fragrance was much in evidence in the odoriferous rooms.

It must be noted that in the two weeks between September 14 and the discovery of the bodies on September 29, Dr. Ruxton was a busy little boy. He was scurrying around the countryside, trying to establish an alibi, ministering to his patients, placing his children, trying desperately to have his house decorated, and keeping three inquisitive women from finding out the truth while making up stories to account for the absence of his wife and nursemaid. All the while he was dissecting two bodies and disposing of the pieces. It was all enough to tire a man. No wonder everyone who saw him during this period remembers his desperate appearance.

After the bodies were discovered near Moffat, Dr. Ruxton became frantic. He contacted everyone he had seen in the previous two weeks asking them to support him in the story he would be telling the police.

Dr. Buck Ruxton was arrested and charged with the murder of Mary Rogerson on October 15, 1935. Two months later he stood trial for murder at the Manchester Assizes.

Once the arrest was made, police swooped down on 2 Dalton Square and almost took the house apart. Floorboards and parts of the wall were removed to the Department of Forensic Medicine at Glasgow University. Stains appearing on both wall and floor were identified as human blood. Dr. Ruxton's hand was examined. It was established that a fruit tin could not have inflicted such a wound. The severe cut was self-inflicted by a sharp knife. A local newspaper to which the doctor subscribed was found wrapped around a portion of Mary Rogerson's body.

Also found with the body was a section of a sheet, which matched perfectly with the other section found in the doctor's house.

Although the doctor maintained his innocence, it is believed that during one of his frequent fits of temper he killed his wife. Mary Rogerson, the nursemaid, may have witnessed the crime and had to be silenced.

Dr. Ruxton was found guilty and sentenced to death. He was hanged at Strangeways Prison on May 12, 1936.

But what of the mysterious Cyclops eye found with the two bodies? Despite many far out theories put forward at Ruxton's trial, it is a mystery which hasn't been solved to this day.

DR. ROBERT CLEMENTS 1947

DR. Robert George Clements was born in Belfast, Ireland. He became an M.D. in 1904, at age 24. The young general practitioner was a bit different than his colleagues right from the beginning. For one thing the good doctor liked the good life. Clements dined in the best restaurants. He attended the theatre regularly, more often than not with a bright-eyed Irish colleen on his arm. The good life necessitated more funds than the doctor earned at his humble practice, so he was often strapped for ready cash. This situation served to gall the man of medicine, but a sure cure was just around the corner. Her name was Edyth Ann Mercier.

Now Edyth was not your average sweet young thing. She was a good ten years Clements' senior. What's more she was plain. But there were compensating factors. Edyth's daddy was an extremely wealthy grain merchant. On the day of his marriage, Dr. Clements came into a tidy sum of cash. Then, as if on cue, Edyth's daddy died of natural causes 18 months after the marriage. He left Edyth £25,000, a princely sum in 1913.

While there is no proof that Dr. Clements had anything whatsoever to do with his father-in-law's death, you should know, in light of future events, that he was Mr. Mercier's doctor during his last illness. Dr. Clements signed the death certificate, stating cancer to be the cause of death.

The Clements' financial status, now substantially improved, allowed the doctor to partake of the good life he so craved. The couple joined several exclusive social clubs, contributed heavily to reputable charities and, in the main, were considered to be an integral part of Belfast's status-conscious society.

Seven years later, the bloom was definitely off the rose. Edyth was aghast to discover that they, or to be more specific, her husband, had gone through their entire fortune. To add insult to injury, nasty rumors were being bandied about, referring to the doctor's unmedical dalliances with younger lady friends.

Coincidental with their financial and domestic difficulties, Edyth fell ill. Her husband told friends that she suffered from sleeping sickness and that the prognosis was not good. Clements was correct. Edyth died in 1920, leaving the doctor so distraught that he personally signed the death certificate, sold his practice and moved to Manchester.

One thing you can say for Robert George Clements—he was a fast worker. No sooner was his shingle swaying in the Manchester breeze than he was the steady escort of a bevy of that city's most eligible rich ladies. A year after Edyth's death, Clements married for the second time. Mary McCleery, the daughter of a wealthy Manchester industrialist, became wife number two. Once more, the doctor was in the chips. Once more, he spent money with, as they used to say, reckless abandon. Once more, his wife grew ill just as the money was running out. Mary lasted until 1925, when she suddenly expired. Dr. Clements signed the death certificate, listing the cause of death as endocarditis.

Three years later, Dr. Clements went to the well for the third time. Katherine Burke was not of the same mould as numbers one and two. Katherine was not wealthy and was acquainted with Clements' previous wives. There is even a possibility that Clements actually cared for Katherine and there is undeniable evidence that his practice had prospered to the extent that he was able to live in the grand manner without outside help.

This state of affairs lasted until 1939. Poor investments in the hotel business reduced Dr. Clements' funds to a dangerously low level. That's when the doctor let it be known that Katherine was suffering from tuberculosis. She died, even after Dr. Clements brought in a young colleague at the last moment. The grieving husband suggested that tuberculosis had carried Katherine away. The young doctor agreed.

For the first time in his murderous career, Dr. Clements was suspected of foul play. A friend of his most recently departed wife was a lady doctor, Dr. Irene Gayus. She personally disliked Clements and when she learned that he had signed the death certificates of his previous two wives, she grew downright ugly. Dr. Gayus ran to the police, suggesting they delay Katherine's burial. However, they were too late. Katherine had been cremated only a few hours before police arrived at the scene.

There is no evidence that Clements had knowledge of this near miss. He went on his merry way. Wife number four was Amy Victoria Barnett, a lady 20 years the doctor's junior. Papa Barnett was loaded. And what's more, he conveniently died in 1940, leaving his daughter and her husband a cool £22,000 and his opulent residence in Southport.

Wouldn't you just know it, seven years later, Dr. Clements was telling his acquaintances that his wife wasn't well at all. He had a colleague, Dr. John Holmes, look in on her, but the doctor couldn't pinpoint the problem. A few evenings later, Dr. Holmes received an urgent call from Dr. Clements that his wife was gravely ill.

Dr. Holmes had the stricken woman admitted to the Astley Bank Nursing Home, where she was immediately examined by Dr. Andrew Brown. Brown noticed that Mrs. Clements' eyes had pinpoint pupils, her skin had turned bluish and she was having difficulty breathing. He thought she was suffering from an overdose of morphine. Next morning, at 9:30 a.m., Amy Victoria Clements died.

Upon hearing the distressing news, Clements suggested his wife had suffered from a brain tumor. Dr. Brown disagreed and insisted on performing an autopsy immediately. Dr. James Houston, a young pathologist who knew the Clements well, assisted Dr. Brown. The brain was examined, but no evidence of a tumor was found. Dr. Houston, for reasons never explained, destroyed the vital organs he removed from the body. However, he later reported that his testing of blood samples indicated that Mrs. Clements' death was caused by myeloid leukemia.

This conclusion did not sit well with Dr. Brown. He contacted the coroner, who in turn contacted police. The local gendarmes took a long look. When they discovered Dr. Clements had been writing prescriptions for large quantities of morphine for patients who had never been treated with the drug, they decided to act. A second autopsy was ordered, and Dr. Houston was notified of this decision.

When police went to question Dr. Clement, they found him unconscious in his kitchen. He died hours later, leaving behind a short note. The note read: "To Whom it May Concern, I can no longer tolerate the diabolical insults to which I have recently been exposed."

The second post mortem proved to be most revealing. Remember that vital organs had been destroyed, so the pathologist had little to work with. However, he was able to establish that death had been caused by an overdose of morphine. A search of Clements' flat turned up large quantities of morphine tablets hidden in bottles.

A few days later, Dr. Houston was found dead in his laboratory. He had taken

300 times the lethal dose of sodium cyanide. Poor Houston, despondent over wrongly certifying that Mrs. Clements had died of leukemia, had ended it all.

On Tuesday, June 25, 1947, an inquest into the weird events leading successively to the deaths of Mrs. Clements, Dr. Clements and Dr. Houston, was held in Southport. Three days later the jury came to the conclusions that; a) Mrs. Clements was murdered by Dr. Clements; b) Dr. Clements committed suicide; and c) Dr. Houston took his own life in a state of depression. It was learned that Dr. Houston had committed a series of medical errors, which had caused him to become severely depressed. The Clements' case was the last straw.

And so ended the case of the doctor who married and poisoned four wives.

DR. FLORENCE WHITTINGHAM
1953

THIS is a love story with an unhappy ending.

It all began in Dunedin, New Zealand, when Dr. John Saunders met Dr. Florence Whittingham. John was the resident medical officer at Dunedin Public Hospital. At 27 years of age, the handsome young medic could look forward to a long and fulfilling career. The nurses at the hospital considered him to be a prize catch.

When Florence, who was the same age as John, arrived at the hospital, the two doctors were in contact with each other on a daily basis. Florence was the hospital's new house surgeon.

It didn't take John long to become infatuated with his new surgeon. The doctors dated. Florence fell in love. In a matter of weeks, John and Florence were inseparable. Around the hospital they were considered a pair who would eventually marry.

John wrote to his mother in Christchurch that he had met and was going steady with an attractive surgeon, whom he would one day bring home for a visit. Mrs. Saunders read a lot into her son's letter. Although she knew John had often dated, this was the first time he had ever mentioned bringing home a girl to meet his mother.

In May 1953, John proposed to Florence. She was thrilled. Theirs would be the ideal marriage. Everything was stacked in their favor. They had similar cultural backgrounds, were the same age and both were totally committed to their medical specialties.

In the weeks following their engagement, they were only separated on those occasions when their medical duties kept them apart. When Florence informed John that she was pregnant, he was ecstatic. He pointed out that because of the pregnancy they should get married as soon as possible.

The happy couple travelled to Christchurch to visit with John's mother.

Mrs. Saunders was almost as excited as her son at the news of his impending marriage to pleasant, attractive Florence. Right up until John told her Florence was expecting his baby.

That's when Mrs. Saunders changed her tune. Was John sure he wasn't marrying because of the baby? Up to that time, John had not even thought that he was being coerced into marriage. After all, he loved Florence. Her pregnancy had been nothing less than a thrilling and happy circumstance. John's mother even suggested that if they really and truly didn't want to marry, she would adopt the baby.

John and Florence left Christchurch in a state of shock. Their happy news was now muddled. A doubt had been placed in John's mind.

Back at the hospital, the two doctors worked together, but there was a subtle change in their relationship. John was no longer the warm, concerned lover. It appeared to Florence that he no longer wanted their child. When she faced him with this accusation, he reproached her for thinking irrationally, but Florence didn't believe he was telling the truth. In July, she procured an abortion. When John was informed of the abortion, he appeared to be relieved. As the weeks went by, he started to ignore Florence. In time, their relationship, which could have lasted a lifetime, was over. In September, John officially called off their engagement.

Florence was devastated. Of necessity, she and John had to work together at the hospital. There were many days when Florence dragged herself to the hospital, performed surgery and dragged herself home. Life was not worth living without John. His reaction to escaping being a husband and father was one of total relief. Soon he was dating other women, in particular nurse Frances Kearney.

News of John's dating came to Florence's attention. It was not easy to take. Only months earlier she had been pregnant with John's baby. They had been planning a life together. Now she had nothing.

Dr. Florence Whittingham purchased a .303 rifle and a box of ammunition. The weapon lay in her room for some weeks, untouched. Maybe she would one day put the fear of God in John's mind. Maybe that would bring him to his senses. On the other hand, it was possible that she would never use the rifle.

The decision was made for her when she heard that John was taking Frances Kearney to a hospital party to be held at Dr. Brian McMahon's apartment. A few days before the party, which was scheduled for December 12, Florence phoned Frances and said, "This is the mother of John Saunders' child speaking."

Frances was astounded, but recognized Florence's voice. She asked if this was Dr. Whittingham. There was a pause and then a sobbing yes. Frances hung up and immediately informed John of the irrational phone call. He suggested they ignore it. That was a mistake.

John took Frances to the party. Florence took along her trusty .303, concealed under her coat. She arrived late and sought out John. Most of those attending the affair were in one room. Suddenly a shot emanating from the hall brought the merrymaking to a sudden halt. The shot was followed by a blood-curdling scream.

The partygoers ran out to the hall. There was Dr. John Saunders on his knees, blood pouring down his shirt. Florence was at his side, babbling to the dying man, "Listen to me John!" But John Saunders was beyond listening. Slowly, he slumped dead to the floor. As he did so, Florence dropped beside him. When she was lifted from his fallen form, a .303 rifle was evident beside his body. Florence screamed, "John's dead! He's dead!" Everyone there knew that.

Dr. Florence Whittingham was taken into custody and charged with murder. Her sensational trial commenced on February 8, 1955. The entire story of love and death was recounted in detail. The prosecution claimed that it was purely and simply a case of premeditated murder. Florence had purchased the weapon, which she had carried to the party with the express purpose of killing John Saunders.

Florence's defence was based on her statement that she had taken the rifle to the party in order to frighten John, not to kill him. The trial lasted six days, after which the jury retired to reach their verdict. They deliberated 12 hours before returning a verdict of guilty, not of murder, but of manslaughter, with a strong recommendation to mercy. In reaching their verdict, they stated that they felt the rifle had discharged accidentally.

Dr. Florence Whittingham was sentenced to the light term of three years imprisonment.

DR. YVES EVENOU 1955

SIMONE Deschamps was a 43-year-old seamstress when she met Dr. Yves Evenou. It was an innocent enough meeting. Simone called on the doctor for a medical. Five years later, the seamstress and the doctor would provide all of France with one of the juiciest trials that country has ever enjoyed.

Simone wasn't beautiful, nor did she have a voluptuous figure. But beneath the seamstress' plain appearance beat the heart of a passionate, love-starved woman who had never fulfilled those urges we all possess in various degrees. Dr. Yves Evenou would change all that.

On the surface, Evenou was a kind and gentle doctor with a fine reputation. Tucked away at home there dwelt his ever loving wife, Marie-Claire, and 12-year-old daughter, Francoise. They had no idea the good doctor was leading a double life. When not in his office or at home, Evenou was seldom without a glass of port in his hand. He loved the ladies and indulged in every perversion known to man with various ladies of the night. Sometimes, the doctor invented unique perversions of his own. Let's face it, he was one wild and crazy guy.

In Simone he met a lady who was easily led. After a few dates, she was not only in love with the medic, but totally under his influence. No perversion was too weird for Simone. Always half sloshed on port, Evenou didn't treat Simone with a great deal of respect. He would often insult her in front of waiters. Despite the humiliations, Simone was madly in love with him and did exactly as she was told.

Probably her most demeaning moments came when Evenou brought home strangers to have intercourse with her while he watched. On other occasions, he would urge her to take off portions of her clothing in public places to satisfy some unfathomable personal sexual desire.

The relationship between the odd couple grew stronger. Simone moved into the apartment building where Evenou lived with his wife and daughter. She occupied an apartment on the first floor. What could be more convenient? The doctor slipped down the stairs at every opportunity to indulge his peculiar sexual urges. Simone never disappointed. For five years the unholy alliance flourished.

Something had to give. It all happened within a period of 24 hours one day in 1955. Dr. Evenou was slugging back his port with Simone at one of their regular watering holes, Madame Porree's Restaurant on Avenue des Allies. He brought up the subject of murdering his wife. The dear woman was ill, which would make the task that much easier. Evenou is reported to have said to Simone, "We can't go on unless she is removed. You must remove her. You have taken her place. You have a duty to me."

Simone, after years of obedience, listened wide-eyed. She agreed. It seemed the logical thing to do. The doctor went on, "Marie-Claire must die today. You must kill her. I will make preparations, of course. I shall see that everything is made ready. I think it would be as well if you stabbed her. Yes, that would be best."

Simone excused herself. Evenou ordered some more port. Twenty minutes later, Simone returned to the restaurant. She smiled as she showed her lover the menacing hunting knife with the horn handle which she had just purchased. Evenou approvingly took the weapon in his hand. It was perfect.

Together, the tipsy doctor and the dressmaker left the restaurant. Evenou told Simone that they must kill his wife that very night. He briefed her on his plan and told her to wait in her apartment. The waiting was the hard part. Simone admitted later that although she was nervous, she never once thought of not going through with the plot to kill Marie-Claire Evenou.

A few floors up, in his own apartment, Evenou enjoyed the last dinner his wife would ever prepare. Although she was ill, Marie-Claire insisted on cooking her husband's meals. After eating, the doctor went for a short walk around the neighborhood. No doubt he felt that he had created the perfect sex partner to share in his perversions. This would be the ultimate perversion. He had trained Simone to such a degree that she would kill for him on command.

Evenou returned to his apartment and called Simone. He said only one word, "Now." Simone had prepared herself as her lover had instructed. She wore only high-heeled red shoes and black gloves. She slipped her overcoat over her nude body and carefully placed the horn handled knife into a pocket. One last touch. Simone applied bright red lipstick as Evenou had suggested. She was ready. She walked up the stairs leading to her lover's apartment, making certain that she wasn't seen by anyone.

Evenou was waiting. He removed the knife from Simone's pocket and placed her coat over a chair. He assured her that everything had been arranged. He had taken the precaution of giving his wife a sleeping pill earlier on. The doctor led Simone to his wife's room. Gently, he pulled down the bedclothes. Then he pointed to his wife's body and told Simone, "Look. There is the heart. Now strike there."

As always, Simone obeyed. Nude except for her black gloves and red shoes, she struck. Maybe her mind was willing, but she hesitated. The knife came down, but it was a slow, sluggish blow which hardly broke the skin.

Marie-Claire awoke with a start. "Yves, Yves!" she cried as she looked up at her husband's smiling face.

The consoling husband responded, "I'm here, you were having a nightmare." Marie-Claire rose to get out of bed. Her husband clutched her in his arms and shouted to Simone to strike. Simone slashed out with the hunting knife. All hesitation had left her. She swung wildly time and time again. In all, she inflicted 11 stab wounds. Finally, Marie-Claire lay still in death.

In a daze, Simone returned to her apartment. She washed her blood-smeared body before turning to the incriminating knife and gloves. They too were dripping blood. Simone washed them carefully and then took needle and thread and sewed them into her mattress.

Dr. Evenou called police, but his story of an intruder didn't stand up under close scrutiny. His love affair with the lady in the ground floor apartment was discovered by police. It didn't take long for Evenou and Simone to confess to the murder, each accusing the other of being the mastermind behind the killing.

Arrested and lodged in prison, awaiting trial, Dr. Evenou took seriously ill. His years of drowning himself in port, coupled with his dissipated lifestyle, had taken its toll. The good doctor died, leaving Simone alone to face the music. And face the music she did, to the fascination of the entire country.

Eighteen months after the crime was committed, Simone, now 48, stood trial for murder. The woman who sewed dresses for a living, who up to five years earlier had led a humdrum existence, stood in real danger of being executed. On the advice of her counsel, Simone revealed her every thought and action from the time she had first met the evil doctor.

The details were so explicit and perverse that the judge often cleared the courtroom before allowing Simone to continue. Her defence rested on the influence the doctor wielded over her. She was depicted as nothing more than a tool in the hands of an evil man who had used her to kill an unwanted wife.

The prosecution demanded Simone's head. They claimed that cunning alone had enabled her to sew the gloves and knife into her mattress.

Simone was found guilty, but displayed great remorse for what she had done. It was this remorse which provided the court with the necessary "extenuating circumstances" required to reduce the sentence from the guillotine to life imprisonment.

And that's how it all ended for the seamstress who, six years earlier, had called on a doctor for a routine medical.

DR. CARLO NIGRISOLI 1964

I am certain that Dr. Carlo Nigrisoli of Bologna, Italy, started out in the practise of medicine convinced that he would uphold every single one of old Hippocrates' tenets. After all, the good doctor came from a long line of distinguished physicians who had practised medicine in Bologna for generations. He had no reason to stray from the straight and narrow.

What went wrong? Iris Azzali, that's what.

Iris strolled into Carlo's clinic one day with a minor ailment. The doctor cured what ailed her, and other things as well. Iris was a willowy, long-legged beauty, with big brown eyes, full seductive lips, and a body that would make the Leaning Tower of Pisa stand up straight and take notice.

From that very first meeting, the older man with a wife and three children at home thought of little else but beautiful, youthful Iris. She, in turn, thought the debonair society doctor so much more intelligent and mature than her regular companions.

How can one put it delicately yet retain a degree of candor? Carlo and Iris met clandestinely at her apartment where their signs of affection soon graduated to physical fulfilment. Oh, what the heck, they hit the sack at every opportunity.

Sure, there were a few anxious moments. Take the time Iris became a tad pregnant. She cried and in general carried on something fierce, but Carlo rose to the occasion. He escorted her to another city, where she obtained an abortion. Presto, her troubles were over.

Now, folks, all this intrigue did not have a good effect on Carlo's wife Ombretta. She realized that Carlo was no longer the loving husband and attentive father he had once been. When Ombretta attempted to discuss her husband's changing attitude toward her, he flew into a rage. Ombretta became nervous and distraught. Something definitely was rotten in the state of Bologna.

The unhappy couple's best friends, Anna and Carlo Frascaroli, soon became aware of the tension between Carlo and Ombretta. Frascaroli, who was also a doctor, had been approached by Carlo, who told him that Ombretta was suffering from nervous exhaustion. Dr. Frascaroli prescribed a series of injections. He began giving the injections himself, but for convenience sake both doctors agreed that Carlo Nigrisoli would continue to give them to Ombretta at their home. Of course, the Frascarolis were totally unaware of Carlo's extracurricular activities with Iris.

Meanwhile, the affair grew warmer. Carlo and Iris couldn't stay away from each other. They took little trips together into the country. Ombretta was miserable. She was losing her husband. The father of her children was no longer interested. On the other hand, Carlo now regarded his wife as an obstacle standing in the way of his happiness with firecracker Iris.

The potentially dangerous triangle exploded on March 14, 1964. It was around midnight when Carlo raced from his bedroom shouting to the servants, "I must get Signora Nigrisoli to the clinic! She has had a heart attack!"

Poor Ombretta was rushed to her husband's clinic, but died without regaining consciousness. Carlo explained, "I had given her a heart stimulant by injection, but it doesn't seem to have succeeded." Carlo was completely distraught, but did muster up enough presence of mind to suggest to the doctors in attendance, "Put on the death certificate that she died from coronary thrombosis." The doctors disagreed with Carlo, feeling that they did not have enough information to be certain of the cause of death.

Suddenly, Carlo extracted a neat little pistol from his inside coat pocket. Raving like a lunatic, he shouted that he would kill himself unless the doctors signed the death certificate. Instead, they calmed him down and called police. In minutes the blubbering Carlo was in a police station answering embarrassing questions. When Italian detectives found out that he had been giving his wife a series of injections, they decided to hold him until the results of the post mortem were revealed.

These results caused a sensation throughout the country. The autopsy showed that Ombretta had died from an injection of curare. Curare is not your average poison, not by a long shot. It's a rare vegetable poison derived from certain South American plants. Some South American Indian tribes treat the tips of their arrows with it for use in warfare. The poison causes paralysis of the muscles, which is quickly followed by an inability to breathe. It has been used medically as a relaxant prior to operations. Dr. Frascaroli stated definitely that he had never used nor prescribed curare for Ombretta's condition.

Dr. Carlo Nigrisoli was charged with his wife's murder. His trial began on October 1, 1964. It was the first trial held in Italy where curare was used as the instrument of death. It was also Italy's first televised murder trial. Adding to the uniqueness of the proceedings, Carlo obtained permission to testify from his cell via a sound system especially set up for that purpose. At no time was he actually in the courtroom, although his voice could be heard and he could hear everything which transpired.

Iris testified, admitting to her affair with the accused man. Dr. Frascaroli related that he had prescribed a nerve tonic for Ombretta to be taken intravenously. Dr. Frascaroli dramatically added that he had instructed Carlo to discontinue the injections a few days before Ombretta died.

It was proven that Carlo continued to give the injections. The prosecution painted the cruel picture of Carlo injecting his wife with curare, which rendered her helpless. He then cleaned up the evidence of his deed and watched as his wife took 20 minutes to die. It was only then that he ran for help.

A well known neurologist, Prof. Domenico, surprised the court when he testified that Ombretta had discovered a hidden bottle of curare in her bathroom on the day before her death. Realizing that her husband might very well be about to murder her, she visited the professor for advice. He told her to go directly to the police, but she wouldn't listen. She insisted on trying every possible method of winning back the affection of her husband. The professor did convince her to take a trip the next day in order to be out of Carlo's reach. The advice came too late. On the day following Ombretta's visit to the professor, she was dead.

On February 14, 1965, the 117-day trial came to an end. Dr. Carlo Nigrisoli was found guilty of murder and sentenced to life imprisonment.

PART 7

MULTIPLE MURDERERS FROM AROUND THE WORLD

DIETER BECK

INGRID Kanike's parents never even knew their 23-year-old daughter had been delayed. She often took the train from her home in Rehme, Germany to Minden. Usually, she arrived home after midnight when her parents were already in bed and left for work in the morning before they got up.

On Friday, April 17, 1961, Ingrid took in a movie in Minden, but she never returned home. On Saturday morning, Oscar Riedel was on his way to work at a local factory near the Rehme railway station. There, lying in a ditch, was the body of a young girl. She had been raped and strangled. Ingrid Kanike would never see her parents again.

Police examined the girl's purse, which was found near her body. It contained the usual items, including some money. Investigators were convinced that nothing had been removed from the purse. They felt that someone had randomly attacked the girl after she had disembarked from the train.

It was established that Ingrid was fearful of walking home alone after midnight and always took a cab. Investigators questioned the 20 people who had arrived on the 12:07 train from Minden. Not one could remember having seen Ingrid. Cab drivers who regularly met the train were questioned. Several recalled Ingrid having been their passenger on previous nights, but they swore they hadn't seen her on the night of the murder. For some reason, on this particular night, Ingrid had chosen to walk from the station to her home rather than take a cab.

The first murder in 20 years in a town of 35,000 caused quite a stir. Girls who normally walked alone at night were now afraid to venture outdoors. Husbands and boyfriends accompanied their mates wherever they went. As time went by, the incident faded from people's minds. The general feeling was that a stranger had plucked a local girl off the streets and, after satisfying his abnormal urges, had moved on.

When the investigation wound down, Ingrid's parents consulted Dutch clairvoyant Gerard Croiset. He told them that the killer worked in a machine factory near Rehme, which was not too helpful as there were several machine factories in the area employing hundreds of men.

Four years after Ingrid's murder, another young woman was killed in a similar fashion. On May 17, 1965, Ursula Fritz, a 26-year-old secretary failed to show up at her place of employment in Herford, about eight miles down the road from Rehme. Her employer figured she had quit her job and made no inquiries. Eight days later, Ursula's landlady decided to use her passkey to open the door to the young woman's room. The rent was overdue and she hadn't seen her roomer for over a week. Once the bedroom door was open, it was obvious why Ursula had not been heard from. She was lying, strangled and raped, on her own bed.

There was no forced entry to the room. In fact, it appeared that Ursula was quite friendly with her killer, which was contradictory to her lifestyle. She had no boyfriends, certainly none that had ever been invited to her room, yet there were two glasses on a coffee table, one of which bore Ursula's fingerprints, while a smeared set of male prints were lifted from the other. Gray serge fibres from a man's suit were found on the bedclothes.

Police in Herford sent out details of the crime to all surrounding towns and cities. It didn't take long before the current crime was connected to the similar murder of Ingrid Kanike, which had taken place four years previously. Was a serial killer on the loose? That was the fear of residents of the surrounding towns.

Despite the many clues pertaining to the most recent murder, police couldn't get a lead to the killer's identity. In desperation they decided to requestion all the cab drivers who had met the 12:07 train from Minden four years earlier.

When one cabbie, August Fennel, gave a statement which conflicted with the one he had given years earlier, police pounced. Fennel admitted that he had lied in his earlier statement. His reason was simple enough. He didn't want to get involved in a murder investigation.

Under threat of being charged with obstructing a police investigation, Fennel admitted that Ingrid had entered his cab when she had disembarked from the 12:07 train. She had been accompanied by a good looking man who had instructed him to stop the cab, saying, "We will walk the rest of the way." Fennel was sure Ingrid had willingly accompanied the stranger. When Fennel was shown photos of men who had been on the train that night, he could not pick out the one who had been in his cab with Ingrid. It appeared to detectives that Ingrid must have met the man on the train.

Once again, police pored over the male passenger list, eliminating those with ironclad alibis, as well as those who were too young or too old. Finally, they were left with four men—Otto Johanns and Emil Bach from Rehme, Carl Mueller from Minden and Dieter Beck from Bielefeld. It was felt that Fennel would have recognized the first two men, whom he knew by sight. The remaining two men, Mueller and Beck, worked at machine tool plants in Rehme, which brought to mind clairvoyant Croiset's opinion that Ingrid Kanike's killer worked at such a factory. Still, there was no proof that either man was involved in the murders.

The killer struck again on February 28, 1968, almost three years after Ursula Fritz's murder. The victim was 21-year-old Anneliese Herschel of nearby Werther. Her body was found by railway track inspector Leopold Beisel beside the tracks about a mile from Bielefeld. Anneliese had been raped and strangled. She was thought to be the third victim of the serial killer who let long periods of time elapse between murders.

Police found a book of matches in the victim's coat, advertising the Igloo Bar, Kon St., Bielefeld. The manager of the bar remembered Anneliese. He stated that she had been in his establishment and had left with a man on the night she was murdered. Police showed photographs of several suspects, including Mueller and Beck, to the bar owner. He picked out the photograph of Dieter Beck as the man who had left his bar with Anneliese. Two other employees independently identified Beck's photo as well.

Dieter Beck was located and taken into custody. He unhesitatingly admitted killing all three women. Dieter had chosen them because they were slightly overweight or not very attractive. He figured they would be easy to meet casually and might even consider themselves fortunate to make the acquaintance of a rather handsome young man. Dieter told police, "I didn't want to kill those girls. It's just something that comes over me and then I can't help myself." Over the years in which he raped and killed three women, Dieter carried on normal sexual relations with several women, all of whom claimed he was a considerate, gentle lover.

In June 1969, Dieter Beck stood trial on three counts of premeditated murder. He was found guilty on all three charges and sentenced to three terms of life imprisonment.

ANDREI CHIKATILO

THE world's most prolific serial killer, a Russian? Impossible! We tend to categorize these reprehensible monsters as American or British phenomena. Berkowitz, Bundy, Gacy, the Yorkshire Ripper, names indelibly carved in our memories. Yet there was one Russian who operated over a longer period of time and killed more of his fellow human beings than any of those infamous predators.

The little boy who grew up in the Ukrainian village of Yablochnoye lived through the ravages of the Second World War. Looking back at his earlier history, there is little to distinguish him from other little boys who were brought up in similar circumstances.

Andrei Chikatilo developed into a big, strong teenager. He did excellent work in school, joined the Communist party and looked forward to a higher education. There was one disturbing physical defect which bothered the young student. He couldn't perform with members of the opposite sex. He tried; he wanted to, but he physically couldn't do the trick. The few teenage girls who participated in Andrei's immature attempts at lovemaking ridiculed their awkward partner. It was humiliating.

Andrei entered a technical college and graduated as a communications engineer. After a short period of time spent in the work force, he was drafted into the army, where he served three uneventful years. In 1960, at age 24, Andrei returned to his home village of Yablochnoye, but the rural Ukrainian village was not for him. He gravitated to a town about 20 miles removed from Rostov, where he found a job as a telephone engineer.

Because of his inability to perform sexually, Andrei tended to avoid women and developed into somewhat of an introvert. His only sister, Tatyana, was concerned. She introduced him to her friend, Fayina. The pair hit it off and in 1963, they married. Their honeymoon was less than a roaring success. Fayina was patient with her inept husband, but it took a week before the marriage was consummated. In the months to follow, the sex act between Andrei and Fayina became a clumsy obligation rather than an act of love. The couple managed to have two children, a boy and a girl. Andrei doted on them both. In his spare time, he attended Rostov University, obtaining a degree in philology and literature in 1971.

With degree in hand, Andrei changed careers, accepting a position as a teacher in the town of Novoshakhtinsk, about a two-hour train ride from Rostov. It was while teaching that he got into trouble for the first time. In 1973, he was accused of fondling a 15-year-old pupil. When the girl screamed, Andrei experienced a degree of pleasure. He was lectured about his behavior and was asked to resign when a second incident occurred.

Andrei was hired to teach at another school in Shakhti. The Chikatilo family moved into a comfortable four-room apartment. No one was aware that the new teacher purposely rode on crowded trains so that he could rub up against young girls and boys. The urges were getting stronger. Andrei made preparations for what was to follow. He rented a dilapidated one-room hovel at 26 Mezhevoi Perevlok on the edge of town.

Andrei roamed the city searching for a likely candidate to participate in his sexual fantasies. He found partners in destitute prostitutes who would sell their bodies for a slug of vodka and something to eat. Unlike his wife, they would do anything he wanted. He liked it best when they screamed in agony and offered resistance.

On December 22, 1978, Andrei picked up nine-year-old Lena Zakotnova. To the little girl, he looked like a kindly grandfather. She consented to visit his one-room hovel. No one saw the pair walk down the dark lane and enter number 26. Lena became the monster's first murder victim. Later he would explain that inflicting pain was no longer enough to satisfy him. He stabbed Lena time and time again, after which he strangled her to death. Andrei carried her body to the River Grushevka and threw it in. Two days later, Lena Zakotnova's body was found a short distance downstream.

Andrei was caught up in the murder investigation. Neighbors had seen him take several girls into his shack. His record at his old school was exposed. As luck would have it, at this time 25-year-old Aleksandr Kravchenko, who had committed a similar crime years earlier and had spent six years in prison, lived a few doors down the lane from Andrei. Kravchenko was questioned extensively and eventually confessed to Lena's murder. At his trial, he claimed to have been beaten by police and recanted his confession. He was tried, found guilty and sentenced to 15 years hard labor. The state appealed the light sentence. They succeeded in having Kravchenko sentenced to death. Years later, in 1984, he was executed by a firing squad.

In March 1981, Andrei was dismissed from his teaching position, but soon was hired as a supply clerk for a large industrial company. The job entailed travel procuring supplies, enabling him to roam far afield in search of victims.

Seventeen-year-old Larisa Tkachenko became Andrei's second victim in September 1981. He met her at a bus stop and lured her to a wooded area near railway tracks, where he pounced on the hapless girl, beat her about the body and strangled her to death. The second murder was easier than the first. Andrei Chikatilo, university graduate, husband and father, was now a sex-starved killing machine. His life revolved around killing. At home, Fayina knew nothing of her husband's strange behavior. He made sure never to return home immediately after a killing. Those he raped, mutilated and strangled in his rented room were disposed of elsewhere. He had plenty of time to wash up the large amounts of blood involved. Andrei liked the sight of blood.

In 1982 he killed a total of seven individuals, among them little children, mature women and young boys. He travelled great distances and often committed his murders hundreds of miles from his home base. Despite the variety of his victims and the widespread locations of the crimes, a pattern eventually emerged. Around 1983 police realized that a number of the murders committed in wooded areas near remote railway stations all bore distinctive mutilations. There were many stab wounds concentrated near the eyes of the victims.

During a two-month period in 1984, Andrei stabbed and strangled 10 people. Once, on a seven-day trip to Tashkent, he killed two women. No one ever suspected the supply clerk who lived and worked hundreds of miles from the scenes of the crimes.

It was easy for Andrei to lure his prey off the train leading into Rostov. Sometimes their bodies were found within days. Sometimes they weren't found until months of hot weather had reduced their bodies into nothing more than skeletons.

Finally, several police agencies combined forces and acknowledged that they had a serial killer of monstrous proportions on their hands. They elicited the aid of the Criminal Biology Dept. of the Russian Ministry of Health, which was given all the physical evidence available. It was ascertained that the killer's semen found on several victims was type AB.

On September 14, 1984, an alert plainclothes police officer grew suspicious of a man who had been attempting to pick up women for hours. Upon being questioned, the man claimed he simply liked talking to members of the opposite sex. When the bag he was carrying was checked, it was found to contain knives and a rope. Still, no crime had been committed. The officer took the man's name and wrote out a routine report for his superior. The man was none other than Andrei Chikatilo.

Major Gennady Bondarenko, head of the Rostov police, had Andrei brought in for further questioning. He had a record of molesting children when he had taught school. A footprint found near one of the victims had been made by the same size shoe as that worn by Andrei.

A blood test indicated that Andrei's blood was type A. Because sperm found on the clothing of several victims was type AB, authorities were convinced that they had the wrong man. It is believed by many that the Russians botched the testing. At any rate, Andrei was absolved of involvement in any of the murders. Secretly, he was amazed that the police had failed to nail him.

Detectives conducting the massive investigation had compiled index cards on over 25,000 individuals. Out of this large number, card number nine was devoted to Andrei Chikatilo. It noted that he was absolved of any complicity in the serial killings because he had the wrong blood type. The murders and mutilations continued.

In November 1990, hundreds of plainclothes police officers travelled on the trains around Rostov. Others were staked out at small railway stations. The blanket manhunt paid off. Sgt. Igor Rybakov spotted a man with a bloodstained cheek leaving a lonely wooded area near a remote station where a body had been found some time earlier. He questioned the man, scrutinized his identification, but had no reason to detain him. Later, Rybakov had second thoughts and filed a report on the incident.

A few days passed before the report was deemed important enough to have the area thoroughly searched. About 50 yards from where the first body had been found, another was discovered, covered with leaves. That did it. Andrei was taken into custody.

In time, Andrei confessed to 52 murders, the most recorded by any serial killer in history. He described in detail his urge to inflict pain and death on his victims. He also confessed to cannibalism and necrophilia. The lengthy trial, which held Russia spellbound, featured the accused, head shaven, confined to a cage for his own protection.

Andrei Chikatilo was found guilty of 52 counts of murder and was sentenced to death. President Boris Yeltsin rejected clemency. On February 14, 1994, the Rostov Ripper was put to death.

REVEREND JIM JONES

WHO can forget the horrific photographs of the more than 900 corpses decomposing in the intense heat of the Guyana jungle?

The man behind the horror story that was soon to make headlines around the world was Reverend Jim Jones.

Jones was born in Lynn, Indiana in 1931, the son of an army veteran who was an enthusiastic member of the Ku Klux Klan.

In 1951, the 20-year-old Jones enrolled at Butler University, a school operated by the Disciples of Christ, and attended on and off for the next 10 years. But in 1953, Jones founded his own interdenominational Christian Assembly of God Church. By 1960 his People's Temple, located in Los Angeles, was a bona fide congregation of the Disciples of Christ, which had a membership of almost a million and a half, mostly living in the Midwest.

From 1961 to 1963, Jones performed missionary work in Brazil, organizing orphanages. There is evidence that he visited Guyana while in South America and, quite possibly, it was during this period that the seeds of his own colony in the jungle took root in his mind.

Upon his return from Brazil, Jones displayed a degree of entrepreneurial acumen by forming two non-profit organizations with headquarters in Indianapolis. The Wings of Deliverance was organized to spread the word of God, while the Jim-Lu-Mar Corp. was formed to purchase every money-making venture available. The latter company's elongated name was made up of his own first name as well as that of his mother, Lynette, and wife, Marceline.

During the '60s, Jones operated out of Ukiah, a small town about 160 km north of San Francisco. His headquarters, known simply as the People's Church, became a money-making machine. The strategically-located church afforded Jones and his followers the opportunity to swoop down on weekends to San Francisco and Los Angeles to spread the word, win followers and raise cash.

Sometimes the groups would return to headquarters richer by as much as $40,000. Members of the congregation turned over their social security cheques to Jones. As the flock grew, so did the routine amount of cash flowing into the church's coffers. Many members, completely enraptured with the charismatic Jones, turned over their entire life savings.

Jones wasn't above slick hucksterism. Photographs of "The Father," as he was now called by his followers, were considered to have healing powers. These bogus medical aids fetched a pretty penny, as did other religious artifacts.

In 1971, Jones purchased a former synagogue and moved the centre of his operations to San Francisco. The People's Temple held its opening service with much fanfare. Scores of gospel singers raised their voices in praise of the Lord. Angela Davis spoke. The People's Temple appeared to be a model of what God-fearing folks could achieve. It boasted a day-care, a carpentry shop and facilities to feed hundreds of the poor each day.

Soon the devoted congregation and its dynamic leader were being lauded by the media as a fine example of an efficiently operated and pure charity. Jones's photograph, depicting him handing over sizable cheques to worthwhile causes, often appeared in the press. His now 8,000-member church also became politically powerful.

In 1973, Jones dispatched 20 members of the People's Temple to Guyana, with the express purpose of finding a site for an agricultural mission. A year later, Father Jones leased 27,000 acres in the jungle near the town of Port Kaituma from the government of Guyana. The commune was called Jonestown after its founder.

As the colony was populated, glowing reports were received by relatives back in the States. Crops were flourishing, housing was more than adequate, and, above all, the individual freedom that the disciples enjoyed was lauded by all. The minister of foreign affairs for Guyana reported on Jonestown, "Peace and love in action."

In the '70s Jones was given numerous honors, including the annual Martin Luther King Jr. Humanitarian Award in 1977.

But there were some ominous rumblings. A few members dropped out of the congregation. Others sued, claiming they were brainwashed, beaten and stripped of their wealth. A handful of journalists made their way to Jonestown. Their stories were far from complimentary. They told of poor living conditions and disillusioned members. After their reports appeared in California papers, many of these journalists were threatened. The Guyanese government investigated and reported, "Not one confirmation of any allegation of mistreatment."

California congressman Leo Ryan, 53, was serving his fourth term when he became interested in the Jonestown commune. He decided to look into the matter.

This was not Ryan's first excursion into a high-profile investigation. It was he who strongly and successfully petitioned for the release from prison of his constituent Patty Hearst.

Ryan's entourage, including aides, lawyers, a Guyanese government official, newspaper reporters and a TV crew from NBC, landed at the closest airstrip, Port Kaituma. Only Ryan and four members of his party were allowed to proceed immediately to Jonestown. The rest followed four hours later.

Initial impressions of the commune were favorable. Food appeared to be plentiful. The Ryan group clapped to gospel music as they finished a pleasant meal. Members of the congregation conversed with Congressman Ryan. They told him they were experiencing the happiest years of their lives. Throughout the informal introduction to Jonestown, benevolent Father Jim Jones presided, volunteering his views when asked.

Only Ryan and the four original party members were allowed to spend the night at the commune. The rest were transported back to Port Kaituma in a dump truck. Next morning they returned to Jonestown and were escorted around the compound by Marceline Jones.

Questioned by the reporters, Jones vehemently denied the allegations by former members of his flock of poor treatment. During the questioning, word drifted down to Jones and his interrogators that several members of the commune wanted to leave with Congressman Ryan and his group. Jones flew into a rage. Tension mounted. But no one prevented the dissident members from leaving.

As Ryan talked to the disturbed Jones, a member of the commune pulled a knife and attempted to stab the congressman. While he was being disarmed, the attacker was wounded.

Finally, Ryan, his entourage of officials, newsmen and defectors, boarded the dump truck for the return trip to the airstrip at Port Kaituma. Later, newsmen were to state that at this point they believed that Jones was an unstable character but they were under the impression that he was sincere in his desire to do good for his fellow man. True, there were some flaws to Jonestown but that was to be expected. Sixteen homesick dissidents out of 900 members was not out of the ordinary. No one seemed to be there against their will, no one appeared to be mistreated.

We can only guess at the state of mind of Jim Jones. Unstable, paranoid Jones believed the adverse publicity generated by the stories the newsmen would file would spell the ruin of his colony in the jungle. He also believed that the dissidents who joined Ryan and his group were only the beginning of a wave of dissension that would sweep Jonestown. He determined to force the world to sit up and take notice.

Two small planes landed at the Port Kaituma airstrip to take the visitors home. The dump truck that had originally carried the Ryan group to the landing strip pulled up with a tractor and flatbed. The truck parked but the tractor towing the flatbed drove up between the two aircraft. Suddenly, the men on the tractor and flatbed opened fire. Airplane tires were punctured. Jonestown defector Patricia Parks lay dead. Also killed in the rain of gunfire were San Francisco Examiner photographer Greg Robinson, NBC cameraman Bob Brown, NBC correspondent Don Harris and Congressman Leo Ryan. Others were wounded, some seriously.

While the Guyanese police looked on from a distance, one of the defectors pointed out that Larry Layton, posing as a defector, had opened fire on his fellow commune brothers.

Back in Jonestown, an unbelievable scenario was taking place. Cyanide was mixed with Kool-Aid and quickly distributed to members of the commune. Mothers forced the liquid down their children's mouths. No one refused to take the poison. Black and white, young and old, people who had fled the ghettos and streets of America for the jungles of Guyana, were committing mass suicide. They had followed their charismatic leader, who had promised them a better life. Instead, he led them to death. All 913 died.

On December 2, 1986, 41-year-old Larry Layton was convicted of conspiring to murder a U.S. congressman. He was sentenced to life imprisonment, the only person ever tried for the incident that took a total of 918 lives.

HENRI LANDRU

HENRI Landru was born in Paris on April 12, 1869, to honest, hardworking parents. His mother was a dressmaker who ran her business from her home on Rue de Puebla, and his father was a book seller. These occupations did not place the Landru family in the highest income bracket, but it did allow them to lead comfortable, if frugal, lives. Henri attended a school run by Jesuits, and was a good, hardworking, intelligent student.

At the age of 15 he was initiated into the delights of sex by the neighborhood prostitute, but despite these attractions, he had eyes only for the daughter of a neighbor who lived not far from him on Rue de Puebla. Her name was Marie Catherine Remy, and in his unique fashion Henri loved her. As a result of his affections she became pregnant, at which point Henri, coincidentally enough, left Paris and joined the French Army.

After three years of military service, Henri desperately wanted out. He wrote to Marie's father, who used his influence to get Landru a discharge. Henri came home, married Marie, met his two-year-old daughter, and got a job as an accountant. Within the next two years, the couple was blessed twice more. Now 26 years old, Henri found himself in a dead-end job, with three children and a wife to support.

In the years between 1900 and 1910, Henri tried his hand at swindling women, using any ruse to gain possession of their money and furniture. It didn't seem to matter what he did, he always got caught, and received a series of short jail sentences for fraud. In between sentences, Henri never forgot Marie—in fact, he remembered her to the extent of another bouncing baby daughter. The Landru family now totalled four children.

Henri's profession was that of con artist and thief, with no gainful employment other than the courting, wooing and fleecing of members of the opposite sex. He had a magnetic personality, but at this point in his life he had not yet perfected the fine art of escaping detection after the fact. From 1910 to 1914, he corrected this flaw in his operating procedure to a degree that put his frauds in the top professional category. He kept meticulous notes and records on every lady, her likes, dislikes, and habits. He categorized the potential degree of difficulty in fleecing them and how big a financial reward was waiting to be plucked. Six days a week, Henri left his wife and four children to go to his work.

Only Henri knew that he was busy building up another life and another role, which he entered fully and completely. Sometimes when he left his family, he would have to stay away for a few days. He always told Marie the length of his business trips, and if he was held up for any reason, he was always considerate enough to phone her. She never questioned his absences, nor did she inquire about the cyclical nature of his income. She had a general idea that her husband was in the used furniture business and had several warehouses which he visited. When he made a profitable deal the family shared in the good fortune, but when he had trouble putting together a lucrative transaction, the exchequer suffered.

Marie was a perfect wife for Henri Landru; she cared for her brood, but more important, she didn't have an inquisitive bone in her body. The family moved frequently; this too she took in her stride without question. She knew her husband would be home at least one day a week, for on that day Henri opened his huge desk and did his bookwork.

At the age of 45, Henri had grown a long, flowing beard that was without a doubt his most outstanding feature. He had a rather long body for a small man, which gave him the appearance of being taller than he really was. His pale complexion contrasted sharply with his bright red beard, and he was bald as a billiard ball, with large, powerful hands for a man of his size and build.

In order to guarantee a constant supply of ladies, Henri used the simple but effective method of placing matrimonial ads in the newspapers. He studied the best ads, and by trial and error he developed the wording that brought the best results.

On Bastille Day, July 14, 1914, the Landrus had just moved into another new home in Clichy. Henri had to go to work soon after they arrived in their new home, and this particular job was to be concluded in a most unique way. Using the name Raymond Diard, he had received a reply to one of his ads from Jeanne Cuchet. Jeanne fell into the exact category that rated an A in Henri's book. She had been married to a commercial traveller, who had unfortunately died of natural causes. She lived with her elderly parents and teenaged son, Andre. Best of all, she had a substantial nest-egg of 5,000 francs.

A tall, thin, plain woman, she was flattered and thrilled to be singled out, and soon became completely infatuated with Henri. An expert at his chosen profession, he knew the words, the topics and above all the manners that appealed to Jeanne. As Monsieur Diard he dined with her parents, careful to agree with her father's views on the conduct of war, and careful to have an extra helping of her mother's biscuits. This milieu was Henri's business office, and in it he labored as patiently and efficiently as any accountant. The couple announced their engagement, received congratulations from the family, and another plum of a set-up was ready to be plucked. The 5,000 francs would go a long way—wouldn't Marie be pleased at the successful conclusion of this piece of business!

In subsequent meetings with his fiancée, he let it be known that he was a qualified engineer who ran a small business currently making lighter flints. Lovestruck Jeanne's life had changed in three short months. It was too bad that her son Andre didn't take to Raymond; but never mind, he would doubtless grow to love him as much as she did. What a trusting man Henri was, thought Jeanne. He insisted that he put his money and hers together in the bank. The happy couple moved into a little apartment, and as soon as the money was safely placed in the bank, Henri cleaned out the account and took off.

Months later, quite by accident, Henri bumped into Jeanne, who was tossing flowers at the feet of passing soldiers during a military parade. One of the flowers landed at his feet, and when he looked up it was into her eyes. It was a tribute to his ingenuity and her stupidity that he was able to make up a story that placated her. He admitted to her that he had lied—he was really married and had two daughters—his divorce would become final any day now—the day he left her he had received word that his wife had balked at the divorce and was coming to Paris with his two daughters—he had held her money for her—it was safe in a Swiss bank.

Bluebeard was able to pull it off, and the pair took up where they had left off months before. In November, three months after his reunion with Jeanne, Henri rented a house in the country. It was a villa called The Lodge at 46 Rue de Mantes in Vernouillet, a small town just outside Paris. Henri took Jeanne to this villa. He usually only worked for profit, and there was nothing further to be had from Jeanne but her life. While lying in bed with Jeanne, Bluebeard leaned over, placed his large hands firmly on her neck, and strangled her to death. He then left for Paris with her bankbook. He had noticed that she had managed to save a paltry 400 francs since her last plucking, and it was not difficult for a man of his experience to extract it from the bank. The next day he was back at Vernouillet, with a body on his hands.

The unheated lodge was cold and damp, and when Henri arrived he was altogether uncomfortable, but repeated trips to the woodhouse soon warmed him up. He piled the logs high in the stove, and the fire caught on his first attempt. Next, operating according to his prearranged plan, Henri cleaned out the bathroom tub, which was in the cellar. Revolted as he was at handling Jeanne's body, he managed to place it into the tub. Ditchdiggers don't necessarily like digging ditches, but it's their job. And this was Henri's. With crude household implements Henri managed to dissect the body in the tub. As he proceeded, he decided he would never be this ill-prepared again, but after all, this was only his apprenticeship. If butchers learned how to dress game, he could learn to become as efficient as a butcher.

Over the next several days, Henri lugged his gruesome cargo piece after piece up the stairs and placed it ever so carefully in the stove. Black smoke billowed out of The Lodge's chimney, and the smoke was accompanied by a repulsive odor. The wind carried it to every nook and cranny of Vernouillet. Later, many villagers stated that they had noticed the smoke, and more particularly the offensive smell. Some even said it smelled like roast beef. One villager complained to an official, who knocked on Henri's front door to question him about the terrible smell emanating from his chimney. Henri told the official that the chimney was defective and promised to have it fixed immediately. This seemed to satisfy the official, and he went away.

Soon afterwards, while walking on the streets of Paris with the signs of war all about him, Henri was accosted by Jeanne's son Andre, in one of those chance meetings which plague murderers.

"Monsieur Diard, where is my mother?"

Henri had to shift into high gear in a hurry. Again it is a tribute to his guile that he convinced the lad that his mother and he were living together in Vernouillet, happy and contented. He placated Andre by telling him that his mother was planning to send for him, and now that they had met in this way he wanted Andre to accompany him to Vernouillet. Henri always liked to put a bit of frosting on the cake. "She is pregnant," he told her anxious son.

They arrived at Vernouillet; Jeanne, it seemed, was not in. Henri offered Andre something to eat. While the young man sat at the table Henri's strong hands firmly clasped his neck and squeezed the life from his body. This time the operation went more smoothly. Henri had bought a hacksaw, meat cleaver and mallet, so it was not long before the black smoke and offensive odor billowed forth from the chimney once again.

In December 1916, Monsieur Diard closed The Lodge at Vernouillet and left it forever.

It is one thing to swindle women one at a time, but it is quite another to be playing many roles simultaneously. Henri always kept extensive notes to remember which lady knew him under which name. He couldn't afford a mistake, because sometimes he had to deal with bank officials, using his many aliases without the slightest hesitation. He even got into the habit of talking to himself, using the alias of the moment in order to implant the proper name in his mind. On many occasions he would rush from one apartment to another, consulting his notebook to refresh his memory as to which name and personality he had to assume.

In the summer of 1917, Henri rented a house in Gambais, not far from Paris. He picked it carefully. The house adjoined a cemetery; there were no inhabitants for miles around. Using the name of Paul Fremyet, he purchased a good stove and connected it to the existing smokestack. Then he set about enticing more women, making sure that they turned over their worldly belongs to him before they turned over their lives. In all, Henri Landru strangled and burned eleven people—young Andre Chuchet and ten gullible women.

One of his victims, Anna Collomb, had invited her sister, Madame Pillot, to Gambais to visit the man she was soon to marry. After returning to Paris, Madame Pillot never heard from her sister again, though she wrote to her at Gambais. In desperation, she wrote to the mayor of Gambais, who answered that he believed he had located the house mentioned in her letter, but that no one had ever heard of her sister's fiancé, Monsieur Fremyet. The mayor stated that the tenant of record of the house in question was a Monsieur Dupont. He volunteered that he had received another inquiry about the house from the sister of one Madame Celestine Buisson. The writer of the letter was Mademoiselle Lacoste, and the mayor suggested that Mme Pillot might find it useful to contact Mlle Lacoste.

The two ladies did meet and compare notes. No one could mistake that red beard. Diard, Fremyet, Dupont, Cuchet, the names went on and on. Landru was readily traced and arrested. The police found him trying to destroy a notebook in which he had the names and addresses of all his victims.

One woman, Fernande Segret, visited the house in Gambais and lived to tell about it from the witness stand. For some unknown reason the mass murderer put the pretty Fernande in the same class as his wife, Marie Catherine. They lived as husband and wife, and she claimed he was normal sexually and in every other way. There was nothing perverted or sadistic about Landru, nor did he ever cheat or swindle her, as she had no worldly goods. But relatives and swindled ladies kept coming forward, and from these women and the detailed files Henri kept in his desk at Clichy it was estimated that he had had intimate relations with close to 300 women in the five years before his trial.

On February 24, 1922, Henri Landru, now known throughout the world as Bluebeard, admonished his keepers for offering him a mug of rum and a cigarette. "You know I neither drink nor smoke," he said. The tired old man of 52 was still receiving over a 100 letters a day from women offering everything from a lock of their hair to proposals of marriage. His loyal and faithful wife visited him in jail, and it was only when he refused to see her that his ties with her were finally severed.

His keepers tied his hands behind his back as was the custom, and Henri walked steadily to the guillotine, taking his brief instructions from the executioner. Then his head tumbled into a basket of bran that had been placed in position for that purpose.

SUSI OLAH

THE tiny Hungarian villages of Nagyrev and Tiszakurt were unlikely locales for murder, but from 1909 to 1930, a series of murders took place in the two villages which made headlines throughout Hungary and all of Europe.

The villages were isolated agricultural communities. In the winter, they were snowbound. The closest railroad was 25 miles away. You get the idea. What went on in the two villages was no one's business but the natives.

The male inhabitants worked hard and played hard. They were forever sloshed on the rather vile wine they produced, mainly for their own consumption. For relaxation and to give a boost to their faltering egos, they often beat up their wives. That is, until Susi Olah arrived on the scene in 1909.

Susi was stout, short and not that good looking. In fact, she was a carbon copy of most of the other ladies who were forever cleaning, cooking and having babies. Susi followed the midwifery profession and was in great demand. Her popularity wasn't due entirely to her dexterity around those with expanding tummies.

You see, the farms in the area were small, the soil poor. In most cases, a peasant couldn't expand his farm because rich men's large estates and imposing walls shut off any expansion. The laws were stacked against the peasants as well. Upon the death of the head of the family, offspring would inherit only a fraction of the father's land. Clearly, the more children born to a family, the grimmer the future. Pregnancy and childbirth were not always happy occasions in Nagyrev and Tiszakurt.

Susi gained in popularity when she added abortion to her midwifery repertoire. One has to keep in mind that doctors were not available in the villages. On occasion, when Susi lost a patient, the only official, a sort of modern medicine man, examined the body. This gentleman always attributed the cause of death to pneumonia, consumption, heart failure and other common fatal maladies.

Of course, this couldn't go on forever. Susi was concerned about the number of women dying while she performed abortions. That's when she got her great idea. Arsenic. Wonderful, deadly arsenic was the solution to all her problems.

Why not let the women give birth and poison the infants after birth? The results would be exactly the same as an abortion without any risk to the mother.

No sooner said than done. Susi soaked arsenic laced flypaper in water. The subsequent solution, placed in the unwanted baby's milk proved to be deadly. Business boomed. Susi's reputation as a purveyor of death spread throughout the two villages. For the equivalent of a few dollars, you could purchase a bottle of the solution and, quick as a Gypsy's fiddle, the unwanted child was gone.

Now, Susi wasn't the only midwife in the area. Her competitors became jealous of her success. Word drifted back to Susi that the competition was restless. Not to worry. Susi held a meeting with the four other midwives. She explained that they shouldn't compete against each other. To solve their mutual problem, they should divide the territory. Everyone agreed that it was a super idea. They arranged to meet again at Susi's home.

A few weeks later the midwives met for the second time. Susi served tea and the most delicious petits fours. Shortly after the meeting, one of the ladies took ill and died. Funny thing, after every meeting one of the women took mysteriously ill and went to her great reward. So much for the competition.

Susi's fame and power grew. She had a husband and son of her own. Up to this point, they add little to the strange tale of the arsenic slinging midwife. Unfortunately, Susi grew tired of her husband. He died suddenly, supposedly of pneumonia. Susi's son smelled a rat. Armed with a revolver, he faced his mother on the village's main street. He aimed and fired. Susi stood unharmed as her son fell to the ground in agony.

The villagers were impressed. Susi apparently had the power of life and death. What they didn't know was that Susi, anticipating the problem with her son, had laced his dinner with arsenic. Suffering stomach pains, his aim was off and, quite by chance, he was overcome by excruciating pain the instant after he fired. Susi's son recovered, but so fearful was he of his mother that he fled the territory, never to return.

The long suffering women of the two villages had a bona fide heroine. Susi became their confidante and leader. The dominance of men over women in the villages gradually disappeared. Under Susi's guidance, an unwanted husband was easily dispatched via her ever faithful arsenic. The stout women of the village, once stuck with unloving husbands, took on lovers. If hubby objected, a little meeting with Susi usually straightened him out—permanently. She didn't charge much for her service, normally the equivalent of $25. For those ladies in better financial circumstances, the price rose to about $200. Kindhearted Susi often dispensed her deadly concoction at no charge to those who didn't have the ability to pay.

For years Susi serviced the women of the area. Men died, women took on new husbands and lovers. A sort of secret sisterhood existed between the women, with Susi acting as high priestess. She expanded her operations, dispensing her "medicine" to women who wanted to rid themselves of the elderly.

Of course there were rumors, insinuations and downright suspicions, but they were all put on hold with the outbreak of World War I. The men of the villages went away to war. Some were killed. The survivors returned to the villages. Shortly after their return, seriously wounded former soldiers took ill and died.

The first news of the drama taking place in the villages reached the outside world when a Mrs. Bulenovenski reported that her 77-year-old mother, Mrs. Purris, was missing. A few weeks later, the elderly woman's body was found beside a river bank. Clearly discernible wheelbarrow tracks were found leading to and from the location of the body. When the wheelbarrow was located, it was traced to Mrs. Bulenovenski.

Well, the goulash hit the fan. Mrs. Bulenovenski was tried, found guilty, and sentenced to life imprisonment. The cat was out of the bag. Now the men of the village knew that evil forces were at work. The women, on the other hand, for the first time realized that one of their own could be punished.

In July 1929, a new pastor came to the village of Tiszakurt. No sooner was the man of the cloth installed in his new pulpit than he heard rumors about Mrs. Ladislas Szabo, who had recently buried her aged father and uncle. The pastor decided to pay Mrs. Szabo a visit. He explained his suspicions to the dear woman, who broke into tears at the mere suggestion that she had had anything to do with the recent deaths.

Between sobs, the woman served the pastor a spot of tea. Almost immediately, he was seized with convulsions. A vacationing doctor and a stomach pump saved the pastor's life. He never bothered Mrs. Szabo after that.

Someone who has never been identified informed police in Szolnok, the closest city, that Mrs. Szabo had certainly murdered her father and her uncle.

The police popped up in Tiszakurt one fine day and questioned Mrs. Szabo in the street in front of her neighbors. The terrified woman confessed, implicating several other women, including Susi Olah. The suspects were questioned. Five women broke down and confessed. They were all taken into custody and the entire group removed to Szolnok.

Susi refused to talk and was released. She made her way to her home village and visited several of her women friends. She told them to keep their mouths shut. Unknown to Susi, the police had let her go, hoping that she would lead them to the other conspirators. The scheme worked. All the women were taken into custody. All except Susi.

When the police called at her home, there was no answer. They found the mass murderer in a clothes closet. She had hanged herself.

Thirty-one women were placed on trial in Szolnok for the arsenic poisonings which had taken place in Nagyrev and Tiszakurt. The trials took place that summer and spring of 1930. The pressure was too much for five of the accused. They took their own lives. Others were found guilty and given jail sentences of from five to 20 years imprisonment.

Today, in the two villages, it is difficult to find a home which wasn't affected by the diabolical wave of killings instigated by Susi Olah.

FRANK ALEXANDER

THE organ music could be heard long into the night. No one complained. After all, the Alexanders were otherwise a quiet, respected family who kept pretty much to themselves. No one knew they were as nutty as fruitcakes.

Harold Alexander was a stonemason who had moved with his family from Hamburg, Germany to Santa Cruz, the capital of Tenerife in the Spanish Canary Islands. Harold, 39, was a handsome man who had managed to eke out a living back in Germany. He had moved his family to Santa Cruz when his wife, Dagmar, received a small inheritance.

Once on the island, the Alexanders sought employment. Sabine and Petra, 15-year-old twins, obtained positions as maids at the home of Dr. Walter Trenkler. A native of Germany, Trenkler thought himself fortunate to have two beautiful young German girls as members of his household. It bothered the doctor somewhat that the girls, whom he knew to be deeply religious, never really became friends with any members of his family. They kept strictly to themselves.

The twins' brother, Frank, 16, worked for a shipping firm. The slender, good-looking boy was introverted to the extreme. While he appeared happy enough to colleagues, no one at the shipping firm got to know him well. He was, however, very attentive to his close-knit family.

Dagmar, Harold and a third daughter, Marina, 18, were not employed. The Alexander family would gather at their flat at 37 Calle Jesus Nazareno at every opportunity. On such occasions the drapes would be closed and organ music could be heard far into the night.

The music stopped on the afternoon of December 16, 1970. That was the day Harold Alexander and his son Frank showed up at the residence of Trenkler and asked to see Sabine. The doctor gulped, but summoned his young employee. As the astonished doctor gaped at father and son, soaked from head to foot with brownish caked blood, Sabine entered the room. Her father's first words were, "Frank and I have just finished killing your mother and your sisters."

Trenkler thought he might have misunderstood, but there was no misunderstanding Sabine's reply, "Oh, that's wonderful, father." Then the 15-year-old girl ran to her father and embraced him. As an afterthought, Harold, peering over his daughter's shoulder, addressed the dumbfounded doctor, "My wife and my other daughters; we have killed them. It was the hour of killing."

Trenkler dashed to the other room and called police, although he had a lingering thought: The Alexander family must have met with an accident. His only other theory was that he was dreaming.

When police arrived, Dr. Trenkler briefed them on the strange conversation which had just taken place. He didn't have to point out father and son, who stood before them caked in blood.

Harold Alexander explained to police that he hadn't actually killed his wife and two daughters. He was busy playing the organ at the time. It was the Prophet, better known as his son, Frank, who had actually carried out the sacrifices. Harold explained that the Prophet had declared The Hour of the Great Killing was at hand. Glory to the Prophet and all his holiness. Harold treated the police as if they were stupid creatures from another planet. It was all so simple. The Prophet had ordered the killings.

Police sent a car to 37 Calle Jesus Nazareno. Harold Alexander had told the truth all right. The police who broke down the door of the Alexanders' flat were physically ill and had to leave the premises. No wonder.

Marina's and Petra's naked bodies were in the living room, hacked beyond recognition. Their sex organs had been slashed away. Blood covered the room from floor to ceiling. The victims' clothing, as well as food and broken furniture, were strewn across the floor. Several bloodied knives and a saw were also found nearby. Even the organ keys were covered with blood. Strips of the girls' skin were tacked up on the walls.

The bedroom held additional horrors. Dagmar's body was mutilated. To add to the grisly scene, the murderer had removed her heart, fastened it with a cord and tacked it up on a wall.

Autopsies were performed on all three victims. Despite the horrendous condition of the bodies, the medical examiner was able to ascertain that, in all three cases, death had been caused by repeated blows to the head with a heavy wooden coat hanger found at the scene. Of all the items in the flat, only the coat hanger bore traces of skin and hair.

Considering Harold's initial statement that his son had carried out the killings alone, it was puzzling how he did it in succession with one hanger. Only the two men in the flat at the time of the murders could answer that query.

Frank said his mother had looked at him in a suggestive manner. He realized immediately it was the hour of killing. He picked up the hanger and struck her several times over the head until she fell unconscious. What was Daddy doing? Why, playing the organ, of course. And what were his two sisters doing? Waiting, what else?

Frank proceeded to club first Marina and then Petra into unconsciousness. Daddy played on. When the three women lay dead, Daddy did stop playing long enough to help with the mutilations. And why had Frank the Prophet killed his mother and his sisters? Replying as if his interrogators were simpletons, Frank said, "The lust of the women had to be punished." Harold agreed with his son's account of the slaughter, always referring to Frank as the Prophet.

Sabine, the surviving daughter, was placed in a convent, where one of the nuns became her confidant. She told the nun her two sisters believed implicitly their brother Frank was a prophet with supreme power over them. The girls and their mother would have sat quietly awaiting death at the hands of the Prophet.

Under sympathetic expert questioning, the Prophet explained that back in Germany when he was very young, he and his father had had an incestuous relationship. That's when Daddy started calling him the Prophet. His sisters often crowded into bed with him as well. Frank was one mixed-up lad. He enjoyed sex with his family, who obeyed his every command. In time, the Prophet's demands and wishes were considered his divine right and were to be followed regardless of the consequences.

The family never learned Spanish and didn't attempt to mix with colleagues or neighbors. The clan would gather, draw the drapes, play the organ and do whatever they did under the auspices of the all powerful Prophet.

Psychiatrists had a field day with the surviving Alexanders. It was more or less agreed that Frank's subconscious and conscious were torn between the deep-rooted belief that he was a divine Prophet and the periodic realization that what he and his family were doing was wrong. The conflict became so strong it exploded into a single episode of violence.

Frank Alexander and his father, Harold, were judged unfit to stand trial.

They were confined to a mental institution, where they remain to this day. Sabine Alexander stayed in the convent to which she was taken immediately after the murders of her mother and sisters.

FRITZ HAARMANN

THIS little tale of terror concerns Fritz Haarmann, a man who was unique in that he had three distinct motives for murder. He received sexual gratification from the act, simply enjoyed killing and also murdered for cold, hard cash.

Fritz was born in Hanover, Germany in 1879. His father was a stoker on the German railway but quit working when Fritz's mother received an inheritance sufficient to support the family of six children, the youngest of whom was our Fritz.

The three Haarmann daughters all took up the profitable but precarious occupation of prostitution. One son, Wilhelm, was institutionalized as a teenager when he attacked a 12-year-old girl. Lest you think that I am leading you to believe that all the Haarmann brood were bad seeds, let me hasten to add that one son led an average, reputable life. And then there was Fritz.

He was an odd kid. No sooner was he able to walk than it was observed that he preferred to play with dolls. Sometimes he dressed in his sisters' clothing. You get the idea.

As he grew into his teens, Fritz developed into a rather good-looking, chubby lad. At 16, he attended a military academy. One day he took a sort of fit while on parade. Some records indicate his fainting spell was the result of sunstroke. After this incident, Fritz left the academy.

At 17, Fritz was accused of indecent acts against children and was sent to the Provincial Asylum at Hildesheim. Six months later, he escaped and spent two years wandering around Switzerland, before returning to Hanover and joining the army. Fritz stayed in the army until 1903. Upon being discharged, he practised every vice imaginable. He stole, committed indecent acts and spent more time in prison than outside. When World War I broke out, Fritz was confined to prison and sat out the entire war. He was released in 1918 into a Germany in turmoil.

In Hanover, Fritz found a city fraught with swindlers, thieves and cutthroats, all intent on exploiting a poorly clothed and hungry populace. The centre of the illicit activity was the Head Railroad Station and the Schieber Market across the street. Here, for a price, one could purchase literally anything from the thousands of little stalls where hawkers merchandised their wares. Among the sellers and buyers were the destitute, the prostitutes, the sneak thieves, the perverts and the fugitives from justice. Hanover truly attracted the dregs.

Fritz took one look and felt right at home. Within six months he had established himself in two professions. He prospered as a butcher and also acted as a police informer to the grossly undermanned Hanover police force. Fritz Haarmann had found his niche. He managed to undercut his competitors' meat prices, making him very popular with his customers. His semi-official police work earned him the nickname of Detective Haarmann.

To the outside world, Fritz even appeared to be performing charitable acts. He was known to befriend homeless boys. On many occasions, he would take a homeless waif and, with the promise of a meal and a mattress, lead the hapless youngster to the warmth of his rooms. The boys never left the butcher's quarters alive.

It is impossible to relate exactly what happened to all of Fritz's victims. It will suffice here to follow the fate of one as representative of all.

Seventeen-year-old Friedel Rothe ran away from home and headed directly for Schieber Market. Two days later, his mother received a brief postcard from him. The Rothes were certain that if they could find their son, they could bring him home. All would be forgiven. A friend of Friedel's told the Rothes that their son had visited a male friend at 27 Cellarstrasse. That's how the Rothes ended up knocking at Fritz Haarmann's door.

With police at their side, the Rothes were shocked to find Haarmann performing a sex act with a young boy. A rather casual search of his rooms uncovered no evidence of the missing Friedel Rothe. We know the search was perfunctory because four years later, at his trial for murder, Fritz remarked, "At the time when the policeman arrested me, the head of the boy Friedel was hidden under a newspaper behind the oven. Later on I threw it into the canal."

In the meantime, Fritz was sent to prison for nine months for indecency. Upon his release, he moved and continued his murderous ways in his new location.

In 1919, he met Hans Grans, a well-built young man with the face of an angel. Fritz and Hans became close friends. Now, with a confederate, it was even easier for Fritz to entice young boys to his quarters for a good time. Certainly, Grans knew of his companion's murderous ways. Later Fritz would accuse Grans of being his willing accomplice in all the murders.

From 1919 to 1923, Fritz, with Grans as an accomplice, brought young boys to his rooms. Here, they were killed. Every stitch of the victims' clothing was sold on the black market, with the exception of certain items young Grans fancied. These he kept for his own use.

Around this time, rumors spread about the district that human flesh was being sold on the open market. Suspicion fell on Fritz Haarmann, mainly because of his association with young boys and also because his meat prices were always the lowest. No one did much about the suspicions. That's all they were—suspicions, nothing more.

How did Fritz kill with impunity over a lengthy period of time? Several conditions existed which favored his nefarious deeds. The disruption of post-war Germany lent itself to a laissez-faire attitude toward criminal activity. The police were desperately understaffed. Finally, there was Fritz's occupation. What was more natural than a bloody apron or a bloody knife in a butcher's premises? Fritz acted quite openly. In hindsight, neighbors remembered him carrying buckets of bloody water through the halls. No one thought much about it. After all, he was a butcher.

On May 17, 1924, youngsters playing on the banks of the Leine River found a human skull. Twelve days later, another skull was found further down the river. In July, boys playing along the river bank found a sack of human bones and a skull. News of the gruesome finds spread like wildfire. There was a killer on the loose. Maybe those rumors about someone selling human flesh were authentic after all.

Citizens gathered by the score to stare at the waters of the Leine River. Police searched the murky depths. They were not disappointed. On the first day they recovered 500 human bones. Doctors agreed that the bones had come from 22 different bodies, all young boys.

Fritz was immediately suspected. Police imported detectives who were not known to the suspect. When Fritz and a young boy were observed arguing on the street, the detectives intervened. Fritz claimed the young man had travelled on a train without a ticket. The youngster charged Fritz with an indecent act. Police seized the opportunity to haul both off to jail while they searched Fritz's rooms.

Blood-smeared pieces of clothing were found and were readily traced to many of the missing boys. One wall of Fritz's room was caked with human blood.

Under extensive questioning, Fritz confessed to "30 or 40" murders. He couldn't remember the exact number. His trial for mass murder brought forth sensational evidence of cannibalism and the butchering of humans. Evidence pointing to the sale of human flesh was suppressed. The German government thought that the conviction of a mass murderer was sufficient.

Hans Grans was found guilty of murder and sentenced to life imprisonment. Fritz Haarmann, one of the most prolific and despicable mass murderers of all time, was found guilty of the murder of 24 young boys. He received the death sentence. In 1925, he was decapitated by a swordsman.

FRITZ HONKA

IT didn't seem to matter how often the tenants in the two bottom flats complained. The night watchman and handyman, Fritz Honka, at 74 Zeiss St. in Hamburg, Germany, didn't take their complaints seriously, even though he admitted that the old house smelled to high heaven.

Klaus Kienzle, who lived in the first floor flat had, at Fritz's suggestion, checked the pipes leading into his bathroom. No clogs or leaks were found. John Fordal, a 46-year-old sailor, who was so drunk most of the time his sense of smell left much to be desired, often complained of the nauseating odor as well. Fritz himself lived in the third-floor flat, which was little more than an attic hovel. Occasionally he sprinkled deodorant throughout the building.

Now I must reveal that 74 Zeiss St. would never be featured in Better Homes and Gardens. The dilapidated structure was located in Hamburg's worst slum. It goes without saying that the occupants of 74 Zeiss were not among the upper rung of German society. The lives of many inhabitants of the area revolved around the popular Golden Glove, a low-life saloon where prostitutes, thieves and pimps, confirmed alcoholics all, hung out until the management closed up in the wee hours each morning.

The alcoholic haze of the area's residents was disrupted somewhat on November 1, 1972, when a woman's head was found in a nearby yard. Police conducted a search of the district. They located two arms and two legs, but no torso. Even though the body parts had been lying in the yard for some months, technicians were able to lift fingerprints, which were instrumental in identifying the unfortunate woman as Susi Braeuer, a 42-year-old licensed prostitute with a police record. Evidently Susi had had a penchant for rolling drunks, which had necessitated her arrest on more than one occasion.

The investigation into Susi's murder involved the questioning of many of her clients, all of whom had nothing but compliments for her in the sex department. They swore they only wanted to love Susi, not kill her. The murder went unsolved.

Meanwhile, as the months turned into years, that annoying odor continued to linger over 74 Zeiss St. Fritz did what he could. He sprayed the attic with more deodorant. The handyman had good reason to keep the odor in check. From time to time virile Fritz, who relished sex of the rougher variety, enticed assorted women to live with him in his attic flat. Eventually, they all moved out, complaining of the vile smell.

No one except her husband paid much attention when Anna Beuschel went missing. Every day like clockwork, Anna showed up at the Golden Glove to get sloshed and to ply her chosen profession. Toothless Anna, well in her 50s, was married to Thomas Beuschel, who was in his 30s and actually held down a legitimate job. No one knew what Thomas saw in the alcoholic prostitute, but he apparently loved Anna and provided her with enough money to stay intoxicated when her business dried up. Each evening on his way home from work, he checked at the Golden Glove to see if Anna was all right. On the evening of August 4, 1974, Anna wasn't there. In fact, she was never seen alive again. Thomas reported her missing to police.

On Christmas Eve 1974, prostitute Rita Roblick, a regular patron of the Golden Glove, didn't show up at her usual table. Hamburg's finest believed there might be a connection between Rita's disappearance and that of Anna Beuschel. Who knows, maybe the four-year-old Susi Braeuer case was connected in some way. All three women were prostitutes who frequented the Golden Glove.

The next lady of the night to go missing was something of a local celebrity. Ruth Schultz was a member of the 50-something gang whose claim to fame involved a penchant for practising her varied talents in public. This behavior was frowned on by authorities, licensed prostitute or not.

For years it was Ruth's habit to have her hasty midday meal on the same park bench each day. Intoxicated or sober, she never missed her ritual of having something to eat on that park bench. On January 10, 1975, when she failed to show up as usual, one of the local merchants, fearing that she might be ill, informed the police. Because she fit the pattern of the other missing women and hung out at the Golden Glove, her disappearance received immediate attention.

On June 17, 1975, in the early morning, John Fordal tipped over a candle in a drunken stupor. The fire raged upward into the attic and onto the roof. Fordal was fortunate to escape the blaze. It took well over an hour for firemen to bring the flames under control. Once the fire was extinguished, they entered Fritz's apartment, fearing that the night watchman may have been trapped inside. Such was not the case. Fritz had been at an all-night drinking party and had missed the fun.

Conscientious fireman Walter Aust sifted through the debris in Fritz's apartment. He made his way behind a cardboard partition which appeared to have escaped the brunt of the fire. Walter peered down and gazed in horror at the mummified torso of what had once been a woman. Later he learned, as did the rest of Germany, that he had found the missing torso of Susi Braeuer. There was more. In that confined storage space, firemen unearthed the bodies of Anna Beuschel, Rita Roblick and Ruth Schultz in various stages of decomposition.

As authorities pondered their gruesome find, the occupant of the death flat showed up to discover police, firemen and medical personnel scrambling about his humble abode. He knew very well why they were there.

Fritz was taken into custody. Faced with the undeniable fact that four bodies had been found only a few feet from his bed, he confessed to strangling the women. He told the police that he liked his sex on the rough side. When the women protested, he strangled them. Fritz had decided to dissect his first victim Susi Braeuer, but found it a difficult task, working as he did with elementary tools in the confined space of his kitchen. After disposing of her head, arms and legs in the field, he placed her torso in the storage space. The next three women were simply put in the storage space behind the cardboard partition. Fritz always feared he would be exposed because of the repugnant odor. He never dreamed his murderous ways would be revealed due to a drunken sailor knocking over a lit candle.

Fritz Honka stood trial for the murders of the four women. He was found guilty and was sentenced to life imprisonment.

BELA KISS

THE tiny village of Czinkota, Hungary, is one of the most beautiful spots in the world. Before the First World War it could have appeared on a postcard, representing all the quaint villages of Central Europe. It has a few commercial establishments—a general store, post office, and blacksmith shop were as near as you got to big business in Czinkota—and nothing exciting ever happened in the village.

Then Bela Kiss and his wife arrived and immediately bought the only imposing house in the area, a huge greystone structure on the outskirts of the village. Bela was about 40 years old, and his wife was fifteen years his junior when they took up residence.

Mr. Kiss immediately impressed the locals with his acts of kindness towards the less fortunate in the village. He made it his business to find out who was ill and who needed assistance; nothing seemed too insignificant for the unselfish Bela to lend a hand.

He owned a dashing red roadster, and many a night it would be seen roaring up the main drag, sometimes to deliver a food basket to a needy citizen, sometimes to bring some much-needed medicine to a sick friend. Everyone agreed that Bela was the greatest thing that ever happened to Czinkota. He seemed not to worry about money at all, though he had no visible means of support. But the villagers must have felt that it was not for them to look a gift horse in the mouth.

Despite his magnanimous gestures, Bela was a shy, introverted man, short of stature but with considerable presence. He sported a black handlebar moustache, which accentuated his oval face, and made him appear somewhat chubby. His wife, Marie, was a real knockout in the looks department, with a voluptuous figure to match. She and Bela hired two girls from the village to act as servants, but they only stayed during the day, returning to their own homes each night. As for Bela, he sometimes left in his red car for a few days, but generally could be found at home, in his great greystone house, living the life of a country gentleman.

It is too bad that such scenes of marital bliss and tranquillity should have to come to an end. In Bela's case, the whole thing came to an abrupt stop when he learned that Marie was seeing an artist, Paul Bihari, on the side. Actually, she was doing more than seeing him; she was sharing his bed. Imagine Bela's disappointment when he found out that the one woman he ever cared about was being unfaithful to him, particularly since it coincided with his purchase of their new home and their good life in Czinkota.

At about the time that this revolting development came to Bela's attention, the village constable paid a social visit to the Kiss residence. Constable Adolph Trauber, who didn't have that much to do in the village anyway, occasionally did a little public relations work to pass the time of day. He wanted to know if there was any way he could be of service to the village's most illustrious resident. Bela said that he would appreciate it if Trauber would keep an eye on the property on those nights when he was away and Marie was left alone in the house, and the constable said that he would be delighted to do so. Trauber, a big, friendly man, immediately liked and admired Bela, and a warm friendship grew between the two men.

In the meantime, every time that red roadster disappeared over the hill, who would show up but Marie's lover, Paul. In a village the size of Czinkota it was impossible to keep tongues from wagging, and the townspeople passed the days wondering about the outcome of the triangle. All agreed that the shabby artist couldn't be half the man kind Mr. Kiss was, but there were a couple of things— the artist was tall, slender, and above all, the same age as Marie.

One day just before Christmas, when the two servants reported for work in the morning, they were surprised to find Bela in his study with his head buried in his arms. They gingerly asked him what was wrong. Bela passed them a letter written to him by his wife to the effect that she had left him for the artist Paul Bihari. Bela, beside himself with grief, informed the two servants that he wouldn't be needing them any more now that he was alone in the big house, and that anyway he wanted to be alone in his sadness.

As the weather grew colder and the grey house remained dark and quiet, the only break in the monotony of village life came when one evening a wagon pulled up at Bela's door and deposited two large metal drums. Then the cold winter descended like a blanket, leaving the villagers with only one piece of gossip to discuss during the long dark evenings—poor Bela's beautiful wife running off with an artist.

Weeks passed into months, and one day it dawned on Constable Trauber that he had not seen his friend Bela since his wife ran away. He decided to pay him a visit. When he knocked at the door, though he pounded long and hard, nobody answered. He broke the lock and entered the dark interior. In the study he found Bela, looking half-starved, his clothes in rags and the house a shambles. It was obvious to Trauber that his friend had not taken care of himself or the house since his wife left him.

"I have nothing to live for, Adolph," said the downhearted Bela.

"Nonsense," said the constable. "First we will get someone to look after you and the house. You are both a mess."

The very next day an old woman knocked on Bela's front door, announcing that she was the widow Kalman and that Constable Trauber had sent her to take care of him and the house, and that was that. Under the widow's supervision Bela once more began to look like his old self. He started to gain weight, and with the improvement in his health, his old cheerful but reserved disposition returned. By spring he appeared to be back to normal.

One fine day, when the snow had melted and flowers were beginning to show their buds, Bela had a little tete-a-tete with the widow. He thanked her profusely for being such a great help to him, but felt that he was sufficiently recovered so that he no longer needed her at night. She could return to her home each evening and come back each morning. The widow didn't know whether to take this new arrangement as an insult or a compliment, but eventually she found out that when Mrs. Kiss lived in the house the two servants had returned to their homes each night, so all things considered she decided not to take offence. At least nice Mr. Kiss was well enough to take care of himself.

Mr. Kiss had some strange ideas, thought Mrs. Kalman. Take the upstairs closet which he always kept locked—she had once asked about cleaning in there, but was told that it wasn't necessary. It was none of her business, mind you, but a body couldn't help but be curious.

Shortly after Bela's little meeting with the widow, he left the village in his smart red car and returned with a lady. The widow Kalman was given to understand that the visit would be more or less a permanent one. The Madame, as Bela

called her, was an overweight blonde in her late fifties. She was just getting settled in when a wagon pulled up to the Kiss residence and deposited another
metal drum. Bela had the delivery man carry it to the upstairs closet which
already held the other two drums.

Kiss, who never ceased to amaze the widow Kalman, then offered to send
her on a week's vacation with full pay. The widow took her boss up on the offer,
and was on her way the same day the proposition was put to her. When she came
back from her unexpected vacation, she noticed that the Madame was nowhere
to be seen. Bela nonchalantly told her that the Madame had left. This puzzled
Mrs. Kalman, because when she had set off on her travels a few days earlier it
had appeared that the Madame would be a permanent resident.

Maybe Bela realized the widow was having some misgivings about her boss,
because he came to her and invited her into his study. The widow, who was
becoming accustomed to their little chats, nevertheless shifted uneasily in an
overstuffed chair. Bela coughed once or twice, and then confessed to Mrs.
Kalman that he liked women and he intended to indulge himself with them. He
was sorry if he shocked her, but out of respect for her he thought it best to let her
know that he planned to invite several ladies to the house in the future. She could,
of course, leave his employ if she wished, but Bela would rather—indeed positively insisted—that she stay. To sweeten the pie, Kiss let it drop that there would
be quite a few paid vacations during the coming months. The widow Kalman
made up her mind. Women or no, she would be happy to remain in his employ.

Next day Bela took off in the red roadster and returned with a six-foot, 300-
pound Amazon. He winked knowingly at the widow Kalman. "Madame will be
with us for some time," he said. Mrs. Kalman nodded understandingly and
started to unpack Madame's bags. She then went on one of her periodic vacations, so she didn't see the wagon when it delivered the fourth steel drum. Upon
her return she inquired after the new Madame, and was told she had left. The
widow Kalman nodded her head and went about her dusting.

One day Constable Trauber, who by now was justifiably proud of butting into
Bela's life and bringing him out of the doldrums, paid his friend a semi-official
visit. Two Budapest widows had mysteriously disappeared of late, and as Bela
had recently entertained two ladies, would he mind answering a few questions?
Evidently a man named Hofmann had enticed the ladies to his flat, and they were

never heard of again. The Budapest police had found the flat, but Hofmann had long since gone. The police felt that the women had been murdered, because both had withdrawn their life savings immediately before their disappearance.

Trauber and his friend had a good laugh. Such gullible women almost deserved whatever fate befell them. The two men had a glass of wine, a good cigar out of Bela's humidor, and spent a pleasant few hours, as good friends will. Bela told Trauber that he had something he had been wanting to show him. He took the constable upstairs and unlocked the closet door. Inside were four metal drums which Bela started to bang on with a stick. They all gave off a dull thud as if they were full of liquid. Bela took the cover off one of the drums and told his friend to look in.

"Petrol," Trauber said.

"Yes," replied Bela. He had a friend who could only pay off his debts in petrol, which was just fine with him. With the sabre-rattling that was going on throughout Europe, Bela explained, it was only a matter of time before the world would be at war and petrol would be better than hard cash. Trauber agreed, as Bela replaced the lid. Bela tapped the other three. "See," he said, "they contain petrol, too. Here, take the keys to this room. If anything ever happens to me, you take the petrol. I wouldn't want my wife and her artist friend to have any claim to it."

The two friends returned to the study to have a few more glasses of wine, Trauber protesting that nothing was about to happen to Bela.

In 1914, the war broke out. Time and again Bela was seen with middle-aged ladies by his side as he roared from Budapest to Czinkota in his red roadster. Mrs. Kalman was taking more and more paid vacations, and the man with the drums kept reappearing at Bela's door. Bela, always an impressive figure around the village, distinguished himself by acting as a voluntary recruiting officer. The young, able-bodied men had to be on their guard if they shirked their duty, because Bela didn't take his job lightly.

Then one day it actually happened to him. He was taken without notice from his house to Budapest to join the army. He never even got a chance to return to his home to tidy up his affairs, and nothing further was heard from him. Often on a cold winter evening the very old, for they and the very young were the only people left in Czinkota in 1914 and '15, wondered how their distinguished little neighbor was making out at the front.

In May 1916, Adolph Trauber received word that Bela Kiss had been killed in action at the front. Constable Trauber had lost a friend, the village its most illustrious citizen, and Hungary a true patriot, in one fell swoop. Having spent many an afternoon in his cups with Bela, Adolph felt that he had suffered a personal loss. He went down to the village square and inscribed Bela's name on the roll of honor. Grief-stricken villagers jointed the constable, and with bowed heads they mourned the passing of Bela Kiss.

Not long after the touching scene in the village square, representatives of the government entered Czinkota looking for the most precious of all commodities—petrol. They looked up Constable Trauber and made their mission known to him. It was only then that the constable remembered the hoard of petrol which Bela had shown him so many months before. He took the soldiers to the austere gray house, and up the stairs to the closet where the petrol was stored. The soldiers tilted the first drum and one peered inside. He said, "My God!" and started to stammer, pointing into the drum. The second soldier took a look, and he too became incoherent. Finally the constable looked into the drum and saw the well-preserved body of a woman, submerged in alcohol.

In all there were seven drums in the closet. All but two contained the bodies of middle-aged ladies; in the sixth was the body of Paul Bihari, and the seventh contained petrol—the same petrol that Adolph had peered into when Bela showed him his secret.

A top detective was dispatched from Budapest to take over the strange case of Bela Kiss. Detective Nagy pasted together the baffling pieces of the case. He searched Bela's house, and found his desk full of letters from women all over Europe.

The mass killer had used the simplest of schemes, that of placing matrimonial advertisements in newspapers and luring rich widows to his home in Czinkota, where he had strangled each of his victims with a rope and pickled them in alcohol. Detective Nagy traced the supplier of the drums and found out that he had delivered many more than the seven that were found. As a result, a thorough search of the entire area was conducted, and several more drums were uncovered.

Each of them contained the well-preserved body of a strangled lady.

When news of Detective Nagy's gruesome find spread, several farms came forward and told of turning up skeletons when they were ploughing fields adjoining Bela's property. In all it seemed that Bela Kiss had murdered 23 women, including his wife, and one man, the artist Paul Bihari.

Then, in 1919, people who knew his face reported seeing him in Budapest. The reports were so positive that Detective Nagy went to the hospital in Belgrade where Kiss had died of his wounds during the war. He was shocked to find out that Bela was a tall, blond, blue-eyed Nordic type. It was obvious that Bela had managed to switch papers with a critically wounded soldier. When the soldier died, Kiss had assumed the dead man's identity, and had been discharged at the war's end.

Cunning little Bela Kiss had made good his escape. Years passed without word of the mass killer, until in 1952, a deserter from the French Foreign Legion told of a companion named Hofmann, who used to amuse his fellow in the desert with stories of how he had loved and strangled woman in Hungary. When Detective Nagy heard these stories he recognized details that had never been made public, and he knew that the teller was in reality Bela Kiss. But by the time Nagy got in touch with officials of the French Foreign Legion, Bela had deserted.

Though some criminologists who have studied the Bela Kiss case believe he emigrated to the United States, he has never been apprehended.

PETER KURTEN

HENRI Landru burned his lady friends. Reg Christie liked to plant bodies in the walls of his flat. George Haigh disposed of his victims in sulphuric acid. All of them either had a certain type of victim or a definite pattern of perpetrating their murders.

Peter Kurten did it all. He didn't care who the victim was and he used any means he saw fit to dispose of his victims. If one man can be held up to the light of criminal history and be described as the worst monster who ever lived, it is Peter Kurten who must be given this rather macabre honor.

Kurten was one of 13 children whose father was a hopeless drunk. The lived in Dusseldorf, Germany, and each night the father would beat up the whole family just for fun. The father once spent three years in prison for having an incestuous relationship with Kurten's 13-year-old sister.

Kurten became inquisitive and aroused at the open sex taking place in the confined quarters at home. At the age of nine he achieved some perverted thrill from torturing dogs. He became fascinated with the sight of blood, and as a teenager received complete sexual gratification from killing animals.

With this training-ground Peter graduated from experimenting with animals to humans. He took to living with prostitutes who let him inflict beatings upon them. In order to feed his sexual habits, he engaged in petty robbery. He was caught and received two years in prison. Rather than suppressing his sexual urges he found that solitary confinement gave him the peace and quiet he required to take part in sadistic daydreaming.

Once released from prison, he made his first attack on a woman. He raped and stabbed her, but she didn't die and probably never reported the incident to the authorities. We only have Kurten's word that this was his first offence against another human being.

After this original attack, Kurten attacked women, girls, and even men. He received sexual satisfaction from the sight of blood, and had no remorse or feelings of any kind for his victims. Because he devoted himself so completely to his sexual gratification, of necessity he had to steal to live. He was continually being caught and sent to prison. In all, he was to spend 20 years behind bars.

On May 25, 1913, when he was 30 years old, he was robbing an inn at Mulheim where the owners lodged above the drinking area. While rummaging through the rooms he discovered 13-year-old Christine Klein asleep in her bed. He strangled her and cut her throat. He returned to Dusseldorf, but came back the next day to Mulheim and lingered in a cafe opposite the Klein's Inn. In this way, he was able to savor the horror and excitement his crime had caused the people in the immediate vicinity.

For the next 17 years, Kurten kept killing and raping. He would have killed more, but he was continually being put in prison for robbery. He got progressively worse until finally the people of Dusseldorf realized a living monster was in their midst.

On the night of August 23, 1929, a suburb of Dusseldorf named Flene was holding its annual fair. At around 10:30, two foster sisters, Gertrude Hamacher, aged five and 14-year-old Louise Lenzen were on their way home from the fair. A pleasant man stopped them and asked the older girl to run back and get him a package of cigarettes. The Dusseldorf monster strangled Gertrude and cut her throat. When Louise returned with the cigarettes he did the same thing to her.

Only 12 hours later a servant, Gertrude Schulte, aged 36, was wondering what to do on her night off. A mild-mannered, pleasant man stopped her and suggested they take in the fair. While walking through a wooded area the man turned on her. He became furious when she resisted his advances. As he had done so often before, he brought out his knife and with quick, sure arcs plunged it into the poor woman's body. Finally the monster literally threw her away. Gertrude Schulte did not die. Her screams caught the attention of a passerby, and she was rushed to a hospital.

It became apparent that the Dusseldorf monster had lost all control of his desires. He was stalking victims on a full-time basis. In short order two servant girls, Ida Reuter and Elisabeth Dorrier, were raped and stabbed to death.

As summer turned to winter, Kurten attacked and wounded a girl of 18, a woman of 37, and a man of 30, all in a half hour. One child, Gertrude Albermann, was found dead with 36 stab wounds.

On the night of May 14, 1930, Maria Budlick arrived in Dusseldorf looking for work. A young man engaged her in conversation at the railway station. He offered to show her the way to a hotel that catered to young women. As they strolled through the well-lit streets all went well, but as they entered the dimly lit area the girl, who had heard all about the Dusseldorf monster, became apprehensive. She tried to get rid of her escort and they started to argue.

Just as the argument was becoming more heated, a man appeared and inquired if everything was all right. The young escort left and an unsuspecting Maria accepted an invitation of something to eat at her new friend's apartment. He took her to a one-room flat in Mettmannerstrasse, where she had a ham sandwich and a glass of milk. Her new friend offered to take her to the women's hotel. Once in an isolated district, Kurten tried to rape her. Maria fought her attacker. As she was about to lose consciousness, Kurten asked her if she knew his address, so that if she ever needed help she would be able to find his flat. Maria said no and in so doing saved her life. He let her go.

Next day, accompanied by the police, Maria identified the flat. While she was pointing out the flat to the police, Kurten strolled up the stairs, walked by the police and Maria, went in his flat and closed the door.

The police arrested their cool suspect. Remember, at this point in time he was suspected of attacking Maria only. Almost immediately, as if to get a great load off his shoulders, Kurten confessed, "I am the Monster of Dusseldorf."

Kurten's trial was the most sensational ever held in Germany up to the time of the Nuremberg war crimes trial. To ensure his security he was placed in a cage. Kurten was exactly the opposite of what one might envision a monster to look like. He was a slight, pleasant-appearing, middle-aged man. He had a remarkable memory, and could give names and dates of his crimes going back years. He liked to describe them all in detail.

Kurten admitted to 68 major crimes, not including those of theft and assault. Officially he was charged with a total of nine murders and seven attempted murders.

Several top psychiatrists declared Kurten to be sane. All agreed he was the most perverted human being they had every examined.

The jury deliberated only an hour and a half before finding Kurten guilty.

On July 21, 1931, Peter Kurten, the Monster of Dusseldorf, was executed.

EDWARD LEONSKI

IN 1942, the citizens of Melbourne, Australia had every reason to believe the seemingly invincible Japanese army would invade their country. Thousands of Allied servicemen were stationed in Australia. Life had taken on a nervous, superficial, carefree attitude.

On May 9, Mrs. Pauline Thompson, the estranged wife of a Melbourne police officer, was found strangled in front of her rooming house on Spring St. A post mortem indicated that tremendous pressure had been applied to Mrs. Thompson's neck by someone with unusually strong hands. Although the victim had not been sexually interfered with, her clothing had been torn to shreds. Mrs. Thompson's handbag was found a short distance away. Her attacker had obviously taken the few pounds the bag contained before tossing it away.

What concerned police was the similarity between Mrs. Thompson's murder and that of Ivy Violet McLeod, which had taken place six days previously. Mrs. McLeod, a 40-year-old domestic, was found in a doorway about three miles from her home. Her neck had the same grotesque indentations as those found on Mrs. Thompson. Although she hadn't been raped, she too had had her clothes ripped into shreds. Both women had been killed where their bodies were found.

Despite the imminent threat of a Japanese invasion, the citizens of Melbourne were well aware that a monster was in their midst. Nine days later, the maniac struck again.

Miss Gladys Lillian Hosking, 41, was employed as a secretary at Melbourne University. Her body was discovered by a gardener in Royal Park on the morning of May 19, 1942. As in the case of the previous victims, Miss Hosking had been viciously mangled by someone intent on something beyond cutting off her air supply.

Because of the threat of invasion, an air raid trench had been dug in the park. Distinctive yellow mud had been excavated from the trench. Miss Hosking's body lay face down in this mud. She hadn't been sexually attacked, but her clothing was torn into tiny strips. Miss Hosking's gloves, shoes, handbag and umbrella were scattered within a 10-yard radius of her body.

Three women had been murdered in strikingly similar circumstances within 15 days. All had been accosted relatively close to their homes. It was obvious that they were not well acquainted with their attacker. He killed on the streets with little regard for his own safety. In the case of Miss Hosking, police surmised that she too had been attacked on the street and had been dragged into the park.

Royal Park was located near Camp Pell, at the time an American Army installation. Investigating officers, who at this point had come up with little to lead them to the killer, decided it was possible that the murderer could be an American soldier. Sure enough, they found a guard who remembered a soldier returning to the camp late on the night of Miss Hosking's death. The guard remembered him because he was covered with yellow mud. When casually questioned by the guard, the soldier said he had fallen over a mound of mud while taking a shortcut through the park.

Homicide officers W. Mooney and F. Adam visited Camp Pell. They slowly walked down rows of canvas tents. When they came to tent number 29, they stopped. There, on the ground at the entrance to the tent, was evidence of yellow mud. Inside the tent, the officers found more of the tell-tale mud adhering to a metal bed. The officers left the camp, taking mud samples with them. Later their suspicions were verified when laboratory analysis proved that the mud taken from in front of the tent and the bed matched perfectly with mud samples from the freshly dug trench in Royal Park.

The two detectives returned to Camp Pell to interrogate the occupants of tent 29. Before doing so, they required clearance from the company commander. He surprised the officers by telling them that he had already received a complaint concerning one of the men in tent 29.

Private First Class Edward Joseph Leonski was continually returning to the camp intoxicated, causing a disturbance in the tent, babbling incoherently, sleeping fitfully and waking up in the middle of the night screaming. Once he had inquired of his buddies whether they had ever heard of Dr. Jekyll and Mr. Hyde. During the day, he pored over details of the murders which appeared in the newspapers.

The detectives were incredulous that Leonski's tentmates hadn't complained sooner. The soldiers explained that Leonski was such a likeable guy when sober, it was very difficult to suspect him of hurting a fly, let alone being a vicious murderer.

When Mooney and Adam finally came face to face with their quarry, they knew what the soldiers had meant. Private First Class Eddie Leonski was a well-built, tall blond 24-year-old with a cherubic face. He was a pleasant, good-natured guy, well liked by everyone. He did, however, have the reputation of turning into a real troublemaker when under the influence of alcohol. The guard who had stopped the soldier covered with yellow mud on the night of Miss Hosking's murder picked Eddie out of a lineup of 12 uniformed men.

The police investigated Leonski's background. Born in New York, Eddie had taken up weightlifting while still a teenager. He had a reputation for having extremely strong hands. Eddie was an honor student who played the piano and sang in the choir. The more police delved into his history, the more he resembled an enlistment poster. Eddie exemplified the all-American boy.

Eddie's father had died while he was still a youngster, but his mother had managed to make ends meet and raised him to be a fine upstanding citizen. Or so she thought. In reality, Eddie was overly devoted to his mother. His accomplishments were for her only. His setbacks affected him because he had let his mother down. When Eddie was called into the army, he cried at the thought of being separated from his mother.

Once in Australia, Eddie began to drink heavily. While under the influence, he would become belligerent and, according to his army buddies, he would undergo a strange transformation. His voice would change dramatically, becoming soft and high-pitched, very much resembling a female voice.

Eddie started off by picking up girls in Australia. He didn't do anything to them. He just liked to drink with them and listen to them talk. He drank at every opportunity, was often absent without leave, and in general was a poor soldier. His army record was in direct contrast to his exemplary behavior in civilian life.

Eddie himself knew something terrible was happening to him. Once, he pleaded with a guard, "Please put me in the guardhouse and keep me there. I'm too dangerous to run around loose."

Slowly Eddie gravitated from just talking to girls to trying to strangle them. He would release his grip before they lost consciousness. Eddie later explained that he didn't really want to kill the girls. Their voices reminded him of his mother. He only wanted to remove their voices. These girls had reported his attacks to the police, but in each case the attack had taken place in the dark and they were not able to provide useful descriptions.

Eddie couldn't explain why he became a murderer. He didn't know any of his victims, but he had struck up a conversation with each of them before clasping his hands around their throats. After killing Mrs. McLeod he knew he had to kill in order to possess the voices of his victims. Eddie couldn't explain his compulsion to rip his victims' clothing. He did say that when he read about his crimes in the newspapers he would cry. Yet, knowing what would happen when he drank, he never hesitated to go on a bender whenever the opportunity presented itself.

Eddie told the authorities of meeting Miss Hosking on the street. He asked her for directions back to camp. She was obliging and walked away with him. As the hapless woman talked, Eddie knew he had to possess her voice. Without warning, he clutched her throat and, as his victim went limp, he dragged her into Royal Park. It was there that he stumbled and fell on the excavated mounds of yellow mud.

Eddie was examined by psychiatrists. They all agreed that he was full of unnatural feelings for his mother and was undoubtedly a fetishist. However, in the strict legal sense, he was found to be sane.

Eddie was tried by a U.S. military court, found guilty and sentenced to death. Just prior to his execution, he sang a song in his cell. He sang in a soft, clear female voice.

Edward Joseph Leonski was hanged for his crimes on November 9, 1942.

KAI METZMANN

WHOEVER coined the phrase that crime doesn't pay never heard of the Metzmann case.

Let's go back to 1987, to the famed German wine country on the eastern slopes of the Palatinate Mountains, to the tiny village of Lambrecht. Among the wealthiest inhabitants of Lambrecht was the Metzmann family.

Willi, the head of the family, was a self-made millionaire. He had started out as a mechanic and ended up owning a prosperous welding equipment company. Willi's wife of 26 years, 48-year-old Renate, worked at her husband's business, as did their 19-year-old son Kai and 25-year-old daughter Silke. They all lived in a luxurious home, complete with expensive cars in the driveway and an extensive riding stable.

The tranquil life of this successful family was shattered forever on the morning of Tuesday, February 24, 1987. On that bitterly cold morning, Kai Metzmann lurched into the village's police station and blurted out, "My folks are all dead!" The boy was near collapse. Officers comforted the lad as best they could before rushing out to the Metzmann residence. Once there, they realized their limitations in handling the first multiple murder ever to take place in their village. They summoned experienced homicide detectives from the closest city.

Inside the Metzmann residence, police found Willi's body in the master bedroom about 12 feet from the bed. On the bed lay the body of his wife Renate. Silke's body was found in the study.

Renate had been shot in the forehead with a 30-calibre rifle. After death she had been stabbed three times with a sword and eight times with a kitchen knife. She had then been beaten about the head with a rifle butt. Police believed Renate had been shot and attacked while she slept. Willi had been shot six times with the same weapon and stabbed with a sword which had gone directly through his body. Silke had been shot twice in the chest, after which she had received a total of over 40 stab wounds inflicted by knife and sword. The estimated time of death for all three victims was between midnight and two in the morning.

Detectives examining the murder scenes and the entire house found large sums of money and jewelry lying about. Obviously robbery had not been the motive for the triple murder.

Kai told investigators that he had arrived home from a party in Neustadt in the morning and had walked in on the slaughtered remains of his entire family. Detectives were sympathetic, but were taking nothing for granted. They noted the names of the other young people who had attended the same party as Kai.

Within hours, at least a half dozen teenagers told police that Kai and his best friend, Jurgen Lischer, hadn't left the party until 8:30 in the morning. Apparently, the party had been quite a blast, with drugs and liquor available in seemingly unlimited quantities. At least 50 young people had attended. The statements of the partygoers, some of whom didn't know Kai that well, effectively eliminated him as a suspect in his family's murder.

Detectives learned that on the way up the entrepreneurial ladder, Willi Metzmann had stepped on a few toes. Boris Andower, a former competitor in the welding business, held a grudge against Willi. He had gone into bankruptcy some years earlier and had always blamed his rival for the demise of his business, although as far as the police could ascertain, Willi had nothing to do with Boris' business failure. Another man, Karl Bursch, had been a foreman in Boris' firm. When the business closed down, he lost his job. He too blamed Willi for his misfortune. Both men were thoroughly investigated. Although they admitted threatening Willi, they swore they were not involved in the murders.

When Boris' home was searched, police found a 30-calibre rifle with blood on the stock. Boris explained away the blood with the unlikely tale that he had killed a chicken in his garage and no doubt had gotten blood on the stock at that time. The weapon was confiscated and the blood analyzed. Well, son of a gun, the blood on the stock turned out to be chicken blood. In time Boris Andower and Karl Bursch were absolved of all complicity in the crime.

Officials believed that it was quite possible that the murders would never be solved. The motive was a mystery. Nothing had been taken from the home. The two men who might have sought revenge, no matter how unfounded, were innocent of any involvement. The murder weapons sword, kitchen knife and rifle, had been in the house at the time of the murders and had been carried away by the killers. Police couldn't figure out why they would take away the weapons.

Detectives reconstructed the crime. From the evidence, it appeared that two killers were involved. They either had a key to the house or had picked the lock to one of the doors. All the occupants had been asleep. The killers entered the master bedroom and shot Renate as she slept. Willi jumped out of bed and was brought down as he attempted to advance towards his adversaries.

The intruders must have pounced on the already dead victims with sword, kitchen knife and rifle butt. Silke, in her bedroom down the hall, must have heard the shots. She ran out of her bedroom into the study and locked the door. While she frantically attempted to phone police, her killers broke down the door and shot her dead. When found, she was beside the telephone, which was lying out of its cradle. The killers then left the house, removing all the murder weapons.

The reconstruction was no doubt accurate, but did little to reveal the identity of the killers. More in desperation than for any other reason, investigators decided to recheck Kai Metzmann. After all, he stood to gain his parents' complete fortune.

The young people who had been at the wild party were questioned again. This time, several admitted that by 10 p.m. everyone was so high on drugs that they had no idea if Kai or Jurgen had been at the party between 11:30 p.m. and 2:30 a.m. Originally, they had been asked if the two suspects had left the party. At that time they had truthfully stated that they hadn't seen Kai or Jurgen leave. Now, with their negative statements, police realized that both young men could have left the party, committed the murders and returned to the party without being missed.

Kai was picked up and questioned. His main interest was to confirm that under the German Juvenile Criminal Code, the maximum sentence for murder for a 19-year-old was 10 years imprisonment with the distinct possibility of parole after five years. Once assured of the law, Kai confessed, implicating his friend Jurgen. They had left the party, killed the Metzmann family, and had returned to the party. They were not missed.

The motive was cold, hard cash. Kai was tired of working for his father. He wanted his freedom from family ties and his parents' money in order to live as he saw fit. Jurgen confessed and corroborated Kai's version in every detail. He had agreed to take part in the murders in return for a portion of the inheritance.

The two killers led police to the Speyer River, where they had tossed the rifle, sword and knife. All the weapons were recovered.

In January 1988, Kai Metzmann and Jurgen Lischer pleaded guilty to pre-meditated murder and were sentenced to 10 years juvenile detention. Both have since been paroled. Kai Metzmann, released at the age of 24, is the richest young killer in Germany.

JEAN-BAPTISTE TROPPMANN

WE are inclined to think multiple murder is a modern phenomenon. Such is not the case. Let's go back in time to 1869, when one of the most despicable killers ever to grace the pages of criminal history made his appearance in Paris, France.

Jean-Baptiste Troppmann was born in the small town of Cernay in Alsace. His father was a mechanic and moderately successful inventor. Jean dropped out of school at age 14 to labor in his father's workshop. When one of his father's inventions was sold to a factory in the Parisian suburb of Pantin, it was necessary for Jean to move to the big city. When a second machine was sold to a firm in Roubaix, young Jean was sent there.

At age 19, Jean met Jean Kinck, a man more than twice his age. To Jean, his new friend oozed success. Kinck owned three homes in Roubaix, a small factory and a pleasant summer home. In addition, his happy marriage to wife Hortense had produced six children: Gustave, 15; Emile, 13; Henri, 10; Achille, 8; Alfred, 6; and Marie, 2.

The very first day Kinck met Jean, he brought him home to meet his family. Thereafter, a close relationship existed between the two men. Despite the difference in their ages, they seemed to enjoy each other's company immensely. Seldom did a day pass that they weren't seen together chatting over an aperitif in a neighborhood cafe. Jean was constantly talking about schemes that would make them both rich. Kinck enjoyed the conversations, but dismissed the ideas as being too far-fetched. Unknown to Kinck, his friend, now in his twenties, had already made up his mind to kill him for his money.

Eventually, Jean came up with a scheme which fascinated Kinck. He claimed he had been put in touch with a gang of coin counterfeiters operating out of a deserted house in Alsace. They were going to disband their business, which had made them wealthy. Jean had offered them 5,000 francs to take over their operation. Kinck's mouth watered. This time he felt Jean's scheme was foolproof. Count him in.

Jean travelled to Bollwiller equipped with a bottle of prussic acid. Kinck joined him there. The two friends set out for the home of Jean's parents in Cernay. Jean arrived alone. He was greeted warmly by his parents, who had no idea their son had poisoned his friend on the way to their home. Jean appeared to be very prosperous. He even had an expensive watch.

Next day, Jean dashed off a note to Mme Kinck. Unfortunately, her husband was unable to write. He had a slight injury to his writing hand and was dictating this note to Jean. In essence, the letter explained their business deal was proceeding famously. Kinck requested that his wife forward 5,500 francs to him in care of the post office in Guebwiller. The moment Hortense received her instructions, she went to the bank, procured the money and posted it as requested.

Jean showed up at the post office, but the stubborn postmaster refused to release the letter because Jean didn't have the proper documentation to accept the mail of Jean Kinck. Jean wrote Hortense in Roubaix, again under the guise of Kinck, advising her that since he was now nowhere near Guebwiller, would she please dispatch Gustave with the proper documentation so Jean could pick up the money at the post office. Gustave left immediately without the all-important letter, but with his mother's promise that she would send it along as soon as she received it from the bank. Furthermore, Kinck instructed Hortense to meet him in Paris with all the children.

The cunning Troppmann went to Paris and checked in at the Railroad Hotel. Hortense waited a few days until she received the necessary documentation, which she sent along to Gustave, but Gustave had lost his patience and had left for Paris to meet his family. Troppmann met him at the station. The boy dashed off a telegram to his mother, advising her all was well. Then he went off with Jean Troppmann.

In September 1869, Gustave Kinck was stabbed and beaten to death. Jean buried him in a shallow grave near Pantin. Having murdered both father and son, Jean found himself in a complicated scenario of letters, instructions and bogus schemes designed to part the Kinck family from their worldly goods. So far, all his machinations had netted him only a few francs and a gold watch from Jean Kinck's pockets.

Undaunted, Jean sent off a further missive to Mme Kinck, again posing as her husband. He beseeched her to carry with her all pertinent documentation pertaining to their homes, cottage and business. With their friend Jean Tropp-mann's assistance, they were about to embark on a new and successful life. Hort-ense, who was pregnant, bundled up the children and headed for Paris. Once there, she went to the Railroad Hotel and inquired if Jean Kinck was registered. Of course Troppmann had registered under her husband's name. Hor-tense was disappointed to learn from Troppmann that her husband and her son Gustave were at Pantin, but not to worry, he would take them there without delay.

And so the strange journey by horse-drawn enclosed cab began. Inside, Hortense and her five children were together with a human monster in the form of Jean Troppmann. At a deserted spot known as Quatre Chemins, Jean motioned the cabbie to pull up. Jean, Hortense and two of her children started off into the darkness. The three boys stayed in the cab. They chatted with the dri-ver. Twenty-five minutes later, Jean returned alone. He told the boys they were staying in a house down the way and instructed the cabbie to return to Paris.

There, in the fields near Pantin, this most diabolical of killers had dug a grave, into which he had placed the bodies of Hortense and the two children. Within a half hour the remaining Kinck children were murdered and buried in the same grave. At last, Jean Troppmann had the birth certificate and ownership documentation belonging to Jean Kinck. He would immediately start selling his victim's worldly goods. Soon he would sail for America and no one would be the wiser.

Next day, a laborer named Langlois spotted fresh blood on a mound of earth, as well as a handkerchief sticking out of the ground. He called police and, within hours of the foul deed, Jean Troppmann's great plans were in the process of crumbling. Gendarmes uncovered the bodies of Hortense and her five children. All had been brutally stabbed and strangled.

At the scene, police recovered a broken kitchen knife, a pick and a spade, all stained with blood. The proprietor of the hotel where Hortense had stayed with her children gave police a description of the man who had registered as Jean Kinck, the woman's husband. Where was Hortense's husband? We all know he and his eldest son were dead and buried, but the police had no idea the Jean Kinck they were looking for was in reality Jean Troppmann.

It was left to a gendarme in Le Havre to sight Troppmann in a cabaret. The officer asked Jean to accompany him to a police station. While crossing a dock,

Jean bolted and fell off the dock into the harbor, hitting his head on the way down. Once back on dry land, it wasn't long before Jean was identified as the man who had posed as Jean Kinck. A few days later, Gustave Kinck's body was uncovered a few yards from those of the rest of the family. Jean Kinck's body was found in Alsace.

Arrogant, defiant Jean stood trial for the murder of the entire Kinck family. The cab driver, the clerks who sold the implements of murder and the postmaster at Guebwiller left little doubt that Jean was the killer. He was found guilty and sentenced to death.

On January 19, 1870, Jean-Baptiste Troppmann's head fell into a basket of bran after Dr. Guillotine's infernal machine had done its job.